THE PREMIUM DESK

TRADING OPTIONS LIKE A RISK MANAGER™

The Professional's Framework for Trading Options

The system real traders use. Now in your hands.
Including AI Tools, Algorithmic Markets & Modern Risk Protocols

By Eddy Alexandre, Master Trader

TRADING OPTIONS LIKE A RISK MANAGER

The Professional's Framework for Trading Options

Published by:
The Premium Desk LLC
Long Island, New York
www.thepremiumdesk.com | info@thepremiumdesk.com

First Edition — 2026

ISBN-13 (Paperback): 979-8-9957316-1-0
ISBN-13 (Hardback): 979-8-9957316-0-3
ISBN-13 (eBook): 979-8-9957316-2-7
ISBN-13 (Audio): 979-8-9957316-3-4

Library of Congress Control Number: 2026940061
Printed in the United States of America
Available in English, Français, and Español

CONTENTS IN BRIEF

Table of Contents

To my mother Philomise Alexandre
and in memory of my father Matthieu L. Alexandre.

To my wife,
and my lovely children.

ACKNOWLEDGMENTS

It is never possible to name every person whose encouragement, challenge, or example shaped a book like this one. Over more than two decades of trading, teaching, and writing, I have been fortunate to be surrounded by people whose generosity of spirit is reflected in every chapter.

To the researchers, data analysts, and editorial contributors who gave their time and skill to help bring this project to its highest standard — Eddy Clarke for his generous and skillful aid with compiling statistical data; Jose G. Minaya for his eagle-eye comments and criticism of earlier drafts; The Premium Desk staff for their assistance with many of my questions about the editorial process; and to the legal, compliance, and technical team members who ensured that everything between these covers is accurate and defensible — my deepest thanks. You know who you are.

To my extended family, my community, and my closest friends who supported me through the long hours that producing a work of this scope requires: your patience and belief made the difference. A special word of gratitude to my staunch supporters who never stopped pushing, never stopped believing, and never let me settle for less than the clearest possible version of this framework.

To The Premium Desk community — the traders, students, and subscribers on every platform who showed up with hard questions, real trades, and genuine curiosity — this book was written for you and because of you. Your feedback over years of live sessions, newsletters, and one-on-one conversations is woven into every page.

Finally, to my wife and my children: the hours this project consumed belong to all of us. That you gave them willingly is a gift I do not take for granted. This book is, in every meaningful sense, ours.

Eddy Alexandre
Long Island, New York • 2026

ABOUT THE AUTHOR

Eddy Alexandre

Eddy Alexandre has been analyzing, trading, and writing about the financial markets since 2000. He is a passionate advocate and promoter of the intersection between finance and technology — what the industry now calls FinTech. His career has been defined by a singular mission: to contribute to the advancement of mass adoption of modern markets technology in the median household, placing the well-guarded wealth-building tools of Wall Street into the hands of everyday investors.

Over more than two decades, Eddy has edited multiple financial newsletters, published numerous white papers on finance and technology, and built educational platforms that have reached tens of thousands of traders worldwide.

Upcoming Books

- Trading Forex Like a Risk Manager;
- Trading Crypto Like a Risk Manager; and
- Trading Futures & Commodities Like a Risk Manager.
- Day Trading Like a Risk Manager

Eddy Alexandre, Master Trader, is the lead author of The Premium Desk Risk Manager Series. He has spent more than two decades doing what most trading books only describe: managing real capital, in live markets, through every condition the market has ever produced. Options. Futures. Volatility events. Extended drawdowns. Euphoric runs. He has been in all of it — not as an observer, but as the person with skin in the game. Over a documented multi-year period, his live trading account averaged 25% monthly in futures and options — a record that has been independently verified and is part of the public record.

Website: **optionspremium.substack.com**

FOREWORD

If you have ever handed over your savings — or your confidence — to a trading program that promised transformation and delivered confusion, this book was written for you.

I know that feeling from the inside. Early in my journey, I invested in countless trading systems, courses, and products. I followed the formulas. I did the work. The results were meager. The outcomes were bewildering. I kept moving from one method to the next, certain the next one would finally be different. It never was — not because I lacked discipline or desire, but because none of those programs told me the fundamental truth about how markets actually work.

The truth, when I finally found it, was not exciting. It was this: markets do not reward speed. They reward system. Not the breakthrough trade. The repeatable process. Not the home run. The consistent return, compounded quietly over time.

And beneath that was an even more counterintuitive discovery — one that separates serious traders from the crowd: the market does not primarily reveal itself in charts. It reveals itself in fundamentals. Ninety percent of every decision I make is rooted in what a business actually is: its strength, its value, its resilience, its position in the economic cycle. Technical analysis earns the remaining ten percent — confirming timing, not dictating direction. Not the other way around.

This is the opposite of how most retail investors are taught to operate. They follow chart cues first and ask fundamental questions later, if at all. They are handed a magnifying glass when what they need is a map. That single inversion — chasing signals instead of understanding substance — is precisely where most of them lose. It was where I lost, before I understood better. It is the gap this book is designed to permanently close.

That realization changed everything. It is the foundation of every page in this book.

When I began teaching, I met that same confusion in the faces of students who had paid a far higher price than I had. Many of them had lost more than money — they had lost months, years, and in some cases the livelihood they had worked a lifetime to build, chasing magic formulas that were never designed to deliver real results. They did not come to me looking for another shortcut. They were done with shortcuts. They were looking for something they could trust, repeat, and stake their financial future on. A real solution — one rooted in understanding, not hope.

Now they have it.

Over two decades of live trading — managing multi-million dollar options positions through bull markets, bear markets, volatility spikes, and every condition the market has seen fit to produce — I have stress-tested these principles with real capital, at real scale, in real conditions. Nothing in this book is borrowed from a textbook. The strategies are the ones I use. The rules are the ones I follow. The mistakes described are ones I have made, witnessed, or both.

The financial markets are the greatest wealth-building infrastructure ever created. In no other arena can a disciplined individual working from a laptop, on their own schedule, without a boss or a building, build a meaningful income stream that compounds over time. But access to that infrastructure without honest education is not an opportunity. It is a trap. Main Street has always had a seat at the table. What Main Street has never been given is the knowledge that Wall Street takes for granted.

This book is my answer to that injustice.

The existing literature on options trading fails in one of two ways: it speaks in the language of finance professionals who already know the dialect, or it is so simplified that it never reaches the depth a serious trader actually needs. Worse, the concepts worth knowing are scattered across dozens of volumes. No single resource takes a trader from first principles all the way through portfolio-level income management. I spent years writing supplements and bridging materials just to give my students a coherent foundation. I decided to stop patching and start building.

This book is what I built.

At its core is a single, honest proposition: you do not need to get rich fast. You need to stop losing, start earning consistently, and build a system that outlasts every market condition. A trader who reads this book and applies it correctly will not triple their account in a month — and I will never tell you otherwise. What they will build is something far more valuable: a repeatable income system, grounded in fundamental understanding, that compounds steadily and survives the difficult periods that every market cycle inevitably produces.

The system begins with a framework I call the Six Directions™: the understanding that every financial instrument moves within a bounded set of possibilities, and that the buyer and seller of any contract occupy fundamentally different positions within that space. From there, it progresses through the mechanics of markets, the language of options, the behavior of price, the role of technical analysis in confirming what fundamentals already suggest, and the psychology of sustaining it all consistently across months and years. It culminates in the Seller's Philosophy™ — a structured approach to income generation built around precision, patience, and process.

The path requires as little as fifteen minutes a day. What it demands is that you follow it completely.

My dream is for Main Street to seize this moment — to close the gap that has separated everyday investors from lasting financial freedom for far too long. This book will be available in English, French, and Spanish, because that breakthrough belongs to a wider world. It is the first in a series; companion editions covering Forex, Cryptocurrency, and Futures & Commodities are to follow.

I am grateful to the thousands of students who have trusted The Premium Desk with their financial education. Your questions made every chapter sharper. Watching you move from confused to confident, from losing to consistently profitable — that is the only result that matters to me.

Read this book from the beginning. Work the examples. Fill in the worksheets. Complete the checklists before you trade. And when you are ready to place your first cash-secured put on a quality stock — check the earnings calendar first.

You have found the system. Now build with it.

Eddy Alexandre, Master Trader
The Premium Desk LLC · Long Island, New York · 2026
www.thepremiumdesk.com | optionspremium.substack.com

HOW TO USE THIS BOOK

This book is built to be read in sequence — especially the first time through. Every chapter builds on what came before. A trader who jumps to income strategies in Part II without reading Part I will encounter terms whose logic they cannot fully understand. The sequence is the system. Part I gives you the complete foundation: market structure, the business cycle, options mechanics, valuation, the Greeks, fundamental analysis, technical analysis, and risk calculation — in precisely the order a professional would learn them. Only when Part I is complete does Part II make full sense.

That said, this book is also designed as a working reference. Once you have read it front to back, you will return to individual chapters repeatedly — to the Ten Indicators before evaluating a new underlying, to the Greeks dashboard when managing a position, to the Rollover Strategies chapter when a trade is approaching T-21™. Every major system and checklist in this book is designed to be self-contained enough to stand alone as a reference.

The Four Parts

PART I — FOUNDATIONS

Chapters 1–10 establish the complete operating environment for the trader using this system: the pre-trading flight check, market structure, business cycles, technical analysis, and the full options mechanics including contracts, valuation, and the Greeks. Do not skip this section. The Six-Condition Framework™ and the T-21 Rule™ are introduced here.

PART II — STRATEGY TOOLKIT

Chapters 10–15 build your strategy library: calculating risk, combining positions, spreads, ETFs, the Ten Indicators quality filter, and the complete income writer's system including the PPD Framework™ (Profit Per Day) and the Wheel. Chapter 9 is the FA headquarters of this book — the 90/10 fundamental-to-technical ratio in full depth.

PART III — MASTERY

Chapters 16–23 address mastery-level market conditions: volatility and the VIX (including skew exploitation and HV/IV gap trading), algorithmic trading, options on futures and commodity futures, swing trading, adjusted options risk, backtesting, personal strategy mastery, and rollover management. This is where the serious practitioner separates from the casual learner.

PART IV — THE COMPLETE TRADER'S EDGE

Chapters 24–29 complete the professional framework: the stair-layered approach, daily and monthly trade management metrics, long/short portfolio construction, the earnings season playbook, risk psychology, and building your first $50K portfolio. This is the capstone of the system.

Key Features Throughout

- Callout Boxes — named rules and principles you will reference repeatedly (the Snowman in Florida, the Seller's Harvest Window, the T-21 Rule, and more);

- Tables — every major concept translated into a structured reference you can use before, during, and after a trade;
- Scoring Worksheets — the Ten-Indicator Worksheet and others are designed to be filled in before every new position;
- Checklists — pre-trade, strategy selection, and exit checklists appear throughout. Use them every time, not just when you are uncertain; and
- Chapter 11: Walking You Through Your First Option Trade — a step-by-step execution walkthrough that bridges theory and live market action.

A Note on the 90/10 Principle

Throughout this book, the ratio 90% Fundamental Analysis to 10% Technical Analysis appears repeatedly. This is not decoration. It is the operating system. Wall Street professionals do not lead with charts. They lead with financials. The chart helps time the entry. The fundamentals determine whether an entry is worth taking at all. Every chapter in this book is written with that hierarchy in mind.

Complete the Appendix reference sheets as you work through each section. They are designed to be your permanent trading desk reference — not homework to be done once and forgotten.

A Note on Trade Examples

All trade examples presented throughout this book are derived from actual executed positions and are supported by brokerage records. Results reflect specific market conditions and are presented for educational purposes only. Position sizing shown in examples reflects the author's own account parameters and risk tolerance and may not be appropriate for all traders.

INTRODUCTION

Trading vs. Saving: Setting the Right Mindset

A REAL TRADE — BEFORE WE EXPLAIN ANYTHING

June 5, 2025. Micron Technology (MU) is trading at $102. The weekly chart shows a clean uptrend above the 26-week EMA, recovering strongly from the April lows. The VIX is low — implied volatility is cheap. MU has passed the Ten Indicators. This is Condition 1: bullish trend, low IV. Strategy: buy a call.

The trade: Buy 1 MU $105 Call, 38 days to expiration, at $2.20. Maximum loss: $220 — the premium paid. No margin. No assignment risk. Sized at 2% of account.

The rule: Close when the option reaches 50–80% gain on premium — $3.30 to $3.96. One exit rule. No guessing. No watching it all day.

That is the system. One condition read. One strategy. One rule. The rest of this book builds the framework that made that decision take under five minutes.

THE SYSTEM WORKING — VERIFIED BROKERAGE RECORD

Five months later, the same system. Same stock. Higher conviction.

November 17, 2025. MU has continued its AI-driven bull run. Still Condition 1. The $185 Call expiring February 20, 2026 is trading at $72.70 deep in the money. Buy 1 contract. Total cost: $7,270. Maximum loss defined. No margin. No assignment risk.

December 30, 2025 — 43 days later. MU has rallied further. The $185 Call is now worth $110.34. Sell to close. Credit received: $11,034.

Realized profit: +$3,764. Return on premium: +51.78%.

Fill date, fill price, realized profit — brokerage-confirmed. That is not a backtest. That is a live account. That is the system.

WHY THIS BOOK. WHY NOW.

Wall Street Now Sells Quant Trading to The Masses — Wall Street Journal, April 22, 2026

On April 22, 2026 — as this book was going to press — the Wall Street Journal reported that JPMorgan, Goldman Sachs, Morgan Stanley, and Citigroup are now competing to sell systematic, rules-based trading programs to retail investors and institutions. Bank trading units now manage over $850 billion in quantitative investment strategies (QIS) globally, up from $362 billion five years ago. The growth driver: fear that traditional, judgment-based investing cannot keep pace in an era of AI and algorithmic markets.

The WSJ article captured the moment with a single pull quote: "Portfolio managers and analysts get bonuses. Computers don't."

Here is what that headline means for you: the same systematic, rules-based approach that Wall Street is now packaging and selling to pension funds and family offices — at management fees and performance fees — is what this book teaches you to run yourself. The Six-Condition Framework IS the systematic rules engine. The pre-trade checklist IS the algorithm. The T-21 rule IS the automatic position management protocol.

The difference: Wall Street charges you to access it. This book gives you the framework to own it.

There is one more thing the article quietly reveals — and it exposes a contradiction worth understanding. The same banks promoting these "quant" strategies as purely mechanical also describe using AI to rapidly digest earnings calls, analyze financial reports, and adjust portfolios based on the results. That is not quant. That is fundamental analysis — just executed faster.

This book does not make that mistake. The Six-Condition Framework is systematic — it removes emotion and guesswork from every trade decision. But it is built on a foundation of fundamental quality: the Ten Indicators screen every underlying for earnings consistency, revenue growth, competitive moat, and balance sheet strength before a single option is sold. You are not a quant ignoring the business. You are a risk manager who combines the discipline of a systematic framework with the judgment of a fundamental analyst. That combination is precisely what the smartest institutional money is now trying to replicate with AI — and what this book teaches you to do with a checklist and fifteen minutes a day.

And here is what separates this book from every other options book on the market: Chapter 17 provides nine battle-tested AI prompts — one for each critical stage of your trading process, from pre-market condition read to post-trade journal analysis. The same AI-powered fundamental analysis that JPMorgan and Goldman Sachs are building into $850 billion worth of institutional programs is available to you right now, for free, using the prompts in this book. The banks need an army of engineers. You need a smartphone and the right question.

Systematic rules. Fundamental foundation. No fees.

Let's start with a question most financial advisors never want you to ask: if saving money is so smart, why are so many people still broke at retirement?

The math is brutal. If you start with $10,000 today and add $500 a month at a modest expected return, a savings plan calculator will tell you it takes over 43 years to reach $1,000,000. Forty-three years. And that's assuming you never miss a payment, never face a medical bill, never lose a job, and inflation doesn't quietly devour half of what you've built.

But what if there were a different approach? What if instead of saving $500 per month into a savings account earning approximately 4.5% APY account, you learned to generate income from the financial markets — using defined-risk strategies that professionals have used for decades? What if you could generate consistent monthly options income — and compound that alongside your savings?

This is not speculation. Options income trading — selling defined-risk premium on quality stocks — has been practiced by institutional investors, hedge funds, and pension funds for over 50 years. The strategies are not secret. The mechanics are well-understood. The edge comes from discipline, risk management, and patience — the exact qualities that most retail traders lack and that this book will build in you, chapter by chapter.

The framework in this book was built from two decades of managing real options positions through every condition the market has produced: the 2008 financial crisis, the 2020 COVID crash and recovery, the 2022 rate-driven bear market, the 2024 AI-driven bull run, and the volatility regimes in between. It was not written from a classroom. It was written from a live account — through drawdowns, recoveries, and the slow development of the discipline required to survive and compound in this market long-term.

The difference between trading and saving is not that one is risky and the other is safe. Both involve risk. Saving risks inflation erosion, opportunity cost, and the probability that your nest egg simply will not be large enough when you need it. Trading risks loss of capital — but with the framework in this book, that risk is defined, managed, and bounded before every trade is placed.

Here is what we are going to build together over 29 chapters: a complete, professional-grade system for trading options with discipline. Not a collection of tips. Not a strategy-of-the-month newsletter. A system — with rules, management protocols, psychological frameworks, and a 90-day implementation plan. By the time you finish this book and work through the exercises, you will have something most retail traders never build: a repeatable, tested, documented process for generating income from the options market.

A word about who this book is for. You do not need a finance degree. You do not need $100,000. You do not need to quit your job. You need three things: (1) enough capital to start — as little as $5,000, though $10,000-$25,000 is ideal for the strategies in this book; (2) enough time to learn — 30-60 minutes per day is sufficient once the system is in place; and (3) the willingness to follow rules even when your emotions tell you to do otherwise. If you have those three things, this book will give you everything else.

One final note before we begin. This book is structured in four parts that build on each other. Part I gives you the foundation: market structure, the business cycle, options mechanics, and the Greeks. Part II gives you the strategy toolkit: risk calculation, position building, income generation, and stock selection. Part III develops mastery: volatility, AI, trading options on futures, swing trading, backtesting, and personal strategy. Part IV completes the edge: advanced structures, portfolio management, the earnings playbook, trading psychology, and your portfolio growth roadmap. Read them in order. Do not skip to the strategy chapters before understanding the foundation — every shortcut in trading education creates a blind spot that the market will eventually exploit.

THE SAVINGS MATH	THE TRADER'S ALTERNATIVE
Starting capital: $10,000 Monthly savings: $500 Interest rate: 4.5% APY Goal: $1,000,000 Time required: **43 YEARS, 8 MONTHS**	Same starting capital: $10,000 Disciplined options income: 30%/yr Goal: $1,000,000 Time required: **A FUNDAMENTALLY DIFFERENT APPROACH**

I don't know about you, but I don't have 43 years. And I'd bet you don't either.

This is not an argument against saving. Saving is discipline, and discipline is the foundation of everything in this book. But saving alone — putting money in a bank account, a 401(k), or even an index fund and forgetting about it — is not a path to financial freedom on any timeline that matters to most people.

Trading is. Specifically, options trading — when done with the risk-first framework in this book — is one of the most capital-efficient tools available to the individual investor. It lets you generate income, hedge existing positions, and build wealth at a pace that saving simply cannot match.

Why Most Traders Fail Before They Even Start

Here's the uncomfortable truth: the majority of people who try trading lose money. Not because the markets are rigged — though the Algos and institutions do have structural advantages we'll address — but because they walk in with the wrong mindset. They come in thinking about profits. They should be thinking about risk.

The gambler asks: "How much can I make?" The risk manager asks: "How much can I lose, and can I survive it?" That single mental shift is the difference between a trader who lasts and one who blows up an account in their first six months.

- Most new traders size positions too large — one bad trade destroys months of gains;
- Most chase volatile stocks without understanding the options chain attached to them;
- Most have no defined exit strategy — they hold losers and cut winners too soon; and
- Most ignore the Greeks, the business cycle, and the cap tier — three things that determine whether a trade has any edge at all.

THE CORE PRINCIPLE

This book is built on one idea: manage risk first, and the profits will follow. Every strategy, every framework, every table and checklist in these pages exists to make you a more disciplined, more durable trader — not a luckier one.

The Psychology of the Risk Manager

Professional traders don't think about making money. They think about not losing it. That sounds counterintuitive — you're here because you want to build wealth, not protect zero. But the path to consistent profits runs directly through loss prevention. Here's why:

A 50% loss requires a 100% gain just to get back to even. Lose half your account, and you now need to double what's left before you're back where you started. This is the mathematics of survival. The risk manager understands this viscerally — every trade decision is made with this asymmetry in mind.

- Protect your principal above everything else — it is your only tool;
- Define your maximum loss before you enter any trade — not while you're in it;
- Remove emotion from your exit decisions — let your plan run, not your gut;
- Treat every win as a lesson and every loss as a more expensive lesson; and
- The market is the ultimate equal opportunity employer — it takes from the undisciplined and gives to the patient.

You are about to learn a system. Not tips, not hot picks, not a Discord alert service. A system — one grounded in how markets actually work, how institutional money actually moves, and how options actually behave across market conditions. Work the system, and the system works for you.

THE FOUNDATION

The Six-Condition Philosophy™

Everything an options trader needs to know about market direction

---

Before you read a single chapter of this book, you need to understand one foundational truth about markets. Not a strategy. Not a Greek. Not a formula. A truth.

The market — any market, any stock, any index, any ETF — can only go one of six ways. That is not an oversimplification. That is the complete reality. Every option strategy ever invented, every position ever opened, every trade ever executed is a response to one of these six conditions. All of them. Without exception.

Direction has three states: the market is going up, going down, or going sideways. Volatility has two states: it is high or it is low. Three directions times two volatility states equals six possible market conditions. That is the entire decision tree for an options trader.

THE MARKET GOES ONE OF SIX WAYS.

You have one response for each. That is the complete system.

#	DIRECTION	VOLATILITY (VIX / IV)	YOUR STRATEGY	YOUR LOGIC
1	UP SLOW ↑ (Bullish)	LOW	Long Call | Bull Call Spread	IV is cheap — buy premium. Calls cost less when volatility is suppressed. The trend is your ally. Pay for upside participation at a low cost basis.
2	UP FAST ↑ (Bullish)	HIGH	Covered Call | Cash-Secured Put | Bull Put Spread	IV is expensive — sell premium in the direction of the trend. Collect elevated credit on bullish structures. The trend increases probability of profit. Theta works for you.
3	DOWN SLOW ↓ (Bearish)	LOW	Long Put | Bear Put Spread	IV is cheap — buy premium on the downside. Puts are affordable. A bear put spread reduces cost while capturing the decline. Do not sell premium into a falling market.
4	DOWN FAST ↓ (Bearish)	HIGH	**Bear Call Spread ONLY (credit spread — call side)**	IV is expensive — sell premium, but on the CALL side only. This is the critical rule: you do not buy puts (IV crush will destroy them). You sell calls. The spread caps your risk. This is the only approved structure for this condition.
5	SIDEWAYS SLOW ↔ (Range Bound)	LOW	Butterfly Spread | Iron Condor	No directional move expected + cheap options = structured range trades. The butterfly concentrates payoff at a target price. The iron condor collects from both

#	DIRECTION	VOLATILITY (VIX / IV)	YOUR STRATEGY	YOUR LOGIC
				sides of the range. Theta is your income source.
6	SIDEWAYS FAST ↔ (Range Bound)	HIGH	ATM Calendar Spread | Diagonal Spread	Elevated IV + no direction = harvest the time decay differential between expirations. Sell expensive near-term IV. Buy relatively cheaper longer-dated IV. The spread earns from the IV differential collapsing over time.

That table is the foundation of everything that follows.

Every chapter that follows — the Greeks, the spreads, the Wheel, the rollover rules, the backtesting framework, the portfolio management tools — all of it exists to help you do one thing: identify which of these six conditions you are in, and execute the correct strategy for that condition with precision.

Not the interesting strategy. Not the complex strategy. Not the strategy you saw on YouTube. The correct one.

The VIX tells you whether volatility is high or low. The chart tells you whether price is going up, down, or sideways. Two data points. Six possible combinations. One decision per combination. That is the system.

Everything else — sentiment indicators, analyst ratings, CNBC headlines, Discord alerts, complex multi-leg exotics — is noise layered on top of a decision that was already made the moment you read the VIX and looked at the chart. The six conditions are not a simplification of the market. They are the market. All other complexity is decoration.

How to use this table every trading day:

Step 1 → Check the VIX.

Step 2 → Look at the chart: up, down, or sideways?

Step 3 → Find your row. Execute that strategy.

Step 4 → Ignore everything that is not in that row.

What this philosophy eliminates:

X Strategy confusion — one condition, one response.

X Overtrading — only trade when condition is clear.

X Emotional decisions — the condition decides, not you.

X Complexity for its own sake — six rows is all you need.

A NOTE ON LANGUAGE

Throughout this introduction we have used plain-language labels: Up Fast, Up Slow, Down Fast, Down Slow, Sideways Fast, Sideways Slow. These are intentional. When you are new to options, the word 'volatility' carries baggage. Fast and slow are things you already understand.

As you move deeper into the book — particularly Chapter 5 (The Greeks) and Chapter 16 (Volatility: The Hidden Driver) — you will learn the professional term: Implied Volatility, or IV. High IV means the market expects fast movement. Low IV means it expects slow. The concept is identical to what you have already learned here. The language just gets more precise.

FAST / SLOW = IMPLIED VOLATILITY

Fast = High IV. The market expects large moves. Options are expensive.

Slow = Low IV. The market expects small moves. Options are cheap.

You will use this every time you trade. When you hear 'check the VIX', that is checking whether the market is in Fast or Slow mode.

Condition	Direction / IV State	Primary Strategy	Min Account
C1	Bullish / Low IV	Long Call · Debit Spread	$2,000
C2	Bullish / High IV	Cash-Secured Put · Wheel	$15,000
C3	Bearish / Low IV	Long Put · Bear Put Spread	$2,000
C4	Bearish / High IV	Bear Call Spread	$5,000
C5	Range-Bound / High IV	Iron Condor	$10,000
C6	Range-Bound / Low IV	Calendar Spread · Diagonal	$5,000

Figure 0.1 — Six-Condition Strategy Map — Minimum account size required per strategy across all six market conditions.

The Six-Condition Account Map — your daily decision framework before every trade.

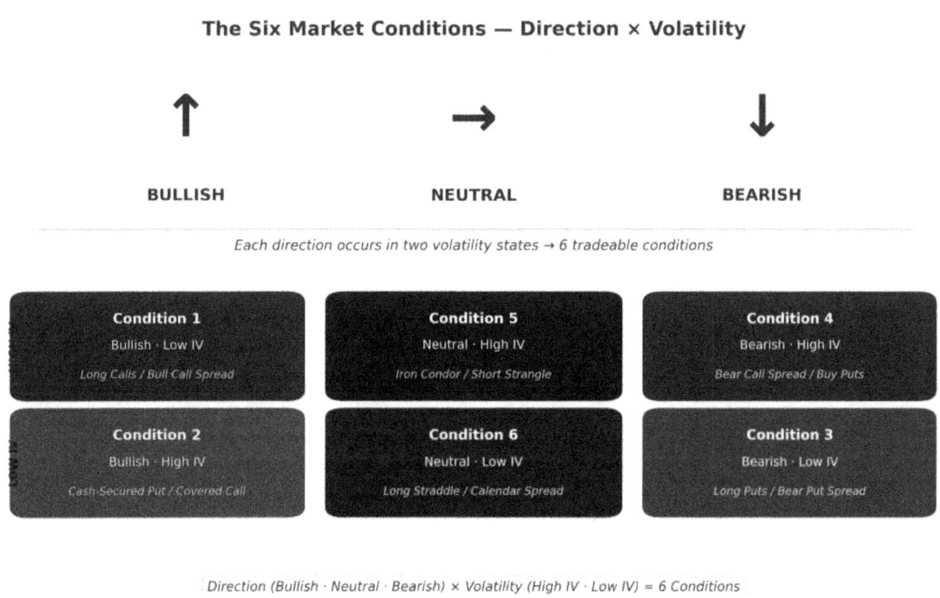

Figure 0.2 — The Six Market Conditions. Direction (Bullish, Neutral, Bearish) × Volatility (High IV, Low IV) = the six conditions that define every trade decision in this book.

Come back to this table every time the market confuses you.

The answer is always in one of six rows.

PART I

THE FOUNDATION OF EVERY TRADEChapters 1–10 establish the complete operating environment: account setup, the Six-Condition framework, options contracts, valuation, the Greeks, market structure, technical analysis, and risk calculation. Every strategy in Parts II through IV assumes mastery of Part I.

THE FOUNDATION OF EVERY TRADE

The condition is the strategy. Every trade begins with a condition read.

THE SIX CONDITIONS — YOUR TRADING MAP (PREVIEW)

Before any strategy in this book, you need one foundational framework: the Six-Condition System. Every market presents itself in one of six states, defined by two inputs — price direction and volatility level. Condition 1: Bullish + Low IV — buy calls or debit spreads. Condition 2: Bullish + High IV — sell puts (CSP), run the Wheel. Condition 3: Bearish + Low IV — buy puts or debit spreads. Condition 4: Bearish + High IV — sell calls or use bear call spreads. Condition 5: Range-bound + High IV — iron condor or short strangle. Condition 6: Range-bound + Low IV — calendar or diagonal spreads. Every chapter teaches you to identify your condition and execute the correct strategy. You do not need to know the strategies yet — just know this map exists.

6-CONDITION FRAMEWORK ▸ ALL SIX CONDITIONS — universal pre-trade filter

The flight check runs before every trade, in every condition. It is the discipline that prevents you from trading the wrong condition, the wrong underlying, or the wrong structure.

No pilot takes off without running through a checklist. It doesn't matter if they've flown the same route a thousand times — the checklist runs every single flight. Not because pilots are incompetent. Because the stakes of skipping it are catastrophic and irreversible.

Pre-Trading Flight Check

1. Account Funded & Margin Set
Cash or margin account verified, buying power confirmed

2. Platform Configured
Charts, option chains, Greeks columns visible

3. Watchlist Built
Stocks screened by cap tier, sector, liquidity

4. Market Condition Assessed
VIX level, trend direction, sector rotation phase

5. Strategy Selected
CSP/CC/Spread/Iron Condor matched to conditions

6. Position Sized
Max 5% of account per trade, max risk calculated

7. Entry Criteria Met
IVR ≥ 30, Delta target, DTE 30-45 days

8. Exit Plan Defined
50% profit target, stop-loss, T-21 management

9. Journal Ready
Trade log open, entry documented before execution

10. Execute
Place the trade — no hesitation, no deviation

Figure 1.1 — The Pre-Trade Flight Check. Every item must be confirmed before submitting an order.

Trading is no different. Before you place your first options trade — before you even open a brokerage account — there is a flight check that every serious trader must complete. This chapter is that checklist. Skip it and you are taking off blind.

You have already seen the six-condition philosophy that anchors this entire book. Before every flight, the pilot checks the weather — direction and intensity. Before every trade, you check the market — direction and volatility. Two inputs. Six conditions. One strategy per condition. Every pre-trade check in this chapter is designed to bring you to that moment of clarity: which of the six conditions am I in right now?

Step 1: Protect Your Principal

Your trading capital is not play money. It is not casino chips. It is the raw material of every trade you will ever make, and without it, you cannot trade at all. Protecting your principal is not a defensive posture — it is the first offensive move of a risk manager.

The first rule before any trade: never risk money you cannot afford to lose completely. This is not legal boilerplate. It is the foundational operating principle of every professional trader. Options positions can go to zero. Understand this before you fund an account.

- Start with capital you have designated exclusively for trading — not rent money, not emergency funds;
- Determine your maximum account drawdown threshold before you start — most professionals use 20-25%;
- If your account drops to that threshold, stop trading, review, and reassess — do not chase losses; and
- Never add to a losing position in hopes of averaging down — this is how small losses become catastrophic ones.

RISK MANAGER'S FIRST LAW

The goal of every trading session is first to preserve capital, second to grow it. A trader who survives a bad month can recover. A trader who blows up an account has nothing left to trade with.

Step 2: Account Setup & Options Permissions

Not all brokerage accounts are created equal when it comes to options. Before you can trade options, your broker requires you to apply for options trading approval — and they tier that approval based on your stated experience, income, and risk tolerance. Understanding these levels is essential, because the level you're approved for determines which strategies in this book you can actually execute.

There are five permission levels. Level 0 is automatic — every new account starts here. You must apply and qualify for each subsequent level:

Level	Permission	Strategies Permitted	Who It's For
Level 0	No Permissions (Automatic)	No options trading — stocks only	Every new account by default
Level 1	Seller — Cash Secured	Selling Cash-Secured Puts & Covered Calls	Income-focused beginners — this is where most of this book lives

Level	Permission	Strategies Permitted	Who It's For
Level 2	Level 1 + Buying Options	Buying calls and puts in addition to Level 1	Directional traders comfortable with defined risk
Level 3	Debit and Credit Spreads in addition to Level 2	Debit and Credit Spreads	Intermediate traders — spreads cap both risk and reward
Level 4	Level 3 + Advanced	All strategies including complex multi-leg structures	Experienced traders — full toolkit, highest margin requirements

THE MOST IMPORTANT LEVEL: LEVEL 1

The majority of this book's income strategies — Selling Cash-Secured Puts and Covered Calls — require only Level 1 approval. A $5,000–$10,000 account at Level 1 is enough to start building systematic income. The goal is not to get the highest level as fast as possible. The goal is to master the strategies at your current level before adding complexity.

- Apply honestly — overstating experience to get a higher level exposes you to strategies you are not ready for;
- Level 4 (naked/uncovered) carries theoretically unlimited loss potential — do not go there before you understand spreads cold;
- Your broker's options application will ask about income, net worth, investment objectives, and trading experience — answer accurately; and
- Margin requirements: Level 3 and Level 4 strategies typically require a margin account — understand how margin amplifies both gains and losses.

2026 REGULATORY UPDATE

On April 14, 2026, the Securities and Exchange Commission (SEC) approved the elimination of the Pattern Day Trader (PDT) rule — a regulation that had restricted retail traders since 2001

Under the old framework, any margin account under $25,000 was limited to three round-trip trades in a rolling five-business-day window.

This applied to options as well: opening and closing the same options position on the same day counted as a day trade.

Traders who exceeded the limit without meeting the $25,000 threshold faced a 90-day account freeze.

That designation no longer exists in law.

The SEC has replaced the PDT rule with a risk-based intraday margin model that assesses actual position exposure in real time, rather than simply counting trades.

Step 3: Rewire Your Brain Before Your First Trade

This is the step most books skip. They go straight to contracts and Greeks and leave you with a technically correct framework sitting on top of a psychologically broken operating system. We're doing it differently.

Your brain is not wired for trading. It was built by evolution to avoid loss more than it pursues gain — a phenomenon behavioral economists call loss aversion. This means your emotional response to a $500 loss is roughly twice as powerful as your response to a $500 gain. Left unmanaged, this will cause you to:

- Hold losing positions far too long — hoping they'll come back;
- Cut winning positions too early — grabbing profits before they materialize fully;
- Trade impulsively after a loss — trying to "make it back" immediately;
- Freeze on entries — paralyzed by analysis after a painful trade; and
- Size up after wins and size down after losses — exactly backwards from what the math requires.

None of this is weakness. It is biology. The risk manager's job is to build a system that overrides these impulses with rules — rules that were written when you were calm, rational, and thinking clearly, to govern your behavior when you are not.

THE 10 DO'S & DON'TS

1. Focus on managing risk
2. Don't avoid losses — manage them.
3. Trade with discipline.
4. Don't try to remove emotions — learn to manage them.
5. Always have a plan.
6. Be patient.
7. Avoid analysis paralysis.
8. Own your results.
9. Never stop learning.
10. Do love the game.

Step 4a: Define Your Trading Plan Before You Trade

A trading plan is not a wish list. It is a written document — your personal operating manual — that defines exactly how you will behave in every market condition. Before you place your first trade, your plan must answer the following:

- What is my maximum risk per trade? (Recommended: no more than 2-5% of account per position);
- What is my profit target? When do I take gains off the table?;
- What is my stop-loss rule? At what point do I exit regardless of my conviction?;
- What strategies am I approved and trained to use? (Start narrow — master two strategies before adding a third);
- What market conditions will I NOT trade in? (e.g., the day before major Fed announcements, during earnings blackout periods); and
- How many positions will I hold at one time? Concentration risk is real — too many open trades dilutes your attention.

Your plan evolves as you gain experience. But you must have one from day one. Markets don't care who you are or what you stand for — all they want is the money of the undisciplined. The plan is your shield.

Step 4b: The 2% Rule — Your Position Sizing Foundation

Before you place a single trade, you need a hard rule for how much of your account you will risk on any one position. Most professionals use the 2% Rule: never risk more than 2% of your total account equity on a single trade. If you are a beginner, start at 1% until you have tripled your trading equity.

This is not arbitrary. Consider what happens over 10 consecutive losing trades — the worst losing streak most traders will ever experience — at 2% risk vs. 5% risk:

Trade #	Account Balance	2% Risk Per Trade	5% Risk Per Trade
Start	**$1,000.00**	**$1,000.00**	**$1,000.00**
Trade 3	—	$960.40	$902.50
Trade 5	—	$941.19	$857.38
Trade 10	—	$833.79	$630.25

After 10 losing trades, the 2% trader has lost 17% of their account. The 5% trader has lost 37%. The 2% trader survives and recovers. The math compounds in both directions — protecting you in the drawdown is as important as growing in the upside.

POSITION SIZE FORMULA

Position Size = Risk Amount ÷ (Entry Price − Stop-Loss Price) | Example: $10,000 account, 2% risk = $200. Buy stock at $50 with stop at $47. Position size = $200 ÷ $3 = 66 shares. This formula applies to stocks and the underlying leg of any options position.

Step 4c: The 20% Drawdown Rule — When to Stop Trading

Every professional trader has a personal drawdown limit — a point at which they stop trading for the month, step back, and review. The recommended threshold is 20%: if your account has dropped 20% from its peak balance, stop trading for the rest of the month.

This rule exists because drawdowns are psychologically dangerous. When you are losing, the temptation to overtrade, increase size, and chase losses is at its highest — and that is exactly when your judgment is at its most compromised. The 20% rule forces a circuit breaker.

- When you hit your 20% threshold: stop trading, do not place new positions;
- Review every losing trade: was it strategy failure, execution failure, or bad luck? Be honest;
- When you return after a reset: reduce your risk exposure by 25% (from 2% to 1.5%) until your account recovers its previous high; and
- Never restore full risk exposure until the account has returned to its prior peak — this forces accountability.

AVOIDING A MARGIN CALL

A margin call happens when your account equity drops below the minimum required by your broker. At 10x leverage, losing 10% triggers a call. At 5x leverage, losing 20% triggers a call. With a $1,000 account at 100:1 leverage, a 1% loss wipes you out. The safest rule: understand exactly how much leverage you are using before any position is opened. When in doubt, use less.

Step 5: Know Your Tools

The options trader's workstation is not just a brokerage account. You need real-time data, charting capability, and the ability to analyze options chains before you pull the trigger on any trade. At minimum, you need:

- A brokerage platform with live options chain data — ThinkOrSwim (TD Ameritrade/Schwab) is the gold standard for active options traders; it's free and built for what we do;
- Real-time charting — TradingView is an excellent browser-based alternative; StockCharts.com provides strong technical analysis tools;
- Access to fundamental data — SEC EDGAR (sec.gov/edgar) provides free access to all 10-K and 10-Q filings for every publicly traded company;
- Implied volatility tracking — your platform should show IV rank and IV percentile for every underlying you trade; and
- A trade journal — a simple spreadsheet where you log every trade: entry, exit, thesis, outcome, lesson learned.

You do not need expensive subscriptions to start. You need real-time data, a reliable platform, and the discipline to use both correctly. The edge is not in the tools — it's in the trader.

Step 6: Apply the Six-Condition Framework Before Every Flight

The final step of your pre-trading flight check is the most important: before you open any position, you must identify which of the six market conditions is currently active. This is not optional. It is not something you do when you are unsure. It is the step that turns a trade idea into a risk-managed decision.

The six-condition framework — the proprietary framework at the heart of this book — tells you that the market can only do one of six things. Three directions (bullish, bearish, range-bound) times two volatility states (high IV, low IV) equals six conditions. One condition is always active. Your job before every trade is to identify which one.

The Six-Condition Check

#	What to Check	What You Are Reading	Your Decision
1	Check the VIX level and IVR on your platform	VIX < 20 and IVR < 25 = LOW volatility. VIX > 20 and IVR > 50 = HIGH volatility. Between 20–25, use IVR to decide.	HIGH = you are approved for credit strategies (conditions 2, 4, 6). LOW = you are approved for debit strategies (conditions 1, 3, 5).
2	Look at the SPY or QQQ daily chart	Is price making higher highs and higher lows above the 50MA and 200MA? Lower highs and lower lows below? Or	UP = conditions 1 or 2. DOWN = conditions 3 or 4. SIDEWAYS = conditions 5 or 6.

#	What to Check	What You Are Reading	Your Decision
		oscillating between defined support and resistance?	
3	Cross-reference your two readings	Combine direction and volatility to identify the exact condition number.	VIX low + up = Condition 1. VIX high + up = Condition 2. VIX low + down = Condition 3. VIX high + down = Condition 4. VIX low + range = Condition 5. VIX high + range = Condition 6.
4	Look up your condition in the Six-Condition Table	The Foundation section of this book contains the complete table. Appendix A contains the 90-Day Trader Development Roadmap and framework reference tools.	Read the approved strategy for your condition. This is the only strategy you should open today. Ignore all other ideas.
5	Run your pre-trade checklist for the chosen strategy	Ten Indicators, earnings check, adjusted options check, position sizing, open interest confirmation — all the steps above.	All five steps complete = you are cleared for takeoff. Any step failing = no trade today. Wait for a clear condition.

The six-condition pre-trade check adds approximately two minutes to your morning routine. Two minutes that eliminate strategy confusion, prevent wrong-environment trades, and ensure that every position you open has the market structure working in its favor — not against it.

THE PILOT'S PROMISE

Every pilot who walks away from their career with a perfect safety record made the same commitment: the checklist runs on every flight. No exceptions. No shortcuts. No overrides because they 'feel good about this one.' The options trader who lasts ten, twenty, thirty years makes the same commitment — the six-condition check runs before every trade. Not most trades. Every trade.

Choosing Your Brokerage: The Options Trader's Platform Checklist

Your broker is the infrastructure your entire trading system runs on. A poor choice here costs you in hidden ways: slow fills, restricted options levels, inadequate tools, and support that disappears when you need it most. Before you open an account, evaluate every candidate against these five non-negotiable criteria.

Criteria	What to Look For	Red Flags
Options Approval Levels	Must offer Level 3 or higher (required for spreads, straddles, and multi-leg positions). Level 4 for naked positions. Apply for the highest level your experience supports.	Broker that caps you at Level 1 (covered calls only) without a path to upgrade. You cannot execute the six-condition system with Level 1 access.
Commission Structure	$0–$0.65 per contract for options. No ticket charges. No per-leg surcharges on multi-leg orders. Compare total cost on a 4-leg iron condor, not just headline rate.	Brokers charging $1.50+ per contract will erode your edge on income strategies. A CSP paying $1.20 premium with $0.65 entry and $0.65 exit leaves only $0.10 of real profit after commissions.
Platform & Tools	Real-time Greeks display on all positions. IV Rank and IVR visible on option chain. P&L graph for multi-leg positions. Mobile app with	Platform that shows only intrinsic value, no Greeks. No paper trading mode. Greeks that update only on refresh, not in real time.

Criteria	What to Look For	Red Flags
	full options functionality. Paper trading mode.	
Execution Quality	PFOF (Payment for Order Flow) disclosure and fill quality reports available. Ability to set limit orders on multi-leg spreads as a single order. Mobile and desktop fills within 1–2 seconds on liquid underlyings.	Broker that routes all flow to a single market maker. Frequent partial fills on spreads. Market orders as the only option on mobile.
Margin & Buying Power	Cash-secured put buying power reserved correctly (full strike × 100 per contract). Margin accounts available for Level 3+. Portfolio margin available for professional accounts.	Brokers that miscalculate buying power on spreads, causing positions to appear to violate risk limits incorrectly — triggering forced liquidation.

Broker Comparison: Options-Specific Features

Broker	Cost/Contract	Best For	Key Feature for Options Traders
TastyTrade	$1.00/leg ($10 max/leg)	Active options traders	Built specifically for options. Best Greeks display, probability cone, IV rank, and position management tools available. The Premium Desk's primary recommended platform.
ThinkorSwim (TD/Schwab)	$0.65/contract	Education + advanced charting	The most powerful charting and backtesting platform available to retail traders. Paper trading mode is the best simulator. Excellent for condition reads and technical analysis.
Interactive Brokers	$0.25–$0.65/contract	High volume, multi-leg	Lowest commissions at scale. Sophisticated order routing. Preferred by traders doing 20+ contracts per trade. IBKR Pro required for full options toolkit.
E*Trade (Power E*Trade)	$0.65/contract	Beginners to intermediate	Clean mobile app, strong options chain display, good customer service. Options education resources built in. Solid choice for first-year traders.
Webull	$0 commissions	Mobile-first beginners	Commission-free but limited options tools. Acceptable for learning basic chain reading. Not recommended for multi-leg strategies.

The most popular platforms among options traders at all levels — from beginner to professional — are TastyTrade (purpose-built for options, lowest commissions, excellent Greeks display), thinkorswim by TD Ameritrade (best charting and analysis tools, complex multi-leg orders), Interactive Brokers (best for margin rates and international access, steeper learning curve), Schwab (best for beginners, strong customer support, recently absorbed TD Ameritrade infrastructure), and E*TRADE (now part of Morgan Stanley; excellent options analytics, Power E*TRADE platform features real-time Greeks, strategy P&L modeling, and a strong mobile interface; well-suited for traders who want institutional research alongside active options trading).

Start with one platform. Learn it completely. The six-condition system runs on discipline and process, not on switching platforms. Once you have executed 50 or more paper trades and 20 or more live trades on one platform, you will know whether its tools serve your system or limit it.

PAPER TRADE FIRST — NON-NEGOTIABLE

Every platform listed above offers paper trading. Use it for a minimum of 90 days before committing real capital. Not because the markets are too hard — but because you need 90 days of condition reads, entry executions, position management, and exits to build the muscle memory that keeps your discipline intact when real money is on the line. The six-condition system executed on paper for 90 days is worth more than any course, signal service, or hot-tip Discord server in existence.

Portfolio Margin: Reduced Requirements for Advanced Accounts

Portfolio Margin is a margin calculation methodology available to qualified options traders that replaces the traditional Regulation-T (Reg-T) fixed-percentage requirements with a risk-based system. Under Portfolio Margin, your margin requirement is determined by evaluating your actual position risk across 10 equally-spaced price intervals within a predetermined stress range — and setting the requirement equal to the worst-case loss among those scenarios. The result: margin requirements that reflect the real risk of your position rather than arbitrary percentages.

Portfolio Margin became available to eligible retail accounts on April 2, 2007. To qualify, you generally need a minimum account value of $100,000 (with a real-time margining system) or $150,000 otherwise. Individual brokers may impose higher minimums. Approval for naked options trading (Level 4) is also required. Your broker can elect not to offer Portfolio Margin even if you qualify — it is an optional program, not a right.

PORTFOLIO MARGIN STRESS RANGES

The CBOE supplies the stress-test ranges daily. As of the current rules:

- +/−15%: Individual stocks, stock options, stock futures, narrow-based index options.
- +/−10%: Broad-based indices that are NOT high capitalization.
- +6%/−8%: High-capitalization broad-based indices (S&P 500, Nasdaq 100, etc.)
- Minimum requirement: $37.50 per contract regardless of calculation result.

This means a naked SPX put is stress-tested against an 8% downward move — significantly less than the standard customer naked margin requirement. Properly hedged positions benefit dramatically.

The practical impact of Portfolio Margin depends on your strategy. Positions where risk is clearly defined by the structure — protected positions, spreads with defined maximum loss — see the greatest reductions. Strategies where risk appears theoretically large but is actually bounded by market reality (like reverse calendar spreads) also benefit significantly. The table below summarizes the margin reduction impact by strategy type:

Reduction Level	Strategies	Why
Most Reduced	Protective put, collar, short calendar (buying near-term, selling longer-term)	Risk is limited — the long option or stock holding is credited. Portfolio margin recognizes the hedge and reduces requirement dramatically.
Potentially Large Reduction	Long strangle, long straddle (especially long-term)	System assumes large price movement possible — long options appear to have low risk

Reduction Level	Strategies	Why
		in stress scenarios, benefiting buyers.
Reasonably Sized Reduction	Covered call, short long-term strangle, index condor, naked index option, short index strangle	Defined or bounded risk recognized. Covered call: only 15% stock decline stressed vs. 50% under Reg-T.
Smallest Reduction	Vertical spreads, long calendars, synthetic long stock	Defined-risk structures already have relatively low Reg-T requirements — less room to improve.

A practical example: Suppose you are considering a covered call on IBM at $106, selling the July 110 call at $1.50. Under standard Reg-T margin, the requirement is 50% of the stock price ($53) minus the premium received ($1.50) = $51.50 per share, or $5,150 per 100 shares. Under Portfolio Margin, the requirement drops to 15% of stock price ($15.90) minus the premium ($1.50) = $14.40 per share — just $1,440 per 100 shares. The same covered call now requires 72% less capital, making covered writing on margin a far more capital-efficient strategy.

PORTFOLIO MARGIN — THE SELLER'S PHILOSOPHY CONNECTION

Portfolio Margin is the capital efficiency layer of the Seller's Philosophy. As you scale your income operation across all six conditions simultaneously — running CSPs, covered calls, iron condors, and calendars in parallel — Portfolio Margin allows you to do so with significantly less capital reserved per position. The leverage is not increased by taking more risk. It is freed by the system correctly recognizing that your hedged, defined-risk book is not as dangerous as position-by-position Reg-T calculation implies. Use the freed capital to add positions — not to increase position size beyond your 2% rule.

Important note: Portfolio Margin gives you more leverage. Leverage is not inherently good or bad — it is a tool. The risk is not in the leverage itself but in how it is used. You can always allocate more than the minimum margin requirement to any position, thereby voluntarily reducing your leverage to whatever level your risk system requires. The 2% Rule applies regardless of how much margin Portfolio Margin frees up. A freed-up $5,000 in buying power is not a signal to increase position size — it is capital available for the next qualifying setup.

To explore Portfolio Margin calculations, the OCC offers a portfolio margin calculator at https://cpm.theocc.com/tims_online.htm. The CBOE maintains additional reference materials and worked examples at https://cboe.com/margin.

The Risk Management Hierarchy: What to Protect and In What Order

When things go wrong — and they will — you need to know what to protect first. Most traders instinctively protect their profits. Professionals protect in a specific order, and that order determines whether they survive the bad periods.

Priority	Protect	How	Why This Comes First
1	**Your Capital**	2% rule per trade. 6% max portfolio risk at any time. Circuit breakers.	Without capital, you cannot trade. Everything else is irrelevant if the account is blown.
2	**Your Discipline**	Trade journal. Sunday review. Morning routine. Circuit breakers.	Without discipline, capital erodes slowly but inevitably. A $100K account with no discipline becomes a $50K account within 12 months.
3	**Your System**	Backtesting. Paper trading. Monthly scorecard. Rule compliance tracking.	Without a tested system, discipline has nothing to execute. You need both the plan and the will to follow it.
4	**Your Psychology**	Behavioral journal. 90-day protocol. Emotional circuit breakers.	Without psychological resilience, system discipline breaks under pressure. This is why most traders fail in year 2, not year 1.
5	**Your Profits**	50% profit targets. PPD (Profit Per Day) tracking. Compound reinvestment rules.	Profits come last — not because they are unimportant, but because they are the natural result of protecting everything above them. Chase profits directly and you lose everything else.

Read the hierarchy from bottom to top and you see how most retail traders think: they focus on profits first, psychology never, and wonder why they cannot make the strategies work. Read it from top to bottom and you see how this book is structured: capital protection, discipline building, system development, psychological resilience, and then — as a consequence of everything else — consistent profits.

THE HIERARCHY IN ONE SENTENCE

Protect your capital so you can build discipline, which allows your system to function, which develops your psychology, which generates your profits. Skip any step and the chain breaks. This is not a philosophy — it is the operating system of every professional trader who has survived more than five years.

IMPORTANT: BINARY OPTIONS ARE NOT TRADITIONAL OPTIONS

Before we begin: you may have seen ads for "binary options." These are not the instruments taught in this book. Binary options are fixed-payout yes/no wagers with no Greeks, no intrinsic/extrinsic value, and no secondary market. The SEC and CFTC have issued formal investor warnings about binary options fraud. This book teaches only standard listed options traded on regulated U.S. exchanges. A full explanation is in the Warning section at the end of this chapter.

6-CONDITION FRAMEWORK ▸ INSTRUMENTS for all six conditions

Calls and puts are the two raw materials. Every strategy in all six conditions — from a long call in condition 1 to a calendar spread in condition 6 — is built from these two instruments in different configurations.

An options contract is a legally binding agreement between two parties. One party buys a right. The other party takes on an obligation. That asymmetry — rights on one side, obligations on the other — is the fundamental architecture of every options trade you will ever make. Before you understand strategies, Greeks, or market cycles, you must understand this.

This chapter lays the complete foundation: what options are, how they're structured, how they're identified, when they expire, and exactly what you are agreeing to when you buy or sell one.

KNOW YOUR OPPONENT

Options trading is an adversarial process — a fight if you will. In other words, whoever is on the other side of your trade has one goal in mind: to take your money. Whether you realize it or not, you have the same goal. You don't have their best interest in mind either. The market is not your friend. It is a sophisticated opponent populated by hedge funds, algorithmic systems, and institutional desks trading with information advantages you do not have. Your edge is discipline, system, and risk management — not luck.

A Brief History of Options Trading

Options have existed for centuries. The first recorded use dates to ancient Greece, where Thales of Miletus purchased rights to use olive presses before the harvest season. In 17th-century Holland, options on tulip bulbs traded during the famous Tulip Mania of 1636-1637.

Modern listed options began on April 26, 1973, when the CBOE opened as the first organized exchange for standardized contracts. On that first day, 911 contracts traded on 16 stocks. That same year, Fischer Black and Myron Scholes published their landmark pricing model. Today, the OCC clears more than 60 million contracts per day as of 2025 — a sixth consecutive annual volume record, with volume having tripled since 2019. On April 4, 2025, a single trading day saw over 100 million contracts change hands for the first time in history. Commission-free trading and real-time data have placed institutional-grade tools in every trader's hands — which is precisely why a systematic framework for using them matters more than ever.

The Four Building Blocks — Everything Starts Here

Before strategies, spreads, or combinations — there are only four fundamental options actions. Every trade in this book, from the simplest cash-secured put to the most complex diagonal spread, is built from some combination of these four:

Action #1	Action #2	Action #3	Action #4
BUY CALLS when stock to go UP — Bullish	BUY PUTS when stock to go DOWN — Bearish	SELL PUTS when stock sideways or UP — Bullish income	SELL CALLS when stock sideways or DOWN — Bearish income

WHY ONLY FOUR?

There are only two types of options (calls and puts) and you can either buy or sell each one — that gives you exactly four possible actions. Every strategy you will ever learn is a combination of two or more of these four. Master the four building blocks and every multi-leg strategy becomes immediately readable.

Listed Options vs. OTC Options

There are two categories of options in the market. The first — and the only kind we trade in this book — are listed options: standardized contracts that trade on regulated U.S. exchanges. There are 17 options exchanges in the United States, all connected through the Options Clearing Corporation (OCC), which acts as the central counterparty guaranteeing every contract.

The second category is over-the-counter (OTC) options — privately negotiated agreements between two parties, off-exchange. OTC options are used by institutions and are not available to retail traders through standard brokerage accounts. Swaps are a common form of OTC derivative — bilateral agreements to exchange cash flows based on a notional amount, such as interest rate swaps or currency swaps, settled privately between institutions without exchange oversight. When OTC instruments malfunction — as happened in 2008 — the lack of centralized clearing means losses cascade without limit. This is why we stay in the listed, standardized, OCC-cleared world.

WHY LISTED OPTIONS ONLY

Listed options are standardized — every contract represents 100 shares, has a defined expiration, and trades on a regulated exchange. The OCC guarantees every trade. This structure gives you the ability to enter, manage, and exit positions at published, transparent prices. OTC derivatives offer none of these protections.

The Two Types of Options Contracts

Every options contract is either a Call or a Put. These are the only two instruments. Everything else — spreads, collars, iron condors, diagonals — is a combination of calls and puts. Master the individual contract first.

Type	What It Gives the Buyer	What It Obligates the Seller	Market Outlook
CALL	The RIGHT to BUY 100 shares at the strike price, on or before expiration	The OBLIGATION to SELL 100 shares at the strike price if assigned	Bullish — buyer profits when price rises
PUT	The RIGHT to SELL 100 shares at the strike price, on or before expiration	The OBLIGATION to BUY 100 shares at the strike price if assigned	Bearish — buyer profits when price falls

Note: You can also use options to limit your total portfolio risk — to protect an existing stock position, to hedge a sector exposure, or to generate income against shares you already own. Options are not just speculative instruments. In the hands of a risk manager, they are the most precise hedging tools in the market.

Contract Mechanics: What's Inside Every Options Contract

Every listed options contract contains five standardized components. Know all five before you read a single options chain:

Component	Definition	Example (AAPL $185 Call, 30 DTE)	Why It Matters
Underlying	The stock or ETF the option is based on.	AAPL (Apple Inc.)	Determines liquidity, IV level, and risk profile.
Strike Price	The price at which you have the right to buy/sell.	$185	Defines your breakeven and max profit/loss.
Expiration	The date the contract ceases to exist.	30 days from today.	Controls theta decay rate and gamma risk.
Type	Call (right to buy) or Put (right to sell).	Call.	Determines directional exposure.
Premium	The price you pay or receive.	$4.20 / $420 per contract.	Your max risk (buyer) or max reward (seller).

Figure 4.1 — Options Contract Anatomy. The five components of every listed options contract.

- Underlying Asset — The stock, ETF, or index the option is based on. The option's price is derived from the underlying's price movement;
- Strike Price — The agreed-upon price at which the underlying can be bought (call) or sold (put). The relationship between the strike price and the current stock price determines the option's moneyness — a concept covered in detail in Chapter 2;
- Expiration Date — The date on which the option contract expires. After this date, the option is worthless if not exercised. Options lose value as expiration approaches — this is the time decay (theta) that sellers rely on;
- Contract Size — Every standard listed options contract represents exactly 100 shares of the underlying. When you see a premium quoted at $3.50, the actual cost of one contract is $3.50 × 100 = $350; and

- Premium — The price of the option itself. The buyer pays the premium to the seller. The seller keeps the premium regardless of outcome — their obligation is what they sold in exchange for it.

Reading the Options Symbol

Every listed options contract has a standardized symbol that encodes all five components. Once you can read the symbol, you can instantly identify any contract on any chain. The format is:

Underlying	Year	Month	Day	C or P	Strike Price
GOOGL	**25**	**01**	**17**	**C**	**00123000**
Alphabet Inc.	2025	January	17th	Call	$123.00 Strike

So GOOGL251017C00123000 is a Alphabet Inc. call option expiring January 17, 2025 with a $123 strike price. Every contract on every platform is encoded this way. Once you're fluent in the symbol, you can move through a chain with precision.

Options Expiration Cycles

Not all options expire on the same schedule. Listed options are grouped into expiration cycles that determine which months have available contracts. All optionable stocks have at least the current month and the following month available. Beyond that, they follow one of three standard quarterly cycles — and the larger and more liquid the underlying, the more expirations are available simultaneously.

Cycle	Quarterly Months	Also Always Available	Notes
Cycle I	January, April, July, October	Current month + next month	Jan/Apr/Jul/Oct cycle
Cycle II	February, May, August, November	Current month + next month	Feb/May/Aug/Nov cycle
Cycle III	March, June, September, December	Current month + next month	Mar/Jun/Sep/Dec cycle

Beyond the standard monthly cycles, there are four expiration types every options trader must understand — and they suit very different strategies:

Type	Frequency (Expiration)	Best For	Warning	Examples
Daily / 0DTE	Every trading day (SPX/SPY/QQQ)	Event trades, scalping. Ultra-high gamma. NOT for income sellers.	100% of premium can vanish in hours. Maximum gamma risk. Professionals only.	SPX 0DTE, SPY 0DTE

Type	Frequency (Expiration)	Best For	Warning	Examples
Weekly	Every Friday expiration	Short-term income, event-driven plays. Fast theta decay works for sellers.	Gamma risk amplified in final 2 days. Exit by Wednesday to avoid expiration whipsaw.	SPY, QQQ, AAPL, most large caps
Monthly	3rd Friday of each month	Primary income strategy window. 30–45 DTE entries. Ideal theta/gamma balance.	Standard: requires more capital per contract than weekly options.	All optionable stocks and ETFs
Quarterly	Last day of March, June, Sept, Dec	Institutional hedging and rebalancing. Less liquid mid-quarter.	Wide bid/ask spreads outside of quarterly roll dates.	Index ETFs, major sector ETFs
LEAPS	Jan expirations 1–3 years out	Stock substitute, long-term directional plays, LEAPS covered calls.	Low daily theta but high Vega — IV crush can hurt even when right on direction.	AAPL Jan 2026, SPY Jan 2027

THE 30–45 DTE SWEET SPOT

The income seller's optimal entry window is 30–45 days to expiration (DTE) — monthly options. This is where theta decay is accelerating but gamma risk has not yet become dominant. You open positions here to ride the fastest portion of the decay curve, and close at 21 DTE to lock in gains before gamma risk rises. The weekly vs. monthly choice is not about preference — it's about which strategy you're running.

Knowing Your Rights & Obligations as an Options Trader

This is the most important concept in the entire chapter. The buyer and the seller of an options contract have fundamentally different roles — different rights, different obligations, and different risk profiles. Confusing them is one of the most dangerous mistakes a new trader can make.

Position	Role	Rights	Obligations & Risk
CALL BUYER	Buyer (Long)	Right to BUY 100 shares at the strike price on or before expiration.	Risk limited to premium paid. No obligation to exercise.
CALL SELLER	Seller (Short)	Collects premium upfront — keeps it regardless of outcome.	OBLIGATION to SELL 100 shares at strike if assigned. Unlimited risk on naked calls.
PUT BUYER	Buyer (Long)	Right to SELL 100 shares at the strike price on or before expiration.	Risk limited to premium paid. No obligation to exercise.

Position	Role	Rights	Obligations & Risk
PUT SELLER	Seller (Short)	Collects premium upfront — keeps it regardless of outcome.	OBLIGATION to BUY 100 shares at strike if assigned. Risk down to zero on naked puts.

The Four Order Actions — BUY/SELL to OPEN/CLOSE

When you log into your brokerage platform and place an options trade, you will see four possible order actions. New traders consistently confuse these. This framework resolves the confusion permanently:

Order Action	Effect	What It Means
BUY TO OPEN	ENTER	You are purchasing an option to initiate a new long position. You now OWN a contract.
SELL TO OPEN	ENTER	You are selling an option to initiate a new short position. You now OWE an obligation.
SELL TO CLOSE	EXIT	You are selling an option you already own to close a long position and lock in profit or loss.
BUY TO CLOSE	EXIT	You are buying back an option you previously sold to close a short position.

Note: BUY TO OPEN and SELL TO OPEN both OPEN a position. SELL TO CLOSE and BUY TO CLOSE both EXIT a position. Additionally, if you choose to exercise your contract rights rather than closing, this creates a new BUY or SELL transaction in the underlying stock — processed through the OCC as a chain reaction.

SAMPLE ORDER TICKETS

Buy to OPEN 1 CALL XYZ March 30 $30 Strike = enter a long call | Sell to CLOSE 1 CALL XYZ March 30 $30 Strike = exit that same long call | Sell to OPEN 1 PUT ABC June 20 $75 Strike = enter a short put (income trade) | Buy to CLOSE 1 PUT ABC June 20 $75 Strike = exit that short put by buying it back. These four transactions cover 90% of everything you will ever do on a brokerage platform.

The Leverage Argument — Why Options vs. Stock

Here is the most concrete illustration of what options actually provide. Suppose AAPL is trading at $126 per share.

- To own 100 shares of AAPL outright: 100 × $126 = $12,600 of capital at risk;
- To control 100 shares via a call option at the $126 strike: premium of approximately $4.65 × 100 = $465.

Would you rather risk $12,600 to own 100 shares of AAPL, or $465 for the right to buy 100 shares at $126 before expiration? Obviously, $465 is cheaper. This is what leverage means in options — you control the same 100 shares for a fraction of the capital. The tradeoff: the option expires. If AAPL doesn't move in your favor before the expiration date, the $465 is lost. The stock holder just holds. The options buyer has a deadline.

THE CRITICAL RISK

The chance that an option goes to zero is 100% — because every option that reaches expiration out of the money expires completely worthless. The stock can always recover. The option has a clock. This is why buying options for income is not the strategy in this book. Selling options — collecting the premium from buyers who need that clock — is.

Covered vs. Naked — Know Which One You Are

Short Sales: How Traders Sell What They Do Not Own

One of the most confusing concepts for new market participants is the short sale — the ability to sell a security you do not currently own. This sounds impossible. How can you sell something you do not have? The answer lies in borrowing. When you sell a stock short, your brokerage firm borrows the shares from another client's account (with that client's permission, typically granted through their margin agreement) and sells them on your behalf in the open market. You now have an obligation: you must eventually return those borrowed shares to the lender by buying them back in the market.

Step	Stage	Who Acts	What Happens
1	Locate & Borrow	Broker	Broker locates shares to borrow on your behalf.
2	Sell Short	Trader	Trader sells the borrowed shares at current market price.
3	Price Declines	Market	Stock falls as expected; position moves in your favor.
4	Buy to Cover	Trader	Trader buys shares back at the lower price to close the position.
5	Return & Profit	Broker	Shares returned to lender. Profit = Sale Price − Cover Price − Borrow Costs.

Figure 4.2 — Short Sale Lifecycle. Five steps from borrow to profit.

The short sale profit mechanism is the mirror image of a long trade. In a long trade, you buy low and hope to sell high. In a short trade, you sell high first, then hope to buy back lower. If you sell 100 shares of XYZ at $68 and the price falls to $55, you buy back (cover) at $55 — returning the shares to the lender and pocketing the $13 per share difference, or $1,300 total on 100 shares, minus commissions and any borrowing fees.

The risk of a short sale is fundamentally asymmetric and deserves clear statement: the maximum profit on a short sale is 100% of the sale price (if the stock goes to zero). The maximum loss is theoretically unlimited — because a stock can rise infinitely. A trader who shorts XYZ at $68 and sees it rally to $120 has already lost $52 per share with no ceiling in sight. This unlimited loss risk is why naked short selling of stocks is considered a high-risk strategy, and why the options market offers a far more controlled alternative: the bear put spread, which caps your maximum loss at the debit paid while providing similar directional benefit.

In the options world, understanding short sales is essential because selling options IS a form of short selling. When you sell a call option, you are short that call — you have sold something (the right to buy shares at the strike price) that you created, not that you owned. The buyer of the call paid you a premium; your obligation is to deliver shares at the strike price if the buyer exercises. The dynamics of risk, margin, and obligation that govern stock short sales also govern short options positions, which is why the covered vs. naked distinction in the next section matters so profoundly.

	Long Position (Bought Stock)	Short Position (Sold Stock Short)
Entry action	Buy shares in the market	Borrow shares, then sell them
Profit when...	Stock price rises	Stock price falls
Maximum profit	Unlimited (stock rises to infinity)	100% of short sale price (stock → $0)
Maximum loss	100% of cost (stock → $0)	Unlimited (stock rises without limit)
Holding period	No forced deadline	Must cover if broker recalls shares
Options equivalent	Long call (bullish, limited loss)	Naked short call (bearish, unlimited risk)

SHORT SELLING AND OPTIONS: THE CONNECTION

Options traders are short sellers every time they sell a call or a put. The premium collected is your proceeds from the short sale. Your obligation — to deliver shares at the strike price (short call) or to buy shares at the strike price (short put) — is your liability as the short party. The key advantage of selling options over shorting stock is that your risk is defined by the contract terms: a short put's maximum loss is the strike price minus the premium received. Stock short selling has no such limit. This is why the Seller's Philosophy in this book is built on short options, not short stock.

Whether a short options position is covered or naked is one of the most important risk distinctions in all of options trading:

- CALL — Covered: You own the shares when you sell a call. Your risk is capped — the worst case is you must sell shares you already own at the strike price;
- CALL — Naked: You do NOT own the shares when you sell the call. Risk is theoretically unlimited — if the stock rockets to $500, you must buy it at market to deliver it at your strike price;
- PUT — Covered (Cash-Secured): You have the full cash to buy 100 shares at the strike price in your account. If assigned, you buy the stock with funds already set aside. Risk: the stock goes to zero after you buy it; and
- PUT — Naked/Uncovered: You do NOT have the cash reserved. If assigned, you will have a new long stock position in your account purchased at the strike price — with money you may not have planned to use.

BEWARE AND BE INTENTIONAL

SELLING PUTS is a tricky transaction. Markets don't care about your intentions. If you sell a put and the stock drops 40%, you are obligated to buy 100 shares at your strike price regardless of what the stock is currently worth. Go into every short put trade knowing exactly what you are committing to own, at what price, and with what capital reserved.

What Happens Between Entry and Expiration

Between the moment you open an options position and its expiration date, you have choices. Understanding them is the difference between a managed trade and a surprise outcome.

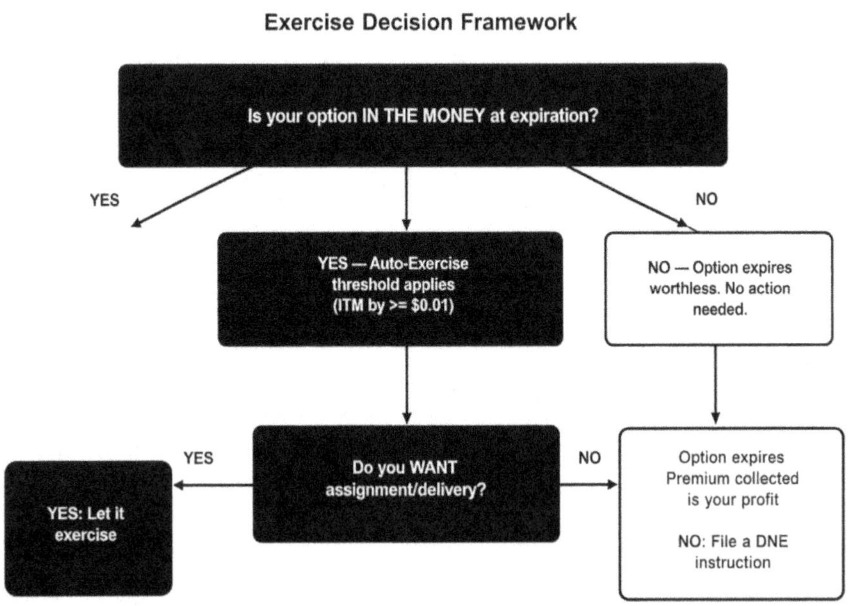

Figure 4.3 — Exercise Decision Framework. Should you exercise, let it expire, or file a DNE?

Figure 4.3 — Exercise Decision Framework. Should you exercise, let it expire, or file a DNE?

Account / Situation	ITM Status	What Happens	Override Option
Customer Account (retail trader)	ITM by $0.01 or more	Automatic — no action required by holder.	File DNE instruction before 4:30 PM ET.
Firm Account (broker/institutional)	ITM by $0.01 or more	Automatic — no action required.	File DNE instruction per firm policy.
OTM at Expiry	Out of the money	Expires worthless automatically.	None needed.
Special Cases (corporate actions)	Adjusted contracts	Review non-standard terms carefully.	Consult broker before expiration.

Figure 4.4 — OCC Auto-Exercise Thresholds. The $0.01 ITM rule and override procedures.

As a BUYER, you have four choices:

- Sell to close — Sell your option before expiration to lock in a profit or cut a loss. This is the most common action for active traders. You never have to hold to expiration;
- Exercise your right — Call buyers can buy 100 shares at the strike price; put buyers can sell 100 shares at the strike price. Most retail traders sell to close rather than exercise;
- Let it expire worthless — If the option is out of the money at expiration, it expires worthless and you lose the premium paid. This is the maximum loss for a buyer;
- Roll the position — Buy back your expiring option and simultaneously sell a new option at a different strike or expiration to extend or adjust your position. Rolling allows buyers to maintain directional exposure when the thesis is correct but timing was off. A roll is a two-legged order: close the existing position and open the replacement in a single transaction to minimize slippage;

As a SELLER, you have three choices:

- Buy to close — Buy back the contract you sold to lock in a profit (premium has decayed) or cut a loss (premium has expanded against you). This is the seller's primary management tool;
- Roll the position — Close the current contract and simultaneously open a new one at a different strike, expiration, or both. Rolling extends your time horizon and adjusts your risk profile;
- Let it expire worthless — The seller's ideal outcome. If the option expires out of the money, the full premium collected is profit. No further action required;

Pricing Factors: What Drives the Premium

Three primary forces determine how much an options contract costs. Understanding all three is essential before you evaluate any trade:

- Time to Expiration — Options with more time until expiration are worth more. All else equal, a 90-day option costs more than a 30-day option on the same strike. This time value melts away daily — a process called theta decay, which accelerates as expiration approaches;
- Strike Price Attractiveness — How close the strike is to the current stock price directly affects the premium. At-the-money (ATM) options (strike = current price) carry the most time value. Deep in-the-money options carry mostly intrinsic value. Deep out-of-the-money options are cheap — but cheap for a reason; and
- The Algos (Artificial Intelligence, Bots, and Algorithmic Systems) — This is the third factor most books omit. AI and algorithmic trading systems are now responsible for more than 80% of all trading volume on any given day. These systems influence options pricing in real time — adjusting implied volatility, skewing bid-ask spreads, and reacting to news, earnings, and technical levels at speeds no human can match. Ignoring the Algos is like driving with your eyes closed. We cover this in detail in Chapter 15.

THE RISK EVERY BUYER MUST ACCEPT

The chance that an out-of-the-money option goes to zero is 100%. Every OTM option that reaches expiration worthless is a complete loss of premium paid. Options are time-limited assets. Unlike a stock that can always recover, an option that expires OTM is gone. This is why this book focuses on selling options — collecting premium from buyers who accept this risk — rather than buying options as a primary income strategy.

Four Market Conditions — Your Pre-Trade Filter

Before you formulate any options strategy, you must identify which of four market conditions you are operating in. This is the first filter, not the last. The condition you are in determines which strategies are appropriate — and which are likely to hurt you:

Condition 1	Condition 2	Condition 3	Condition 4
HIGH Implied Volatility (IV) — premiums are expensive. Sellers get paid more. Best time to sell.	LOW Implied Volatility (IV) — premiums are cheap. Buyers get better value. Spreads become attractive.	SIDEWAYS / Range-Bound — stock not trending. Income strategies and neutral spreads excel.	DIRECTIONAL — stock moving strongly up or down. Directional strategies (calls, puts, spreads) align.

Always identify the condition before selecting the strategy — not after. Selling premium in a low-IV environment generates less income and provides less cushion. Buying directional options in a high-IV environment means you are overpaying for the contract. Condition determines strategy. Strategy does not determine condition.

Expiration Types Compared: Which to Use and When

Not all expirations are created equal. Each type has structural characteristics that make it better or worse for specific strategies. Choosing the wrong expiration for your strategy is like putting diesel in a gasoline engine — it will not work the way you expect.

Type	DTE Range	Theta Decay	Best For	Worst For	Liquidity
0DTE (Same day)	0	Extreme	Scalping, gamma plays for experienced traders only	Any income strategy. Any new trader.	Very high on SPY/QQQ. Low on individual stocks.
Weekly	1-7	Very fast	Short-term directional bets. Quick income on liquid names.	Strategies needing time to develop. Multi-leg structures.	High on 50+ names. Thin on most.
Monthly	21-45	Moderate — ideal	Income selling (CSP, CC, IC). This is the bread-and-butter DTE for 90% of this book's strategies.	Very long-term thesis. LEAPS-style trades.	Highest across all names.
Quarterly	60-90	Slow	Calendar spreads. Diagonal spreads. Post-earnings 10-week income window.	Short-term income (theta too slow to generate meaningful daily income).	Good on liquid names. Thin on small caps.
LEAPS	270-1095	Very slow	Stock replacement. Long-term directional thesis. Covered call substitute (diagonal).	Income selling (too slow). Quick trades.	Moderate. Wide bid-ask on many names.

For the strategies in this book, you will use monthly expirations 80% of the time, quarterly 15%, and LEAPS 5%. Weeklies and 0DTE are specialty tools — powerful in the right hands, destructive in the wrong ones. Master monthly expirations first. Everything else is advanced.

Who Buys What — and Why: The Seller's Clock vs the Buyer's Runway

This is one of the most frequently asked questions in options trading, and the answer is more precise than most books acknowledge. Sellers and buyers do not use the same expiration types. They use different timeframes for a fundamental reason: they are on opposite sides of the time decay equation.

THE SELLER: Sellers want time decay to work for them as fast as possible. Theta — the daily erosion of an option's time value — accelerates in the final 30 days before expiration. A seller writing a weekly contract collects premium that evaporates in 5 days. A monthly seller does the same in 30 days. Both are operating in the steepest part of the decay curve, recycling capital efficiently and repeatedly. A quarterly expiration is too slow — the seller waits too long to realize the gain.

THE BUYER: Buyers need the opposite. A buyer purchasing a weekly option has 5 days for their thesis to play out. One bad day, one gap against the position, and the premium is gone. Monthly gives 30 days to be right. Quarterly gives 60–90 days — enough runway to survive short-term noise, weather a temporary move against the position, and still profit from the directional thesis. The buyer is paying for time, and quarterly delivers the most time per dollar of premium relative to the decay rate.

THE CORE PRINCIPLE: Time is the currency of options trading. Sellers sell time; buyers buy it. Your choice of expiration defines which side of the time decay equation you are on — and determines the entire structure of your trade.

THE SELLER'S CLOCK vs THE BUYER'S RUNWAY

SELLERS write expirations where time works fastest:

- Weekly (1–7 DTE) — Primary. Maximum Theta. Capital recycled every week.
- Monthly (21–45 DTE) — Secondary. Ideal Theta/Gamma balance for income strategies.
- Quarterly — Avoided. Too slow. Premium decays too gradually to be efficient.
- BUYERS purchase expirations where time works slowest:
- Monthly (21–45 DTE) — Primary. Enough time for the thesis. Manageable decay.
- Quarterly (60–90 DTE) — Secondary. Maximum runway. Survives short-term noise.
- Weekly — Avoided. Too fast. One bad day destroys the position.
- The Core Principle: Sellers eat premium FAST. Buyers need premium to last.

This framework resolves the confusion most new traders experience when they see both monthly and quarterly options available and wonder which to choose. The answer is not about which expiration is 'better' — it is about which side of the trade you are on. Establish that first. Everything else follows.

A Warning on Binary Options

BINARY OPTIONS ARE NOT TRADITIONAL OPTIONS

Binary options are a fundamentally different instrument from every strategy taught in this book. They function as fixed-payout yes/no wagers — not as contracts granting the holder the right to buy or sell an underlying asset. Unlike traditional options, binary options have no Greeks, no intrinsic/extrinsic value structure, and no secondary market for position management. They are frequently offered on unregulated offshore platforms, and the SEC and CFTC have both issued formal investor warnings citing widespread losses, platform fraud, and identity theft. The word "option" in "binary option" is misleading. This book does not teach, endorse, or reference binary options strategies in any form. If you encounter a platform promoting binary options trading, treat it as a red flag and move on.

6-CONDITION FRAMEWORK ▸ INFRASTRUCTURE — the rails that execute all six conditions
The 17 exchanges, the OCC, and the NBBO are what make execution possible across all six conditions. This chapter explains why your fills are fair and your positions guaranteed — regardless of which condition you trade.

Every listed options contract you trade was created by the market itself — not by a company, not by an exchange, and not by your broker. Understanding how options come into existence, who guarantees them, and how they are cleared is foundational knowledge that directly informs how you think about counterparty risk, assignment, and exercise. Most retail traders skip this chapter. The ones who understand it trade with significantly more confidence.

Understanding Stock Indexes: What You Are Trading When You Trade Index Options

Before trading options on the S&P 500, QQQ, or any index ETF, you need to understand exactly what an index is — and what it is not. An index is a number that represents the composite value of a group of items. In the case of a stock index, that number is determined by the market prices of the stocks that make up the index. As stocks in the index rise in price, the value of the index rises. As stocks fall, the index falls. Importantly, because the index is made up of many individual stocks, some stocks can rise while others fall — and the overall index value may remain unchanged even while its component prices are moving in opposite directions.

Index Type	Calculation Method	Key Example	Options Implication
Price-Weighted Index	Sum of stock prices divided by a divisor.	Dow Jones Industrial Average.	Higher-priced stocks have more influence.
Market-Cap Weighted	Each stock weighted by market capitalization.	S&P 500, Nasdaq Composite.	Largest companies dominate index moves.
Equal-Weighted Index	Each stock gets equal weight.	S&P 500 Equal Weight (RSP).	Small stocks matter as much as large ones.
Float-Adjusted Index	Uses only publicly traded shares.	Most modern index funds.	Excludes locked-up institutional shares.

Figure 5.1 — How a Stock Index Is Calculated. Price-weighted vs. cap-weighted methodology.

Index	Type	Components	Options Volume	Best Strategies
SPX / SPY	Broad-Based	500 large-cap U.S. stocks	Highest — billions in daily notional.	Iron condors, credit spreads, all conditions.
QQQ	Broad-Based	100 Nasdaq technology stocks	Very high.	Growth-focused; Conditions 1 & 2.

IWM	Broad-Based	2,000 small-cap U.S. stocks	High.	Risk-on/off plays; higher beta than SPY.
XLK	Narrow/Sector	Tech sector S&P 500 stocks	Moderate.	Sector rotation; Conditions 1 & 3.
GLD / SLV	Commodity ETF	Gold / Silver spot price proxy	Moderate.	Macro hedges; IV spike plays.

Figure 5.2 — Broad-Based vs. Narrow-Based Indexes. Volume and options tradability by index type.

Stock indexes are classified as either broad-based or narrow-based. A broad-based index represents the market as a whole or a large portion of it. The S&P 500 (500 stocks), the Russell 2000 (2,000 small-cap stocks), and the Nasdaq 100 (100 large technology and growth stocks) are all broad-based. A narrow-based index represents a specific market segment — such as the Dow Jones Transportation Index (20 transportation companies) or the S&P Utilities Index (31 electrical energy companies).

Figure 3.1 — What Is an Index — How index values are calculated and the key differences between broad-based and narrow-based indexes.

What Is an Index — How index values are calculated and the difference between broad and narrow indexes.

There are two primary methods for calculating an index. A price-weighted index (like the Dow Jones Industrial Average) calculates its value as the simple average of the stock prices of its components. In a price-weighted index, a $200 stock has twice the influence of a $100 stock regardless of the company's total market size. A capitalization-weighted index (like the S&P 500) weights each component by its total market capitalization — share price multiplied by shares outstanding. This means larger companies have proportionally more influence on the index's movement. Most modern indexes use capitalization weighting because it more accurately reflects the true economic weight of each company.

WHY INDEX UNDERSTANDING MATTERS FOR OPTIONS TRADERS

When you trade SPY options, QQQ options, or options on /ES futures, you are not trading a single stock — you are trading a position on the aggregate direction and volatility of the entire index. This has three critical implications: (1) Single-stock earnings events do not directly affect your index position (though large-cap earnings can move the index). (2) Index options are typically European-style, which means no early assignment risk. (3) Index options on SPX and /ES are cash-settled at expiration — no shares change hands, only the cash difference. These structural advantages make index options the preferred vehicle for professional income sellers.

How Options Are Created

A listed options contract is created the moment a buyer and a seller agree on a transaction. Unlike stocks, which have a fixed number of shares outstanding, options have no fixed supply. Every time a new buyer and a new seller open a position, a new contract is created. This is called open interest — the total number of outstanding contracts that have been opened but not yet closed or exercised.

- When you Buy to Open and the counterparty Sells to Open — a new contract is created. Open interest increases by 1;
- When you Sell to Close and the counterparty Buys to Close — an existing contract is extinguished. Open interest decreases by 1; and

- When you Buy to Open against someone else's Sell to Close — no new contract is created. Open interest stays the same.

This is why open interest is one of the most important liquidity signals in options trading. High open interest means many contracts are outstanding at that strike — the market is active, spreads are tighter, and you can enter and exit at fair prices. Low open interest means the strike is thinly traded — you may struggle to get a fair fill or exit quickly.

OPEN INTEREST VS. VOLUME

Volume is how many contracts traded today. Open interest is how many contracts are currently outstanding. Volume resets to zero each day. Open interest accumulates over time and tells you the depth of the market at each strike. Always check both before trading — volume without open interest can be misleading.

The Options Clearing Corporation (OCC)

The Options Clearing Corporation is the central counterparty for every listed options contract traded in the United States. It is the most important institution in the options market that most traders have never heard of — and understanding its role eliminates an entire category of risk that new traders worry about unnecessarily.

Step	Who Acts	What Happens	Time Frame
1	You (Trader)	Submit limit order to buy/sell an options contract via broker.	Instant — order enters queue.
2	Broker OMS	Routes order to best exchange via NBBO scan across all 17 exchanges.	Milliseconds — automatic routing.
3	Exchange (e.g., CBOE)	Matches buyer and seller; execution confirmed.	Milliseconds — electronic matching.
4	OCC	Becomes buyer to every seller and seller to every buyer.	Instant — OCC guarantees trade.
5	Clearing	OCC nets positions across all member firms daily.	End of trading day — T+1 settlement.
6	Settlement	Premium debit/credit applied to your account.	T+1 — funds clear next business day.

Figure 5.3 — The OCC Trade Lifecycle. From order submission to settlement.

When you buy a call option from another trader, you are not actually exposed to that trader's credit or reliability. The moment the trade executes, the OCC steps between you and the other party, becoming the buyer to every seller and the seller to every buyer. Your counterparty is the OCC — not the person on the other side of the trade. The OCC is backed by a multi-billion dollar clearing fund maintained by all its member firms.

- The OCC guarantees performance on every listed options contract traded on a U.S. exchange;

- This guarantee means you never have to worry about your counterparty defaulting on their obligation — the OCC is always there; and
- The OCC clears contracts for all 17 active U.S. options exchanges — CBOE, Nasdaq PHLX, NYSE Arca, and others — through a single central clearing infrastructure.

COMING IN 2026: IEX OPTIONS — THE 18TH EXCHANGE

On September 18, 2025, the SEC approved IEX Options — the 18th U.S. options exchange — despite opposition from Citadel Securities. IEX Options features a 350-microsecond speed bump on all incoming orders, designed to curb latency arbitrage and level the playing field for retail traders. MEMX also plans a second venue in late 2026, which would bring the total to 19 exchanges. More competition means tighter spreads and better fills for every retail options trader.

- The OCC is regulated by both the SEC (for its securities clearing function) and the CFTC (for its futures-related functions)

The Options Participants: Who Is on the Other Side?

Every options trade has a buyer and a seller. In the listed options market, these participants fall into three broad categories — understanding who you are trading with shapes how you think about price discovery, IV behavior, and market dynamics.

Participant	Role in the Market	Impact on Options Trader
Market Makers	Provide continuous bid/ask quotes on every strike and expiration. They are obligated to make a market. They profit from the bid/ask spread and hedge their delta exposure continuously.	They set the prices you see. Tight spreads = active market maker. Wide spreads = thinly traded strike. Never fight a wide bid/ask — use limit orders and be patient.
Institutional Traders	Hedge funds, prop desks, pension funds, and asset managers using options for hedging, income, and directional exposure. They move large size and their flow can shift IV.	Large institutional flows cause IV spikes and unusual options activity. Watching for large unusual volume at specific strikes is a real signal — institutions don't place large bets randomly.
Retail Traders	Individual traders like you. Generally buyers of options more than sellers. Often trade emotionally, concentrate near earnings, and overpay for OTM lottery tickets.	You are competing with the other side — but your edge is defined-risk discipline and time horizon. Most retail losses come from oversizing, not bad analysis.
Algorithmic Systems (Used by all three categories)	High-frequency trading systems and algo bots that react to price, flow, and order imbalance in microseconds. They dominate intraday volume and set the tone for IV behavior.	Algos can cause sudden, sharp price moves that feel irrational. Chapter 15 covers this in depth. For now: don't fight sudden algo-driven moves — wait for them to resolve, then trade.

Exercise and Assignment: The Mechanics

Exercise is the act of a buyer enforcing their right — buying shares (call) or selling shares (put) at the strike price. Assignment is what happens to the seller when a buyer exercises — the seller is required to fulfill their obligation.

- American-style options (most equity options) can be exercised any time before expiration — not just at expiry;

- European-style options (SPX, XSP, some index options) can only be exercised at expiration — no early exercise risk;
- Most retail traders never exercise early — they sell to close instead. But sellers can be assigned early at any time;
- Early assignment most commonly occurs when: (1) the option is deep in the money and has very little time value remaining, or (2) there is an ex-dividend date where a call buyer benefits from exercising to capture the dividend; and
- If you are short an option and get assigned, your broker will automatically execute the stock transaction at your strike price — you will own shares (short put assignment) or be forced to sell shares (short call assignment).

ASSIGNMENT IS NOT A DISASTER

Assignment on a cash-secured put means you buy 100 shares at the strike you agreed to. If you selected that strike deliberately — at a price you were willing to own the stock — assignment is the plan working correctly, not a failure. The risk manager defines assignment as a known outcome before entering the trade, never as a surprise.

Trading Rules: The Non-Negotiables

The market is an adversarial process. Whoever is on the other side of your trade has one goal: to profit at your expense. This is not personal — it is the structure of any zero-sum financial market. The risk manager's trading rules exist to give you a systematic advantage over the undisciplined majority.

- Trade listed options only — standardized, OCC-cleared, exchange-traded. No OTC, no swaps, no exotic structures;
- Use limit orders exclusively — never market orders on options. A market order on a thinly traded option can fill at a price 10–20% away from the midpoint;
- Check open interest before entering — if the open interest at your strike is below 100, reconsider the trade or widen to a more liquid strike;
- Never trade options on stocks you do not understand — the options market is efficient; if you don't know why a stock moves, you don't know why your option will move; and
- Always know your max loss before entry — not approximately, exactly. Write it down.

Trading Places: The 17 U.S. Options Exchanges

When you place an options trade, you are not trading in one place. You are trading on one of 17 regulated U.S. options exchanges, all competing for your order simultaneously. Your broker's smart order routing system scans every exchange in real time and sends your order to the one offering the best price at that moment. Understanding who these exchanges are — and how they connect — gives you a complete picture of where your money actually goes.

#	Exchange	Operator	What You Need to Know
1	CBOE Options Exchange	Cboe Global Markets	The largest and oldest U.S. options exchange. Founded in 1973 as the first listed

#	Exchange	Operator	What You Need to Know
			options marketplace. Home of SPX, VIX, and RUT index options. When traders talk about 'the options market,' they usually mean CBOE.
2	C2 Options Exchange	Cboe Global Markets	Cboe's fully electronic second exchange, running parallel to CBOE. Offers identical products with different fee structures. Created to provide competition within Cboe's own ecosystem and attract different order flow.
3	Cboe BZX Options	Cboe Global Markets	Cboe's equity options exchange — focused on equity and ETF options. High-speed, fully electronic. Known for tight spreads on high-volume underlyings like AAPL, SPY, QQQ.
4	Cboe EDGX Options	Cboe Global Markets	Electronic exchange targeting taker-maker fee models — pays traders to take liquidity rather than provide it. Appeals to high-frequency and algo traders. Cboe's fourth exchange in its multi-exchange family.
5	NYSE Arca Options	NYSE / ICE	The options arm of NYSE, running on a fully electronic platform. Handles a massive volume of equity and ETF options. One of the primary venues for SPY, QQQ, and major index ETF options. Tight, competitive markets.
6	NYSE American Options	NYSE / ICE	Formerly AMEX (American Stock Exchange) — one of the original options exchanges. Now fully electronic under NYSE ownership. Historically important as the second exchange to list equity options after CBOE in 1975.
7	Nasdaq PHLX	Nasdaq	The Philadelphia Stock Exchange — the oldest stock exchange in the U.S. (founded 1790), now running as a modern electronic options exchange under Nasdaq. Specializes in equity options and is a major venue for retail order flow.
8	Nasdaq ISE	Nasdaq	International Securities Exchange — the first fully electronic U.S. options exchange when launched in 2000. Now Nasdaq-owned. Known for its price-time priority model. Major venue for equity and ETF options.
9	Nasdaq GEMX	Nasdaq	Nasdaq's third options exchange, targeting maker-taker fee structures. Primarily electronic. Competes for flow from broker-dealers and market makers using competitive pricing incentives.
10	Nasdaq MRX	Nasdaq	Nasdaq's fourth options exchange, formerly ISE Mercury. Provides an additional venue for equity options trading with distinct fee schedules to attract different participant types.

#	Exchange	Operator	What You Need to Know
11	MIAX Options	Miami International Holdings	Miami International Exchange — a modern, fully electronic exchange launched in 2012. Known for aggressive market maker incentive programs and tight spreads. Rapidly grew to be a major volume exchange.
12	MIAX Pearl Options	Miami International Holdings	MIAX's second exchange, launched 2017. Operates with a different fee model from its parent to attract complementary order flow. Part of MIAX's growing multi-exchange strategy.
13	MIAX Emerald	Miami International Holdings	MIAX's third exchange, launched 2019. Rounds out MIAX's multi-exchange family. Competes primarily on pricing incentives for market makers and professional traders.
14	MEMX Options	Members Exchange	Launched by a consortium including Morgan Stanley, Goldman Sachs, and Citadel Securities. Fully electronic, focused on competitive pricing. A significant entrant challenging established exchange operators.
15	MIAX Sapphire	Miami International Holdings	MIAX's fourth options exchange. Housed in Miami's new financial district trading floor. Continues MIAX's aggressive multi-exchange expansion.
16	Nasdaq BX Options	Nasdaq	Nasdaq's additional options venue using a maker-taker pricing model. Part of Nasdaq's multi-exchange portfolio strategy.
17	Cboe EDGX Options	Cboe Global Markets	Cboe's fourth options exchange targeting taker-maker fee models appealing to high-frequency and algo traders.

Four groups dominate the exchange landscape: Cboe Global Markets (4 exchanges), Nasdaq (4 exchanges), NYSE/ICE (2 exchanges), and MIAX (3 exchanges). This is not an accident — regulators encourage multi-exchange competition because it tightens spreads and improves price discovery for all participants. Every group of exchanges competes directly for your order flow.

WHY 17 EXCHANGES BENEFIT THE RETAIL TRADER

When thirteen exchanges compete for your order simultaneously, they are all racing to offer you the best price. This competition is the reason bid/ask spreads on heavily traded options like SPY and AAPL are often just $0.01–$0.02 wide. On a thin, single-exchange market, the same contract might trade $0.10–$0.20 wide. Multi-exchange competition is one of the most powerful structural advantages the modern retail options trader has over traders of twenty years ago.

How Your Order Gets There: NBBO and Smart Order Routing

The National Best Bid and Offer (NBBO) is the best available bid price and the best available ask price across all 17 exchanges at any given moment. When you place a limit order to buy an option at the midpoint, your broker's Order Management System (OMS) checks the NBBO and routes your order to the exchange currently offering the best fill. This process happens in microseconds — by the time you click 'submit,' your order has already been evaluated against all 13 venues.

The NBBO is published continuously by OPRA — the Options Price Reporting Authority — a consolidated feed that aggregates quote data from all 17 exchanges into a single stream. Every broker, every platform, every algorithmic system that trades options subscribes to OPRA. When you see a bid and an ask on your trading platform, you are seeing the NBBO — the best prices available anywhere in the market at that exact moment.

Step	Who Acts	What Happens
1 — You Submit	Retail Trader	You click 'submit' on a limit order to sell 1 SPY $450 put for $2.35 credit. Your order enters your broker's Order Management System.
2 — NBBO Check	Broker OMS	Your broker's system queries OPRA in real time. OPRA returns the current best bid ($2.34) and best ask ($2.36) across all 17 exchanges — the NBBO.
3 — Route Decision	Smart Router	The OMS compares all 13 exchange quotes. It identifies which exchange is currently showing $2.35 on the bid — or closest to it — and routes your order there. If multiple exchanges show the same price, it uses fee structures and fill probability to decide.
4 — Exchange Match	Exchange (e.g. CBOE)	Your order arrives at the exchange. If a market maker or another participant is willing to buy at $2.35, the trade executes immediately. If not, your order rests on the order book until matched.
5 — OCC Clears	OCC	The moment the trade executes, the OCC steps in as central counterparty. The OCC becomes the buyer of your put and records the new open interest. The premium ($235) is credited to your account.
6 — Confirmation	Broker	Your broker receives the fill confirmation from the exchange and posts it to your account. Your margin is reserved. The position appears in your portfolio.

THE MIDPOINT IS YOUR FRIEND

On liquid options, the NBBO spread is tight — $0.01 to $0.05. Always start your limit order at the midpoint between the bid and ask. If SPY is $2.34 bid / $2.36 ask, enter your order at $2.35. You will fill at mid on liquid contracts most of the time. Never use a market order on options — you hand control of your fill price to the market maker, who will use every cent of the spread against you.

The Complete Options Ecosystem: All Participants

The options market is not just buyers and sellers. It is a structured ecosystem with distinct participants at every level — each with a different role, different incentives, and a different impact on the prices you see and the fills you receive. Understanding the full ecosystem makes you a sharper trader.

Participant	Level	Primary Role	Impact on You as Retail Seller
Retail Traders	1	Individual traders using standard brokerage accounts (Schwab, TD, TastyTrade, IBKR). Buy and sell listed options for income, hedging, or directional plays.	You. The edge you build comes from discipline, defined risk, and systematic execution — not from information advantages. You trade in the same market as institutions but with different time horizons.
Broker-Dealers	2	Registered firms that execute trades on behalf of clients. They route your orders to exchanges and are members of the OCC. Broker-dealers include full-service firms, discount brokers, and clearing firms.	They determine your commission structure, margin requirements, and order routing quality. Choosing a broker with smart routing and low commissions directly impacts your net PPD.
Designated Primary Market Makers (DPMMs)	3	Exchange-assigned specialists with obligation to maintain continuous two-sided markets on specific underlyings. DPMMs are required to quote bid and ask at all times during market hours — they cannot step away.	DPMMs are the reason you can always get a fill. Their obligation to quote creates the liquidity you rely on. On less liquid underlyings, the DPMM may be the only market maker — watch the spread as a signal of their confidence.
Market Makers (MMs)	3	Firms that provide continuous bid/ask quotes to profit from the spread and hedging activity. Unlike DPMMs, standard MMs have more flexibility in where and when they quote. They manage large delta-hedged books.	MMs set the prices you trade against. Wide spreads mean the MM is uncertain about the underlying's direction and charging you for the risk. Tight spreads mean high confidence and strong liquidity. Always trade where MMs are active.
Institutional Traders	4	Hedge funds, asset managers, pension funds, and prop trading desks. They use options for portfolio hedging, income generation, and complex directional trades. They move large size — 100 to 10,000 contracts at once.	Large institutional flow causes IV spikes and creates unusual options activity. When you see 10,000 contracts bought at an OTM strike with no news, an institution is positioning. This is a real signal — follow the money, don't fight it.
High-Frequency Traders (HFTs)	4	Algorithmic firms executing thousands of trades per second on tiny price discrepancies between exchanges. They dominate intraday volume and play a key role in keeping exchange prices synchronized via arbitrage.	HFT keeps the 17 exchanges in sync. Without it, the same option could trade at different prices on CBOE vs. PHLX. Their arbitrage activity is why the NBBO stays tight and your fills are accurate across venues.
The OCC	5	Central counterparty clearing house for all 17 exchanges. Becomes buyer to every seller and seller to	The OCC eliminates counterparty risk entirely. You never worry about who is on the other side of your trade. The OCC guarantees your position will be honored

Participant	Level	Primary Role	Impact on You as Retail Seller
		every buyer the moment a trade executes. Maintains a multi-billion dollar clearing fund.	— assignment, exercise, and expiration all run through OCC infrastructure.
The SEC & CFTC	5	Regulatory bodies overseeing the options market. SEC governs securities options (equity and ETF). CFTC governs futures-linked products. FINRA oversees broker-dealers. Exchanges must register with and report to regulators.	Regulation is why listed options are safe to trade. Position limits, margin requirements, exchange rules, and the OCC clearing fund all exist because regulators require them. The guardrails are part of the product.

Exchange Trading Rules: What Governs Every Trade

Every U.S. options exchange operates under a unified regulatory framework established by the SEC and enforced through exchange rulebooks. These rules are not bureaucratic formality — they directly protect you from the most dangerous outcomes a trader can face. Knowing the rules is part of knowing the market.

Rule / Principle	What It Means for the Retail Options Trader
Standardization	Every listed options contract represents 100 shares, has a defined expiration date, and trades at standardized strikes. There is no negotiation on contract terms — the exchange sets them. This is why you can always find a counterparty: every contract is identical to every other contract of the same type.
Price-Time Priority	On most exchanges, orders at the same price are filled in the order they arrived — first in, first out. This is why limit orders placed early at the midpoint often fill before orders placed later at the same price. Time is a competitive advantage even at the retail level.
Position Limits	The SEC sets maximum position limits on options in individual underlyings — typically 25,000 contracts on the same side of the market (calls or puts) for equity options. This prevents any single participant from cornering a market or creating systemic risk. Retail traders never approach these limits, but institutions must manage to them carefully.
Exercise & Assignment Deadlines	Options holders must notify their broker by 5:30 PM ET on expiration day to exercise their contract. If an option is in the money by $0.01 or more at expiration, the OCC automatically exercises it unless the holder files a 'do not exercise' notice. As a seller, you can be assigned at any time on American-style options — this is the rule that makes assignment management a core discipline.
Margin Requirements	Short options positions require margin — reserved capital that ensures you can fulfill your obligation if assigned. For cash-secured puts, this means holding the full strike price × 100 in cash. Margin requirements are set by both the exchange and your broker. Broker margin requirements are often stricter than exchange minimums.
Halt Rules	Options trading on any underlying can be halted when the underlying stock is halted — for earnings releases, circuit breakers, regulatory halts,

Rule / Principle	What It Means for the Retail Options Trader
	or major news. During a halt, you cannot trade, close, or adjust your options position. This is a key risk for short-dated positions around earnings — hence the rule: never sell-to-open before an earnings report.
Best Execution Obligation	Broker-dealers are legally required to seek the best available execution for your orders — including routing to the exchange offering the best price. This is enforced by SEC Rule 605/606 and FINRA. Your broker must document its routing decisions and make them available to you on request. You can see where your orders were routed and whether you received the NBBO.
No Wash Sale on Options	The IRS wash sale rule applies to options — if you sell an option at a loss and repurchase a substantially identical option within 30 days before or after, the loss is disallowed. This is a critical tax rule for active sellers who roll positions frequently. Your CPA should understand options wash sale treatment.

THE INFRASTRUCTURE IS YOUR ADVANTAGE

Most retail traders never think about the 17 exchanges, the OCC, or the NBBO. They place orders, get fills, and move on. But understanding the infrastructure gives you something important: confidence. You know that your $235 premium credit cannot be taken back. You know your counterparty cannot default. You know the exchange must give you the best price available. You know your broker is legally required to route your order optimally. The infrastructure of the U.S. options market — built over 50 years — works in your favor from the moment you place your first trade.

Order Types for Options Traders: Getting the Fill You Deserve

The order type you use is not an afterthought — it is the final line of defense in your risk management system. A market order in a thin options chain is one of the most reliable ways to destroy edge before a trade even begins.

Order Type	When to Use	Options-Specific Guidance
Limit at Midpoint	Always — standard entry for all six conditions	Set limit at (bid+ask)/2. If unfilled after 2 minutes, move toward market in $0.05 increments. A mid fill is a fair fill — you split the spread equally with the market maker.
Market Order	Never for options	In options, a market order guarantees a fill at whatever price the market maker chooses. In a wide spread chain this can cost $0.30–$1.00+ above mid — often 20–40% of your entire expected profit, gone before the trade begins.
Good Till Cancelled (GTC)	Closing orders — profit targets and stops	Set GTC limit orders for your 50% profit target and stop immediately after entry. This removes emotional override of your planned exit and allows hands-off management.

Order Type	When to Use	Options-Specific Guidance
All-or-None (AON)	Multi-leg spreads (conditions 4, 5, 6)	Prevents partial fills that leave you with undefined risk. Always use the broker spread ticket or AON for condors, butterflies, and calendars — never leg in separately.
Trailing Stop	Directional debit (conditions 1, 3)	Once a long call or put reaches 50% profit, set a 25% trailing stop. Locks in profit while letting the winner run toward maximum profit if the trend continues. Unlike credit spreads — where you close at 50% to avoid gamma risk — long directional positions benefit from running as far as the move allows, protected by the trailing stop.

Fill Quality: What a Good Fill Looks Like

Fill Quality	What It Means
Filled at mid or better	Excellent. You split the spread or better. This is the target for every order.
Filled within $0.05 of mid	Acceptable. Minor friction. Within tolerance for chains with $2.00+ premiums.
Filled at the ask (for buys)	Poor. You paid the full spread. Consider moving to a more liquid underlying.
Partial fill only	Chain lacked sufficient OI. Reduce size or try a different strike. Never convert a partial to a market order.
Not filled after 5+ minutes	Market has moved. Reassess. Adjust limit $0.05 toward market, or cancel and re-read the condition.

THE FILL QUALITY RULE

Your theoretical edge is calculated at the midpoint. Every cent above mid on entry and below mid on exit is friction eroding your statistical advantage. On a $2.00 credit trade with a $0.20 spread, filling at the bid instead of mid costs you $0.10 — that is 5% of maximum profit before the position has breathed once. Patient limit orders are risk management.

Exercise and Assignment: What Actually Happens to Your Account

Figure 3.2 — Auto-Exercise Decision Tree — When options are automatically exercised at expiration and the ITM threshold that triggers it.

Auto-Exercise Decision Tree — When options are automatically exercised at expiration.

Auto-exercise is one of the most important mechanics in options trading — and one of the most misunderstood by new traders. At expiration, the OCC automatically exercises any option that is in the money by $0.01 or more per share (i.e., $1.00 or more per contract). This happens without any action required from the option holder. You do not need to call your broker. You do not need to submit an exercise notice. If your long call or put is a penny in the money at expiration, the OCC exercises it automatically on your behalf.

The auto-exercise threshold of $0.01 per share was established by the OCC to protect option holders from losing the intrinsic value of their contract through inaction. Prior to this rule, holders who forgot to exercise ITM options by the expiration deadline would forfeit their intrinsic value — a costly and entirely avoidable mistake. The OCC's auto-exercise rule eliminates this error for most retail traders.

The consequences of auto-exercise are immediate and concrete. If you hold a long call on AAPL with a $180 strike and AAPL closes at $182.50, your call is $2.50 ITM. The OCC auto-exercises it. Monday morning, 100 shares of AAPL appear in your account at a cost of $18,000 (100 shares × $180 strike). If you do not have $18,000 in your account to cover this purchase, your broker will either force-liquidate the shares or require a margin deposit immediately. This is not a theoretical risk — it happens to unprepared traders every expiration Friday.

THE DO-NOT-EXERCISE NOTICE

You can override auto-exercise by submitting a Do-Not-Exercise (DNE) notice to your broker before the expiration deadline (typically 4:30 PM ET on expiration Friday, though broker deadlines vary). You would submit a DNE if your long option is barely ITM and the transaction costs of exercising (commissions, bid/ask on the stock) would exceed the intrinsic value. Always confirm your broker's DNE deadline — missing it means unwanted stock positions in your account Monday morning.

For option sellers, the flip side of auto-exercise is automatic assignment. If you are short a call that is $0.01 or more ITM at expiration, the OCC assigns you automatically. Your short call position becomes an obligation to deliver 100 shares at the strike price. If you do not own the shares (naked call), your broker will either purchase them in the open market at current prices — which may be substantially above your strike — or force-close the position. For short put sellers, automatic assignment means you are required to purchase 100 shares at the strike price. This is the planned outcome for the Wheel strategy — assignment is not an emergency, it is the designed alternative.

The window between 3:00 PM and 4:00 PM ET on expiration Friday is known as the 'exercise by exception' window. During this period, the underlying stock price can move significantly after the options market closes at 4:00 PM (S&P options expire at 4:15 PM, while equity options expire at 4:00 PM). A stock option that appears OTM at 4:00 PM can become ITM by 4:15 PM if a news event occurs after market close but before the OCC's exercise cutoff. This creates a phenomenon called pin risk, discussed next.

Pin Risk: The Hidden Danger Near the Strike at Expiration

Pin risk occurs when the underlying stock price closes at or very near your short option's strike price at expiration. In this situation, you cannot know with certainty whether your short option will be exercised against you. If the stock closes exactly at your strike, the option is technically at-the-money — neither ITM nor OTM. The option holder has until 5:30 PM ET to submit an exercise notice, and they may choose to exercise or not based on after-hours price movements. As the short party, you are in a position of uncertainty: you may or may not receive an assignment notice on Monday morning.

The practical protection: always close short options positions that are within $0.50 of the current stock price before 3:00 PM on expiration Friday. The cost of closing a nearly worthless position (often $0.05 or less) is far smaller than the operational chaos of an unexpected Monday assignment. This rule is especially critical for cash-secured put sellers running the Wheel — a surprise assignment at an inconvenient time can disrupt the entire position management cycle.

Note for new traders: pin risk, gamma risk near expiration, and early assignment mechanics can feel abstract at this stage. You will manage these situations practically in Chapter 23 (Rollover Strategies), which gives you exact protocols for every assignment scenario. For now, focus on understanding that assignment is not an emergency — it is the planned alternative outcome of selling a put on a stock you are willing to own.

Most traders understand exercise and assignment conceptually but are shocked when it actually happens in their account. Here is the exact sequence of events for each scenario — including the timeline, the cash flows, and the common surprises.

Event	What Triggers It	What Happens in Your Account	Timeline	Common Surprise
Call Exercised (you are long the call)	You choose to exercise your right to buy 100 shares at the strike.	Cash debited: strike price x 100. 100 shares appear in your account Monday morning.	Exercise notice Friday after 4 PM. Shares settle T+1 (Monday).	You need enough cash or margin to receive 100 shares. A $200 strike = $20,000 needed. Many traders forget this.
Call Assigned (you are short the call)	The call buyer on the other side exercises. The OCC randomly assigns a short call holder.	100 shares removed from your account (if covered) OR short stock position created (if naked). Cash credited: strike x 100.	Assignment notice Saturday. Reflected Monday morning.	If you do not own the shares, you now have a SHORT STOCK position. This has unlimited risk until you buy to cover.
Put Exercised (you are long the put)	You choose to exercise your right to sell 100 shares at the strike.	100 shares removed from your account. Cash credited: strike x 100.	Same timeline as call exercise.	You must own the shares to exercise. If you do not, your broker may auto-close the put instead.
Put Assigned (you are short the put / CSP)	The put buyer exercises. The OCC assigns you.	Cash debited: strike x 100. 100 shares appear in your account.	Assignment notice Saturday. Shares settle Monday.	This IS the Wheel entry point. If you sold a quality CSP, this is the planned outcome. Do not panic.
Early Assignment (before expiration)	American-style options can be exercised any time. Usually happens near ex-dividend dates or deep ITM options.	Same as above but mid-cycle. Your position disappears from your options account and becomes a stock position.	Can happen any business day. Usually overnight.	Dividend-related early assignment on covered calls is the most common surprise. Check ex-dates before selling CCs.

The single most important takeaway: assignment is not an emergency. If you sold a CSP on a quality stock and got assigned, you now own shares of a company you already evaluated and approved. Follow the Assignment Recovery protocol in Chapter 9 and begin the Wheel. The only assignment that should concern you is an unexpected early assignment on a covered call near an ex-dividend date — check the calendar before every CC entry.

ASSIGNMENT READINESS CHECK

Before selling any option that could result in assignment, ask yourself: (1) Do I have the cash or margin to receive 100 shares at the strike price? (2) Am I genuinely willing to own this stock at this price? (3) Do I have a post-assignment plan? If any answer is no, you should not sell that option. The premium is not worth the surprise.

> **6-CONDITION FRAMEWORK ▸ PRICING — how fair value is determined in all six conditions**
> Buying premium (conditions 1, 3, 5) requires low IV to get fair entry. Selling premium (conditions 2, 4, 6) requires high IV to collect maximum credit. Valuation is what separates a well-priced trade from an overpriced one.

A contract is only worth what someone will pay for it. But in options, that price is not random — it is built from two distinct and measurable components: intrinsic value and extrinsic value. Every option premium you ever see on a chain is the sum of these two things. Understanding what drives each one is what separates traders who know what they're buying from traders who are just guessing.

The Two Components of Every Option Premium

Component	What It Is	Key Characteristic
Intrinsic Value	The real, in-the-money value of the option — what it would be worth if exercised right now	Always zero or positive. Never negative. Exists only when the option is in the money.
Extrinsic Value	Everything else in the premium — time value, implied volatility, and market expectations	Also called Time Value. Decays to zero at expiration regardless of stock price. This is what sellers collect.

The formula is simple: Option Premium = Intrinsic Value + Extrinsic Value. The challenge — and the opportunity — is that these two components behave very differently over time and across market conditions.

Intrinsic Value: The Real Worth

Intrinsic value is the amount by which an option is in the money. It is the concrete, exercise-right-now value of the contract. There is no speculation in intrinsic value — it's pure math based on where the stock is trading vs. where the strike is set.

- Call Option Intrinsic Value = Current Stock Price − Strike Price (if positive; otherwise zero);
- Put Option Intrinsic Value = Strike Price − Current Stock Price (if positive; otherwise zero).

Example: AAPL is trading at $240. A call option with a $220 strike has $20 of intrinsic value — the right to buy at $220 something that is currently worth $240. That $20 is real, hard value baked into the contract. A call with a $260 strike has zero intrinsic value — it is out of the money.

Extrinsic Value: The Time Premium

Extrinsic value — also called time value — is the portion of the premium that exists purely because time remains before expiration. As long as there is time left, there is a chance the stock can move in a favorable direction. The market prices that possibility into the contract. This is why options with more time cost more.

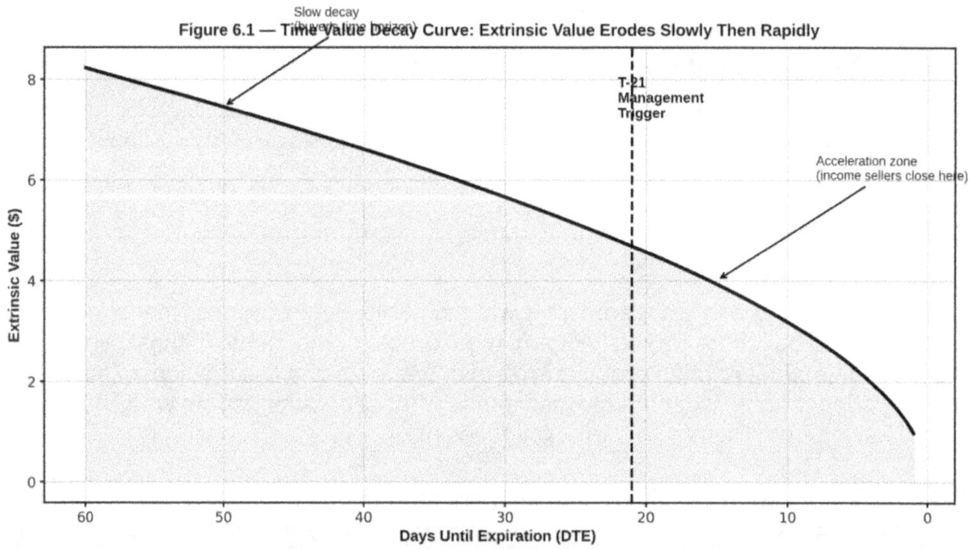

Figure 6.1 — Time Value Decay Curve. Extrinsic value erodes slowly then accelerates in the final 30 days.

But here is the critical insight for traders: time value does not decay in a straight line. It melts slowly at first, then accelerates dramatically as expiration approaches. Eddy Alexandre's analogy is perfect: the time value is melting away like a snowman in Florida — slowly at first, then fast.

TIME VALUE DECAY CURVE

90 DTE —————————— 45 DTE —————————— 30 DTE ——— 7 DTE —— EXP

Slow decay ↘ Accelerating decay ↘↘ Rapid decay ↘↘↘.

Best time to SELL options: 30–60 DTE • Best time to close short positions: 50–75% profit

The practical implication: option writers benefit most from the accelerating decay in the final 30 days before expiration. This is why the 30–45 DTE (days to expiration) entry zone is the sweet spot for most income strategies — you capture the steepest part of the decay curve while still having enough time to manage the trade if it moves against you.

Options Moneyness: ITM, ATM, OTM

Moneyness describes the relationship between an option's strike price and the current price of the underlying stock. It determines how much intrinsic value the option has, how it will behave as the stock moves, and which valuation component dominates the premium. Every option on every chain falls into one of three categories:

Strike	Moneyness (Call)	Call Bid	Call Ask	Intrinsic	Extrinsic	Delta
$170	Deep ITM	$21.40	$21.60	$20.00	$1.50	0.91

$180	ITM	$13.10	$13.30	$10.00	$3.20	0.76
$185	Slightly ITM	$8.80	$9.00	$5.00	$3.90	0.63
$190	ATM	$5.50	$5.70	$0.00	$5.60	0.50
$195	Slightly OTM	$3.20	$3.40	$0.00	$3.30	0.37
$200	OTM	$1.70	$1.90	$0.00	$1.80	0.25
$210	Deep OTM	$0.45	$0.55	$0.00	$0.50	0.10

Figure 6.2 — Option Chain Ladder. ITM, ATM, and OTM strikes with live bid/ask, IV, and delta for AAPL.

Strike	Moneyness	Intrinsic Value	Extrinsic Value	Delta Range	Best Used For
< $185	Deep ITM	High ($5+)	Low	0.75–0.99	Stock replacement; high cost, low leverage.
$185–$189	ITM	Moderate	Moderate	0.60–0.75	Balanced exposure; costs more, higher probability.
$190	ATM	$0	Highest	~0.50	Pure time value; maximum extrinsic cost.
$191–$195	OTM	$0	Moderate	0.25–0.49	Income sellers target; balanced risk/reward.
$196–$204	OTM	$0	Low	0.15–0.25	Directional bets; lower cost, lower probability.
> $205	Deep OTM	$0	Minimal	< 0.15	Lottery tickets; low cost, very low probability.

Figure 6.3 — Moneyness Ladder: Call Contract. For calls, strikes above the stock price are ITM — they have intrinsic value. Strikes below are OTM — pure time value only.

Strike	Moneyness	Intrinsic Value	Extrinsic Value	Delta Range	Best Used For
> $195	Deep ITM	High ($5+)	Low	-0.75 to -0.99	Bearish stock replacement; high delta, expensive.
$191–$195	ITM	Moderate	Moderate	-0.60 to -0.75	Directional put play; high probability.
$190	ATM	$0	Highest	~-0.50	Maximum extrinsic; pure time value.
$185–$189	OTM	$0	Moderate	-0.25 to -0.49	Income sellers target; CSP sweet spot.

$176–$184	OTM	$0	Low	-0.15 to -0.25	Premium selling zone; low probability of touch.
< $175	Deep OTM	$0	Minimal	> -0.15	Far OTM protection; very low premium.

Figure 6.4 — Moneyness Ladder: Put Contract. For puts the relationship inverts — strikes above are ITM, strikes below are OTM. Internalizing this asymmetry makes every options chain readable at a glance.

Moneyness	Condition (Call)	Condition (Put)	Premium Makeup	Behavior
ITM — In the Money	Strike BELOW stock price	Strike ABOVE stock price	Intrinsic + Extrinsic	Moves most with the stock (high delta). More expensive. Behaves like a stock position.
ATM — At the Money	Strike = stock price	Strike = stock price	Pure Extrinsic Value	Maximum time value. Highest sensitivity to IV changes. Sweet spot for many strategies.
OTM — Out of the Money	Strike ABOVE stock price	Strike BELOW stock price	Pure Extrinsic Value	No intrinsic value. Cheaper premium. Requires larger stock move to profit. High leverage, high risk.

The table above describes the logic. The diagrams below make it spatial. This is the most important visual in options education — the Moneyness Framework Ladder — showing exactly where ITM, ATM, and OTM fall on the price scale for calls and puts. Note carefully: ITM and OTM are OPPOSITE for calls vs. puts.

CALL CONTRACT — Moneyness Ladder	**PUT CONTRACT — Moneyness Ladder**
Resistance (Top) $90 ———— ITM (In-The-Money) ✓. $85 / $80 / $75 / $70 ——— ITM [+] Breakeven (BE) ———— transition zone **★ Stock Current Price $60 ——— ATM (At-The-Money)** $55 / $50 / $45 / $40 ——— OTM [-] Support (Bottom) $35 ———— OTM (Out-of-The-Money) X	Resistance (Top) $90 ———— OTM (Out-of-The-Money) X. $85 / $80 / $75 / $70 ——— OTM [-] **★ Stock Current Price $65 ——— ATM (At-The-Money)** Breakeven (BE) ———— transition zone $55 / $50 / $45 / $40 ——— ITM [+] Support (Bottom) $35 ———— ITM (In-The-Money) ✓

THE KEY ASYMMETRY

For a CALL: the strikes ABOVE the current price are ITM, strikes BELOW are OTM. For a PUT: it is exactly reversed — the strikes BELOW the current price are ITM, strikes ABOVE are OTM. This is because a call gives you the right to BUY, so you want the price to be above your strike. A put gives you the right to SELL, so you want the price to be below your strike. This single distinction, once internalized, makes every options chain readable at a glance.

AAPL is trading at $240. You are looking at a call option with a $220 strike, expiring in 55 days, priced at $22.30.

- Intrinsic Value: $240 − $220 = $20.00 (the option is $20 in the money);
- Extrinsic Value: $22.30 − $20.00 = $2.30 (time value remaining with 55 days to expiration); and
- Total Premium: $22.30 × 100 shares = $2,230 per contract.

Why is there $2.30 of extrinsic value on top of the $20 of intrinsic value? Because with 55 days left, there is still time for AAPL to move higher — and the market is pricing that possibility into the contract. As those 55 days tick down toward zero, the $2.30 melts away. At expiration, if AAPL is still at $240, the option is worth exactly $20 — pure intrinsic value, zero extrinsic.

PREMIUM = CONTRACT PRICE × 100

Always multiply the quoted premium by 100 to get the actual dollar cost of the contract. A $3.50 premium = $350 per contract. A $22.30 premium = $2,230 per contract. This is one of the most common sources of sticker shock for new options traders — and the most avoidable.

Implied Volatility & The Premium

Implied volatility (IV) is the market's forward-looking expectation of how much the underlying stock will move, expressed as an annualized percentage. It is embedded entirely in the extrinsic value component of the premium. When IV is high, premiums are expensive — both calls and puts cost more across every strike and expiration. When IV is low, premiums are cheap.

IV is not historical — it does not measure how much the stock has moved. It measures how much the market expects it to move. This distinction is critical because IV can spike suddenly on news events, earnings announcements, or macro shocks — even when the stock hasn't moved yet. When IV spikes, option premiums inflate overnight.

- High IV environment → Premium sellers have the advantage — collect elevated premiums, benefit as IV reverts;
- Low IV environment → Premium buyers have the advantage — cheap options, better reward-to-risk on directional plays;
- IV Rank (IVR) — Measures current IV relative to the past 52 weeks. IVR above 50 means IV is elevated vs. history — generally favorable for sellers; and
- IV Percentile — Similar to IVR but measures the percentage of days in the past year that IV was lower than today.

THE VALUATION RULE

Before entering any options trade, check three things: (1) Where is the stock relative to your strike — ITM, ATM, or OTM? (2) How much time value are you paying or collecting? (3) Is IV elevated or depressed relative to its historical range? These three answers determine whether the trade has edge.

Valuation Through the Six-Condition Lens

Valuation is not abstract. Every six-condition strategy has a specific valuation requirement that must be met before entry. The table below maps each condition to its valuation test — the specific check that confirms the option is priced correctly for your strategy before you execute.

#	Condition	Strategy	Valuation Test — What to Check Before Entry
1	**Bullish / Low IV**	Long call / bull call spread	IV Rank < 25. Check: is the debit you are paying less than 30% of the distance to your profit target? Example: Bull call spread with $10 width — max profit $10. Debit should be ≤ $3.00. If IV has been rising recently, wait — the premium cost may not yet reflect normal low-IV levels.
2	**Bullish / High IV**	CSP / bull put spread	IV Rank > 50. Credit collected must be ≥ 15% of spread width (for spreads) or ≥ 0.5% of reserved capital (for CSPs). Example: $10 spread must collect ≥ $1.50. CSP with $50 strike must collect ≥ $0.25. If premium is below these thresholds, IV is not truly elevated — wait.
3	**Bearish / Low IV**	Long put / bear put spread	IV Rank < 25. Same rule as condition 1 in reverse: debit paid ≤ 30% of spread width. Check: is IV rising (which would make your debit more expensive and disadvantage you)? If VIX is climbing, consider waiting until IV stabilizes.
4	**Bearish / High IV**	Bear call spread	IV Rank > 50. Credit collected ≥ 15% of spread width. Short call must be above all significant resistance levels on the chart. Do not sell into a level the stock is actively testing — the strike must be in clear air above the market.
5	**Range / Low IV**	Butterfly / iron condor	IV Rank < 30. For iron condors: net credit collected ≥ 25% of the total width of one spread. The strike-to-strike width must reflect actual chart support/resistance — not arbitrary round numbers. Probability of profit at entry should be ≥ 65% as shown on your platform.
6	**Range / High IV**	Calendar / diagonal	IV Rank > 50 on near-term leg. The IV differential between the short-dated and long-dated option must be positive (near-term IV > far-term IV). If this differential is zero or inverted, the calendar spread has no valuation edge — do not enter.

VALUATION IS THE FINAL GATE

The six-condition framework tells you which strategy to use. Valuation tells you whether to use it today or wait. An excellent strategy at the wrong price is a mediocre trade. Running the valuation test on every position before entry — five additional minutes per trade — is the discipline that separates trades with edge from trades with hope.

Black-Scholes: The Engine Behind Every Options Price

Every options price on every exchange in the world is anchored to some version of the Black-Scholes pricing model, developed by Fischer Black and Myron Scholes in 1973. You do not need to be able to derive the formula — but understanding its six inputs will make you a dramatically more effective options trader because they explain exactly why premiums change the way they do.

The Black-Scholes model takes six inputs and outputs a fair value for the option. Your platform calculates this continuously as market conditions change. The six inputs are:

Input	What It Is	How Changes Affect Premium
Current Stock Price	Where the underlying trades right now	Higher stock price → call premiums rise, put premiums fall. This is Delta at work.
Strike Price	The agreed exercise price of the contract	The further OTM the strike, the lower the premium. The more ITM, the higher.
Time to Expiration	Days remaining until expiration	More time = more premium. As time decays, extrinsic value melts. This is Theta.
Implied Volatility	Market's expected future movement	Higher IV = HIGHER premiums on all options at all strikes. The most powerful driver of premium changes. This is Vega.
Risk-Free Rate	Current interest rate (typically 3-month T-bill)	Higher rates modestly increase call premiums and decrease put premiums. This is Rho.
Dividends	Expected cash dividends before expiration	Ex-dividend date causes put premiums to rise and call premiums to fall. Critical for covered call timing.

Of these six inputs, Implied Volatility is the only one that is not directly observable — it must be extracted from market prices by working the Black-Scholes formula backward. This is why IV is sometimes called 'the market's estimate' of future movement: it is derived from what traders are collectively paying for options, not from the stock's historical behavior.

How Implied Volatility Drives Premium Across Strikes and Expirations

One of the most important practical skills in options trading is understanding exactly how IV changes affect premiums across different strikes and expiration dates — because the effect is not uniform. IV expansion inflates near-term options premiums more aggressively than longer-dated ones. And IV expansion inflates ATM options more than deep OTM options. These two asymmetries are where your edge lives.

IV Scenario	Effect on Near-Term Options	Effect on Far-Term Options
IV rises 10 percentage points	ATM premium increases 15-25%. Near-term options have higher Vega sensitivity per dollar of premium.	ATM premium increases 8-15%. Longer-dated options have higher absolute Vega but lower percentage sensitivity.
IV collapses post-earnings	ATM premium can drop 30-50% overnight regardless of stock price move. This is IV crush.	ATM premium drops 10-20%. Far-term options lose less because earnings was only one expiration cycle.
IV gradually expands (rising uncertainty)	Premium sellers benefit: collect elevated near-term premium that reverts when uncertainty resolves.	LEAPS buyers benefit less: far-term IV expands more slowly and is less affected by near-term uncertainty events.
IV compressed at historic lows	Near-term options are cheap — favorable for directional buyers. Premiums may not justify selling.	Far-term options are also cheap — ideal for LEAPS buyers. The full time value is available at a discount.

The practical implication: when IV expands suddenly (earnings announcement, macro shock, VIX spike), the traders who benefit most are those who already sold near-term options BEFORE the spike — they collected premiums at elevated IV and now benefit from IV contraction as well as time decay. The traders who try to sell into the spike are fighting an already-inflating premium and often overpay for the risk they are taking.

THE IV TIMING RULE

The best time to sell premium is when IV is elevated but has not yet peaked. The second best time is immediately after a spike begins to deflate. The worst time is at the peak of an IV spike — you are selling into maximum fear, and if the underlying continues to move, your elevated premium provides only partial protection. Sell into rising IV, not peak IV. Let the first 30% of any IV spike pass before entering short premium positions.

Bridging Valuation to the Greeks: What You Are Really Measuring

Chapter 5 introduces the Greeks — the sensitivity measures that quantify how your position changes in response to each of the inputs in the Black-Scholes model. Before you meet them in depth, here is the essential bridge: every Greek is simply the rate of change of the option's premium with respect to one of the Black-Scholes inputs.

Greek	Black-Scholes Input	What It Measures	Why Options Traders Care
Delta (Δ)	Stock Price	Rate of premium change per $1 move in the stock	Determines directional exposure and probability of expiring ITM. Strike selection tool.
Gamma (Γ)	Stock Price (2nd order)	Rate of change of Delta as stock moves	Risk accelerator near expiration. High Gamma = rapid Delta change. Manage at T-21.
Theta (Θ)	Time to Expiration	Daily premium decay in dollars	The income seller's friend. Theta is the daily collection check. Accelerates near expiry.
Vega (V)	Implied Volatility	Premium change per 1% change in IV	Determines how much your position profits or loses when IV moves. Short options have negative Vega.
Rho (ρ)	Risk-Free Interest Rate	Premium change per 1% rate change	Minor effect for most equity options. Significant for LEAPS in rapidly changing rate environments.

This table is your bridge from Chapter 4 to Chapter 5. Every concept in Chapter 5 flows directly from the Black-Scholes framework introduced here. When Chapter 5 tells you that Theta accelerates near expiration, you now know why: time to expiration is one of the six pricing inputs, and as it shrinks toward zero, its rate of change on the premium accelerates non-linearly. The Greeks are not arbitrary numbers — they are the calculus derivatives of a pricing model you now understand.

Intrinsic vs. Extrinsic: A Real-Money Breakdown

Every option's price is the sum of two components. Understanding which component you are paying for — and which component is decaying — changes how you evaluate every trade.

AAPL at $190	Strike	Option Price	Intrinsic	Extrinsic	Moneyness
Call	$170	$23.50	$20.00	$3.50	Deep ITM
Call	$180	$15.20	$10.00	$5.20	ITM
Call	$190	$8.00	$0.00	$8.00	ATM
Call	$200	$3.40	$0.00	$3.40	OTM
Call	$210	$1.10	$0.00	$1.10	Deep OTM
Put	$200	$12.80	$10.00	$2.80	ITM
Put	$190	$7.50	$0.00	$7.50	ATM
Put	$180	$3.00	$0.00	$3.00	OTM

Key insight: the ATM options ($190 strike for both call and put) have ZERO intrinsic value — they are 100% extrinsic. This means every dollar you pay for an ATM option will decay to zero by expiration unless the stock moves. The deep ITM $170 call, by contrast, is $20 intrinsic and only $3.50 extrinsic — it behaves much more like the stock itself. As a buyer, you are paying for time. As a seller, you are harvesting it.

HOW TO READ THIS CHAPTER

Chapter 5 has 21 sections organized in three progressive layers. Layer 1 (Delta through Rho): Essential for all traders — read these first and fully understand each Greek before continuing. Layer 2 (Greeks in management, delta-neutral basics, straddles): Read after your first few live trades when you want deeper management understanding. Layer 3 (Portfolio delta, adjustments, IV crush, week-in-the-life): Advanced management — return to these once you are actively running a live portfolio. Do not try to absorb all 21 sections at once. Fluency with the Greeks comes from use, not memorization.

6-CONDITION FRAMEWORK ▸ **GREEK PRIORITY SHIFTS by condition — this is the core insight**
Conditions 1 & 3 (buy premium): Delta and Gamma are primary — you need the move. Conditions 2 & 4 (sell premium): Theta and Vega are primary — you need decay and IV contraction. Conditions 5 & 6 (range): Theta dominates. Always know which Greeks are working FOR you.

Every options position you hold is in motion. Even when the underlying stock sits perfectly still, your option is changing — losing time value, shifting sensitivity, responding to volatility. The Greeks are the instruments on your risk dashboard that measure exactly how and why your position is moving. Ignoring them is like flying without instruments. Flying by the Greeks is what separates traders from gamblers.

There are five primary Greeks: Delta, Gamma, Theta, Vega, and Rho. Each measures a different dimension of an option's sensitivity to market variables. You will use all five, but Delta and Theta will govern the majority of your daily trade management decisions.

Delta (Δ) — Directional Sensitivity

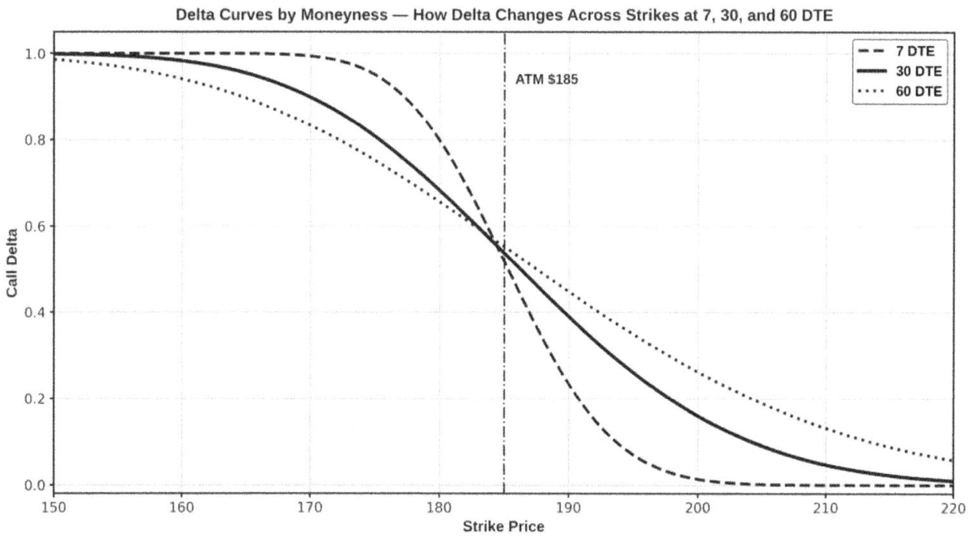

Figure 5.1 — Delta Curves by Moneyness — How delta changes across strike prices for calls and puts at different points in time.

Delta measures how much the option's price changes for every $1 move in the underlying stock. It is the most important Greek for position management and the one you will check first on every trade.

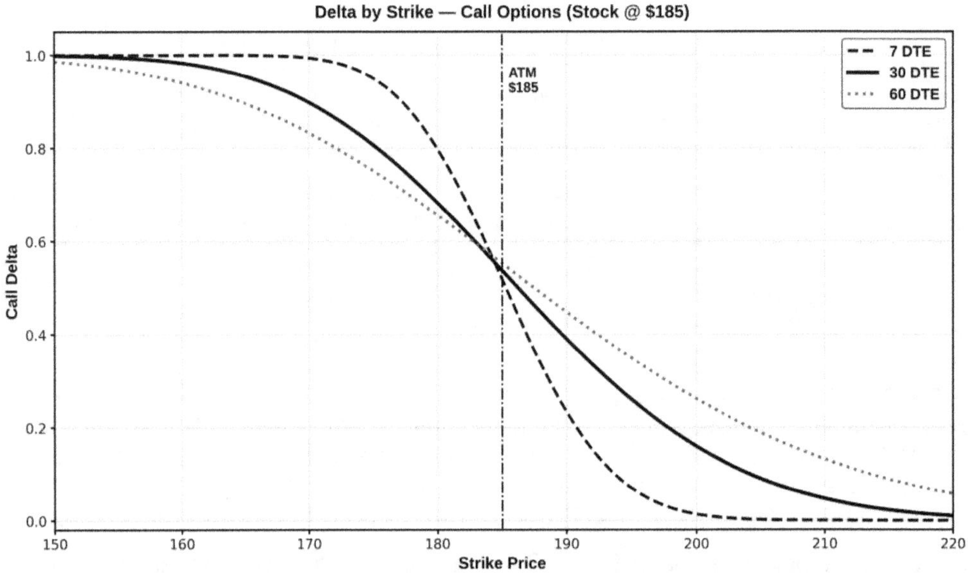

Figure 7.1 — Delta by Strike. How delta varies across strikes at different DTEs.

Position	Delta Range	Direction	What It Means
Long Call	0 to +1.0	Positive	Gain $0.50 per $1 rise in stock (0.50 delta). Option moves with the stock.
Short Call	0 to -1.0	Negative	Lose value as stock rises — seller wants stock to stay flat or fall.
Long Put	-1.0 to 0	Negative	Gain value as stock falls. -0.50 delta = gains $0.50 per $1 drop.
Short Put	0 to +1.0	Positive	Gain as stock stays flat or rises. Assigned if stock drops through strike.
Long Stock	+1.0	Positive	Always delta 1 — moves dollar for dollar with the stock.

Figure 7.2 — How Delta Changes with Price. The gamma effect at 30 DTE vs. 7 DTE.

Position	Delta Range	Direction	What It Means
Long Call	0 to +1.0	Positive	Gain $0.50 per $1 rise in stock (for 0.50 delta). Option moves with the stock.
Short Call	0 to −1.0	Negative	Lose value as stock rises — seller wants stock to stay flat or fall.

Position	Delta Range	Direction	What It Means
Long Put	−1.0 to 0	Negative	Gain value as stock falls. −0.50 delta = gains $0.50 per $1 drop.
Short Put	0 to +1.0	Positive	Gain as stock stays flat or rises. Assigned if stock drops through strike.
Long Stock	+1.0	Positive	Always delta 1 — moves dollar for dollar with the stock.

- ATM options have a delta near 0.50 — the option moves roughly $0.50 for every $1 in the stock;
- Deep ITM options approach delta 1.0 — they behave almost exactly like owning the stock;
- Deep OTM options approach delta 0 — they barely respond to stock movement until they get closer to the money; and
- Delta also approximates the probability that the option expires in the money — a 0.30 delta option has roughly a 30% chance of expiring ITM.

DELTA AS PROBABILITY

A 0.16 delta short put has approximately an 84% probability of expiring worthless — meaning you keep the premium. This is why most professional premium sellers target short strikes between 0.15 and 0.30 delta. It balances a high probability of profit with a premium that's still worth collecting.

Gamma (Γ) — The Rate of Delta Change

Gamma measures how fast delta changes as the stock moves. It is the Greek of acceleration — and it is the primary source of risk for short option positions near expiration.

- High Gamma = Delta is changing rapidly with each dollar move in the stock;
- ATM options near expiration have the highest Gamma — a small stock move can dramatically shift the option's delta;
- For option buyers: Gamma is your friend — a big move in your direction can rapidly accelerate your gains; and
- For option sellers: Gamma is the enemy near expiration — it creates whipsaw risk that can turn a winning trade into a loser overnight.

This is why experienced sellers manage and close positions before expiration rather than holding to expiry — the Gamma risk in the final week is simply too unpredictable to hold for the last few dollars of premium. Close at 50–75% profit and redeploy. Don't fight Gamma in the final 7 days.

Gamma of the Gamma — The Sixth Risk Measurement

ADVANCED CONCEPT

This section covers the sixth and most arcane risk measurement. It is included for completeness and for those managing large multi-leg positions. New traders may read it once for awareness and return to it after gaining experience with the first five Greeks.

You now know that as the stock moves, the delta changes — by the amount of the gamma. But there is a deeper layer: the gamma itself also changes as the stock moves. The gamma of the gamma measures exactly how much the gamma will change for each one-point move in the underlying price. It is the rate of change of the rate of change — the Greek of Greeks.

The formal definition: the gamma of the gamma is the amount by which the gamma will change when the stock price changes by one point. If a call has a gamma of 0.05 and the stock moves up one point, and the gamma decreases to 0.04, then the gamma of the gamma is −0.01. A negative gamma of the gamma means your gamma is shrinking as the stock rises — which is the normal behavior for options moving deeper in-the-money.

Option State	Gamma of Gamma	What It Means
Deep OTM	Near zero	Delta barely moving — gamma of gamma irrelevant. Position risk is low.
OTM approaching ATM	Positive and rising	Gamma is growing as strike nears — delta will accelerate faster with each move. Monitor closely.
ATM	Turns negative	Gamma has peaked and begins to shrink. This is the most dangerous zone for short sellers — gamma is at maximum but about to shift.
Slightly ITM	Most negative	Gamma is shrinking rapidly. Delta is approaching 1.0 — the option behaves more like stock. Short positions face maximum delta exposure.
Deep ITM	Approaches zero (negative)	Gamma near zero. Delta locked near 1.0. Gamma of gamma stabilizes — but the damage to a short position is already done.

For premium sellers operating within the Six-Condition system, the gamma of the gamma is most relevant in two specific situations:

- Condition 3 (Neutral High IV — Iron Condor): when the underlying drifts toward one of your short strikes, the gamma of that wing is growing — and the gamma of the gamma tells you how fast that gamma is accelerating. A large positive gamma of the gamma on an approaching strike means your risk is compounding faster than a static gamma reading suggests;
- Condition 2 (Bullish High IV — Cash-Secured Put): understanding that gamma of the gamma peaks while the option is still OTM — before the strike is tested — explains why defending a short put early, before it goes ATM, is always the correct risk-management posture. By the time the option goes ATM, gamma has already peaked, but the delta damage is now maximum.

The T-21 Rule reflects gamma of the gamma in practice. In the final 21 days, short options have both high gamma and rapidly changing gamma — the gamma of the gamma is at its most dangerous. Every point the stock moves against you in the final three weeks generates a larger delta change than the same move would have generated at 45 DTE. This is the mathematical reason why the T-21 exit rule exists: not just to capture theta, but to exit before the gamma of the gamma turns your position into a runaway delta machine.

GAMMA OF THE GAMMA — SELLER'S RULE

When your short strike is being tested, do not just check the gamma. Check whether the gamma is growing or shrinking. If the underlying is approaching your strike from below (for short calls) or from above (for short puts), the gamma of the gamma is positive — meaning your gamma is increasing and your delta exposure is compounding with every move. This is the mathematical signal to either close, roll out, or add a hedge. Waiting until you are ATM is waiting until gamma has already peaked and the delta damage is done.

Theta (Θ) — Time Decay

Theta measures how much the option's value decreases each day due to the passage of time, all else being equal. It is expressed as a dollar amount per day per contract. A Theta of −0.05 means the option loses $5 in value each day (0.05 × 100 shares).

→ See Figure 6.1 — Time Value Decay Curve (Chapter 4 — Options Valuation)

- Long options have negative Theta — time works against buyers, eroding the value of their premium daily;
- Short options have positive Theta — time works for sellers, the premium they collected decays into profit;
- Theta accelerates as expiration approaches — decay is fastest in the final 30 days (the steepest part of the decay curve); and
- The 30–45 DTE entry zone maximizes Theta collection while maintaining enough time to manage the position.

DTE Range	Theta Decay Rate	Strategy Implication
90+ DTE	Slow — small daily decay	Ideal for LEAPS buyers. Sellers: too little Theta to collect efficiently.
45–60 DTE	Moderate — accelerating	Sweet spot for opening short premium positions. Good balance of Theta vs. Gamma risk.
21–30 DTE	Fast — significantly accelerating	Sellers close positions here to lock in gains. Buyers look to roll or exit.
0–7 DTE	Extreme — Gamma risk is dominant	Danger zone for sellers. Max Gamma exposure. Close or roll — do not hold.

The acceleration is not abstract — it is measurable. Here are real AAPL theta values at three different points in a contract's life, all for the same $135 Call:

Days to Expiration	Theta (cents/day)	What It Means
55 DTE	7.081¢ / day	Option loses $7.08/day — slow melt. Seller benefits gradually.
20 DTE	9.675¢ / day	Same option now losing $9.68/day — 37% faster than at 55 DTE.
5 DTE	11.462¢ / day	Final burn — $11.46/day. Nearly double the rate vs. 55 DTE.

THE SNOWMAN IN FLORIDA

Theta is melting away like a snowman in Florida. At first it melts slowly. Then time decay accelerates and it melts fast. The seller's optimal window — 30 to 45 DTE — is the moment just before the melt accelerates. You open the position to capture that acceleration. You close it at 21 DTE before Gamma risk rises to dangerous levels.

Option Premium Decay — Empirical Tracking Table

The table below shows real, observable premium behavior over the life of a single contract. This is not theoretical — it is what happens to the option's price, day by day, as time passes. The stock price is unchanged throughout. Only time is moving. Watch what that does to the premium:

Day	DTE Remaining	Option Premium	Daily $ Decay	Total Decay	% of Premium Lost
Day 1 (Open)	45 DTE	$4.50	—	$0.00	0%
Day 5	40 DTE	$4.22	$0.056	$0.28	6.2%
Day 10	35 DTE	$3.91	$0.062	$0.59	13.1%
Day 15	30 DTE	$3.55	$0.072	$0.95	21.1%
Day 20	25 DTE	$3.11	$0.088	$1.39	30.9%
Day 25	20 DTE	$2.58	$0.106	$1.92	42.7%
Day 30	15 DTE	$1.94	$0.128	$2.56	56.9%
Day 35	10 DTE	$1.19	$0.150	$3.31	73.6%
Day 40	5 DTE	$0.52	$0.134	$3.98	88.4%
Day 45 (Exp.)	**0 DTE**	**$0.00**	**$0.104**	**$4.50**	**100%**

Notice the acceleration: the first 15 days consume only 21% of the premium. The final 15 days consume the remaining 43%. The decay is not linear — it is exponential toward expiration. This is why the writer closes at 21 DTE: by that point, you have captured over half your maximum profit (57%), with the most dangerous portion of the gamma risk still ahead.

THE SELLER'S HARVEST WINDOW

Opening at 45 DTE and closing at 21 DTE gives the seller the best of both worlds: the theta acceleration zone (days 25–35) is fully captured, gamma risk from the final 2 weeks is avoided, and capital is freed for the next cycle. The premium left on the table at 21 DTE is the insurance cost against the gamma risk you don't take.

Theta Across the Full Option Lifecycle — 150 DTE to Expiration

The table below tracks a single at-the-money call option from 150 days out all the way to expiration, holding all other factors constant. The stock price does not move. Only time passes. This is the theta curve in its purest form — and the acceleration in the final 30 days is the core reason for the T-21 rule.

Days Until Expiration	Theta (daily loss)	Option Premium	Observation
150 DTE	−0.016	$4.85	Slow melt — seller earns $1.60/day per 100 shares
120 DTE	−0.019	$4.34	Slight acceleration — still the buyer's time horizon
90 DTE	−0.021	$3.72	Decay steady — LEAPS zone ends here
60 DTE	−0.026	$3.03	Acceleration building — income sellers start watching
30 DTE ★	**−0.040**	**$2.14**	**⚠ ACCELERATION BEGINS — seller's entry sweet spot**
20 DTE ⚠	**−0.043**	**$1.71**	**★ T-21 CLOSE ZONE — 55% of premium already captured**
10 DTE	−0.060	$1.21	Gamma rising — sellers who remain face whipsaw risk
5 DTE	−0.085	$0.86	Extreme decay — 5× faster than at 150 DTE

Days Until Expiration	Theta (daily loss)	Option Premium	Observation
1 DTE	-0.191	$0.19	Final-day destruction — theta at maximum velocity

Underlying: ABC @ $45 | 45-Strike ATM Call | 35% Implied Volatility | All other factors held constant

The critical insight: from 150 DTE to 60 DTE, theta moves only from −0.016 to −0.026 — a modest change over 90 days. But from 30 DTE to 1 DTE, theta explodes from −0.040 to −0.191 — a 377% increase in decay rate over just 29 days. The option loses more premium in its final day alone than it lost in its first 30 days of life. This is not a linear curve. It is a cliff.

★ **For option writers (sellers):** The T-30 row marks where acceleration begins. The T-21 row is your action threshold — the point at which you close the position to bank the majority of your gains while gamma risk is still manageable. Open at 30–45 DTE. Close at T-21. That window is where the math lives.

★ **For option buyers:** Time is your enemy past T-30. Every day you hold without a significant move, theta erodes your premium at an accelerating rate. Enter with enough time for your thesis, and never hold through the final 30-day cliff unless the trade is actively working.

Vega (V) — Implied Volatility Sensitivity

VEGA OR TAU?

There is no letter in the Greek alphabet called "vega." Some strategists prefer to use the real Greek letter tau (τ) to refer to this risk measurement. The term "vega" will be used in this book, but the reader should note that "tau" means the same thing. Vega is the amount by which the option price changes when the volatility changes.

Vega measures how much the option's price changes for every 1% change in implied volatility. Unlike the other Greeks, Vega is not a Greek letter — it is sometimes called tau (τ) by purists — but it behaves like one, and every options trader must understand it because IV can move dramatically even when the stock price barely budges.

- Long options have positive Vega — a rise in IV increases the value of your option (good for buyers);
- Short options have negative Vega — a rise in IV increases the value of the option you sold, working against you (bad for sellers);
- Vega is highest for ATM options and for options with more time to expiration — longer-dated positions are more sensitive to IV changes; and
- Earnings events, Fed announcements, and macro shocks all cause IV to spike — then rapidly collapse (IV crush) after the event passes.

IV crush is one of the most common ways new traders lose money around earnings. They buy an option before earnings, the stock moves in their direction, but the option loses value because IV collapses after the announcement. The stock moved right, but Vega crushed the premium. Understanding this is non-negotiable before trading through any catalyst event.

IV CRUSH WARNING

Never buy options immediately before an earnings announcement without understanding IV rank. If IV is elevated (IVR above 50), the premium you pay is inflated. Even if the stock moves your way, IV collapse after earnings can neutralize or destroy your gain. Sell premium into high IV events — don't buy it.

Rho (ρ) — Interest Rate Sensitivity

Metric	What It Measures	For Sellers	For Buyers	Trader Action
Rho ρ (Interest Rate)	Change in option price per 1% change in rates.	NEUTRAL for 30–60 DTE. Negligible impact on income trades.	CALLS: positive (rates up = value up). PUTS: negative (rates up = value down).	Standard trades: ignore Rho. LEAPS (1–3 yr): monitor if rates shift >1% during hold period.

Figure 5.6 — Rho (ρ): Interest Rate Sensitivity — Seller vs. Buyer perspective. Standard equity trades: negligible. LEAPS in rate-shift environments: monitor closely.

Greek	Measures	Seller Uses It For	Buyer Uses It For	Priority
Delta	Price sensitivity per $1 move.	Strike selection — keep short delta 0.15–0.25.	Entry timing — buy high delta (0.5+).	#1 — check every trade.
Gamma	Rate of delta change.	Risk alarm — high gamma means rapid loss at expiry.	Acceleration tool — high gamma = fast profit.	#2 — watch near T-21.
Theta	Daily time decay in $.	Daily income — collect $X/day while you wait.	Enemy — theta erodes premium paid.	#1 income trades.
Vega	IV sensitivity per 1% change.	Sell high IV — vega works in your favor.	Buy low IV — vega gives leverage.	#2 — before earnings.
Rho	Rate change per 1% rates.	Irrelevant for 30–60 DTE trades.	Minor positive for calls.	#5 — LEAPS only.

Figure 5.2 — Greeks Dashboard — The five risk measures displayed simultaneously for a single options position.

Rho measures how much the option's price changes for every 1% change in interest rates. Of the five Greeks, Rho has the least day-to-day impact on most retail options strategies — but it becomes meaningful in two specific scenarios: LEAPS positions (longer-dated options are more Rho-sensitive) and high interest rate environments where the cost of carry matters.

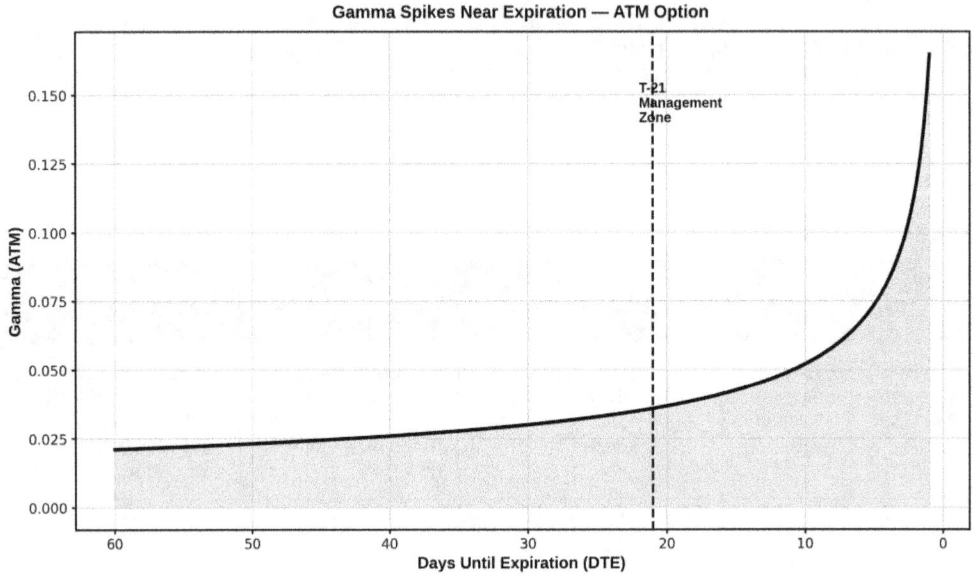

Figure 7.3 — Gamma Spikes Near Expiration. ATM gamma accelerates sharply inside 21 DTE.

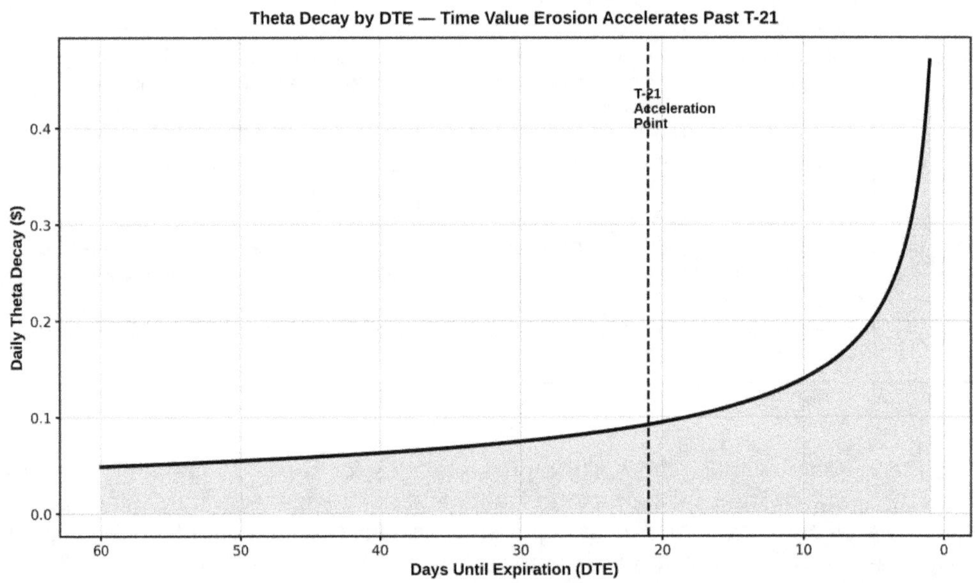

Figure 7.4 — Theta Decay by DTE. Time value erosion accelerates past the T-21 mark.

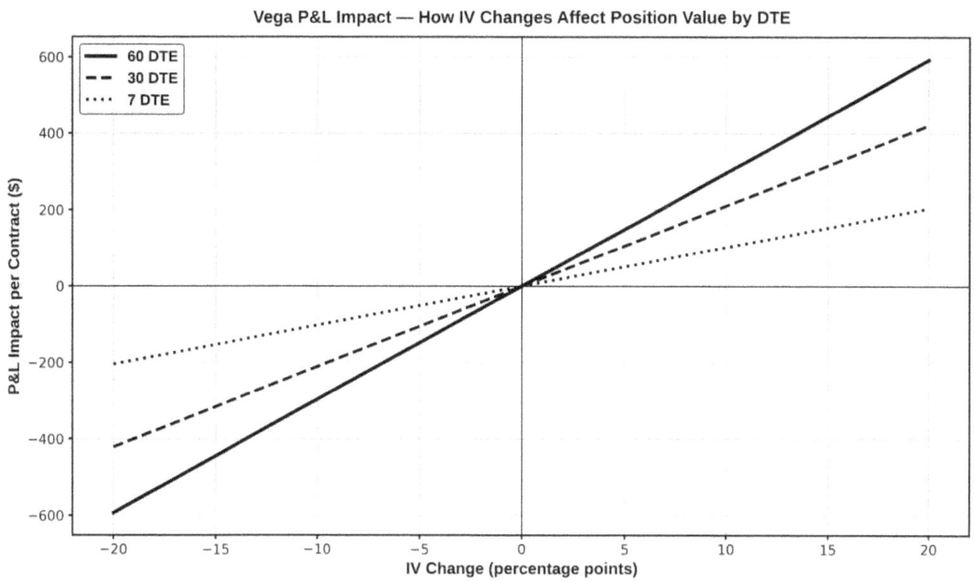

Figure 7.5 — Vega P&L Impact. How IV changes affect position value by DTE.

Greek Impact Summary — Options Seller vs. Buyer

Delta Δ	Price sensitivity	Low delta (near 0.20)	High delta (near 0.80)	Directional exposure
Gamma Γ	Delta rate of change	Low gamma (far from expiry)	High gamma (near expiry)	Risk acceleration
Theta Θ	Daily time decay	HIGH theta (collect decay)	Low theta (buy time cheap)	Income engine
Vega V	IV sensitivity	LOW vega (sell when IV high)	High vega (buy before IV rise)	Volatility edge
Rho ρ	Interest rate effect	Neutral	Slight positive (calls)	Rate environment

Figure 7.6 — Greek Impact Summary. Seller vs. Buyer perspective for all five Greeks.

- Call options have positive Rho — rising rates slightly increase call values (higher cost of carrying stock);
- Put options have negative Rho — rising rates slightly decrease put values;
- For standard 30–60 DTE positions: Rho is largely irrelevant to daily trade management; and
- For LEAPS (1–3 year expirations): Rho becomes a meaningful factor if rates shift significantly during your holding period.

The Greeks in Real-Time Trade Management

Knowing the Greeks individually is the start. Using them together in real time is the skill. Here is how a risk manager reads the Greeks dashboard on an open position:

Greek	Watch When...	Alert Signal	Management Action
Delta	Stock moves significantly	Delta moves toward 1.0 on short options (assignment risk)	Adjust strike, roll position, or close to reduce directional exposure
Gamma	Within 21 DTE on any short position	Gamma spikes as expiration approaches	Close or roll before Gamma becomes unmanageable — don't hold to expiry for last few dollars
Theta	Daily — especially on long positions	Theta eroding faster than stock is moving in your favor	Exit long options that aren't moving — time is actively working against you
Vega	Before any catalyst event (earnings, Fed)	IV spike before event; IV crush after	Avoid buying premium into high IV. Sell premium before events; close before IV collapses

THE GREEKS HIERARCHY

For most trades: Delta tells you if you're right on direction. Theta tells you if time is on your side. Vega tells you if volatility is working for or against you. Gamma tells you when to get out. Rho tells you almost nothing on short-dated trades. Manage in that order.

ADVANCED: THE DELTA-NEUTRAL FRAMEWORK

Limiting directional risk and engineering positions that earn from volatility — not prediction

Limiting Directional Risk

Every trade you place carries delta — directional exposure. When you buy a call with a delta of 0.50, you are expressing a bullish view equivalent to owning 50 shares of the underlying. If the stock moves against you, the delta works against you. This is the core challenge of all directional trading: you must be right on direction, magnitude, AND timing simultaneously.

The delta-neutral framework solves the direction problem entirely. Instead of betting on which way the market moves, you engineer a position where net delta equals zero — or very close to it. A delta-neutral position does not care whether the stock goes up or down. It cares about HOW MUCH it moves, and how quickly. This reframes your entire edge: from prediction to volatility harvesting.

This is not a passive approach. Delta-neutral is an active risk management architecture — one that requires you to understand delta at a deeper level than 'how much does my option move with the stock.' You need to understand portfolio delta, how delta changes as the position ages, and how to maintain neutrality through adjustment.

Directional Trading — Delta at Work FOR You	**Delta-Neutral — Direction Eliminated**
You buy a call. Delta = +0.50.	Long call (+0.50) + short 50 shares (−0.50) = net delta 0.
Stock rises \$2 → option gains ~\$1.00 ✓.	Stock rises \$2 → position flat ≈ \$0.
Stock falls \$2 → option loses ~\$1.00 ✗.	Stock falls \$2 → position flat ≈ \$0.
You need to be right on direction.	**You earn from volatility and time — not direction.**

Neutral View vs. Neutral Position: A Critical Distinction

This distinction is one of the most important conceptual clarity moments in all of options trading. Most traders confuse having a neutral view — 'I don't know which way the market is going' — with having a neutral position — 'My book has zero net delta.' They are completely different.

	NEUTRAL VIEW	NEUTRAL POSITION (Delta-Neutral)
What it means	You have no strong opinion on which direction the stock will move in the near term. Your forecast is: 'I don't know — up or down both seem equally possible right now.'	Your position has been mathematically engineered so that net portfolio delta equals zero. Dollar-for-dollar, the position does not gain or lose value from small directional moves.
How it feels	A feeling or a forecast. Gut-level market read.	A mathematical state. Achieved by combining options and/or shares so net delta = 0.
Can you have one without the other?	Yes — you can have a neutral view but still own a call (net delta +50). You 'feel' neutral but are directionally long.	Yes — you can have a neutral position but expect a large move in one direction. A delta-neutral straddle is neutral now but is designed to profit from a big move — up or down.
Six-condition link	Conditions 5 and 6 (range-bound) reflect a neutral VIEW — the trader does not expect a large directional move.	Conditions 5 and 6 strategies (iron condor, butterfly, calendar) aim to build delta-NEUTRAL POSITIONS — so theta, not delta, drives the P&L.
Management requirement	None — it is just a market opinion.	Active — delta drifts as the stock moves and as time passes. Must be monitored and re-balanced through adjustments.

THE PREMIUM DESK DEFINITION

A neutral view is what you bring to the trade. A neutral position is what you build with the trade. The first is analysis. The second is architecture. You can be wrong on your view and still profit — if your position is properly delta-neutral and volatility behaves as expected. Architecture trumps forecast.

Capitalizing on a Big Move: The Straddle

The straddle is the purest expression of the delta-neutral framework for conditions 5 and 6. You simultaneously buy a call and a put at the same strike, same expiration, on the same underlying. The call has a positive delta. The put has a negative delta. At the ATM strike, both deltas are approximately 0.50 — so the net position delta is close to zero at entry.

What the straddle is expressing is not a directional view — it is a volatility view. You believe the stock will make a significant move, but you do not know which direction. You are buying exposure to movement itself.

STRADDLE EXAMPLE — AAPL earnings play

AAPL at $195. Earnings in 5 days. IV elevated (IVR = 72). You don't know if the report will beat or miss.

Buy AAPL $195 Call (DTE = 7) | Cost: $4.20 | Delta: +0.51.
Buy AAPL $195 Put (DTE = 7) | Cost: $3.90 | Delta: −0.49
Total debit: $8.10 ($810 per contract) | Net delta at entry: +0.51 − 0.49 = +0.02 ≈ 0

Breakeven upside: $195 + $8.10 = $203.10 | Breakeven downside: $195 − $8.10 = $186.90.

AAPL reports: stock gaps to $210 (+7.7%) → Call worth ~$15.00. Put worth ~$0.30. Total: $15.30. Profit: $7.20 (+89%).
AAPL reports: stock drops to $180 (−7.7%) → Put worth ~$14.50. Call worth ~$0.25. Total: $14.75. Profit: $6.65 (+82%).
AAPL moves only $3 → both options decay. Total loss: ~$4.00 (−49%). Direction was right. SIZE OF MOVE was wrong.

THE STRADDLE'S ENEMY IS NOT DIRECTION — IT IS STILLNESS

A straddle does not lose because the stock went the wrong way. It loses because the stock did not move enough to overcome the cost of buying both options. Every day that passes without a significant move, theta decays both legs simultaneously. You are paying for movement. If you do not get movement, you pay with time.

Reducing Cost: The Strangle

The strangle solves the straddle's cost problem by moving both strikes out of the money. Instead of buying the ATM call and ATM put (the most expensive pair of strikes), you buy an OTM call and an OTM put. The premium paid is lower. The breakeven points are wider. The probability of maximum profit is lower — but the strategy costs less to enter and requires a larger move to profit.

Metric	ATM Straddle	OTM Strangle	Difference
Strikes	Buy $195 Call + $195 Put	Buy $200 Call + $190 Put	10-point spread
Total premium paid	$8.10 ($810 / contract)	$4.80 ($480 / contract)	41% cheaper
Breakeven upside	$203.10	$204.80	Move needs to be larger
Breakeven downside	$186.90	$185.20	Move needs to be larger

Metric	ATM Straddle	OTM Strangle	Difference
Net delta at entry	≈ 0 (ATM both sides)	≈ 0 (OTM both sides, symmetric)	Both start near-neutral
Max loss scenario	Stock sits at $195 at expiry	Stock sits between $190–$200 at expiry	Strangle has wider 'dead zone'
Best for	High-conviction move expected but direction unknown	Elevated IV + expecting move but willing to wait — lower cost basis	—

The choice between straddle and strangle comes down to two factors: cost tolerance and conviction on size of move. If you believe a major move is imminent and want maximum participation, the straddle's ATM strikes give you the best delta capture on the move. If you are less certain of timing or magnitude and want to reduce cost, the strangle's OTM strikes give you a lower cost basis with wider exposure.

Calculating Portfolio Delta for Combination Positions

When you hold multiple options positions — or a mix of options and shares — your total directional exposure is the sum of all individual deltas, weighted by the number of contracts or shares held. This is your portfolio delta, and it is the number you must track at all times in a delta-neutral strategy.

Position	Quantity	Delta per Unit	Net Delta Contribution
Long AAPL $195 Call	2 contracts	δ = +0.51	2 × 100 × +0.51 = +102
Long AAPL $195 Put	2 contracts	δ = −0.49	2 × 100 × −0.49 = −98
Long AAPL shares	None	—	0
NET PORTFOLIO DELTA			**= +102 − 98 = +4 (nearly neutral)**

The formula is always the same: Net Portfolio Delta = Σ (Contracts × 100 shares × Delta per option). For long shares, each share contributes +1.0 delta. For short shares, each share contributes −1.0 delta. For short options, the delta contribution is reversed — a short call with delta 0.30 contributes −30 delta per contract.

Position	Quantity	Delta per Unit	Net Delta Contribution
Long MSFT $420 Call	3 contracts	δ = +0.45	3 × 100 × +0.45 = +135
Short MSFT $430 Call	3 contracts	δ = −0.28	3 × 100 × −0.28 = −84
Short MSFT shares	50 shares	δ = −1.00	50 × −1.00 = −50

Position	Quantity	Delta per Unit	Net Delta Contribution
NET PORTFOLIO DELTA			= +135 − 84 − 50 = +1 (effectively neutral)

THE DELTA ACCOUNTING RULE

Every position in your book has a delta. Shares have delta. Calls have delta. Puts have delta. When you run a delta-neutral strategy, you are an accountant as much as a trader. You track every unit of delta, every session, against the neutral target. Most modern brokers display net portfolio delta in your positions dashboard. Use it. Check it every morning before the open.

Monitoring the Two Key Greeks in a Delta-Neutral Position: Delta and Gamma

In a delta-neutral position, the two Greeks that dominate your daily management are Delta and Gamma. Every other Greek matters — but these two determine whether your position remains neutral or drifts into significant directional exposure.

You have already met Delta — it measures your rate of change relative to the underlying's price. Gamma is the rate of change of delta itself. It is the acceleration. Gamma tells you how fast your carefully constructed neutral position is going to drift away from neutral as the stock moves.

Greek	What It Measures in a Delta-Neutral Position	What to Do When It Moves
DELTA (δ)	Your net directional exposure. Target = 0. In practice, maintaining |delta| < 10 per contract is acceptable for most positions.	If delta drifts significantly positive: buy puts or short shares to re-neutralize. If delta drifts significantly negative: buy calls or long shares to re-neutralize.
GAMMA (Γ)	The rate at which delta changes as the stock moves. High gamma = delta changes rapidly. Low gamma = delta changes slowly. Gamma is highest at ATM and nearest to expiration.	High gamma near expiration means your delta can swing dramatically on a single session's move. In conditions 5 and 6 (range trades), high gamma near expiration is a warning signal — re-evaluate or close the position before gamma becomes unmanageable.
Gamma risk in practice	A straddle with 5 DTE has very high gamma. A single $3 move in the underlying can shift net delta from 0 to +60 or −60 in one session.	This is why the T-21 rollover rule exists: close or roll short-premium positions before gamma danger zone. Gamma is the clock running out on your neutral position's stability.

The relationship between Delta and Gamma is the relationship between position and velocity. Delta tells you where you are directionally right now. Gamma tells you how fast that position is changing. A delta-neutral position with low gamma is stable — it will remain close to neutral even with moderate stock movement. A delta-neutral position with high gamma is unstable — it can drift far from neutral on a single volatile session.

Creating a Delta-Neutral Straddle: Full Construction Walkthrough

The delta-neutral straddle is the signature structure for conditions 5 and 6 when you believe a significant volatility event is coming but cannot identify direction. Here is the complete construction and daily management protocol.

DELTA-NEUTRAL STRADDLE — SPY Example

Setup: SPY at $520. FOMC announcement in 8 days. IVR = 68. You expect a sharp move but cannot predict direction.

Six-Condition read: Range-bound + High IV → Condition 6 → ATM Calendar or Straddle approved.

Step	Action	Detail
1	Select expiration	Choose DTE 10–14 days. Captures the Federal Open Market Committee (FOMC) event with enough time for the move to materialize. Avoid DTE < 7 — gamma risk too high relative to reward.
2	Buy ATM Call	SPY $520 Call (9 DTE). Premium: $5.20. Delta: +0.51. Gamma: 0.068. Theta: −$0.38/day.
3	Buy ATM Put	SPY $520 Put (9 DTE). Premium: $4.80. Delta: −0.49. Gamma: 0.068. Theta: −$0.35/day.
4	Calculate net delta	Net delta = +0.51 − 0.49 = +0.02. Nearly neutral. Total cost: $10.00 ($1,000 per straddle).
5	Set breakevens	Upside BE: $520 + $10.00 = $530.00. Downside BE: $520 − $10.00 = $510.00. SPY must move more than $10 to profit.
6	Set daily delta check	If SPY moves more than $3 in one session → recalculate net delta. If net delta exceeds ±25, re-evaluate need to adjust.
7	Set profit target	Target 50–75% of max gain. If the position doubles in value after the FOMC announcement, take 75% off and let the remainder run.
8	Set loss rule	If the total position value drops to $4.00 (40% of cost) with more than 4 days remaining → close. Theta decay is destroying value faster than a move can recover it.

Understanding Trade Adjustments: When and How

No delta-neutral position stays neutral by itself. As the underlying moves, delta changes — and the position drifts from neutral into directional exposure. This is not a failure. It is physics. The question is not whether adjustment will be needed. The question is when and how to adjust with discipline.

There are two adjustment philosophies. The first is mechanical: you set a delta threshold — for example, ±25 delta per contract — and adjust any time the position breaches it, regardless of your market view. The second is discretionary: you monitor delta drift and adjust only when the drift is accompanied by a deterioration in the original thesis (e.g., the stock is trending, not ranging). The Premium Desk uses mechanical adjustment thresholds as the default — because discretionary adjustments invite the very emotional decision-making that the six-condition system is designed to eliminate.

Situation	What Happened	Adjustment Action	Result
Straddle drifted long (delta > +30)	Stock has rallied. Call delta expanded. Net delta now +35. Position behaving like a long call.	Sell shares (short 30–35 shares per contract pair) to re-neutralize. Or buy an additional put to offset the extra call delta.	Net delta returns to near 0. Position is neutral again. If stock continues higher, call profit accelerates.
Straddle drifted short (delta < −30)	Stock has fallen. Put delta expanded. Net delta now −38. Position behaving like a long put.	Buy shares (30–38 shares per contract pair) to re-neutralize. Or buy an additional call to offset the extra put delta.	Net delta returns to near 0. If stock continues lower, put profit accelerates.
High gamma near expiration	5 DTE. Gamma has doubled. Delta swings ±15 on each $1 move. Position is difficult to manage.	Close or roll the straddle forward. Add 14–21 DTE to reduce gamma. Do not hold ATM straddles through expiration week unless profiting strongly.	Gamma risk eliminated. Position manageable again.
Thesis broken — stock trending	Stock has been grinding higher for 3 sessions. Range condition is dissolving. Condition may be shifting from 5/6 to 1 or 2.	Close the straddle entirely. Re-read the six-condition table. If condition has changed, deploy the appropriate new-condition strategy.	Capital preserved. No need to fight a position whose thesis no longer applies.

Deciding When to Adjust a Trade: The Three-Question Protocol

Before making any adjustment to a delta-neutral position, run the three-question protocol. This prevents over-adjustment — one of the most common and expensive mistakes in delta-neutral management. Adjusting too frequently generates unnecessary transaction costs and can turn a well-structured position into an over-engineered mess.

Q	Ask Yourself	If YES — adjust. If NO — wait.
1	Has net portfolio delta breached my threshold? (e.g., |delta| > 25 per contract pair)	YES: The position has drifted beyond acceptable neutrality. Adjustment is mechanically triggered. Execute without second-guessing. NO: Delta is still within tolerance. Watch, do not touch.
2	Has the original condition changed? (Ranging stock has begun trending, or low IV has become high IV)	YES: The thesis is broken. Close the entire position and re-read the six-condition table. Deploy the correct strategy for the new condition. NO: Condition intact. Adjustment only if delta threshold was breached.
3	Does the cost of adjustment (commissions + slippage) reduce expected profit by more than 10%?	YES: Consider a larger, less frequent adjustment or an alternative adjustment method (e.g., share-based rather than option-based). NO: Proceed. Transaction cost is acceptable relative to the value of re-neutralization.

DELTA-NEUTRAL IN THE SIX-CONDITION SYSTEM

Conditions 5 and 6 are the natural home of delta-neutral strategies. Condition 5 (range-bound, low IV): use butterfly or iron condor — these are inherently delta-neutral at entry and earn from theta as the stock stays in range. Condition 6 (range-bound, high IV): use calendar spreads, straddles, or strangles — earn from IV contraction and time decay across two expirations. In both cases, your job after entry is not to predict — it is to maintain neutrality and let the structure earn from the passage of time and the compression of volatility.

The Black-Scholes Intuition: What It Really Tells Options Traders

You do not need to derive the Black-Scholes formula to trade options professionally. But you do need to understand what it is computing — because it is computing the number you see every time you look at an option price. Black-Scholes says: given the current stock price, the strike price, the time to expiration, the risk-free rate, and the volatility of the underlying, what is a fair price for this option?

Of those five inputs, four are known and fixed at any moment. Only one is unknown: volatility. This is why implied volatility is derived backwards from the market price — the market tells you what it is paying, and you solve for what volatility assumption justifies that price. When IV is high, the market assumes large future moves and prices options expensively. When IV is low, the market assumes calm and prices options cheaply.

Input	Effect on Option Price	Six-Condition Relevance
Stock Price vs Strike	ITM options more expensive. OTM options less expensive.	Conditions 1 and 3: buy OTM options when cheap (low IV), allow stock movement to push them toward ITM. Intrinsic value grows as the trade works.
Time to Expiration	More time = higher price. Less time = lower price (theta decay).	Sellers (conditions 2, 4, 5, 6) benefit as expiration approaches. Buyers (conditions 1, 3) need enough time for the move before decay dominates.
Implied Volatility	Higher IV = higher option price. Lower IV = lower option price.	The key axis of the six-condition framework. High IV → sell premium (conditions 2, 4, 6). Low IV → buy premium (conditions 1, 3, 5).
Risk-Free Rate (Rho)	Higher rates = slightly higher calls, slightly lower puts.	Minor on short-dated options. Relevant for LEAPS. Rising rates moderately reduce long put values — factor in for long-dated bearish positions.
Dividends	Expected dividends reduce call price, increase put price.	Covered call writers (condition 2): dividend ex-dates create early assignment risk. Check ex-dividend dates before selling calls. Never sell through an ex-date without understanding assignment consequences.

IV Crush: The Phenomenon That Destroys Unprepared Buyers

IV crush is the rapid collapse of implied volatility immediately after a binary event — most commonly earnings. The uncertainty inflating premium disappears instantly when results are known. IV drops 30–60% in a single session. You can be right on direction and still lose money because IV collapse destroys extrinsic value faster than price movement builds intrinsic value.

IV CRUSH EXAMPLE — AAPL Earnings

AAPL at $195 before earnings. IV = 55% (IVR = 80). You buy the $200 call for $3.50. Delta = 0.38. Vega = 0.18.

Earnings: AAPL beats and rises to $202 (+3.6%). Direction: correct.

IV drops from 55% to 25% (crush of 30pts). Vega loss: 0.18 × 30 = −$5.40.

Delta gain from $7 move: 0.38 × 7 = +$2.66. Net result: −$2.74. Call drops from $3.50 to ~$0.76.

Six-condition lesson: IVR = 80 means condition 2, not condition 1. Selling premium was correct. Buying was a framework violation.

THE IV CRUSH RULE

Never buy premium (conditions 1 or 3) when IVR is above 50. You are overpaying for extrinsic value that will evaporate the moment the market resolves its uncertainty. High IVR means sell premium. If you must express direction in high-IV, use a debit spread — it has far less vega exposure than an outright long option.

Managing Greeks in Real Time: A Week in the Life of Five Positions

Monday morning. You have five open positions. Your portfolio Greeks read: total delta -45, total theta +$38/day, total vega -$280. What does this tell you, and what should you do?

The delta of -45 means your portfolio will lose approximately $45 for every $1 the S&P 500 rises (assuming your positions are correlated with the broad market). This is slightly more directional than ideal — a net delta between -20 and +20 is the neutral zone for income portfolios. You are short delta, meaning you profit if the market goes down and lose if it goes up. If the market is in Condition 1 (bull trending), this negative delta is working against the trend. Action: consider closing your most negatively-delta position or adding a small bullish position to bring delta closer to neutral.

The theta of +$38/day means you are earning $38 every calendar day from time decay across all positions. This is your PPD — Profit Per Day. If your monthly income target is $800, you need $800 ÷ 30 = $27/day. At $38/day you are above target. The theta is working. No action needed on the theta front — but log it in your Sunday review to track whether your PPD is trending up or down over time.

The vega of -$280 means that if implied volatility across your positions increases by 1 percentage point, your portfolio will lose approximately $280. You are short vega — which means you benefit from IV contraction and are hurt by IV expansion. If VIX is at 14 and the VIX term structure is in contango, this short vega position is favorable — IV is more likely to stay low or contract further. But if VIX is at 22 and the term structure has flattened, your short vega position is exposed to a potential spike. Action in the second scenario: add a long vega position (buy a cheap OTM put on SPY) to reduce your vega exposure.

Wednesday. The market drops 2% on unexpected inflation data. Your portfolio delta of -45 actually benefits — you gain approximately $90 from the market decline (the S&P dropped about $10, and your delta is -45 × -$10 ÷ 5 ≈ $90 on your correlated positions). But your vega is now working against you: VIX jumped from 14 to 19, a 5-point increase, costing you 5 × $280 = $1,400 in vega losses. Your theta collected $76 over two days. Net impact: +$90 (delta) - $1,400 (vega) + $76 (theta) = -$1,234. The vega hit dominated everything else.

This is why managing Greeks is not about any single Greek — it is about the INTERACTION between all of them. Your delta was fine. Your theta was fine. Your vega was the vulnerability. If you had spent $150 on a SPY put hedge on Monday (reducing your vega exposure by 40%), your Wednesday loss would have been approximately -$690 instead of -$1,234 — still negative, but manageable. The $150 hedge investment would have saved $534 in losses. This is the math of risk management in practice.

Friday. VIX has settled back to 16. Your vega losses partially recovered. Your theta has collected another $76 over two days. One position hit its 50% profit target and you closed it, locking in $210. The week ends with your portfolio down about $800 from Wednesday's shock but recovering through theta decay and one winner. You log the week in your journal, noting: 'Vega exposure was too high for current VIX environment. Next week: add long vega hedge when VIX is below 15 and my net vega exceeds -$200.' This is how Greeks management evolves from theory to practice — one week at a time, one lesson at a time.

Time Decay in Practice: Watching $1,000 Evaporate

Time decay is the income trader's best friend and the option buyer's worst enemy. But most traders do not truly understand HOW it works until they see it happen to real money. Here is a 30-day time decay profile for a $10.00 ATM option on a $200 stock — showing exactly how much value disappears each week.

DTE	Option Value	Value Lost	% Remaining	Daily Decay	Cumulative Loss
30	$10.00	—	100%	$0.15/day	$0
25	$9.25	$0.75	92%	$0.18/day	$75
21	$8.50	$0.75	85%	$0.22/day	$150
14	$6.80	$1.70	68%	$0.30/day	$320
10	$5.50	$1.30	55%	$0.40/day	$450
7	$4.20	$1.30	42%	$0.55/day	$580
5	$3.10	$1.10	31%	$0.70/day	$690
3	$1.90	$1.20	19%	$0.90/day	$810
1	$0.60	$1.30	6%	$1.30/day	$940
0	$0.00	$0.60	0%	—	$1,000

Study this table carefully. In the first 9 days (30 to 21 DTE), the option lost $1.50 — about $0.17/day. In the LAST 3 days (3 to 0 DTE), it lost $1.90 — about $0.63/day. Time decay accelerated nearly 4x. This is why income writers target the 45-to-21 DTE window: they capture the majority of time decay while avoiding the gamma risk of the final week.

For option buyers, the message is equally clear: if your thesis has not played out by 14 DTE, you have already lost 32% of your premium to time alone. Holding and hoping from 14 DTE to expiration is not a strategy — it is a donation to the option writer on the other side of your trade.

THE TIME DECAY MATH

An option that costs $10.00 at 30 DTE loses $1.50 in the first third of its life, $3.00 in the middle third, and $5.50 in the final third. The seller who enters at 30 DTE and closes at 21 DTE captures only 15% of the premium — but takes on only 10% of the gamma risk. The seller who holds to expiration captures 100% of the premium but takes on 90% of the gamma risk in the final week. This is why the T-21 management rule exists.

Greeks in Action: How Each Greek Affects Your Real Positions

Understanding the Greeks in isolation is step one. Step two is understanding how they interact on your actual positions. Here is a complete scenario analysis showing how each Greek affects a short put position on AAPL at different points in its lifecycle.

Position: Sell 1× AAPL $180 put at 35 DTE for $4.50 premium. AAPL at $190 at entry.

Scenario	AAPL	Delta	Theta/Day	Vega	Position Value	Your P&L
Entry (35 DTE)	$190	-0.20	+$8	$-0.12	$4.50	$0
Stock flat (21 DTE)	$190	-0.18	+$12	$-0.08	$2.80	+$170
Stock up 5% (21 DTE)	$200	-0.08	+$6	$-0.04	$1.20	+$330
Stock down 3% (21 DTE)	$184	-0.35	+$15	$-0.15	$4.00	+$50
Stock down 5% (21 DTE)	$180.50	-0.48	+$18	$-0.18	$5.50	-$100
IV spikes +10 pts	$190	-0.22	+$7	$-0.14	$5.70	-$120
IV drops -10 pts	$190	-0.17	+$9	$-0.09	$3.30	+$120
T-21 — close at 50%	$188	-0.22	+$11	$-0.10	$2.25	+$225 EXIT

Key observations from the table: (1) Theta is your ally every single day — even when the stock moves against you, theta is collecting $8-$18/day. (2) Delta risk increases sharply as the stock approaches your strike — at $180.50, your delta is -0.48 vs. -0.20 at entry. This is gamma accelerating your directional exposure. (3) A 10-point IV spike costs you $120 even if the stock does not move — this is vega risk, and it is why you never sell puts when IVR is already low. (4) The T-21 exit at 50% profit captures $225 of the $450 max profit with only 40% of the time elapsed.

The Greeks Cheat Sheet: What to Monitor and When

Greek	Monitor When	Danger Signal	Safe Range	Your Action
Delta	Daily	Portfolio delta > 30% of account notional	10-20% net delta	Rebalance: add opposite direction or hedge
Gamma	Last 10 DTE	Gamma > 0.05 on short options	Gamma < 0.03	Close or roll before gamma accelerates
Theta	Daily	Portfolio theta below your PPD target	Meeting or exceeding PPD	Add new income positions if below target
Vega	When VIX moves >2 pts	Large vega on short positions when VIX is spiking	Net short vega in high IV; net long in low IV	Reduce short vega in VIX spikes; increase in low VIX

Greek	Monitor When	Danger Signal	Safe Range	Your Action
Rho	Rate decisions only	Large LEAPS positions before FOMC	Minimal for 30-45 DTE positions	Only relevant for LEAPS; factor into diagonal pricing

FIRST-TIME READER NOTE

This chapter references options strategies by name — covered calls, cash-secured puts, iron condors. If these are new to you, do not worry. You are not expected to know them yet. This chapter is about understanding which stocks are worth trading before you learn how to trade them. Every strategy mentioned is fully explained in Chapters 2–15. Simply note that larger, more liquid stocks support more complex strategies.

6-CONDITION FRAMEWORK ▸ ALL SIX — determines eligible underlyings per condition
Large-caps are approved for all six conditions. Small-caps are restricted to conditions 1 and 3 (directional debit, low volatility) only. Cap tier is the first filter before reading the condition.

Before you place a single options trade, you need to understand the size of the arena you're entering. Market capitalization — the total market value of a company's outstanding shares — is one of the most overlooked yet consequential variables in options trading. It determines liquidity, volatility, option chain depth, bid/ask spreads, and ultimately your real-world ability to enter and exit trades at a fair price.

This chapter maps the five cap tiers, their inherent characteristics, and the specific risks each tier creates for the options trader. Knowing this before you ever look at a chart is foundational risk management.

The Five Market Cap Tiers

Cap Tier	Market Cap Range	Examples	Key Risks for Options Traders
Mega Cap	$200B+	Apple, MSFT, NVDA, Amazon	Liquidity illusion, low vol = smaller premiums, macro-sensitivity, index rebalancing risk
Large Cap	$10B–$200B	Delta, Salesforce, FedEx	Sector-specific shocks, earnings vol spikes, activist investor risk
Mid Cap	$2B–$10B	Etsy, Revvity, Wingstop	Lower option liquidity, wider bid/ask spreads, higher beta, earnings gaps
Small Cap	$300M–$2B	Carvana, BigBear.ai, BARK	Thin options chains, manipulation risk, news-driven gaps, low open interest
Micro Cap	Under $300M	Many OTC/Pink Sheet names	Often no listed options, extreme volatility, illiquid chains, pump-and-dump exposure

RISK MANAGER'S NOTE

Cap size does not equal quality. A mega-cap can crater on a single earnings miss. A small-cap can double in a day. The issue is NOT the move — it's whether your options chain has enough liquidity to let you manage the trade when it happens.

Mega Cap ($200B+) — The Institutions' Playground

Mega caps like Apple, Microsoft, NVIDIA, and Amazon offer the most liquid options chains in the market — tight bid/ask spreads, deep open interest across multiple strikes and expirations, and weekly options that allow surgical precision. For the options trader, this is the highest-quality trading environment.

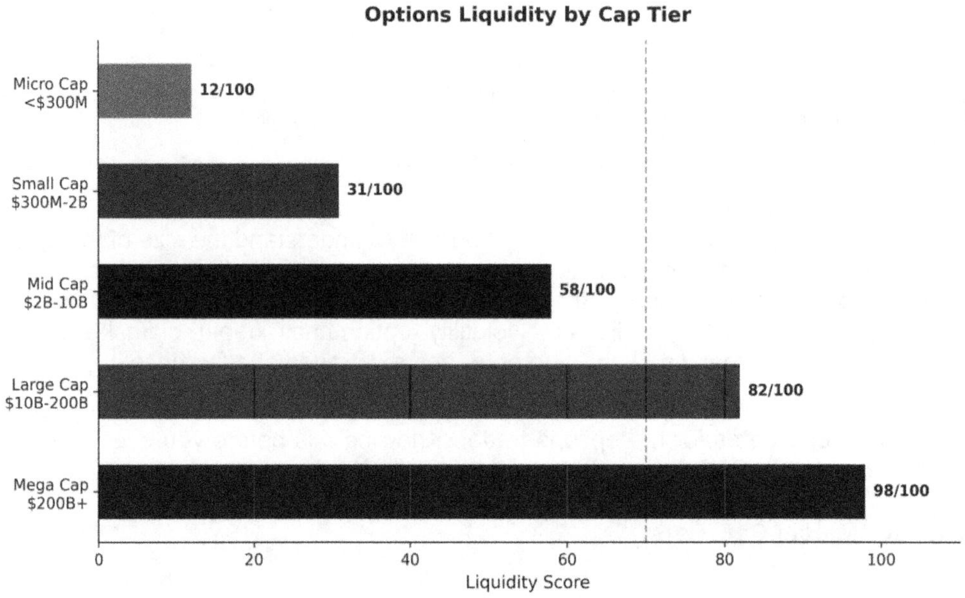

Figure 2.1 — Options Liquidity by Cap Tier. Liquidity score by tier for options tradability.

Cap Tier	Long Call/Put	CSP	Covered Call	Iron Condor	Spreads	Calendar
Mega Cap	√	√	√	√	√	√
Large Cap	√	√	√	√	√	—
Mid Cap	√	√	√	√	—	—
Small Cap	√	CSP (caution)	—	—	—	—
Micro Cap	Avoid options	—	—	—	—	—

Figure 2.2 — Available Strategies by Cap Tier. Strategy eligibility narrows as cap size decreases.

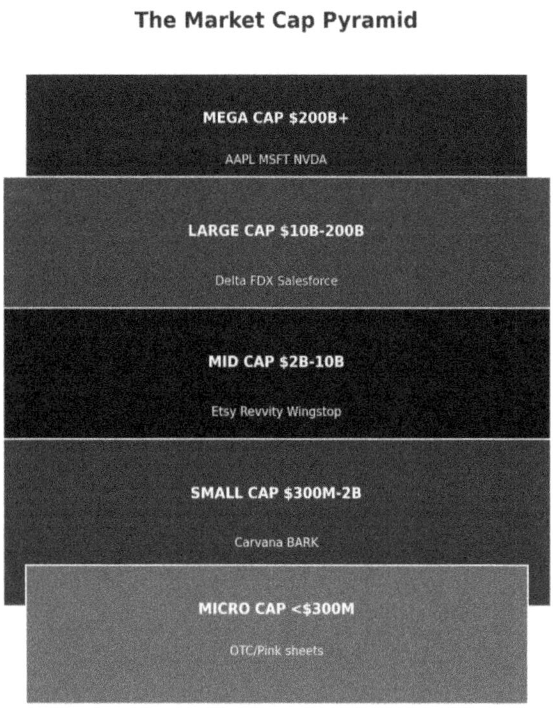

Figure 2.3 — The Market Cap Pyramid. Each tier carries distinct liquidity and options characteristics.

But mega cap comes with its own traps. Because they are so widely held — by ETFs, index funds, pension funds, and sovereign wealth funds — they are subject to mechanical rebalancing flows that can move the stock regardless of fundamentals. A mega cap can experience sharp, algorithm-driven moves triggered by macro data, Fed speeches, or index rebalancing events. Additionally, implied volatility in mega caps is often suppressed because the market is so efficient, meaning option premiums may seem cheap — until a macro event explodes IV overnight.

- Premium levels may be lower in calm periods, limiting income strategies;
- Rebalancing-driven moves can gap through technical levels;
- Size creates a false sense of safety — mega caps are not immune to 20–30% drawdowns;

Large Cap ($10B–$200B) — The Workhorse Tier

Large caps offer good liquidity with more meaningful premium levels than mega caps. Sector-specific risks are more concentrated here. A pharmaceutical large cap can gap 25% on a clinical trial failure. An airline large cap is deeply sensitive to fuel prices, labor, and macro travel demand. Large caps are where many experienced traders prefer to operate: liquid enough to manage, volatile enough to generate premium income, and available in a wide variety of sectors.

- Watch for sector concentration risk — large caps often represent their sector;
- Activist investor risk: a single 13D filing can reprice the stock overnight; and
- Earnings vol spikes create opportunities — but also traps for the undisciplined.

Mid Cap ($2B–$10B) — Higher Beta, Wider Spreads

Mid cap stocks occupy the transition zone between the institutional world and the retail world. Option chains exist but are shallower. You may find yourself trading strikes where open interest is thin and the market maker widens the spread to compensate for their risk. Position sizing becomes even more important here because slippage — the cost of entering and exiting between bid and ask — can meaningfully erode your edge.

Mid caps tend to have higher beta (more movement relative to the broad market) and can experience larger percentage gaps on earnings or news. This creates both opportunity and danger.

- Always check open interest at your intended strike before committing;
- Use limit orders — never market orders — in mid cap options;
- Higher beta means your delta exposure moves faster as the stock moves;

Small Cap ($300M–$2B) — Thin Ice Territory

Small cap options are for experienced traders only. The chains are thin, spreads are wide, and open interest at many strikes may be single or double digits. A single large order from an institution can move the stock against you before you can adjust. News-driven gaps — both up and down — are common and violent, and the stock may not have analyst coverage that would give you warning.

- Avoid market orders entirely — you will pay a severe penalty;
- Check daily dollar volume, not just share volume — small caps can have illusory activity;
- If you trade small cap options, use defined-risk strategies only (spreads, not naked positions);

Micro Cap (Under $300M) — Options Trader's Dead Zone

Most micro cap stocks do not have listed options at all. Those that do often have chains so thin they are functionally untradeable for serious position sizes. Micro caps are prone to manipulation, pump-and-dump schemes, and sudden delisting risk. If you see micro cap options in your screener, treat them as a red flag, not an opportunity.

- Assume no reliable options market exists until proven otherwise;
- Any premium that looks 'too good' in a micro cap reflects the risk of complete loss; and
- The risk manager's rule: if you can't get a fair fill, the trade doesn't exist.

How Cap Tier Affects Your Options Strategy

The table above gives you the foundation. The practical implication is this: match your strategy complexity to your cap tier. In mega and large caps, multi-leg strategies work because the liquidity supports them. In mid caps, stick to spreads and be careful with legs. In small caps, if you trade at all, use simple long puts or long calls with defined risk — never naked positions, never iron condors with wide strikes you can't close.

> **RISK MANAGER'S RULE**
>
> Before entering any options trade, ask three questions about the cap tier: (1) Can I get in at a fair price? (2) Can I get out when I need to? (3) What moves this stock in ways that have nothing to do with the chart? If you can't answer all three, reduce size or step away.

Choosing the Right Broker for Options Trading

→ See "Choosing Your Brokerage: The Options Trader's Platform" in Chapter 1 (Pre-Trading Flight Check) for the complete broker selection criteria, comparison table, and platform recommendations including thinkorswim, TastyTrade, Interactive Brokers, Schwab, and E*TRADE.

Account Types: Which to Open and Why

The account type you open determines your maximum options permissions and tax treatment. Most options traders need at minimum a margin account with Level 3 options approval to access the full six-condition strategy set.

Account Type	Options Level	What It Unlocks — Six-Condition Access
Cash Account	Level 1–2	Covered calls only (condition 2 partial). Long calls and puts (conditions 1 and 3). No spreads. No CSP without sufficient cash reserved. Sufficient for conditions 1 and 3. Cannot execute conditions 4, 5, or 6 fully.
Margin Account	Level 3	Full access to all six conditions. Cash-secured puts (condition 2), spreads of all types (conditions 4, 5, 6), multi-leg structures. This is the minimum account type for the complete six-condition system.
IRA / Roth IRA	Level 2–3 (varies by broker)	Limited margin. No naked positions. Spreads allowed at some brokers with Level 3. Tax-advantaged — options income inside a Roth IRA grows tax-free. Ideal for the income seller (conditions 2 and 4).
Portfolio Margin	Level 4–5	Reduced margin requirements based on portfolio-level risk, not position-level. For accounts above $100,000+. Not needed until you are running a multi-position book across all six conditions simultaneously.

The Pre-Trading Mental Checklist

Beyond the technical flight check, there is a psychological readiness check that every trader must run before each session. Physical and mental state directly impacts decision quality. This is not soft advice — it is risk management. A decision made under fatigue, emotional stress, or distraction carries hidden risk that no checklist can compensate for.

	Mental Check	If the Answer is NO — Your Action
☐	Am I well-rested? (Less than 6 hours of sleep impairs risk assessment comparably to mild intoxication)	Do not open new positions today. Manage existing positions only, and only for risk reduction — not optimization.
☐	Am I emotionally neutral? (Not angry, anxious, elated, or recovering from a recent significant loss or win)	Wait 24 hours before opening new positions. Extreme emotional states — both positive and negative — lead to oversized, underdisciplined positions.

	Mental Check	If the Answer is NO — Your Action
☐	Do I have uninterrupted time to monitor the position through the entry session?	Use limit orders only, set 30 minutes minimum for position entry, and ensure you can monitor for the first 30 minutes after the order fills.
☐	Have I already read the condition today? (VIX + chart — two minutes, done before anything else)	Do the condition read now, before looking at individual stocks or scanning for setups. The condition determines the strategy. The strategy determines the stock.
☐	Is today a high-risk calendar day? (FOMC, CPI, earnings for my underlying)	No new positions within 48 hours of a binary event for the underlying in question. Manage existing positions. Do not add exposure before unpredictable events.

THE MOST EXPENSIVE TRADE IS THE ONE YOU WEREN'T READY TO MAKE

The market does not care whether you slept well. It does not care whether you just had an argument, whether your account took a hit yesterday, or whether you are excited about a setup you found at midnight. Risk management begins before the market opens. It begins with the decision to trade — or not trade — today.

Building Your Options Watchlist by Cap Tier

Knowing the cap tiers is academic until you build an actual watchlist organized by tier. Here is a framework for constructing a 20-stock options watchlist that balances opportunity across tiers while respecting the liquidity and risk constraints of each.

Tier	Allocation	# of Names	Example Names	Watchlist Criteria
Mega Cap	50%	10	AAPL, MSFT, AMZN, GOOGL, NVDA, META, JPM, V, UNH, JNJ	Weekly options available. Bid-ask < $0.10. OI > 10,000 at target strikes. These are your core income names.
Large Cap	30%	6	AMD, PYPL, SQ, COIN, BA, GS	Monthly options liquid. Bid-ask < $0.20. OI > 2,000. Higher beta = higher premium but more volatile Wheel.
Mid Cap	15%	3	ETSY, DKNG, SOFI	Monthly options only. Bid-ask < $0.40. OI > 500. Vertical spreads preferred. Size down 50% vs. mega cap.
Small Cap	5%	1	Use ETFs instead: IWM, ARKK	Individual small caps too illiquid for options. Use small-cap ETFs for exposure with tradeable options chains.

Review and update your watchlist monthly. Remove any name whose fundamentals have deteriorated (check the Ten Indicators in Chapter 14). Add names that have recently passed all ten indicators. Your watchlist is a living document — not a permanent list. The market changes; your watchlist should change with it.

One rule above all: never trade options on a stock that is not on your watchlist. If you hear a tip, see a tweet, or get excited about a stock you have not researched — it does not go into your broker. It goes onto your watchlist for evaluation next Sunday. Impulse entries on unresearched stocks are the fastest way to give money back to the market.

Putting Cap Tier to Work: A Practical Trade Example

Theory without experimentation is incomplete. Here is how cap tier selection plays out in a real trade decision — the same setup evaluated across three different tiers, showing how the numbers and risk profile change entirely based on cap size.

The setup: sell a cash-secured put 10% below the current stock price with 30–35 DTE, targeting a 2–3% return on reserved capital. The stock is in a confirmed uptrend, above its 50-day and 200-day moving averages. Same thesis, same structure — different cap tier.

Cap Tier	Example	Strike	Premium	Key Risk
Mega Cap	AAPL @ $200	$180 put	$1.80 ($180)	IV often suppressed — thin premium. Macro/rebalancing flows can gap through your strike with no fundamental cause.
Large Cap	MSFT @ $420	$378 put	$3.20 ($320)	Earnings vol spikes. Macro events can gap 8–12%. Strong premium, good liquidity. Best risk/reward tier.
Mid Cap	ETSY @ $65	$58 put	$2.10 ($210)	Bid/ask spread $0.20–0.40 wide. Lower open interest — harder to close at a fair price. Higher beta amplifies drawdowns.

The mid-cap put ($210) is close in premium to the large-cap put ($320) — but the risk profile is dramatically worse. Bid/ask spread alone costs $20–40 on entry and exit. Lower open interest means an urgent roll may not get a fair fill. The mega-cap delivers the cleanest execution but lowest return. Large cap is the sweet spot for income traders: strong premium, tight spreads, manageable risk.

Practical cap tier rule for income traders: use mega and large cap for consistent, liquid income strategies. Use mid cap only when the options chain confirms high open interest and tight spreads. Avoid small and micro cap for income strategies entirely — execution friction destroys the statistical edge.

CAP TIER SELECTION RULE

Before any options income trade, check three numbers: open interest at your target strike (minimum 500 contracts), bid/ask spread (maximum $0.30 wide for positions under $5.00 premium), and average daily volume (minimum 1,000 contracts/day). If any of these three fail, move to a higher cap tier. The trade you cannot exit cleanly is worse than no trade at all.

Position Sizing by Cap Tier: Matching Risk to Liquidity

Position sizing is not just about how much capital you are willing to risk per trade. It must also account for the liquidity of the underlying — because in an illiquid market, your theoretical position size and your realizable exit size are not the same number. The cap tier determines the maximum position size a disciplined risk manager should deploy.

Cap Tier	Max Contracts (per position)	Max % Account (per position)	Sizing Rationale
Mega Cap ($200B+)	10–20 contracts	5% of account	Deep liquidity supports larger size. Market maker depth is sufficient for 20-contract exits without moving the market. Mega cap is the only tier where sizing up is consistently safe.
Large Cap ($10–200B)	5–10 contracts	3–4% of account	Strong liquidity, occasional spread widening on high-volatility days. Size conservatively on high-IV days when spreads widen. The sweet spot for income strategies.
Mid Cap ($2–10B)	2–5 contracts	2% of account	Thinner chains require smaller size. A 5-contract mid-cap position may be difficult to close cleanly in one fill. Always verify OI at your strike before sizing up.
Small Cap ($300M–2B)	1–2 contracts	1% of account	Minimum size only. Wide spreads and thin OI make multi-contract exits risky. If you cannot close 1 contract at a fair price, the small-cap is not appropriate for income strategies.
Micro Cap (<$300M)	0 contracts	0%	Do not trade options on micro caps. The liquidity premium you would have to pay on every fill destroys any statistical edge before the trade begins.

Liquidity Scoring: A Pre-Trade Filter by Cap Tier

Before entering any position, run a three-point liquidity score on the specific options chain you intend to trade. This is separate from the Ten Indicators in Chapter 14 — those evaluate the underlying stock's quality. This evaluates the quality of the options market for that stock on that specific day.

	Liquidity Check	GREEN (proceed)	YELLOW (reduce size)	RED (do not trade)
1	Open Interest at target strike	OI > 1,000 contracts	OI 200–1,000 contracts	OI < 200 contracts
2	Bid/ask spread as % of midpoint premium	< 5% of midpoint	5–12% of midpoint	> 12% of midpoint
3	Average daily options volume for the chain	> 2,000 contracts/day	500–2,000 contracts/day	< 500 contracts/day

3 GREEN checks	Full approved position size. Execute at the midpoint. Proceed normally.

1–2 YELLOW checks	Reduce to 50% of normal position size. Use limit orders only. Verify you can exit before entering.
Any RED check	Do not trade this underlying today. Move to a higher cap tier or a different underlying in the same sector.

Cap Tier and the Six-Condition Framework: Which Tiers Work in Which Conditions

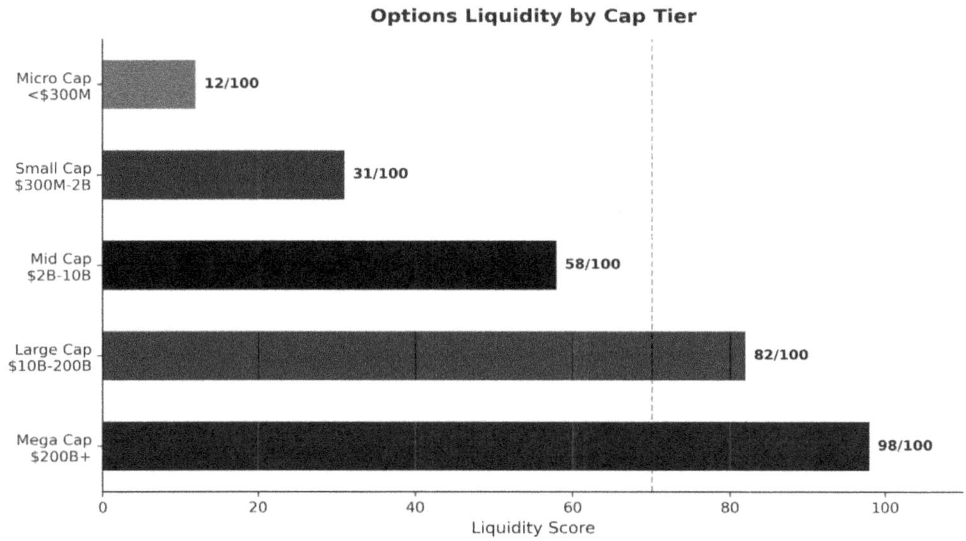

Figure 6.1 — Market Cap Tier Liquidity — Options liquidity, spread width, and strategy availability by company size tier.

Market Cap Tier Liquidity — Options liquidity and strategy availability by company size.

Not every cap tier is appropriate for every six-condition strategy. The more complex the structure — and the more legs that need to be opened and closed at fair prices — the higher the cap tier requirement. This table maps the intersection of condition and cap tier eligibility.

Condition & Strategy	Mega Cap	Large Cap	Mid Cap	Small Cap	Micro Cap
1 — Long Call / Bull Call Spread	√ Full	√ Full	√ Reduced	√ Minimum	X No
2 — CSP / Covered Call	√ Full	√ Full	√ Reduced	X No	X No
3 — Long Put / Bear Put Spread	√ Full	√ Full	√ Reduced	√ Minimum	X No
4 — Bear Call Spread	√ Full	√ Full	√ Reduced	X No	X No
5 — Butterfly / Iron Condor	√ Full	√ Full	X No	X No	X No

Condition & Strategy	Mega Cap	Large Cap	Mid Cap	Small Cap	Micro Cap
6 — Calendar / Diagonal	✓ Full	✓ Full	✗ No	✗ No	✗ No

THE CAP TIER RULE FOR MULTI-LEG STRATEGIES

Conditions 5 and 6 require multi-leg structures — iron condors, butterflies, calendars. These structures require opening 2–4 legs simultaneously and closing them cleanly when your target is reached. Multi-leg execution in thin markets (mid cap and below) is where slippage and wide spreads turn a profitable strategy into a break-even or worse. The rule is simple: if the strategy has more than two legs, it requires large cap liquidity or better. No exceptions.

FIRST-TIME READER NOTE

The Business Cycle chapter uses options strategy terms as examples — cash-secured puts, covered calls, iron condors, T-21 rolls, IVR. These are all explained in detail in Chapters 8–15. As you read this chapter, simply understand that different market environments favor different strategies. This chapter teaches you to read the economic weather. Chapters 8–15 teach you what to do in each weather type.

6-CONDITION FRAMEWORK ▸ ALL SIX — the macro backdrop that sets the dominant condition
Cycle phase tells you which of the six conditions is most likely dominant right now. Expansion favors 1 and 2. Peak/recession favors 3 and 4. Transitions and crisis favor 5 and 6.

If market capitalization tells you the size of the arena, the business cycle tells you the weather. And sector rotation is how the smartest money in the world repositions itself as that weather changes — often months before the mainstream financial press catches on.

For the options trader, understanding sector rotation is not academic. It directly informs which sectors to trade, which direction to bias your positions, and which options strategies align with where institutional money is flowing. Combined with cap tier selection from Chapter 6, this framework becomes one of the most powerful meta-strategies in your toolkit.

Bulls, Bears, and What They Mean for Your Trades

Before we map the cycle, let's establish the vocabulary precisely. A bull market is a market in which a majority of stocks are increasing in value — investors believe the economy is expanding and they are buying in anticipation of continued growth. A bear market is a market in which a majority of stocks are decreasing in value — investors believe the economy is heading for a downturn and they are selling or holding cash.

What most new traders miss: even during a bear market, some stocks offer genuine opportunities. Energy stocks, oil and gas companies, and real estate investment trusts (REITs) can perform well while the broad market falls. The trader's job is to identify the trend — then sell into it, buy into it, or hedge against it — not to wait for conditions to become universally favorable.

KEY DISTINCTION

Bull and bear markets are not about any single day or week. They reflect the predominant direction of the majority of stocks over a sustained period. A one-day rally inside a bear market is a bear market rally. A one-day selloff inside a bull market is a pullback. The business cycle is the framework that tells you which one you are actually in.

The Four Phases of the Business Cycle

- Expansion — GDP growing, unemployment falling, consumer confidence rising. Credit is available. Risk appetite is high;

- Peak — Growth at its highest. Inflation rising. Fed begins tightening. Excesses appear in asset prices;
- Recession/Contraction — GDP declining, layoffs rising, credit tightening. Risk appetite collapses; and
- Trough/Recovery — Bottom of the cycle. Forward-looking investors begin repositioning before the data confirms recovery.

The key insight for traders: the stock market is a leading indicator. Sectors begin rotating before the economic data confirms the new phase. This is why understanding cycle transitions — not just current conditions — is where the edge lives.

Figure 3.1 — The Business Cycle

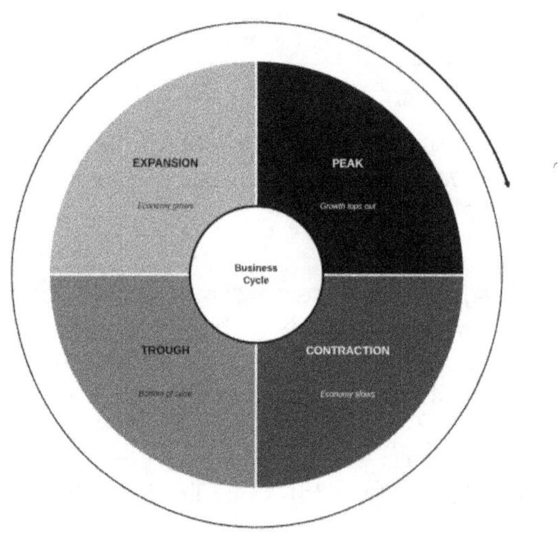

Figure 3.1 — The Business Cycle Wheel. Each phase drives distinct sector leadership and strategy selection.

> **THE NBER TIMING PROBLEM**
>
> The National Bureau of Economic Research (NBER) officially declares recessions — but always months after the fact. The NBER identified December 2007 as the expansion peak, but didn't announce it until December 2008 — by which time the market had already been falling for 15 months. The trough wasn't officially declared until September 2010. Lesson: you cannot wait for official confirmation. Read the market, read the sectors, and act on what price and rotation are telling you — not what the data committee confirms a year later.

Sector Rotation: How Institutional Money Moves

The foundational work on sector rotation was written by Sam Stovall, chief investment strategist for Standard & Poor's, in his 1996 book Sector Investing. Stovall's model showed that market cycles tend to lead business cycles: markets reach their tops just before the economy peaks, and the start of a new bull market can be seen just before the broader economy begins its recovery. This framework — now standard across institutional portfolio management — is the map options traders use to position ahead of rotation.

Figure 3.2 — Sector Rotation

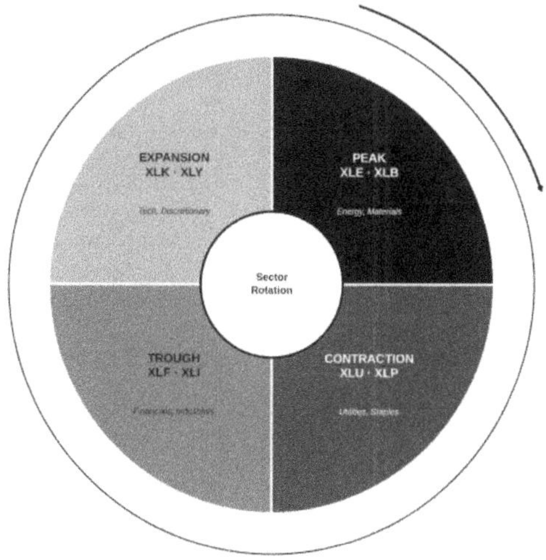

Figure 3.2 — Sector Rotation by Cycle Phase. Where institutional capital flows through each stage.

Sector rotation is the institutional practice of shifting capital from sectors that have peaked in a given cycle phase into sectors poised to outperform the next phase. It is not random — it follows a historically repeatable pattern across economic cycles. The 11 GICS sectors and their SPDR ETFs give the options trader a direct, liquid way to participate in or hedge against these rotations.

The Global Industry Classification Standard (GICS), developed jointly by S&P and MSCI, defines exactly 11 sectors. These are the official categories used by index providers, institutional funds, and the SPDR sector ETFs (the XL-series) that give options traders direct, liquid access to each sector. Every stock in the S&P 500 belongs to one of these 11 — no more, no less. Knowing them cold is foundational to sector rotation trading.

#	GICS Sector (Official)	SPDR ETF	Cycle Sweet Spot	Typical Beta	Options Trader Notes
1	**Information Technology**	XLK	Mid to Late Expansion	1.2-1.5	Deepest options chains; richest IV around earnings; mega-cap weighting ensures large-cap liquidity throughout the chain
2	**Health Care**	XLV	Late Expansion / Recession	0.6-0.8	Defensive anchor; lower beta compresses premiums; binary risk on FDA events inside biotech holdings
3	**Financials**	XLF	Early Expansion	1.0-1.2	Yield curve sensitive; earnings vol spikes create premium-selling setups; watch regional bank ETF KRE for tail risk
4	**Consumer Discretionary**	XLY	Early to Mid Expansion	1.1-1.4	Amazon and Tesla dominate index weighting; high beta; earnings gaps

#	GICS Sector (Official)	SPDR ETF	Cycle Sweet Spot	Typical Beta	Options Trader Notes
					are common; strong premium-selling environment
5	**Consumer Staples**	XLP	Recession / Late Cycle	0.4-0.6	Ultra-low beta; dividend yield supports price floor; ideal for cash-secured put income strategies in down cycles
6	**Communication Services**	XLC	Early Expansion	0.9-1.1	Alphabet and Meta drive the sector; sensitive to ad spend and streaming trends; moderate IV environment
7	**Industrials**	XLI	Mid Expansion	1.0-1.2	Broad manufacturing, transport, and defense exposure; earnings move in sync with GDP; clean cycle rotation signal
8	**Energy**	XLE	Mid to Late Expansion	1.2-1.6	Commodity-driven; IV spikes sharply on oil supply disruptions; collars essential for managing late-cycle energy exposure
9	**Materials**	XLB	Mid Expansion	1.0-1.3	Inverse to the dollar; copper prices lead sector direction; earnings can gap on commodity moves; use spreads
10	**Real Estate**	XLRE	Early Expansion / Recovery	0.8-1.0	Rate-sensitive with inverse relationship to rising rates; put debit spreads serve as effective rate-spike hedges
11	**Utilities**	XLU	Recession / Contraction	0.3-0.5	Lowest beta of all 11 GICS sectors; low IV means cheap protective puts; pure defensive play; inverse to rate moves

GICS NOTE

Sub-industries like Semiconductors, Biotechnology, Airlines, and Regional Banks are not separate GICS sectors — they are industries within the 11 official sectors. When you see them referenced in rotation analysis, they are sub-plays within their parent sector, tradeable via specialized ETFs like SOXX, XBI, JETS, and KRE.

Business Cycle Phase	Sectors That Lead	Sectors to Avoid	Options Strategy Fit
Early Expansion	Financials, Consumer Discretionary, Tech	Utilities, Staples, Telecom	Long calls / bull call spreads on leaders; CSPs on pullbacks
Mid Expansion	Industrials, Materials, Energy	Financials, Real Estate	Covered calls on industrials for income; diagonal spreads
Late Expansion / Peak	Energy, Materials, Health Care	Tech, Consumer Discretionary	Defensive collars; sell calls against existing longs; put debit spreads

Business Cycle Phase	Sectors That Lead	Sectors to Avoid	Options Strategy Fit
Recession / Contraction	Utilities, Staples, Health Care	Industrials, Materials, Tech	Long puts / bear put spreads; short calls; calendar spreads on low-vol names
Early Recovery (Trough)	Consumer Discretionary, Financials	Energy, Utilities	Sell cash-secured puts on beaten-down leaders; long call spreads

KEY INSIGHT

Sector rotation doesn't happen overnight. Transitions often take 3–6 months. The options trader's advantage is using defined-risk positions — spreads and calendars — to capture the directional drift without being destroyed by day-to-day noise.

The Macro Events Calendar: What Every Options Trader Must Watch

The business cycle is the slow-moving tide. Macro events are the individual waves. Understanding the cycle tells you which sectors to favor and which strategies to run. Understanding the macro events calendar tells you specifically when to hold, when to act, and when to step aside entirely. Missing either layer leaves money on the table — or worse, puts capital at unnecessary risk.

The following recurring macro events move markets, sectors, and implied volatility in predictable ways. Not always on the same day or in the same direction — but predictably in terms of the type and duration of volatility they generate. This is your standing calendar as an options trader.

Event	Frequency (Expiration)	What It Measures	Market Impact	Options Trader Action
Federal Reserve FOMC Meeting	8× per year (every 6–7 weeks)	Fed Funds Rate decision + forward guidance on rate path	Largest single recurring market mover. Rate holds: low volatility. Rate changes or hawkish/dovish pivot: sharp sector rotation within hours. Rate-sensitive sectors (XLF, XLRE, XLU) react immediately.	Close or hedge rate-sensitive short premium positions before FOMC. Elevated IV in the 3–5 days before FOMC — do not sell premium into it. Wait for the decision, let IV deflate, then re-enter.
Consumer Price Index (CPI)	Monthly — typically 2nd or 3rd Tuesday	Year-over-year and month-over-month inflation: food, energy, shelter, goods	Hot CPI (above expectations): rate hike fears spike → Technology and Growth sell off, Financials benefit short-term. Cool CPI: risk-on rally → broad market lifts, Utilities and Staples underperform.	Do not hold short premium positions in rate-sensitive sectors (XLK, XLRE, XLU, XLF) into a CPI print. Wait for the number — then enter with the direction confirmed.

Event	Frequency (Expiration)	What It Measures	Market Impact	Options Trader Action
Producer Price Index (PPI)	Monthly — typically 1–2 days after CPI	Wholesale/producer-level inflation — leads CPI by 1–3 months	A leading indicator for CPI. Rising PPI signals future consumer inflation before it shows up in CPI. Materials and Energy sectors respond directly to PPI surprises.	Use PPI as your 30-day warning system for upcoming CPI volatility. Rising PPI + rising CPI = sustained rate pressure = sustained headwind for growth sectors.
Non-Farm Payrolls (NFP)	Monthly — 1st Friday of every month	US job creation excluding farm workers — the broadest employment measure	Strong NFP: rate expectations rise → growth stocks pressured, Financials benefit. Weak NFP: recession fears → Defensive sectors (XLP, XLU, XLV) outperform. NFP day is one of the highest-volatility trading days of the month.	Mark the first Friday of every month on your calendar without exception. Avoid opening new short premium positions on NFP Friday. Evaluate all open positions the day before — roll or close anything within 5% of its strike.
Unemployment Rate	Monthly — same release as NFP	Percentage of labor force actively seeking work	Confirms NFP direction. Rising unemployment = recession signal → rotate into defensives immediately. Falling unemployment in late cycle = inflationary pressure → Fed may tighten further.	Track the trend, not the number. Unemployment rising three consecutive months is a cycle phase transition signal — adjust sector rotation exposure accordingly.
Fed Chair Press Conference	After every FOMC meeting	Forward guidance on Fed policy — often more market-moving than the rate decision itself	Forward language is the variable. 'Higher for longer,' 'data-dependent,' 'restrictive territory' — each phrase has a defined market interpretation. Algos parse every word within milliseconds.	Do not trade in the 30 minutes after the press conference begins. Wait for the initial volatility to resolve (typically 2–4 hours). The real direction often reverses the initial reaction.
GDP (Advance, Preliminary, Final)	Quarterly — 3 releases per quarter	Gross Domestic Product — the broadest measure of economic output	Negative GDP for two consecutive quarters = technical recession. Markets typically price in recession expectations 3–6 months before official GDP data confirms it. Watch the trend, not the headline.	GDP releases are rarely surprises for prepared traders — markets have already priced the likely outcome from leading indicators (PMI, employment, consumer confidence). Use GDP as confirmation of cycle phase, not

Event	Frequency (Expiration)	What It Measures	Market Impact	Options Trader Action
				as a primary trade trigger.
ISM Manufacturing PMI	Monthly — 1st business day of month	Purchasing Managers Index: factory orders, production, employment	Above 50 = expansion. Below 50 = contraction. PMI is a leading indicator — it often turns before GDP data confirms the cycle shift. Industrials and Materials sectors are most sensitive.	PMI above 55 for 2–3 consecutive months in early cycle = strong signal to add Industrials and Materials exposure. PMI falling below 50 = early warning to begin reducing cyclical sector exposure and rotating toward defensives.

Leading vs. Lagging Indicators: The Trader's Distinction

Every macro data point falls into one of two categories: leading indicators (they predict where the economy is going) or lagging indicators (they confirm where it has been). Options traders must prioritize leading indicators — because by the time lagging indicators confirm a cycle shift, the market has already moved.

Leading Indicators — Act On These	Lagging Indicators — These Confirm, Not Signal
ISM Manufacturing PMI (turns before GDP)	GDP growth rate (confirms 3–6 months after markets)
Yield curve shape (inverts 12–18 months before recession)	Unemployment rate (peaks 6–12 months after recession begins)
Sector Bullish Percent Index — BPI (turns before price)	Corporate earnings (reported 45 days after the quarter ends)
Credit spreads — investment grade vs. junk (widen before stress)	CPI inflation (reflects prices set 30–90 days ago)
Consumer confidence surveys (leading by 3–6 months)	Fed rate decisions (respond to data that is already old)
Copper price — 'Dr. Copper' leads industrial activity	NBER recession declaration (announced 12+ months after the fact)

The Yield Curve: Your Macro Compass

The yield curve is the single most reliable macro predictor available to options traders. It shows the relationship between short-term and long-term interest rates across US Treasury bonds. The shape of the curve tells you what the bond market — the largest, most sophisticated market in the world — believes about the future of the economy.

Yield Curve Shape	What It Signals	Sectors That Benefit	Options Trader Response
Normal (upward sloping: 10-year yield > 2-year yield)	Healthy expansion expected. Economy growing. Credit available.	Financials (XLF), Industrials (XLI), Consumer Discretionary (XLY)	Standard income strategy environment. Full position sizing on cyclical sector CSPs.
Flat (10-year ≈ 2-year yield)	Uncertainty — transition between cycle phases. Growth slowing but not recessionary yet.	Defensives beginning to outperform. Health Care (XLV) and Staples (XLP) starting to attract institutional flows.	Reduce position sizes. Widen short strikes. Avoid new cyclical sector exposure. Start building defensive sector income positions.
Inverted (2-year yield > 10-year yield)	Recession warning — bond market pricing in rate cuts ahead as growth slows. Historically accurate 12–18 months in advance.	Utilities (XLU), Consumer Staples (XLP), Health Care (XLV)	Defensive rotation: shift income strategies to low-beta sectors. Buy protective puts on broad market ETFs. Reduce or eliminate cyclical sector exposure.
Steepening from inversion (yield curve re-steepening)	Recovery approaching — the most actionable signal for options traders. Bond market pricing in future growth before equity markets fully react.	Financials (XLF) first, then Consumer Discretionary and Technology	Early recovery entry signal. Begin opening CSPs on beaten-down sector leaders. This is the best premium-selling opportunity of the full cycle.

THE YIELD CURVE RULE

Check the 2-year vs. 10-year Treasury yield spread weekly. You can find it on any financial data site under '10Y-2Y Treasury Spread' or on the St. Louis Fed's FRED database (ticker: T10Y2Y). When the spread goes negative: begin defensive rotation immediately — do not wait for GDP data or NBER confirmation. The bond market is smarter, faster, and better-capitalized than any individual trader. Follow it.

Bridging the Cycle to Your Rolls: Macro Timing for Position Management

The business cycle does not just tell you which sectors to trade — it tells you how aggressively to manage your open positions. In early expansion, you can afford to hold positions longer and roll proactively with confidence. In late expansion and early contraction, you should be tightening management discipline, rolling earlier, and reducing the number of simultaneous positions.

Cycle Phase	Position Management Style	Roll Trigger	Maximum Simultaneous Positions
Early Expansion	Confident. Cyclicals leading. IV low-moderate. Standard sizing.	T-21 proactive rolls. Roll Out at same strike. Take 50–75% profit targets.	Full capacity — up to your personal maximum (typically 5–8 for retail traders)

Cycle Phase	Position Management Style	Roll Trigger	Maximum Simultaneous Positions
Mid Expansion	Measured. Rotation to Industrials and Energy. Watch PMI and commodity signals.	T-21 still the trigger. Begin tightening profit targets to 50% closes.	Maintain full capacity but avoid adding new mid-cap positions — liquidity risk rises
Late Expansion / Peak	Cautious. Defensive rotation beginning. IV starting to expand.	Roll earlier — consider T-28 trigger. Widen short strikes. Reduce position size 25%.	Reduce to 60–70% of maximum. No new speculative positions. Collars on existing longs.
Recession / Contraction	Defensive. Utilities, Staples, Health Care only. High IV environment.	T-35 trigger. Consider closing for 40% profit — do not wait for 50%. Avoid new income trades on cyclicals.	Reduce to 40–50% of maximum. Capital preservation priority. Hedge all longs.
Trough / Early Recovery	Opportunistic. Beaten-down sector leaders showing elevated IV. Best CSP premium of the cycle.	Standard T-21. Widen strikes aggressively — IV is high, so you can sell further OTM for the same premium.	Begin rebuilding toward full capacity. Focus on Financials and Consumer Discretionary first.

THE MACRO TIMING RULE

Your roll decisions should never be made in isolation from the macro environment. A T-21 roll that is aggressive and profitable in early expansion can be dangerous in late expansion when the underlying sector is deteriorating. Read the cycle phase before you read the options chain. The macro environment is the context inside which every roll decision lives — ignore it at your cost.

The 11-Sector Rotation Playbook

Which sectors lead in each phase — and which to AVOID — gives you a structural edge.

Phase	Leaders	Options Play	Laggards	Avoid
Early Expansion	XLF, XLY, XLK	Bull call spreads. CSPs on cyclicals.	XLU, XLP	Selling puts on defensives.
Mid Expansion	XLK, XLI, XLB	Iron condors. Wheel on mega-cap. Max income.	XLV, XLRE	Overconcentration in one sector.
Late Expansion	XLE, XLB, XLI	Reduce positions. Build hedges.	XLK, XLY	Adding growth longs.
Peak to Recession	XLU, XLV, XLP	Defensive CSPs. Long puts. Cash 30-50%.	XLE, XLF	Catching falling knives.
Trough to Recovery	XLF, XLY	Small positions. LEAPS on cyclicals.	XLU, XLP	Moving too fast.

The Avoid column prevents more losses than the Leaders column generates. Rotate when BPI shifts — not when media declares the shift (always 4-6 weeks late).

Sector Rotation in Real Time: A Verified Trade

The energy sector is one of the most responsive to business cycle positioning. When crude oil inventories tighten, energy infrastructure spending increases, and the cycle enters the early expansion phase, energy stocks become Condition 1 candidates with clean technical setups and underpriced options. The following trade is documented from a live account.

VERIFIED TRADE — CVE (Cenovus Energy)

January 14, 2026. Cenovus Energy (CVE) is in a confirmed uptrend. The business cycle signals early expansion. Energy sector showing institutional rotation inflows. VIX suppressed — Condition 1.

Trade: Buy 1 CVE Feb 20, 2026 $16 Call at $2.45. Total cost: $245. Maximum loss: $245.

January 28, 2026 — 14 days later. CVE has moved. The $16 Call is worth $3.70. Sell to close.

Realized profit: +$125. Return on premium: +51.02% in 14 days.

The business cycle identified the sector. The Six-Condition Framework identified the trade. $245 at risk. 51% return. Brokerage-confirmed.

This is what sector rotation trading looks like in practice. The edge is not in predicting which sector will move. The edge is in reading the cycle phase, identifying the sectors that typically lead in that phase, and waiting for a clean Condition 1 setup within those sectors before deploying premium. The cycle does the heavy lifting. The framework does the selection. The trade does the work.

This was an actual trade taken under the framework described.

Business Cycles in Recent History

2020 Trough to Recovery (March-June): The COVID crash took the S&P 500 down 34% in 23 days. VIX hit 82. Then the Fed announced unlimited QE. Within weeks, the BPI bottomed and began climbing. Financials and Consumer Discretionary led the recovery — exactly as the cycle model predicts. The trader who sold CSPs on XLF and XLY at IVR above 90 captured the highest premium opportunity of the decade.

2021 Late Expansion (January-November): GDP growth exceeded 5%. Inflation began rising above 2%. Energy surged 54% for the year while Technology grew more volatile. The rotation model called for reducing tech and increasing energy — exactly what outperformed.

2022 Peak to Recession (January-October): The yield curve inverted in April. The BPI rolled over. VIX averaged 25+ all year. The S&P dropped 25%. Utilities gained 1.6% while Technology lost 28%. The defensive rotation alone saved portfolios from catastrophic losses.

2023-2024 Recovery to Expansion: The Fed paused hikes. Inflation declined. The yield curve began re-steepening. The BPI rose above 50 in Technology and Financials. The recovery signal from late 2022 led to the AI-driven rally of 2023-2024. Traders who accumulated LEAPS calls on quality tech captured massive gains.

The pattern is always the same: the signals appear in the data months before the headlines. The BPI moves before stocks. The yield curve inverts before recession. Your edge is reading the present correctly while most traders are still reacting to the past.

★ Sector Rotation Options Strategies — The Playbook

STRATEGY 1: The Rotation Rider — Bull Call Spread on Incoming Leader Sector

When macro data and price action confirm a new cycle phase is beginning, the incoming leader sector typically shows relative strength before the broader market moves. Use a bull call spread on the sector ETF (e.g., XLF in early recovery, XLE in mid expansion) to capture upside with defined risk.

- Setup: Buy ATM call, sell OTM call (same expiration, 30–60 DTE);
- Target: 50–75% of max profit — take it and rotate again;
- Risk: Defined to the debit paid — ideal for uncertain cycle transitions;
- Cap tier overlay: Prefer large cap names within the sector for the underlying if not using ETF;

STRATEGY 2: The Fade Trade — Bear Put Spread on Exiting Sector

As a sector peaks and institutional money begins to rotate out, relative weakness often develops before the fundamental story turns negative. The fade trade captures this with a bear put spread — directional downside exposure with defined risk.

- Setup: Buy ATM or slightly OTM put, sell deeper OTM put (same expiration, 30–45 DTE);
- Sector signals to watch: Sector ETF breaks below 50-day EMA while broad market holds;
- Watch for: Rising implied volatility in the sector — it confirms institutional repositioning;
- Risk management: If the sector reverses above your breakeven within 5–7 sessions, close the trade;

STRATEGY 3: The Income Rotation — Cash-Secured Puts on Beaten-Down Sector Leaders

At the trough of a sector's rotation cycle, beaten-down large and mega cap names within that sector often display elevated implied volatility — perfect for premium selling. This strategy generates income while positioning for the next leadership phase.

- Setup: Sell OTM cash-secured puts 15–20% below the current price on sector leaders;
- Best applied: 2–3 months before the sector is expected to re-emerge as a leader;
- Risk: If the sector continues lower, you are assigned stock at your strike — understand this exposure;
- Cap tier rule: Only use this strategy on large or mega cap names — the liquidity protects your exit;

STRATEGY 4: The Defensive Collar — Protecting During Late-Cycle Sector Exposure

If you hold a position in a sector that has had a strong run and the cycle is showing late-expansion signals, a collar protects gains without requiring you to sell the position and trigger a tax event. This is defensive sector rotation risk management.

- Setup: Own the stock (or ETF) → Buy OTM put for downside protection → Sell OTM call to finance the put;
- Result: Your upside is capped, but your downside is floored — ideal for late-cycle holdings;
- Timing: Apply when sector ETF makes a new high while breadth begins to diverge;

STRATEGY 5: The Diagonal Calendar — Riding Slow Rotation with Time Decay

Sector rotations rarely move in straight lines. They grind, pause, and retest. The diagonal spread captures this slow drift while using theta decay as a secondary profit mechanism — you sell shorter-dated options against a longer-dated long position.

- Setup: Buy 90-day call on the incoming sector leader ETF → Sell 30-day call at a higher strike;
- Result: You collect premium from the short call while your long call participates in the rotation;
- Roll: As the short call expires, sell the next month's call at a new strike that reflects where the sector has moved;
- Best environment: Confirmed rotation with steady, non-explosive price movement;

Reading the Rotation: Tools & Signals

Sector rotation doesn't announce itself. You have to read it from a combination of price action, relative strength, and macro data. These are the primary signals to track:

- Relative Strength (RS) vs. SPY: Is XLF outperforming XLK on a 3-month basis? That's a rotation signal;
- Sector ETF vs. 50-day Exponential Moving Average: A sector ETF reclaiming its 50-day EMA after a downtrend is a rotation alert;
- Sector BPI (Bullish Percent Index): Rising BPI in a sector while overall BPI is flat confirms underlying accumulation;
- Yield Curve Shape: A steepening yield curve favors Financials and Industrials; an inverted curve favors Utilities and Staples;
- Commodity Prices: Rising oil confirms Energy rotation. Rising copper confirms Industrial and Materials rotation;
- Dollar Direction: A strong dollar is typically a headwind for Materials and Energy; a weak dollar is a tailwind;

Combining Cap Tier + Sector Rotation for Maximum Precision

The most powerful application of this framework is combining the cap tier lens from Chapter 6 with the sector rotation map from this chapter. Here's how the two work together in practice:

- Identify the current cycle phase and the sectors poised to lead;
- Within the leading sector, focus on large cap or mega cap names for the best options liquidity;
- Use mid cap names within the sector for higher-beta, higher-premium opportunities — with tighter sizing; and
- Avoid small and micro cap names in sector plays unless you have a specific, defined-risk thesis.

PUTTING IT TOGETHER

Cycle suggests early expansion → Financials and Consumer Discretionary beginning to rotate in → XLF large-cap leader JPMorgan breaking above resistance → bull call spread on JPM or bull call spread on XLF itself → 45 DTE, defined risk. This is the full framework in one trade.

Business Cycle Phase → Six-Condition Dominant Environment

The business cycle does not just determine which sectors to focus on — it tells you which of the six conditions is structurally most likely to persist. The chart and VIX will always provide your daily condition read, but knowing which conditions dominate each cycle phase helps you set position sizing, strategy aggressiveness, and planning horizons.

Cycle Phase	Typical VIX	Dominant Condition	Practical Six-Condition Strategy
Early Expansion	20–30 (declining from cycle peak)	**2 transitioning to 1**	Begin with condition 2 (CSPs, bull put spreads) as IV is still elevated from the prior recession phase. As VIX falls below 20 and IVR drops, shift toward condition 1 (long calls, bull call spreads). Size up as the trend confirms.
Mid Expansion	12–18 (sustained low)	**1 dominant, 5 in pauses**	Condition 1 is your primary setting — trend is up, IV is low. Long calls and bull call spreads are cheap and the trend provides consistent wins. During brief consolidations, condition 5 (iron condors) can be layered as a secondary income source.
Late Expansion / Peak	18–25 (rising)	**2 dominant, 4 appearing**	Shift toward condition 2 (premium selling with trend). Rising VIX provides better premium. Begin layering collar hedges on core longs. Watch for first confirmed lower high on SPY — the signal that condition 4 is emerging. Start reducing directional debit exposure.
Recession / Contraction	25–45 (elevated)	**4 dominant (bear + high IV)**	Condition 4 environment: bear call spreads on index ETFs and sector ETFs. High IV provides excellent credit on OTM call spreads. Directional put buying (condition 3) is tempting but expensive — IV crush is a constant risk. Prefer credit structures. Keep positions defined-risk only.
Trough / Recovery Begin	25–35 (declining from peak)	**2 or 4 → transition to 2**	The transition is the most valuable moment. As VIX peaks and begins contracting, condition 2 setups appear before the trend clearly confirms bullish. CSPs on quality large-caps at deep discounts from their highs offer extraordinary risk/reward. This is when the premium seller's patience is rewarded.

THE CYCLE IS YOUR MACRO CONDITION FILTER

The business cycle does not override your daily condition read — it informs it. When the cycle says Late Expansion, be more attentive to condition 4 setups appearing. When the cycle says Trough, be ready for the first condition 2 signal with extra eagerness. The cycle gives you direction. The VIX and the chart give you the precise condition. Both working together is the complete six-condition system operating at full power.

> **6-CONDITION FRAMEWORK ▸ CONDITIONS 1–6: Risk calculation changes with every condition**
> Risk in condition 1 (long call) is the premium paid. Risk in condition 4 (bear call spread) is spread width minus credit. Risk in condition 6 (calendar) is the debit paid. This chapter shows you how to calculate it for each.

Risk management is not a philosophy. It is arithmetic. Before you place any options trade, you must be able to calculate four concrete numbers: your breakeven price, your maximum risk, your maximum reward, and your reward-to-risk ratio. If you cannot calculate all four before entering a trade, you are not trading — you are guessing with money.

This chapter gives you the formulas, the frameworks, and the discipline model to size every position correctly and enter every trade with a complete picture of what you stand to gain and what you stand to lose.

Breakeven: The Number That Actually Matters

Breakeven is the price at which your trade neither profits nor loses — the exact point where your premium paid equals the intrinsic value of your position. Everything above breakeven for a long call, or below it for a long put, is profit. Everything on the wrong side is loss. Know this number before you enter.

Position	Breakeven Formula	Example
Long Call	Strike Price + Premium Paid	Strike $100 + $3.50 premium = $103.50 breakeven. Stock must exceed $103.50 to profit.
Long Put	Strike Price − Premium Paid	Strike $100 − $3.50 premium = $96.50 breakeven. Stock must fall below $96.50 to profit.
Short Call	Strike Price + Premium Received	Strike $105 + $2.00 received = $107.00. Stock must stay below $107 to keep full premium.
Short Put	Strike Price − Premium Received	Strike $95 − $2.00 received = $93.00. Stock must stay above $93 to keep full premium.
Bull Call Spread	Lower Strike + Net Debit Paid	Buy $100 call, sell $105 call, net debit $2.00 → breakeven at $102.00.
Bear Put Spread	Higher Strike − Net Debit Paid	Buy $100 put, sell $95 put, net debit $2.00 → breakeven at $98.00.

One critical nuance on breakeven for option buyers vs. sellers: for a buyer, the breakeven is adjusted upward (call) or downward (put) by the premium paid, because you need the stock to move enough to recover the cost of the contract. For a seller, it works in reverse — you receive the premium upfront, so your breakeven is the strike adjusted by what you collected. The premium received is your cushion.

Maximum Risk & Maximum Reward

- Long Call / Long Put: Maximum Risk = premium paid × 100. Maximum Reward = unlimited (long call) or down to zero (long put). Risk is fully defined at entry;
- Short Call (naked): Maximum Risk = unlimited — the stock can theoretically rise without limit. Maximum Reward = premium received × 100. This is why naked calls are only for Tier 3 traders with deep experience;
- Short Put (naked): Maximum Risk = (strike price − premium received) × 100 — the stock can fall to zero. Maximum Reward = premium received × 100;
- Bull Call Spread: Maximum Risk = net debit paid × 100. Maximum Reward = (spread width − net debit) × 100. Both fully defined at entry; and
- Bear Put Spread: Maximum Risk = net debit paid × 100. Maximum Reward = (spread width − net debit) × 100. Both fully defined at entry.

DEFINED RISK IS NOT OPTIONAL FOR BEGINNERS

Until you have mastered position management across at least 50 live trades, every position you take should have a defined maximum risk. Spreads, not naked options. The difference between a defined-risk spread and a naked position is the difference between a bad trade and a wipeout.

Reward-to-Risk (R/R): Your Edge Filter

The reward-to-risk ratio tells you how much you stand to gain for every dollar you risk. It is your primary filter for deciding whether a trade is worth taking. A trade with a 1:1 R/R requires you to be right more than 50% of the time just to break even on your portfolio. A trade with a 3:1 R/R can be profitable even if you're only right 30% of the time.

The risk manager's minimum standard: never take a trade where the potential reward is less than the potential risk — 1:1 is the floor, 2:1 or better is the target for directional trades. Premium selling strategies flip this — they collect smaller rewards more frequently — but the math must still work in your favor across a sufficient sample of trades.

Strategy	Max Risk	Max Reward	R/R Ratio	Win Rate Needed to Break Even
Long Call / Put	$350 (debit)	Unlimited / large	3:1+ target	~25–33%
Bull / Bear Spread	$200 (debit)	$300 (max profit)	1.5:1	~40%
Cash-Secured Put	$9,500 (stock)	$500 (premium)	1:19 (seller)	~95% prob ITM needed
Iron Condor	$400 (net)	$100 (premium)	1:4 (seller)	~80% prob needed
Covered Call	Cost of stock	Premium + upside	Varies	Premium adds cushion

The Win-Rate Conversion Table — The Trade That Changes Your Thinking

Most new traders focus obsessively on win rate — trying to be right as often as possible. The R/R table below reveals why that instinct is wrong. With the right R/R ratio, you can lose far more trades than you win and still profit. This is one of the most paradigm-shifting tables in trading education:

Strategy	Strike / Entry	Premium	Breakeven Formula	Breakeven Price
Long Call	$185 strike	$4.80 debit	Strike + Premium	$189.80
Long Put	$185 strike	$4.75 debit	Strike − Premium	$180.25
Cash-Secured Put	$180 strike	$3.20 credit	Strike − Premium	$176.80
Covered Call	Stock @ $183	$3.50 credit	Stock Cost − Premium	$179.50
Bull Call Spread	180/190	$3.00 net debit	Lower Strike + Net Debit	$183.00
Iron Condor	175/180/190/195	$2.80 net credit	Both wings +/− Credit	177.20 / 192.80

Figure 10.1 — Breakeven by Strategy. Formulas and real numbers for the six core structures.

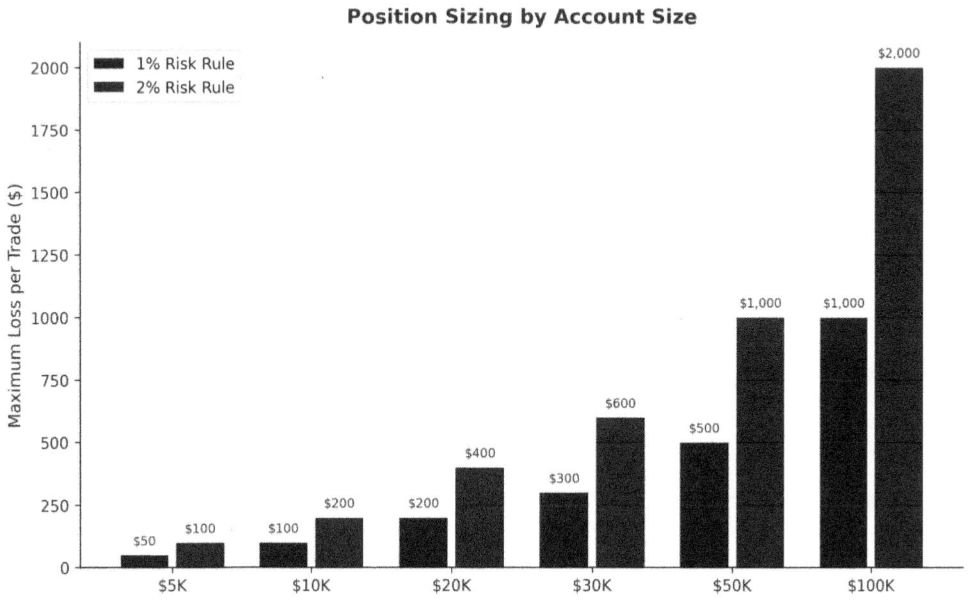

Figure 10.2 — Position Sizing by Account Size. Maximum loss per trade at 1% and 2% risk rules.

R/R Ratio	Losses Required to Break Even	Wins Required	What This Means
1:2	66 losses	33 wins	Win only 33% of the time to break even

R/R Ratio	Losses Required to Break Even	Wins Required	What This Means
1:3	75 losses	25 wins	Win only 25% of the time to break even
1:4	80 losses	20 wins	Win only 20% of the time to break even — see worked example below
1:5	83 losses	17 wins	Win only 17% to break even
1:8	88 losses	11 wins	Win only 11% — still breakeven with 1:8 R/R
1:10	91 losses	9 wins	Win only 9% of the time to break even at 1:10 R/R

The 1:4 R/R worked example: Risk $50 per trade (stop-loss). Profit target $200 per trade (4× the risk). On a $5,000 account with 1% risk, your stop is $50 and your target is $200. Run 100 trades: 80 losses × $50 = $4,000 lost. 20 wins × $200 = $4,000 gained. You're at breakeven — with a 20% win rate. One additional win makes you profitable. This is why R/R ratio, not win rate, is the holy grail of trade management.

RISK MANAGEMENT IS THE HOLY GRAIL

Risk management, combined with systematic position sizing, is the holy grail of professional trading. It is the difference between a professional and a hobbyist. After learning the trading strategies, converting them into real-world results takes discipline to sustain growth — and that discipline lives entirely in your R/R framework.

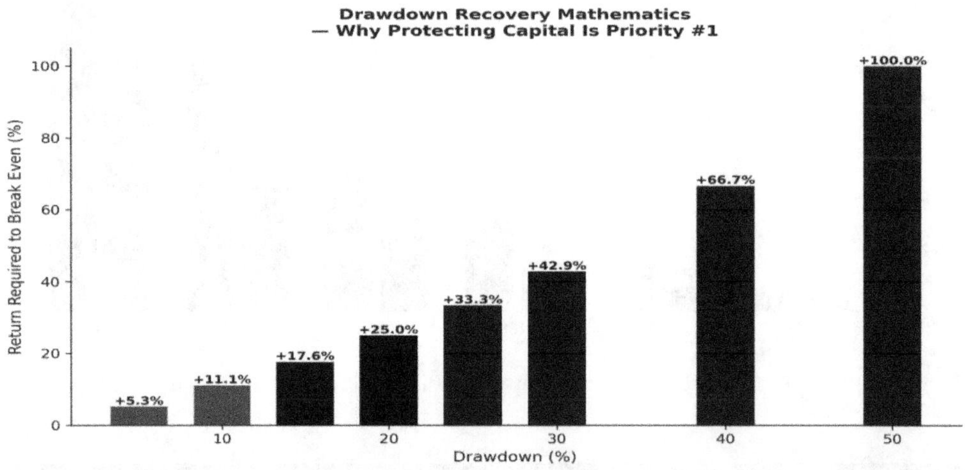

Figure 8.1 — Drawdown Recovery Math — The gain required to recover from each level of loss. A 50% loss requires a 100% gain to break even.

Drawdown Recovery Math — How much gain is required to recover from each level of loss.

Drawdown Recovery: The Math That Demands Respect

The second table every trader must memorize is the drawdown recovery table. It shows how much gain is required to recover from a given loss — and why losses compound against you more severely than gains compound for you:

Account Loss	Gain Required to Recover	The Lesson
5% loss	**5.2% gain to recover**	Small loss, manageable recovery — protect early.
10% loss	**11.1% gain to recover**	Already requires more than you lost to get back.
25% loss	**33.3% gain to recover**	A bad quarter requires a great half-year to undo.
50% loss	**100% gain to recover**	Half your account gone = must double remaining capital.
75% loss	**300% gain to recover**	Three-quarters gone = nearly impossible recovery path.
100% loss	GAME OVER	**Don't let small losses turn into large ones. Ever.**

THE FIRST RULE OF TRADING

Don't let a small profit turn into a loss. Don't let a small loss turn into a large loss. These two rules, applied consistently, do more to protect your account than any indicator, screener, or strategy ever will.

Position Sizing: How Much to Risk Per Trade

Even a perfect trade thesis is worthless if the position size is wrong. Oversizing is the single most common reason talented traders blow up accounts — not bad analysis, not bad strategy, but too much capital concentrated in a single position that moves against them.

The risk manager's position sizing framework is built on one simple rule: never risk more than 2–5% of your total trading capital on any single position. This rule does not feel exciting. It is designed not to feel exciting. It is designed to keep you in the game long enough for your edge to compound.

- Account of $10,000 → maximum risk per trade: $200–$500;
- Account of $25,000 → maximum risk per trade: $500–$1,250;
- Account of $50,000 → maximum risk per trade: $1,000–$2,500;
- Never adjust position size based on conviction — the strongest convictions produce the biggest emotional blind spots; and
- If a trade requires a larger position to be 'worth it' — the trade is not worth it at your current account size.

The Protection Analysis Framework

Before entering any trade, run through this four-question framework. It forces you to define all critical numbers in advance — when you are calm, rational, and thinking clearly — rather than in the heat of a moving market.

#	Question	What to Write Down Before You Trade
1	What is my maximum risk?	The exact dollar amount I will lose if this trade goes fully against me. Not a range — a number.
2	What is my profit target?	The price or percentage gain at which I will close this trade. Written before entry, honored at that level.
3	What is my stop trigger?	The price level or loss threshold that triggers my exit — no questions asked, no rationalizing.
4	What is my position size?	Number of contracts, calculated from my 2–5% max risk rule. Not adjusted based on how much I like the trade.
5	What could make me wrong?	The one or two scenarios that would invalidate my thesis. If either happens, the trade closes — thesis broken.

THE TRADER'S MATH

Markets don't care who you are or what you stand for. All they want is the money of the undisciplined. Skillfully applying your trading plan requires practice, patience, and experience — it is a journey. But the math has to work before the journey begins.

Six-Condition Risk Calculation Reference

#	Strategy	Max Risk Formula	Max Reward Formula	Risk Calculation Walk-Through
1	Long Call (Cond. 1)	Premium paid × 100	Unlimited (theoretically)	AAPL $240. Buy $250 call at $4.20. Max risk: $4.20 × 100 = $420. Max exposure at expiry if AAPL drops below $250 — full $420 lost.
2	Bull Put Spread (Cond. 2)	(Spread width − credit) × 100	Credit received × 100	SPY $520. Sell $490/$480 spread. Credit: $1.25. Max risk: ($10 − $1.25) × 100 = $875. Max reward: $1.25 × 100 = $125.
3	Bear Put Spread (Cond. 3)	Net debit paid × 100	(Spread width − debit) × 100	QQQ $280. Buy $270/$260 spread at $3.00 debit. Max risk: $3.00 × 100 = $300. Max reward: ($10 − $3.00) × 100 = $700.
4	Bear Call Spread (Cond. 4)	(Spread width − credit) × 100	Credit received × 100	SPY $437. Sell $460/$470 spread. Credit: $1.45. Max risk: ($10 − $1.45) × 100 = $855. Max reward: $1.45 × 100 = $145.
5	Iron Condor (Cond. 5)	Wider spread width − total credit × 100	Total net credit × 100	SPY $520. Put spread + call spread. Total credit: $1.80. Max risk: ($10 − $1.80) × 100 = $820. Break-evens: $488.20 (lower) / $551.80 (upper).

Figure 8.2 — Risk Calculation Framework — The complete risk and reward calculation process for any options position before entry.

Risk Calculation Framework — Complete risk/reward calculation process for any options position.

Risk calculation is not one-size-fits-all across the six conditions. How you calculate and interpret maximum risk, probability of profit, and expected value differs fundamentally depending on whether you are buying or selling premium. This section provides the complete risk math for all six conditions in a format you can run before every trade.

#	Strategy	Max Risk Formula	Max Reward Formula	Risk Calculation Walk-Through
1	**Long Call (Cond. 1)**	Premium paid × 100	Unlimited (theoretically)	AAPL $240. Buy $250 call at $4.20. Max risk: $4.20 × 100 = $420. This is your total exposure. If AAPL drops below $250 at expiry, you lose the full $420. Nothing more.
2	**Bull Put Spread (Cond. 2)**	(Spread width − credit) × 100	Credit received × 100	SPY $520. Sell $490/$480 put spread. Credit: $1.25. Max risk: ($10 − $1.25) × 100 = $875. Max reward: $1.25 × 100 = $125. Always verify: risk/reward acceptable vs. probability of profit.
3	**Bear Put Spread (Cond. 3)**	Net debit paid × 100	(Spread width − debit) × 100	QQQ $280. Buy $270/$260 put spread at $3.00 debit. Max risk: $3.00 × 100 = $300. Max reward: ($10 − $3.00) × 100 = $700. Break-even: $270 − $3.00 = $267 at expiry.
4	**Bear Call Spread (Cond. 4)**	(Spread width − credit) × 100	Credit received × 100	SPY $437. Sell $460/$470 call spread. Credit: $1.45. Max risk: ($10 − $1.45) × 100 = $855. Max reward: $1.45 × 100 = $145. Short strike must be above all chart resistance.
5	**Iron Condor (Cond. 5)**	Wider spread width − total credit × 100	Total net credit × 100	SPY $520. Put spread ($490/$480) + call spread ($550/$560). Total credit: $1.80. Max risk: ($10 − $1.80) × 100 = $820 (one side only — max loss occurs only if stock breaks past one short strike to the long strike). Break-evens: $490 − $1.80 = $488.20 (lower). $550 + $1.80 = $551.80 (upper).
6	**Calendar Spread (Cond. 6)**	Net debit paid for the spread × 100	Variable — depends on IV differential at near-term expiry	SPY $520. Sell 30-DTE $520 call. Buy 60-DTE $520 call. Net debit: $2.10. Max risk: $2.10 × 100 = $210. Max reward: approximated by the IV differential × 100 on the day before near-term expiry — typically 1.5–2.5× debit paid if conditions hold.

CALCULATE BEFORE YOU CLICK

Write down three numbers before submitting any options order: (1) Max loss in dollars. (2) Max gain in dollars. (3) Break-even price at expiration. If any of these three are unclear, do not submit the order. Clarity about risk is not optional — it is the precondition for every trade in the six-condition system.

Portfolio Risk Aggregation: Seeing Your Total Exposure

Individual position risk is necessary but insufficient. You also need to see how all your positions interact. Five perfectly sized individual positions can still create dangerous portfolio-level exposure if they are all in the same sector, all short delta, or all expiring on the same date.

Position	Type	Sector	Delta	Theta/Day	Max Loss	Expiry
AAPL CSP	Income	Tech	-12	+$8	$1,800	Mar 21
MSFT BPS	Income	Tech	-8	+$6	$500	Mar 21
JPM CSP	Income	Finance	-15	+$10	$2,200	Apr 18
SPY IC	Income	Index	-3	+$14	$400	Mar 21
NVDA BCS	Direction	Tech	+18	-$4	$1,200	Apr 18
PORTFOLIO	**—**	**—**	**-20**	**+$34**	**$6,100**	**—**

This portfolio has three problems visible only at the aggregate level: (1) Tech concentration: 3 of 5 positions are in Technology. A single sector event (antitrust ruling, chip export ban) hits 60% of the portfolio. (2) Expiration clustering: 3 positions expire March 21. If the market drops the week before expiration, all three face simultaneous gamma risk. (3) Total max loss: $6,100 is 12.2% of a $50K account — above the 6% portfolio risk limit recommended in Chapter 1.

The fix: replace one of the two Tech income positions with a Healthcare or Financials position. Stagger the March expirations — roll one to April. And either reduce position sizes by 20% each or add a SPY put hedge to bring total portfolio risk below 6%.

Expected Value: The Professional's Risk Filter

Expected value (EV) is the single most important calculation a risk manager makes before entering any trade. It answers the only question that matters over a large sample of trades: on average, how much do I make or lose per trade if I execute this setup repeatedly? A positive EV trade makes money over time even when it loses more often than it wins. A negative EV trade loses money over time even when it wins frequently. The goal is not to be right — it is to take positive EV positions consistently.

The formula: EV = (Win Rate × Average Win) − (Loss Rate × Average Loss). Every variable in this formula is known before you enter the trade. Win rate comes from your backtest. Average win and average loss come from your defined profit target and maximum risk. If you do not have a backtest, use conservative estimates — 50% win rate, defined targets, defined stops — and calculate whether the structure itself has positive EV regardless of directional accuracy.

Strategy	Win Rate	Avg Win	Avg Loss	EV per Trade	Assessment
Bull Call Spread (C1)	55%	$185	$115	(0.55×$185)−(0.45×$115) = +$50	✓ Positive EV — take every qualified setup
Cash-Secured Put (C2)	72%	$220	$580	(0.72×$220)−(0.28×$580) = +$7	✓ Marginally positive — requires strict discipline to realize
Bear Put Spread (C3)	45%	$280	$120	(0.45×$280)−(0.55×$120) = +$60	✓ Positive EV despite sub-50% win rate — large wins

Strategy	Win Rate	Avg Win	Avg Loss	EV per Trade	Assessment
					offset frequent small losses
Iron Condor (C5)	65%	$190	$310	(0.65×$190)−(0.35×$310) = +$15	✓ Positive EV — management at T-21 critical to maintaining this edge
OTM Naked Call (no hedge)	80%	$80	$1,200	(0.80×$80)−(0.20×$1,200) = −$176	✗ Negative EV — frequent wins mask catastrophic tail risk
FOMO Momentum Buy	40%	$150	$200	(0.40×$150)−(0.60×$200) = −$60	✗ Negative EV — feels exciting, destroys capital systematically

THE EV RULE

Never enter a trade without calculating its expected value first. If you cannot calculate the EV — because you have no defined profit target, no defined stop, or no win rate estimate — the trade does not meet the minimum standard for entry. EV is not a prediction. It is the mathematical description of your edge. A trader with positive EV and iron discipline will be profitable over 100+ trades regardless of short-term outcomes. A trader without EV is gambling with sophisticated-sounding strategies.

Theta Risk in Dollar Terms: What Time Costs You Per Day

Theta is expressed as a daily dollar decay per contract. Most traders check their theta as a percentage or ignore it entirely. Professional risk managers translate it immediately into a daily dollar cost that is benchmarked against the position's income or directional thesis. A position with theta of −$8 per day means you are paying $8 per calendar day for the right to hold that position. After 10 days without movement, you have consumed $80 of the position's value through time alone.

For option sellers, theta is income — you receive it daily as the short option decays. For option buyers, theta is an expense — you pay it daily as your long option loses time value. Understanding theta in dollar terms changes how you manage both sides of the book.

Position Type	Daily Theta in $ Terms	Risk Management Implication
Long Call / Long Put (buyer)	−$5 to −$25 per contract per day depending on DTE and strike. Accelerates toward expiration.	Calculate total daily theta cost across all long positions. If your total daily theta bill exceeds 0.1% of account value per day, your long book is consuming capital too fast. Reduce size or close positions approaching T-21.

Position Type	Daily Theta in $ Terms	Risk Management Implication
Short Put CSP (seller)	+ $8 to +$40 per contract per day. Maximum collection in 30–45 DTE window.	Your theta income is your business revenue. Calculate weekly theta collection vs. weekly position risk. Target: theta income covers at least 20% of the position's maximum risk per month.
Iron Condor (net seller)	+ $15 to +$60 per day (net of all four legs). Peaks at ATM strikes approaching expiration.	Iron condor theta income accelerates in the final 21 days — but gamma risk accelerates faster. The T-21 exit rule closes the position before gamma consumes the theta benefit.
Bull Call Spread (debit buyer)	−$3 to −$12 per day net (long leg theta minus short leg theta credit).	The short leg partially offsets the theta cost of the long leg — the key structural benefit of spreads over single-leg long options. Calculate the net daily theta cost and set a maximum holding period based on it.
Calendar Spread (long theta)	+ $5 to +$25 per day (near-term decays faster than far-term).	Calendar spreads are long theta — time works in your favor. But they are also long vega. A drop in IV hurts the calendar even as theta helps it. Monitor both daily.

Vega Risk in Dollar Terms: What an IV Move Costs You

Vega measures how much your option position changes in value for every one percentage point move in implied volatility. Like theta, most traders read vega as an abstract Greek number. Risk managers translate it into dollar terms immediately: a vega of 0.15 means your position gains or loses $15 per 1% move in IV. If IV expands from 20% to 25% (a 5-point move — common during earnings or macro events), a position with vega of 0.15 changes by $75 per contract.

Vega risk is directional: long options have positive vega (benefit from rising IV), short options have negative vega (hurt by rising IV). For premium sellers running CSPs, covered calls, and iron condors, every position is short vega — meaning an IV spike creates immediate mark-to-market losses even if the underlying has not moved.

Scenario	Vega Exposure	Dollar Impact	Risk Management Response
VIX spikes 5 points on a CSP portfolio (3 contracts, vega −0.12 each)	Net portfolio vega: −0.36 (3 × −0.12)	Dollar loss from IV spike alone: −$180 (5 × $36). Position may show loss even if stock has not moved.	Do not close. The IV spike is a mark-to-market loss, not a realized loss. If the stock has not violated your strike, the position is intact. The IV will contract — often within days.

Scenario	Vega Exposure	Dollar Impact	Risk Management Response
Pre-earnings IV expansion on a long call (vega +0.18, IV expands 8 points)	Net positive vega: +0.18	Dollar gain from IV expansion: +$144 (8 × $18). Position profits from fear even before direction.	Consider closing before earnings if the IV gain is sufficient. Do not hold through earnings with a long vega position — IV crush after the event destroys the vega gain regardless of direction.
IV crush after earnings on a short straddle (vega −0.45 per leg, total −0.90)	Net negative vega: −0.90	IV drops 12 points after earnings. Dollar gain from IV crush: +$108 (12 × $9 per vega unit). The position profits.	This is the earnings IV crush trade working correctly. IV contraction after the event is the anticipated profit. Close at 50% of max profit when available.
Calendar spread in rising IV environment (long vega +0.08 net)	Net positive vega: +0.08	IV rises 6 points. Dollar gain from vega: +$48. Calendar profits from both theta and vega simultaneously.	Ideal environment for calendars. Monitor the term structure — if both near and far-term IV are rising equally, the calendar's vega advantage diminishes. The spread needs near-term IV to rise more than far-term.

THE VEGA STRESS TEST

Before entering any short premium position, run one stress test: if IV expands 10 points overnight (a common move during a market crisis), what is the dollar impact on this position? Multiply: position vega × 10 × number of contracts × 100. If the answer exceeds 3% of your account value, the position is over-sized for the vega risk it carries. Reduce contracts until the 10-point IV stress test produces a dollar impact below 3% of account.

Correlation Risk: When Your Diversified Portfolio Is Not Diversified

The most dangerous illusion in portfolio construction is the appearance of diversification without the reality of it. A portfolio with 5 positions across 5 different stocks feels diversified. But if 4 of those stocks are large-cap technology companies — AAPL, MSFT, NVDA, GOOGL, and META — the portfolio has a single risk factor: tech sector performance. When the tech sector drops 8%, all five positions move in the same direction simultaneously. The portfolio's actual risk is not 5 independent positions — it is one large correlated bet expressed in five contracts.

Correlation risk compounds in two ways. First, losses accumulate faster than individual position risk suggests — if 4 correlated positions each lose $200 simultaneously, the combined loss is $800, not $200. Second, margin requirements and portfolio stress can spike simultaneously across correlated positions, potentially triggering forced closes at the worst possible moment.

Correlation Source	How It Appears	Hidden Risk	Structural Fix
Sector concentration	5 positions in Tech — AAPL, MSFT, NVDA, GOOGL, AMD	Single sector shock hits all 5 simultaneously. Appears diversified by company but is undiversified by factor.	Maximum 20% of deployed capital in any single GICS sector. Enforce this across all open positions regardless of company name.
Market cap concentration	All positions in large-cap S&P 500 components	High beta correlation to SPY. Portfolio effectively tracks the index with options leverage. A broad market correction hits all positions.	Mix cap tiers deliberately. At least one position from outside the S&P 500 large-cap universe reduces broad market correlation.
DTE concentration	All positions expiring in the same month	A single catalyst event (FOMC, CPI, geopolitical) affects all positions simultaneously at their most vulnerable gamma point.	Stagger expirations: no more than 40% of positions in the same expiration month. Spread DTE across 30, 45, and 60-day cycles.
Direction concentration	All positions short puts or long calls — fully bullish book	A sudden market reversal turns the entire portfolio against you simultaneously. No natural hedge.	Maintain at least 20% short delta exposure (via puts or bear spreads) as a permanent portfolio hedge regardless of condition.
Volatility concentration	All positions short vega (CSPs, iron condors, covered calls)	A VIX spike creates simultaneous mark-to-market losses across every position. The portfolio has no long vega offset.	Run at least one long vega position (calendar spread, long call in C1) to offset aggregate short vega exposure in income books.

THE CORRELATION AUDIT

Once per week, look at your open positions and answer five questions: Are more than 20% of my positions in the same sector? Are all my positions directionally aligned (all bullish or all bearish)? Do more than 40% of my positions expire in the same month? Am I entirely short vega with no long vega offset? Is my aggregate delta within my defined range? If any answer is yes — you have a correlation risk that individual position management cannot see. Fix the book structure, not the individual trades.

PORTFOLIO RISK CHECK

Every Sunday, calculate three numbers: (1) Total portfolio delta — your directional exposure. (2) Total max loss if every position hits its worst case simultaneously — this must stay below 6% of account. (3) Sector concentration — no sector above 30% of exposure. If any number is out of range, fix it Monday morning before opening new positions.

> 6-CONDITION FRAMEWORK ▸ **PRE-CONDITION filter — qualify the underlying before reading the market**
> The Ten Indicators screen happens BEFORE you read the condition. A stock that fails the Ten Indicators is not eligible for any of the six strategies, regardless of market condition. Quality first. Condition second. Strategy third.

This chapter operates at the intersection of two disciplines. The first half establishes the Fundamental Analysis Framework — the institutional method for determining whether a company is worth trading at all. The second half delivers the Ten Indicators — your practical scoring system for executing that framework before every position. Together, they form the quality-first foundation of the 90% fundamental, 10% technical approach that underlies every strategy in this book.

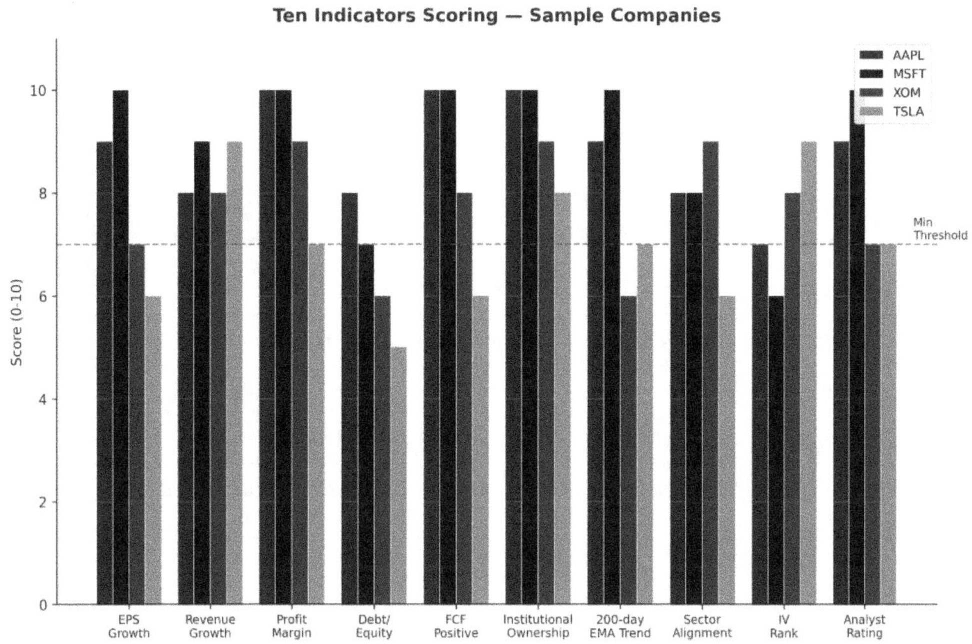

Figure 8.1 — Ten Indicators by Company. Comparative scoring across four sample stocks.

Score	Class	Eligible Strategies	Position Sizing	Highest Conviction
9–10	A+	All strategies including CSPs, CCs, naked puts.	Full size — up to 2% rule maximum.	Ideal Wheel candidate; all conditions approved.
8	A	All defined-risk strategies; CSP, CC, spreads, condors.	Full size.	Solid setup; all six conditions.
6–7	B	Defined-risk spreads; iron condors; CSP with caution.	Reduced to 75% of normal size.	Conditions 2, 5 preferred; avoid naked premium.

4–5	C	Defined-risk spreads only; no CSP, no CC, no naked.	Half size — 50% of normal.	Conditions 5, 6 only; no directional bias.
< 4	D	Do not trade options on this underlying.	No position.	Wait for better setup or find another stock.

Figure 8.2 — Score Class & Strategy Eligibility. A+ through D — what each class can trade.

THE PREMIUM DESK PHILOSOPHY

90% Fundamental Analysis · 10% Technical Analysis.

Wall Street professionals do not lead with charts. They lead with financials. The chart helps time the entry. The fundamentals determine whether an entry is worth taking at all.

Section A — The Fundamental Analysis Framework

Fundamental analysis determines the intrinsic value of a company's security by examining economic data, industry conditions, and company financials — then comparing that value to current market price. The framework moves through four layers: macroeconomics, industry, company situation, and financial statements.

Step	Layer	What You Are Evaluating
1	**Macroeconomic Analysis**	GDP, inflation, interest rates, trade policy, and government fiscal actions that affect all sectors simultaneously.
2	**Industry Analysis**	Market size, competitive landscape, major players, capacity & output, demand trends, and regulatory environment.
3	**Situational Analysis**	Management quality, corporate governance, business model, competitive moat, market share, and SWOT position.
4	**Financial Analysis**	Revenue & EPS growth, profit margins, balance sheet strength, free cash flow, and valuation multiples vs. peers.

The Four Steps in Depth

Step 1 — Macroeconomic Analysis

The first step is understanding the broad economic environment. No company exists in a vacuum — economic cycles, interest rates, inflation, and government policy affect every sector and every stock simultaneously.

- GDP Growth: Rising GDP indicates expansion and generally supports higher corporate earnings and stock valuations;
- Interest Rates: Higher rates increase borrowing costs and compress valuations by reducing the present value of future earnings. Rising rate environments penalize high-debt companies most severely;
- Inflation: Moderate inflation signals healthy demand. High inflation erodes purchasing power and squeezes margins — especially for companies that cannot pass costs to customers;

- Government Policy: Tax policy, trade tariffs, and regulatory changes can dramatically shift an industry's cost structure overnight. Always check the regulatory risk section of any 10-K;

Step 2 — Industry Analysis

Zoom into the specific industry. Industries have their own cycles, competitive dynamics, and structural tailwinds or headwinds that must be understood before evaluating any individual company within them.

- Industry Life Cycle: Is the industry emerging (high growth, high risk), mature (stable, predictable), or declining? Emerging industries offer the highest growth potential but the most uncertainty. Declining industries generate cash but offer limited upside;
- Porter's Five Forces: Competitive rivalry, threat of new entrants, supplier power, buyer power, and threat of substitutes. A company operating in an industry with weak competitive forces — high barriers, few substitutes, fragmented buyers — has structural pricing power; and
- Peer Benchmarking: Compare margins, growth rates, and valuation multiples across the peer group. A stock that looks expensive in isolation may look cheap when its margins are 2x the industry average.

Step 3 — Situational Analysis

Drill down to the specific company — its competitive position, management quality, and strategic circumstances that make it unique within its industry.

WHAT IS A MOAT?

A moat is a durable competitive advantage that protects a company's profits from competitors — just as a water-filled moat protected a medieval castle. The term was popularized by Warren Buffett. Types: network effects (Visa, Meta), switching costs (Microsoft, Salesforce), cost advantages (Walmart), intangible assets (patents, brands), and regulatory moats (utilities). Wide-moat companies sustain above-average returns for years — making them the safest underlyings for premium-selling strategies.

- Competitive Moat: Durable advantages — brand, patents, network effects, switching costs — that protect against competition. The wider the moat, the more sustainable the earnings growth and the more defensible the options income position;
- Management Quality: Executive track record, capital allocation decisions (do they buy back stock at high prices or low prices?), and alignment with shareholder interests (insider ownership, compensation structure);
- Business Model: How does the company make money? Recurring revenue models (subscriptions, SaaS, licensing) command higher valuations than transactional models because they provide earnings visibility;
- SWOT Analysis: Strengths, Weaknesses, Opportunities, and Threats specific to this company at this moment in time. A company with strong strengths and limited threats is a better options underlying than one fighting on all fronts;

Step 4 — Financial Analysis

The final step: scrutinize the financial statements to quantify what the business is actually worth. This step translates all qualitative insights into numbers that can be compared, ranked, and tracked.

- Revenue & EPS Growth: Is the top line growing consistently? Are earnings per share expanding or contracting? Require at least 5% YoY revenue growth and positive EPS growth;
- Profit Margins: Gross, operating, and net margin reveal how efficiently the company converts revenue to profit. Rising margins signal pricing power or operational leverage — both are positive;
- Balance Sheet Strength: Total debt, cash reserves, and debt-to-equity ratio measure financial leverage and solvency risk. High debt in a rising-rate environment is a structural risk to earnings;
- Free Cash Flow: Cash after capital expenditures — the true measure of a company's ability to fund growth, dividends, and buybacks. A company with growing FCF can self-fund without diluting shareholders; and
- Valuation Multiples: P/E, P/B, EV/EBITDA, and PEG ratio allow comparison against fundamentals and industry peers. Always compare to the company's own historical averages, not just the S&P 500 average.

Macro + Micro Convergence: How Intrinsic Value Is Built

Fundamental analysis synthesizes two categories of forces into a single output — the intrinsic value of the stock. Macro-economic forces set the operating environment. Micro-economic company factors determine how well the company navigates that environment. The intersection of the two produces the intrinsic value estimate.

MACRO-ECONOMIC FACTORS		MICRO-ECONOMIC FACTORS	Signal
Economy (GDP, rates, inflation)	↔	Management (Executive Team)	
Industry (competitive forces)	↔	Business Policies (moat, model)	
Market Share (sector trends)	↔	Earnings (revenue, margins, FCF)	→ Intrinsic Value

Intrinsic Value: The Goal of Fundamental Analysis

Fundamental analysis converges on a single output: the intrinsic value of the stock — the estimated true worth independent of current market price. The gap between intrinsic value and market price is the margin of safety. Value investors require 20–30% margin of safety before buying.

UNDERVALUED	OVERVALUED
Market price BELOW intrinsic value Intrinsic Value > Market Price **[BUY SIGNAL]** Margin of safety in your favor.	Market price ABOVE intrinsic value Intrinsic Value < Market Price **[AVOID or EXIT]** No margin of safety.

Section B — Key Metrics for Fundamental Analysis

Metric	Definition	What It Tells You
P/E Ratio	Price ÷ Earnings Per Share	How much investors pay per $1 of earnings. Compare to industry peers — never evaluate in isolation.
Dividend Yield	Annual Dividend ÷ Stock Price × 100	Income return. Very high yields may signal financial distress, not generosity.
EPS	Net Income ÷ Shares Outstanding	Profit per share. Consistently growing EPS signals operational leverage.
Debt-to-Equity	Total Debt ÷ Shareholders' Equity	Financial leverage. High D/E increases risk, especially in rising rate environments.
Free Cash Flow	Operating Cash Flow − CapEx	Real cash generated. FCF reveals whether profits are real.
PEG Ratio	P/E ÷ Earnings Growth Rate	PEG below 1.0 suggests potential undervaluation relative to growth.

Two additional metrics complete the essential toolkit — often overlooked but critical for options traders:

Metric	Definition	What It Tells You
Cash Reserves	Total Cash + Cash Equivalents	The financial cushion. Strong cash reserves allow investment, dividends, buybacks, and weathering downturns without issuing dilutive equity.
Market Share & Growth Outlook	% of Industry Revenue + Projected Revenue CAGR	Growing market share in an expanding industry is one of the strongest signals of competitive strength — and sustained earnings growth.

WHAT IS CAGR?

CAGR — Compound Annual Growth Rate — is the annualized rate of return that shows how fast a company's revenue, earnings, or stock price has grown over a period, as if it grew at a steady rate each year. Formula: CAGR = (Ending Value / Beginning Value)^(1/Years) − 1. A revenue CAGR of 15%+ over 5 years signals a high-growth company. Used throughout Chapter 9 to evaluate earnings and revenue momentum.

Financial Ratio Categories: The Complete Analytical Framework

Beyond the eight primary metrics above, financial analysis organizes ratios into four functional categories — each revealing a different dimension of company health. A stock may look attractive on profitability but dangerous on solvency. Always check all four dimensions before drawing conclusions.

Profitability	Solvency	Operational Efficiency	Valuation
• Gross Profit Margin • Net Profit Margin • Return on Equity (ROE) • Operating Margin	• Liquidity Ratio • Quick Ratio • Gearing Ratio • Debt-to-Equity Ratio	• Asset Turnover • Inventory Turnover • Receivables Turnover • Revenue per Employee	• Price-to-Eamings (P/E) • Price-to-Book (P/B) • Price-to-Sales (P/S) • Dividend Yield

A low P/E may look attractive until you discover the company carries crushing debt (solvency failure). A high ROE may look impressive until you see it is driven by excessive leverage rather than operating efficiency. Always compare metrics against industry peers and the company's own historical averages before drawing conclusions. One metric alone never tells the full story.

Section C — Fundamental vs. Technical Analysis

Dimension	Fundamental Analysis	Technical Analysis
Definition	Value calculated from economic factors, financial statements, and competitive analysis	Uses price movements and chart patterns to predict future price direction
Data Source	Economic reports, earnings filings, industry statistics, SEC filings	Chart analysis, historical price/volume data, momentum indicators
Time Horizon	Days, weeks, months, or years	Seconds to a few weeks
Primary Strength	Deep understanding of company health. Identifies durable long-term value.	Real-time decisions from price/volume.
Primary Limitation	Labor-intensive. Not designed for short-term timing.	Does not evaluate business quality.

> ★ **Combined Approach:** Use FA to identify an undervalued stock with strong financials. Use TA to time your entry — waiting for a support retest, double bottom, or reversal candle. FA gives you the conviction. TA gives you the discipline to wait for the right price.

Section C — Fundamental vs. Technical Analysis: The 90/10 Rule

Fundamental analysis and technical analysis serve different functions. Fundamental analysis answers: is this company worth owning? Technical analysis answers: is now the right time to enter? In the Six-Condition framework, these questions are answered sequentially, not simultaneously.

The 90/10 ratio is the operating principle: 90% of your decision to trade a stock is based on fundamental analysis (does this company pass the Ten Indicators?), and 10% is based on technical analysis (is the entry timing optimal?). Wall Street professionals lead with financials — earnings quality, balance sheet strength, sector positioning. The chart helps them time the entry. The fundamentals determine whether the entry is worth taking at all.

The practical implication: never buy a technically perfect chart setup on a fundamentally broken company. A beautiful cup-and-handle pattern on a company with declining earnings, rising debt, and shrinking margins is a trap. The Ten Indicators in this chapter are your fundamental filter. The technical tools in Chapter 10 are your timing tools. Run the fundamental filter first. If the stock fails, no technical setup justifies entry. If it passes, use technicals to find the optimal entry within the confirmed trend.

THE 90/10 RULE IN PRACTICE

Before opening any options position: Step 1 — Run the Ten Indicators. Does the stock score 70 or above? If no, stop. If yes, continue. Step 2 — Check the technical picture. Is the stock in a confirmed trend matching your intended strategy? Is entry timing clean? Only when both steps confirm should you open the position. Skipping Step 1 and going straight to technicals is the most common shortcut that destroys accounts.

Section D — Financial Documents for Fundamental Analysis

Every fundamental analysis begins with a company's financial filings. All are available free at edgar.sec.gov. The analyst who reads the full 10-K — including the Risk Factors and footnotes — catches problems before the market does.

Document	Purpose & Key Line Items
Cash Flow Statement	Tracks cash inflows and outflows across operations, investing, and financing. Key line: Free Cash Flow (Operating CF minus CapEx). Answers: Is the company generating real cash, or just paper profits?
Balance Sheet	Snapshot of assets, liabilities, and shareholders equity at a point in time. Key lines: Cash, Total Debt, Shareholders Equity, Book Value. Answers: How financially strong is the company?
Income Statement	Shows revenue, expenses, and profit over a period. Key lines: Revenue, Gross Profit, Operating Income, Net Income, EPS. Answers: Is the company profitable and are margins expanding?
Annual Report (10-K)	Comprehensive yearly filing including audited financials, business description, risk factors, and MD&A. The most complete picture of any public company. Always read the footnotes — management often buries risks there.
Quarterly Report (10-Q)	Unaudited quarterly update used to track progress toward annual goals and identify emerging trends before the year-end 10-K.
Proxy Statement (DEF 14A)	Discloses executive compensation, board composition, and shareholder votes. Used to assess management quality and alignment with shareholder interests — key for Indicator 8 (Insider Ownership).
Earnings Releases	Quarterly press releases summarizing key financial results, often including forward guidance. The primary driver of short-term price moves around earnings dates.

Where to Find These Documents

- SEC EDGAR (edgar.sec.gov) — official repository of all U.S. public company filings. Free. Contains every 10-K, 10-Q, DEF 14A, and Form 4 (insider transactions) for every public company;

- Macrotrends.net — free historical financial data. Essential for EPS trends, revenue growth, margins, and dividend history — used throughout the MSFT walkthrough in this chapter;
- Company Investor Relations pages — earnings releases and annual reports in investor-friendly format;
- Bloomberg, FactSet, or Wisesheets — professional-grade aggregators. Wisesheets integrates with Excel for automated fundamental data pulls; and
- Brokerage research portals — Schwab, IBKR, TD, and TastyTrade provide pre-digested fundamental dashboards with screeners and analyst ratings.

THE EDGAR ADVANTAGE

SEC EDGAR is free and contains every filing for every U.S. public company. Most retail traders never read a 10-K. Analysts who do find problems before the market does. The risk factors section and footnotes are where the real story lives. A 15-minute read of the 10-K risk factors on any stock you plan to sell puts on will tell you more than any chart.

Every options strategy in this book is built on top of one foundational assumption: the underlying stock or ETF is worth trading. A technically perfect options structure on a fundamentally broken company is not a strategy — it is a ticking clock. The ten indicators in this chapter are your quality filter. Run every potential underlying through this framework before you trade it. The indicators do not guarantee a winner. They filter out the land mines.

These ten indicators apply primarily to individual stocks. ETFs are evaluated differently — by the quality and breadth of their underlying holdings, their liquidity, and their sector alignment with the current business cycle phase.

The Ten Indicators

1. The Company Has Rising Profits

Earnings growth is the engine of stock price appreciation. A company that consistently grows its earnings per share (EPS) over sequential quarters is demonstrating operational leverage — it is generating more profit from each dollar of revenue. Look for companies with three or more quarters of sequential EPS growth, and compare growth rates to the sector average. Above-average earnings growth is the first indicator of a quality options underlying.

- Check: quarterly EPS trend — is it rising sequentially? Year-over-year?;
- Tool: SEC EDGAR earnings filings, earnings call transcripts, FactSet, Bloomberg;
- Red flag: one-time gains inflating EPS. Look at operating income, not just net income;

2. The Company Has Rising Sales

Revenue growth is the top-line signal. A company can grow earnings temporarily through cost-cutting, buybacks, or one-time events — but sustainable earnings growth requires revenue growth. Rising sales tell you the company's market is expanding and that customers are choosing this company's products over competitors'. Revenue growth that outpaces the sector average is a primary indicator of competitive advantage.

- Check: quarterly revenue trend — sequential and year-over-year growth rates;
- Compare to sector peers: is this company gaining or losing market share?;
- Red flag: revenue growth driven entirely by acquisitions rather than organic growth;

3. The Stock Is at a Bargain Price (Price vs. Value)

A great company at an inflated price is a poor options trade — especially for income strategies where your profit is capped by the premium you collect. Price vs. Value analysis asks: is the stock trading at a reasonable multiple relative to its earnings growth rate? The PEG ratio (Price/Earnings divided by Earnings Growth Rate) is the most direct measure — a PEG below 1.0 suggests the stock may be undervalued relative to its growth.

- Key metrics: P/E ratio, PEG ratio, Price-to-Sales (P/S), Price-to-Free Cash Flow;
- Compare multiples to the 5-year historical average and to sector peers;

- For CSP and Wheel strategies: bargain price provides additional margin of safety at your strike;

4. Dividends Are Growing

Dividends are the long-term investor's best friend — and an underappreciated signal for options traders. A company that consistently raises its dividend is demonstrating confidence in its future cash flows. Growing dividends require growing free cash flow, which requires a business with durable pricing power and operational efficiency. For the Wheel strategy, dividend-paying stocks add an additional income stream on top of options premium.

- Check: dividend history — consecutive years of increases (Dividend Aristocrats have 25+ years);
- Payout ratio: dividend as a percentage of earnings — below 60% is sustainable, above 80% is at risk;
- Warning: high dividend yield can signal a falling stock price, not generosity — always check the trend;

5. The Market Is Growing

Even the best-run company struggles to grow in a shrinking market. The total addressable market (TAM) for a company's products and the direction of that market is as important as the company's internal metrics. A company serving a growing market has the wind at its back — pricing power, new customer acquisition, and expansion opportunities all become easier. A company fighting for share in a declining market is rowing upstream.

- Evaluate: is the company's industry growing, stable, or contracting?;
- Look for secular megatrends driving demand (digital transformation, healthcare aging, clean energy, AI infrastructure);
- Align with Chapter 7's sector rotation framework — entering a sector in an early-to-mid expansion phase captures market growth tailwinds;

6. The Company Is in a Field with a High Barrier to Entry

Barriers to entry protect a company's profits from competition. Without barriers, above-average returns attract competitors, who erode margins until returns normalize. Companies with high barriers — network effects, proprietary technology, regulatory moats, high switching costs, or significant capital requirements — can sustain above-average returns for years or decades. These are Warren Buffett's 'moat' businesses, and they make the best underlying candidates for long-term income strategies.

- High-moat examples: enterprise software (switching costs), pharmaceuticals (patents), utilities (regulatory moat), payment networks (network effects);
- Low-moat examples: airlines, restaurants, commodity producers — competition easily erodes margins;
- The stronger the moat, the more confidently you can sell puts at discounts — the stock is less likely to undergo permanent impairment;

7. The Company Has a Low Political Profile

Companies with high political visibility face a risk that does not appear in any earnings model: regulatory action, antitrust investigation, congressional scrutiny, or sanctions. Big Tech antitrust cases, pharmaceutical pricing investigations, and energy sector regulation are all examples of political risk materializing as sudden stock price gaps that destroy income positions. Low-profile companies operating in well-understood, non-controversial industries are generally safer as options income underlyings.

- Red flags: ongoing regulatory investigations, congressional hearings, major government contract dependencies;
- This is not a political statement — it is a risk management filter. Political headlines move stocks in ways that have nothing to do with earnings or fundamentals;
- When in doubt: use sector ETFs rather than individual high-profile names to diversify this risk;

8. The Stock Is Optionable

This one seems obvious — but it has layers. An optionable stock is not just one that has listed options. It is one with a liquid options chain: tight bid/ask spreads, open interest in the hundreds or thousands at the strikes you intend to trade, and multiple expiration dates available. A stock that technically has options but has zero open interest at your target strike is not tradeable for your strategy. Confirm full chain liquidity before committing capital.

- Check: open interest at your intended strike > 100 minimum, ideally > 500;
- Bid/ask spread should be no more than 10% of the option premium on standard strikes;
- Weekly options available? This expands your income strategy frequency from monthly to weekly cycles;

9. The Stock Is Benefiting from Favorable Megatrends

A megatrend is a structural shift that affects an unusually large segment of the marketplace over a multi-year or multi-decade period. Megatrends are the rising tide that lifts entire industries. Companies positioned at the intersection of multiple megatrends can sustain growth well beyond what their current financial metrics would suggest. Identifying megatrend beneficiaries early — and running income strategies on them — is one of the highest-conviction ways to compound the Wheel strategy.

- Current megatrends: Artificial Intelligence infrastructure, Aging demographics (healthcare), Energy transition (clean energy), Digital finance (fintech, crypto infrastructure), Deglobalization (domestic manufacturing, defense);
- The megatrend test: will this industry be meaningfully larger in 10 years than it is today? If yes — the secular tailwind supports holding the underlying through short-term volatility;
- Megatrend alignment is not a substitute for fundamental quality — it amplifies the thesis of an already-strong company;

10. The Company Has Low Liabilities

Debt can consume an otherwise excellent company. Too much leverage amplifies both gains and losses — in a rising rate environment or an economic contraction, highly indebted companies face cash flow pressure, refinancing risk, and potential covenant violations that can send a stock down 40–60% with little warning. For income traders running the Wheel, owning shares of a highly leveraged company at an assigned strike during a credit event can produce losses that overwhelm years of collected premium.

- Key metrics: Debt-to-Equity ratio (below 1.0 is conservative), Interest Coverage ratio (earnings before interest / interest expense > 3× is healthy);
- Net debt position: does the company have more cash than debt? Net cash companies have maximum financial flexibility; and
- Compare to sector norms: some sectors (utilities, financials) structurally carry higher debt — evaluate relative to peers, not absolute numbers.

THE TEN-INDICATOR CHECKLIST

Before running any options income strategy on an individual stock, score it on the 10 indicators. 8–10 indicators met: High-conviction underlying — full position size, full strategy toolkit available. 5–7 indicators met: Acceptable underlying — reduce position size, use defined-risk structures only. Below 5 indicators: Do not use for income strategies. Trade directional debit spreads only, if at all. Remember: ETFs bypass most of this checklist — the diversification does the quality filtering for you.

The Ten-Indicator Scoring Worksheet

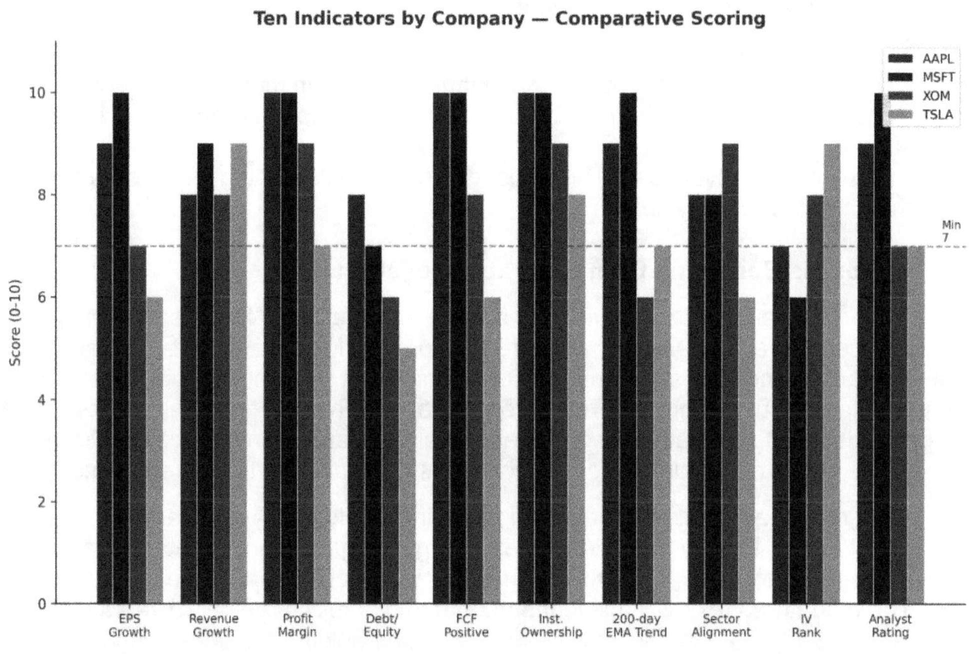

Figure 9.1 — Ten Indicators Scoring System — How to score a stock across all ten criteria to determine eligibility as an options underlying.

Ten Indicators Scoring System — How to score a stock across all ten indicators to determine eligibility.

Use this worksheet for every stock you are considering trading. One point per indicator met. Score before every new position — not just when you first discover a stock. Conditions change. A company that scored 9/10 six months ago may score 6/10 today if earnings have reversed or debt has risen. Re-score every quarter minimum.

#	Indicator	Quick Check	Score (0 or 1)
1	Rising Profits	EPS growing sequentially for 3+ quarters. Operating income trend positive.	__ /1
2	Rising Sales	Revenue growing YoY and sequentially. Market share stable or increasing.	__ /1
3	Bargain Price	PEG ratio below 1.5. P/E below sector average or justified by growth rate.	__ /1
4	Growing Dividends	Dividend raised at least once in past 2 years. Payout ratio below 70%.	__ /1
5	Growing Market	TAM expanding. Industry in secular growth phase. Sector BPI trending up.	__ /1
6	High Barrier to Entry	Moat identifiable: patents, network effects, regulatory protection, switching costs.	__ /1
7	Low Political Profile	No active regulatory investigation, antitrust scrutiny, or congressional targeting.	__ /1
8	Optionable (Liquid Chain)	Open interest > 500 at target strike. Bid/ask spread < 10% of premium. Weekly options available.	__ /1
9	Megatrend Alignment	Company positioned in a secular growth megatrend (AI, healthcare aging, clean energy, fintech).	__ /1
10	Low Liabilities	Debt-to-Equity < 1.0. Interest Coverage > 3×. Net debt position manageable.	__ /1
	TOTAL SCORE		**___ / 10**

Score → Six-Condition Eligibility: What Your Score Allows

The Ten-Indicator score does not just determine whether to trade — it determines which of the six conditions you are allowed to apply to this specific underlying. A low-quality stock is never eligible for income strategies regardless of what the VIX says.

Score	Rating	Eligible Six-Condition Strategies
8–10 / 10	**A-CLASS — Full Access**	ALL SIX CONDITIONS available at full position size. This underlying is the backbone of your income book. Run the Wheel, sell spreads, buy directional debit — all strategies are approved at normal sizing.

Score	Rating	Eligible Six-Condition Strategies
6–7 / 10	**B-CLASS — Restricted Access**	Conditions 1, 2, 3 available at reduced size (50% of normal position). Defined-risk structures only — no naked positions. No Wheel on this stock. Monitor the failing indicators — if they resolve, upgrade to A-class.
4–5 / 10	**C-CLASS — Directional Debit Only**	Conditions 1 and 3 only, at minimum size. Long calls or long puts with capped risk. No income strategies. The quality is insufficient to accept the obligation of short premium positions.
Below 4 / 10	**INELIGIBLE — Do Not Trade**	No conditions approved for individual stock strategies. If you want exposure to this sector or theme, use an ETF instead. The ETF's diversification compensates for what the individual stock lacks in quality.

QUALITY FIRST. CONDITION SECOND. STRATEGY THIRD.

This is the Premium Desk sequence — and the order is non-negotiable. You never skip step one to get to step three faster. A perfectly read six-condition trade on a low-quality underlying is a structurally flawed trade. The quality filter is the foundation. The condition read is the blueprint. The strategy is the execution. All three must align.

The Ten-Indicator Screen: Three Real Stocks Compared

Apply the indicators to actual stocks — one that passes, one that fails, one borderline.

Indicator	MSFT (Pass)	RIVN (Fail)	INTC (Border)
1. Rising Profits	8 qtrs EPS growth ✓	Negative EPS X	Declining but recent beat ~
2. Rising Sales	Revenue +12% YoY ✓	Revenue growing but cash burn ~	Revenue flat X
3. Bargain Price	P/E 32x justified ✓	No P/E (neg earnings) X	P/E 25x, below avg ✓
4. Growing Dividends	12yr consecutive ✓	No dividend X	Dividend cut X
5. Market Growth	Cloud + AI +20% ✓	EV market competitive ~	Foundry uncertain ~
6. Barrier to Entry	Enterprise lock-in ✓	Low — dozens of rivals X	Fab manufacturing ✓
7. Low Political Risk	Moderate ✓	EV subsidies volatile X	CHIPS Act beneficiary ✓
8. Optionable	Weekly, tight, massive OI ✓	Available but wider ~	Good liquidity ✓
9. Megatrends	AI, cloud, enterprise ✓	EV transition ~	Semiconductor demand ✓
10. Low Liabilities	Debt/eq 0.35 ✓	Debt/eq 1.8 X	Debt/eq 0.47 ✓

MSFT: 10/10 — ideal Wheel candidate. RIVN: 2/10 — do NOT sell puts. INTC: 6/10 — use spreads only, size down 50%.

QUALITY FILTER RULE

7+ indicators = CSP and Wheel eligible. 5-6 = spreads only. Below 5 = do not trade. Being wrong on MSFT costs time. Being wrong on RIVN costs capital.

Step-by-Step Scoring Walkthrough: Microsoft (MSFT)

The Ten Indicator screen takes 15–20 minutes per stock when you first learn it. After 30 stocks, it takes 8 minutes. After 100 stocks, it takes 5. The speed comes from knowing where to find each data point. Below is a complete walkthrough using Microsoft as the example, showing exactly what to look for and how to assign each score. Use this as your template for every new stock you evaluate.

Data sources used in this walkthrough: SEC EDGAR (for 10-K/10-Q filings), Macrotrends.net (historical financials), Yahoo Finance (current ratios and dividend history), Barchart or CBOE (options chain liquidity).

Indicator 1 — Rising Profits (EPS Growth)

Where to look: Macrotrends.net → search MSFT → 'EPS Diluted.' Check the last 8 quarters of EPS. You need a consistent upward trend — not every quarter, but the clear direction.

What you find for MSFT: EPS has grown from $2.35 (Q1 FY2022) to $3.30 (Q1 FY2024). Every fiscal year shows higher EPS than the prior year. The trend is unambiguous. Cloud and AI segments are driving margin expansion.

- SCORE: 1 point. EPS growth is clear, consistent, and supported by structural tailwinds.

Indicator 2 — Rising Sales (Revenue Growth)

Where to look: Same Macrotrends page → 'Revenue.' Check year-over-year growth rate. Require at least 5% YoY revenue growth for a mature company; more for a growth-oriented name.

What you find for MSFT: Revenue grew from $198B (FY2022) to $212B (FY2023) to $245B (FY2024). That is approximately +7% and +15% in consecutive years — accelerating growth, not decelerating. Azure cloud revenue grew 28% YoY. Revenue quality is high: recurring subscription and cloud revenue comprises over 60% of total.

- SCORE: 1 point. Revenue growth is accelerating, high-quality, and diversified across segments.

Indicator 3 — Bargain Price (Valuation)

Where to look: Yahoo Finance → MSFT → Statistics tab → P/E ratio, Forward P/E, PEG ratio. Compare to S&P 500 average and sector peers.

What you find for MSFT: P/E of ~35x versus S&P 500 average of ~22x. This appears expensive — but context matters. MSFT's PEG ratio (P/E divided by growth rate) is approximately 1.8, which for a company with MSFT's margin profile and recurring revenue base is acceptable. More importantly, the stock is trading at a modest premium to its own 5-year average P/E of ~32x, not an extreme premium.

Judgment call: For Indicator 3, you are not looking for deep value — you are looking for reasonable valuation given quality. MSFT is not dirt cheap, but it is not wildly overpriced. For a quality compounder with dominant market position and accelerating cloud growth, a P/E in the mid-30s is defensible.

- SCORE: 1 point. Valuation is premium but justified by quality and growth. Not a bargain, but not a danger zone.

Indicator 4 — Growing Dividends or Buybacks

Where to look: Macrotrends → 'Dividend per Share' history. Or Yahoo Finance → 'Dividends & Splits.' Look for 5+ consecutive years of dividend growth. Also check buyback history if the company does not pay dividends.

What you find for MSFT: Microsoft has increased its dividend every year since 2003 — over 20 consecutive years of dividend growth. Current annual dividend: $3.00/share, yielding approximately 0.8% at today's price. While the yield is modest, the consecutive growth record signals financial strength and management commitment to shareholder returns. Additionally, MSFT repurchased $9.7B in stock in FY2024.

- SCORE: 1 point. 20+ years of consecutive dividend growth plus significant buybacks. Maximum quality on this indicator.

Indicator 5 — Participation in Market Growth (Megatrends)

Where to look: Company's investor relations page and recent earnings calls. Identify which secular growth themes the company participates in. Megatrends include: cloud computing, AI/machine learning, cybersecurity, digital transformation, healthcare technology, renewable energy, aging population.

What you find for MSFT: Microsoft is arguably the most directly exposed large-cap company to the AI megatrend through its OpenAI partnership and Azure AI services. Additionally: cloud computing (Azure, #2 global), enterprise software (Office 365, Teams), gaming (Xbox, Activision), and cybersecurity. Four distinct megatrend exposures in a single company.

- SCORE: 1 point. Multiple high-conviction megatrend alignments. This is an A+ on Indicator 5.

Indicator 6 — Competitive Moat (Barrier to Entry)

Where to look: Annual report (10-K) 'Competitive Strengths' section, and your own assessment of switching costs. Ask: if a competitor entered this market tomorrow with unlimited funding, how long would it take to replicate what this company has built?

What you find for MSFT: Microsoft's moat is extraordinary. Enterprise lock-in from Office 365, Teams, and Azure Active Directory creates switching costs measured in years, not months. The average enterprise Microsoft deployment involves hundreds of integrated workflows. Azure's 60,000+ active customers include most of the Fortune 500 — they will not migrate. Windows remains the dominant enterprise OS. Xbox Game Pass is the only platform with a full-stack gaming ecosystem. This is one of the widest moats in the public markets.

- SCORE: 1 point. Exceptional competitive moat across multiple business units.

Indicators 7–10 — Completing the MSFT Scorecard

#	Indicator	MSFT Finding	Score
7	**Low Political Risk**	US-domiciled, highly regulated (good — regulation protects incumbents), bipartisan support for domestic tech. Main risk: EU antitrust scrutiny on Activision deal (resolved). CHIPS Act beneficiary through Azure data centers.	1 / 1
8	**Insider Ownership**	Satya Nadella holds significant MSFT stock, compensated heavily in stock rather than cash. Bill Gates still a major holder. Board members collectively own meaningful shares. Insider selling is normal-rate (diversification), not alarming.	1 / 1
9	**Optionable (Liquidity)**	MSFT has the deepest options chain of any non-index security. Average daily options volume exceeds 400,000 contracts. Weekly options available. Bid/ask spreads are 1-2 cents wide at major strikes. Perfect options liquidity.	1 / 1
10	**Low Liabilities**	Debt-to-equity: 0.35. Interest coverage ratio: 40x+ (earnings easily cover interest payments). Net cash position when netting debt against cash holdings. Balance sheet is fortress-grade.	1 / 1

MSFT FINAL SCORE: 10 / 10 Classification: A-CLASS — Full Access. All six strategies eligible at full position size.	**Approved Strategies:** Wheel Strategy ✓ Cash-Secured Put ✓ Covered Call ✓ Bull/Bear Spreads ✓ Iron Condor ✓

This is what a 10/10 stock looks like. It does not have to be MSFT specifically — but every stock in your income book should look like MSFT across these ten dimensions. When you find yourself rationalizing a 5/10 stock because 'the premium is too good to pass up,' remember: MSFT passes every indicator AND offers liquid options at every strike. There is no reason to trade inferior quality.

Print or copy this worksheet for every new stock you evaluate. Complete it before allowing yourself to open the options chain. The discipline of completing the worksheet — even when you already 'know' the answer — is what separates systematic quality control from wishful thinking.

#	Indicator	Your Findings (Write Here)	Score 0 or 1	Data Source
1	**Rising Profits**		___ / 1	Macrotrends.net → EPS Diluted
2	**Rising Sales**		___ / 1	Macrotrends.net → Revenue
3	**Bargain Price**		___ / 1	Yahoo Finance → Statistics
4	**Growing Dividends / Buybacks**		___ / 1	Macrotrends → Dividend History
5	**Megatrend Alignment**		___ / 1	10-K: Business Overview
6	**Competitive Moat**		___ / 1	10-K: Competition section
7	**Low Political Risk**		___ / 1	News search + 10-K: Risk Factors
8	**Insider Ownership**		___ / 1	SEC Edgar Form 4 filings
9	**Optionable / Liquid Chain**		___ / 1	CBOE or your platform chain
10	**Low Liabilities**		___ / 1	Macrotrends → Debt-to-Equity

Ticker: ___________ Date: ___________ Price: $__________ Sector: ___________.	**TOTAL ___ / 10**	8-10: A-Class 6-7: B-Class 4-5: C-Class <4: Ineligible	Classification: ___________ Approved strategies: ___________________

QUALITY FIRST. CONDITION SECOND. STRATEGY THIRD.

This is the Premium Desk sequence — and the order is non-negotiable. You never skip step one to get to step three faster. A perfectly read six-condition trade on a low-quality underlying is a structurally flawed trade. The quality filter is the foundation. The condition read is the blueprint. The strategy is the execution. All three must align.

Figure 9.12 — Candlestick Anatomy: The Four Data Points Encoded in Every Candle

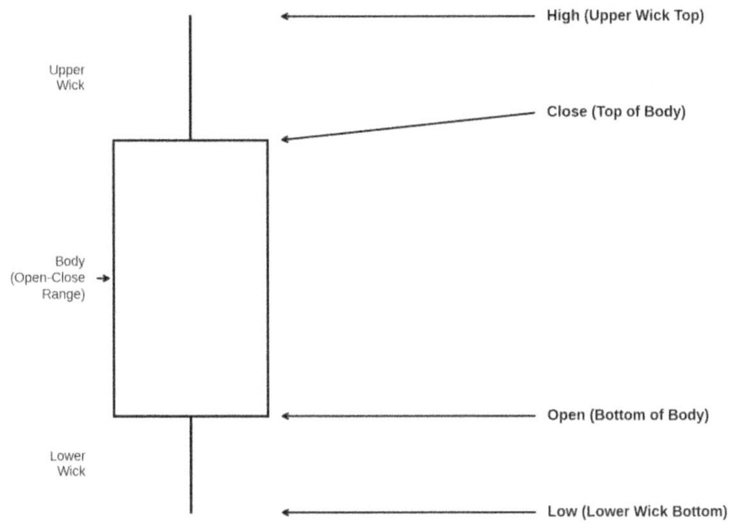

Figure 9.11 — Candlestick Anatomy. The four data points encoded in every candle: open, high, low, close.

> **6-CONDITION FRAMEWORK ▸ IDENTIFIES DIRECTION — the first axis of the six-condition read**
> Chart analysis answers the direction half: uptrend (conditions 1-2), downtrend (3-4), or range (5-6). VIX answers the volatility half. Together they lock in your condition. This chapter teaches you to read one axis.

Technical analysis is not about predicting the future. It is about reading the present — identifying where price has been, where it is struggling, and where the weight of buying or selling pressure is concentrated. For the options trader, technical analysis is a timing tool: it tells you when to enter a position, where to anchor your strikes, and when the trade thesis is still intact vs. broken.

The key distinction from pure stock trading: you are not just picking a direction. You are picking a direction AND a time frame AND a magnitude of move. All three must be correct for a long options trade to profit. Technical analysis sharpens each of those three decisions.

Charts: The Language of the Market

A price chart is the complete record of every decision made by every participant in a market, compressed into a visual format. Candlestick charts are the standard for active options traders — each candle shows the open, high, low, and close for a given time period, and their patterns reveal the battle between buyers and sellers at every price level. Before you can read patterns, you must be fluent in the alphabet: the individual candles themselves.

OHLC: The Four Data Points of Every Price Bar

Every candlestick — whether on a 1-minute chart or a monthly chart — encodes exactly four data points, collectively known as OHLC:

Open — the first traded price when the session or time period begins. The open tells you where consensus stood at the start. A gap between the prior close and the current open signals overnight sentiment shift — bullish if gapping up, bearish if gapping down. For options traders, opening gaps directly affect delta exposure on existing positions.

High — the highest price reached during the session. The high represents the maximum point of buyer aggression. When a high touches or exceeds a known resistance level, it tells you buyers attempted to break through. Whether they succeeded determines the signal: a close near the high confirms buyer control; a close well below the high (long upper wick) signals seller rejection at that level.

Low — the lowest price reached during the session. The low represents the maximum point of seller aggression. When a low touches or penetrates a known support level, it tells you sellers tested that floor. A close well above the low (long lower wick) confirms buyers defended the level — this is one of the highest-probability CSP entry signals in candlestick analysis.

Close — the last traded price when the session ends. The close is the single most important data point. It represents final consensus — where the market settled after all the intraday battles. The relationship between the close and the open defines the candle's color and body: close above open = bullish (filled/green), close below open = bearish (hollow/red). The close relative to the high and low defines the wick pattern, which reveals conviction.

> **THE OHLC HIERARCHY**
>
> Professional traders read candles in a specific order: Close first (who won?), then Open-to-Close range (by how much?), then High and Low (how far did the losers push before being rejected?). This hierarchy — Close → Body → Wicks — is the foundation of every candlestick pattern in this chapter. Master OHLC reading and every pattern becomes intuitive rather than memorized.

Time frames for options traders: Use the daily chart for trade direction and strike selection. Use the weekly chart to confirm the larger trend. Use the 4-hour or 1-hour chart for entry timing on shorter-dated trades only.

The Four Candlestick Definitions Every Options Trader Must Know

Every candlestick encodes four pieces of data: the open, the high, the low, and the close. The body of the candle represents the distance between the open and close. The wicks (or shadows) represent the high and low extremes reached during the session. A bullish candle closes higher than it opened — represented by a filled (dark) body. A bearish candle closes lower than it opened — represented by an open (white/hollow) body. In most B&W printed references, bullish candles are filled and bearish candles are outlined; on color screens, green = bullish, red = bearish.

The power of candlestick analysis is not in individual candles — it is in the sequence. A single candle tells you what happened in one session. A string of candles tells you who is winning the battle between buyers and sellers, and at what price levels the tide turned. The patterns below are not memorization exercises. Each one represents a specific supply/demand dynamic that repeats across markets and timeframes.

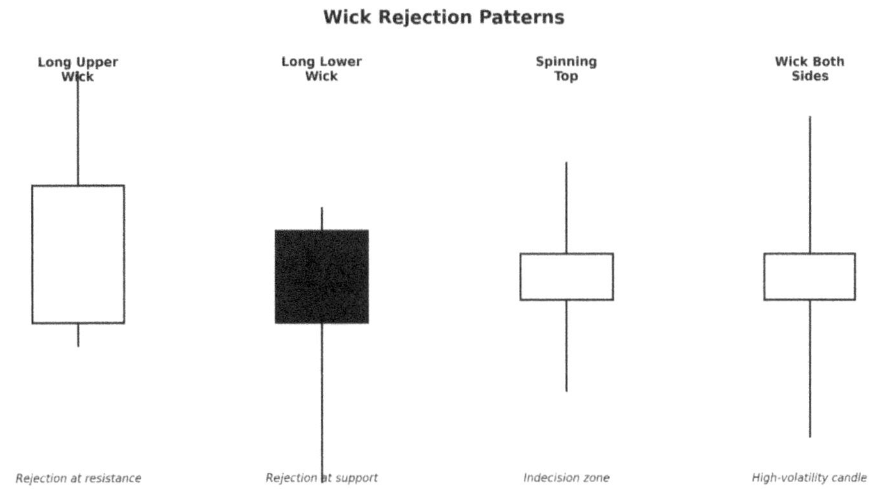

Figure 9.1 — Wick Rejection Patterns.

Bullish Candle Types: Reading Buyer Strength

The shape of a bullish candle tells you precisely how much control buyers had during the session. A large body with no wicks (Marubozu) means buyers dominated from the opening bell to the close — maximum conviction. A large body with small wicks means buyers won decisively but faced brief opposition. A small body with long wicks means the session was contested — buyers ultimately prevailed but the result was close. Understanding this spectrum lets you grade the quality of every bullish candle you see.

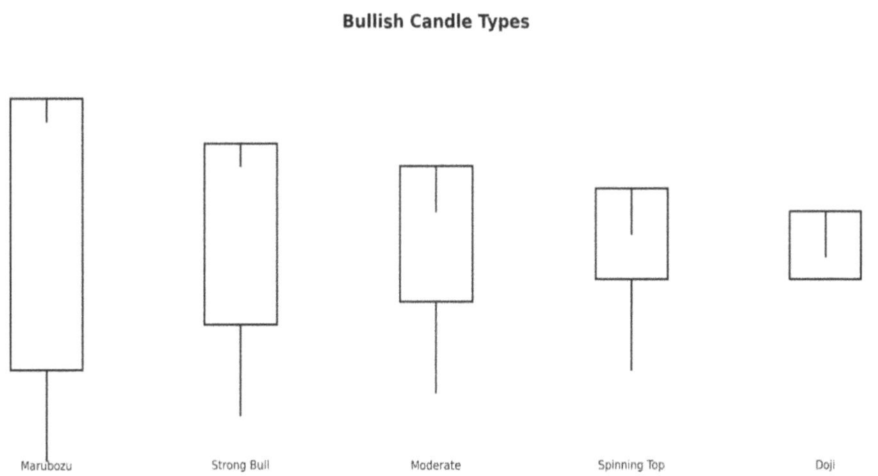

Figure 9.2 — Bullish Candle Types. From Marubozu to spinning top — reading the degree of buyer control.

Options application: a Marubozu or large bullish body closing ABOVE a resistance level on elevated volume is a Condition 1 entry signal. The wick pattern tells you whether the breakout has conviction (small wicks = buyers still in control) or is at risk of reversal (large upper wick = sellers already testing the new level). Strike selection for a long call should be ATM or one strike OTM on a confirmed large-body breakout candle.

THE MARUBOZU RULE

A full green Marubozu — no upper wick, no lower wick — is the strongest single-session bullish signal in candlestick analysis. It means buyers controlled the session from the first tick to the last. When you see a Marubozu closing above a key resistance level on above-average volume, the breakout has maximum conviction. This is a Condition 1 entry candidate. Size appropriately and do not wait for a pullback that may not come.

Bearish Candle Types: Reading Seller Strength

The bearish candle spectrum mirrors the bullish exactly. A full bearish Marubozu means sellers controlled the session completely — open to close, no buyer interference. A large bearish body closing below a support level with minimal lower wick is a breakdown confirmation: sellers tested the level, broke it, and held it. A small bearish body inside the range of previous candles is a pause, not a reversal — sellers are present but not yet in control. Do not act on small inside bearish candles at the end of uptrends without additional confirmation.

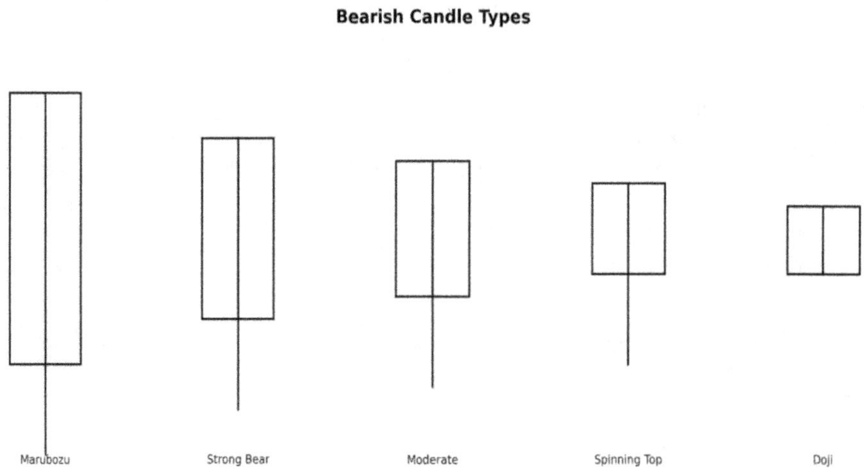

Figure 9.3 — Bearish Candle Types. The mirror of bullish candles — reading seller conviction.

THE BREAKDOWN CANDLE RULE

A large bearish body closing BELOW a known support level on elevated volume is a Condition 3 or 4 signal. The support level that was previously a floor has become a ceiling. Exit any bullish CSP or covered call positions on the underlying immediately. A debit put spread targeting the next support level down is the options play. Do not buy the close of a breakdown candle hoping for a bounce — wait for a failed retest of the broken level from below.

Reading the Wicks: Where the Real Battle Happened

The wick is the most underread element of candlestick analysis. While most traders focus on the body (where price closed relative to where it opened), the wick tells you where price went and was rejected. A long upper wick means price was pushed up significantly during the session but sellers stepped in hard and drove it back down before the close. This is bearish — sellers won the battle at higher prices. A long lower wick means price was pushed down but buyers stepped in and absorbed all the selling, pushing price back up before the close. This is bullish — buyers defended lower prices aggressively.

The most important rule about wicks: their signal value increases dramatically when they occur at known technical levels. A long lower wick sitting exactly on a major support level tells you buyers are defending that level with conviction. This is the highest-probability CSP entry signal in candlestick analysis — the wick proves buyers are there. A long upper wick at resistance confirms sellers are defending that level. Place your iron condor's short call strike above that wick high.

THE WICK RULE FOR STRIKE PLACEMENT

Long lower wick at support = CSP entry candidate. Your short put strike goes at or just below the support level the wick touched. Long upper wick at resistance = covered call or bear call spread entry. Your short call strike goes at or just above the resistance level the wick touched. The wick is the market showing you exactly where the counterparty stepped in. Align your short strike with that level.

Doji Patterns: When Neither Side Wins

A Doji forms when the open and close are at virtually the same price — the body is a horizontal line or near-zero width. Doji candles mean the session ended in a draw: buyers pushed price up, sellers pushed it back, and neither side gained ground by the close. The shape of the doji tells you more about the nature of the stalemate. The Standard Doji has roughly equal wicks on both sides. The Gravestone Doji has a long upper wick and no lower wick — price rallied then was completely rejected, a bearish signal at market tops. The Dragonfly Doji has a long lower wick and no upper wick — price sold off then was completely recovered, a bullish signal at market bottoms. The Long-Legged Doji has very long wicks on both sides, indicating extreme indecision after a volatile session.

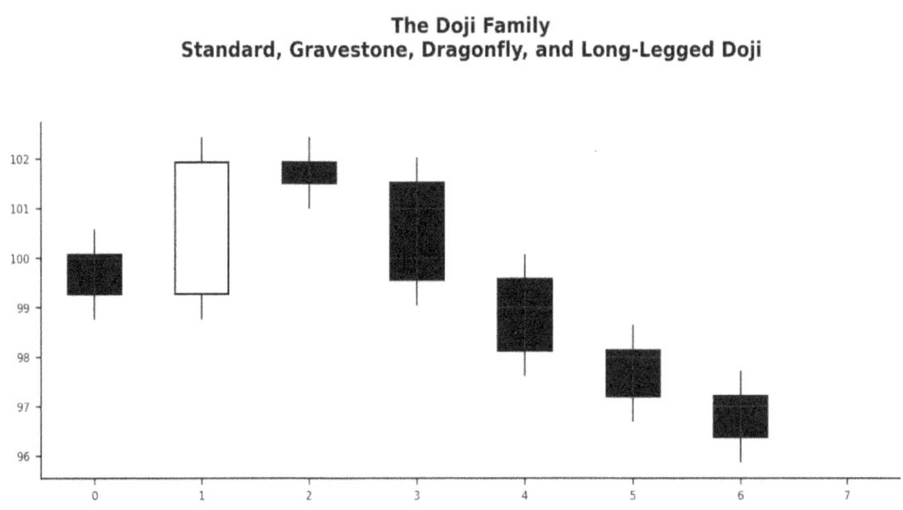

Figure 9.4 — The Doji Family. Standard, Gravestone, Dragonfly, and Long-Legged Doji.

Critical principle: a single Doji is context, not a signal. What makes the Doji powerful is its LOCATION within the trend. A Gravestone Doji after a 5-session rally at a known resistance level is a high-probability reversal signal. The same Gravestone Doji in the middle of a consolidation range is noise. Always ask: what happened in the 3–5 sessions before this Doji, and where does the Doji sit relative to the nearest technical level?

Engulfing Patterns: The Strongest 2-Candle Reversal Signal

The engulfing pattern is the most reliable two-candle reversal signal in candlestick analysis. A Bullish Engulfing occurs when a large bullish candle completely engulfs the body of the prior bearish candle — the bullish candle opens below the prior close and closes above the prior open. This means buyers not only reversed all of the prior session's losses but went further, establishing new closing highs. The larger the bullish candle relative to the bearish candle it engulfs, the stronger the signal.

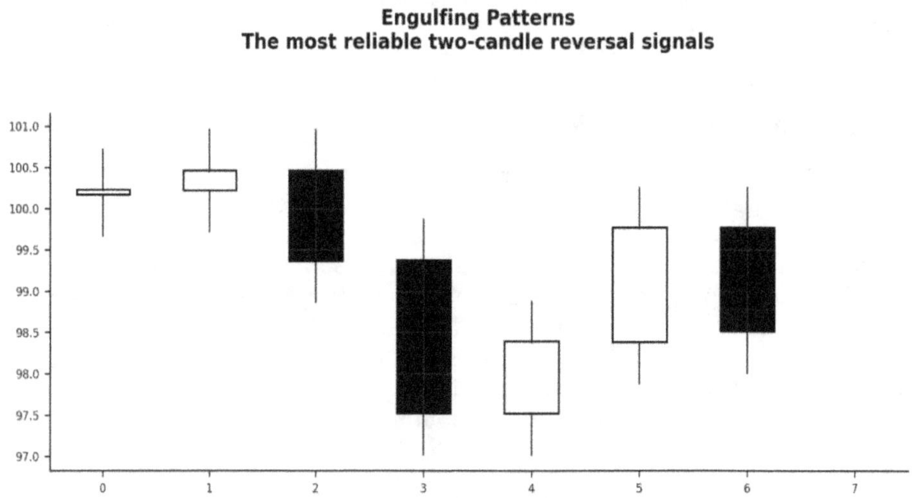

Figure 9.5 — Engulfing Patterns. The most reliable two-candle reversal signal.

A Bearish Engulfing is the mirror image: a large bearish candle completely swallows the prior bullish candle. This means sellers reversed all prior session gains and pushed price to new closing lows. The engulfing pattern is most powerful when it occurs: (1) after a clear multi-session trend in the opposite direction, (2) at a known support or resistance level, and (3) on above-average volume confirming institutional participation. An engulfing pattern in the middle of a range or on light volume is a lower-probability signal.

ENGULFING + VOLUME = HIGH CONVICTION

An engulfing pattern on volume that is at least 1.5x the 20-day average volume is one of the highest-probability short-term reversal signals in technical analysis. For CSP sellers: a bullish engulfing at a major support level on high volume is the cleanest single-candle entry signal you will find. For spread traders: a bearish engulfing at resistance on high volume is a Condition 3 or 4 signal to enter a debit put spread or bear call spread targeting the next support level.

Hammer & Shooting Star: Single-Candle Reversal Signals

The Hammer and Shooting Star are two of the most widely recognized single-candle reversal patterns. Both are defined by a very small body positioned at one extreme of the session range, with a very long wick extending in the opposite direction. The Hammer occurs at the end of a downtrend: the session sold off sharply (the long lower wick) but buyers stepped in and recovered nearly all losses before the close, leaving a small body near the session high. The message: sellers tried hard, buyers absorbed everything.

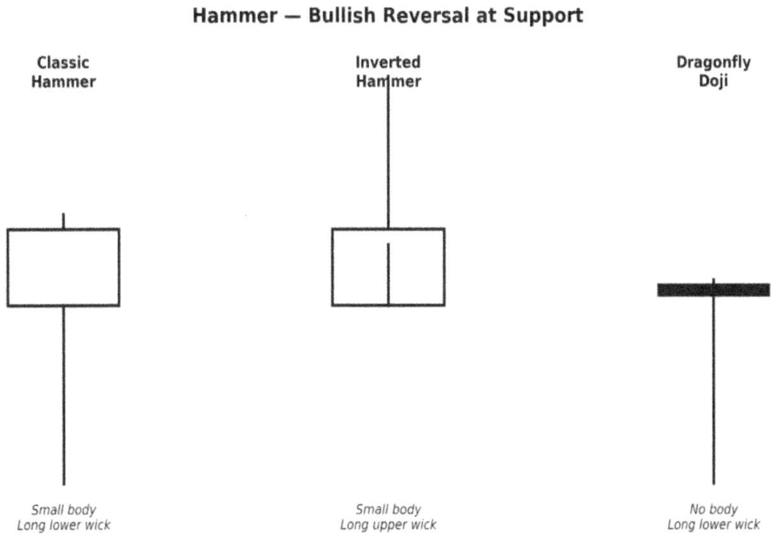

Figure 10.1 — Hammer and Shooting Star Candlesticks — Reversal signals at support and resistance. Wick length indicates rejection strength.

The Shooting Star is the bearish equivalent, appearing at the end of an uptrend. The session rallied sharply (the long upper wick) but sellers stepped in at the highs and pushed price back down near the session low. The message: buyers tried hard, sellers absorbed everything at elevated prices. For the options trader, the Hammer at a support level is a CSP entry signal (buyers are defending that price). The Shooting Star at a resistance level is a covered call or bear spread entry signal (sellers are defending that ceiling).

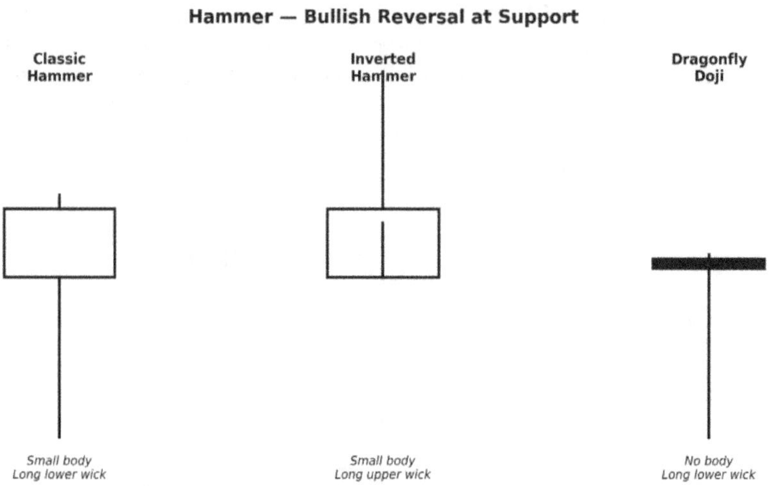

Figure 9.6 — Hammer Patterns. Three bullish reversal candles at support — Classic, Inverted, Dragonfly.

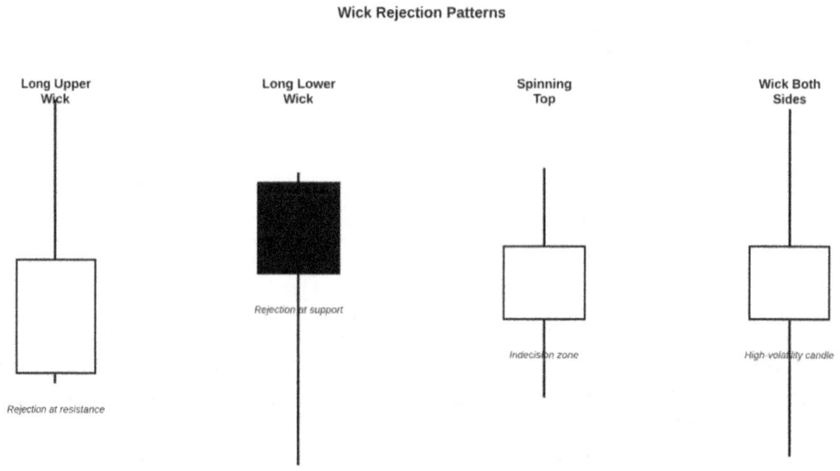

Figure 9.7 — Shooting Star Patterns. Three bearish reversal candles at resistance.

Morning Star & Evening Star: 3-Candle Reversal Patterns

The Morning Star and Evening Star are three-candle reversal patterns that represent one of the highest-probability reversal signals in candlestick analysis. The Morning Star appears at the bottom of a downtrend and consists of: (1) a large bearish candle confirming the downtrend, (2) a small-bodied candle (star) that gaps below the prior close, showing indecision and momentum loss, and (3) a large bullish candle that closes deep into the body of the first candle, confirming the reversal. The three-candle sequence tells a complete story: sellers in control → battle → buyers take over.

The Evening Star is the bearish mirror: a large bullish candle, then a small star that gaps above, then a large bearish candle closing deep into the first bullish body. For options traders, the Morning Star at a major support level on elevated volume is one of the cleanest Condition 1 setups available — long call or bull call spread targeting a move to the next resistance level. The Evening Star at a major resistance level is a Condition 3 setup. The three-candle confirmation reduces false signals significantly compared to single-candle patterns.

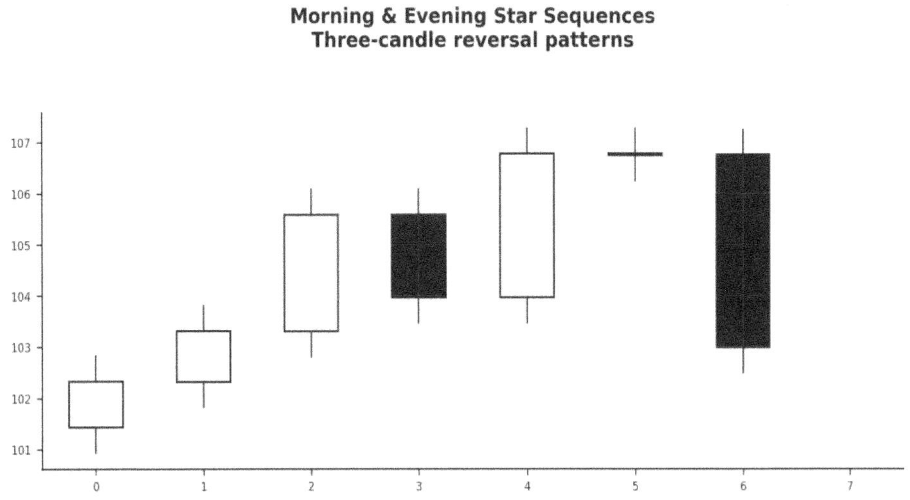

Figure 9.8 — Morning & Evening Star Sequences. Three-candle reversal patterns with entry timing.

Harami Patterns: Inside Bar Reversals

The Harami (Japanese for 'pregnant') is a two-candle pattern where a small candle is completely contained within the body of the prior larger candle. The Bullish Harami occurs in a downtrend: a large bearish candle is followed by a small bullish candle whose body fits entirely inside the prior bearish body. The small candle signals that selling momentum is exhausting — the bears cannot extend the move. The Bearish Harami is the mirror: a large bullish candle followed by a small bearish inside candle, signaling bull exhaustion.

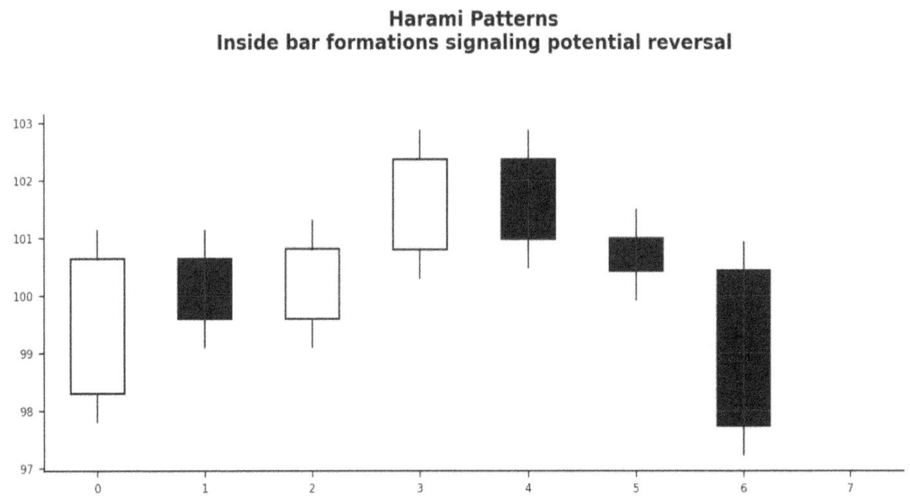

Figure 9.9 — Harami Patterns. Inside bar formations signaling potential momentum pause.

The Harami is a warning signal, not an action signal. It says momentum is potentially ending, but confirmation is required. Wait for the candle after the Harami: if it closes decisively in the new direction (bullish candle after Bullish Harami), act. If it continues the original trend, the Harami was noise. For premium sellers, a Harami at your short strike price is a signal to monitor the position closely — it suggests directional pressure may be reversing.

Three White Soldiers & Three Black Crows: Trend Confirmation

These three-candle patterns are not reversals — they are trend confirmation signals. Three White Soldiers is a sequence of three consecutive large bullish candles, each opening within the prior body and closing higher than the prior close. It signals powerful, sustained buying pressure across multiple sessions. This is the pattern that confirms a trend change has occurred and the new direction has momentum. Three Black Crows is the bearish mirror: three consecutive large bearish candles each closing lower. Both patterns are most significant when they appear after a period of consolidation or at a key technical level.

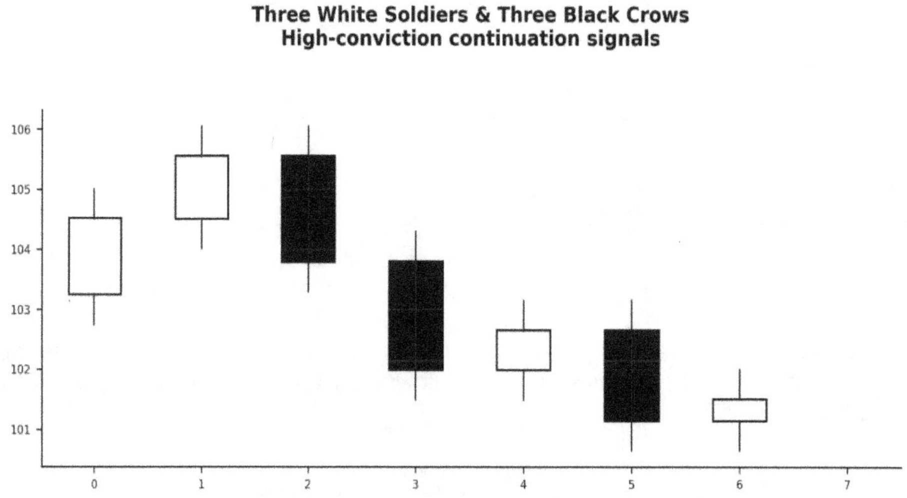

Figure 9.10 — Three White Soldiers & Three Black Crows. High-conviction continuation patterns.

> **THREE SOLDIERS + BREAKOUT = POSITION SIZE UP**
>
> When Three White Soldiers appears immediately after a breakout above a major resistance level that has held for months or years, this is one of the highest-conviction entry signals in all of technical analysis. The breakout happened, the follow-through is confirmed across three full sessions, and institutional buyers are clearly present. For Condition 1 trades, this is a signal to use full position size — not a scaled entry. The conviction pyramid applies: if you were at Tier 1 waiting for confirmation, the third soldier candle is your Tier 2 and 3 entry trigger.

Support & Resistance: Where the Market Remembers

Support is a price zone where the downtrend tends to pause due to greater buying interest — it is a floor. Resistance is just the opposite: where the uptrend is expected to pause or meet selling pressure — it is a ceiling. Once price reaches a key support or resistance level, there are two and only two outcomes: it bounces back, or it violates the level. Traders bet on the next move from these levels. If wrong, they close at a small stop-loss. If right, they ride the considerable move that follows.

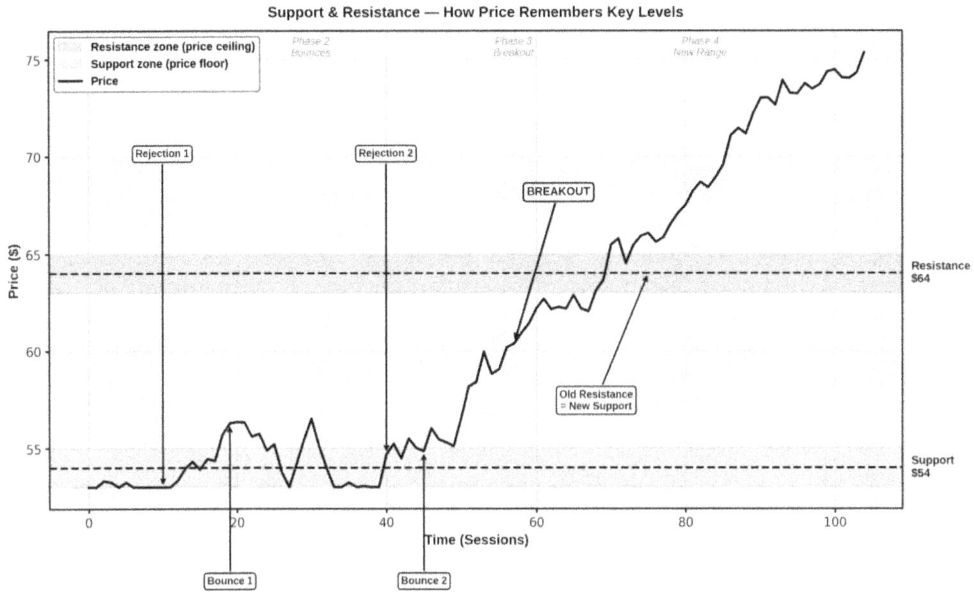

Figure 10.2 — Support & Resistance. Price is rejected twice at resistance, bounces twice at support, then breaks out — and old resistance becomes new support.

- Support becomes resistance after it breaks — former buyers are now trapped and will sell rallies to break even;
- Resistance becomes support after it breaks — former sellers cover and new buyers step in;
- For options traders: anchor your short strikes BELOW support (for puts) and ABOVE resistance (for calls). Let the chart's structure define your risk zones;

Three rules for identifying strong, reliable support and resistance:

- Rule 1 — Zoom out. You cannot find strong S/R on a 5-minute chart. You need to go out as far as several months of daily data. The further you zoom out, the stronger the level you identify. Support and resistance should not be set on 5-minute charts unless you are day-trading.
- Rule 2 — Use daily and weekly charts as your primary frames. For options traders running 30–45 DTE positions, daily chart S/R is your primary reference. Weekly chart S/R is your ultimate backstop; and
- Rule 3 — Count the touches. The more times a price level has been tested and held, the stronger it is. A level tested 4 times is stronger than one tested twice. Connect at least 2–3 touchpoints to confirm a support line (connecting dips) or resistance line (connecting spikes).

STRIKE PLACEMENT RULE

Never place your short strike inside a known support or resistance zone. Place it beyond — where the stock would need to break a significant technical level to reach your strike. The technical level is your first line of defense.

Why S&R Levels Hold: Memories, Pain & Regret

Support and resistance levels are not random lines on a chart. They exist because masses of traders have memories — and those memories create emotional commitments that drive buying and selling behavior at specific price levels. Understanding the psychology behind S&R transforms it from a charting technique into a window into crowd behavior.

Three groups of traders create S&R levels and defend them long after the initial move:

- Trapped longs: Traders who bought near a resistance level and are holding losses. When price rallies back to their entry, they sell to break even — creating fresh resistance at that exact level. Their pain becomes the ceiling;
- Trapped shorts: Traders who sold short near a support level and are holding losses. When price falls back to their entry, they buy to cover — creating fresh support at that level. Their regret becomes the floor;
- Traders who missed the move: Those who watched a breakout and wished they had bought. They wait for a pullback to the old level — and when it comes, their buying reinforces the new support. Old resistance becomes new support precisely because a new group of committed buyers has taken over;

This crowd psychology explains three phenomena that confuse new chart readers:

- Why S&R levels flip: when support breaks, the trapped longs who could not sell at breakeven become trapped with larger losses, and now sell any rally — converting their former floor into a ceiling;
- Why levels are tested multiple times before breaking: each test brings in more defenders, but also exhausts the buying pressure that has been defending the level; and
- Why breakouts from well-tested levels are explosive: by the time a level breaks after five tests, the trapped traders on the wrong side are all forced to cover simultaneously.

The Three Factors That Determine S&R Strength

Not all support and resistance levels are equally powerful. Three factors determine how strongly a level will hold — and how explosive the move will be if it breaks:

Factor	What It Measures	Options Trader Application
Length (Time)	How long price spent in the congestion zone. A 2-week range = minor level. A 2-year range = major level. More time = more traders with emotional commitment.	Weekly S/R from multi-month bases = strongest strike anchors. Daily S/R from 2–3 week ranges = reliable but less powerful. Intraday levels = noise unless you are scalping.
Height (Price Range)	How tall the congestion zone is as a percentage of price. A 1% zone = minor S/R. A 3% zone = intermediate. A 7%+ zone = major barrier that can stop major trends.	A 7%+ wide congestion zone above your short call strike gives you a double wall of protection. A 1% zone barely slows a determined trend. Size the protection to the height of the zone.
Volume (Commitment)	How much trading occurred in the congestion zone. High volume = strong emotional commitment from many participants. Low volume =	A support level formed on high-volume accumulation is where institutions bought. It will be defended again. A level formed on thin volume may look like support but has no army

Factor	What It Measures	Options Trader Application
	weak commitment, easier to break.	behind it. Check volume before trusting any S/R level.

S&R STRENGTH FORMULA

Strong S&R = Length (time) × Height (price range) × Volume (commitment). A level that is old, wide, and heavily traded is a fortress. A level that formed quickly on thin volume is a suggestion. The strongest options trade setups are those where your short strike sits beyond a fortress-level S&R — where the stock would need to break through years of institutional memory to reach your position.

Fibonacci Retracement — The Magic Numbers

Fibonacci retracement is a technical indicator that identifies potential support and resistance barriers during a pullback. Unlike static S/R levels, Fibonacci levels are dynamically calculated from a stock's most recent significant high-to-low move. The identifying of potential pullback levels doesn't rely on any previous price action — it is based on a mathematical sequence that appears throughout nature and markets alike.

The five most important Fibonacci levels that every options trader must know:

Fib Level	What It Means for Options Traders
23.6%	Shallow retracement — trend is very strong. Minor pullback. Good entry for strong uptrend continuation plays.
38.2%	Moderate pullback — healthy trend consolidation. Strong support in uptrends. Common short put strike anchor zone.
50.0%	Psychological midpoint — not a Fibonacci number but universally respected as support/resistance. High-volume reaction expected.
61.8%	The 'Golden Ratio' — the most powerful Fibonacci level. If a pullback reaches 61.8%, the trend is being seriously tested. Strong reversal or breakdown likely here.
78.6%	Deep retracement — trend is weakening significantly. A break of 78.6% often signals a full trend reversal. Strike placement below 78.6% is aggressive.

Most charting platforms (TradingView, ThinkorSwim, Barchart) have Fibonacci retracement tools built in. Draw the tool from the most recent swing low to swing high (for an uptrend pullback). The levels appear automatically. For options strike selection: the 38.2% and 61.8% levels are your most reliable support zones for placing short put strikes — the market has a strong historical tendency to find buyers at these levels.

Moving Averages: The Trend Filter

An exponential moving average (EMA) smooths price data over a defined period, creating a dynamic line that filters out noise and reveals the underlying trend direction.

For options traders, moving averages serve as trend filters and dynamic support/resistance levels — not entry signals on their own, but critical context for every trade.

Exponential Moving Average	Period	What It Shows	Options Trader Application
20-day EMA	20 sessions	Short-term trend; closely tracks recent price action	Options strike buffer for 30-DTE trades. Reclaim of 20-day EMA = short-term bullish entry signal.
50-day EMA	50 sessions	Intermediate trend; institutional reference level	Key inflection point for sector rotation signals. Sector ETF reclaiming 50-day EMA = rotation alert.
200-day EMA	200 sessions	Long-term trend; the line between bull and bear market	Above 200-day = bullish bias on all trades. Below 200-day = bearish bias, reduce long exposure.
EMA (Exponential)	Variable	Weights recent prices more heavily — faster to react	Use 8/21 EMA crossover for shorter-dated entry timing. More responsive than EMA to recent momentum.

MACD: Momentum Confirmation

The MACD (Moving Average Convergence Divergence) is a momentum oscillator that measures the relationship between two exponential moving averages — typically the 12-day and 26-day EMA — and plots that relationship as a histogram. For options traders, MACD is a momentum confirmation tool, not a standalone signal.

- MACD crossing above the signal line from below — bullish momentum confirmation. Use to time entry on bullish setups (bull call spreads, CSPs);
- MACD crossing below the signal line from above — bearish momentum confirmation. Use to time entry on bearish setups (bear put spreads, bear call spreads);
- MACD histogram shrinking while price is still trending — momentum is fading. Consider tightening stops or rolling positions;

MACD divergence is the highest-value signal the indicator produces — and the one most books describe without fully explaining:

- Bearish MACD Divergence: Stock makes HIGHER highs, but MACD makes LOWER highs. The price is advancing but momentum is weakening — the rally is losing its engine. This often precedes a retracement. A bullish position entered here is lower probability;
- Bullish MACD Divergence: Stock makes LOWER lows, but MACD makes HIGHER lows. Selling pressure is exhausting even as price falls — often the setup before a reversal. Good timing indicator for CSP or bull put spread entries;

The Centerline Rule — The Most Misunderstood Divergence Requirement

Most traders identify MACD divergences incorrectly because they miss one critical structural requirement: for a true divergence to exist, the MACD-Histogram must cross its zero line between the two bottoms (bullish) or two peaks (bearish). Without the centerline crossing, there is no divergence — there is only a trend weakening.

- Bullish divergence requirement: Price makes lower low → MACD-Histogram rallies ABOVE the zero line → Price makes second lower low → MACD-Histogram makes a shallower low (second bottom does not need to cross zero again). The centerline crossing between the two bottoms 'breaks the back of the bear.';
- Bearish divergence requirement: Price makes higher high → MACD-Histogram declines BELOW the zero line → Price makes second higher high → MACD-Histogram makes a shallower peak. The centerline crossing between the two peaks 'breaks the back of the bull.';
- The buy signal fires when MACD-Histogram ticks UP from its second bottom — not when it crosses zero. This allows entry before the main move begins; and
- The sell signal fires when MACD-Histogram ticks DOWN from its second peak — not when it crosses zero. Same principle, earlier entry.

If you cannot find the centerline crossing between two bottoms or two peaks, you do not have a divergence — you have a trend. Trade with it, not against it. Valid divergences that meet the centerline rule are infrequent but among the most powerful signals in technical analysis. When one appears, it warrants sizing up.

DIVERGENCE CENTERLINE RULE

Before acting on any MACD divergence, verify: did the histogram cross its zero line between the two reference points? If not, the divergence is invalid. A pattern of lower MACD lows without a centerline crossing simply confirms a strong downtrend — not an imminent reversal. The centerline crossing is what 'resets' the pattern and makes the second bottom or peak meaningful.

The Dual EMA System: The Value Zone for Precision Entry

The most actionable exponential moving average framework for options traders is not the 50MA/200MA institutional trend system — those are condition filters, not entry timing tools. For entry timing, the Dual EMA system using a fast and slow exponential moving average creates what traders call the Value Zone: the space between the two lines where price is neither overextended nor undervalued. This zone is where the highest-probability options entries occur.

The setup uses two EMAs in a 2:1 ratio — typically a 13-day EMA (fast) and a 26-day EMA (slow). The slow EMA represents the longer-term consensus of value. The fast EMA represents the shorter-term consensus. Value lives between them. When price pulls back into the value zone during an uptrend, it has returned to fair value — an ideal entry for CSPs and bull call spreads. When price rallies into the value zone during a downtrend, it has returned to fair value from below — an ideal entry for bear call spreads.

- In an uptrend (slow EMA rising): pullbacks into the value zone between the fast and slow EMA are CSP entry windows. Price has retreated from overextension to value — buyers typically step back in at this zone;

- In a downtrend (slow EMA declining): rallies into the value zone between the fast and slow EMA are bear call spread entry windows. Price has recovered from oversold to value — sellers typically step back in at this zone;
- In a range (slow EMA flat): the value zone marks the middle of the range. Entries at the channel extremes (above fast EMA for short calls, below for short puts) are preferred over value-zone entries;
- EMA slope confirmation: A rising slow EMA confirms an uptrend regardless of short-term price noise. A flat slow EMA signals a range. A declining slow EMA signals a downtrend. Always check the slow EMA slope before deploying the value zone entry; and
- The 2:1 ratio is not magic — it is a yardstick. Using 26/13 across all timeframes (weekly, daily, intraday) keeps your analysis consistent and prevents the confusion that comes from using different parameters on different charts.

THE VALUE ZONE ENTRY RULE

Do not enter bullish premium positions (CSPs, bull call spreads) when price is far above the value zone — you are buying at market mania. Do not enter bearish premium positions when price is far below the value zone — you are chasing market depression. Wait for price to return to the value zone, confirm the slow EMA slope, and enter in the direction of the tide. Patience at the value zone beats chasing every time.

RSI: Overbought, Oversold, and Divergence

The Relative Strength Index (RSI) measures the speed and magnitude of price changes on a 0–100 scale. Traditional interpretation: above 70 is overbought, below 30 is oversold. For options traders, the overbought/oversold reading is less useful than the divergence signal — it is one of the most reliable early warning systems in technical analysis.

IMPORTANT: Do not confuse RSI with Relative Strength (RS). They are completely different indicators. RSI is an oscillator on a 0–100 scale that measures a stock's price momentum against itself. Relative Strength (RS) measures how a stock or ETF is performing compared to a benchmark index such as the S&P 500. The naming similarity has caused confusion for decades — know which one your platform is showing you.

- RSI above 70 — stock may be extended. Avoid buying calls or initiating new bullish debit spreads. Consider selling covered calls or initiating bear call spreads;
- RSI below 30 — stock may be oversold. Avoid buying puts or adding to bearish positions. Consider selling cash-secured puts or initiating bull put spreads;
- Bearish RSI divergence: Price makes a new high, RSI makes a lower high — momentum is weakening. Bullish entry is higher risk; consider protective structures; and
- Bullish RSI divergence: Price makes a new low, RSI makes a higher low — selling pressure is exhausting. Opportunity window for CSPs or bull call spreads on quality names.

Relative Strength (RS): The Stock Selection Filter

Relative Strength — distinct from RSI — is the comparison of one security's performance against a benchmark. The strongest trading candidates are those that are outperforming the broader market. By focusing on stocks and ETFs that are leading the market rather than lagging it, you increase your probability of profitable results.

The strongest trading candidates show all of the following:

- Solid fundamentals — earnings growing faster than average, operating in a growing economy;
- Leading stock in a strong sector — sector is in the right phase of the business cycle (Chapter 7);
- Approaching a technical buy signal on its price chart — not already extended; and
- Performing better than the S&P 500 on a 1-month, 3-month, and 6-month basis.

RS Calculation: Divide the stock's price by the index value to plot a ratio. Rising ratio = outperforming. Falling ratio = underperforming. Most platforms (TradingView, StockCharts PerfChart) show this visually — you can chart up to 12 symbols simultaneously against the S&P 500.

Rate of Change (ROC): Trend Velocity

The Rate of Change indicator measures how fast a stock's price is moving — not just the direction, but the velocity. It calculates the percentage change in price over a specified lookback period (typically 12 or 14 days) and plots it as an oscillator around a zero line.

- ROC above zero and rising — price is accelerating upward. Confirms trend strength. Favorable for bullish setups;
- ROC above zero but declining — upward momentum is slowing. Possible topping action. Reduce long exposure or tighten stops;
- ROC crossing below zero — trend has turned negative. Exit bullish positions. Begin evaluating bearish or neutral setups; and
- ROC divergence from price — same principle as MACD divergence. Price making new highs with ROC making lower highs = bearish warning.

ROC is particularly useful as a trend-following confirmation for the sector rotation strategies in Chapter 7 — a sector ETF with rising ROC confirms the institutional buying that precedes a full rotation.

Bollinger Bands: Volatility Visualization

Bollinger Bands place two standard deviation bands above and below a 20-day exponential moving average. When the bands are narrow (a squeeze), volatility is compressed and a breakout is likely imminent. When the bands are wide, volatility is expanded and mean reversion may follow. For options traders, Bollinger Bands are a volatility timing tool as much as a price tool.

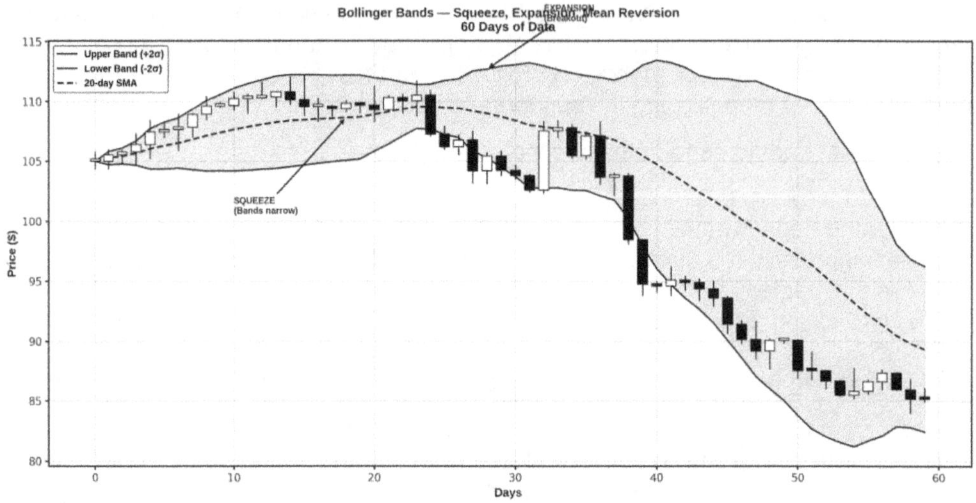

Figure 9.12 — Bollinger Bands. Squeeze, expansion, and mean-reversion signals.

- Bollinger Band squeeze → IV is likely low → favorable time to buy options or enter calendar spreads before expansion;
- Price touching the upper band consistently in an uptrend → trend confirmation, not automatic reversal signal;
- Price touching the lower band after extended downtrend with RSI divergence → potential reversal setup for CSP or bull call spread;
- Band walk: Price hugging the upper or lower band for multiple sessions signals a strong trend — do not fade it with mean-reversion trades;
- Momentum + Bollinger combination: When both momentum (MACD/ROC) and price are at the upper Bollinger Band simultaneously, the trend is at maximum extension — high-probability zone for pullback or pause;

Bullish Percent Index (BPI): Market Breadth

The Bullish Percent Index measures the percentage of stocks in a given index or sector that are on a Point & Figure buy signal. It is a breadth indicator — it tells you not just where the index price is, but how many stocks are participating in the move. This distinction is critical for sector rotation analysis.

- BPI above 70% — sector is overbought on a breadth basis. Premium selling setups become more favorable; avoid initiating new long debit spreads;
- BPI below 30% — sector is oversold on a breadth basis. Begin watching for CSP opportunities on sector leaders as rotation back in begins;
- Rising BPI in a sector while the broad market BPI is flat — confirms underlying accumulation in that sector. This is a sector rotation entry signal; and
- Falling BPI in a sector that is still making price highs — breadth divergence. The move is narrowing. Defensive structures (collars, put spreads) are warranted.

The New High–New Low Index: Market Leadership Breadth

The New High–New Low Index (NH-NL) is one of the most powerful leading indicators of broad market direction. It tracks the leaders — stocks reaching new 52-week highs minus stocks hitting new 52-week lows on any given day. The logic is simple: when the army's officers are advancing (new highs rising), the troops will follow. When the officers are retreating (new lows expanding), the army will turn and run.

NH-NL = New 52-Week Highs − New 52-Week Lows. Most data services and charting platforms provide this data. Plot it as a line below a daily SPY or SPX chart, with a horizontal reference line at zero.

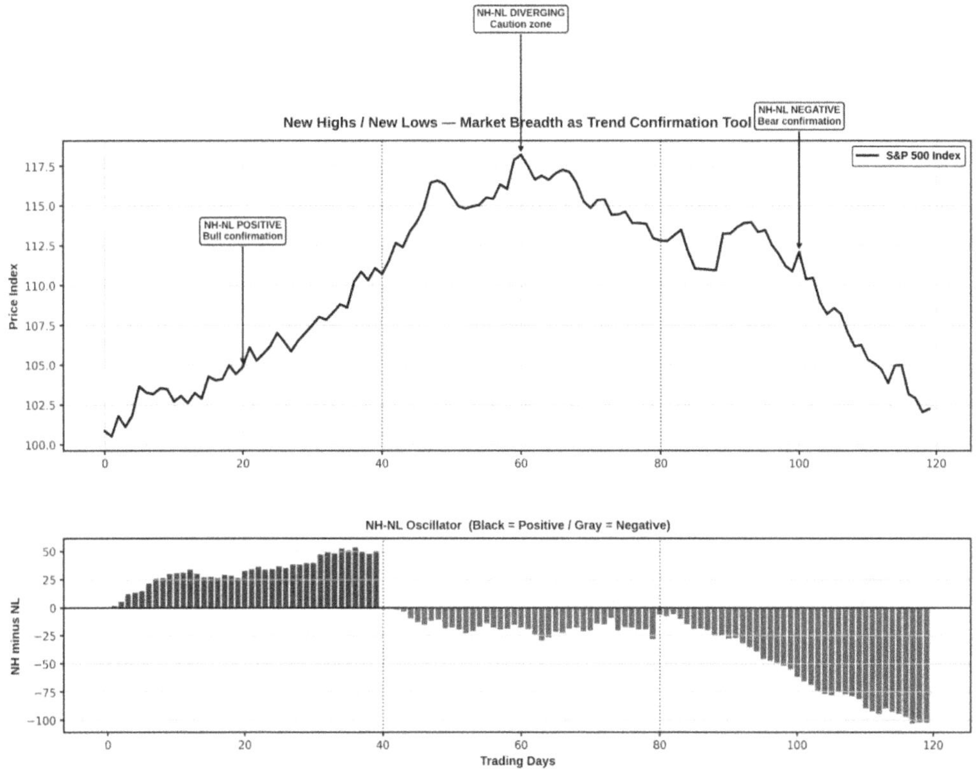

Figure 10.2 — New Highs / New Lows Breadth Indicator — Market-wide participation as a trend confirmation and divergence detection tool.

New Highs/New Lows Breadth Indicator — Market-wide participation as a trend confirmation tool.

Three NH-NL Signals for Options Traders

Signal	What It Means	Options Strategy Implication
Zero Line Position	NH-NL above zero: bullish leadership dominant. NH-NL below zero: bearish leadership dominant. Can remain on one side for months during sustained trends.	Add Condition 1 or 2 confirmation: when NH-NL is above zero and rising, CSPs and bull call spreads on quality names have the broad market as a tailwind. When negative, hold fire on new bullish positions.
Trend Direction	When market rallies and NH-NL rises together: trend confirmed, likely to continue. When market rallies but NH-NL shrinks or turns flat: fewer stocks are participating — a warning sign of distribution.	A CSP opened when NH-NL is rising has a stronger macro backdrop than one opened when NH-NL is declining. If NH-NL diverges from price for 3+ sessions, reduce new bullish position size by 50%.

Signal	What It Means	Options Strategy Implication
Divergence from Price	Most powerful signal. If the market makes a new high but NH-NL makes a LOWER high: bearish divergence — leadership is deteriorating even as index rises. If market makes new low but NH-NL makes HIGHER low: bullish divergence — decline is losing its leadership.	Bearish NH-NL divergence while holding bullish positions: begin defensive rolling (shorten DTE, widen strikes, take partial profits). Bullish NH-NL divergence in a downtrend: prepare first CSP list — reversal probability is rising.

NH-NL AS A POSITION SIZING FILTER

Before opening any new options position, check NH-NL. If NH-NL is positive and trending higher: deploy full intended position size. If NH-NL is positive but declining: deploy 75% size. If NH-NL is near zero or negative: deploy 50% size or wait. If NH-NL is sharply negative and declining: stand aside on new bullish positions entirely. The broad market environment is the context inside which every individual trade lives. NH-NL tells you the quality of that context — before you commit capital.

Breakouts: The Momentum Entry — and the Professional Fading Framework

A breakout occurs when price moves decisively above a resistance level or below a support level on elevated volume. Breakouts are high-conviction entry signals for options traders because they confirm that the balance of power has shifted — buyers have overwhelmed sellers at resistance, or vice versa.

- Volume confirmation is essential — a breakout on light volume is suspect and prone to false breakout reversal;
- For call entries: wait for the daily candle to close above resistance — closing above is the confirmation, not an intraday touch;
- For put entries: wait for the daily candle to close below support — intraday breaks are frequently reversed by end of day;
- Retest entries: after a breakout, price often returns to test the broken level as new support/resistance. This retest entry offers better pricing and confirmation that the level has flipped;

The Professional Edge: Fading False Breakouts

Markets spend far more time in trading ranges than in trends. The majority of breakouts from those ranges are false — price pierces the boundary, triggers stop-loss and buy-stop orders of range traders, then reverses back inside. Retail traders chase breakouts. Professional traders do the opposite: they wait for the breakout to stall, confirm the reversal, and enter against the failed move with a tight stop and a target in the middle of the prior range.

- True breakout confirmation requires ALL THREE: (1) daily close beyond the level, (2) volume significantly above average, AND (3) momentum indicators (MACD, RSI) confirming — not diverging. Without all three, the breakout is suspect;
- False breakout signals: volume below average on the breakout day, close back inside range within 1–3 sessions, OR momentum indicators show divergence from the move;

- The options fade trade: A failed upside breakout → bear call spread with short strike just above the failed high. A failed downside breakdown → bull put spread with short strike just below the failed low. The failed extreme becomes the natural strike anchor; and
- Wait for two consecutive daily closes back inside the range before entering the fade. One close is a test. Two closes is confirmation.

THE PROFESSIONAL FADING RULE

Professionals know that most breakouts fail and are followed by reversals — this is why they trade against deviations from the range rather than chasing them. When a breakout fails and price closes back inside the prior range for two sessions: initiate the fade trade. Bear call spread above the failed high. Bull put spread below the failed low. The failed extreme is where sellers (or buyers) are well-organized. Let their strength work for you.

Managing a failed breakout on existing positions: two clean protocols:

- Protocol 1: If price pulls back below the resistance level it just broke — exit immediately. The breakout failed. Take the small loss;
- Protocol 2: If price falls back to the midpoint of the prior trading range — the breakout has definitively failed. That midpoint is your stop-loss exit on any position opened on the breakout.

The Three-Timeframe Framework for Options Traders

Professional traders never analyze a market in a single timeframe. Every instrument moves simultaneously in multiple timeframes — what looks like an uptrend on one chart can be a pullback in a larger trend on another. Options traders face a more complex version of this problem than stock traders: they must correctly identify not just direction but also velocity, timing, and magnitude — all of which appear differently depending on which chart you are looking at.

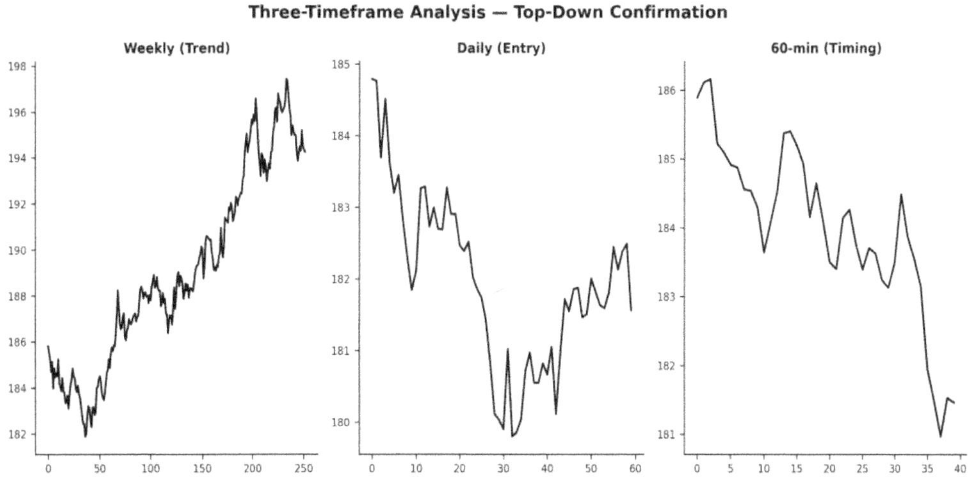

Figure 9.13 — Three-Timeframe Analysis.

The solution is a systematic three-timeframe approach where each chart serves a distinct and non-overlapping purpose. The three timeframes for a standard 30–45 DTE options position are the Weekly, Daily, and Intraday (4-hour or 1-hour chart). Think of them as tide, wave, and ripple — you trade in the direction of the tide, use the wave to time entry, and use the ripple to execute precisely.

Timeframe	Role	What You Read	Decision Made
Weekly Chart	**THE TIDE Strategic Direction**	26-week EMA slope (up/down/flat). MACD-Histogram direction. Major S/R levels. Sector trend from rotation analysis (Ch. 3).	BULL / BEAR / NEUTRAL condition. Strike range (ATM vs OTM). DTE selection (45 days for income, 60–90 for LEAPS). Whether to sell or buy premium.
Daily Chart	**THE WAVE Tactical Entry**	RSI divergence or overbought/oversold. MACD crossover or divergence. Dual EMA value zone. Chart pattern confirmation. Volume on key candles.	EXACT STRIKE PRICE. Entry timing (enter now or wait for pullback to value zone). Stop-loss reference level. Which spread structure fits the setup.
Intraday (4H or 1H)	**THE RIPPLE Precision Execution**	Price relative to intraday EMA. IV level at time of order (check mid-price vs mark). Bid/ask spread width. Order book depth at strike.	LIMIT ORDER PRICE. Whether to place order now or wait for better fill. GTC close order level (50% profit target). Avoid opening in final 30 minutes of session.

The sequence is non-negotiable: always begin with the weekly chart. Never glance at the daily first — it will bias your analysis and make you see patterns that confirm what you already want to do. The weekly chart gives you the unbiased strategic view. Only after committing to a weekly direction do you drop to the daily to time the entry. Only after confirming the daily setup do you drop to the intraday for execution.

Three-Timeframe Application by Strategy

Strategy	Weekly Signal Required	Daily Entry Signal	Intraday Execution
Cash-Secured Put (CSP)	Weekly EMA rising. MACD-H positive. NH-NL above zero.	Price pulls into value zone (fast/slow EMA). RSI 40–55. No bearish divergence.	Place limit order at mid-price when bid/ask spread ≤ $0.30. Set GTC buy-to-close at 50%.
Covered Call	Weekly EMA rising or flat. Underlying you own is above 200-day EMA.	Price at or near upper Bollinger Band or resistance. RSI above 60 but not diverging.	Place limit at mid. Avoid opening day before earnings or ex-div. Set GTC at 50% profit.
Bull Call Spread	Weekly uptrend confirmed. MACD-H rising. NH-NL rising above zero.	Pullback to value zone or confirmed pattern breakout with volume.	Buy spread for ≤60% of max profit. Target: sell when spread = 80% of width. Stop: 100% of debit.
Bear Call Spread	Weekly EMA declining. MACD-H negative or turning down. NH-NL below zero.	Rally into value zone in downtrend. Bearish candle at resistance. RSI overbought.	Sell spread for ≥40% of width. Set GTC at 50% profit. Stop: 200% of credit received.
Iron Condor	Weekly EMA flat. Range-bound condition	Price between S/R levels. Bollinger Band squeeze	Sell condor for ≥30% of width. Manage at 21 DTE

Strategy	Weekly Signal Required	Daily Entry Signal	Intraday Execution
	(Conditions 5/6). VIX stable.	resolved or ongoing. RSI neutral (40–60).	(T-21 rule). Adjust if either wing breached.

THE THREE-TIMEFRAME RULE

Weekly chart sets the direction. Daily chart times the entry. Intraday chart executes the order. If the weekly and daily are in conflict — stand aside. Do not enter any position when timeframes are giving contradictory signals. Wait for alignment. The best trades are the ones where all three screens are telling the same story. Those are the setups you size up. Those are the setups you let run.

THE TECHNICAL CHECKLIST

Before entering any options trade, run this 60-second check: (1) Is price above or below the 200-day EMA? (Determines directional bias.) (2) Is MACD and/or ROC confirming momentum in your trade direction? (3) Is RSI neutral (40–60) or showing divergence? (4) Is RS vs. SPY rising or falling? (5) Where is your strike relative to the nearest Fibonacci level and S/R? (6) Is NH-NL above zero and rising? (7) What does the weekly chart say — does the daily entry align with the tide? Seven questions. Ninety seconds. Better trades.

Technical Signal Mapping: What Each Indicator Tells You About the Six Conditions

Quick reminder of the framework: each of the six conditions is defined by two inputs — price direction (bullish, bearish, or range-bound, read from the chart) and volatility level (high or low, read from the VIX). The technical indicators in this section confirm which direction input applies. Chapter 16 covers the volatility input. Together they give you a complete condition read in under two minutes.

Technical indicators do not generate trade ideas in isolation. Their job in the six-condition system is to confirm the direction axis of your condition read — and to warn you when the chart signal is in conflict with the macro backdrop. The table below maps every indicator covered in this chapter to the specific conditions they confirm or warn against.

Indicator	Conditions Confirmed	Warning Signal	How to Use in the Daily Read
Moving Averages (50MA, 200MA)	1 & 2 (price above both MAs). 3 & 4 (price below both MAs). 5 & 6 (price between or touching both MAs).	Price crossing back through the 50MA after a breakout = condition change alert. Re-read the chart before opening any new positions.	First check every morning. Are you above or below the 200MA? Above = bullish bias (conditions 1–2). Below = bearish bias (conditions 3–4). At = range suspicion (conditions 5–6).
MACD	Conditions 1 & 2 (MACD line above signal, histogram positive). Conditions 3 & 4 (MACD below signal, histogram negative).	MACD divergence (price new high, MACD lower high) warns of condition 1→5 transition. Exit or reduce long delta exposure.	Confirms momentum direction after the EMA check. Do not trade condition 1 if MACD is declining even with price still above MAs.
RSI	All conditions. RSI above 50 confirms bullish conditions. RSI below 50 confirms bearish	RSI > 70 in conditions 1/2 = overbought. Warning to avoid new long debit entries. RSI < 30 in conditions 3/4 = potential	Check as the third EMA/MACD. Specifically useful for timing pullback entries in condition 1: enter

Indicator	Conditions Confirmed	Warning Signal	How to Use in the Daily Read
	conditions. RSI between 45–55 confirms range.	reversal — tighten stops on bearish positions.	when RSI pulls back to 45–50 in an uptrend.
Relative Strength vs. SPY	Rising RS confirms condition 1 and 2 setups on individual stocks and sector ETFs — shows institutional buying. Falling RS confirms conditions 3 and 4.	RS turning flat in a confirmed uptrend = early warning of condition 1 weakening. Begin reducing delta exposure if RS flattens for 3+ days.	Use for ETF selection in conditions 1 and 3. In condition 1 (bullish, low IV), buy calls or spreads on the ETF with the highest RS vs. SPY — that is where the money is flowing.
Bollinger Bands	Squeeze (narrow bands) confirms conditions 5 or 6 — the range before the move. Wide bands confirm conditions 1, 2, 3, or 4 — active trend.	Band breakout from a squeeze is a condition change warning — conditions 5/6 may be transitioning to 1, 2, 3, or 4. Wait for confirmation before changing strategies.	Check bandwidth daily when in conditions 5 or 6. Narrowing bandwidth = time to manage existing range positions. Expanding bandwidth = exit iron condors if the expansion goes against you.
BPI (Bullish Percent Index)	BPI above 60 and rising confirms conditions 1 and 2. BPI below 40 and falling confirms conditions 3 and 4. BPI flat between 40–60 confirms conditions 5 and 6.	BPI diverging from price (price rising, BPI falling) is one of the most reliable warnings of a condition 1→5 or 5→3 transition. Reduce position size when this divergence persists.	Check sector BPI for any ETF you are trading in conditions 1 or 2. Confirms that the sector, not just the ETF, is being bought broadly by institutions.

Use this table as your morning review sheet alongside the six-condition quick reference in Appendix F. Run through each indicator in order: MAs first, MACD second, RSI third, RS fourth, Bollinger Bands fifth, BPI sixth. The condition that all six indicators point toward is the high-confidence condition read. When indicators conflict, wait — a clear condition will emerge within one to three sessions.

WHEN INDICATORS CONFLICT

Conflicting technical signals are not a signal to trade — they are a signal to wait. If EMA says bullish but MACD is declining and BPI is flat, the condition is transitional. Transitional conditions are the most dangerous for options positions. Wait for clarity. One session of patience is worth more than three sessions of cleanup on a wrong-condition trade.

Exponential Moving Average Systems for Condition Identification

Moving averages are not just trend indicators — in the six-condition framework, they are the primary tool for confirming the direction component of your condition read. The relationship between price, the 50-day EMA, and the 200-day EMA tells you with high reliability whether you are in conditions 1-2 (bullish), 3-4 (bearish), or 5-6 (range).

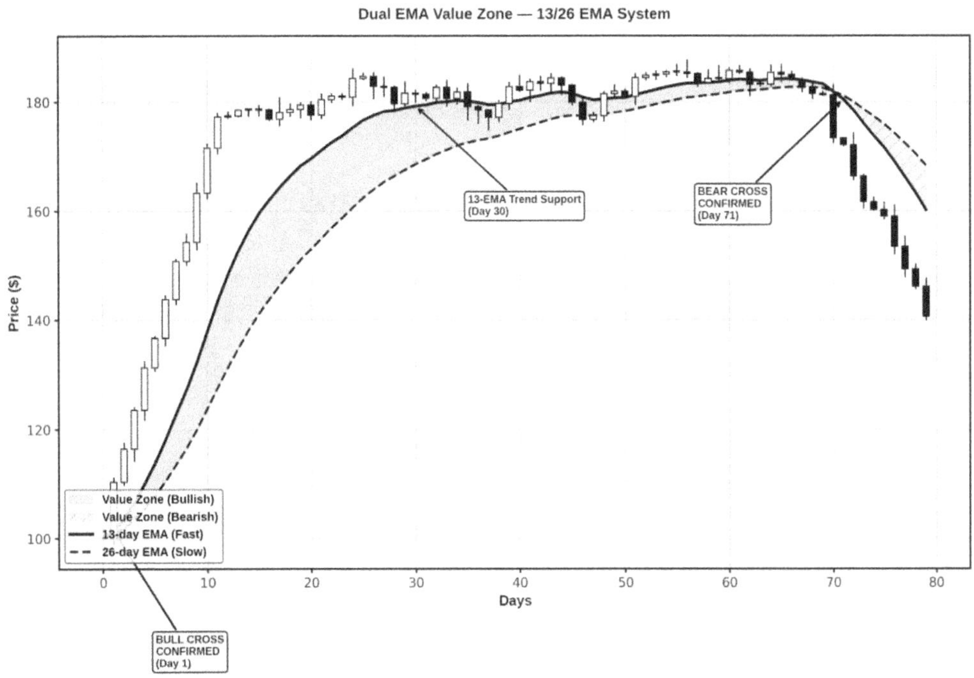

Figure 9.14 — Dual EMA Value Zone. The 13/26 EMA system showing the value zone and bull/bear cross signals.

EMA Relationship	Six-Condition Signal	Options Trader's Action
Price > 50MA > 200MA (all aligned bullish)	BULLISH confirmed → Condition 1 or 2 depending on VIX	Cross-reference VIX. High IV → sell CSP or bull put spread (condition 2). Low IV → buy calls (condition 1).
Price crossed above 50MA, 50MA still below 200MA (early recovery)	TRANSITIONAL bullish — not yet confirmed	Wait for 50MA to cross above 200MA (golden cross) before deploying full bullish strategies. Smaller size, defined risk only.
Price < 50MA < 200MA (all aligned bearish)	BEARISH confirmed → Condition 3 or 4 depending on VIX	Cross-reference VIX. High IV → bear call spread only (condition 4). Low IV → buy puts or bear put spread (condition 3).
Price crossed below 50MA, 200MA still above (early decline)	TRANSITIONAL bearish — not yet confirmed	Reduce or hedge existing bullish positions. Wait for price to establish below both MAs before deploying full bearish strategies.
Price oscillating between 50MA and 200MA (compressed range)	RANGE-BOUND → Condition 5 or 6 depending on VIX	High IV → calendar or diagonal (condition 6). Low IV → butterfly or iron condor (condition 5). The MAs act as the range boundaries.
50MA = 200MA (flat, compressed, converging)	INFLECTION POINT — major move imminent	Straddle or strangle candidates. Market will break out — direction unknown. Size small, defined risk, wait for the break before committing directional capital.

Chart Pattern Catalog: 9 Patterns Every Options Trader Must Master

Chart patterns are the visual fingerprints of supply and demand. They are not predictions — they are probability maps. Each pattern below is organized in the same format: what it looks like, what the psychology is driving it, how to confirm it, and most importantly, which options strategy it sets up. For every pattern, the entry rule is the same — require the confirmation signal before committing capital.

Pattern 1 of 9 — Head & Shoulders (Bearish Reversal)

Anatomy: The Head & Shoulders is the most widely recognized bearish reversal pattern in technical analysis. It consists of three peaks: a left shoulder (a rally that peaks and pulls back), a head (a higher rally that peaks and pulls back to roughly the same level as the first trough), and a right shoulder (a lower rally that peaks and pulls back again). The line connecting the two troughs between the peaks is called the neckline.

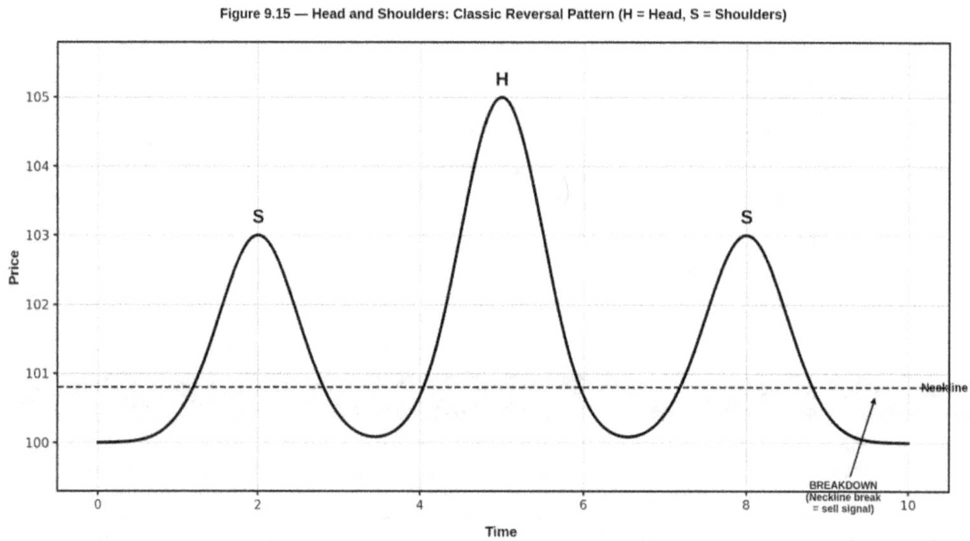

Figure 9.15 — Head and Shoulders. The classic reversal pattern with neckline break entry.

Psychology: Institutional sellers enter at the head — price cannot make a new high from the right shoulder. Each rally brings in buyers, but fewer and fewer. At the right shoulder, buying exhausts before reaching the head's high. This pattern of lower highs with a flat neckline is the signature of a market where sellers are gradually overwhelming buyers.

- Confirmation rule: Wait for a daily CLOSE below the neckline on above-average volume. Intraday breaks do not count;
- Failure mode: If price closes back above the neckline after the break, the pattern has failed. Exit any bearish position immediately — failed Head & Shoulders patterns often produce sharp upside reversals; and
- Measurement target: The distance from the head's peak to the neckline, measured BELOW the neckline breakpoint.

HEAD & SHOULDERS — OPTIONS PLAY

Right shoulder = the ideal entry zone. As price approaches the neckline from the right shoulder, enter a bear call spread with the short strike just above the right shoulder high. This positions you to profit before the neckline break while limiting risk if the pattern fails. On neckline confirmation: add a long put or bear put spread targeting the measured move. DTE: 45–60 days. Short call strike: above right shoulder peak.

Pattern 2 of 9 — Double Bottom (Bullish Reversal)

Anatomy: The Double Bottom forms a W-shape. Two distinct troughs appear at approximately the same price level, separated by a recovery peak. The neckline is drawn at that recovery peak between the two bottoms. The second bottom confirms that sellers cannot push price lower than the first test — buyers are defending that level.

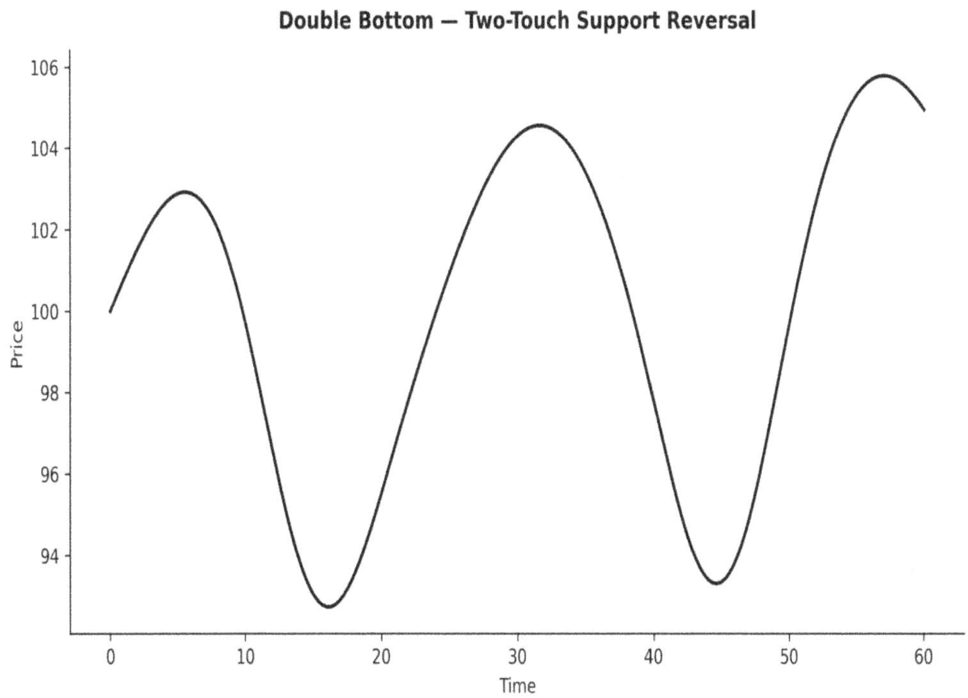

Figure 9.16 — Double Bottom. Two-touch support reversal with confirmation break.

Psychology: The first bottom is a capitulation low — sellers overwhelm buyers and price drops sharply. A recovery follows as value buyers step in. When price tests that low again and holds, it confirms two things: (1) the prior low was not a random level but a genuine area of demand, and (2) selling pressure has exhausted itself.

- Confirmation rule: The pattern is not confirmed until price closes ABOVE the neckline (the peak between the two bottoms) on elevated volume. Many traders enter early at the second bottom — this is a statistically inferior entry with higher failure risk;
- Bullish RSI divergence at the second bottom — price makes an equal low, RSI makes a higher low — is the highest-conviction version of this pattern. It tells you selling momentum is already weakening even as price retests the level; and
- Measurement target: Distance from the neckline to the bottom level, added to the neckline breakout price.

DOUBLE BOTTOM — OPTIONS PLAY

Two entry windows: (1) Aggressive — sell a cash-secured put at or just below the second bottom as it forms, using the pattern level as structural support. (2) Conservative — wait for neckline break, then enter a bull call spread targeting the measured move. The neckline retest (price returns to the broken neckline from above) is the highest-probability, lowest-risk entry. Short put strike: at or below double-bottom level. DTE: 30–45 days.

Pattern 3 of 9 — Double Top (Bearish Reversal)

Anatomy: The Double Top is the mirror image of the Double Bottom — an M-shape consisting of two peaks at approximately the same price level, separated by a trough. The neckline is drawn at the trough. When price tests a prior high and cannot exceed it, sellers are matching or exceeding buyer demand at that level.

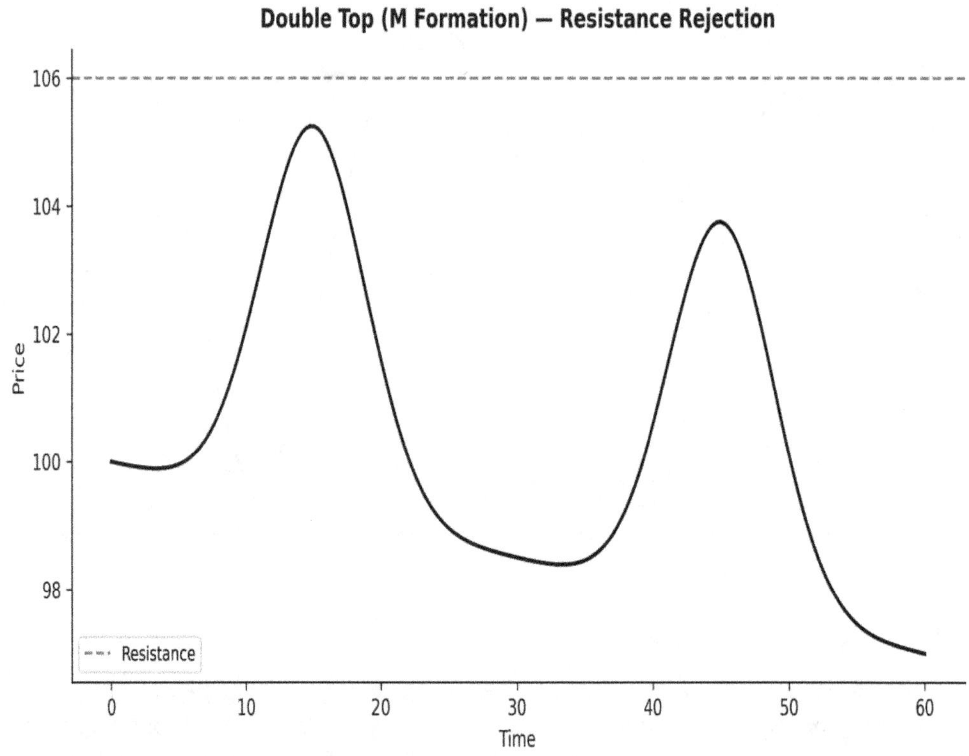

Figure 9.17 — Double Top (M Formation). Two failed attempts at resistance — bearish reversal with breakdown entry.

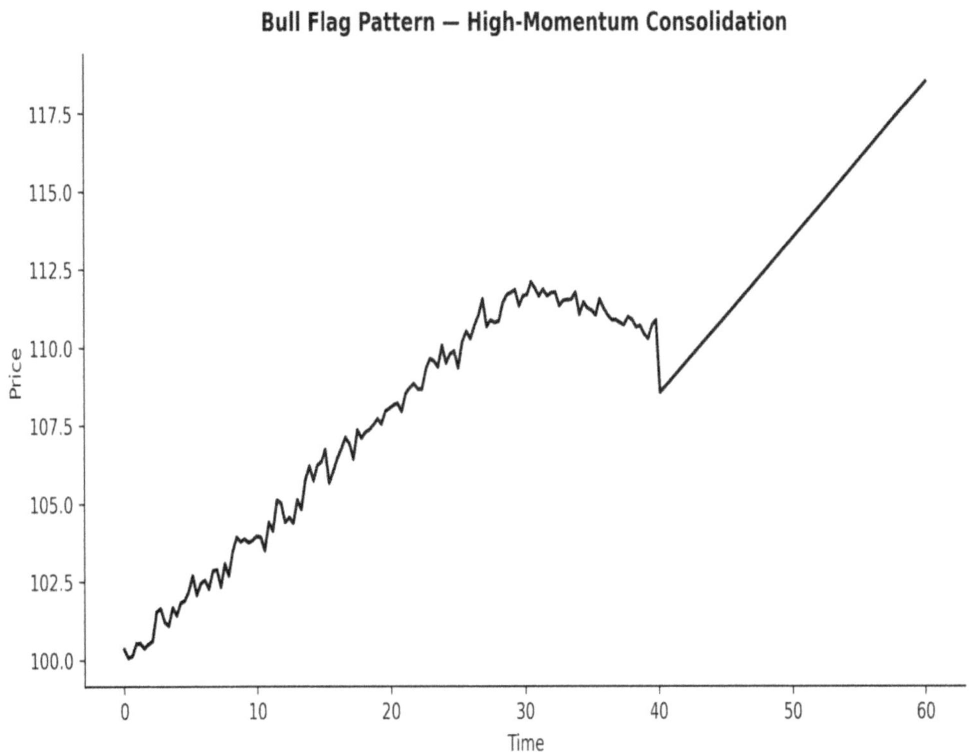

Figure 9.18 — Bull Flag Pattern. High-momentum consolidation followed by continuation breakout.

Psychology: The first top brings in profit-taking from prior holders and new sellers who recognize resistance. Price recovers partially, attracting a second wave of buyers — but when this second wave reaches the prior high and stalls, it signals that sellers are well-organized at that price. Buying interest is diminishing at the point where it should be strongest.

- Confirmation rule: Daily close BELOW the neckline on elevated volume. This is not optional — the pattern can look complete multiple times before actually breaking;
- Bearish MACD divergence (price makes equal high, MACD makes lower high) at the second top significantly increases pattern reliability; and
- Measurement target: Distance from the peak to the neckline, measured below the neckline breakdown point.

DOUBLE TOP — OPTIONS PLAY

The second top forms at known resistance — this is where to initiate a bear call spread. Short call strike: just above the double-top resistance level. This position profits whether the pattern completes or the stock simply stalls at resistance. On neckline breakdown confirmation: layer in a long put or bear put spread targeting the measured move. Avoid naked short calls — the pattern can produce a failed breakdown (false reversal) that triggers a sharp squeeze. DTE: 45–60 days.

Pattern 4 of 9 — Bull Flag (Bullish Continuation)

Anatomy: The Bull Flag consists of two components: the flagpole (a sharp, strong rally on heavy volume) and the flag (a shallow consolidation in a slight downward-slanting parallel channel on declining volume). The flag is the pause after the initial thrust — it is not a reversal, it is digestion. Weak holders are shaken out while strong holders accumulate more.

Psychology: After a sharp move, some participants take profits — this creates the pullback. But the underlying buying pressure that caused the initial move has not exhausted. The parallel channel of the flag forms as the stock consolidates between the buyers who see it as an entry and the profit-takers who create the resistance. When profit-taking exhausts, the buyers take over again and the next leg launches.

- Volume signature: Heavy volume on the flagpole, declining volume during the flag. Volume should EXPAND again on the breakout above the flag's upper channel line. A volume-less breakout is a failed flag;
- Time in the flag: The flag should form over 3–15 trading sessions. A consolidation lasting longer than three weeks loses its character as a flag; and
- Measurement target: The flagpole's length added to the breakout point from the flag.

BULL FLAG — OPTIONS PLAY

The flag's lower channel line is the stop reference. Buy calls or enter a bull call spread when price breaks above the upper channel of the flag on volume. This is one of the cleanest directional entry signals for options because: (1) the entry is defined, (2) the stop is defined (below the flag), and (3) the target is mathematically derived. DTE: 30–45 days. Strike selection: long call near ATM on the breakout day.

Pattern 5 of 9 — Cup & Handle (Bullish Continuation — LEAPS Pattern)

Anatomy: The Cup & Handle features a rounded U-shaped base (the cup) followed by a smaller, tighter consolidation with a slight downward drift (the handle). The cup typically takes weeks to months to form. The depth should be 15–30% for high-quality stocks. The rim of the cup — the prior high — is the key resistance level. The handle typically retraces 10–15% from the cup's rim.

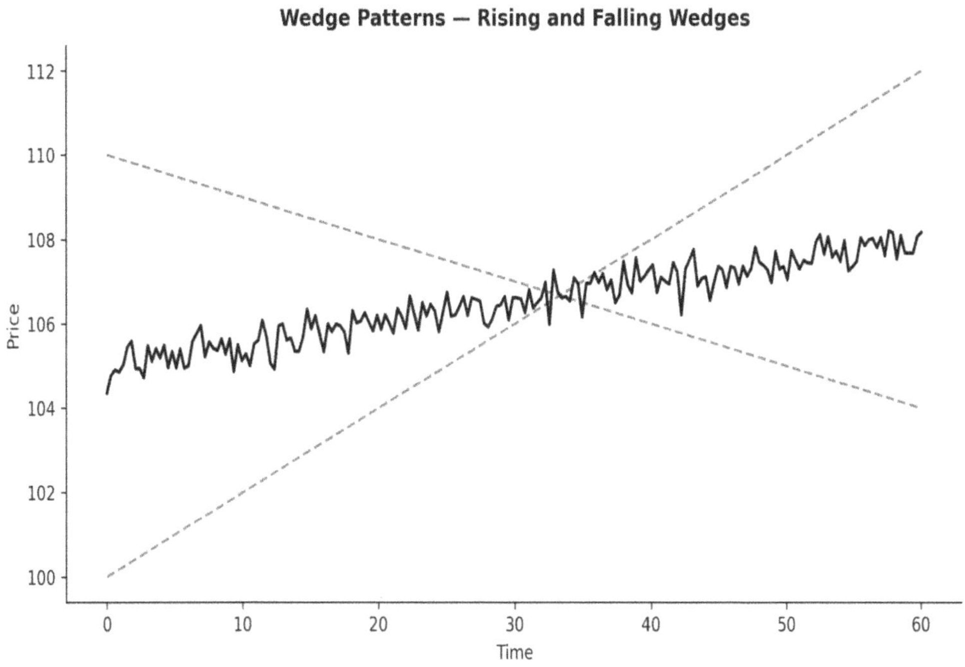

Figure 9.19 — Wedge Patterns. Rising and falling wedges — counter-trend patterns with high reliability.

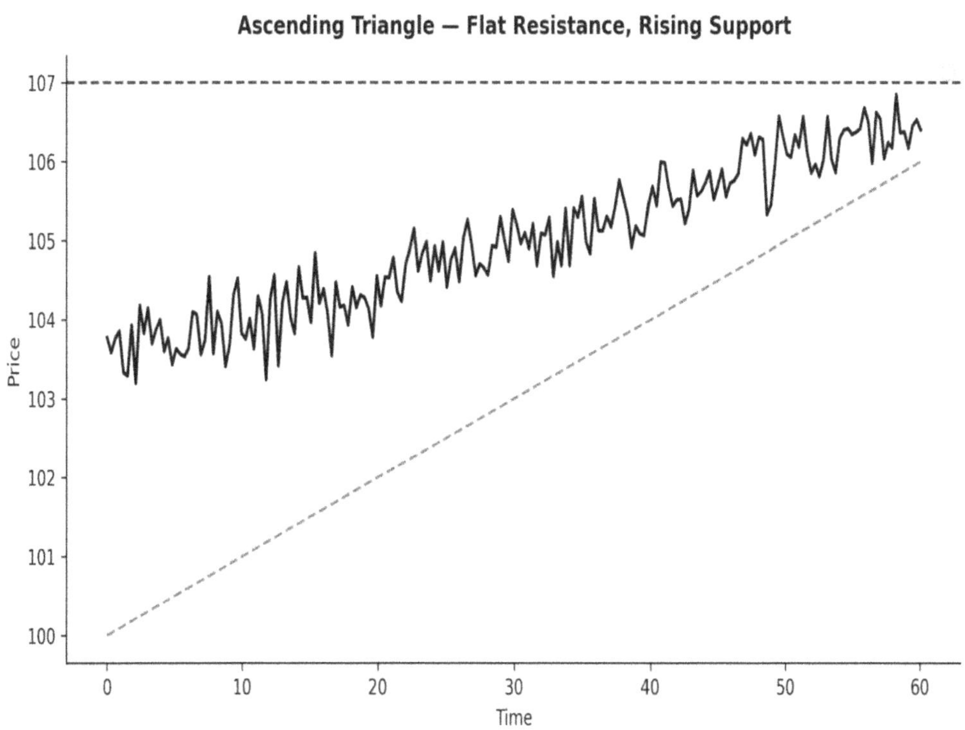

Figure 9.20 — Ascending Triangle. Flat resistance with rising support — bullish continuation breakout pattern.

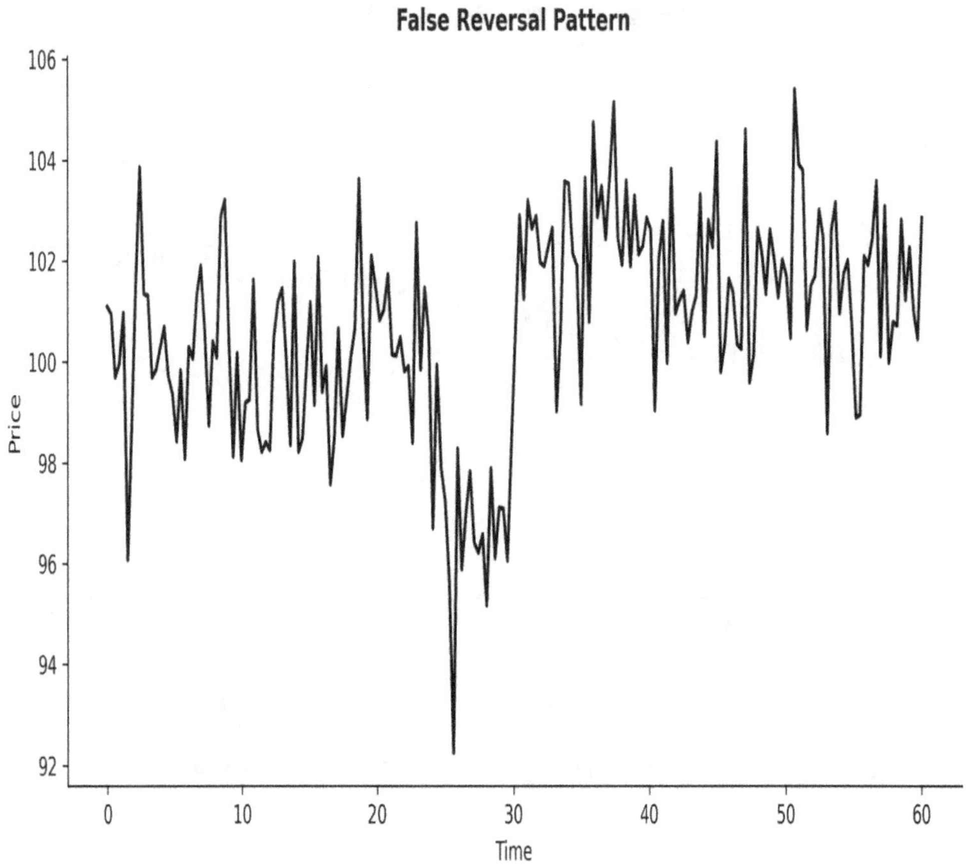

Figure 9.21 — False Reversal Pattern. Apparent reversal that fails — how to confirm before committing.

Pattern	Type	Signal	Key Characteristic	Options Play
Hammer	Reversal	Bullish at support	Long lower wick, small body.	Buy calls or bull put spread at confirmed support.
Shooting Star	Reversal	Bearish at resistance	Long upper wick, small body.	Buy puts or bear call spread at confirmed resistance.
Engulfing Bullish	Reversal	Strong buy signal	Large bull candle swallows prior bear candle.	Aggressive call entry; high-conviction C1 setup.
Engulfing Bearish	Reversal	Strong sell signal	Large bear candle swallows prior bull candle.	Put entry or bear spread; C3/C4 confirmation.
Doji	Indecision	Neutral — wait for confirmation	Open ≈ Close; near-equal wicks.	Hold. Do not initiate without directional confirmation.
Morning Star	Reversal	Bullish 3-candle	Bear, doji, then bull candle sequence.	Enter calls on third candle close confirmation.

Evening Star	Reversal	Bearish 3-candle	Bull, doji, then bear candle sequence.	Enter puts on third candle close confirmation.
Three Soldiers	Continuation	Strong bullish	Three consecutive higher-close bull candles.	Trend confirmation; add to existing long position.
Three Crows	Continuation	Strong bearish	Three consecutive lower-close bear candles.	Trend confirmation; add to existing short/put position.

Figure 9.22 — Candlestick Pattern Summary. The nine most reliable reversal and continuation patterns at a glance.

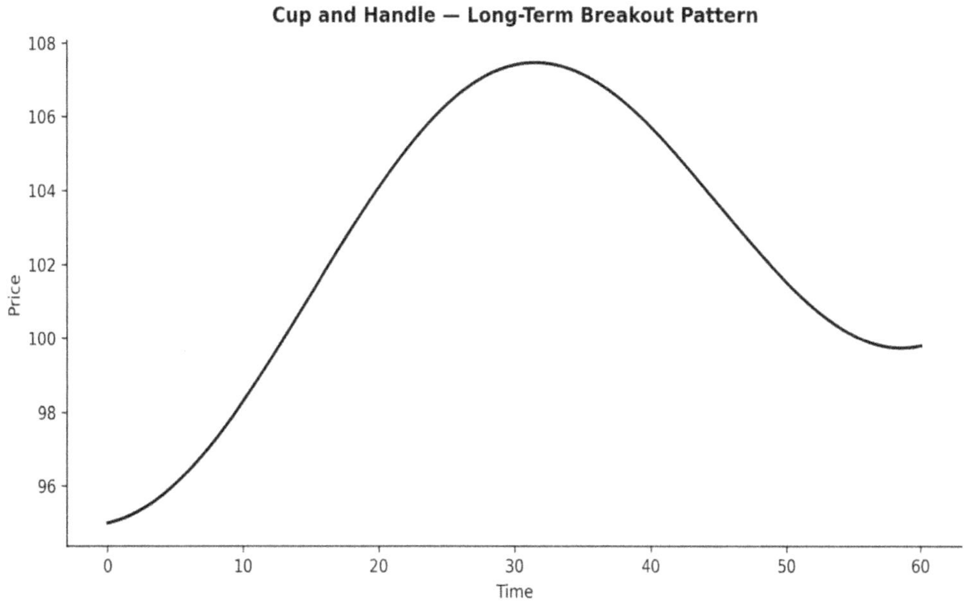

Figure 9.23 — Cup and Handle. Long-term consolidation pattern preceding a breakout continuation.

Psychology: The cup is an institutional accumulation pattern. As price declines, institutional buyers gradually absorb selling pressure — the rounded bottom reflects this gradual, patient accumulation rather than a sharp capitulation. The handle is the final distribution of impatient holders who sell as the stock approaches the prior high. After the handle, only committed holders remain — and when the rim breaks, the move is often sustained.

- Volume signature: Volume should dry up in the right side of the cup and during the handle. Volume should expand significantly on the rim breakout;
- The handle must form in the upper half of the cup — if it forms in the lower half, the pattern is invalid; and
- Measurement target: The depth of the cup added to the breakout point at the rim.

CUP & HANDLE — OPTIONS PLAY

This is the premium LEAPS setup. The rounded base signals institutional accumulation, providing a high-probability support foundation for a long-dated position. Enter a long call LEAPS (6–12 months) as price forms the handle — IV is often low during the handle's quiet consolidation, giving you cheap long-dated premium before the breakout. Alternatively, sell cash-secured puts at the handle's low during formation. Stop reference: below the cup's right side low. This is one of the few patterns where LEAPS are clearly superior to standard options.

Pattern 6 of 9 — False Breakout (The Bull Trap)

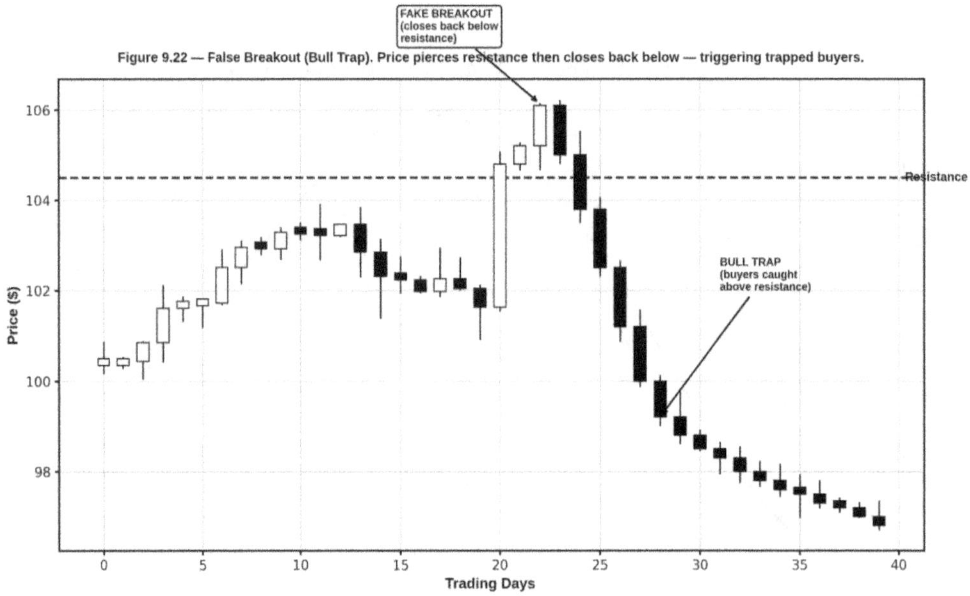

Figure 9.22a — False Breakout (Bull Trap). Price pierces resistance then closes back below — triggering trapped buyers.

Anatomy: A false breakout occurs when price pierces above a resistance level — triggering buy signals in pattern-following systems — but then CLOSES back below that resistance level within the same session or within 1–3 sessions. From above, it looks like a breakout. By the end of the day or week, it is a trap.

Psychology: Breakout traders and automated algorithms buy when price touches resistance. Institutional sellers — who have been accumulating short positions at that resistance level — are waiting for exactly this moment. They distribute their inventory into the buying pressure triggered by the breakout, then drive price back down. The result: retail buyers are long at the worst possible entry; institutions are short at the best possible entry.

- Identification rule: Intraday touch of resistance does NOT constitute a breakout. A breakout is confirmed ONLY by a daily close above resistance. If price closes below the level — regardless of the intraday spike — the breakout has failed;
- The false breakout as a bearish signal: A failed breakout at resistance is not neutral. It is bearish. It tells you sellers are organized and willing to absorb all buying at this level. This is actionable information; and
- Volume test: A breakout on very high volume that then reverses is a more dangerous false breakout — it means institutional distribution is heavy. The higher the volume on the failure, the more committed the sellers are.

FALSE BREAKOUT — OPTIONS PLAY

When a breakout fails and price closes back below the prior resistance level: initiate a bear call spread with the short strike at or just above the failed resistance level. The failed breakout creates a natural resistance ceiling — sellers will defend that level again. This is one of the cleanest bear call spread setups available. DTE: 30–45 days. Avoid buying puts directly on the failed candle — the initial spike can cause IV expansion that makes puts temporarily expensive.

Pattern 7 of 9 — False Reversal (The Bear Trap)

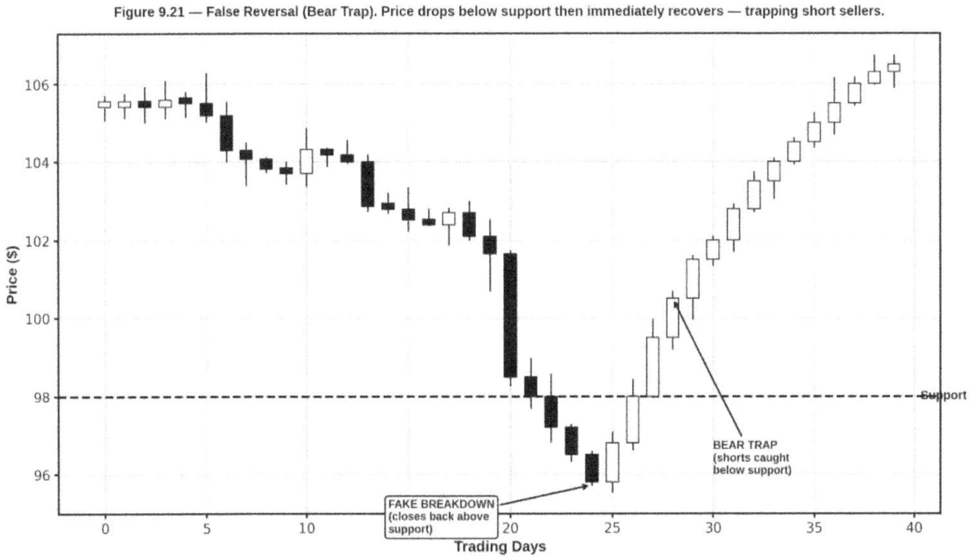

Figure 9.21a — False Reversal (Bear Trap). Price drops below support then immediately recovers — trapping short sellers.

Anatomy: A false reversal occurs within an established trend when price produces a countertrend move that appears to signal a change of direction — a bounce in a downtrend or a pullback in an uptrend — but then resumes the original trend with renewed force. For options traders in downtrends, the false reversal most commonly appears as a bullish-looking bounce that triggers premature put-selling entries.

Psychology: In a downtrend, trapped buyers from higher levels are desperate to exit on any relief rally. Short sellers take partial profits. This creates a temporary bounce that looks bullish. Countertrend traders enter. Then the original sellers — who never covered their full positions — step back in and the downtrend resumes. The countertrend players are now trapped alongside the original buyers.

- The reversal confirmation requirement: A TRUE reversal in a downtrend requires at minimum a higher high AND a higher low. A single bullish candle or a short bounce that fails to make a higher high is not a reversal — it is a counter-trend move within a continuing downtrend;
- The structure test: Draw the downtrend line. A true reversal requires a clean break ABOVE that trendline, followed by a retest and hold. A bounce that fails

to break the trendline — regardless of how sharp it is — is a false reversal until proven otherwise; and

- Most expensive application: Selling puts into a false reversal. The stock looks like it is bottoming, you sell puts for income — then the downtrend resumes and you are assigned shares on the way to new lows.

FALSE REVERSAL — THE RULE

NEVER sell puts into a downtrending stock based solely on a single bullish candle or short bounce. Require ALL THREE of the following before switching from bearish to bullish strategies: (1) Price breaks above the downtrend line. (2) Price makes a higher high relative to the prior countertrend peak. (3) Price makes a higher low — does not return to test the prior swing low. Until all three conditions are met, the downtrend is intact. Stay bearish or stay out.

Pattern 8 of 9 — Ascending Triangle (Bullish Breakout)

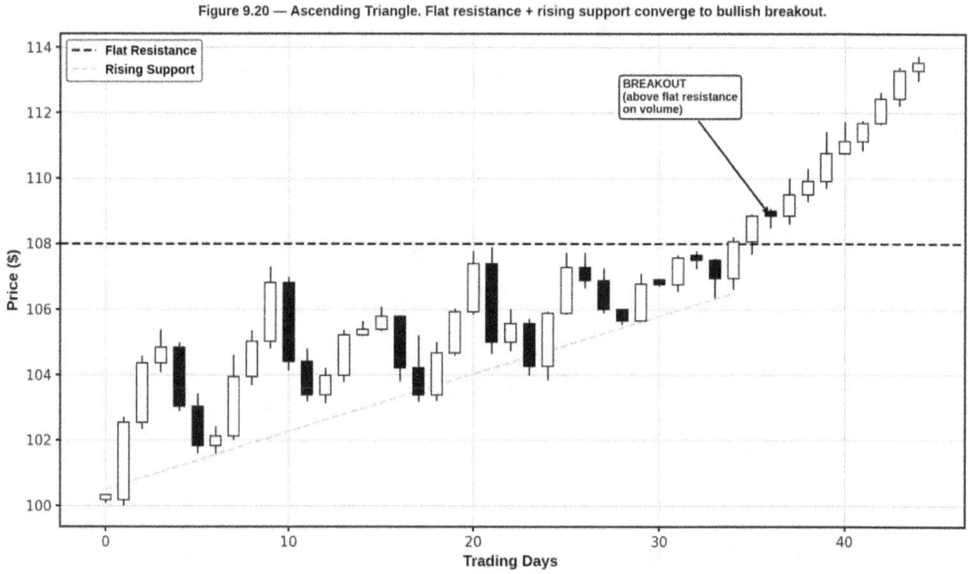

Figure 9.20a — Ascending Triangle. Flat resistance with rising support — bullish breakout.

Anatomy: The Ascending Triangle has two defining trendlines: a flat horizontal line connecting multiple peaks at a consistent resistance level, and an upward-sloping line connecting a series of higher lows. The two lines converge toward an apex. Price oscillates within this coiling structure, making less and less room — until a breakout resolves the tension.

Psychology: The flat resistance line represents a seller — perhaps a large holder distributing inventory at a consistent price. But the rising lows tell you buyers are increasingly aggressive, willing to pay more each time rather than waiting for a deeper pullback. The buyers' urgency is increasing while the seller remains. Eventually, the seller's inventory exhausts and buyers overwhelm the resistance.

- Volume signature: Volume typically declines as the pattern develops (consistent with the coiling) and then expands sharply on the breakout — this is the Bollinger squeeze equivalent in price structure;
- The built-in timer: The breakout typically occurs between 2/3 and 3/4 of the distance to the apex. If price reaches the apex without breaking, the pattern is failing — the urgency of the buyers is waning; and
- Measurement target: The height of the triangle at its widest point added to the breakout level.

ASCENDING TRIANGLE — OPTIONS PLAY

Two entry strategies: (1) Pre-breakout — as the pattern narrows (typically at the 2/3 point toward apex), IV often compresses. Buy a call debit spread in anticipation of the breakout. The maximum loss is the debit paid if the pattern fails. (2) On breakout — enter a bull call spread on the confirmed close above the flat resistance. The resistance level, now flipped to support, is your stop reference. DTE: 30–45 days. The coiling phase is also a candidate for a long straddle if you expect the move but not the direction.

Pattern 9 of 9 — Rising & Falling Wedge (Reversal Patterns)

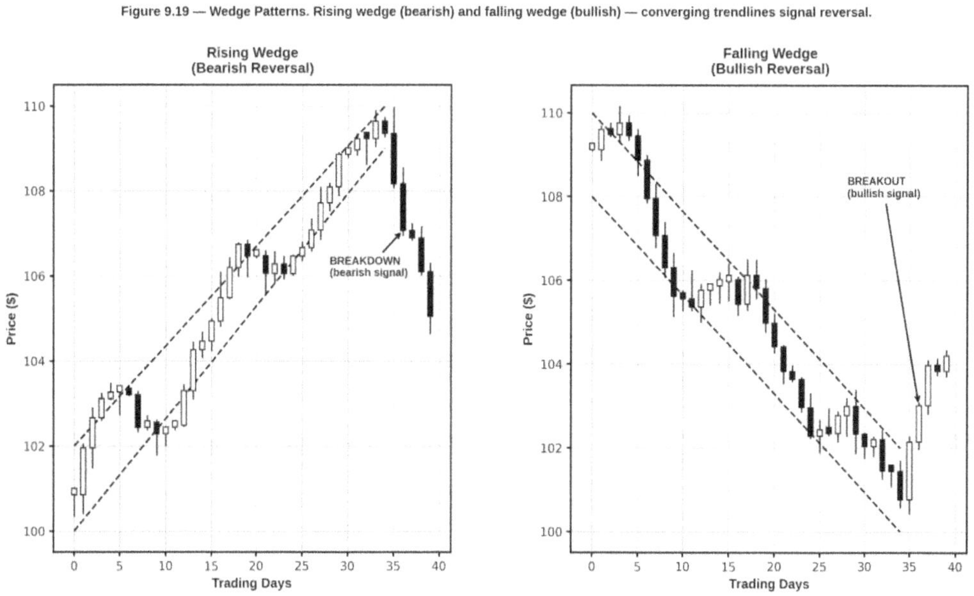

Figure 9.19 — Wedge Patterns. Rising wedge (bearish) and falling wedge (bullish) — converging trendlines signal reversal.

Anatomy: Wedge patterns are defined by two converging trendlines that slope in the SAME direction — unlike a triangle (where one is flat) or a channel (where they are parallel). In a Rising Wedge, both the upper and lower trendlines slope upward but converge — the highs are getting smaller relative to the lows. In a Falling Wedge, both slope downward but converge — the lows are getting smaller relative to the highs.

Rising Wedge (Bearish Reversal):

Psychology: Price is making higher highs AND higher lows — so at a glance, it looks like a healthy uptrend. But the tightening range reveals the truth: buyers are running out of steam. Each successive high is smaller than the last relative to the effort. Sellers are gradually stepping in closer and closer to the prior high. When the lower trendline breaks, the reversal is often sharp because everyone who bought into the apparent uptrend is now holding a loss at once.

- Confirmation: Break BELOW the lower rising trendline on expanded volume;
- Options play: Bear call spread with the short strike above the upper trendline. As the wedge narrows, IV often compresses — the false calm before the break. This is an opportunity to sell premium at relatively cheap IV into a pattern that historically resolves sharply downward;

Falling Wedge (Bullish Reversal):

Psychology: Price is making lower highs AND lower lows — which looks bearish. But the tightening range reveals the opposite: sellers are losing momentum. Each successive low is less severe than the last. Buyers are stepping in progressively earlier, not waiting for deeper pullbacks. When price breaks above the upper falling trendline, the move can be explosive because all the bearish positioning that built during the wedge is suddenly wrong.

- Confirmation: Break ABOVE the upper falling trendline on expanded volume, OR simply a break that holds for two consecutive daily closes; and
- Options play: Bull call spread or CSP after the break above the upper trendline is confirmed. The most recent swing low within the wedge is the stop reference. The falling wedge is also one of the better setups for a long call in low-IV environments — IV is often cheap during the wedge's quiet compression.

WEDGE vs. CHANNEL — KNOW THE DIFFERENCE

A wedge converges — the two trendlines approach each other toward an apex. A channel is parallel — the two lines maintain the same distance. Channels are continuation patterns (trade with the trend, buying dips and selling rips). Wedges are reversal patterns (the trend is deceiving — the breakout goes against the wedge's slope direction). Misidentifying a wedge as a channel causes traders to buy into a rising wedge and get trapped at the top.

Pattern Quick Reference: All 9 Patterns

Pattern	Type	Condition Signal	Options Strategy
Head & Shoulders	Reversal	Bearish → Cond. 3/4	Bear call spread at right shoulder; long put on neckline break
Double Bottom	Reversal	Bullish → Cond. 1/2	CSP at second bottom; bull call spread on neckline break
Double Top	Reversal	Bearish → Cond. 3/4	Bear call spread at second top; bear put spread on neckline break
Bull Flag	Continuation	Bullish → Cond. 1/2	Long call or bull call spread on breakout from flag; flag low = stop
Cup & Handle	Continuation	Bullish → Cond. 1/2	LEAPS call during handle formation; CSP at handle low
False Breakout	Trap / Reversal	Bearish → Cond. 3/4	Bear call spread with short strike at failed resistance level

Pattern	Type	Condition Signal	Options Strategy
False Reversal	Trap / Continuation	Trend continues	Do NOT sell puts. Require 3 structural confirmations before switching
Ascending Triangle	Breakout	Bullish → Cond. 1/2	Bull call spread on flat-top breakout; short put at rising trendline
Rising Wedge	Reversal	Bearish → Cond. 3/4	Bear call spread above upper trendline; profit from IV compression
Falling Wedge	Reversal	Bullish → Cond. 1/2	Bull call spread on upper trendline break; CSP at wedge lows

PATTERN + VIX = CONDITION

Chart patterns give you direction. VIX gives you volatility. Together they give you the condition. Do not act on a chart pattern without checking the VIX first. A perfect cup-and-handle forming in a VIX 30 environment means condition 2, not condition 1 — you sell premium into the bullish setup, not buy it. The pattern tells you the direction. The VIX tells you the strategy.

The Options Trader's Technical Indicator Quick Reference

You do not need twenty indicators. You need five, used consistently. Here is the complete quick reference for the indicators that matter most for options entry timing.

Indicator	Type	Time Frame	Buy/Sell Signal	Options Application
50-Day EMA	Trend	Intermediate	Price above = bullish. Below = bearish. Cross = trend change.	CSPs when stock above 50-day. Do not sell puts into a stock below its 50-day EMA.
200-Day EMA	Trend	Long-term	The institutional dividing line. Above = bull market. Below = bear.	Wheel candidates must be above 200-day. Period. Non-negotiable quality filter.
RSI (14)	Momentum	14 periods	Below 30 = oversold (potential bounce). Above 70 = overbought. Divergence is the key signal.	RSI divergence + support = CSP entry. RSI overbought + resistance = time to close or hedge.
MACD	Momentum	12/26/9	Signal line cross = momentum shift. Histogram expansion = acceleration.	MACD positive crossover confirms pullback entry for bull spreads. Negative crossover = close directional longs.
Bollinger Bands	Volatility	20-day, 2σ	Touch lower band = potential support. Touch upper = potential resistance. Band squeeze = breakout imminent.	Band squeeze = enter straddle or strangle. Touch lower band + RSI < 30 = high-probability CSP entry.
Volume	Confirmation	Daily	Volume confirms price moves. Low-volume moves are suspect. High-volume reversals are reliable.	Never enter a swing trade on a low-volume breakout. Require volume > 50-day average on entry day.
Fibonacci	Support/Resistance	Any	38.2% and 61.8% retracements are the	Sell CSPs at 38.2% pullback on quality uptrend

Indicator	Type	Time Frame	Buy/Sell Signal	Options Application
			primary levels. 50% is psychological.	names. Set stops below 61.8% — if that breaks, the trend is over.

The most powerful combinations: (1) 50-day EMA + RSI divergence + Fibonacci 38.2% = highest-probability CSP entry for income traders. (2) MACD crossover + volume surge + Bollinger breakout = highest-probability swing entry for directional traders. (3) Stock below 200-day EMA + RSI < 30 + high volume = potential turnaround — but use defined-risk spreads only, never naked exposure.

THE TECHNICAL ENTRY RULE

No options position should be entered on a single indicator. Require at least two confirming signals from different indicator TYPES (one trend + one momentum, or one momentum + one volatility). A single indicator is a hypothesis. Two confirming indicators from different categories is evidence.

PART II

BUILDING YOUR STRATEGY TOOLKITChapters 11–15 build your complete strategy library. Every strategy maps to one of the six conditions. Before entering any trade, confirm your condition read — then select only the structure built for that condition.

Can you identify the current six-condition read without looking at a reference card? · Can you read a candlestick chart and identify the trend, S/R levels, and a Fibonacci retracement zone? · Can you explain what Delta, Theta, and Vega mean in plain English? · Can you calculate the intrinsic and extrinsic value of any option from the chain?

If yes to all four: you are ready for Part II. If not: return to the chapter that covers the gap before proceeding. The strategies in Part II assume fluency in Part I — not familiarity.

Remember: The market goes one of six ways. Every strategy in this Part maps to one of those six conditions.

Remember: The market goes one of six ways. Every strategy in this Part maps to one of those six conditions.

PART I FOUNDATION CHECK — Before continuing, confirm you can answer these:

Can you identify the current six-condition read without looking at a reference card? · Can you read a candlestick chart and identify the trend, S/R levels, and a Fibonacci retracement zone? · Can you explain what Delta, Theta, and Vega mean in plain English? · Can you calculate the intrinsic and extrinsic value of any option from the chain?

If yes to all four: you are ready for Part II. If not: return to the chapter that covers the gap before proceeding. The strategies in Part II assume fluency in Part I — not familiarity.

Chapter 11 Walking You Through Your First Option Trade

AFTER CONDUCTING YOUR RESEARCH as prescribed by this book — Ten Indicators confirmed, condition read, strategy selected — here is the exact sequence for placing your first live options trade.

Two complete walkthroughs: a Long Call (directional/Condition 1) and a Cash-Secured Put (income/Condition 2). Read both regardless of which strategy you plan to use first.

There is a specific kind of paralysis that grips traders before their first live options order. You have read every chapter. You understand the Greeks. You can recite the Six Conditions. You know your strategy. And yet — the moment you open the order ticket with real money on the line — your hand hesitates over the Submit button. Your eyes scan the numbers one more time. You wonder if you missed something.

That hesitation is not weakness. It is your brain correctly recognizing that this is real and that the stakes are different from paper trading. The antidote is not to eliminate the hesitation — it is to replace it with a process. A process is executable even when confidence wavers. A process does not require you to feel good to work. This chapter gives you the process.

We will walk through two complete trades from first click to confirmed fill: a Long Call on Micron Technology (MU) representing a Condition 1 directional setup, and a Cash-Secured Put on Apple (AAPL) representing a Condition 2 income setup. These are not theoretical examples — they follow the exact sequence of clicks, decisions, and confirmations you will use on any live platform.

BEFORE YOUR FIRST LIVE TRADE

You must have paper-traded for a minimum of 30 consecutive trades before placing your first live order. Not 30 days — 30 trades. This requirement is not negotiable. It is about building the muscle memory of process execution: checking the chain, selecting expiration, calculating position size, setting the limit, and entering the order ticket without hesitation. The 31st trade should feel mechanical, not emotional. If it does not, return to paper for another 15 trades.

Condition 3 — The trend is down and options are cheap. Buy directional exposure.

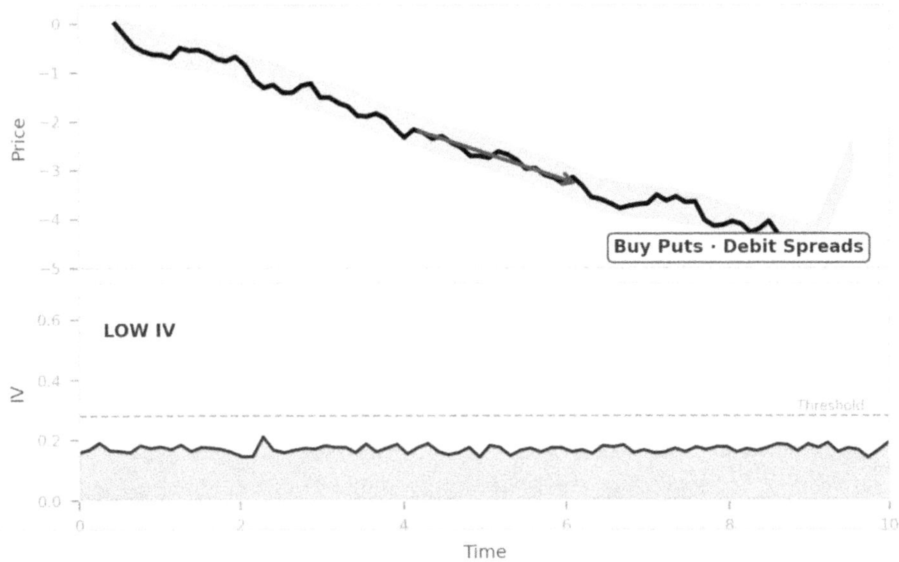

Figure 3. C3 — Bearish + Low IV: Recommended strategy — Buy Puts · Debit Spreads

Figure C1.1. C1 — Bullish + Low IV: Recommended strategy — Buy Calls · Debit Spreads

Reading the Risk Graph

How to read a risk graph in 30 seconds: the horizontal axis is the stock price at expiration. The vertical axis is your profit or loss in dollars. Where the line crosses zero is your breakeven. Above zero is profit territory. Below is loss territory. The shape tells you the structure: an upward slope means unlimited upside (long call). A flat line that drops is capped profit with defined loss (short put). A tent shape is maximum profit in the middle (iron condor). Once you can read a risk graph, you can evaluate any options structure in seconds.

The risk graph (also called a profit/loss diagram or risk profile) is the single most important visual tool in options trading. It shows you the profit or loss of a position across every possible stock price at expiration. Learn to read one instantly — you should never enter a multi-leg trade without seeing its risk graph first.

- The horizontal axis is the underlying stock price at expiration;
- The vertical axis is the profit (above the zero line) or loss (below the zero line);
- The point where the P&L line crosses zero is the breakeven price — or, for a spread, the two breakeven prices;
- A flat line at the bottom means maximum loss is capped — a defined-risk position;
- A line that continues downward without stopping means unlimited risk — a naked position; and
- The peak of the curve shows maximum profit and at what stock price it is achieved.

Before placing any multi-leg trade, ask: Does this risk graph match my thesis? Does the profit zone cover the price range I expect the stock to be in at expiration? Is my maximum loss one I can absorb without emotional damage to my trading? If the answer to any of these is no, redesign the position or don't trade it.

→ See Figure 11.3 — Long Call Risk Graph (Chapter 11 — Walking You Through Your First Option Trade)

→ See Figure 11.6 — Long Put Risk Graph (Chapter 11 — Walking You Through Your First Option Trade)

ALWAYS PROFILE BEFORE YOU TRADE

Your brokerage platform will show you the risk graph for any position before you submit the order. Use it every time. The 60 seconds it takes to examine a risk profile is the cheapest risk management tool you have. The cost of skipping it can be measured in dollars — many of them.

Position Sizing by Account Size: The 2% Rule Applied

Here is how the 2% rule applies at different account sizes — showing exactly what you can and cannot trade.

Account	2% Risk	Strategy	Max Loss	Contracts
$10,000	$200	BPS $2 wide	$200 - premium	1 contract
$10,000	$200	BPS $5 wide	$500 - premium	0 (TOO RISKY)
$25,000	$500	CSP on $45 stock	$4,500 managed	1 contract
$25,000	$500	Iron Condor $3 wide	$300 - premium	1-2 contracts
$50,000	$1,000	Wheel on $95 stock	$9,500 managed	1 contract
$50,000	$1,000	BPS $5 wide	$500 - premium	2 contracts
$100,000	$2,000	Wheel on $180 stock	$18,000 managed	1 contract
$100,000	$2,000	Iron Condor $5 wide	$500 - premium	3-4 contracts

Critical insight: a $10,000 account CANNOT safely trade a $5-wide spread. The max loss exceeds the 2% budget. This is not a suggestion — it is math. Small accounts must use narrower spreads or smaller underlyings. Trading a strategy your account cannot afford is a mathematical guarantee of destruction.

Walkthrough 1: Long Call — Condition 1 (Bullish, Low IV)

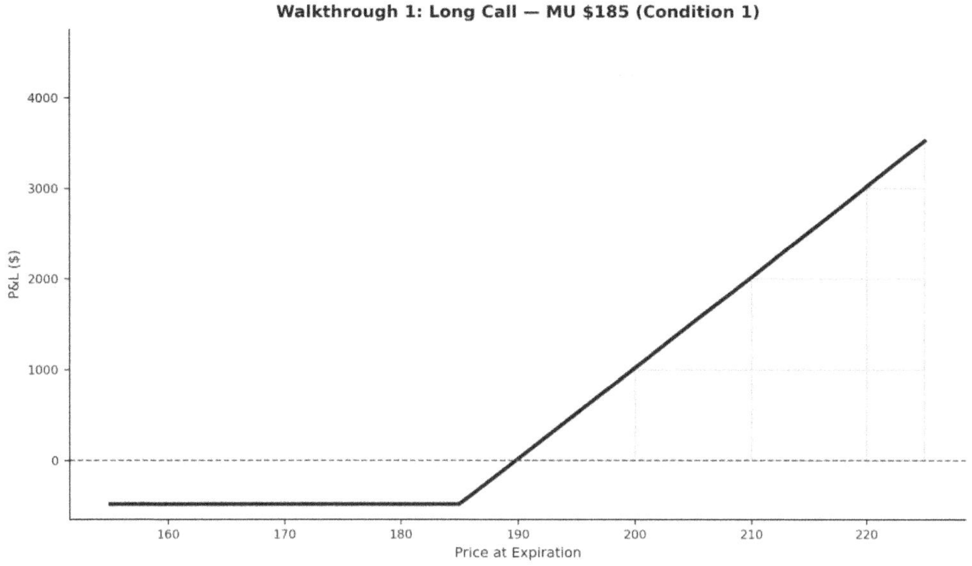

Figure 11.1 — First Trade Walkthroughs — Step-by-step execution of a Long Call (Condition 1) and a Cash-Secured Put (Condition 2).

Setup: Micron Technology (MU) has passed all Ten Indicators. The weekly chart shows a clean uptrend above the 26-week EMA. VIX is at 16 — low implied volatility, Condition 1. Strategy: buy a call to participate in the directional move.

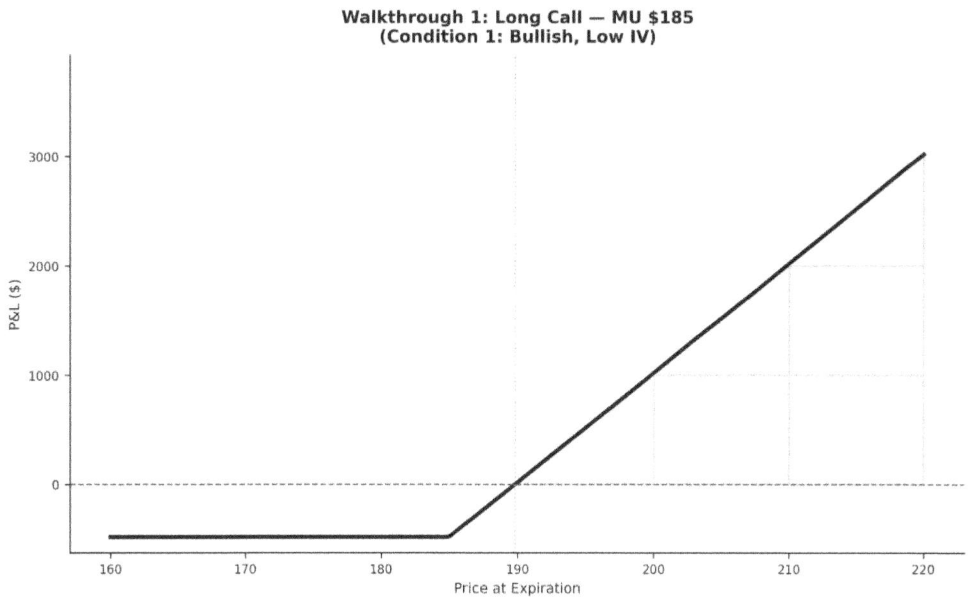

Figure 11.1 — Long Call Walkthrough (MU). Entry, breakeven, and P&L profile for Condition 1.

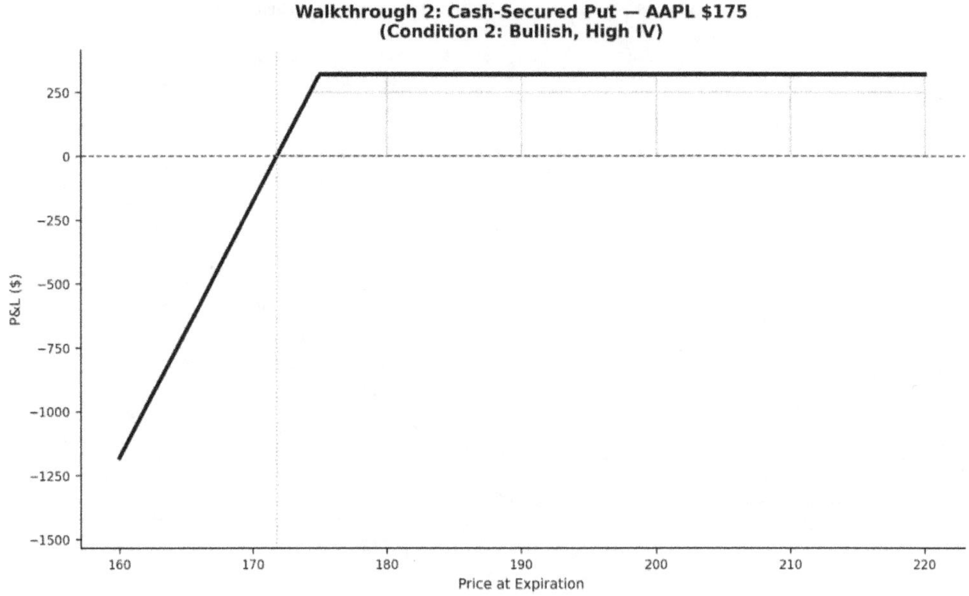

Figure 11.2 — Cash-Secured Put Walkthrough (AAPL). Entry, breakeven, and P&L profile for Condition 2.

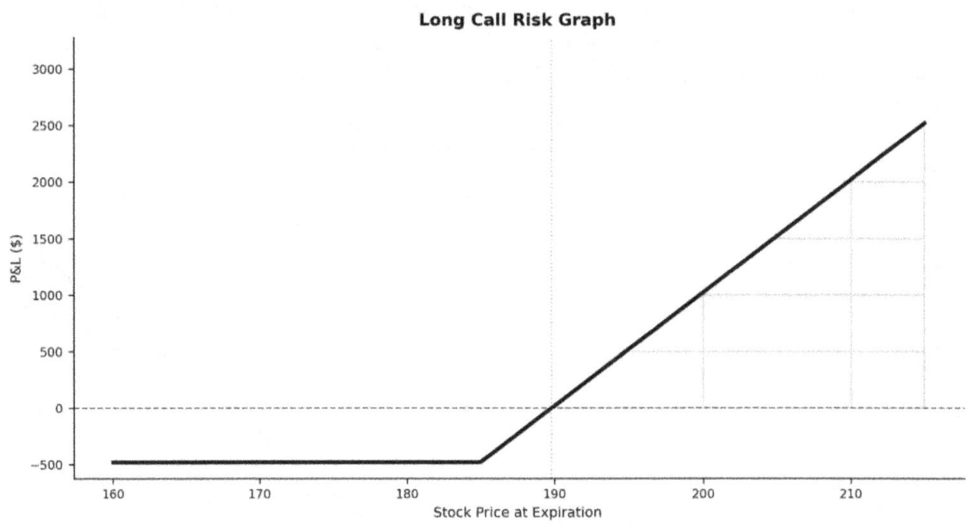

Figure 11.3 — Long Call Risk Graph. P&L profile from entry to expiration — max loss capped at premium paid.

Step A — Locate the Ticker and Open the Chain

In your platform's search bar, type MU and select Micron Technology. Click the OPTIONS tab to open the Option Chain — the table showing every available contract organized by expiration date and strike price. Calls appear on one side, Puts on the other. You will see Bid, Ask, Volume, Open Interest, and the Greeks for each strike.

Strike	Bid	Ask	Volume	OI	Delta
100	4.20	4.30	1,842	12,300	0.52
105	2.15	2.25	3,601	28,450	0.38
110	0.85	0.95	5,220	41,800	0.22

MU Call Option Chain — 38 DTE. MU trading at $102. Prices are illustrative.

Step B — Select Expiration, Strike, and Entry Price

Expiration: select the monthly expiration 38 days out. This is our standard 30-45 DTE window. For directional buys, we need enough time for the thesis to develop — never buy calls with less than 30 DTE unless you are specifically trading a short-term catalyst.

Strike: with MU at $102, the $105 Call (Delta 0.38) is our selection. Slightly OTM, reasonable premium of $2.25, and a Delta that gives meaningful participation in the move without the high cost of an ITM option.

- $100 strike (ITM, Delta 0.52): Higher cost $4.25, higher probability, lower leverage. Use for high-conviction setups;
- $105 strike (OTM, Delta 0.38): $2.25, balanced leverage. Standard Condition 1 selection; and
- $110 strike (Deep OTM, Delta 0.22): $0.90, speculative. Only for small-allocation lotto plays.

Entry price: set a limit order at the MIDPOINT between bid and ask. ($2.15 + $2.25) / 2 = $2.20. Start there. If no fill after 5 minutes, move $0.05 toward the ask. Maximum: pay the ask if necessary, but only after attempting mid.

Step C — Build and Submit the Order Ticket

Order Field	What to Enter
Action	BUY TO OPEN
Ticker / Underlying	MU
Option Type / Strike	Call / $105
Expiration	Monthly, 38 DTE
Quantity	1 contract
Order Type	LIMIT — never market on options
Limit Price	$2.20 (the midpoint)
Time in Force	DAY
Total Debit	$220 (your maximum risk — confirmed)

Read the ticket aloud one time before clicking Submit: 'Buying 1 MU $105 Call expiring in 38 days for $2.20 limit. Maximum risk $220. Confirmed.' Click Submit. The order is now PENDING in the market.

Once filled: immediately set your post-fill management. Profit target: 50-80% gain, meaning close when the option reaches $3.30-$3.96. Maximum loss: full premium paid, $220 — already defined. No stop-loss required for a debit spread. Mark your T-21 date in your calendar.

WHAT TO DO AFTER THE FILL

Close your platform. Do not watch every tick. Check the position once at market close each day — not during the session. Constant monitoring does not improve outcomes; it multiplies emotional interference. The position does not need you watching it. Set your daily 4:00 PM review and honor it.

Condition 2 — The trend is up but options are expensive. Sell premium with a bullish bias.

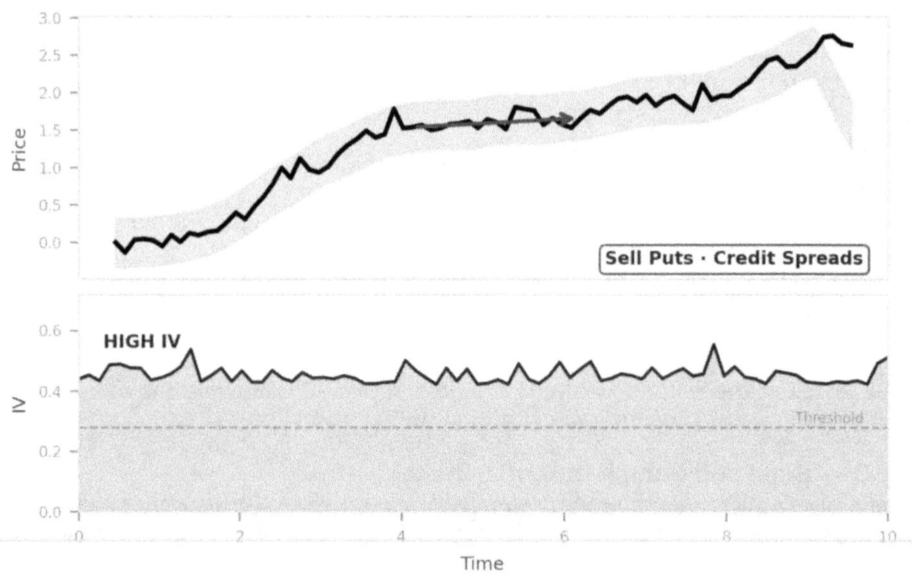

Figure 2. C2 — Bullish + High IV: Recommended strategy — Sell Puts · Credit Spreads

Figure C2.1. C2 — Bullish + High IV: Recommended strategy — Sell Puts · Credit Spreads

Walkthrough 2: Cash-Secured Put — Condition 2 (Bullish, High IV)

Setup: Apple (AAPL) has passed all Ten Indicators. Weekly uptrend intact. VIX is at 28 — elevated implied volatility, Condition 2. Strategy: sell a cash-secured put to collect elevated premium with the bullish trend as our tailwind and the IV environment working in our favor as sellers.

Key mindset shift: in Walkthrough 1 we were BUYERS hoping for a directional move. Here we are SELLERS — we collect premium upfront and profit if the stock stays above our strike, moves up, OR even falls slightly. Three ways to win versus one.

CSP Step A — Confirm Cash and Select the Strike

A Cash-Secured Put requires cash equal to the strike price x 100 in your account. For an AAPL $185 CSP: you need $18,500 reserved. Confirm this before selecting a strike. AAPL is trading at $193. Our target: sell the $185 Put at Delta ~0.28, giving AAPL an $8 buffer (4.1%) below current price.

- Check the earnings calendar FIRST: no earnings within the expiration window. This is mandatory, non-negotiable;
- Delta target for income CSPs: 0.25-0.35. This is the sweet spot between meaningful premium and adequate safety margin.

Strike	Bid	Ask	Volume	OI	Delta
190	3.80	3.95	4,210	38,900	-0.38
185	2.10	2.25	6,840	55,200	-0.28
180	1.05	1.15	8,120	71,300	-0.18

AAPL Put Option Chain — 38 DTE. AAPL at $193. Prices are illustrative.

CSP Step B — Calculate the Trade Metrics Before Submitting

This calculation takes 30 seconds and must be done before every CSP entry. No exceptions.

Metric	AAPL $185 Put @ $2.20 Credit
Premium Collected	$2.20 x 100 = $220 received upfront
Capital Reserved	$185 x 100 = $18,500 (held for potential assignment)
Return if Expired Worthless	$220 / $18,500 = 1.19% in 38 days
Annualized Return	1.19% x (365 / 38) = ~11.4% annualized
Breakeven at Expiration	$185 - $2.20 = $182.80
Buffer to Breakeven	$193 - $182.80 = $10.20 or 5.3% downside
Profit Target (50%)	Close when put value drops to $1.10
T-21 Management Date	17 days from entry date

Order ticket: SELL TO OPEN, 1 contract, AAPL $185 Put, monthly 38 DTE, Limit at $2.20 (midpoint between $2.10 bid and $2.25 ask), DAY order. Once filled, $220 is immediately credited to your account. Immediately set a Buy to Close GTC order at $1.10 (50% profit). Set T-21 calendar reminder.

THE CSP OWNERSHIP TEST

Before submitting any cash-secured put, ask yourself this question aloud: If AAPL fell to $182.80 tomorrow and I was assigned 100 shares, would I be comfortable owning them at that price? Yes means submit. Any hesitation means find a different underlying or a lower strike. The premium is never worth owning a stock you do not want to own.

This example reflects a real trade executed and recorded in real time. Position sizing shown here reflects my own account parameters and may not be appropriate for all traders.

Condition 6 — The market is range-bound and options are expensive. Collect premium and theta.

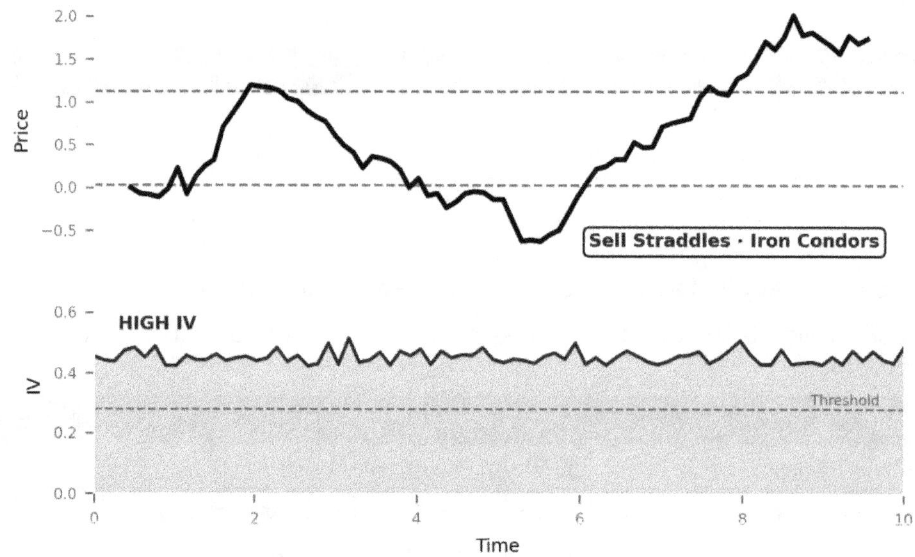

Figure 6. C6 — Neutral + High IV: Recommended strategy — Sell Straddles · Iron Condors

Figure C4.1 — Condition 4: Bearish + High IV → Sell Calls / Credit Spreads

Walkthrough 3: Bear Put Spread — Condition 3 (Bearish, Low IV)

A confirmed downtrend with low implied volatility calls for a debit spread — you buy premium rather than sell it, because IV is cheap enough to make buying worthwhile and the direction is clearly defined. The bear put spread is the Condition 3 instrument: buy an ATM or slightly OTM put, sell a further OTM put to offset the cost, and define your maximum loss as the debit paid.

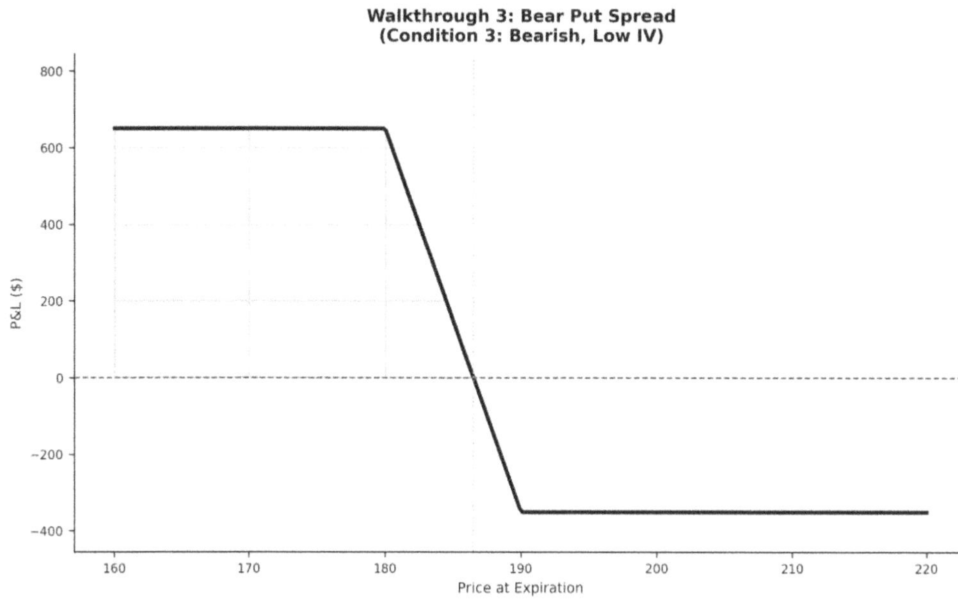

Figure 11.4 — Bear Put Spread Walkthrough. Condition 3 bearish trade with real strikes.

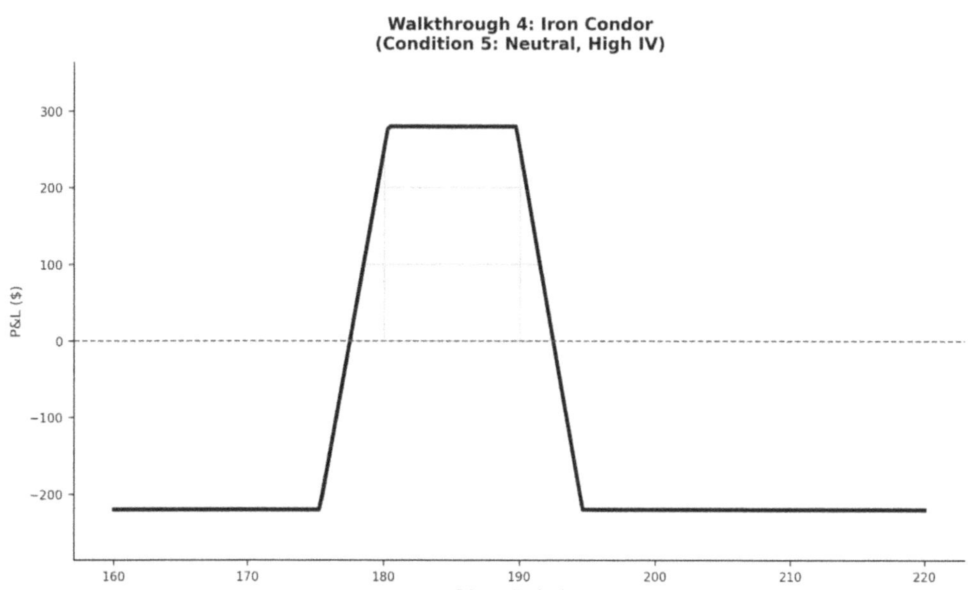

Figure 11.5 — Iron Condor Walkthrough. Condition 5 neutral trade with profit zone shown.

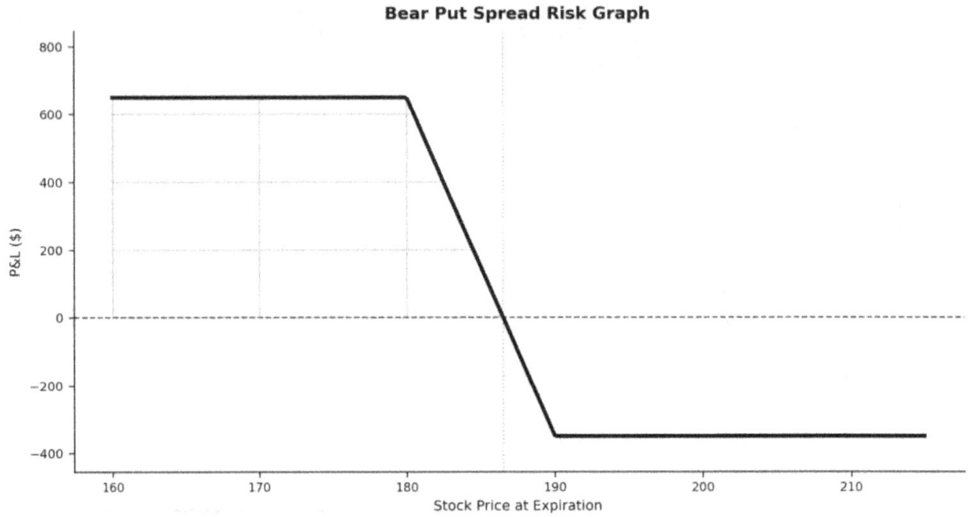

Figure 11.6 — Bear Put Spread Risk Graph. Defined risk, defined reward bearish position.

Example: QQQ is below its 200-day EMA, MACD is negative, VIX is at 16 (low IV). Buy the $380 put for $6.20, sell the $370 put for $3.00. Net debit: $3.20. Maximum profit: $6.80 (if QQQ closes below $370 at expiration). Breakeven: $376.80. Maximum loss: $3.20 (debit paid). This trade has no assignment risk, fully defined loss, and profits from any sustained move below $376.80 over the next 30–45 days.

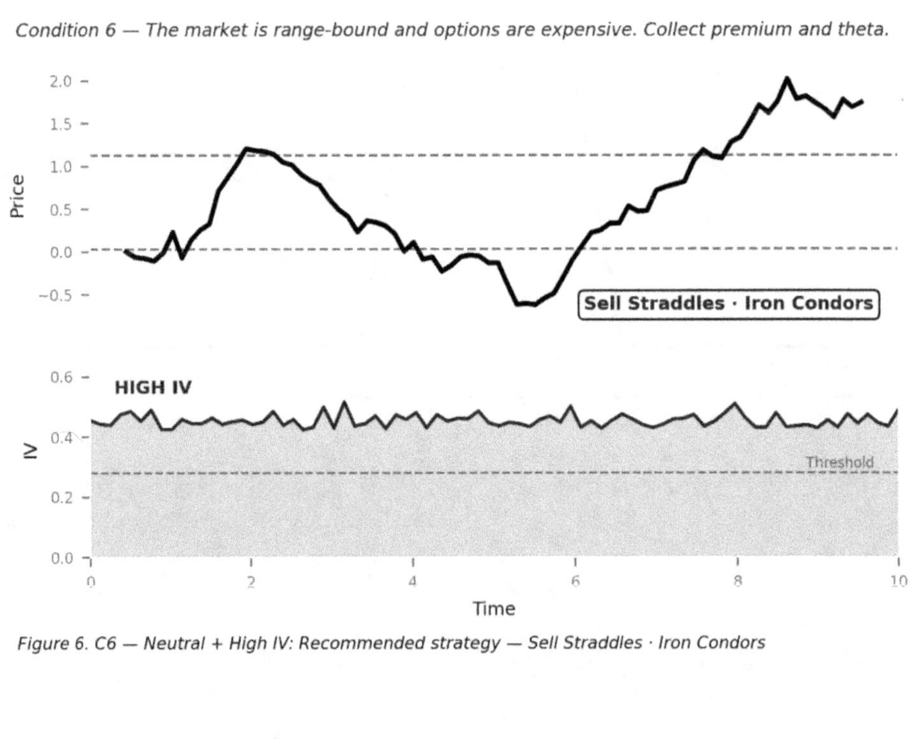

Figure 6. C6 — Neutral + High IV: Recommended strategy — Sell Straddles · Iron Condors

Figure C4.1. C4 — Bearish + High IV: Recommended strategy — Sell Calls · Credit Spreads

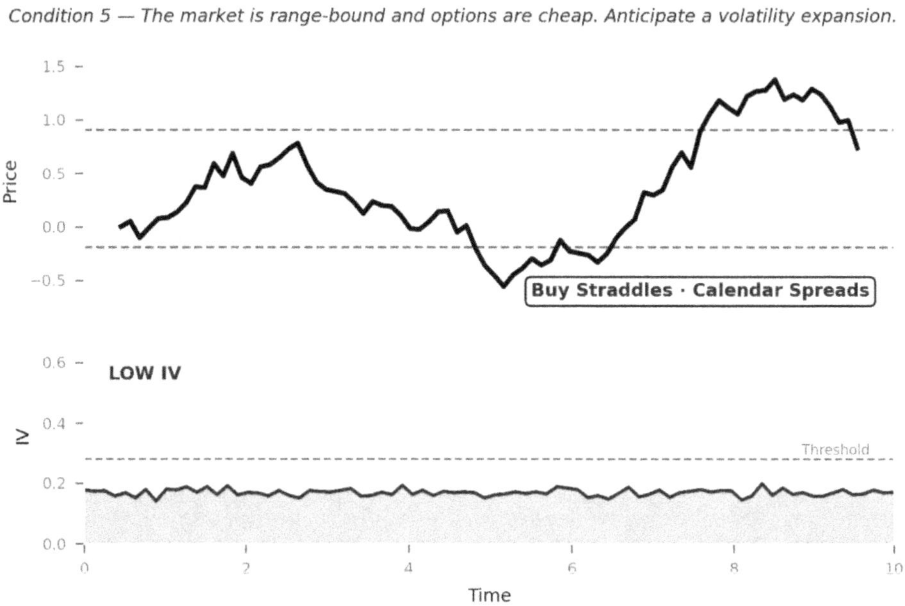

Figure 5. C5 — Neutral + Low IV: Recommended strategy — Buy Straddles · Calendar Spreads

Figure C5.1. C5 — Neutral + Low IV: Recommended strategy — Buy Straddles · Calendar Spreads

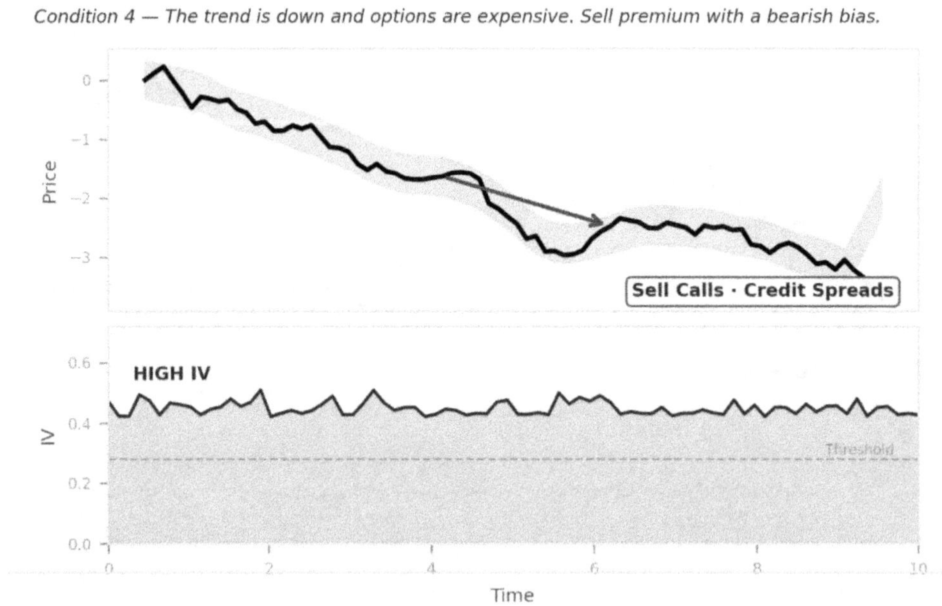

Figure 4. C4 — Bearish + High IV: Recommended strategy — Sell Calls · Credit Spreads

Figure C6.1. C6 — Neutral + High IV: Recommended strategy — Sell Straddles · Iron Condors

Walkthrough 4: Bear Call Spread — Condition 4 (Bearish, High IV)

A confirmed downtrend with elevated implied volatility calls for a credit spread on the short side — you sell premium rather than buy it, because IV is expensive enough to make selling the better risk-adjusted play. The bear call spread is the Condition 4 instrument: sell an OTM call near resistance, buy a further OTM call to cap your risk, and collect a net credit. The trade profits if the stock stays below your short call strike through expiration.

Setup: QQQ is below its 50-day and 200-day EMA, making lower highs for 4 consecutive weeks. MACD is negative. VIX is at 28 — elevated implied volatility. IVR is 72. Condition 4 confirmed: Bearish + High IV. The recent bounce has brought QQQ to resistance at $390 — the same level it failed to break twice in the past month.

Decision Point	Action
Condition verification	VIX: 28. IVR: 72 (HIGH). QQQ below 50MA and 200MA, lower highs confirmed. → Condition 4 ✓
Earnings calendar check	No QQQ components reporting within DTE window. ETF has no earnings risk. ✓
Short strike selection	$390 — current resistance level. Two failed breakout attempts. Delta: 0.28. IV: 31%.

Decision Point	Action
Long strike (hedge)	$395 — $5 above short strike. Caps maximum loss. Delta: 0.18.
DTE	35 days — within the 30–45 DTE income window. ✓
Premium collected	Sell $390 Call at $2.15. Buy $395 Call at $1.10. Net credit: $1.05 per share = $105 per spread.
Maximum risk	($395 − $390 − $1.05) × 100 = $395 per spread. Defined. ✓
Maximum reward	$1.05 × 100 = $105 per spread if QQQ stays below $390 at expiration.
Reward-to-risk ratio	$105 / $395 = 0.27:1. Requires high win rate — appropriate for C4 where the trend is your ally.
Breakeven	$390 + $1.05 = $391.05. QQQ must close above $391.05 to produce a loss.
Order ticket	SELL TO OPEN 1 QQQ $390 Call / BUY TO OPEN 1 QQQ $395 Call. Same expiration. Net credit limit: $1.05. GTC.
Post-fill management	Profit target: close at 50% of credit ($0.525 buy-to-close). Stop: close if spread widens to 2× credit ($2.10). T-21 rule: evaluate roll or close at 21 DTE regardless.

CONDITION 4 CRITICAL RULE

In a bearish, high-IV environment the most intuitive trade is to buy puts — the market is going down, so buy downside protection. But high IV makes those puts expensive, and even if you are right on direction, IV contraction after the move can destroy your profit. The bear call spread solves both problems: you collect the elevated IV premium on the short call, define your risk with the long call, and profit from both the directional move AND the IV contraction. Counterintuitive. Correct.

Condition 4 — The trend is down and options are expensive. Sell premium with a bearish bias.

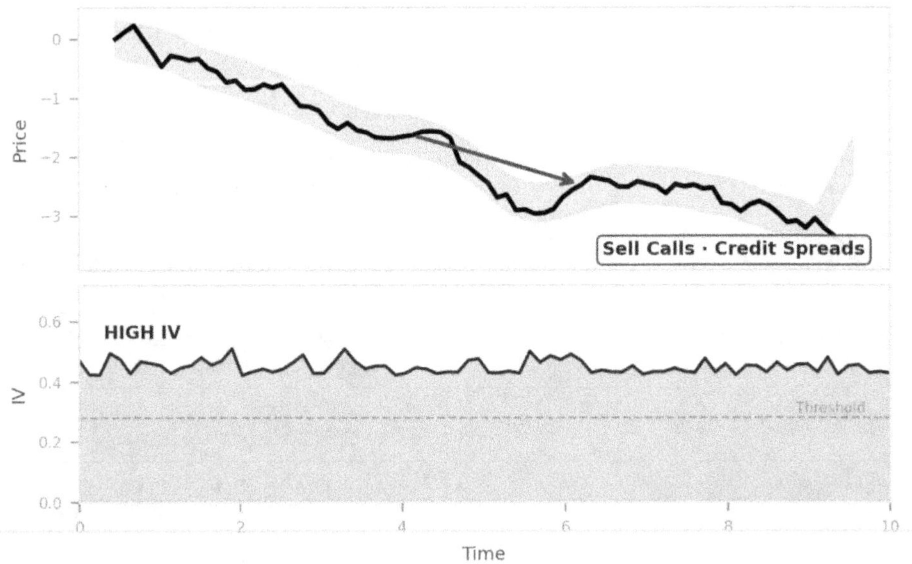

Figure 4. C4 — Bearish + High IV: Recommended strategy — Sell Calls · Credit Spreads

Figure C6.1 — Condition 6: Neutral + High IV → Sell Straddles / Iron Condors

Walkthrough 5: Calendar Spread — Condition 6 (Neutral, Low IV)

When the market is range-bound and implied volatility is low, the calendar spread is the precision instrument. You sell a near-term option at the strike you expect the stock to remain near, and simultaneously buy a longer-dated option at the same strike. The near-term option decays faster than the longer-dated one — you collect the differential decay as income while the stock stays within its range. Unlike the iron condor, the calendar profits from a rise in IV — making it the ideal Condition 6 structure when IV is cheap and expansion is anticipated.

Setup: SPY has been trading in a tight 8-point range between $490 and $498 for three weeks. No significant macro events in the next 30 days. VIX is at 14 — suppressed. IVR is 18. Near-term options are cheap. Condition 6 confirmed: Neutral + Low IV. The ATM strike is $494.

Decision Point	Action
Condition verification	VIX: 14. IVR: 18 (LOW). SPY flat, oscillating $490–$498, no directional confirmation. → Condition 6 ✓
Strike selection	$494 ATM call — center of the current trading range. Maximum theta decay at the money.
Short leg (sell)	Sell 1 SPY $494 Call, 30 DTE. Premium received: $3.80. This leg decays fastest.

Decision Point	Action
Long leg (buy)	Buy 1 SPY $494 Call, 60 DTE. Premium paid: $6.10. This leg decays slower — it is our protection.
Net debit	$6.10 − $3.80 = $2.30 per share = $230 total. This is your maximum risk.
Profit potential	Maximum profit occurs if SPY is exactly at $494 at 30-day expiration. Near-term call expires worthless ($380 received), long-term call retains significant value. Est. max profit: $180–$220.
Vega advantage	Calendar is long vega: if IV expands from 14% to 18%, long leg gains more than short leg loses. IV expansion is your ally in Condition 6.
Order ticket	BUY CALENDAR: Sell 1 SPY $494 Call 30 DTE / Buy 1 SPY $494 Call 60 DTE. Net debit limit: $2.30. GTC.
Post-fill management	Profit target: close when the spread value reaches $3.80 (65% return on debit). Stop: close if SPY breaks outside $488–$500 range. T-21 rule: at 21 DTE on the short leg, evaluate rolling to next month.
What kills this trade	SPY breaks decisively out of the range — either direction. A strong directional move hurts the calendar. The position assumes continued consolidation. If the condition changes to C1, C2, C3, or C4 — exit.

THE CALENDAR SPREAD INSIGHT

The calendar spread is the only strategy in this book that profits from three simultaneous factors: (1) the stock staying near the strike — time decay differential, (2) a rise in IV — long vega position, (3) the passage of time — the short near-term leg decays faster than the long leg every single day. When all three align — as they do in Condition 6 — the calendar is among the highest-probability income structures available. When any one of the three is violated — particularly a directional breakout — exit immediately.

Walkthrough 6: Iron Condor — Condition 5 (Range, High IV)

When the market is range-bound and implied volatility is elevated, the iron condor is the optimal structure. You collect premium from both sides of the range simultaneously, with defined risk on both wings. The trade profits from time decay and volatility contraction — you do not need a move in either direction. You need the stock to stay inside your short strikes.

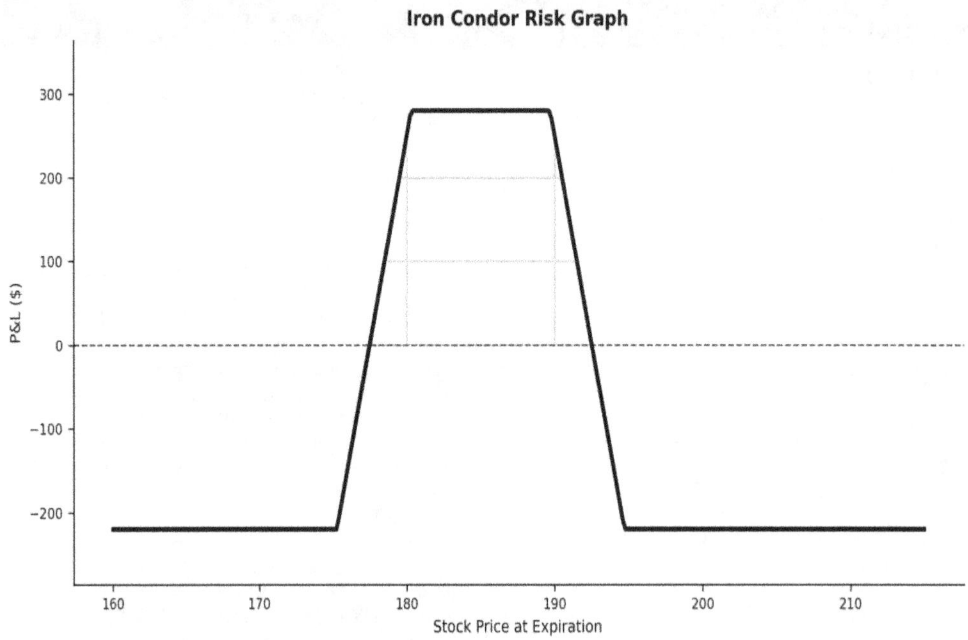

Figure 11.7 — Iron Condor Risk Graph. Premium collected upfront, profit if stock stays in the profit zone.

The Seven Most Common First-Trade Mistakes

Mistake	What It Looks Like	Prevention
Using a market order	Fill at ASK or worse on a wide-spread option, immediately losing 5-10% of potential profit	Set platform default to Limit Order. Never override for options.
Wrong expiration selected	You select the nearest weekly instead of the monthly you intended	Read the expiration date aloud before confirming: 'June 21, 38 DTE — confirmed.'
Bid/ask confusion	You try to buy at the bid (no fill) or the midpoint gets filled adversely	Buying: limit starts at mid, moves toward ask. Selling: limit starts at mid, moves toward bid.
Wrong quantity	You enter 10 contracts thinking it means 10 shares of exposure	Always calculate true dollar exposure: contracts x 100 x premium. For every first-month trade: 1 contract maximum.
No exit plan at entry	Position fills, you have no profit target or stop defined	Set GTC exit order immediately after every fill. Before closing the platform.
Constant position monitoring	You check P&L every 20 minutes and override your plan on temporary adverse moves	Check once at 4 PM market close. Remove the app from your phone if necessary for the first 30 days.
Selling into earnings	AAPL has earnings in 12 days, you sell a 30 DTE put through the announcement	Earnings calendar check before every CSP and covered call. This rule has no exceptions.

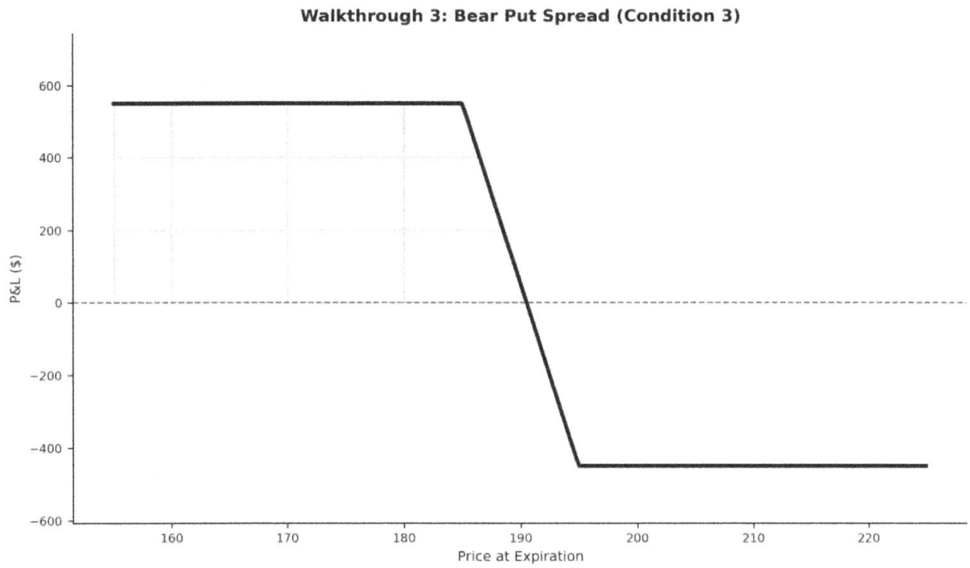

Figure 11.2 — Bearish and Neutral Trade Walkthroughs — Bear Put Spread (Condition 3) and Iron Condor (Condition 5) execution.

Bearish and Neutral Trade Walkthroughs — Step-by-step execution of bear put and iron condor trades.

Condition 1 — The trend is up and options are cheap. Buy directional exposure.

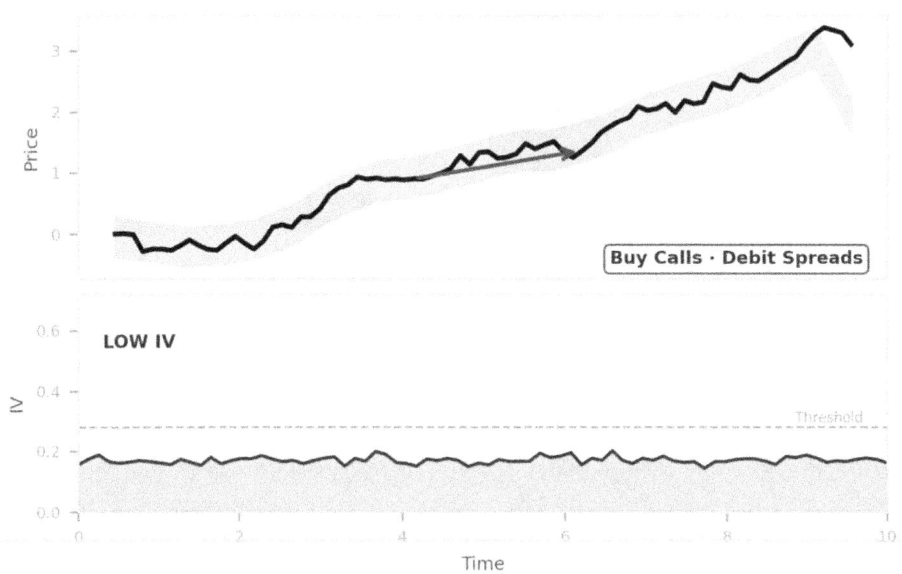

Figure 1. C1 — Bullish + Low IV: Recommended strategy — Buy Calls · Debit Spreads

Figure C3.1. C3 — Bearish + Low IV: Recommended strategy — Buy Puts · Debit Spreads

The System in Action — Verified Trade Record

The following trades were executed live using the Six-Condition framework, Ten Indicator screening, and the T-21 Rule. Every entry and exit is brokerage-verified.

Trade	Strike	Entry Price	Exit Price	Return %	P&L
MU Long Call #1	$185 Call	$4.80	$7.28	+51.78%	+$248
MU Long Call #2	$310 Call	$3.85	$13.02	+238.44%	+$1,007
MU Long Call #3	$340 Call	$5.60	$7.05	+25.89%	+$145
MU Long Call #4	$420 Call	$6.15	$6.99	+13.66%	+$84
TOTAL SERIES	4 trades	—	—	+79.6% avg	+$22,829

Figure 11.8 — MU Verified Call Series. Four brokerage-verified trades with entry, exit, and return.

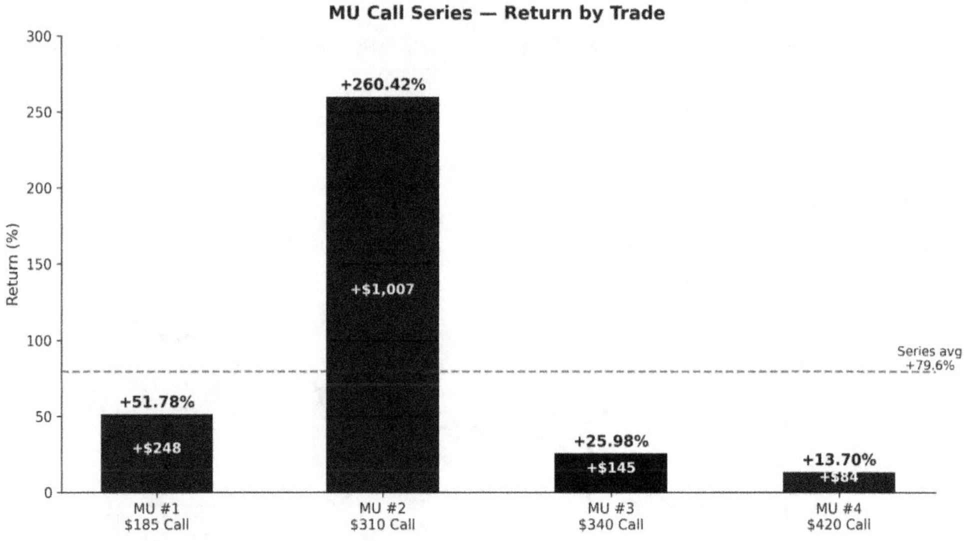

Figure 11.9 — MU Series Returns. +260.42% peak / +$22,829 total closed P&L.

The following trades were executed live using the Six-Condition framework, Ten Indicator screening, and the T-21 Rule. Every entry and exit is brokerage-verified.

Example: SPY is oscillating between support at $490 and resistance at $510. VIX is at 24 (Condition 5: range, elevated IV). Sell the $510 call/$515 call spread for $1.40. Sell the $490 put/$485 put spread for $1.40. Total credit: $2.80. Maximum profit: $280 per iron condor (if SPY stays between $490 and $510 at expiration). Maximum loss on either side: $220 ($500 spread width minus $280 credit). Breakeven levels: $487.20 on the downside, $512.80 on the upside.

THE IRON CONDOR ENTRY RULE

Never enter an iron condor when IVR is below 40. Below that level, you are collecting too little premium relative to the risk you are taking on both wings. The iron condor is an income-from-volatility trade — if volatility is not elevated, the income does not justify the defined risk. Wait for IVR above 40, ideally above 50, before deploying the condor.

The Order Ticket: Mechanics of Submitting Your First Trade

Knowing the strategy is not enough. You need to know exactly how to translate a trade plan into a brokerage order. Every options platform has the same core fields, and every field has a correct answer before you submit.

Order Field	What You Select	Why It Matters
Action	Buy to Open / Sell to Open	Buy = pay debit. Sell = collect credit. Never confuse with closing orders.
Underlying	Ticker symbol (e.g. AAPL)	Confirm the exact underlying. Options on similar tickers can differ in liquidity.
Expiration	Select the date (e.g. Jan 17)	Match to your planned DTE. Avoid the front week unless intentional.
Strike	The specific strike price	Double-check. One click selects the wrong strike in fast markets.
Option Type	Call or Put	Verify this matches your strategy direction before submitting.
Quantity	Number of contracts	Start with 1 contract for first trades. Each contract = 100 shares.
Order Type	Limit order (always)	Never submit a market order on options. The spread will fill you poorly.
Limit Price	Mid-price of bid/ask	Start at the mid. Move $0.05 toward the ask if unfilled after 2 minutes.
Time in Force	Day or GTC	Use Day for entries. Use GTC only for profit-target close orders.

THE LIMIT ORDER RULE

Options traders who submit market orders consistently get poor fills. The bid-ask spread on options can be wide — sometimes $0.20 to $0.50 per contract. A market order guarantees you fill at the worst side of that spread. A limit order at the mid-price costs nothing extra in time (most liquid options fill at mid within 30–60 seconds) and saves you real money on every trade across hundreds of positions per year. Always use limit orders.

First Trade Review Checklist

Before submitting any options order, run this checklist. Every item must be confirmed.

	Pre-Trade Check	Status
1	Underlying has passed the Ten Indicators screen (Chapter 9)	☐ Confirmed
2	Market condition identified using the Six-Condition framework	☐ Confirmed
3	Strategy matches the identified condition	☐ Confirmed
4	No earnings announcement within the option DTE window	☐ Confirmed

	Pre-Trade Check	Status
5	Expiration selected in the 30-45 DTE window (income sellers)	☐ Confirmed
6	Strike price and delta confirmed per strategy rules	☐ Confirmed
7	Limit order set — NOT market order	☐ Confirmed
8	Position size within 2% account risk rule (Chapter 1)	☐ Confirmed
9	T-21 management date noted in trading journal	☐ Confirmed
10	Exit target and maximum loss defined before entry	☐ Confirmed
11	GTC exit order queued to submit immediately after fill	☐ Confirmed
12	Three-timeframe check: weekly / daily / intraday aligned	☐ Confirmed

THE FILL QUALITY RULE

Your theoretical edge is calculated at the midpoint. Every cent above mid on entry and below mid on exit is friction eroding your statistical advantage. On a $2.00 credit trade with a $0.20 spread, filling at the bid instead of mid costs you $0.10 — that is 5% of maximum profit before the position has breathed once. Patient limit orders are risk management.

6-CONDITION FRAMEWORK ▸ CONDITIONS 2, 4, 5, 6 — multi-leg structures for non-directional markets
Single-leg positions serve conditions 1 and 3. Multi-leg combinations serve all others. Spreads cap risk on the credit strategies of conditions 2 and 4. Complex structures serve the range conditions 5 and 6.

A single options contract — a lone call or put — is a powerful instrument. But the real versatility of options emerges when you combine them. Multi-leg positions let you define both your maximum risk and your maximum reward simultaneously, express nuanced market views that a single contract cannot capture, and generate income in sideways markets where directional trades go nowhere.

This chapter covers the architecture of combined positions: how they're built, how they're profiled, and the risk graph — the visual tool that shows you exactly what a combined position does across every possible stock price at expiration.

The A-B-C Building Framework — How All Combinations Are Assembled

Every multi-leg options position — no matter how complex it looks — is built from the same four building blocks introduced in Chapter 10: Buy Call, Buy Put, Sell Call, Sell Put. The A-B-C framework gives you a systematic way to construct any combination by stacking these actions in sequence:

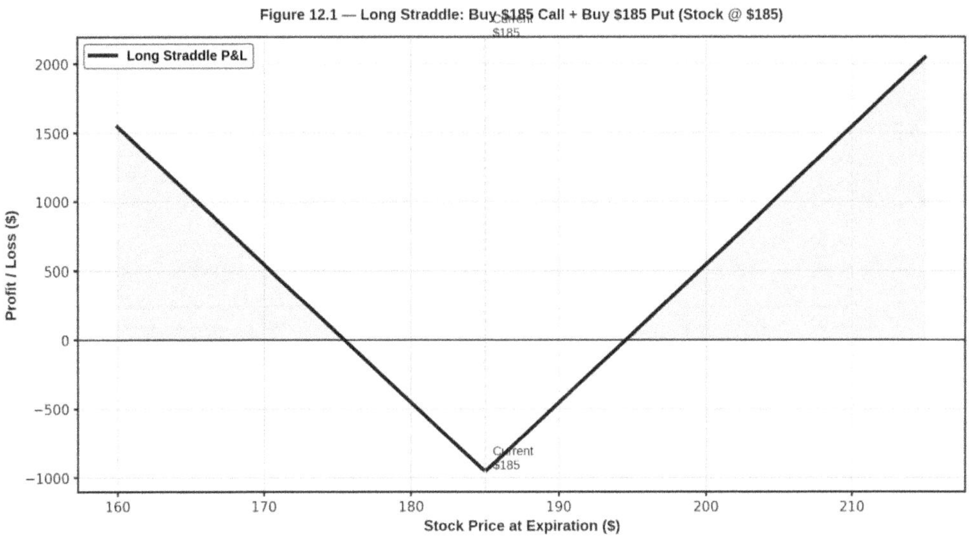

Figure 12.1 — Long Straddle. Profit on large move either direction.

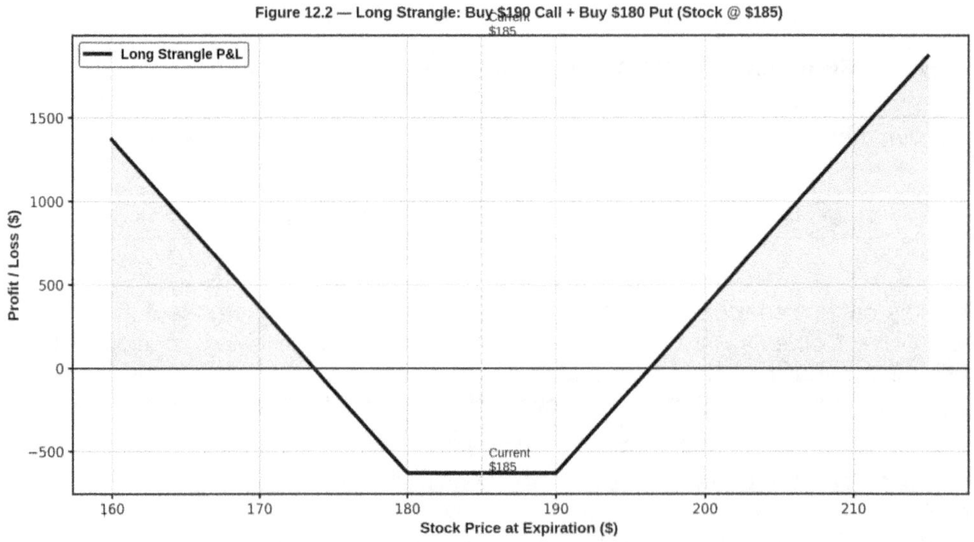

Figure 12.2 — Long Strangle. Lower cost, wider breakevens than straddle.

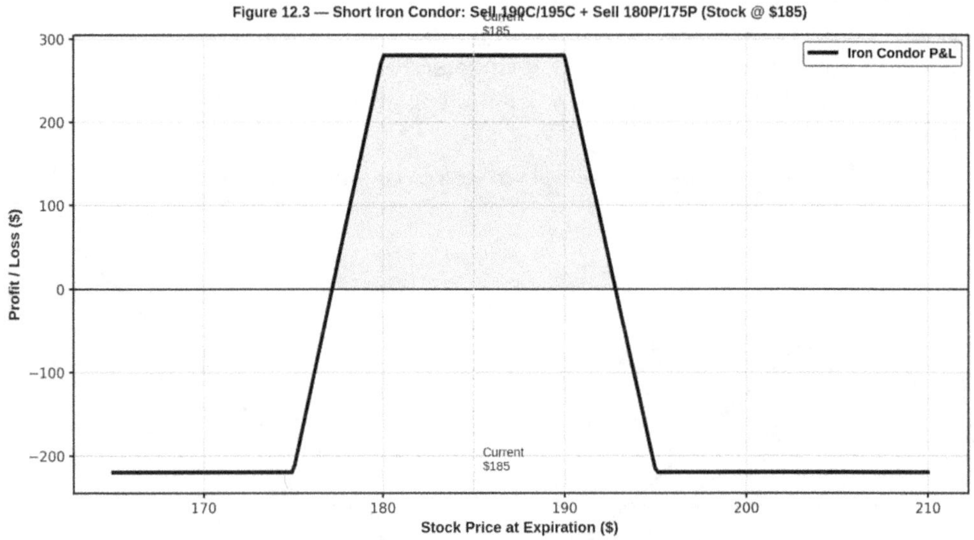

Figure 12.3 — Short Iron Condor. Profit if stock stays in the profit zone.

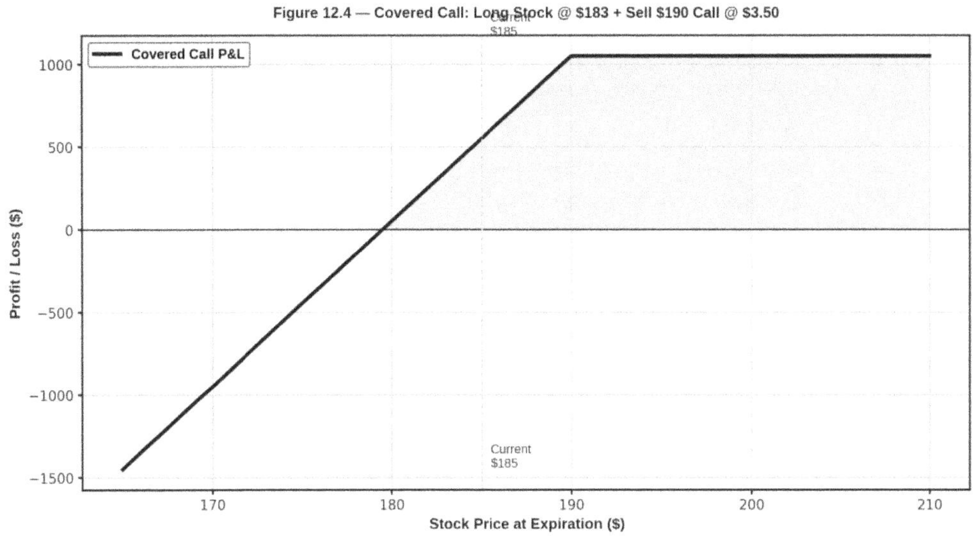

Figure 12.4 — Covered Call. Long stock plus short OTM call — income overlay.

Leg	Action	Purpose	Example
A	The PRIMARY leg — your directional or income core	Establishes the trade thesis. Long call = bullish. Short put = income. This is the reason for the trade.	Sell 1 OTM Put at $90 strike → income trade thesis, bullish-neutral
B	The SECONDARY leg — modifies cost or risk of A	Finances the primary leg, adds a hedge, or creates a spread. Reduces cost basis or caps risk.	Buy 1 OTM Put at $85 strike → caps maximum loss on A. Creates a bull put spread.
C	The TERTIARY leg — adds a third dimension	Adds directionality, generates additional income, or creates a more complex payoff structure.	Sell 1 OTM Call at $100 strike → adds covered call income to the position.

The A-B-C framework reveals something important: a two-leg position (A+B) is a spread. A three-leg position (A+B+C) is a combination or collar. A four-leg position (two spreads combined) is an iron condor or iron butterfly. Every strategy name you will ever encounter maps back to these building blocks. Once you understand how each leg functions, you can reverse-engineer any multi-leg position — and construct custom positions that exactly match your risk profile.

BUILD FROM THE INSIDE OUT

Always construct combinations starting with the primary leg (A). Ask: what is my core thesis? Then add B to define your risk boundary. Then, only if appropriate, add C to further engineer the payoff. Adding legs without a clear purpose for each one is how traders build positions they don't understand — and can't manage when the market moves against them.

The Two Dimensions of Combination Strategies

All combination strategies are built along two axes. Understanding these axes tells you what every multi-leg position is designed to do before you look at a single number.

- Directional Bias — Is the strategy designed to profit from a stock move up, down, or sideways? Every combination has a built-in directional assumption. Matching that assumption to your market thesis is the first design decision;
- Volatility Bias — Is the strategy designed to profit from expanding volatility (long vol) or contracting volatility (short vol)? Long options positions benefit from IV expansion. Short options positions benefit from IV contraction. Your view on IV is the second design decision.

Combination strategies are tools to offset directional bias, reduce cost basis, generate income, or hedge existing exposure. The risk manager uses them not to maximize the size of a bet — but to precisely engineer the risk profile they want.

Stock + Options Combinations

The simplest multi-leg positions pair a stock holding with one or more options contracts. These are foundational strategies that every options trader should master before moving to pure options combinations.

Strategy	Components	Market Outlook	Risk Profile
Covered Call	Long 100 shares + Short 1 OTM Call	Neutral to mildly bullish	Income from premium. Upside capped at strike. Downside is stock loss minus premium received.
Married Put	Long 100 shares + Long 1 OTM Put	Bullish with downside insurance	Unlimited upside. Downside floored at put strike minus premium paid. Best hedge for a stock position.
Protective Put	Existing stock position + Long Put	Bullish but hedged	Same as married put but applied to existing position. Locks in a sell price regardless of how far stock falls.
Collar	Long stock + Long OTM Put + Short OTM Call	Neutral — capital preservation	Put finances call (or vice versa). Upside capped, downside floored. Ideal for late-cycle holdings.

Pure Options Combinations

Pure options combinations use only contracts — no stock. These allow you to express precise directional and volatility views with fully defined risk on both sides, without owning the underlying shares. They are the core toolkit of the active options trader.

Strategy	Components	Market Outlook	Risk Profile
Long Straddle	Long ATM Call + Long ATM Put (same strike, same exp.)	Big move expected — direction unknown	Profit if stock moves significantly either way. Loss if stock stays flat — both premiums decay.
Long Strangle	Long OTM Call + Long OTM Put (different strikes)	Big move expected — cheaper than straddle	Same as straddle but requires larger move to profit. Lower cost, lower probability.
Short Straddle	Short ATM Call + Short ATM Put (same strike)	Stock stays flat — IV contraction expected	Collect both premiums. Unlimited risk in both directions. High IV environment only.
Short Strangle	Short OTM Call + Short OTM Put (different strikes)	Stock stays in a range — IV high	Wider profit zone than straddle. Still carries unlimited risk — use only with defined-risk wrapper.
Bull Call Spread	Long lower-strike Call + Short higher-strike Call	Moderately bullish	Defined risk (debit paid). Defined reward (spread width - debit). Best when IV is moderate.
Bear Put Spread	Long higher-strike Put + Short lower-strike Put	Moderately bearish	Defined risk (debit paid). Defined reward (spread width - debit). Best in elevated IV.
Iron Condor	Short OTM Call + Long further OTM Call + Short OTM Put + Long further OTM Put	Range-bound, low movement	Collect premium on both sides. Profit zone between short strikes. Risk defined by wing width.

The Six-Condition Position Combination Matrix

Every combined position in this chapter maps to at least one of the six conditions. Before building any multi-leg structure, confirm which condition you are in — then select only the combination built for that condition. Using a strangle in condition 1 (bullish, low IV) is not a risk-managed trade; it is a mismatch between structure and environment. The matrix below gives you the approved pairings.

#	Condition	IV	Approved Multi-Leg Structure	Why This Structure Fits This Condition
1	**Bullish ↑**	LOW	**Bull Call Spread (debit)**	Low IV makes debit spreads cheap. Pay a small debit for defined upside participation. The short call leg funds the long call — reduces cost without eliminating profit potential.
2	**Bullish ↑**	HIGH	**Bull Put Spread (credit)**	High IV inflates put premiums. Selling an OTM put spread collects elevated credit with the trend behind you. You profit from the stock staying above your short put strike AND from IV contracting after entry.
3	**Bearish ↓**	LOW	**Bear Put Spread (debit)**	Low IV makes put debit spreads affordable. The trend confirms the direction. The short put leg reduces cost. Maximum risk is the debit paid — fully defined from entry.

#	Condition	IV	Approved Multi-Leg Structure	Why This Structure Fits This Condition
4	**Bearish ↓**	**HIGH**	**Bear Call Spread (credit)**	High IV makes call premium rich. Sell an OTM call spread to collect credit on the bearish side. The trend is behind the position. You profit from the stock staying below your short call strike AND from IV contraction.
5	**Range ↔**	**LOW**	**Long Butterfly / Iron Condor (debit or net credit)**	Low IV environment with range-bound price. Butterfly concentrates payoff at one target price. Iron condor collects from both sides of the range. Both profit from the stock NOT moving — the opposite of directional debit trades.
6	**Range ↔**	**HIGH**	**Calendar Spread / Diagonal Spread**	High IV on the near-term leg, normal IV on the far-term leg. Sell the expensive near-term IV. Buy the relatively cheaper far-term IV. Profit from the IV differential collapsing as the near-term option decays faster.

Notice the symmetry: every condition has exactly one primary multi-leg structure. This is not arbitrary — it is the result of aligning structure to the two market forces driving that condition. Conditions 1 and 3 are debit structures because IV is low and you need the move to earn. Conditions 2 and 4 are credit structures because IV is high and the premium writer has the statistical edge. Conditions 5 and 6 are range structures because no directional move is expected.

THE COMBINATION RULE

Never combine options legs into a structure without first identifying which condition you are in. A straddle in condition 2 (bullish, high IV) is not a hedge — it is an expensive lottery ticket on the short leg's IV. A bull call spread in condition 4 (bearish, high IV) is a debit trade fighting the trend. Match the structure to the condition. Every time.

The Buy-Call Combination: A Worked Example

Here is a complete worked example of the Buy Call Combination strategy — a three-leg structure that combines a long call, a short call, and a long put. This is one of the foundational institutional combinations, sometimes called an A-B-C trade.

- A — Buy to Open 1 Call XYZ at the current price (long call, directional participation);
- B — Sell to Open 1 Call XYZ at a higher strike (short call, caps upside, collects premium to offset cost);
- C — Buy to Open 1 Put XYZ at or below current price (long put, insurance leg — protects against adverse move);

The result: if the stock rises moderately, the long call appreciates while the short call limits but defines the upside. The long put acts as insurance against a sharp drop. If the market reacts unexpectedly, the put contract makes money going down, partially offsetting losses on the call side. This is not a speculation — it is a structured position with insurance built in from the start.

Example using XYZ at $80:

- Buy 5 XYZ Calls, X-date exp, $60 Strike @ $5 Premium: 5 contracts × $500 = $2,500 paid out;

- Sell 5 XYZ Calls, X-date exp, $75 Strike @ $5 Premium: $5 contracts × $500 = $2,500 collected (when VIX > 30); and
- Buy 1 XYZ Put, X-date exp, $60 Strike @ $5 Premium: 1 contract × $500 = $500 paid out — the insurance leg.

Net position: $2,500 paid − $2,500 collected + $500 insurance = $500 net cost for the full structure. Your upside is the spread between $60 and $75 strikes across 5 contracts, with the put protecting your downside. This is how professional traders build cost-efficient, hedged positions — not by buying naked calls and hoping.

Multi-Leg P&L Profiles: Visualizing Combined Positions

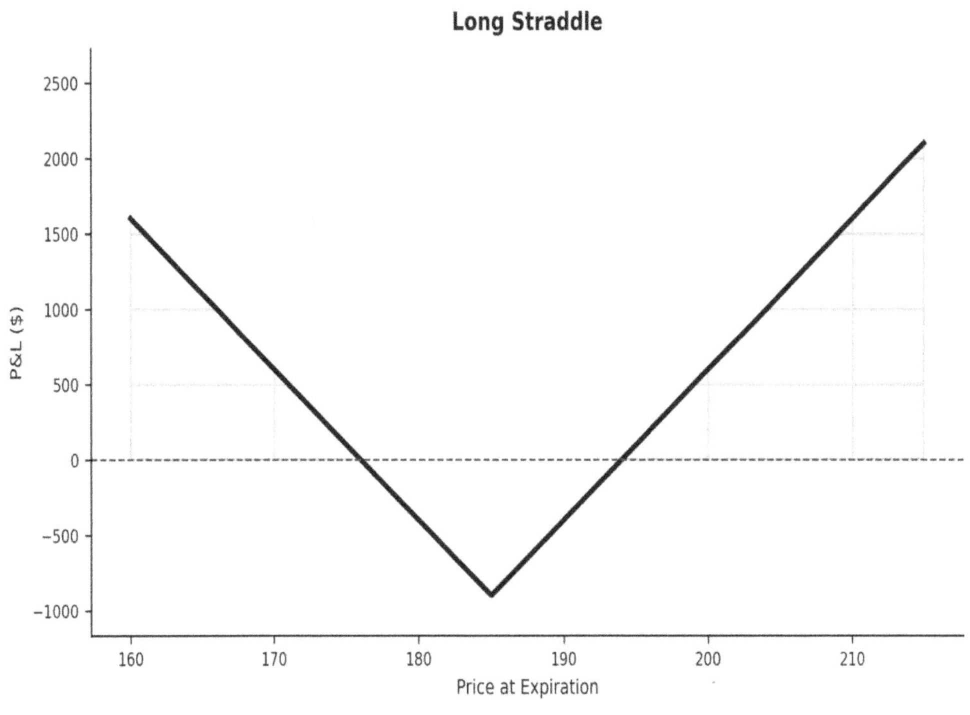

Figure 12.1 — Combined Positions Overview — How multi-leg positions create different risk and reward profiles than single-leg trades.

Combined Positions Overview — How multi-leg positions create different risk/reward profiles.

When you combine options positions, the resulting P&L profile is the mathematical sum of each leg's individual profile. Understanding these combined shapes allows you to instantly recognize the risk and reward architecture of any multi-leg position before you open it — without needing to see the exact numbers.

Combination	Shape of P&L	Max Profit	Max Loss
Long Call + Long Put (Straddle)	V-shape (profits in both directions from center)	Unlimited upside, high downside profit	Total premium paid — occurs if stock stays exactly at strike at expiry
Bull Call Spread (Long lower call + Short higher call)	Capped ramp up	Spread width minus debit paid	Debit paid — occurs if stock finishes below lower strike
Bear Put Spread (Long higher put + Short lower put)	Capped ramp down	Spread width minus debit paid	Debit paid — occurs if stock finishes above higher strike
Bull Put Spread (Short higher put + Long lower put)	Capped income plateau	Credit received — collected if stock stays above short strike	Spread width minus credit — if stock drops below long strike
Iron Condor (Bull put + Bear call spread)	Plateau in center, losses on both wings	Net credit received — if stock stays between short strikes	Wider wing width minus credit — if stock breaches either short strike significantly
Long Call Butterfly (Buy 1 low call, sell 2 mid calls, buy 1 high call)	Tent shape, peaks at middle strike	Spread width minus debit, realized at middle strike at expiry	Debit paid — if stock finishes at either extreme strike

Combination Risk Tables: Real Numbers for Common Structures

The P&L shape tells you the architecture. The numbers tell you the trade. Here are three complete combination risk tables using real stock prices and current market premiums, showing exactly what each multi-leg position costs, earns, and risks.

IRON CONDOR — SPY $520 (Condition 5: Range-bound, Low IV)

Sell $530 Call / Buy $535 Call + Sell $510 Put / Buy $505 Put | DTE: 30 | IVR: 22.

Credit received: $1.85 ($185/spread). Max profit: $185 if SPY stays between $510–$530 at expiry.

Max loss: $315 ($500 spread width − $185 credit) per side if SPY closes beyond $505 or $535.

Probability of max profit (stock stays in range): ~62%. Target: close at 50% credit ($92.50) after ~14–16 days.

Six-condition verification: Range-bound (chart oscillating $510–$530) + Low IV (IVR=22) = Condition 5. Iron Condor approved.

THE COMBINATION POSITION RULE

Always know the maximum loss before you know the maximum profit. The architecture of a multi-leg position is designed to cap your loss — but only if all legs are placed and managed correctly. A misplaced leg, an unfilled second leg, or an improperly sized condor can expose you to losses far beyond the designed maximum. Use the broker's spread order ticket, verify all legs filled, and know your exact P&L boundaries before the position goes live.

Multi-Leg Thinking: How Professionals Build Positions

Retail traders think in single options. Professionals think in structures. Every multi-leg position is built from four blocks (long/short call, long/short put). Here are the six core structures:

Structure	Blocks	Max Profit	Max Loss	View
Bull Put Spread	Short put + Long put (lower)	Credit	Width - credit	Bullish/neutral
Bear Call Spread	Short call + Long call (higher)	Credit	Width - credit	Bearish/neutral
Iron Condor	Bull put + Bear call	Total credit	Wider side - credit	Range-bound
Straddle	Long ATM call + Long ATM put	Unlimited	Premium paid	Big move, direction unknown
Strangle	Long OTM call + Long OTM put	Unlimited	Premium paid	Big move, cheaper entry
Collar	Stock + Long put + Short call	Call strike - stock	Stock - put strike	Protect existing shares

The first three (bull put, bear call, iron condor) are credit strategies — you get paid at entry. The last three are debit or mixed. For income trading, you primarily use the first three.

STRUCTURE SELECTION

Before building any multi-leg position, answer: (1) Bull, bear, or neutral? (2) Am I willing to pay or do I want to get paid? Your answers map directly to the six structures above.

> 6-CONDITION FRAMEWORK ▸ **CONDITIONS 2 (bull put spread), 4 (bear call spread), 5 & 6 (iron condor, calendar)**
> Advanced structures are not complexity for its own sake — each one is the precision tool for a specific condition. Master the condition first. Then master the structure built for it.

Spreads are the risk manager's primary trading vehicle. They replace unlimited-risk naked positions with defined-risk structures that let you express precise market views — bullish, bearish, or neutral — while capping your maximum loss at a known amount from the moment you enter. If there is one chapter in this book that transforms how you approach every trade, this is it.

A spread is created by combining a long option and a short option of the same type (both calls or both puts) on the same underlying, with different strikes, different expirations, or both. The short leg reduces — or eliminates — the cost of the long leg. In exchange, it caps the maximum profit. That trade-off is the essence of professional risk management.

Vertical Spreads: Defined Risk, Defined Reward

Vertical spreads use the same expiration but different strike prices. They are the most commonly used spread structure because they are simple, liquid, and create a clean defined-risk P&L profile. Every options trader should be able to build and manage vertical spreads instinctively.

Figure 13.1 — Vertical Spread: Max Loss and Max Profit are Both Defined

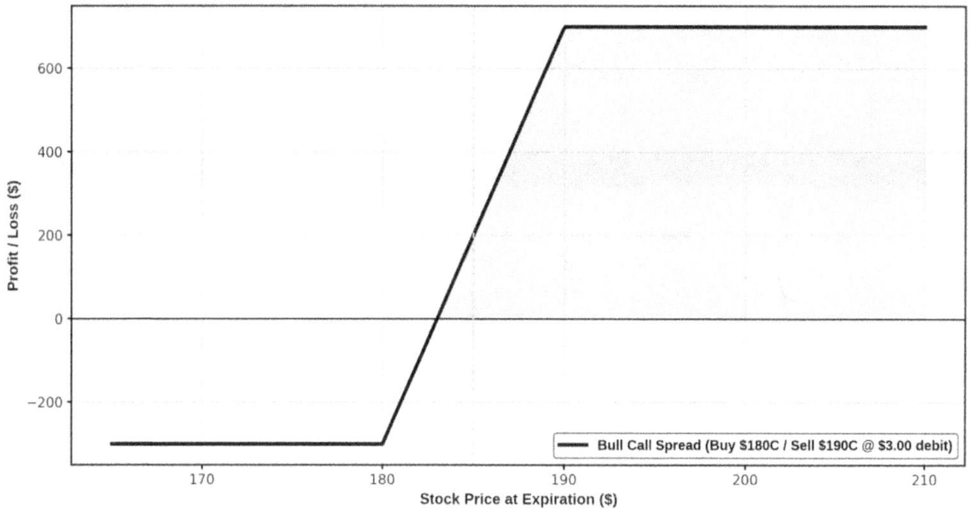

Figure 13.1 — Vertical Spread Risk Graph. Maximum loss and maximum gain both capped.

→ See Figure 11.7 — Iron Condor Risk Graph (Chapter 11 — Walking You Through Your First Option Trade)

Spread	Construction	Outlook	Max Risk	Max Reward
Bull Call Spread	Buy lower-strike call + Sell higher-strike call (same exp)	Bullish	Net debit paid	Spread width − net debit
Bear Put Spread	Buy higher-strike put + Sell lower-strike put (same exp)	Bearish	Net debit paid	Spread width − net debit
Bull Put Spread	Sell higher-strike put + Buy lower-strike put (same exp)	Bullish	Spread width − credit received	Net credit received
Bear Call Spread	Sell lower-strike call + Buy higher-strike call (same exp)	Bearish	Spread width − credit received	Net credit received

Debit spreads (bull call, bear put) are paid for upfront — you pay a net debit and your maximum risk is that debit. Credit spreads (bull put, bear call) collect premium upfront — you receive a net credit and your maximum risk is the spread width minus what you collected. Both are fully defined at entry. This is what makes them the risk manager's preferred vehicle.

DEBIT VS. CREDIT SPREAD SELECTION

Use debit spreads when IV is low — you're paying for the spread, so cheap premiums work in your favor. Use credit spreads when IV is high — you're collecting premium, so elevated IV means more income. Match the spread type to the IV environment, not just the directional thesis.

Spread Trade Examples — Real Strikes, Real Numbers

Figure 13.1 — Spread Examples: Debit vs. Credit Spreads Side-by-Side

Component	Bull Call Spread (Debit)	Bull Put Spread (Credit)
Direction	Bullish	Bullish
IV Preference	Low IV (buy cheap)	High IV (sell expensive)
Entry	Net debit paid	Net credit received
Max Profit	Spread width - debit	Credit received
Max Loss	Debit paid	Spread width - credit
Breakeven	Lower strike + debit	Short strike - credit
Best Condition	Condition 1	Condition 2

Figure 13.1 — Spread Examples — Side-by-side comparison of debit and credit spread structures across bullish, bearish, and neutral conditions.

The structures shown in the figures above become intuitive when you work through real examples. Here are worked trades for each spread type with concrete entry prices:

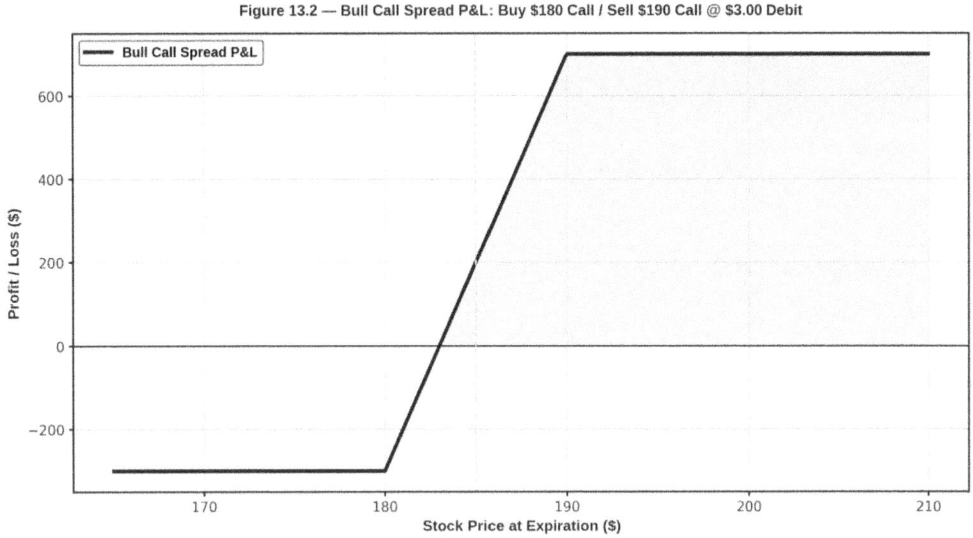

Figure 13.2 — Bull Call Spread P&L. Buy lower strike, sell higher strike — defined risk bullish.

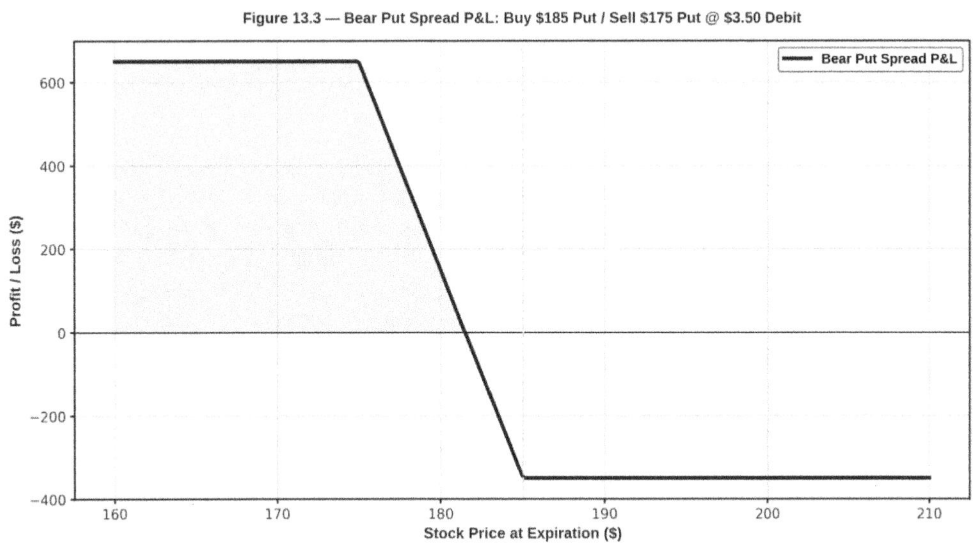

Figure 13.3 — Bear Put Spread P&L. Buy higher strike, sell lower strike — defined risk bearish.

Spread Type	Entry (Buy + Sell)	Net Debit / Credit	Outlook
Call Credit Spread (Bearish)	Sell 1 Feb $55 Call @ $3.25 Buy 1 Feb $60 Call @ $0.85	Net Credit: $2.40 ($240 per contract)	Bearish — keep credit if stock stays below $55
Put Credit Spread (Bullish)	Sell 1 Feb $35 Put @ $4.60 Buy 1 Feb $25 Put @ $1.90	Net Credit: $2.70 ($270 per contract)	Bullish — keep credit if stock stays above $35
Call Calendar	Sell 1 Jan $135 Call Buy 1 Mar $135 Call	Net Debit (Mar costs more)	Neutral near-term — stock stays

Spread Type	Entry (Buy + Sell)	Net Debit / Credit	Outlook
			near $135 through Jan exp
Put Calendar	Sell 1 Jan $150 Put Buy 1 Mar $150 Put	Net Debit (Mar costs more)	Neutral near-term — stock stays near $150 through Jan exp
Call Diagonal	Sell 1 Jan $130 Call Buy 1 Mar $150 Call	Net Debit (different strikes)	Mildly bullish — capture upside drift with Theta on short leg
Put Diagonal	Sell 1 Jan $155 Put Buy 1 Mar $155 Put	Net Debit (different exp)	Mildly bearish — use when expecting gradual decline

Notice that credit spreads immediately show you the direction — the spread that receives a net credit is the one where your directional thesis is that the stock stays away from the sold strike. The spread that costs a debit is where you need movement. When in doubt: credit spreads = income from staying put. Debit spreads = income from moving.

A calendar spread (also called a time spread or horizontal spread) uses the same strike price but different expiration dates. You sell the near-term option and buy the longer-term option. The trade profits from the differential in time decay — the short-term option decays faster than the long-term option, creating a net gain as time passes.

- Construction: Sell near-month option (same strike as long leg) + Buy far-month option — both calls OR both puts;
- Market outlook: Neutral to mildly directional. The stock should stay near the strike through the near-month expiration;
- Max risk: Limited to the net debit paid for the spread. The long leg always costs more than the short leg receives;
- Max reward: Occurs when the stock is exactly at the strike on the near-month expiration date — both legs have maximum relative value differential; and
- Roll mechanic: When the short leg expires, sell the next month's option at the same strike. This generates additional income and extends the trade.

Calendar spreads are particularly effective when IV is low at entry — you want IV to expand during the life of the trade, which increases the value of your long option faster than the short. If IV is already elevated at entry, the long leg is expensive and the trade is less attractive.

Diagonal Spreads: The Hybrid Structure

A diagonal spread combines the features of both vertical and calendar spreads — different strikes AND different expirations. It is the most flexible spread structure and allows the trader to fine-tune both the directional and time dimensions of a position simultaneously.

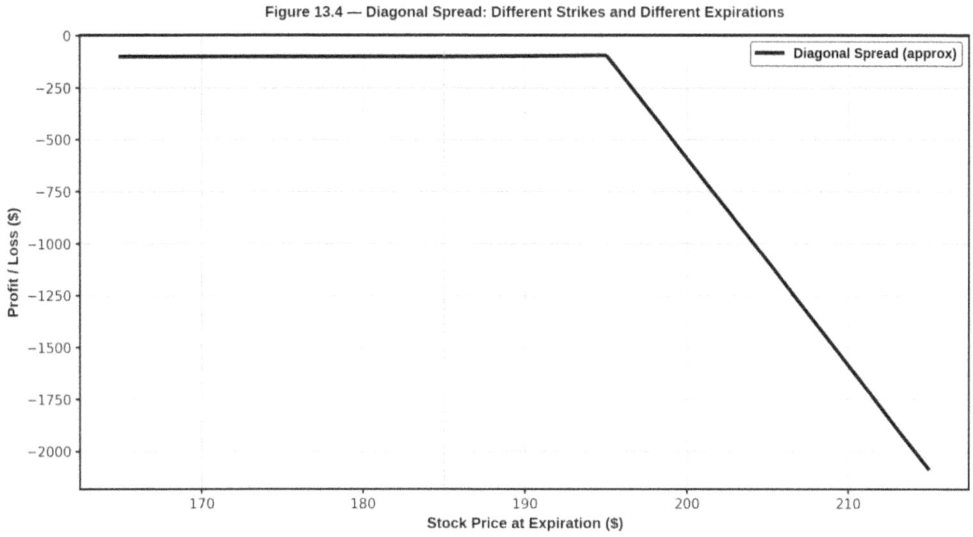

Figure 13.4 — Diagonal Spread Structure. Different strikes and different expirations in one position.

- Construction: Buy a longer-dated option at one strike + Sell a shorter-dated option at a different (typically further OTM) strike;
- The long leg is usually 60–90 DTE; the short leg is usually 30 DTE or less;
- As the short leg expires, roll it to the next month — collecting additional premium on each cycle;
- Best environment: Confirmed directional trend with moderate, steady movement — not explosive volatile moves; and
- Sector rotation application: Diagonal spreads on incoming sector ETF leaders capture slow rotational drift while Theta works in your favor on the short leg.

The beauty of the diagonal is that you can run it as a repeating income machine — buy one long-dated call on a sector ETF in a confirmed uptrend, then sell monthly calls against it at successively higher strikes as the ETF grinds higher. Each month's short call reduces your cost basis further. This is the strategy described in Chapter 7's Sector Rotation Playbook as Strategy 5.

Writes: Collecting Premium as the Primary Strategy

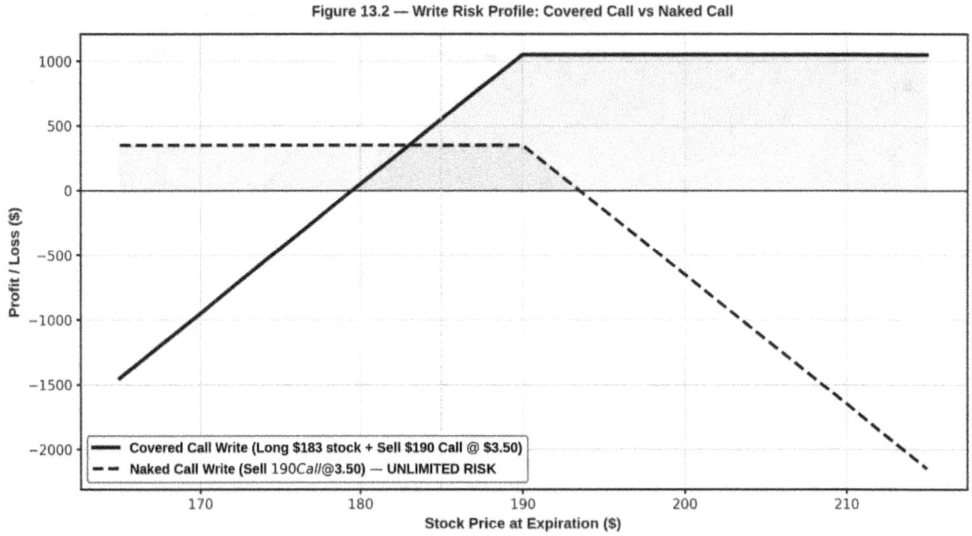

Figure 13.2 — Write Risk Profile — The risk and reward curve for a covered call write at various expiration prices.

A write is simply the act of selling an option without a corresponding offsetting position — or as part of a stock-backed position. Writes are the foundation of premium income strategies and the core of what Chapter 15 covers in detail. Here we define the basic structures:

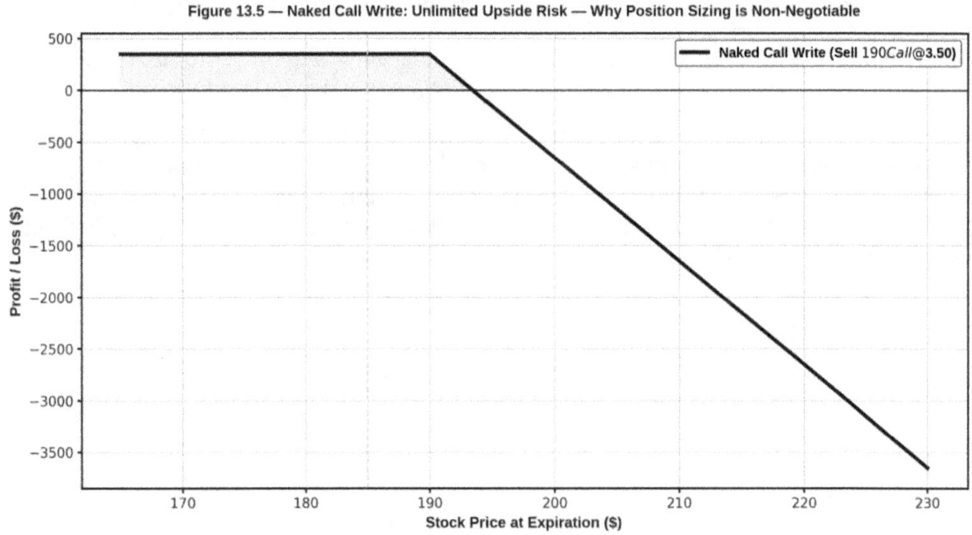

Figure 13.5 — Naked Call Write. Unlimited upside risk — why position sizing is non-negotiable.

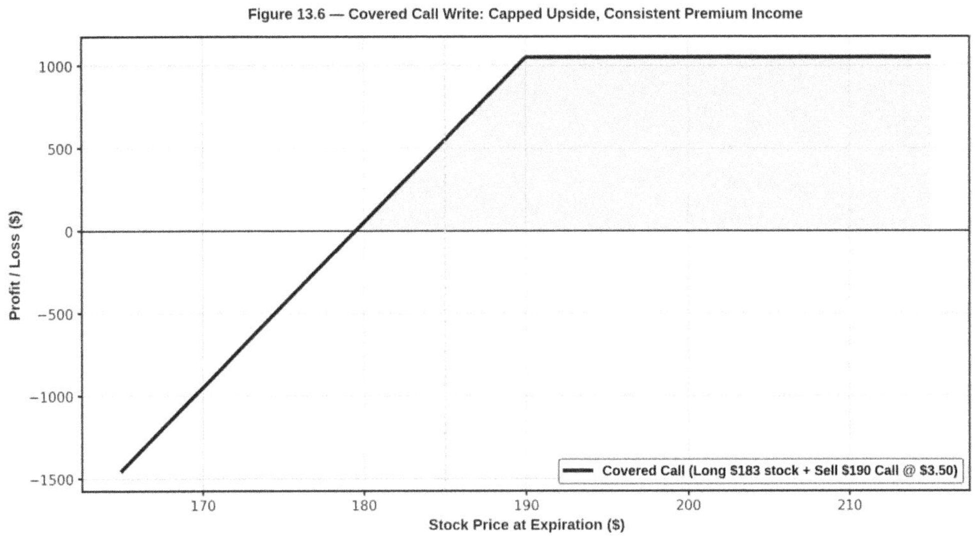

Figure 13.6 — Covered Call Write. Capped upside but consistent premium income.

- Covered Call Write: Sell a call against 100 shares you already own. The stock is your collateral. Generates income. Caps upside at the strike. Best in neutral-to-mildly bullish environments;
- Cash-Secured Put Write: Sell a put with enough cash in your account to buy 100 shares at the strike if assigned. Generates income. You want the stock to stay above the strike. Best on quality names in high-IV environments; and
- Naked Call Write (Tier 3 only): Sell a call without stock collateral. Generates the highest premium. Carries unlimited upside risk. Only for experienced traders with defined position management plans.

THE WRITE RULE

Any time you sell a naked option — a write without a defined-risk hedge — you are accepting unlimited or very large risk in exchange for a fixed premium. The premium received is certain. The risk you are accepting is not. Always know which side of that trade your account can afford to be on.

Spreading Time with Calendars: The Full Framework

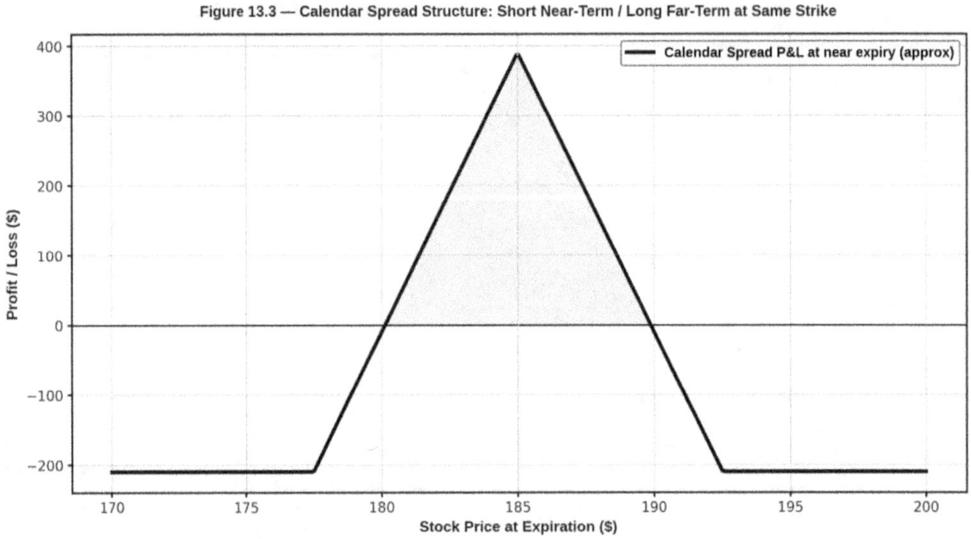

Figure 13.3 — Calendar Spread Structure — Long and short legs at different expirations on the same strike. Near-term decay funds the long leg.

Calendar Spread Structure — Long and short legs at different expirations on the same strike.

Calendar and diagonal spreads have a critical warning that most books bury in fine print: a Calendar or Diagonal Spread that uses a long option for the later month and a short option for the closer month is equivalent to taking a naked short position on the front-month leg alone — and is not consistent with good risk management if the spread is not properly structured.

Best practice: calendar spreads and diagonal spreads that use a long option for the later month leg of the spread are limited-risk positions. The long option is always your protection. You should never allow the short leg to expire while holding the long leg without a roll plan.

- Call calendar and diagonal spreads have unlimited reward potential after the short option expires — but require active management;
- Put calendar and diagonal spreads have limited but high reward potential after expiration of the short option;
- The beauty of spreads: you can, based on your risk profile, level of expiration, and trade goals, mix and match the components of each leg to suit your needs;

Mix and Match: Building Your Spread to the Market

You can create vertical spreads for a debit or a credit. To help keep the outcomes and risk/reward result clear: consider the outlook for the more-expensive option. A Short Call in a bearish outlook keeps a credit into your account. The Short Call option in a Bear Spread is more expensive — so this is a credit spread. The practical implication:

- Bullish thesis + high IV → Bull Put Spread (credit) — collect premium, stock stays above short strike;
- Bullish thesis + low IV → Bull Call Spread (debit) — pay a small debit, participate in upside movement;
- Bearish thesis + high IV → Bear Call Spread (credit) — collect premium, stock stays below short strike;

- Bearish thesis + low IV → Bear Put Spread (debit) — pay a small debit, participate in downside movement;
- Neutral thesis + high IV → Iron Condor or Short Strangle with defined-risk wings — collect premium from both sides; and
- Neutral thesis + low IV → Calendar Spread — sell near-term time decay, hold longer-dated position.

THE SPREAD SELECTOR

Match your spread type to TWO inputs: (1) your directional thesis (bullish / bearish / neutral) and (2) the current IV environment (high / low). These two inputs together determine which spread structure gives you the best edge. Never select a spread based on direction alone.

Full Trade Walk-Through: Bull Put Spread (Condition 2)

Figure 13.4 — Bull Put Spread Walkthrough: Entry, Management, and Exit

Step	Action	Rule
1 — Screen	Confirm Condition 2: Bullish + High IV	IVR > 50, stock above 50-day EMA
2 — Select	Sell OTM put, buy lower put	Short strike 0.25-0.30 delta, 10pt spread
3 — Entry	Sell $185P / Buy $175P at $3.20 credit	Net credit = $320 per contract
4 — Manage	T-21: evaluate roll or close	If untested, close at 50% profit = $160
5 — Exit	Close spread by buying it back	Never hold to expiration on credit spreads

Figure 13.4 — Bull Put Spread Walkthrough — Entry, management, and exit sequence for a Condition 2 credit spread.

Theory locks in when you see the numbers. Here is a complete bull put spread built in condition 2 — bullish trend, high IV. Every number flows from the six-condition read. This is not a hypothetical exercise: it is the exact process you run in your brokerage platform each time condition 2 is confirmed.

Market Condition	Primary Strategy	Alternative	Advanced
Bullish + Low IV	Long Call	Bull Call Spread	Call Diagonal
Bullish + High IV	CSP	Bull Put Spread	Covered Call
Bearish + Low IV	Long Put	Bear Put Spread	Put Diagonal
Bearish + High IV	Bear Call Spread	Bear Put Spread	Short Calls
Neutral + High IV	Iron Condor	Short Strangle	Iron Butterfly
Neutral + Low IV	Calendar Spread	Long Straddle	Butterfly

Figure 13.7 — Spread Selector.

Parameter	Value	Notes
Underlying	XYZ @ $190	Condition 2: Bullish, High IV.
Short Put (Sell)	$185 Put	OTM — 7 points below stock.
Long Put (Buy)	$175 Put	Protection wing — 10pt spread.
Net Credit	$3.20 per contract	32% of spread width collected.
Max Profit	+$320 per contract	If stock stays above $185.
Max Loss	-$680 per contract	If stock falls below $175.
Breakeven	$181.80	Short strike − Net credit.
DTE	35 days	30–45 DTE entry target.
Probability of Profit	~68%	Based on delta of short put.

Figure 13.8 — Bull Put Spread Trade Parameters. Complete trade setup with all key metrics.

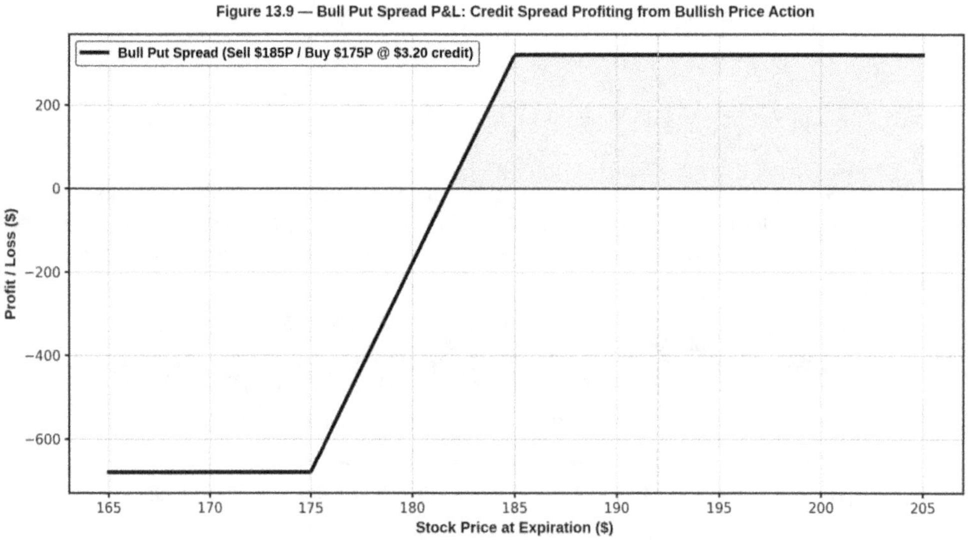

Figure 13.9 — Bull Put Spread P&L. Credit spread profiting from stock staying above short strike.

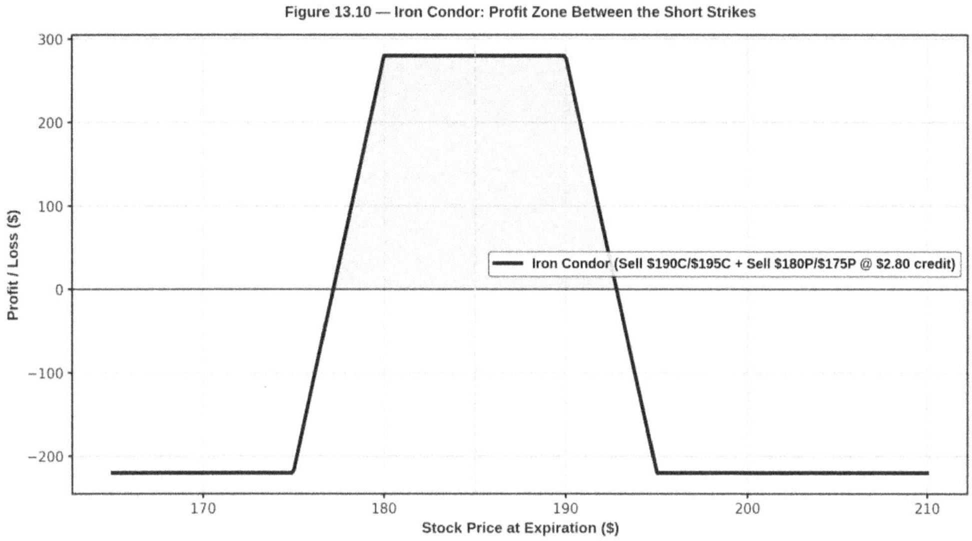

Figure 13.10 — Iron Condor Deep Dive.

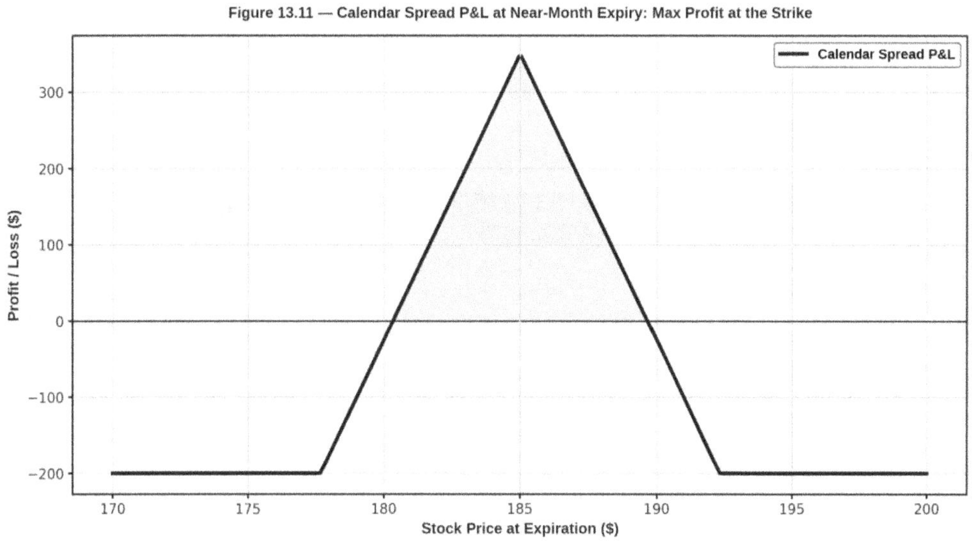

Figure 13.11 — Calendar Spread P&L at Near-Month Expiry. Maximum profit near ATM.

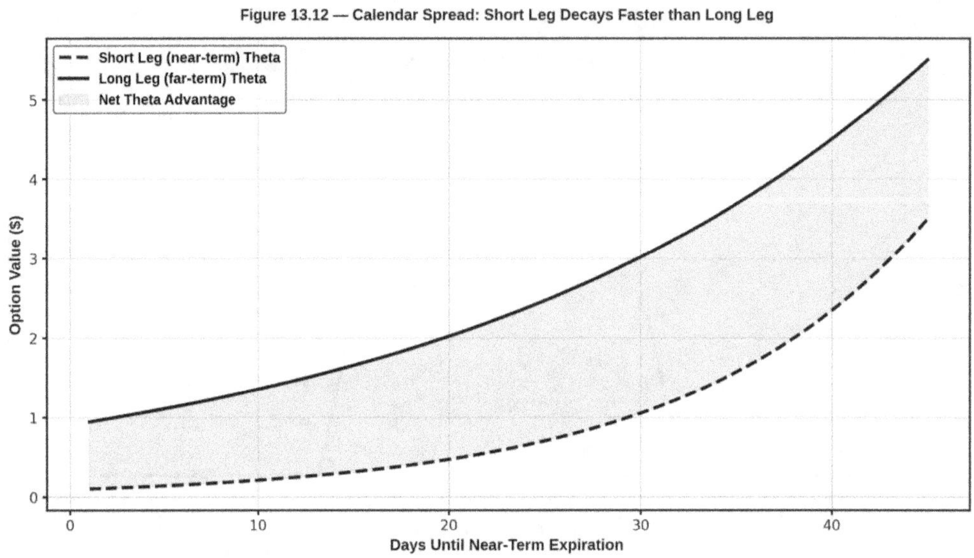

Figure 13.12 — Calendar Spread: Theta Decay. Short leg decays faster — the source of the edge.

Underlying: SPY (S&P 500 ETF) currently trading at $520. The six-condition read this morning: SPY is above its 50MA and 200MA, making higher highs over the past 3 weeks. VIX is at 22.4 and IVR is at 68. Condition 2 confirmed: Bullish + High IV. Approved strategy: Bull Put Spread.

Step	Action	Numbers
1. Confirm the condition	VIX + chart direction check	VIX: 22.4. IVR: 68 (HIGH). SPY above 50MA + 200MA, higher highs. → Condition 2. ✓
2. Select strike location	OTM put strike 5–8% below current price, 30–45 DTE	SPY at $520. Short put at $490 (~5.8% OTM). 35 DTE (next monthly expiry). Delta of short put: 0.22.
3. Build the spread	Sell the $490 put. Buy the $480 put (protection leg)	Sell SPY $490 put → receive $2.85 credit. Buy SPY $480 put → pay $1.60 debit. Net credit: $1.25 per share ($125 per contract).
4. Calculate risk/reward	Max risk = spread width − credit. Max reward = credit collected.	Max reward: $125 (if SPY stays above $490 at expiry). Max risk: ($10 spread − $1.25 credit) × 100 = $875 per contract. Risk/reward ratio: 1 : 0.14 (typical for OTM spreads — offset by high probability).
5. Probability check	Delta of short strike ≈ probability of being tested	Delta 0.22 → ~22% chance stock closes below $490 at expiry. Probability of full profit: ~78%. This is the statistical edge of selling OTM spreads in high-IV environments.
6. Position sizing	2% max account risk rule	Account: $50,000. 2% = $1,000 max risk. Max risk per contract: $875. → 1 contract is within limits. ($875 < $1,000).
7. Set profit target and stop	50% of credit = close early. 200% of credit = stop loss.	Profit target: close when spread value drops to $0.62 (collected $0.63 in gains = 50% of $1.25). Stop loss: close if spread widens to $3.75 (paid $2.50 more than credit = 200% loss).

Step	Action	Numbers
8. Enter the order	Limit order for the spread as a single package	Enter as a credit spread limit order at $1.25 net credit. Do NOT leg into spreads separately. Single-ticket execution avoids leg risk.
9. T-21 check (if held)	At 21 DTE: evaluate roll or close	If position still open at T-21 and showing profit: close for 50%+ gain or roll to next month for additional credit. If at a loss and price near strike: evaluate roll down for defensive credit collection.
10. Log the trade	Journal entry before order submission	Condition: 2. Underlying: SPY. Strategy: Bull Put Spread. Short strike: $490. Long strike: $480. DTE: 35. Credit: $1.25. Max risk: $875. Thesis: SPY uptrend, VIX elevated, IVR 68. Profit target: $0.62 remaining value. Stop: $3.75 spread value.

SPREAD RESULT

SPY closed at $508 on expiration day — well above the $490 short put. The spread expired worthless. Full $125 credit collected. Account risk: 0. The ten-step process ran in under 5 minutes. That is condition 2 executed with discipline.

Iron Condor: The Condition 5 & 6 Powerhouse

The iron condor is the go-to structure for conditions 5 and 6 — when the market is range-bound. It is simply two vertical credit spreads placed simultaneously: a bull put spread below the market and a bear call spread above it. You collect premium from both sides. You profit if the stock stays inside your two short strikes through expiration.

The iron condor earns maximum profit when the stock stays between the two short strikes at expiration. The structure has four legs, but it is entered as a single order and managed as a single position. Your maximum loss is capped on both sides by the wings — the long options you buy to protect each short.

Component	Action	Strike	Purpose
Put Wing — Long	Buy put	$475	Protection if stock breaks sharply lower. Caps max loss on downside.
Put Wing — Short	Sell put	$490	Generates credit. Defines lower boundary of profit zone.
Call Wing — Short	Sell call	$550	Generates credit. Defines upper boundary of profit zone.
Call Wing — Long	Buy call	$565	Protection if stock breaks sharply higher. Caps max loss on upside.
Net Result	Collect net credit from all four legs. Profit if SPY stays between $490 and $550. Max profit = total net credit. Max loss = spread width on either side minus total credit. Profit zone: $60 wide ($550 − $490).		

Iron condor management is about the wings. If one side of the condor is tested — meaning the stock moves toward one of your short strikes — the threatened wing must be managed first. Common adjustments: close the threatened wing and replace it at a new strike (roll the wing); close the entire condor for a partial loss; or add a directional hedge to offset the tested side.

The width of the wings (distance between your short and long strikes) determines your max risk per side. Wider wings = more credit collected + more max risk. Narrower wings = less credit + less max risk. The professional approach: keep wings equal width on both sides and adjust wing width based on your account risk tolerance, not on the premium available.

IRON CONDOR RULE

Never adjust a condor by 'taking off the winning side.' If your put spread is fully profited because the stock rose, do not close the puts to release margin — the puts are your safety net if the stock reverses. Close the entire condor together, or roll the tested call side. Managing the two sides independently creates unbalanced risk.

The Iron Condor Deep Dive: Building and Managing the Six-Condition Range Trade

The iron condor is the signature structure for condition 5 (range-bound, low IV) and one of the highest-probability income strategies in the options toolkit. It earns from time decay when a stock stays within a defined range. Understanding its construction, adjustment triggers, and exit rules is essential for any trader who operates in range-bound markets.

Step	Action	Detail
1	Confirm Condition 5	VIX < 20 (IVR < 30). Chart oscillating in defined range. Bollinger Bands compressing. BPI flat. No binary events within DTE window.
2	Select underlying	Large or mega cap only. OI > 1,000 at target strikes. Liquid chain confirmed. ETFs (SPY, QQQ, IWM) are ideal — index-level diversification removes individual stock event risk.
3	Select expiration	30–45 DTE. Long enough for theta to work, short enough that range assumptions remain valid. Avoid condors with < 21 DTE — gamma risk makes the position difficult to manage.
4	Select short strikes	Sell the call at the strike nearest to the top of the recent range, 1 standard deviation above current price. Sell the put at the strike nearest the bottom of the range, 1 standard deviation below. Target: 15–20 delta on each short strike.
5	Select long strikes	Buy the call 5 points above the short call. Buy the put 5 points below the short put. This defines your maximum loss and margin requirement. Wider wings = more credit but more margin. Narrower wings = less credit but lower capital at risk.
6	Verify credit received	Minimum acceptable credit: 25% of the wing width. A 5-point condor should collect at least $1.25 in credit ($125/spread). Below this, the risk/reward does not justify the trade.

Step	Action	Detail
7	Set profit target	Close the entire condor at 50% of credit received — do not wait for expiration. On a $1.85 credit condor, close when value drops to $0.92. This defensive close secures profit before gamma risk accelerates in the final weeks. This typically occurs in 14–20 days on a well-constructed condor.
8	Set adjustment triggers	If either short strike is tested (stock approaches within $2 of the short call or put): roll that side outward to re-center the range, OR close the tested side and take the partial loss. Never ignore a tested strike and hope it resolves.

The Broken Wing Butterfly: Asymmetric Risk for Directional Bias

Figure 13.5 — Broken Wing Butterfly: Asymmetric Structure with No Downside Risk

Component	Standard Butterfly	Broken Wing Butterfly
Structure	Buy 1 lower / Sell 2 middle / Buy 1 upper (equal width)	Buy 1 lower / Sell 2 middle / Buy 1 wider upper
Max Profit	At middle strike	At middle strike (same)
Downside Risk	Limited loss	Zero or credit received
Upside Risk	Limited loss	Slightly higher
Best Use	Very low IV, pinning	High conviction + income

Figure 13.5 — Broken Wing Butterfly — Asymmetric butterfly structure that collects a net credit with defined risk on one side only.

The standard butterfly is symmetric — equal wing widths on both sides of the body strike. The broken wing butterfly (BWB) deliberately widens one wing, skewing the structure to reflect a slight directional bias while maintaining the range-bound income architecture. It is a hybrid between a butterfly and a directional credit spread.

Figure 13.14 — Standard Butterfly: Symmetric Profit Tent Centered at Middle Strike

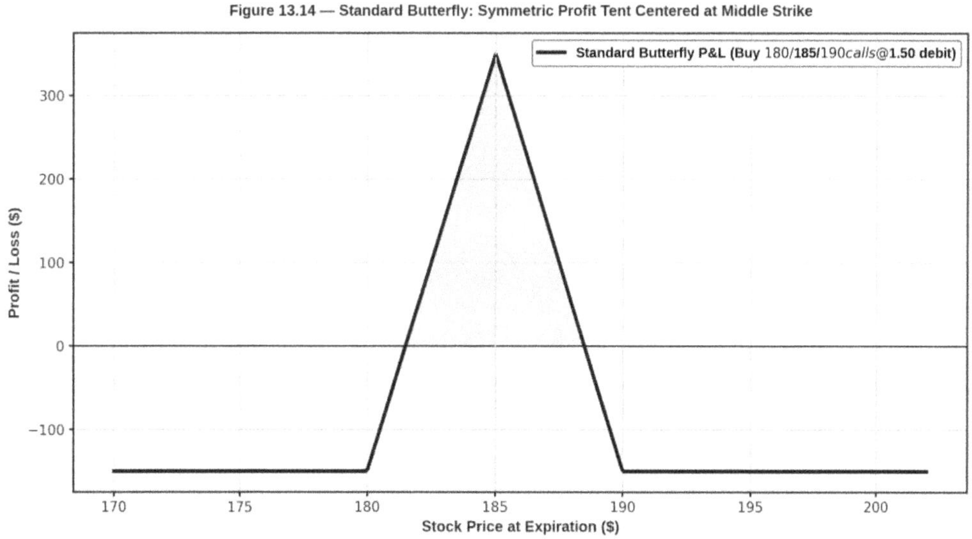

Figure 13.14 — Standard Butterfly. Symmetric profit tent centered on ATM strike.

Figure 13.15 — Broken Wing Butterfly: Asymmetric Structure with No Downside Risk

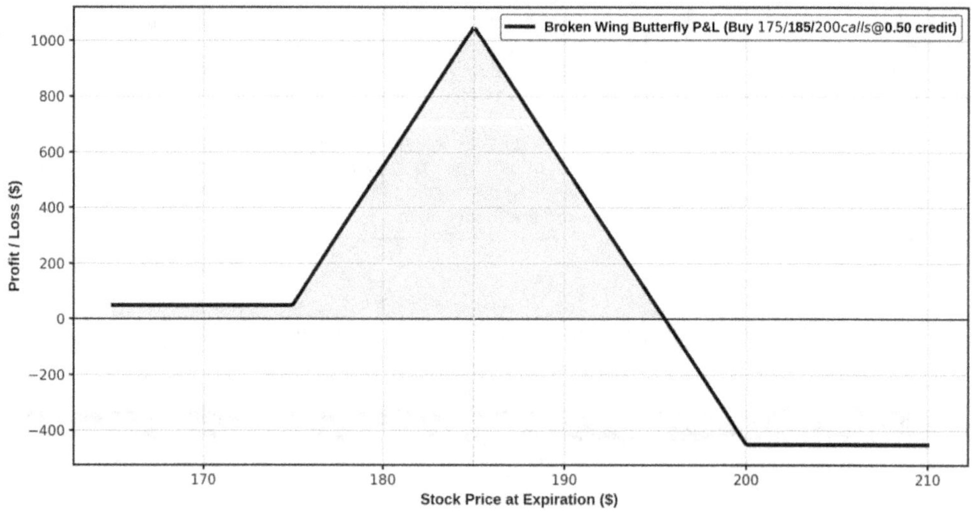

Figure 13.15 — Broken Wing Butterfly. Asymmetric structure with net credit at entry.

	Standard Butterfly	Broken Wing Butterfly (Bullish bias)
Structure	Buy \$195 call + Sell 2× \$200 calls + Buy \$205 call (5-point wings each side)	Buy \$195 call + Sell 2× \$200 calls + Buy \$207 call (5-point lower wing, 7-point upper wing)
Cost	Debit of \$0.80 (\$80)	Credit of \$0.15 (\$15) — the structure pays YOU to enter
Max profit	\$4.20 at \$200 at expiry	\$4.35 at \$200 at expiry (slightly higher due to wider upper wing)
Max loss on downside	\$0.80 (debit paid)	\$0.15 credit received — no loss if stock falls below \$195
Max loss on upside	\$0.80 (debit paid)	\$1.85 if stock closes above \$207 (wider upper wing creates larger upside risk)
Six-condition use	Condition 5 — perfect range-bound, neutral bias	Condition 5 with mild bullish bias — you think the range will hold but skew slightly upward. The credit entry reduces cost basis to near zero on the downside.

ADVANCED STRUCTURES EXIST TO SERVE THE CONDITION — NOT THE OTHER WAY AROUND

The broken wing butterfly, the ratio spread, the diagonal — these are precision instruments. They are not more sophisticated versions of the same trade. They are different tools for different conditions and different biases within those conditions. Never deploy an advanced structure because it is interesting. Deploy it because the condition demands it and the risk/reward justifies it. The six-condition framework tells you when each tool belongs in your hands.

Calendar Spreads: Profiting from Time Without Direction

A calendar spread sells near-term and buys longer-term at the same strike. Profit comes from differential time decay — the short option decays faster. If the stock stays near the strike, the short option loses value while the long retains most of its value.

Example — MSFT at $410: Sell 30-DTE $410 call ($8.50). Buy 60-DTE $410 call ($14.00). Net debit: $5.50 ($550). Max risk: $550. Max profit: ~$5.00-$6.00 if MSFT is at $410 at near-term expiry. Profit zone: ~$400-$420.

MSFT at Near Expiry	Short Call	Long Call (est.)	Net P&L
$395 (-3.7%)	$0.10	$5.20	-$0.40 loss
$400 (-2.4%)	$0.30	$7.00	+$1.20 profit
$405 (-1.2%)	$1.50	$8.80	+$1.80 profit
$410 (flat)	$3.00	$10.50	+$2.00 MAX
$415 (+1.2%)	$5.50	$11.80	+$0.80 profit
$420 (+2.4%)	$10.00	$13.00	-$2.50 loss

The calendar's sweet spot is neutral conditions (Conditions 3-4). It profits when the stock goes nowhere — the opposite of a directional trade. Perfect complement to your directional strategies.

Chapter 14 **Trading with ETFs**

> **6-CONDITION FRAMEWORK ▸ ALL SIX CONDITIONS — ETFs as the cleanest vehicle for each**
> ETFs offer index-level diversification, high liquidity, and predictable behavior in each of the six conditions. SPY, QQQ, and sector ETFs are the go-to underlyings for executing the six-condition system at scale.

Exchange-Traded Funds are one of the most powerful tools available to the options trader — and one of the most misunderstood. An ETF is not just a basket of stocks. In the context of options trading, ETFs are precision instruments: they give you defined, liquid exposure to an entire sector, index, or asset class, with options chains deep enough to support every strategy in this book.

For the risk-first trader, ETFs solve a problem that individual stocks cannot: they eliminate single-stock binary risk. A pharmaceutical stock can gap 40% down on an FDA rejection. The healthcare sector ETF — XLV — will absorb that move across 60+ holdings. You participate in sector-level thesis without betting on a single company's fate.

What Is an ETF?

An ETF is a fund that trades on a stock exchange exactly like an individual stock — you can buy it, sell it, and trade options on it using the same order entry process as any equity. Unlike a mutual fund, ETFs price continuously throughout the trading day and can be bought or sold at any moment the market is open.

Most ETFs are designed to track an index or a specific sector. When you buy SPY, you are buying exposure to all 500 stocks in the S&P 500 index in one instrument. When you buy XLF, you are buying exposure to the entire Financials sector. This is the core utility for options traders: a single, liquid, optionable instrument that represents a broad market thesis.

- ETFs are not derivatives — they are not futures, not options, not swaps. They are registered securities that own the underlying assets they track;
- ETFs trade on major U.S. exchanges. Buying and selling uses the same order process as stocks — same order types, same brokers, same margin rules;
- ETF options work identically to individual stock options — same contract structure (100 shares), same Greeks, same expiration cycles; and
- Most popular ETFs offer weekly options — SPY, QQQ, IWM, and all SPDR sector ETFs have weekly expirations available.

Index ETFs vs. Sector ETFs vs. Thematic ETFs

Not all ETFs are created equal for options trading. The three categories differ significantly in liquidity, options chain depth, and bid/ask spread quality.

Factor	ETF	Individual Stock
Earnings Risk	None — no binary events.	High — IV spikes at earnings.
Corporate Action Risk	None — no adjusted options.	Splits, mergers can adjust contracts.

Diversification	Built-in — basket of stocks.	Single company concentration.
Liquidity	Very high (SPY, QQQ, IWM).	Varies — check open interest.
IV Level	Generally lower, more stable.	Higher IV = more premium but more risk.
Options Chain	Weekly + monthly available.	Varies by ticker.
Best Use	Condition-based income strategies.	Verified Ten-Indicator setups only.

Figure 14.1 — ETF vs. Individual Stock. Liquidity, volatility, and premium comparison.

Category	Examples	Options Quality	Best Use
Broad Index ETFs	SPY, QQQ, IWM, DIA	Best in market — tightest spreads, deepest chains, weekly options, high volume	Macro directional plays, hedging entire portfolios, income strategies on the broad market
GICS Sector ETFs	XLK, XLF, XLE, XLV, XLY, XLP, XLI, XLB, XLRE, XLU, XLC	Excellent — SPDR series has institutional-level liquidity across all 11 sectors	Sector rotation plays, cycle-aligned directional trades, income strategies by sector
Sub-Sector ETFs	SOXX (semiconductors), XBI (biotech), KRE (regional banks), JETS (airlines)	Good — decent chains on major names, watch bid/ask on smaller sub-sectors	Targeted sub-sector thesis, earnings-event plays on concentrated industry exposure
Thematic / Niche ETFs	ARK funds, commodity ETFs, international ETFs	Fair to Poor — chains can be thin, spreads wide, open interest low	Use with caution. Always check OI before trading. Avoid market orders entirely.

ETF-Specific Risks Options Traders Must Know

ETFs carry a distinct risk profile from individual stocks. For the options trader, these differences materially affect how you size positions, select strategies, and manage trades.

- Tracking Error — An ETF may not perfectly replicate its index due to fees, rebalancing timing, and cash drag. For options purposes, this is minor on major ETFs but can be meaningful on leveraged or inverse products;
- Leveraged ETF Decay — 2x and 3x leveraged ETFs (e.g., TQQQ, SOXL) suffer volatility decay over time — they are designed for single-day holds, not multi-week options trades. The options on these instruments are highly complex and carry extreme Gamma risk. Avoid until you are deeply experienced;
- Index Rebalancing Events — ETFs that track cap-weighted indexes (SPY, QQQ) periodically rebalance their holdings. This creates mechanical buying and selling flows that can temporarily distort prices and IV — particularly in mega-cap components;

- Dividend Risk — Many ETFs pay quarterly dividends. Holding short calls through an ex-dividend date can create unexpected early assignment risk, as call buyers may exercise to capture the dividend. Always check the ex-dividend calendar before opening short call positions on dividend-paying ETFs; and
- Premium Compression — Broad index ETFs like SPY have lower implied volatility than individual stocks, which means lower premiums per contract. You will need more contracts to generate the same income as a single-stock trade — which means more capital at risk.

THE ETF RULE

For sector rotation trades: use the SPDR sector ETFs (XL-series). For broad market income: use SPY or QQQ. For sub-sector thesis: verify OI and bid/ask before trading. For leveraged ETFs: treat as a separate, advanced instrument requiring its own study. Never assume ETF = safe.

ETF Options Strategies: The Practical Framework

The strategies below represent the most effective ETF-specific applications for options traders. Each maps directly to a market condition and a specific ETF category.

Figure 14.2 — ETF Strategy Matrix: Strategy Selection by ETF Type and Six-Condition Environment

Strategy	ETF Type	Market Condition	Notes
Bull Call Spread	Sector ETF (XLF, XLE)	Condition 1 — Bullish Low IV	Sector rotation entry; 30-60 DTE, defined risk
Bear Put Spread	Sector ETF (XLU, XLP)	Condition 3 — Bearish Low IV	Defensive rotation; buy puts on weak sectors
Cash-Secured Put	Broad Index (SPY, QQQ)	Condition 2 — Bullish High IV	Market pullback dip; sell OTM put for income
Covered Call	Broad Index or Sector	Condition 2 — Sideways mildly bullish	Income on existing ETF; cap upside at strike
Iron Condor	SPY, QQQ	Condition 5/6 — Neutral	Low vol range-bound; collect both sides
Protective Put	Any held ETF	Condition 4 — Late cycle macro risk	Floor downside; partial hedge on portfolio

Figure 14.2 — ETF Strategy Matrix. Strategy selection by ETF type and Six-Condition environment.

Strategy	ETF Type	Market Condition	Notes
Bull Call Spread	Sector ETF (XLF, XLE, XLK)	Confirmed sector rotation entry	30–60 DTE. Capture sector upside with defined risk. Exit at 50–75% max profit.
Bear Put Spread	Sector ETF (XLU, XLP)	Defensive rotation — recession signals	30–45 DTE. Directional downside on outgoing sector. Watch for IV confirmation.
Cash-Secured Put	Broad Index (SPY, QQQ)	Market pullback in uptrend	Sell OTM put during market dip. Collect premium; prepared to own shares at strike.
Covered Call	Broad Index or Sector ETF	Sideways to mildly bullish	Generate income on existing ETF long position.

Strategy	ETF Type	Market Condition	Notes
			Best in low-IV, calm markets.
Iron Condor	SPY, QQQ	Low-vol, range-bound market	Sell call spread + put spread on SPY or QQQ. Collect credit from both sides. Profit if index stays range-bound.
Protective Put	Any held ETF position	Late-cycle or elevated macro risk	Buy OTM put to floor downside on existing ETF holding. Partial hedge cost vs. full exit.

ETF Research Resources

Avoiding analysis paralysis is critical given the broad range of ETFs available. Identify your objective first, then find the ETF that fits it best. These resources give you independent, reliable ETF data:

Resource	Website	Best For
Nasdaq	www.nasdaq.com/etfs	Excellent summary of ETF information and performance analysis
ETF Database	www.etfdb.com	Comprehensive ETF screening tool — filter by sector, volume, options availability
State Street Global Advisors	www.sectorspdr.com	Definitive source for all 11 SPDR sector ETFs — data, charts, and sector analysis
BlackRock iShares	www.ishares.com	Listing of widely held BlackRock ETF products — strong for fixed income and international

---

Sector ETF Rotation System: Trading the Six Conditions at the Sector Level

Individual ETFs track sectors. Sectors rotate through the business cycle. The combination of these two facts creates a powerful system: you can apply the six-condition framework not just to the broad market (SPY, QQQ) but to individual sectors as they enter and exit their favorable cycle phases. This is sector ETF rotation — and it is one of the cleanest ways to run the six conditions with minimal single-stock risk.

Sector ETF	Ticker	Cycle Phase Favored	Six-Condition Application
Tech	**XLK**	Expansion (mid-to-late)	Conditions 1 and 2. High IV during earnings seasons makes condition 2 (CSP, covered call) ideal. Sells on strength in expansion. Condition 4 (bear call spread) during contraction.
Health Care	**XLV**	Recession / Defensive	Conditions 2 and 5. Stable dividend payers — covered call income (condition 2). Low-beta range-bound character in recession favors iron condors (condition 5).
Financials	**XLF**	Early expansion	Conditions 1 and 2. Banks benefit from rising rate environment in early expansion. Strong income-selling opportunity at cycle bottom with elevated IV.
Energy	**XLE**	Mid expansion / Peak	Conditions 1 and 2 during commodity runs. Condition 4 (bear call spread) when oil peaks and cycle turns. Highly volatile — condition 3 available on confirmed downtrends.
Utilities	**XLU**	Recession / Late cycle	Conditions 5 and 6. Ultra-stable range-bound behavior. Calendar spreads (condition 6) on XLU are one of the cleanest time-decay harvesting trades in a high-IV defensive environment.
Consumer Discretionary	**XLY**	Mid expansion	Conditions 1 and 2. Correlates strongly with consumer spending cycle. Excellent covered call income as consumer confidence peaks. Condition 3 available when retail sales data turns.
Consumer Staples	**XLP**	Recession / Defensive	Conditions 2 and 5. Predictable cash flows and dividend growth — the ideal covered call income vehicle in any market condition. Low beta reduces risk of sudden strike tests.
Industrials	**XLI**	Early-to-mid expansion	Conditions 1 and 2. Infrastructure spending and manufacturing recovery. Bull put spreads (condition 2) as the sector begins its cycle upswing.

Multi-Sector Options Trades: The System Applied Across Industries

One of the most powerful demonstrations of the Six-Condition Framework is its sector-agnostic nature. The framework does not care whether you are trading semiconductors, energy, mining, or biotech. It reads the condition, identifies the setup, and selects the strategy. The following three trades were executed within the same two-week window across three completely different sectors — all using the same system.

VERIFIED MULTI-SECTOR TRADE LOG — JAN–MAR 2026 TRADE 1: CVE (Cenovus Energy — Oil & Gas) Bought Jan 14, 2026 • $16 Call Feb 20 • Entry: $2.45 Sold Jan 28, 2026 • Exit: $3.70 Hold: 14 days • P&L: +$125 • Return: +51.02%

TRADE 1: CVE (Cenovus Energy — Oil & Gas) Bought Jan 14, 2026 • $16 Call Feb 20 • Entry: $2.45 Sold Jan 28, 2026 • Exit: $3.70 Hold: 14 days • P&L: +$125 • Return: +51.02% TRADE 2: CDE (Coeur Mining — Silver/Gold) Bought Jan 14, 2026 • $19.5 Call Jan 30 • Entry: $2.75 Sold Jan 21, 2026 • Exit: $3.10 Hold: 7 days • P&L: +$35 • Return: +12.73% TRADE 3: IBRX (ImmunityBio — Biotech) Bought Jan 20, 2026 • $4.5 Call Feb 20 • Entry: $3.30 Position moved against — ROLLED to Mar 20 at $1.78 Closed Mar 19, 2026 • Exit: $4.10 on roll leg Roll leg return: +130.3% • Net position: Profitable Three sectors. Three setups. Same system. All brokerage-confirmed.

TRADE 2: CDE (Coeur Mining — Silver/Gold) Bought Jan 14, 2026 • $19.5 Call Jan 30 • Entry: $2.75 Sold Jan 21, 2026 • Exit: $3.10 Hold: 7 days • P&L: +$35 • Return: +12.73%

TRADE 1: CVE (Cenovus Energy — Oil & Gas) Bought Jan 14, 2026 • $16 Call Feb 20 • Entry: $2.45 Sold Jan 28, 2026 • Exit: $3.70 Hold: 14 days • P&L: +$125 • Return: +51.02% TRADE 2: CDE (Coeur Mining — Silver/Gold) Bought Jan 14, 2026 • $19.5 Call Jan 30 • Entry: $2.75 Sold Jan 21, 2026 • Exit: $3.10 Hold: 7 days • P&L: +$35 • Return: +12.73% TRADE 3: IBRX (ImmunityBio — Biotech) Bought Jan 20, 2026 • $4.5 Call Feb 20 • Entry: $3.30 Position moved against — ROLLED to Mar 20 at $1.78 Closed Mar 19, 2026 • Exit: $4.10 on roll leg Roll leg return: +130.3% • Net position: Profitable Three sectors. Three setups. Same system. All brokerage-confirmed.

TRADE 3: IBRX (ImmunityBio — Biotech) Bought Jan 20, 2026 • $4.5 Call Feb 20 • Entry: $3.30 Position moved against — ROLLED to Mar 20 at $1.78 Closed Mar 19, 2026 • Exit: $4.10 on roll leg Roll leg return: +130.3% • Net position: Profitable

TRADE 1: CVE (Cenovus Energy — Oil & Gas) Bought Jan 14, 2026 • $16 Call Feb 20 • Entry: $2.45 Sold Jan 28, 2026 • Exit: $3.70 Hold: 14 days • P&L: +$125 • Return: +51.02% TRADE 2: CDE (Coeur Mining — Silver/Gold) Bought Jan 14, 2026 • $19.5 Call Jan 30 • Entry: $2.75 Sold Jan 21, 2026 • Exit: $3.10 Hold: 7 days • P&L: +$35 • Return: +12.73% TRADE 3: IBRX (ImmunityBio — Biotech) Bought Jan 20, 2026 • $4.5 Call Feb 20 • Entry: $3.30 Position moved against — ROLLED to Mar 20 at $1.78 Closed Mar 19, 2026 • Exit: $4.10 on roll leg Roll leg return: +130.3% • Net position: Profitable Three sectors. Three setups. Same system. All brokerage-confirmed.

Notice what the IBRX trade demonstrates beyond the profit. The February leg moved against the position. Rather than accepting the full loss, the position was rolled defensively to March at a significantly lower premium ($1.78), the thesis was maintained, and the stock recovered. The roll leg closed at $4.10 — a 130.3% return on the rolled position. The roll defense converted what would have been a loss into a net profitable outcome. That is Chapter 23 applied in real time.

The CDE trade closed in 7 days at a modest +12.73%. That is not a spectacular return — it is a disciplined one. The position hit its target, the system said close, and the capital was redeployed. Seven days. Clean. No emotion. That is what the system produces at scale: not every trade is a home run. The system produces consistent, managed results across a portfolio of positions in different sectors simultaneously.

As with all examples in this book, these trades are drawn from real, executed positions.

VIX-Based ETF Strategies: Trading Volatility Itself

Beyond sector ETFs, there is an entire class of exchange-traded products designed to give exposure to volatility itself. These are the VIX-related ETPs — products like UVXY, SVXY, VXX, and VIXY. For experienced traders, these products allow you to directly express a view on volatility regime change: the shift from low-IV to high-IV environments and back.

Product	Direction	What It Tracks	Six-Condition Application + Critical Warning
VXX / VIXY	Long volatility	Short-term VIX futures (1-2 month rolling)	Profits when VIX spikes (conditions 3/4 — fear events). CRITICAL: these products experience severe contango drag — they lose value consistently in calm markets due to the cost of rolling futures forward. Never hold long-term. Use only as short-duration fear hedges.
UVXY	Long 1.5× volatility	Leveraged VIX futures	Amplified version of VXX. Only for experienced traders expressing a view on an imminent volatility spike. The leverage

Product	Direction	What It Tracks	Six-Condition Application + Critical Warning
			and contango drag accelerate both gains and losses. Position size: maximum 0.5% of account.
SVXY	Short volatility	Inverse VIX futures	Profits when VIX falls (conditions 1/2 — calm expanding markets). Gains from contango as short VIX futures roll forward. CRITICAL: a VIX spike from 15 to 40 (as in Feb 2018) can cause SVXY to lose 80-90% in a single session. Defined-risk exposure only — buy calls on SVXY rather than holding shares.

ETFs ARE THE CLEANEST VEHICLE FOR THE SIX-CONDITION SYSTEM

Every six-condition strategy works more cleanly on ETFs than on individual stocks for one reason: diversification eliminates single-event risk. An ETF cannot gap 30% on an earnings miss, an FDA ruling, or an activist investor filing. The range holds more reliably. The IV behaves more predictably. For income sellers especially (conditions 2, 4, 5, 6), ETFs are the highest-quality vehicles available. Build your watchlist around the sector ETFs above and the broad market ETFs (SPY, QQQ, IWM) — then apply the six conditions to each as the cycle evolves.

Diagonal Spreads: Calendar + Direction

A diagonal buys slightly ITM longer-term and sells OTM shorter-term — essentially a covered call substitute. Buy 90-DTE $185 AAPL call ($14.50). Sell 30-DTE $200 call ($3.50). Net: $11.00.

Advantage: you control 100 shares of AAPL for $1,100 instead of $19,000. If AAPL drops 20%, max loss is $1,100 — not $3,800. Same income characteristics as a covered call with a fraction of the capital and defined max loss.

CALENDAR & DIAGONAL ENTRY RULE

Enter calendars when IVR is below 30 (cheap long-dated options). Enter diagonals when IVR is 30-50 (moderate IV makes the short leg attractive). Never enter either when IVR above 60 — high IV inflates both legs and increases risk of IV contraction destroying the position.

ETF Options Strategies: Putting the Instruments to Work

Understanding what ETFs are is only half the job. The other half is knowing which options strategies work best on which ETF types — and why. The structural characteristics of index ETFs, sector ETFs, and sub-sector ETFs each favor different approaches.

Strategy 1 — The Sector Rotation Iron Condor

The iron condor is the natural income strategy for sector ETFs in range-bound or low-conviction environments. Because sector ETFs are diversified across dozens of holdings, they move less violently than individual stocks — their price action is smoother and more mean-reverting at the edges. This makes them ideal for defined-range income trades.

Example on XLF (Financials) trading at $42.00, 30 DTE:

Leg	Action	Strike	Purpose
Short Call	Sell $44.00 Call	Collect premium	Ceiling of profitable range — XLF must stay below $44
Long Call	Buy $45.50 Call	Define max upside risk	Caps loss if XLF breaks above $44
Short Put	Sell $40.00 Put	Collect premium	Floor of profitable range — XLF must stay above $40
Long Put	Buy $38.50 Put	Define max downside risk	Caps loss if XLF breaks below $40

Net credit: approximately $0.85–$1.10 per spread pair. Maximum risk: $1.50 per side minus credit received. Profit zone: XLF stays between $40.00 and $44.00 through expiration. The sector ETF's diversification is your structural edge — a single bad bank earnings report will not spike XLF 15% the way it would a regional bank stock.

Strategy 2 — The Sector CSP for Cycle-Aligned Income

When the business cycle and sector rotation align — expanding economy, Financials leading, BPI rising — a cash-secured put on the relevant sector ETF captures income with the macro tailwind behind it.

- Identify the current business cycle phase using the BPI and sector rotation model (Chapter 7);
- Select the SPDR sector ETF aligned with that phase: XLK in early expansion, XLE in late expansion, XLU in contraction;
- Sell the 0.25–0.30 delta put at 30–35 DTE — this is your cycle-aligned income position; and
- Close at 50% profit or roll at T-21 — same management rules as individual stock CSPs.

The sector ETF CSP has one structural advantage over the individual stock CSP: no binary event risk. No earnings, no FDA approval, no CEO resignation. The risk is macro — sector-level or market-level moves — which are more predictable, slower-moving, and more recoverable than individual stock blow-ups.

Strategy 3 — The Index Hedge for Portfolio Protection

For traders who hold a portfolio of long positions (stocks, CSP assignments, covered call positions), index ETF puts provide cost-effective portfolio-level protection. Rather than buying puts on every individual holding, a single long put position on SPY or QQQ provides broad downside coverage.

The calculation: if your portfolio has $50,000 in long equity exposure and you want to hedge 20% downside, you need a put that profits approximately $10,000 if the market drops 20%. One SPY put 10% out-of-the-money (when SPY is at $500) controls $50,000 of notional value and profits sharply in a correction. The cost: approximately 0.5–1.0% of portfolio value per quarter — a defined insurance premium.

ETF LIQUIDITY RULE

Before trading options on any ETF: (1) open interest at your target strike must exceed 1,000 contracts, (2) bid/ask spread must be under $0.20 for liquid index ETFs or under $0.40 for sector ETFs, (3) average daily options volume must exceed 10,000 contracts for index ETFs or 2,000 for sector ETFs. The 11 SPDR sector ETFs (XLK, XLF, XLE, XLV, XLY, XLP, XLI, XLB, XLRE, XLU, XLC) all pass. Most thematic ETFs do not.

The Complete Sector ETF Options Guide

Not all sector ETFs are equally tradeable for options strategies. Some have excellent options liquidity with tight spreads and deep open interest. Others have wide spreads that make income strategies unprofitable after slippage. Here is the definitive guide to which sector ETFs work for options trading and which to avoid.

Tier 1 — Excellent Options Liquidity (use for all strategies including income selling): SPY (S&P 500), QQQ (Nasdaq 100), IWM (Russell 2000), XLF (Financials), XLK (Technology), XLE (Energy), XLV (Healthcare). These ETFs have weekly options, bid-ask spreads under $0.05 for ATM options, and open interest exceeding 50,000 contracts at popular strikes. You can enter and exit positions at any time without significant slippage.

Tier 2 — Good Options Liquidity (use for CSPs, spreads, and iron condors): XLY (Consumer Discretionary), XLP (Consumer Staples), XLI (Industrials), XLB (Materials), XLU (Utilities), XLC (Communication Services). Monthly options liquid with spreads under $0.15. Sufficient for income strategies but always use limit orders — market orders on Tier 2 ETFs can cost you $0.05-$0.10 per contract in slippage.

Tier 3 — Limited Options Liquidity (use for directional trades only, not income): XLRE (Real Estate), specific thematic ETFs (ARKK, TAN, KWEB). Wider spreads ($0.20-$0.50), lower open interest, sometimes only monthly expirations available. Income strategies lose their edge after accounting for bid-ask slippage. Use these for defined-risk directional trades only.

Tier 4 — Avoid for Options Trading: Most leveraged ETFs (TQQQ, SOXL), most country-specific ETFs (EWJ, FXI), most commodity ETFs (GLD, SLV — exceptions for SPY/QQQ-level liquid names). Extremely wide spreads, low open interest, and complex pricing that does not align with standard options models. The premium looks attractive but the execution cost destroys the edge.

The Six-Condition ETF Playbook

ETFs are the cleanest vehicle for executing the six-condition system at scale. Unlike individual stocks, ETFs carry no earnings binary risk, no single-company fundamental risk, and no adjusted options risk from corporate actions. They are the professional's preferred underlying for income strategies — and the beginner's best starting point for learning condition-specific execution.

The following playbook maps the six conditions to the most liquid, appropriate ETFs for each strategy. Use this as your starting menu — the ETFs that have passed every liquidity and suitability test for each condition.

#	Condition	Strategy	Best ETF(s)	Why This ETF Fits This Condition
1	**Bullish / Low IV**	Long call / bull call spread	**SPY, QQQ, XLK**	The broadest uptrend participation. SPY for S&P 500 beta. QQQ for tech-weighted growth exposure in early/mid expansion. XLK for technology sector leadership. Deep option chains allow precise strike selection.
2	**Bullish / High IV**	CSP / bull put spread	**SPY, QQQ, XLF, XLV**	Income strategies on the most liquid, most recovery-prone ETFs. XLF (Financials) and XLV (Healthcare) offer higher IV during macro uncertainty while remaining fundamentally resilient. Both have weekly options for 52-paycheck cycle.
3	**Bearish / Low IV**	Long put / bear put spread	**QQQ, XLK, XLY**	High-beta sectors fall faster and further in downtrends. QQQ and XLK lead the market in rallies and corrections. Bear put spreads on these ETFs in confirmed downtrends capture maximum directional movement for the debit paid.
4	**Bearish / High IV**	Bear call spread (credit)	**SPY, QQQ, IWM**	Bear call spreads on broad index ETFs during high-IV bearish phases. IWM (Russell 2000) shows higher beta in corrections and elevated IV. Bear call spreads on IWM during bear markets collect excellent credit with broad protection from the downtrend.
5	**Range / Low IV**	Iron condor / butterfly	**SPY, QQQ**	Broadest range-bound behavior occurs in major index ETFs during consolidation phases. SPY iron condors are the most liquid, most forgiving structures for range-bound condition 5 setups. The defined range can often be read directly from support/resistance on the weekly chart.
6	**Range / High IV**	Calendar / diagonal	**SPY, QQQ, GLD, SLV**	Calendar spreads work best when the underlying has predictable IV term structure. SPY and QQQ are the standards. GLD (Gold ETF) and SLV (Silver ETF) offer elevated IV during macro uncertainty events with range-bound price — ideal calendar setups during geopolitical risk-off periods.

THE ETF ADVANTAGE IN THE SIX-CONDITION SYSTEM

ETFs bypass the Ten-Indicator score requirement (Chapter 14), eliminate earnings binary risk, and carry no adjusted-options risk. For every condition, an ETF exists that provides the optimal expression of that strategy. New traders should begin their six-condition practice exclusively on SPY and QQQ before moving to sector ETFs and individual stocks. The ETF tracks the condition cleanly. The individual stock adds idiosyncratic noise.

Volatility ETFs: Trading the VIX Itself

One of the most powerful — and most misunderstood — tools in the ETF universe is the family of volatility ETFs and ETNs that track or respond to VIX-related indices. These instruments allow options traders to express a direct view on volatility itself, independent of direction. In the six-condition system, volatility ETFs are specialized tools for conditions 2, 4, and 6 — where elevated IV is the defining feature.

Understanding how these products work — and more importantly how they decay — is essential before trading them. Volatility ETFs are not buy-and-hold instruments. They are tactical tools with specific entry and exit conditions tied directly to the VIX cycle.

Ticker	Type	Direction	How Options Traders Use It
VXX	ETN	Long VIX (short-term futures)	Buys VIX front-month and second-month futures. Suffers severe contango decay in calm markets — loses value every day the VIX is stable or falling. Use only as a short-term hedge in Conditions 3 and 4 when VIX is rising. Never hold long-term.
UVXY	ETF	1.5× Long VIX	Leveraged long VIX exposure. Amplifies both gains during spikes and decay during calm. Suitable only for short-duration hedges during Conditions 3 or 4 — measured in days, not weeks. Extremely high daily decay in contango.
SVXY	ETF	−0.5× Short VIX	Inverse VIX at half leverage. Profits when VIX declines from elevated levels — a Condition 2 or 6 instrument. Enter after a VIX spike when reversion is expected. Exit before the next fear event. Do not hold through FOMC or earnings season.
VIXY	ETF	Long VIX (short-term futures)	Similar to VXX. Tracks S&P 500 VIX Short-Term Futures Index. Same contango decay problem. Use as defined-risk hedge via buying puts on VIXY — not as a long stock position.
VIXM	ETF	Long VIX (mid-term futures)	Tracks mid-term VIX futures (4–7 months). Less contango decay than VXX. More suitable for multi-week volatility hedges in Condition 4 portfolios. Lower response to acute VIX spikes.

THE CONTANGO TRAP

VIX futures-based ETFs like VXX and UVXY lose value every day through a structural cost called contango — the market's continuous rolling of near-term futures into higher-priced next-month contracts. This roll cost averages 5–10% per month in calm markets. VXX has declined over 99% since inception when adjusted for splits. It is a short-term tactical tool — not an investment. If you want long-term volatility exposure, buy options on SPY instead of holding VXX.

The VIX ETF Six-Condition Use Cases

Cond.	VIX is...	Volatility ETF Action
3 or 4	Rising / High	Buy VXX calls or UVXY calls as a defined-risk hedge against a short portfolio. Size at 2–5% of portfolio value maximum. Exit when VIX reaches your target or after the catalyst event has passed.
2 or 6	Falling from spike	Sell VXX or buy SVXY calls — profit from volatility mean reversion. Enter only after VIX has already peaked and begun declining. The best entry is 24–48 hours after the fear peak, not during it.
1 or 5	Low / Stable	No volatility ETF positions. Contango decay will destroy long VIX positions. SVXY is also dangerous here — a sudden spike from low VIX can cause sharp losses in inverse instruments.

Volatility ETFs are an advanced tool. They reward traders who understand the VIX cycle and punish traders who treat them like regular stocks or ETFs. Master the six-condition framework first, trade SPY and QQQ options for at least six months, and only then consider adding VIX-linked instruments to your toolkit.

The Wheel Strategy: Conditions 1 and 2 in Sequence

The Wheel is not a single strategy — it is two of the six-condition strategies executed in sequence, linked by the assignment event between them. Understanding the Wheel as a six-condition flow (not a standalone strategy) is what separates disciplined Wheel traders from those who get assigned on poor underlyings and hold them forever.

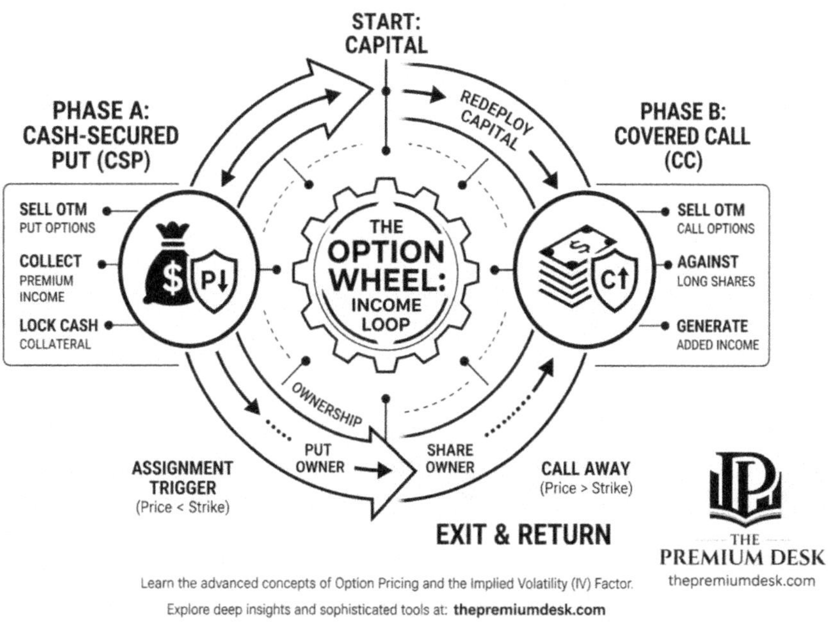

Figure 13.13 — The Option Wheel: Income Loop. Phase A: Cash-Secured Put (CSP) → Assignment Trigger (Price < Strike) → Phase B: Covered Call (CC) → Call Away (Price > Strike) → Exit & Return. The complete two-phase income cycle.

Chapter 15 Options for Income: The Seller's Edge

HOW TO USE THIS CHAPTER

Chapter 15 has 34 sections covering the full income trading system from beginner to advanced. Your reading roadmap: First-time traders — read sections 1–8 (through The SCR Framework) plus The Core Income Strategies through The Wheel on ETFs. After your first 10 live trades — return for Advanced Wheel Mechanics, Wheel Failure Modes, and Assignment Recovery. After 3+ months live — the final third (Double Wheel, Five Stages, Assignment Journal) will fully click. Do not try to absorb all 34 sections at once. The system is designed to be learned in stages with live market experience filling the gaps.

6-CONDITION FRAMEWORK ▸ CONDITIONS 2 & 4 — the premium seller's home conditions

The Wheel, the CSP, and the covered call are condition 2 and condition 4 strategies. When the market is directional and IV is high, the seller has every structural advantage: trend probability, elevated premium, and time working as income.

"The Seller does not hope. The Seller prepares."

— The Premium Desk

This chapter is written for one person: the trader who has decided to stop asking what the market will give them and start telling the market what they need. That is the Seller's mindset. And the moment that shift happens — the moment a trader sits down, defines their annual income target, divides it by 260 — the number of trading days in a year — and writes down a daily number — they have crossed from speculator to professional income operator.

That daily number is your PPD: Profit Per Day. It is the organizing principle of everything that follows in this chapter. Not a metric. Not a comparison tool. A target — your target — that your portfolio reports to work every single day to earn.

The Decision That Changes Everything: Defining Your PPD

Before a single strategy is discussed, before a single stock is screened, before a single strike is selected — you must answer one question: what does this portfolio need to generate every day for your life to work?

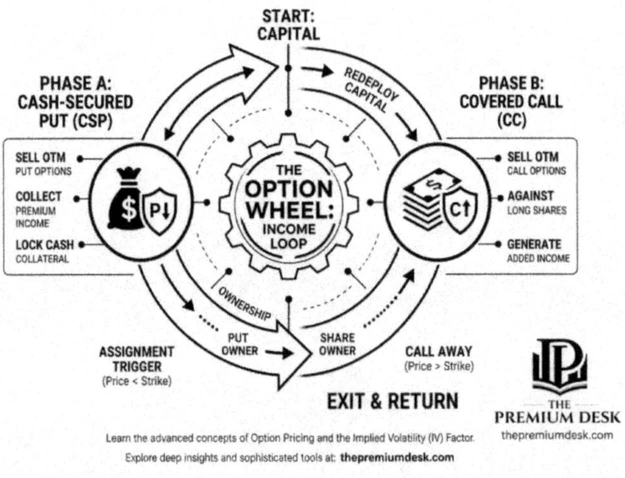

Figure 15.1 — The Four Building Blocks of Income Trading.

This is not a trading question. It is a financial planning question. Answer it honestly and specifically. Not 'as much as possible.' A number.

Annual Income Target	÷ 260 Trading Days	= Your PPD Target
$36,500 / year	÷ 260	**$140/day**
$60,000 / year	÷ 260	**$231/day**
$100,000 / year	÷ 260	**$385/day**
$150,000 / year	÷ 260	**$577/day**
$200,000 / year	÷ 260	**$769/day**

Write your PPD number down. That number is now the mission. Every position you open, every strike you select, every sizing decision you make will be evaluated against one question: does this help me hit my PPD? The Seller's portfolio is not a collection of trades — it is a machine engineered to produce one number, every day, reliably.

THE PPD DECISION

Your PPD is not aspirational. It is operational. Once you define it, it becomes the fixed constraint around which every other decision in this chapter — capital requirements, position sizing, stock selection, DTE, delta — is calibrated. The Seller does not trade to make as much as possible. The Seller trades to make exactly what they planned. That precision is the edge.

The Buyer vs. The Seller: Two Completely Different Games

To understand why the Seller has such a structural advantage, you must first understand the Buyer's world — because the Seller's income comes directly from the Buyer's premium payment. Every dollar the Seller collects is a dollar the Buyer has paid and cannot recover regardless of outcome.

	The Buyer	The Seller
Starting Capital	Small account — $5K to $20K typical. Leverage is the appeal.	Minimum $200,000. Sized to absorb full assignment on any position without distress.
Premium	Pays it. Gone the moment the trade is placed — win or lose.	Collects it. Belongs to the Seller permanently from the moment the trade is placed.
Obligation	None — the Buyer owns a right, not an obligation.	Defined — the Seller has agreed to buy stock at the strike if assigned.
Time	The enemy. Every day the stock doesn't move costs the Buyer money.	The ally. Every day that passes, theta works for the Seller. Time is income.
Preferred Expiration	Monthly or longer — 30, 60, 90+ days. The Buyer needs time for the stock to move AND to recover the premium paid. Short expirations leave no room for error.	Weekly — 7 days or less. Theta burns fastest in the final 7 days. The Seller eats the full soda bottle in one week, banks the premium, and

	The Buyer	The Seller
		opens a fresh trade. 52 paychecks a year.
Motivation	Maximize return. Chase the big move. Accept high risk for high reward.	Hit the PPD target. Collect premium consistently. The Wheel handles the rest.
What they need to win	The stock must move significantly in the right direction before expiration.	The stock must simply not collapse through the strike. Sideways is a win. Up is a win. Mildly down is often still a win.
Exercise reality	~50% of Buyers statistically lack the capital or margin to exercise even when they are right. They bought a right they can never use.	Collects the full premium from every Buyer — including the ~50% who will never exercise. The Seller wins from them by default.
Assignment rate	N/A	~10% of positions end in actual assignment. 90% of trades simply expire or are closed for profit — no stock changes hands.

🥤 The Soda Battle 🥤

Trading Options Like a Risk Manager

The bottle of soda is theta. It was paid for by the Buyer. It is drunk by the Seller. Every single day. Which side are you on?

The bottle of soda is theta. It was paid for by the Buyer. It is drunk by the Seller. Every single day. Which side are you on?

The Buyer	The Seller
😟	😎

The Buyer paid for a full bottle of soda. Every day that passes without a big move, someone takes a sip. The Buyer watches the bottle get emptier with each passing hour — theta draining what they paid for, relentlessly, whether the market is open or closed.

The stock must move far and fast — before the bottle is empty.

The Seller collects that same bottle of soda the moment the trade is placed. Every day that passes, they drink it — theta filling their glass, one sip at a time, whether the stock moves or not. Sideways market? Another sip. Quiet Friday? Another sip.

Time does not cost the Seller. Time pays the Seller.

The bottle of soda is theta. It was paid for by the Buyer. It is drunk by the Seller. Every single day.

Which side are you on?

52 Paychecks a Year: Why the Seller Sells Weekly

The Seller's preferred expiration is weekly — 7 days or less. This is not impatience. It is mathematics. Theta decay is not linear. It accelerates sharply in the final 7 days before expiration, meaning the Seller collecting a weekly premium is capturing the steepest, fastest portion of the decay curve on every single trade. Instead of waiting 30 days to collect one full premium, the Seller opens and closes positions every week — eating the theta fast, banking the premium, and redeploying immediately.

The 52-Week Income Calendar — Monthly Expirations with Income Targets

Dark = Higher IV (preferred entry) · Light = Lower IV (use spreads or calendars)

Figure 15.2 — The 52-Week Income Calendar. Monthly expirations with income target tracking.

Verified Sector Trades — The Framework Applied

Beyond the MU series, the same Six-Condition system produced verified gains across sector names — confirming the framework works equally on individual stocks and sector ETFs.

The Buyer's preferred expiration is the opposite: monthly, or longer. The Buyer needs time — time for the stock to move enough to overcome the premium paid, time to recover if the initial move goes the wrong way, time to be right. A Buyer who buys a 7-day call needs the stock to move immediately and significantly. A Buyer with 60 days can absorb a slow start, a pullback, and still recover. The longer expiration is the Buyer's safety net. For the Seller, that same time is lost income — every extra day of runway is a day the Seller does not need and the Buyer is paying for.

Expiration	The Buyer's Perspective	The Seller's Perspective
Weekly (0–7 DTE)	Extremely risky — needs an immediate, large move. Premium is cheaper but there is almost no time to recover if wrong. Only experienced directional traders use weeklies as buyers.	Ideal. Theta burns at maximum speed. Open Monday, collect premium, close Friday. 52 opportunities per year on the same underlying. Fast, clean, repeatable.
Monthly (30–45 DTE)	Standard entry. Enough time for the thesis to develop. Theta cost is manageable relative to potential gain. Most retail Buyers operate here.	Also viable — the 30–45 DTE window is the income sweet spot where theta is accelerating but gamma risk is still manageable. Close at T-21 or 50% profit. The Seller captures the best part of the decay curve and exits before gamma dominates.
60–90 DTE	Preferred by traders who want more time and lower daily theta cost. More expensive in absolute premium but buys significant runway.	Less efficient for the Seller — capital is tied up longer for proportionally less daily theta. Better used for LEAPS-backed diagonal spreads than pure income CSPs.
LEAPS (180+ DTE)	The Buyer's maximum time advantage — used for long-term directional plays where the Buyer expects a sustained move over many months.	The Seller does not sell LEAPS as income vehicles. Too much time, too little theta per day, too much vega exposure. LEAPS belong to the Buyer's toolkit.

THE SELLER'S WEEKLY RHYTHM

The Seller's calendar is simple: every week is a paycheck. Open a CSP on Monday or Tuesday on a quality stock with no earnings before Friday. Collect the premium. Manage if needed. Close at 50% profit or let it expire worthless by Friday. Deploy the freed capital into next week's trade. Fifty-two times a year, the Seller sits on the right side of theta decay — drinking the soda bottle while the Buyer watches it drain. The Buyer hopes for a move. The Seller just needs another week to pass.

THE PREMIUM IS YOURS

The moment a Buyer pays for an options contract, that premium belongs to the Seller — permanently, unconditionally, regardless of what happens next. The Seller has zero obligation to return it. The Buyer may profit if the stock moves in their favor, but they must profit enough to overcome the premium they already surrendered. The Seller starts every trade ahead. This is not a small advantage. It is the entire business model.

The Buyer May Win More — But Only the Seller Can Plan

Here is the honest truth about the Buyer: they can make extraordinary returns. A well-timed long call can produce 200%, 500%, even 1,000% in weeks. The Seller will never match that on a single trade — and that is precisely the point. Because the Buyer cannot plan. They cannot sit down in January and write a budget for the year based on options trading income. They cannot tell their family what the portfolio will generate this month. Every Buyer trade is a question mark — directionally uncertain, time-decaying against them, dependent on a move that may or may not come.

The Seller can plan. The Seller knows their PPD target. They know approximately how many positions they need open to hit it. They know which stocks they are watching, what strikes align with their thesis, and what their monthly income will look like if the system runs as designed. The Seller runs a business with a budget, a pipeline, and a payroll. The Buyer runs a series of bets — some brilliant, most forgotten.

THE SELLER'S PLANNING ADVANTAGE

Ask any serious Buyer what their portfolio will generate next month. They cannot answer. Ask a disciplined Seller running the SRC system with a defined PPD target. They can answer to within a reasonable range — because their income does not depend on the market moving. It depends on time passing. And time always passes. That predictability — the ability to plan, budget, and build a financial life around a trading income — is the Seller's greatest advantage. Not the statistics. Not the premium math. The certainty.

Why $200,000 Is the Seller's Starting Line

The $200,000 minimum is not a gatekeeping rule — it is a structural requirement for the Seller's model to function as designed. Here is why that number exists:

- Assignment capacity: when a $100 stock is put to you at the $90 strike, you need $9,000 to take delivery of 100 shares. Running 5–8 simultaneous CSP positions on quality large-cap names requires $45,000–$80,000 in reserved capital just for assignment coverage — before your other positions, your cash buffer, or your covered call inventory.
- Premium volume: at a realistic 2–3% monthly return on deployed capital, a $200,000 account generates $4,000–$6,000/month. That is $133–$200/day in PPD — meaningful income. A $25,000 account at the same return generates $500–$750/month — $17–$25/day. The strategy works, but the income does not replace a salary.
- Psychological capacity: the Seller's edge depends on not being forced to make decisions under financial pressure. A $200,000 account that absorbs a $9,000 assignment barely blinks. A $30,000 account that absorbs the same assignment has just deployed 30% of its capital into a single stock position. The size creates the calm. The calm creates the discipline.
- The path to $200,000: this is the role of the growth strategies in this book. You build the account with defined-risk directional trades — bull call spreads, long calls on sector leaders, diagonal spreads during confirmed rotations. When you reach $200,000, you transition. Not before. Trying to run the Seller's income model on a small account produces underwhelming results that breed impatience and bad decisions.

The 10% Assignment Reality — Why Assignment Is the Plan, Not the Problem

Statistically, only approximately 10% of options positions result in actual assignment. The remaining 90% expire worthless or are closed before expiration. The Seller's entire risk management model is built around this number: 90% of the time you collect premium and move on. 10% of the time you acquire stock. And that 10% is not a failure — it is Phase 2 of the Wheel.

But the 10% only works in the Seller's favor if the assignment lands on the right stock. This is why A-class stock selection is non-negotiable. The Seller does not sell puts on anything — they sell puts on companies they would genuinely be proud to own. Companies with strong balance sheets, durable competitive advantages, consistent earnings, and enough institutional support that a temporary decline is recoverable. When you are assigned 100 shares of Apple, Microsoft, or JPMorgan at a price 10–15% below where they were trading when you sold the put — you have not lost. You have acquired a world-class asset at a discount, with a cost basis further reduced by the premium you already collected.

THE SELLER'S SELECTION RULE

Never sell a put on a stock you would not be genuinely happy to own at the strike price. Not 'okay with.' Not 'could live with.' Happy to own — as a long-term position, at that price, right now. If you would not buy the stock outright at the strike, do not sell the put. The Wheel only works when assignment is welcome. If assignment feels like a punishment, the trade should never have been opened.

The SCR Framework: How the Seller Hits PPD Every Month

PPD defines the target. The SRC™ framework — Systematic, Repeatable, Consistent — is the operating system that delivers it. Income trading must be SRC because PPD is not achieved through one great trade. It is achieved through hundreds of well-executed average ones. The Seller who runs a clean, disciplined system across three years will generate more income than the Seller who chases premium and breaks rules — even if the rule-breaker wins more on individual trades.

Before we build the SRC system, one contrast worth making: the lucky trade. During the COVID-19 pandemic, Zoom Video Communications gained 564% as the world moved to remote work overnight. If you caught it long, it was the trade of a lifetime. The Seller was not in that trade. The Seller was collecting $180 on their MSFT covered call that month — and $180 the month after — and $180 the month after that. Three years later, the Seller has collected $6,480 in systematic premium on that one position. The Zoom trader has a great story. The Seller has a business.

SRC vs. LUCKY TRADES

The goal of income trading is not to catch the next 500% move. The goal is SRC profits: Systematic, Repeatable, and Consistent — the kind that generate a monthly paycheck from your portfolio in bull markets, bear markets, and everything in between. Lucky trades are the cherry on top. They are not the strategy. The Seller's edge is not in any single trade. It is in the accumulation of hundreds of well-managed ones that collectively hit the PPD target, month after month, year after year.

- Systematic — Every trade follows the same entry criteria: target delta range, DTE window, underlying selection rules, and position sizing formula calibrated to your PPD target. No improvisation.
- Consistent — You execute the system in every qualifying market environment. You do not skip cycles because you feel uncertain. Uncertainty is the normal operating condition. The system was designed for it.

- Repeatable — The strategy must work across hundreds of trades to express its statistical edge. Any single trade is irrelevant. The system's profitability — and your PPD — lives in the aggregate.

Whether you trade cash or margin will affect your absolute return. A margin account amplifies both gains and losses. For the Seller, the cleaner model is cash — the return on reserved capital is honest, the assignment capacity is genuine, and the psychological pressure of margin calls never enters the equation. When you are ready for margin, the return on margin (ROM) can push annual returns from 30% toward 60% — but only after the cash-based system is fully proven.

Finding Your Trades — The 5-Step Stock Strategy

Before executing any income strategy, you need a repeatable process for finding qualified candidates. This 5-step system ensures every trade you consider has already passed the most important filters before you even look at the options chain:

- Step 1: Find stocks with NO earnings announcement before your expiration date — earnings events create unpredictable IV spikes that destroy premium selling strategies
- Step 2: Find stocks with HIGH implied volatility (IV) in the 30–50% range — this is your premium sweet spot. Above 50% means the stock is whipsawing too violently. Below 30% means premiums are too thin to be worth the capital deployed.
- Step 3: Find stocks in an uptrend OR moving sideways with strong support — the stock's chart must support your thesis that it will stay above your strike
- Step 4: Check your risk profile and protection analysis — run the Protection Analysis worksheet from Chapter 3 on every candidate before proceeding
- Step 5: Place the trade — only after all four prior steps are confirmed

Your primary screening tool is Barchart.com. Here is the exact filter setup for finding cash-secured put candidates:

Barchart Filter	Setting
Exchange	Any (AMEX, NYSE, NASDAQ all checked)
Strike Implied Volatility	30% to 50% — this is your premium target range
Days to Expiration (DTE)	7 to 21 days
Security Type	Stocks only (check Stocks, uncheck ETFs for this screen)
Option Type	PUT (only — you are looking for put-selling candidates)
Stock Price Range	$30 to $250
Volume / Open Interest	Set to 0 — let the flipcharts do the visual filtering
Earnings Date	Exclude any stock with earnings before your expiration
Action	Select FLIPCHARTS — review highest-ranking stocks visually, one by one

TradingView's stock screener can be used the same way — filter by Change % (below -2%), Volume (above 1M), Symbol Type (Common Stock), and Price ($30–$250) to surface the same pullback candidates. The process is identical to Barchart; use whichever platform you prefer.

IV Rank and IV Percentile: Your Precision Entry Signal

The VIX tells you the market's fear level. But for individual stocks and sector ETFs, you need a tool that measures implied volatility relative to that specific ticker's own history. This is where IV Rank and IV Percentile become your primary entry filter for premium-selling strategies.

IV Rank (IVR): Where Is IV Relative to Its 52-Week Range?

IV Rank answers one question: is implied volatility high or low right now compared to where it has been over the past year? Formula:

IVR = (Current IV − 52-Week IV Low) ÷ (52-Week IV High − 52-Week IV Low) × 100

Example: 52-week IV low = 18%, 52-week IV high = 72%, current IV = 54%. IVR = (54−18)÷(72−18)×100 = 67. An IVR of 67 means current IV is in the 67th percentile of its own 52-week range — elevated, and favorable for selling premium.

IVR	Interpretation	Premium Selling Edge	Strategy Bias
0–25	IV near yearly low	Poor — premiums thin, edge minimal	Buy options, debit spreads, calendar spreads
25–50	IV below average	Moderate — standard income trades acceptable	CSPs, covered calls at reduced size
50–75	IV elevated — above average	Good — statistical edge for premium sellers	CSPs, iron condors, credit spreads at full size
75–100	IV near yearly high	Excellent — maximum premium opportunity	Aggressive premium selling, wider strikes, full position

IV Percentile: A More Robust Signal

IV Percentile answers a different question: on what percentage of trading days over the past year was IV lower than it is today? Unlike IVR — which can be distorted by a single outlier spike — IV Percentile uses the full distribution of daily readings. It is more robust when a stock has had one extreme volatility event that inflates the 52-week high.

Example: A stock spiked to 150% IV during a single crisis event but spent 340 of the last 365 days between 20–45% IV. Current IV is 42%. IVR reads very low (because the 52-week high is 150%). IV Percentile reads 90+ (because 42% exceeds nearly every other day's reading). IV Percentile correctly identifies this as an elevated premium-selling environment. IVR misleads.

Rule: use IVR as your primary filter, IV Percentile as confirmation. When both read above 50, the environment is confirmed. When they diverge significantly, investigate — a recent extreme event may be distorting IVR.

Finding IVR on Your Platform

On ThinkOrSwim (TD Ameritrade/Schwab): Today's Options Statistics section on any ticker page shows both IV Rank and IV Percentile. On Barchart.com: the Options Overview tab displays both metrics. On TastyTrade: IVR is prominently shown on every ticker page. On Market Chameleon: free, detailed IV history and percentile charts for any stock.

THE IVR ENTRY RULE

Only sell premium when IVR is above 50. This single filter eliminates the most common premium-selling mistake: entering when IV is historically low, collecting thin premiums, then watching IV expand after entry — hurting all short premium positions through Vega. High IVR means you are getting paid well for the risk. Low IVR means you are not. When IVR is below 50, wait or use debit structures instead.

THE VIX FEAR RULE

Fear is your best friend when selling options. VIX above 30 = HIGH fear = HIGH premiums = collect MORE premium as a seller. VIX below 20 = LOW fear = LOW premiums = less income per trade. The rule: when the VIX is high, sell options aggressively. When the VIX is low, be more selective — the premium may not justify the risk. VIX is covered in depth in Chapter 9.

The Only Two Strategies the Seller Uses — And Why

Before introducing any strategy in this chapter, one rule must be stated clearly and without qualification. It is not a guideline. It is not a suggestion for beginners. It is the non-negotiable boundary that defines the entire Seller's model:

⚠ THE SELLER'S HARD RULE ⚠

The Seller operates by three rules — and three only:

1. **Cash-Secured Put (CSP) — to enter a position**
2. **Covered Call — after assignment, to work the Wheel**
3. **Never sell-to-open before an earnings report**

That is the complete list. Nothing else.

No naked calls. No naked puts. No short strangles. No short straddles. No undefined-risk structures of any kind. These expose the Seller to theoretically unlimited loss — a loss that can exceed the entire account in a single overnight gap move. The Seller's model is built on certainty: you know your maximum risk before the trade is placed. The moment unlimited risk enters the equation, certainty is gone — and with it, the ability to plan, size correctly, and sleep.

The cash-secured put is defined risk by construction: your maximum loss is the strike price minus the premium collected, and you have the cash reserved to cover it. The covered call is defined risk by construction: you already own the shares. There is no scenario where either strategy produces a loss larger than what the capital committed can absorb. This is not a conservative choice — it is the professional choice. Experienced institutional sellers use defined-risk structures because blowing up an account is the one outcome that ends the game permanently.

WHY ONLY THESE THREE RULES

Every other premium-selling strategy adds complexity, undefined risk, or both. Iron condors, short strangles, naked calls — they may produce higher theoretical returns per dollar in ideal conditions. But the Seller's edge is not in maximizing return on any single trade. It is in staying in the game across hundreds of trades and years. One undefined-risk position that gaps overnight can erase twelve months of consistent CSP income. And earnings? Earnings is the one event that can gap any stock — including your best A-class names — 15, 20, 30% in a single overnight session. No premium justifies that binary risk. The rule is absolute: check the earnings calendar before placing every trade. If earnings fall before your expiration, wait. The premium will still be there after the report. Your account may not be if you don't wait.

The Core Income Strategies

→ See Figure 6.4 — Moneyness Ladder: Put Contract (Chapter 4 — Options Valuation)

Figure 15.2 — Put Contract Moneyness Ladder. The Cash-Secured Put targets OTM strikes below the stock price — collecting premium while staying outside intrinsic value territory. Assignment happens when the stock falls below your short strike.

STRATEGY 1: Cash-Secured Put (CSP)

The cash-secured put is the foundational income strategy for the risk-first trader. You sell an OTM put on a stock or ETF you are willing to own at a price below the current market. You collect premium upfront. If the stock stays above your strike through expiration, the put expires worthless and you keep the premium. If the stock falls below your strike, you are assigned — you buy 100 shares at the strike price you agreed to.

- Setup: Sell 1 OTM put, 30–45 DTE, at a strike 10–20% below the current price on a quality underlying
- Cash requirement: Have enough cash in your account to buy 100 shares at the strike price — this is the 'cash-secured' requirement
- Exit rule: Buy to close at 50% of the premium received. Do not hold to expiration for the last few dollars — the Gamma risk is not worth it
- Cap tier rule: Use only on mega cap and large cap names where the options chain is liquid and assignment at the strike is genuinely acceptable
- IV timing: Sell CSPs when IV is elevated (IVR above 30) — you collect more premium for the same risk

CSP SELECTION CRITERIA

Ask three questions before selling any CSP: (1) Would I be happy owning this stock at this strike price? (2) Does the company have strong enough fundamentals that a temporary decline is recoverable? (3) Is there a known catalyst (earnings, FDA, macro event) that could gap the stock through my strike before I can manage it? If the answer to #3 is yes — wait for the event to pass.

STRATEGY 2: Covered Call (CC)

The covered call is the mirror image of the CSP in terms of risk profile. You own 100 shares of stock (or an ETF) and sell an OTM call against it. You collect premium monthly. Your upside is capped at the call strike, but you reduce your cost basis on the stock with every premium collected. Over time, a disciplined covered call program dramatically lowers the effective cost of your stock positions.

- Setup: Own 100 shares + sell 1 OTM call, 30–45 DTE, at a strike 5–15% above the current price
- Premium collected reduces cost basis — after enough cycles, your effective cost can approach zero
- Exit rule: Buy to close at 50% of premium received, or roll up and out if the stock runs through your strike
- Rolling: If the stock rises above your call strike before expiration, buy to close and sell the next month's call at a higher strike — collect more premium and preserve your position
- Best environment: Sideways to mildly bullish market. Avoid selling covered calls in strongly trending bull runs — you cap your gains at the worst time

STRATEGY 3: The Wheel — CSP into Covered Call

The Wheel combines the CSP and the covered call into a single continuous income cycle on the same underlying. It is the most complete expression of the Seller's Edge for a focused position.

- Phase 1 — Sell cash-secured puts on a quality stock until assigned
- Phase 2 — Once assigned, immediately begin selling covered calls against the shares
- Phase 3 — If the covered call is exercised (shares called away), return to Phase 1 and sell cash-secured puts again
- The Wheel works best on: stocks you genuinely want to own, with liquid options chains, in sectors aligned with the current business cycle phase
- The Wheel fails on: weak fundamentals, thin options chains, or stocks in confirmed downtrends — the cost basis keeps rising as the stock keeps falling

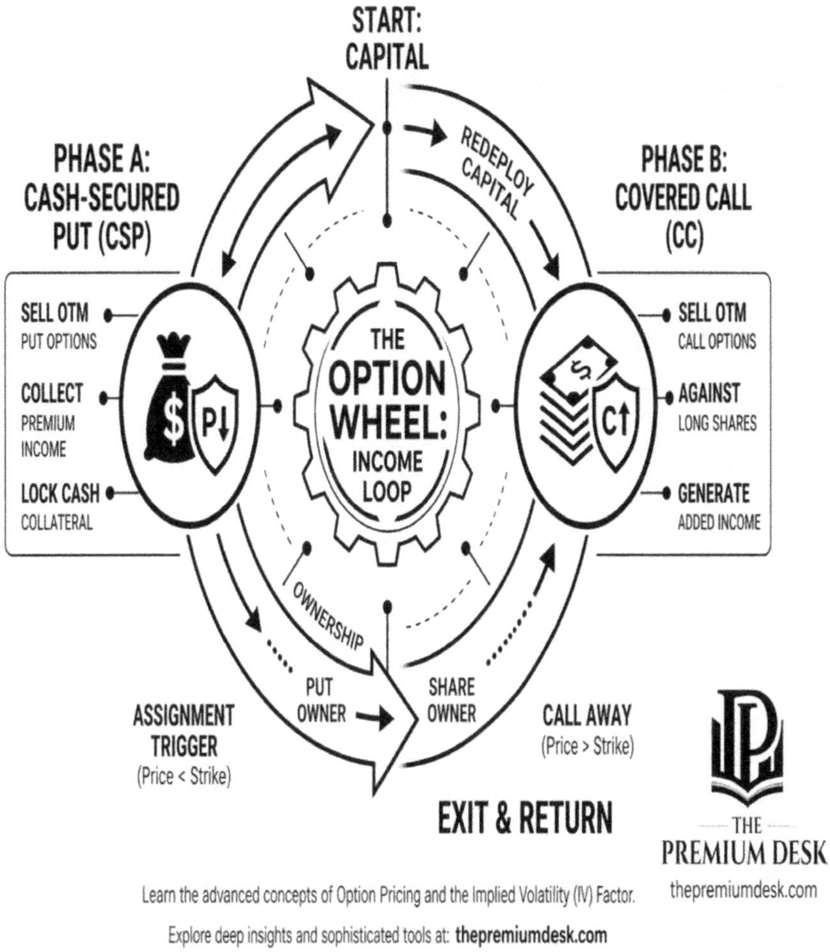

Figure 15.2 — The Wheel Cycle — The complete Cash-Secured Put to Covered Call income loop. Each cycle reduces effective cost basis.

THE INCOME TRADER'S CREED

Trading requires discipline. Losses are part of trading — strikeouts are part of baseball. Success is trading in general needs: Determination

The right strategy.

The paper mindset.

The ultimate belief that this process works across hundreds of trades. The income trader does not trade for excitement. They trade for consistency.

SCR IN ACTION: WORKED EXAMPLES

How to Trade Like a Seller — Win, Lose, and Still Come Out Ahead

The following two examples use the same underlying stock — XYZ Corp, trading at $100 — to show you what the SCR framework looks like in real life. In Example A, the trade wins cleanly. In Example B, the trade loses initially — and then you watch the seller turn that loss into a profit using the Wheel. Both are equally important. The income trader must be comfortable with both outcomes because the system is built to profit from the sequence, not just the individual trade.

EXAMPLE A The Clean Win — Cash-Secured Put Expires Worthless	
Underlying	XYZ Corp — quality large-cap stock you are willing to own
Stock Price	$100.00 per share at trade entry
Strategy	Sell 1 Cash-Secured Put — 35 DTE
Strike Selected	$90 Put (10% OTM — below a clear support level on the chart)
Premium Received	$2.50 per share × 100 shares = $250 collected upfront
Cash Reserved	$9,000 set aside (enough to buy 100 shares at $90 if assigned)
IVR at Entry	52 — IV is in the upper half of its annual range. Favorable for sellers.
Profit Target	Close at 50% of premium received = buy back at $1.25 or less

What Happens: XYZ Holds Above $90 Through Expiration

Over the 35-day life of the trade, XYZ moves sideways — it dips briefly to $95 on a market dip but never threatens the $90 strike. Theta does its job. The put premium decays from $2.50 to $1.20 by day 18.

Day	XYZ Price	Put Premium	Unrealized P&L	Action
0	$100.00	$2.50	—	SELL TO OPEN 1 $90 Put — collect $250
7	$97.50	$2.10	−$40	Monitoring. Put cost increased slightly. No action.
14	$95.00	$1.60	+$90	Stock dipped — premium decayed despite move. Theta working.
18	**$96.00**	**$1.20**	**+$130**	**At 52% profit. CLOSE — BUY TO CLOSE at $1.20. ✓ Target hit.**
35	$98.00	$0.00	+$250	(If held to expiry — put expires worthless. Full $250 kept.)

✓ EXAMPLE A RESULT — CLEAN WIN

Premium collected: $250 | Premium paid to close: $120 | Net profit: $130 in 18 days
Cash reserved ($9,000) is now free to deploy in the next trade.
Annualized return on reserved capital: ($130 ÷ $9,000) × (365 ÷ 18) = ~29.3% annualized.

EXAMPLE B The Wheel in Motion — Assignment, Recovery, and Profit

Underlying	XYZ Corp — same stock, same thesis: quality name you are willing to own
Stock Price	$100.00 per share at trade entry
Strategy	Sell 1 Cash-Secured Put — 35 DTE
Strike Selected	$90 Put (10% OTM)
Premium Received	$2.50 per share × 100 = $250 collected upfront
Cash Reserved	$9,000 set aside to buy shares if assigned
IVR at Entry	55 — IV elevated, favorable for sellers

Phase 1: The Market Drops — Assignment Occurs

A sector-wide selloff hits XYZ hard. The stock drops from $100 to $84 by expiration. The $90 put is now $6 in the money. The put buyer exercises their right — you are assigned 100 shares of XYZ at $90. Your account: $250 premium received − $9,000 stock purchase = net stock cost basis of $87.50 per share ($90 strike − $2.50 premium collected).

At Assignment	Your Position	Your Effective Cost Basis
XYZ trading at $84.00 Put assigned at $90 strike	Long 100 shares of XYZ Purchase price: $90.00/share	**Strike $90.00 − $2.50 premium = $87.50 Unrealized loss vs. market: $3.50/share ($350 total)**

THIS IS NOT A LOSS — THIS IS PHASE 2

Assignment on a quality stock at a price you agreed to in advance is not a failure. It is the plan executing correctly. You now own 100 shares of XYZ at an effective cost of $87.50. The market is at $84. Your job now is to sell covered calls against those shares every month until the position profits. The Wheel begins.

Phase 2: The Wheel — Three Covered Call Cycles

You now own 100 shares of XYZ at an effective cost basis of $87.50. XYZ is trading at $84. Every month, you sell a covered call against your shares. Each premium collected reduces your cost basis further. You do not panic. You do not sell the shares at a loss. You work the system.

Cycle	XYZ Price	Call Strike	DTE	Premium Collected	Cumulative Premium	Cost Basis After Cycle
1	$84.00	$87 Call	35 DTE	$1.80 ($180)	$430 total	$87.50 - $1.80 = $85.70
2	$86.50	$89 Call	35 DTE	$1.60 ($160)	$590 total	$85.70 - $1.60 = $84.10
3	**$90.00**	**$92 Call**	**35 DTE**	**$1.50 ($150)**	**$740 total**	**$84.10 - $1.50 = $82.60**

Cycle-by-Cycle Breakdown

Cycle 1 — XYZ at $84, Sell $87 Call, 35 DTE, $1.80 Premium

XYZ is still below your cost basis. You sell the $87 call — slightly OTM — collecting $180. If the stock rises above $87 by expiration, your shares get called away at $87. If it stays below, the call expires worthless and you keep the $180 and still own the shares. Either outcome reduces your effective cost basis.

- Call expires worthless (XYZ stays at $84–$86): Keep $180. New cost basis: $85.70. Try again next month.
- Call exercised (XYZ rises above $87): Shares sold at $87. Net result: $87 sale + $180 call premium + $250 original CSP premium − $9,000 stock purchase = sell at $87 with $430 in total premium collected → effective exit at $91.30. Profit even if called away above cost.

Cycle 2 — XYZ at $86.50, Sell $89 Call, 35 DTE, $1.60 Premium

The stock has recovered to $86.50. You move your call strike up to $89 — giving the stock room to run while still collecting premium. $160 collected. Cost basis now $84.10. You are narrowing the gap between your cost basis and the market price every single month — without the stock needing to do anything dramatic.

- Call expires worthless: Keep $160. Cost basis now $84.10. Position improving with each cycle.
- Call exercised at $89: Shares sold at $89 + $590 total premium collected → effective exit price = $92.90. Solid profit.

Cycle 3 — XYZ at $90, Sell $92 Call, 35 DTE, $1.50 Premium

XYZ has recovered to $90 — back to where you originally sold the put. You sell the $92 call, collecting $150. Cost basis is now $82.60. At this point the stock is trading ABOVE your effective cost basis. You are in profit on the position even before this call is resolved.

- Call expires worthless: Keep $150. You own XYZ at an effective cost of $82.60 while the stock trades at $90. Unrealized profit: $7.40/share ($740).
- Call exercised at $92: Shares called away at $92 + $740 total premium → effective exit = $99.40/share. Full recovery and profit.

EXAMPLE B — FULL P&L SUMMARY

From Assignment to Full Recovery

Original CSP premium collected: **+$250**
Covered Call — Cycle 1 premium: **+$180**
Covered Call — Cycle 2 premium: **+$160**
Covered Call — Cycle 3 premium: **+$150**

Total premium collected across all cycles: $740

Effective cost basis after all premium: **$82.60/share**
XYZ market price at end of Cycle 3: **$90.00/share**

Unrealized profit if holding shares: +$7.40/share = +$740 total

If shares called away at $92 (Cycle 3 call exercised):
Total profit: $740 premium + ($92 − $90) × 100 = $740 + $200 = **+$940 net profit**

A trade that looked like a loss at assignment became a $940 profit over 4 months.

THE SELLER'S RECOVERY RUBRIC

How to Turn a Losing Trade into a Winning Trade as a Premium Seller

Step	Situation	Seller's Action	Why It Works
1	You sell a CSP on a quality stock at a strike 10–15% below market	Select strike below clear chart support. Collect premium upfront. Set cash aside equal to 100 shares at the strike.	You are paid to agree to buy something you want, at a price lower than today's market. The premium is yours regardless of outcome.
2	Trade goes your way — put expires worthless	Buy to close at 50% of premium received (don't hold to expiry for last few dollars). Free up cash. Repeat the cycle.	You captured the fastest-decaying portion of the premium. Theta worked for you. Return the capital to work immediately in the next cycle.
3	Trade goes against you — stock drops, you are assigned	Accept the shares. Calculate your true cost basis (strike minus all premium collected). Do NOT panic sell at a loss.	Assignment is the plan working. You own a quality stock at a price below where it was when you agreed to buy it. You are not a victim — you are a disciplined buyer.
4	You now own the shares below market — begin the Wheel	Immediately sell an OTM covered call against your 100 shares. Target a strike above your cost basis if possible. Collect premium.	Every dollar of covered call premium collected reduces your cost basis further. The stock doesn't need to rise — time alone is reducing your risk with each passing month.
5	Covered call expires worthless — stock still below original entry	Sell another covered call at the same or slightly higher strike. Collect another month of premium. Repeat.	The market may be stuck, but your cost basis is falling. Three months of covered call premium can reduce your cost basis by

Step	Situation	Seller's Action	Why It Works
			$4–6/share on a $90 stock — that's meaningful cushion.
6	Stock recovers — covered call is exercised or position is profitable	If call is exercised: shares sold at strike + all premium collected = full recovery and profit. If holding shares: sell when effective cost basis is well below market price.	The Wheel has completed its cycle. A trade that produced a paper loss at assignment generated real income every month and exited at a net profit. This is the SCR system in action.
7	Return to Step 1 — Repeat	Take the recovered capital and begin the next CSP cycle on the same or a new quality underlying.	The SCR framework compounds. Each completed Wheel cycle builds track record, confidence, and account value. The income is not in any single trade — it is in the sequence.

Advanced Wheel Mechanics: Strike Selection by Cycle Phase

The Wheel is not a static system — it is a dynamic one. The best Wheel traders calibrate their strike selection, their DTE window, and their aggressiveness to the current business cycle phase. Selling the same delta in a late expansion market as you would in an early recovery is leaving money on the table in one environment and taking excessive risk in the other.

Cycle Phase	IVR Environment	CSP Strike Delta	DTE Target	Covered Call Delta	Wheel Aggression
Early Expansion	Low to Moderate (IVR 30–55)	0.25–0.30 — closer to ATM for higher premium	30–35 DTE	0.25–0.30 — give stock room to run	Moderate — market rising, premiums thin, be selective
Mid Expansion	Moderate (IVR 40–60)	0.20–0.25 — standard income zone	30–45 DTE	0.20–0.25 — standard covered call zone	Full — optimal environment for the Wheel
Late Expansion / Peak	Moderate to High (IVR 55–75)	0.15–0.20 — wider cushion as vol rises	35–45 DTE — longer to absorb vol	0.20–0.25 — tighter — don't cap upside in late rally	Cautious — reduce position count by 25%
Recession / Contraction	High (IVR 70–100)	0.10–0.15 — maximum cushion, far OTM	45 DTE — maximum time buffer	0.15–0.20 on quality mega-cap only	Defensive — mega and large cap only, 50% of normal size
Trough / Early Recovery	Very High (IVR 75–100)	0.20–0.25 — IV is high, same premium further OTM	35–45 DTE	0.20–0.30 — collect elevated premium on recovery	Opportunistic — best CSP premiums of the cycle, increase size

The trough / early recovery phase deserves special attention. This is the only phase where the Wheel is simultaneously most risky on paper and most rewarding in practice. Stocks are beaten down, IV is high, and premium is rich — but the news is terrible and sentiment is bearish. The income trader's advantage is that the news is already priced in. You are not buying hope; you are selling puts on quality companies at prices that already reflect worst-case scenarios, collecting premiums that price in continued distress. This is the highest-edge Wheel environment of the full cycle.

The Wheel on ETFs: Sector Rotation Income

Volatility Skew Strategies for Options on Futures and Commodity Futures Options

The Seller's Philosophy extends naturally to options on futures and commodity futures options — where volatility skew creates additional premium-selling opportunities that are structurally different from equity options. In commodity markets, the skew is often inverted relative to equities: for grain and agricultural futures, implied volatility on OTM calls can be significantly elevated above ATM volatility because supply shocks drive violent upside price spikes. This creates ideal conditions for OTM call ratio writes — where the seller captures the skew premium in addition to the standard time value decay.

For futures options, the skew selection rule is: identify the strikes where implied volatility is highest relative to historical volatility, then construct the ratio write to sell those overvalued strikes in larger quantity while buying fewer contracts at a less overvalued strike. The result is a structure where you are receiving more premium than a simple naked write — with the long leg providing protection against violent one-directional moves. The full framework for commodity futures options writing and the put-call ratio timing method is developed in Chapter 18.

Most traders run the Wheel on individual stocks. Professional income traders also run the Wheel on sector ETFs — and for good reason. ETF Wheels eliminate single-stock binary risk, never have earnings announcements, and benefit directly from the sector rotation framework in Chapter 7. The trade-off: lower premiums per contract compared to volatile individual names, but smoother, more predictable behavior that allows more aggressive strike selection.

- Best ETFs for the Wheel: SPY, QQQ, IWM (broad index), XLF, XLK, XLV, XLE, XLY (sector ETFs with highest options volume). Avoid thematic or leveraged ETFs — they fail the liquidity and risk tests.
- ETF Wheel advantage: no single-stock event risk. No CEO departure, no FDA rejection, no earnings gap. The ETF absorbs individual company shocks across dozens of holdings. Your short put on XLF is not threatened by one bad bank quarter — it takes a sector-wide crisis to challenge it.
- ETF Wheel strike selection: use the sector rotation calendar (Chapter 7) to time your entries. Open CSPs on sector ETFs that are in the early-to-mid phase of their cycle leadership. Roll into covered calls only after assignment — and continue selling calls until the sector shows late-cycle signals, at which point close the position and rotate to the next incoming leader.

ETF WHEEL RULE

When running the Wheel on a sector ETF, apply a rotation exit rule that does not apply to individual stocks: if the sector moves from mid-cycle to late-cycle leadership while you are holding assigned shares, prioritize selling the assigned shares at a profit over continuing the covered call cycle. The macro rotation is more important than the remaining covered call premium. Take the profit and redeploy into the next incoming leader sector.

Credit Spreads as Capital-Efficient Income

The cash-secured put requires setting aside 100% of the potential purchase price as reserved capital — $9,000 for a $90 strike put. For traders with limited capital or those who want to run more simultaneous positions, the bull put spread (also called a put credit spread) offers the same directional thesis at a fraction of the capital requirement. The trade-off: capped maximum profit vs. an uncapped one on the CSP.

Construction: sell the higher strike put, buy the lower strike put at the same expiration. The bought put caps your maximum loss. The difference between the strikes minus the net credit received is your maximum risk — and that maximum risk is the only capital you need to reserve.

Structure	CSP (Cash-Secured Put)	Bull Put Spread ($5 wide)
Trade	Sell $90 put on $100 stock	Sell $90 put, Buy $85 put on $100 stock
Premium collected	$2.50 ($250)	$1.20 ($120) — net credit after buying the $85 put
Capital reserved	$9,000 (full strike × 100)	$380 (spread width $500 - $120 net credit)
Maximum loss	$8,750 ($9,000 - $250 premium)	$380 (the capital reserved — fully defined)
Return on capital	$250 ÷ $9,000 = 2.8%	$120 ÷ $380 = 31.6% on capital at risk
Maximum loss scenario	Stock goes to zero	Stock falls below $85 at expiration
Assignment risk	Yes — must own 100 shares if assigned	No — maximum loss is capped at $380
Best use	When you genuinely want to own the stock at the strike	When you want premium income without the capital commitment or assignment obligation

The credit spread's 31.6% return on capital versus the CSP's 2.8% looks like a clear winner — but these are not comparable on a risk-adjusted basis. The CSP's capital is mostly intact at assignment (you own shares worth $84 on a stock where you paid $90), while the credit spread's capital is fully at risk and gone if the stock breaches the lower strike. The right choice depends on your capital situation and whether you want the assignment obligation. Many experienced income traders use CSPs on their highest-conviction names and bull put spreads for broader portfolio exposure.

PPD: Profit Per Day — The Wheel Trader's True Scorecard

Most traders evaluate Wheel trades the wrong way. They compare total premium collected — $300 on one trade versus $250 on another — and conclude the first is better. But if the $300 trade runs 45 days and the $250 trade runs 15 days, the second trade is generating nearly twice the capital efficiency. The number that tells you the truth is PPD: Profit Per Day.

PPD normalizes every trade for time. It answers the only question that matters for a capital-efficient income portfolio: how much am I earning per day for every dollar I have deployed?

The PPD Formula

PPD = Net Premium Collected ÷ Days Held

PPD on Reserved Capital = (Net Premium ÷ Capital Reserved) ÷ Days Held × 100.

Two versions: the raw PPD (dollars per day) tells you how efficiently you extracted value from the trade. PPD on reserved capital (% per day) normalizes across positions of different sizes and lets you compare a $50 stock trade against a $200 stock trade on equal footing.

PPD in Practice: Why the 50% Profit Close Rule Exists

The 50% profit target is not arbitrary. It exists because of PPD. Here is why closing at 50% profit almost always produces a better PPD than holding to expiration — even when expiration would deliver more total premium.

Scenario	Premium Collected	Days Held	PPD	PPD on $9,000 Capital
Hold to expiration (35 DTE)	$3.00 ($300 full premium)	35 days	$8.57/day	0.095%/day — annualizes to ~34.7%
Close at 50% profit (day 18)	$1.50 ($150 net)	18 days	$8.33/day	0.093%/day — nearly identical PPD
Close at 50% + redeploy (new trade, day 19–53)	$1.50 + $1.50 = $300 total	35 days total	$8.57/day across both trades	0.095%/day — same annualized return, with half the Gamma risk
Hold to expiration, position goes against you (day 25)	$0 or worse — stop triggered	25 days	$0 or negative	PPD destroyed — illustrates the asymmetry of holding late

The table reveals the core insight: closing at 50% profit and immediately redeploying produces the same PPD as holding to expiration — but with dramatically less risk in the final third of the trade's life, when Gamma accelerates and a single adverse day can erase weeks of decay. The last 50% of premium takes 50–60% of the time to collect, while carrying 80%+ of the Gamma risk. PPD exposes this trade-off in a single number.

Using PPD to Compare and Rank Trade Candidates

Before entering any Wheel trade, calculate the projected PPD and compare it against your alternatives. This is the selection discipline that separates income traders who run their portfolio as a business from those who trade on feel.

Candidate	Stock Price	Strike	Premium (50% target)	Days to 50%*	PPD on Capital
AAPL CSP	$195	$175 put	$1.60 ($160)	~18 days	$160 ÷ $17,500 ÷ 18 = 0.051%/day
MSFT CSP	$420	$390 put	$3.80 ($380)	~20 days	$380 ÷ $39,000 ÷ 20 = 0.049%/day
XLF CSP	$42	$39 put	$0.55 ($55)	~14 days	$55 ÷ $3,900 ÷ 14 = 0.101%/day
NVDA CSP	$800	$720 put	$8.50 ($850)	~16 days	$850 ÷ $72,000 ÷ 16 = 0.074%/day
SPY CSP	$500	$470 put	$2.20 ($220)	~17 days	$220 ÷ $47,000 ÷ 17 = 0.028%/day

* Estimated days to 50% profit based on historical theta decay rates at 30–35 DTE. Actual results vary.

In this example, XLF produces the highest PPD on capital (0.101%/day) — not because it collects the most premium in absolute terms, but because the strike price requires far less reserved capital while delivering proportionally strong premium relative to its size. NVDA, despite an $850 absolute premium, ties up $72,000 in reserved capital. SPY, despite being the 'safest' trade, produces the lowest PPD because the premium-to-capital ratio is weakest.

PPD ranking turns trade selection from a feel-based decision into a math-based one. Run this calculation on every candidate before you enter. The highest-PPD trade that passes all other quality filters is the one you execute.

THE PPD RULE

Never enter a Wheel trade without calculating its projected PPD on reserved capital. Your minimum acceptable PPD threshold should be set based on your monthly income target — work backwards: if you need $3,000/month on $100,000 deployed, you need 0.10%/day average PPD across your portfolio (3,000 ÷ 100,000 ÷ 21.7 trading days per month). Any trade generating below half your target PPD should be passed over for a better opportunity — or not traded at all.

SPREAD VS. CSP DECISION RULE

Use a CSP when: (1) you genuinely want to own 100 shares of this stock at this price, (2) you have the capital to reserve without compromising other positions, and (3) the underlying is mega or large cap with strong fundamentals. Use a bull put spread when: (1) you want income without assignment obligation, (2) you are working with a smaller account and need capital efficiency, or (3) you want to run more simultaneous positions than a CSP portfolio would allow. Never use a spread to trade an underlying you would not also use for a CSP — the spread caps your loss but not the thesis risk.

Building Your Income Portfolio: The Sizing Math

Most traders approach income trading as a series of individual trades. Professional income traders approach it as a portfolio — a collection of coordinated positions sized to generate a target monthly income with defined maximum drawdown exposure. Here is how the math works from the top down.

Step 1 — Define your monthly income target. Be specific. Not 'make money trading' — a precise dollar amount. Example: $2,000/month in net premium income after all transaction costs.

Step 2 — Calculate required capital. At a sustainable 2–3% monthly return on deployed capital, $2,000/month requires $67,000–$100,000 in deployed capital. This is the capital actively working in positions — not your total account. Keep 20–30% in cash reserve for margin requirements, assignments, and new opportunities.

Step 3 — Determine position count. Divide your deployed capital by your average capital per position. At $9,000 per CSP position (average $90 strike on quality names) with $70,000 deployed: 70,000 ÷ 9,000 = approximately 7–8 simultaneous positions. This is your maximum — not your target. Start with 3–4 and build as your management skills scale.

Account Size	Deployed Capital (75%)	Monthly Target (2.5%)	Avg Position Size	Max Simultaneous Positions
$25,000	$18,750	$469/month	$5,000–$6,000 (lower-priced names)	3–4 positions
$50,000	$37,500	$938/month	$7,000–$9,000	4–5 positions
$100,000	$75,000	$1,875/month	$8,000–$10,000	7–8 positions
$200,000	$150,000	$3,750/month	$9,000–$12,000	12–15 positions
$500,000	$375,000	$9,375/month	$10,000–$15,000	25–35 positions (requires systematic management tools)

Two critical rules govern deployed capital management:

- Never have more than 20% of your total deployed capital in a single sector. If XLF, JPM, and BAC are all in your CSP portfolio simultaneously, a Financials sector shock hits all three at once. Diversify across at least four sectors at all times.
- Always maintain at minimum 20% of total account value in cash — this is your assignment buffer, your dry powder for high-conviction setups, and your psychological safety net that prevents panic decisions when one position moves against you.

Wheel Failure Modes: When the System Breaks

The Wheel is one of the most resilient income strategies in existence — but it has specific failure conditions that must be understood before they occur. The trader who knows when the Wheel breaks can exit cleanly. The trader who learns about failure modes from experience pays tuition.

Failure Mode	Why It Destroys the Wheel	Early Warning Signals & Action
Fundamental deterioration — the company's business breaks while you are wheeling it	The Wheel requires the stock to eventually recover. If earnings are collapsing, management is in crisis, or the business model is disrupted, the stock may never return to your cost basis. Covered call premium alone cannot compensate for a structurally declining stock.	Warning: three consecutive earnings misses, declining revenue, rising debt-to-equity while you are holding assigned shares. Action: sell the shares at a loss immediately when these signals appear. Do not Wheel a broken company.
Assignment at the top of a sector cycle — buying when macro headwinds begin	Being assigned shares of an Energy stock at cycle peak means you are entering a covered call cycle just as the sector rotation model says to rotate out. Premium income cannot offset a 30–40% sector decline.	Warning: sector BPI turning lower, commodity prices reversing, yield curve flattening while you hold cyclical sector shares. Action: sell covered calls aggressively at lower strikes to accelerate exit. Accept the call-away as soon as possible — don't fight the macro.
Over-concentrating the Wheel on one underlying or sector	Running multiple CSP positions on the same stock, or three Wheel positions in the same sector, turns a diversified income strategy into concentrated directional risk. One sector event wipes the entire portfolio simultaneously.	Warning: more than 20% of deployed capital in one sector or one underlying. Action: close or roll the most ITM position and redeploy into a different sector.
Running the Wheel on a name that fails the Ten Indicators	The Wheel's safety net is the quality of the underlying. If you are assigned on a stock with rising debt, declining earnings, or no competitive moat — the recovery thesis is weak. Premium income cannot substitute for fundamental quality.	Warning: Ten Indicators score below 6. Action: do not open Wheel positions on names that score below 7. Close any existing Wheel on a name whose fundamentals have deteriorated to below 6 since entry.
Selling covered calls too far in-the-money after assignment	After being assigned, the temptation is to sell an ITM call to collect maximum premium and escape the position quickly. But selling deep ITM covered calls locks in a loss — you cap upside at a price below your cost basis and collect premium that doesn't compensate for the difference.	Warning: you are considering a covered call strike below your effective cost basis. Action: only sell covered calls at strikes above your effective cost basis. Accept a slower recovery — premium income + stock appreciation must bring you to breakeven or profit, not just premium income alone.

The Psychology of Income Trading: Managing Ordinary Days

The biggest psychological challenge of income trading is not the losing trades — it is the ordinary days. The income trader's week is mostly unremarkable: positions decay, no catalysts fire, nothing needs managing. This is success. But the human brain is wired for stimulation, novelty, and action — and the boredom of a smoothly running income portfolio is one of the most underestimated threats to long-term performance.

Boredom creates phantom urgency. It makes traders open new positions they do not need, adjust positions that do not require adjustment, and override rules they wrote specifically to prevent impulsive decisions. The trader who makes money consistently is not necessarily the most skillful one — it is the one who can sit on their hands when there is nothing to do.

- Recognize boredom as a risk factor, not a neutral state. If you are checking your positions more than twice per day when no alerts have triggered, you are operating in a boredom risk zone. Log it in your trade journal under 'behavioral observation.'
- Have a defined non-trading activity for flat markets. Study a new strategy, review your trade journal, read a company's most recent 10-K, research a new sector. The mind needs engagement — give it something productive that is not opening new positions.
- Track 'phantom trades' — positions you considered opening but did not. Once per month, review these against your entry criteria. If you were right to stay out of most of them, your discipline is working. If most would have been profitable, investigate whether your filters are too restrictive.

THE INCOME TRADER'S PSYCHOLOGICAL EDGE

The most dangerous days in income trading are not the days when the market crashes. Those days demand action and provide clarity. The dangerous days are the Tuesdays in February when nothing happens, the account is flat, and you have been staring at the same five positions for two weeks. On those days, the enemy is inside the account — not in the market. Discipline on ordinary days is what separates income traders who compound for years from ones who blow up their consistency on a slow afternoon.

Assignment Recovery: What to Do When the Wheel Puts You in the Stock

Assignment is not failure — it is the planned outcome of a cash-secured put on a quality name. But the hours immediately following assignment are where most Wheel traders make their worst decisions. They panic-sell, freeze, or immediately write a covered call at a terrible strike.

The first rule: do nothing for 24 hours after assignment. Monday morning's opening price will determine which recovery path applies.

Scenario	Stock Opens	Covered Call Response	Why This Works
A — Shallow Dip (1-3%)	Near cost basis	Sell CC at cost basis, 30 DTE	Called away at breakeven + premium = full Wheel profit
B — Moderate (3-8%)	Below cost basis	Sell CC one strike below cost basis	Accept small loss on shares, keep income flowing. Two cycles recover most positions.
C — Deep Dip (8-15%)	Well below basis	Wait for bounce to 20-day EMA, then sell CC	Writing into a falling knife locks terrible strikes for 30 days. Patience saves months.
D — Thesis Broken (15%+)	Fundamental issue	Close the stock position. No CC. The Wheel stops.	A 15%+ drop on earnings or guidance cuts means this is no longer a Wheel candidate.

The critical distinction is between C and D. In Scenario C, the stock dropped but the thesis is intact — growing earnings, strong balance sheet, reason to recover. In Scenario D, the thesis itself is broken. Learning this distinction is the most important skill in Wheel management.

The Double Wheel: Accelerating Recovery with Two Premium Streams

When assigned shares below your cost basis, you have a second accelerator: sell CSPs below current market price simultaneously with your covered call. Two premium streams instead of one.

Example: Assigned 100 MSFT at $420. Stock now at $400. Cost basis after original CSP premium: $415.

- Covered call layer: Sell $415 call at 30 DTE — collecting ~$4.50. If called away, exit at breakeven + $4.50 profit.
- CSP layer: Sell $385 put at 30 DTE — collecting ~$3.20. If assigned again, average cost drops to ~$399.
- Combined income: $7.70/share per cycle (~1.9% of stock price in 30 days). Two streams compound recovery dramatically.

DOUBLE WHEEL CAPITAL

The Double Wheel requires buying power for a second assignment. Only run it when you have the capital AND genuinely want more shares at the lower price. Never double down on a broken thesis.

Advanced Wheel Management: The Five Stages Every Position Passes Through

A Wheel position is not a single trade — it is a lifecycle. Understanding where your position sits in that lifecycle determines every management decision. Most traders treat the Wheel as two separate events (sell put, then sell call). Professionals see it as a five-stage cycle, and they manage differently at each stage.

Stage 1 — The Premium Harvest (CSP Active). You have sold a cash-secured put on a quality stock at 30-35 DTE. The position is working as intended: theta is decaying, the stock is above your strike, and you are collecting income. Your job at this stage is to do nothing except monitor your T-21 date and the stock's relationship to your strike. The most common mistake at Stage 1 is adjusting a position that does not need adjusting. If the stock is above your strike and nothing has changed fundamentally, leave it alone. The Wheel works by not being touched.

Stage 2 — The Decision Point (T-21 Management). Your position has reached 21 days to expiration. This is the moment where passive holding transitions to active management. Three paths are available: (a) if the position is at or above 50% profit, close it — you have captured the majority of available theta with minimal remaining risk. (b) If the position is profitable but below 50%, evaluate whether to hold to 50% or roll to the next cycle for additional credit. (c) If the position is losing, execute your stop-loss protocol — close if the stock has broken below support, or roll defensively if the thesis remains intact and you can collect net credit.

Stage 3 — Assignment Transition. You have been assigned shares. The stock closed below your strike at expiration, and 100 shares now appear in your account Monday morning. This is not an emergency. This is the planned alternative outcome. Your 24-hour protocol activates: do not trade the shares or write a covered call until you have assessed the opening conditions (refer to the Assignment Recovery section earlier in this chapter). The first covered call you write after assignment sets the trajectory of your entire recovery — getting it wrong means months of suboptimal positioning.

Stage 4 — The Covered Call Harvest. You are now in the second half of the Wheel: selling covered calls against your assigned shares. The management rules are the same as Stage 1 (T-21 monitoring, 50% profit target), but the psychology is different. Many traders write covered calls too aggressively (too close to current price) because they want to 'get rid of the shares' — this is loss aversion disguised as strategy. Write calls at strikes that make mathematical sense for your cost basis, not strikes driven by emotional urgency to exit.

Stage 5 — The Cycle Reset. Your covered call expires in the money, your shares are called away, and you receive the strike price in cash. The Wheel is complete. You now return to Stage 1 with the same stock (if the thesis remains valid) or with a new stock from your watchlist. Before re-entering, update your journal: total premiums collected across all stages, total time in the Wheel cycle, effective annualized return, and any lessons learned. This data compounds into your most valuable trading asset over time.

The complete cycle — CSP entry through call-away — typically takes 60-120 days depending on market conditions and whether assignment occurs. A trader running 3-4 Wheel positions simultaneously will have positions at different stages at all times, creating a steady flow of premium income regardless of whether individual positions are in the harvest phase or the recovery phase. This diversification of stage — not just diversification of stocks — is what makes the Wheel a portfolio-level income system rather than a collection of individual trades.

The Income Trader's Annual Calendar

Income trading is not random. It follows a predictable annual rhythm driven by earnings seasons, volatility cycles, and expiration calendars. The professional income trader maps their entire year around this rhythm.

January: Earnings season begins (banks report first). Reduce income positions on stocks reporting. Sell premium on stocks that already reported clean results. VIX typically elevated from year-end rebalancing — good premium environment. Annual tax-loss harvesting adjustments from December may create January bargains.

February-March: Post-earnings income window. VIX typically declining. This is the highest-quality income period of Q1. Enter Wheel positions on stocks that reported strong Q4 results. Monitor for late-season earnings surprises. March quarterly expiration creates opportunities for roll management.

April: Q1 earnings begin. Same protocol as January: defend first, then enter post-earnings. Tax deadline (April 15) — ensure your trading records from the prior year are complete and filed. Spring sector rotation often begins here as funds rebalance for Q2.

May-June: Post-Q1 earnings income window. Historically lower VIX period (the 'sell in May' seasonal pattern reduces volatility). Premium income may be lower due to compressed IV — adjust expectations downward by 15-20% versus Q1. June quarterly expiration.

July: Q2 earnings. Midsummer liquidity can be thinner — wider bid-ask spreads on some names. Be selective: focus on mega-cap names where liquidity remains strong even in July. This is not the time to trade small-cap or mid-cap options.

August-September: Post-Q2 income window, but September is historically the worst month for equities. Begin building hedge positions in late August. Reduce overall position count in September. September quarterly expiration often coincides with increased volatility.

October: Q3 earnings. October is historically volatile but also marks the beginning of the 'best six months' seasonal pattern (November through April). This is where aggressive income traders begin increasing position size for the strong seasonal period ahead.

November-December: Post-Q3 income window plus the year-end rally period. VIX often declines into December as institutional selling subsides. Tax-loss harvesting creates selling pressure in losers and buying pressure in winners. December is an excellent month for Wheel entries on high-quality names that have been sold for tax reasons — you are selling puts on stocks that institutions are temporarily selling for non-fundamental reasons. This is structural edge.

The Assignment Journal: Tracking Recovery

Field	What to Record	Why It Matters
Assignment Date	Date + expiration cycle	Tracks recovery duration — useful for future sizing decisions
Original CSP Strike	The put strike you sold	True cost basis starts here, minus premium received
Adjusted Cost Basis	Strike minus all premiums (CSP + CCs)	Should decrease every cycle. If not, CC strikes are wrong.
Current Stock Price	Updated weekly	Determines which recovery scenario (A-D) applies
Recovery %	(Original basis - Adjusted basis) / (Original basis - Current price)	Target: 100% within 3-4 cycles via premium income
Thesis Check	Still intact? Y/N + one sentence why	Forces re-evaluation every cycle. The moment this is N — close.

The journal converts a stressful event into a measurable recovery project. Most traders overestimate recovery time. The data almost always shows quality names with disciplined Wheel management recover faster than expected.

THE SELLER'S EDGE IN ONE SENTENCE

As a premium seller, you do not need to be right on the direction. You need to be right on the quality of the stock — because if you are willing to own it at your strike, no market drop can permanently hurt you. Time, premium, and the Wheel do the rest.

PART III

MASTERY: RISK, AI & THE PROFESSIONAL EDGE

THE TRANSITION FROM STRATEGY TO MASTERY

Parts I and II gave you the system. Part III develops the judgment to apply it under real-world conditions that textbooks cannot fully anticipate: extreme volatility events, algorithmic markets that behave differently from human-driven ones, the psychology of sustained losing streaks, and the discipline required to customize a strategy to your own personality and risk tolerance. The trader who masters Part III is not just following rules — they are understanding why the rules exist, which is the only foundation for knowing when a rule must flex and when it must hold.

Mastery is not more strategies — it is executing the right one of six with increasing precision.

> **6-CONDITION FRAMEWORK ▸ IDENTIFIES VOLATILITY — the second axis of the six-condition read**
> Volatility is the axis that splits every direction into two possible strategies. High or low IV determines whether you buy or sell premium. The VIX is the primary volatility signal. This chapter teaches you to read it precisely.

Price is visible. Volatility is hidden. Every options trader who focuses on price alone is trading with one eye closed. Volatility — the rate and magnitude of price change — is the variable that determines whether you overpay for protection, undercollect on income, or walk into an earnings trade perfectly positioned. It is the engine underneath every options premium, and it must be understood before any strategy in this book can be applied with full competence.

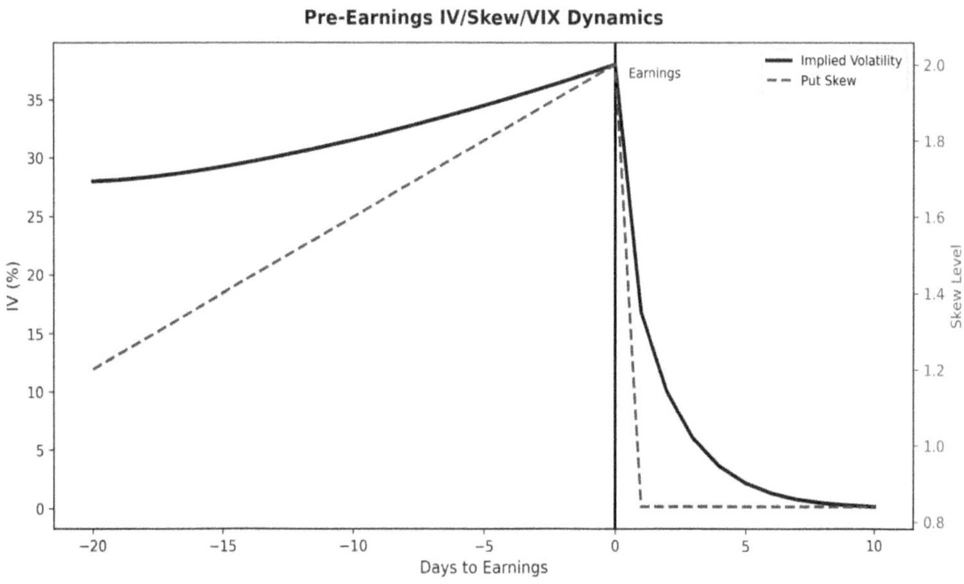

Figure 16.1 — IV Skew and VIX Relationship — How implied volatility skew shifts across strikes as market fear rises.

IV Skew and VIX Relationship — How implied volatility skew shifts as market fear rises.

Historical Volatility vs. Implied Volatility

There are two distinct types of volatility every options trader must be able to distinguish instantly. Confusing them is one of the most expensive mistakes in options trading.

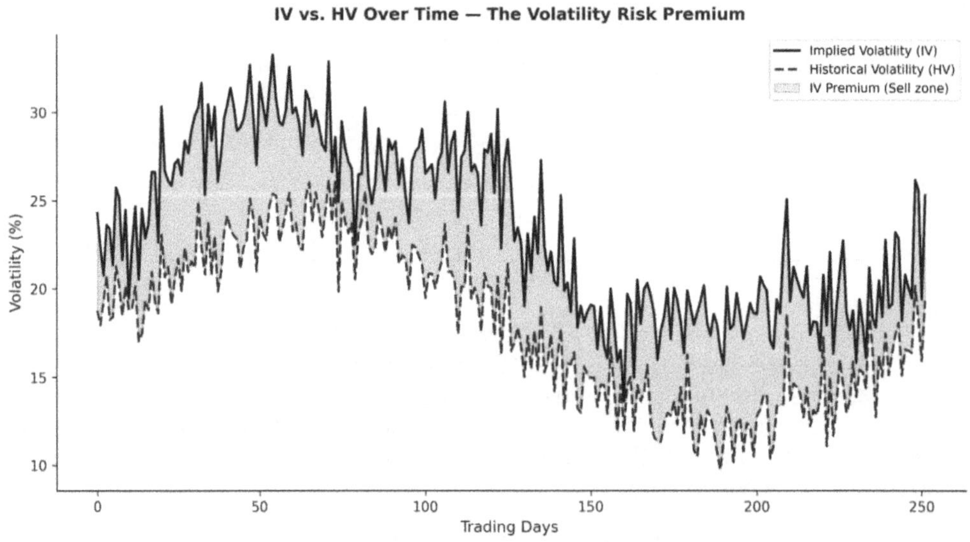

Figure 16.1 — IV vs. HV Over Time. The persistent volatility risk premium — sell when IV spikes above HV.

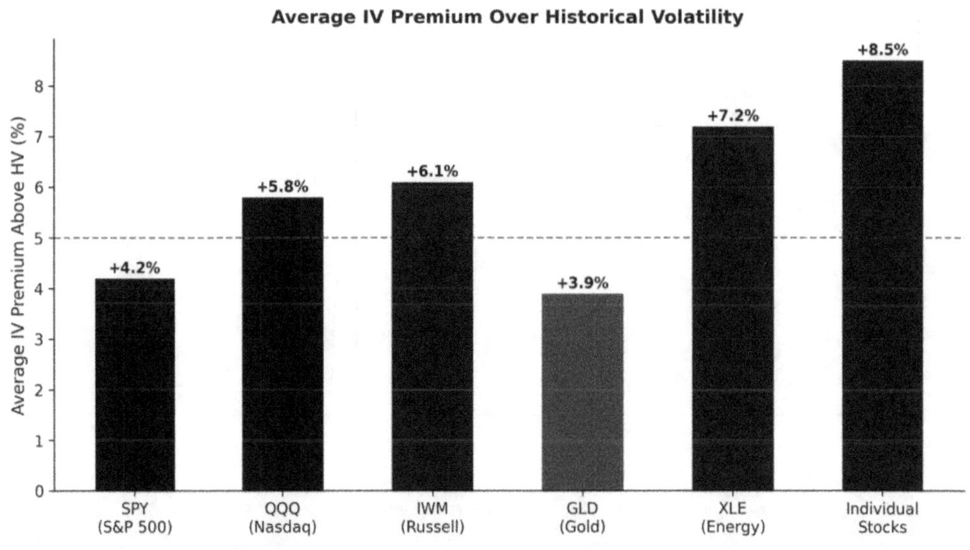

Figure 16.3 — Average IV Premium by Asset. Options consistently overprice realized volatility.

	Historical Volatility (HV)	Implied Volatility (IV)
What it measures	How much the stock HAS moved — backward-looking, statistical	How much the market EXPECTS the stock to move — forward-looking, market-derived
Source	Calculated from actual price data over a defined historical period	Extracted from current options premiums using an options pricing model (Black-Scholes)
Direction	Backward — tells you what happened	Forward — tells you what the market is pricing in

	Historical Volatility (HV)	Implied Volatility (IV)
Use for traders	Benchmark — compare current IV to HV to assess whether options are cheap or expensive	Primary trading signal — high IV = sell premium, low IV = buy premium or spreads
Key metric	20-day HV, 30-day HV, 60-day HV are the most commonly referenced periods	IV Rank (IVR) and IV Percentile measure IV relative to its own historical range

The relationship between HV and IV is the key signal: when IV is significantly above HV, the market is paying more for expected movement than the stock has historically delivered — options are expensive, and selling premium has statistical edge. When IV is below HV, options are cheap relative to actual movement — buying options or entering debit spreads is more favorable.

The VIX: The Market's Fear Gauge

The CBOE Volatility Index (VIX) measures the 30-day implied volatility of S&P 500 options. It is the single most widely watched volatility indicator in the world, and it is essential context for every options trade you make — because it tells you the overall temperature of the market's fear and uncertainty.

VIX Level	Market State	Options Trading Implication
Below 15	Calm, complacent market	Premiums are cheap. Avoid heavy premium selling — low reward for the risk. Favorable for debit spreads, calendar spreads, LEAPS.
15 – 20	Normal market conditions	Balanced environment. Standard income strategies (CSPs, covered calls, vertical credit spreads) are effective.
20 – 30	Elevated uncertainty	Premium selling becomes more attractive. Wider credit spreads, higher CSP premiums. Size down slightly — larger moves are expected.
30 – 40	High fear — market stress	Rich premium environment for sellers. Use defined-risk structures only. Excellent time for iron condors, cash-secured puts on quality names during panic.
Above 40	Extreme fear / crisis mode	Maximum premium — but maximum risk. Size very small. Use spreads, never naked. Wait for VIX to begin declining before deploying heavily.

- The VIX and the S&P 500 have an inverse relationship — when the market falls, VIX typically rises. When the market rallies, VIX typically falls;
- VIX spikes are usually sharper and faster than VIX declines — fear arrives quickly, complacency returns slowly;
- A VIX spike into the 30–40 range that is not accompanied by a fundamental market breakdown is often a mean reversion opportunity — premium sellers historically profit from deploying during panic and closing as VIX returns to normal;

IV Rank and IV Percentile: Relative Volatility

Knowing the current IV level is not enough. You need to know whether that IV is high or low relative to where it has been. This is the purpose of IV Rank and IV Percentile — two metrics that every serious options trader must check before entering any premium-selling trade.

- IV Rank (IVR) = (Current IV − 52-week low IV) ÷ (52-week high IV − 52-week low IV) × 100. An IVR of 0 means IV is at its lowest point of the past year. An IVR of 100 means IV is at its highest;
- IVR above 50 → IV is in the upper half of its annual range → premium selling has statistical edge;
- IVR below 25 → IV is near its annual low → premium is cheap → favor debit spreads, calendar spreads, or no trade; and
- IV Percentile measures the percentage of days in the past year that IV was lower than today — a slightly different calculation but used the same way as IVR.

THE IV RULE

Never sell premium without checking IVR first. Selling a cash-secured put when IVR is 15 means you are collecting a fraction of what you could collect if you waited. Premium selling in low IV environments generates poor income for the risk taken. Wait for IVR above 30 at minimum — above 50 is ideal.

Volatility Skew: What the Market Is Really Pricing

Volatility skew refers to the fact that options at different strikes have different implied volatilities — they do not all share the same IV. This phenomenon exists because the market prices downside risk (put options) more expensively than upside risk (call options), reflecting the real-world asymmetry of crashes vs. rallies.

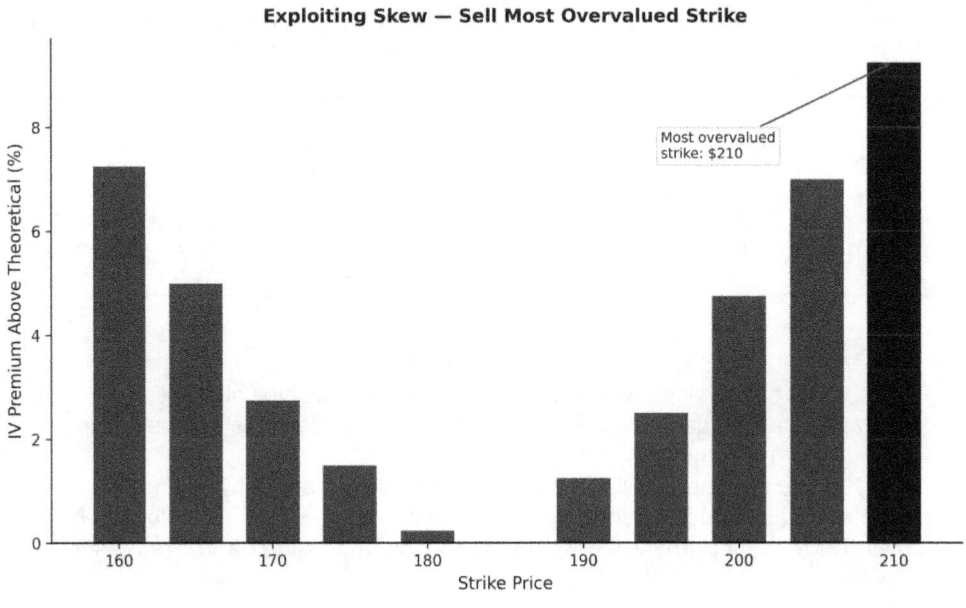

Figure 16.4 — Sell Most Overvalued Strike. Identifying the highest IV premium strike to sell.

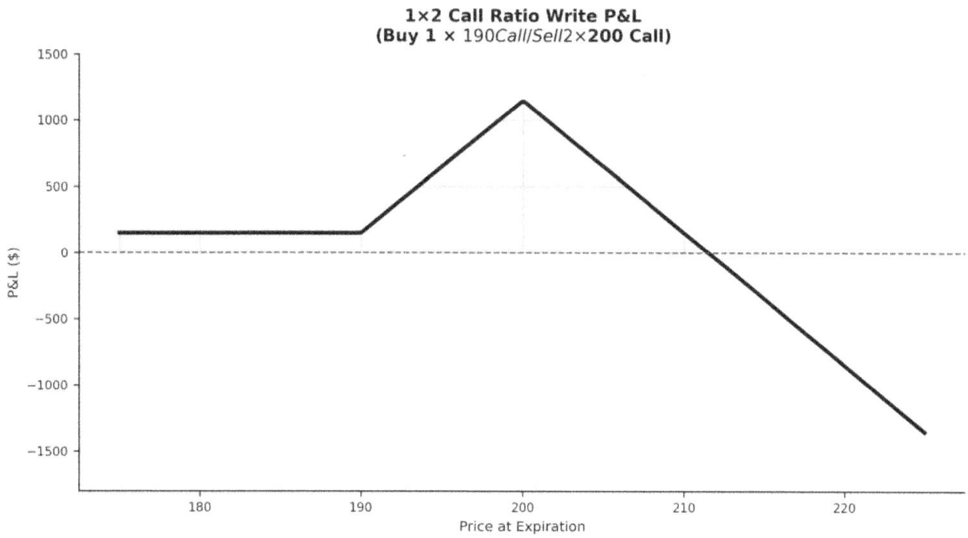

Figure 16.5 — 1×2 Call Ratio Write P&L. Skew exploitation with net credit entry.

- Put skew (normal) — OTM puts have higher IV than OTM calls at the same distance from the money. The market pays more to insure against crashes than to speculate on rallies;
- For premium sellers: this means OTM puts generate more premium per unit of delta than equivalent OTM calls — which is why cash-secured puts often produce better income than covered calls in many environments;
- Term structure skew — near-dated options often have higher IV than far-dated options during stress events. After the event passes, near-dated IV collapses faster — calendar spreads profit from this dynamic;
- Smile pattern — in some underlyings (especially index options), both OTM puts AND OTM calls have elevated IV relative to ATM — creating a 'smile' shape. This reflects demand for protection in both directions;

Bollinger Bands as a Volatility Tool

Introduced in Chapter 14 as a price tool, Bollinger Bands are equally powerful as a volatility visualization instrument. The width of the bands directly reflects current realized volatility — and the squeeze/expansion cycle creates actionable signals for options traders independent of price direction.

- Bollinger Band squeeze (bands narrowing) → HV is contracting → IV is likely low → favorable window to buy options before expansion;
- Bandwidth indicator measures the width of the bands as a percentage of the middle band. Extremely low bandwidth historically precedes significant moves;
- Band expansion after a squeeze → volatility expansion underway → switch from buyer to seller as IV rises and premium expands;
- Price touching the outer band repeatedly without the band widening → trend is real and sustainable → do not attempt mean-reversion trades;

Volatility Across the Business Cycle

Volatility is not constant — it cycles with the economy just as sectors rotate. Understanding where volatility typically sits in each phase of the business cycle allows the options trader to align their strategy selection with the macro environment.

- Early Expansion — VIX declining from recession highs. IV compressing. Transition from premium selling toward directional debit trades as premiums become less rich;
- Mid Expansion — Low VIX, calm markets, compressed IV. Ideal for calendar spreads and diagonal income strategies. Debit spreads cheap and efficient;
- Late Expansion / Peak — VIX beginning to rise as uncertainty increases. Premium selling returns to favor. Collars and protective puts become essential for late-cycle long positions; and
- Recession / Contraction — High VIX, elevated IV, rich premiums. Best environment for defined-risk premium selling on quality names. Size small, spreads only.

VOLATILITY IS THE VARIABLE

Price tells you where the stock is. Volatility tells you how much it is expected to move. Strike selection, strategy choice, position sizing, and entry timing all depend on volatility. A trader who reads price but ignores volatility is navigating with half a map.

The VIX as the Six-Condition Decision Axis

Here is the single most important practical application of everything in this chapter: the VIX reading is one of your two inputs to the six-condition framework. Chart direction gives you the row (up, down, sideways). The VIX gives you the column (high or low volatility). Two numbers. One strategy. Every trading day.

But reading the VIX correctly requires more than glancing at the number. It requires understanding where the VIX is relative to its recent range — not just its absolute level. A VIX of 20 means something very different after a period of sustained 12-level readings than it does after a spike down from 35. This is why IV Rank (IVR) is the operational tool, not the raw VIX number alone.

VIX Level	IVR Reading	Volatility Assessment	Six-Condition Implication — Your Strategy Tier
VIX < 15	IVR < 25	LOW — premium is cheap. Market is calm and complacent. Options priced at discounts relative to realized movement.	BUY premium. Conditions 1, 3, 5. Long calls (condition 1), long puts (condition 3), butterfly/condor (condition 5). Low-cost entry for directional debit and range structures.
VIX 15–20	IVR 25–50	TRANSITIONAL — volatility normalizing. Neither strongly cheap nor expensive. Be selective.	Evaluate the trend carefully. If direction is clear and confirmed, lean toward debit. If direction is unclear, wait for VIX to resolve higher or lower before committing to a strategy tier.
VIX 20–30	IVR 50–75	HIGH — premium is elevated. Market pricing in meaningful uncertainty. Options	SELL premium. Conditions 2, 4, 6. CSP/covered call/bull put spread (condition 2), bear call spread (condition

VIX Level	IVR Reading	Volatility Assessment	Six-Condition Implication — Your Strategy Tier
		are expensive relative to historical norms.	4), calendar/diagonal (condition 6). Collect elevated credit.
VIX > 30	IVR > 75	VERY HIGH — fear spike. Market in crisis or near-crisis mode. Premium at maximum levels.	SELL premium at maximum discipline. Defined-risk only. Size at 25–50% of normal. Conditions 2, 4 (income/bearish credit). Let the first volatility wave peak before deploying. The best credits are paid at the height of fear.
VIX > 40	IVR > 90	EXTREME — systemic fear. Correlations spike to 1. Every stock moves with the index.	Pause. Observe. Deploy only on the highest-quality underlyings with the deepest OTM strikes. The premium is extraordinary — but assignment risk is real. One contract, maximum conviction only.

The Two-Step Condition Read: Chart + VIX

Every trading session, before you look at individual stocks or strategies, run the Two-Step Condition Read. It takes under two minutes. It tells you which of the six conditions is active. It is the most important two minutes of your trading day.

Step	Action	What You Are Identifying
1	Check the VIX (raw number and IVR)	Is the market's volatility high or low right now — relative to its recent history? This is your column selector: HIGH (conditions 2, 4, 6) or LOW (conditions 1, 3, 5).
2	Look at the SPY/QQQ daily chart	Is price making higher highs and higher lows (uptrend → conditions 1-2), lower highs and lower lows (downtrend → conditions 3-4), or oscillating in a defined range (sideways → conditions 5-6)?
3	Cross-reference the two readings	VIX low + uptrend = Condition 1. VIX high + uptrend = Condition 2. VIX low + downtrend = Condition 3. VIX high + downtrend = Condition 4. VIX low + sideways = Condition 5. VIX high + sideways = Condition 6.
4	Open the six-condition table	Find your condition number. Read the approved strategy. That is your strategy for today. Everything else is noise.

THE TWO-MINUTE EDGE

Most retail traders spend an hour reading financial news before they trade. Professional traders spend two minutes on the VIX and the chart. The news tells you stories. The VIX and the chart tell you the condition. The condition tells you the strategy. Stories are entertainment. Condition reads are money.

IV Rank vs. IV Percentile: Which to Use and When

Both IV Rank (IVR) and IV Percentile measure implied volatility relative to its historical range — but they measure different things and can give different signals on the same underlying at the same moment. Understanding the difference ensures you read your volatility tool correctly.

	IV Rank (IVR)	IV Percentile
Formula	(Current IV − 52-week low IV) ÷ (52-week high IV − 52-week low IV) × 100	Percentage of days in the past year where IV was BELOW current IV
Range	0–100 (0 = at 52-week low, 100 = at 52-week high)	0–100 (50 = IV higher than exactly half of all days this year)
What it answers	Where is current IV relative to the extremes of the past year?	How often was IV lower than it is right now?
Best for	Quick screening — 'Is IV elevated or suppressed right now?'	Precision — 'How unusual is this IV level historically?'
Limitation	Distorted if there was one extreme spike in the 52-week window. A single VIX 40 day keeps IVR suppressed for months afterward.	Requires calculation across daily closing IV for the full year — not always shown on all platforms.
Premium Desk preference	Use IVR > 50 as the primary signal for selling premium. IVR < 25 as the primary signal for buying premium.	Use IV Percentile as the confirmation check when IVR gives an ambiguous reading between 35–50.

Practical rule: check IVR first on every position you are considering. If IVR is above 50, you are in sell-premium territory (conditions 2, 4, 6). If IVR is below 25, you are in buy-premium territory (conditions 1, 3, 5). If IVR is between 25 and 50, use IV Percentile to confirm — and if both are ambiguous, wait one more session for the reading to clarify before committing capital.

Volatility Events Calendar: Pre-Scheduling Your Six-Condition Reads

Certain calendar events reliably cause IV to spike before they occur and collapse immediately after. Knowing these events in advance allows you to pre-schedule your volatility reads and position yourself for the IV behavior rather than reacting to it. Build this calendar at the start of every month.

Event	Frequency (Expiration)	Volatility Pattern + Six-Condition Response
Earnings Announcement	**Every quarter per stock**	IV spikes 5–10 days before, then collapses the morning after. BEFORE: straddle/strangle for condition 5 or 6 (range high IV). Day after IV crush: sell premium on remaining elevated IV. Never hold short premium through the announcement.
FOMC Meeting	**8 times per year**	VIX rises 1–3 days before as traders hedge. VIX drops sharply after the announcement regardless of content. BEFORE: avoid opening new short premium in index positions. AFTER: conditions 2 or 4 available as IV normalizes.

Event	Frequency (Expiration)	Volatility Pattern + Six-Condition Response
CPI/PPI Data	**Monthly**	Macro data prints can gap index ETFs 1–2% in either direction. IV elevated the day before. Avoid selling index condors or strangles in the 48 hours before CPI. Open after.
OpEx (Monthly Options Expiration)	**Third Friday of each month**	Max pain gravity and dealer hedging create unusual intraday moves. Do not open new positions on expiration Friday. Use the low-IV post-expiration Monday to open new 30–45 DTE income positions.
Quarterly Earnings Season	**4× per year (Jan, Apr, Jul, Oct)**	Broad IV rises as the season begins and compresses as it ends. The first two weeks of earnings season (mega-cap reporters) are highest-IV. The final weeks of the season are lowest-IV — ideal for buying premium on next-quarter setups.
VIX Expiration	**Every month (Wednesday before third Friday)**	VIX futures settle on Wednesday morning before monthly OpEx. Professional VIX positioning can cause unusual SPX options moves in the 24 hours before settlement. Avoid adding new SPX/SPY positions Tuesday evening.

Volatility Skew: Anatomy of the Market's Mispricing

Volatility skew is the single most important structural concept for the premium seller to master — more important than any individual strategy, because it determines which strikes are worth selling and which are not. Skew refers to the fact that implied volatility is not uniform across all strike prices. Options at different strikes on the same underlying and expiration carry different levels of implied volatility. The resulting curve, when plotted by strike, is never flat. It tilts, slopes, and sometimes smiles — and every shape tells you something different about where the market is mispricing risk.

In equity options, the skew almost always slopes downward from left to right: OTM puts carry significantly higher implied volatility than ATM options, which in turn carry higher IV than OTM calls. This is not random. It reflects the structural demand from institutional investors who buy put options as portfolio insurance. When large institutions are perpetually bidding up OTM puts, the implied volatility on those puts is perpetually inflated above what realized volatility would justify. This is the put skew — and it is one of the most persistent mispricings in financial markets.

In commodity futures options, the skew can be inverted. For grain markets (corn, soybeans, wheat), OTM calls frequently carry higher implied volatility than puts — a call skew driven by the ever-present risk of supply disruptions, drought, freezes, and USDA report surprises. Energy markets exhibit complex bidirectional skews depending on geopolitical conditions. Metals skew can run in either direction depending on macro regime. Understanding which direction the skew runs in your specific market is not academic — it determines which side of the chain to sell.

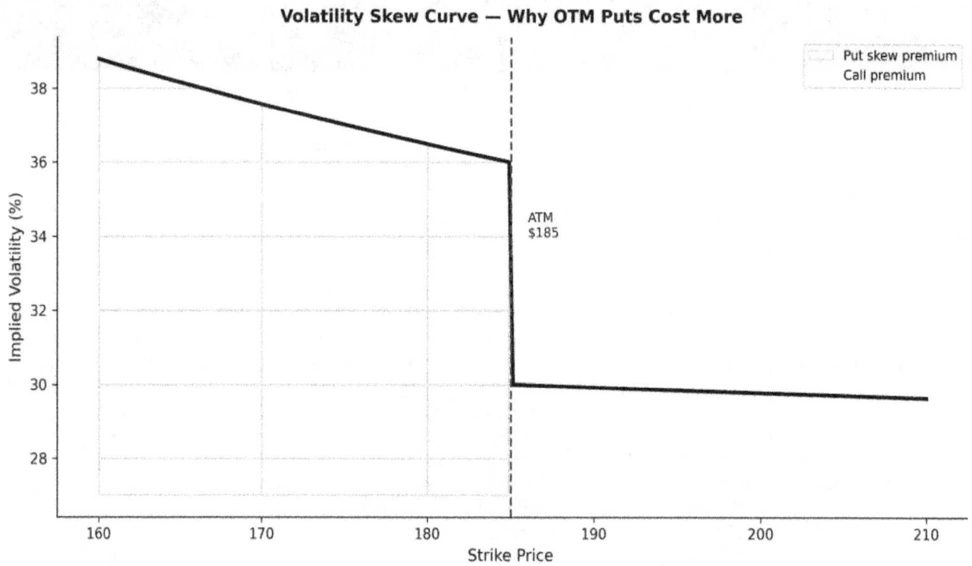

Figure 16.2 — Volatility Skew Curve — Why OTM puts carry higher IV than OTM calls in equity options. The skew premium.

Volatility Skew Curve — Why OTM puts carry higher IV than OTM calls in equity options.

THE SKEW EDGE FOR SELLERS

When the implied volatility of your short strike is higher than the implied volatility of the ATM option, you are selling the most overvalued part of the chain. This is the skew edge. Experienced sellers do not mechanically sell at a fixed delta every cycle — they identify where the skew is most elevated, check that IV is above HV, and sell at that intersection. The skew tells you where the market is paying the most for protection. Your job is to provide that protection at a profit.

THE IV EXPANSION RESPONSE PROTOCOL

When your short premium position is losing value due to IV expansion: (1) Check whether the stock has breached your strike — if NOT, IV expansion is marking you to market, not creating a real loss. (2) Check whether the underlying trend is still intact — if YES, the position is working as designed. (3) Check whether an earnings or macro event is the cause — if YES, assess whether to close before the event or hold through it. (4) Only close at a loss if: the strike has been breached AND the trend has reversed. IV expansion alone is not a reason to close.

Volatility Skew: Why Puts Cost More Than Calls

If implied volatility were uniform across all strikes, the IV of a $190 put and a $210 call — both equidistant from a $200 stock — would be identical. In reality, they are not. OTM puts almost always have higher IV than equidistant OTM calls. This asymmetry is called the volatility skew, and understanding it gives you an edge in strike selection and strategy construction.

The skew exists because institutional portfolio managers buy OTM puts as insurance against market crashes. This persistent demand inflates put premiums relative to calls at equivalent strikes. The practical effects for options traders:

- Selling OTM puts (CSPs) collects more premium per unit of risk than selling OTM calls at equivalent delta — because skew inflates put premiums. This is a structural advantage for income sellers running CSPs and bull put spreads;
- Buying OTM calls for directional plays is generally cheaper than buying OTM puts at equivalent distance — because puts carry the skew premium. Condition 1 debit trades (bull call spreads) benefit from this asymmetry;
- Iron condors: the put spread side typically collects more credit than the call spread side at equivalent wing distances. Many professional condor traders intentionally place the put wing closer to the stock than the call wing to equalize the credit — adjusting for skew; and
- Skew steepens during fear events (VIX spikes, market selloffs) and flattens during calm bull markets. A very steep skew signals institutional hedging activity — the smart money is buying downside protection. Take note.

READING THE SKEW IN YOUR PLATFORM

Most options platforms display IV by strike in the options chain. Look at the IV column for the put side: notice how IV increases as you move from ATM toward the OTM puts (lower strikes). That increasing IV as strikes get lower is the volatility skew. When you see the skew steepen suddenly — OTM put IV jumping significantly higher than ATM — institutional fear is entering the market. This is often a leading indicator of broader market weakness. Monitor it weekly.

The Ratio Write: Selling the Steepest Part of the Skew

The ratio write is the structural expression of skew exploitation.

Rather than selling one option at the most overvalued strike, the ratio write sells a greater number of contracts at that strike while buying fewer contracts at a less overvalued strike.

The result: you capture the skew premium and the raw IV premium simultaneously, with the long leg providing partial protection against a violent directional move.

First, identify the strike with the highest implied volatility relative to historical volatility — this is your short leg. Then identify the nearest strike with significantly lower IV — this is your long leg.

Sell two (or three) of the high-IV strike for every one long-leg contract you buy. If the skew is steep enough, you will either collect a net credit immediately, or construct the position at zero cost with the skew providing built-in edge.

In both cases, your maximum profit zone centers on the short strike — the most overvalued point in the chain.

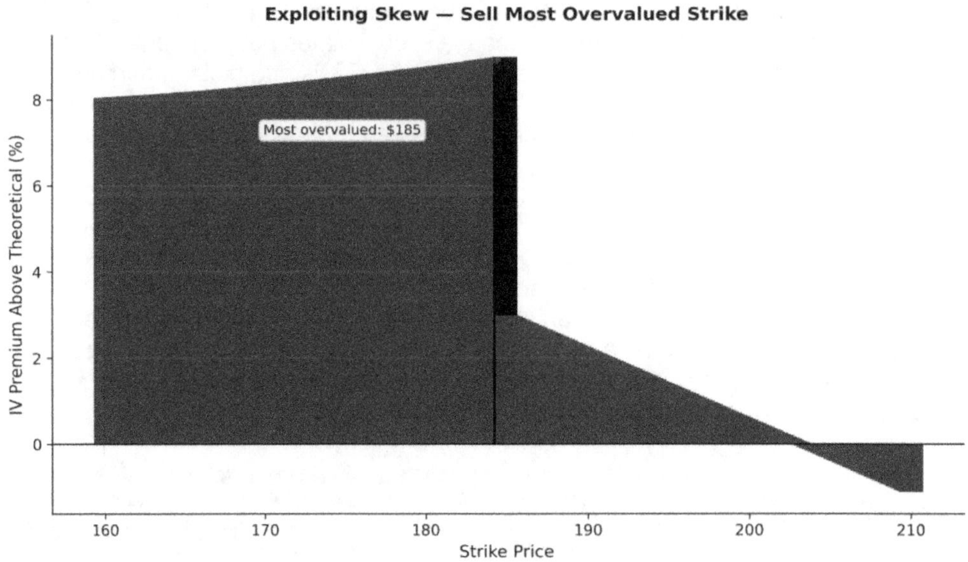

Figure 16.3 — Skew Ratio Write Strategy — Exploiting the volatility skew differential by selling the overpriced wing at a higher ratio.

Skew Ratio Write Strategy — Exploiting the volatility skew differential with a ratio write.

RATIO WRITE SELECTION CRITERIA

Three conditions must be present before entering a ratio write: (1) Current IV is in the top 40th percentile of its 52-week range or higher. (2) Current IV is at least 20–30% above recent historical volatility. (3) The OTM strike carries materially higher IV than the ATM option — the skew is present and measurable. If only two of three conditions are met, use a simple credit spread instead. All three conditions together is the ratio write signal.

HV vs. IV Gap: The Market Imbalance That Creates Writer Profits

IV vs. HV Gap — The persistent volatility risk premium: where premium sellers find their edge.

The most powerful setup for premium sellers is not simply high implied volatility — it is the condition where implied volatility is significantly elevated above historical volatility. When IV is well above HV, the market is pricing in fear that exceeds what recent realized price behavior justifies. The premium seller collects the difference between what the market fears and what the market actually delivers.

The framework is simple: implied volatility is your income, historical volatility is your risk. When the IV Rank (IVR) is above the 50th percentile of its historical range and IV is at least 1.3x HV, you are in a favorable selling environment. When IVR drops below 30 or IV falls below HV, the premium environment has compressed and short positions no longer offer favorable risk-adjusted returns.

IVR Level	HV Level	Skew Condition	Writer's Action
>70th pct	Low to Moderate	Wide IV/HV gap — maximum overvaluation	Sell aggressively: CSPs, covered calls, ratio writes
50th–70th	Moderate	Moderate skew — normal premium environment	Sell selectively: standard income positions

IVR Level	HV Level	Skew Condition	Writer's Action
30th–50th	Moderate to High	Compressed IV — thin premium	Reduce size; favor defined-risk spreads
<30th	High	IV below HV — market underpricing risk	Avoid short premium; favor long premium setups

The practical pre-trade check: before any premium-selling entry, run two numbers:

- What is the current IVR for this underlying?;
- How does current IV compare to the 20-day historical volatility?.

If IVR is above 50 and IV is at least 1.3x HV, the conditions favor selling. If IVR is below 30 or IV is below HV, wait for better conditions.

THE IMBALANCE IS YOUR INCOME

When implied volatility sits in the top quartile of its historical range while historical volatility is in the bottom quartile, the gap between them is your profit opportunity. The market is paying you more than the realized risk justifies. This imbalance corrects through mean reversion over time — and the premium you collected during the overvaluation period is yours to keep.

Trading the VIX: The Fear Index as a Profit Instrument

The VIX is not just a volatility reading — it is one of the most powerful timing instruments available to the premium seller. The CBOE Volatility Index measures the 30-day implied volatility of S&P 500 index options. It is calculated in real time from a weighted average of SPX option prices across a wide range of strikes, designed to reflect the market's consensus expectation of near-term volatility. Because it is derived from implied volatility — which is driven by fear, uncertainty, and demand for protection — the VIX is widely known as the market's fear gauge. Its inverse correlation with the S&P 500 is approximately −0.39 over long periods, meaning: when stocks fall, the VIX typically rises, and vice versa.

For the premium seller, this inverse relationship is not just interesting — it is the core tactical signal. When the VIX spikes above 25 or 30, it means institutional investors are aggressively buying put protection, driving up implied volatility across the entire options chain. Those elevated premiums represent overpriced fear. The seller's job is to sell that fear at a price that exceeds what the market will ultimately deliver in realized volatility. Fear is consistently overpriced. Realized moves are consistently smaller than what the options market prices in. This is the structural edge that every premium seller is exploiting every time they sell an option with IVR above 50.

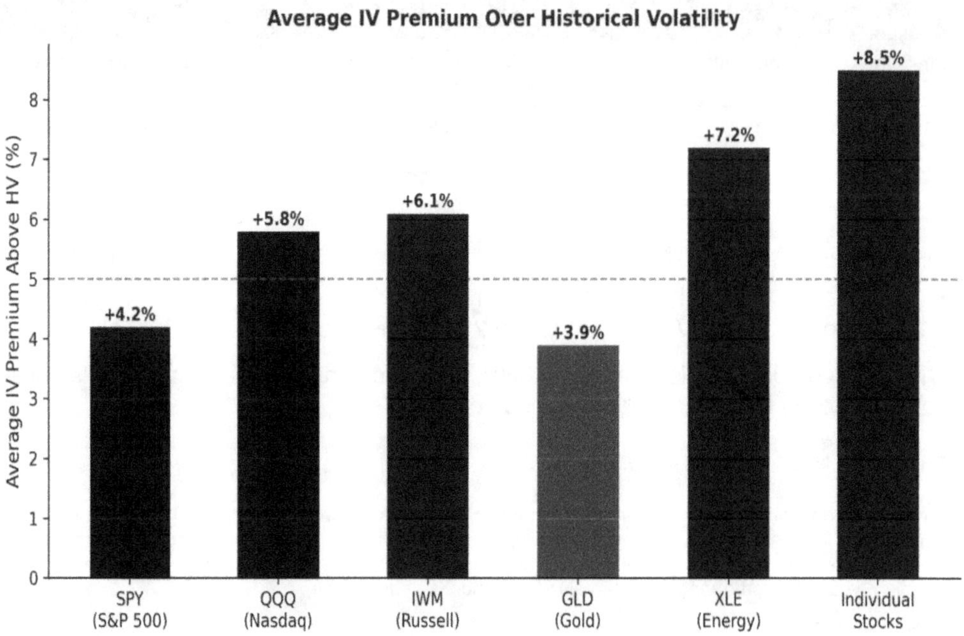

Figure 16.5 — VIX and Fear Correlation — How the VIX moves with market stress and what levels signal premium-selling opportunity.

VIX and Fear Correlation — How the VIX moves with market stress and what levels signal opportunity.

THE FEAR INDEX IS YOUR INCOME SIGNAL

When the VIX spikes above 25 and IVR on your target underlying climbs above 60, the market is paying you a significant premium to take on risk that statistically overestimates what will actually occur. You are not predicting direction. You are identifying the gap between feared volatility and likely realized volatility — and selling it. This is the entire business model of the professional premium seller, stated precisely.

VIX Futures and Term Structure: Contango, Backwardation, and What They Tell You

The CBOE introduced VIX futures in 2004 (ticker symbol UX). VIX futures allow traders to take a direct position on future implied volatility levels — not on the underlying S&P 500, but on volatility itself. This distinction is critical: a VIX futures contract settles into the VIX index value at expiration, not into a deliverable stock or basket. Understanding how VIX futures are priced relative to the spot VIX index is essential for anyone using the VIX as a trading or timing instrument.

Unlike stock index futures, VIX futures prices do not necessarily track the spot VIX index closely on a day-to-day basis. Because the VIX index itself cannot be easily replicated by purchasing its components — you cannot buy the VIX directly — there is no simple arbitrage mechanism forcing VIX futures to mirror the spot index. The futures price reflects where the market believes volatility will be at the futures expiration date, not where it is today. This creates the term structure: a curve showing the price of VIX futures contracts at successive expiration months.

The term structure takes two primary forms. In normal, calm markets, VIX futures trade in contango — front-month futures trade near the spot VIX, and further-dated futures trade at progressively higher prices. This upward slope reflects the market's expectation that volatility will revert toward higher long-run levels from today's low reading. Contango is the typical state during bull markets. In fear events or crises, the term structure inverts into backwardation — spot VIX spikes dramatically, but futures traders expect the spike to mean-revert, so front-month futures trade below the elevated spot VIX. Backwardation signals extreme fear that the market expects to dissipate.

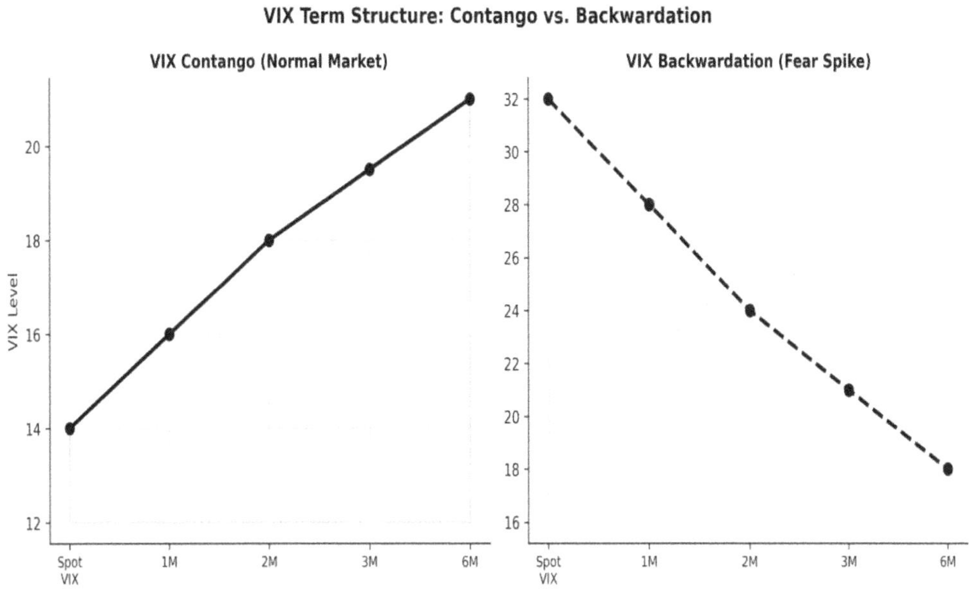

Figure 16.6 — VIX Term Structure — Contango vs. backwardation and what each signals about near-term market expectations.

VIX Term Structure — Contango vs. backwardation and what each signals about market expectations.

Four rules govern how VIX futures behave that every trader using them must internalize:

- Contango time decay: when the VIX term structure is in contango, VIX futures prices will inevitably decline toward spot as time passes. This is why products like VXX and UVXY have historically declined over time — they hold near-term VIX futures that roll down the contango curve daily;
- Backwardation spike: when the VIX spikes into backwardation (near-term futures above long-term), futures prices will decline even if the VIX stays elevated — because backwardation is not a stable state;
- VIX futures are not the VIX: VIX futures prices converge to the spot VIX only at expiration. Before expiration, futures can trade significantly above or below spot based on the expected path of volatility; and
- Settlement is cash-only: VIX futures settle in cash to the Special Opening Quotation (SOQ) — a calculated value based on SPX option opens on the expiration morning. This settlement can be dramatically different from the previous night's VIX closing price.

THE FOUR VIX FUTURES RULES (SOURCE: CBOE)

1. In contango, VIX futures prices decline over time even with no change in the index. 2. VIX futures prices almost never change as quickly as the spot VIX index. 3. Futures and index prices converge at expiration. 4. VIX futures must be evaluated independently of the spot index. These four rules govern every VIX-related trading decision. A trader who ignores rule 2 will be perpetually surprised that a sharp VIX spike did not produce the futures profit they expected.

Reading the VIX for Premium Selling: A Practical Framework

As a premium seller, your relationship with the VIX is not as a trader of VIX products — it is as a reader of market conditions. The VIX tells you the temperature of the options market. Your job is to sell premium when the market is running a fever (high IV, elevated VIX, fear-driven pricing) and to reduce activity or wait when the market is calm (low IV, low VIX, complacency-driven pricing). The VIX is the primary input to this decision.

When the VIX is below 15, the market is complacent. Options premiums across all underlyings compress. The risk/reward of selling premium becomes unfavorable: you collect little credit while still accepting the full assignment and management risk of a short position. This is not the environment to be aggressively short premium. When the VIX moves into the 20–30 range, the environment normalizes and selective premium selling becomes attractive. When the VIX spikes above 30 — particularly with rapid upward movement — you are in the ideal environment: premiums are rich, implied volatility substantially exceeds what realized volatility will likely deliver, and the skew is at its steepest. This is the moment to be a seller. Fear is at its most overpriced.

The VIX term structure provides an additional timing dimension. When the term structure is in steep contango — near-month futures well below further months — the market is calm and complacency is high. This reinforces the caution signal. When the term structure flattens or inverts into backwardation, fear has arrived. But the key insight from the VIX futures behavior is this: at the peak of a fear event, when the spot VIX is at 35 or 40, the futures market is already pricing in mean reversion. The fear is being sold by futures traders who know it will dissipate. The premium seller should be doing the same thing in the options market — selling the overpriced fear premium to the panicking crowd that is buying protection at any price.

VIX Level	Market Regime	Premium Strategy	Avoid	Notes
VIX < 15	Low volatility / Complacency	Long calls; Calendar spreads.	Naked puts; iron condors.	IV too cheap to sell; buy premium instead.
VIX 15–20	Normal range / Balanced	CSP; Covered calls; Bull put spreads.	Short straddles.	Sweet spot for income strategies.
VIX 20–30	Elevated / Fear building	Iron condors; Credit spreads.	Naked calls.	Wider strikes; collect rich premium.
VIX 30–40	High fear / Volatile	OTM puts (CSP); Defined-risk only.	Undefined risk positions.	Size down 50%; short duration only.
VIX > 40	Panic/Crisis / Extreme fear	Protective puts; cash only.	All short premium strategies.	Stand aside or buy protection.

Figure 16.7 — VIX Strategy Selection Table — Which premium-selling strategy to deploy at each VIX level.

VIX Strategy Selection Table — Which premium-selling strategy to deploy at each VIX level.

THE VIX IMBALANCE TRADE

The single most powerful expression of the HV/IV imbalance philosophy is this: when the VIX spikes dramatically above its recent historical range, and realized volatility over the past 20–30 days has been moderate, the gap between what the market is pricing (implied) and what it has been delivering (historical/realized) is at its maximum. That gap is your income. Sell deep OTM put spreads on SPY or SPX. Collect the elevated premium. Hold through the mean reversion. The crowd is buying protection at a 40% premium to what the risk actually warrants. You are the counterparty. This is not a speculation on direction. It is a statistical arbitrage of the fear premium.

THE VOLATILITY CALENDAR IS PART OF YOUR TRADING PLAN

At the start of every month, map every FOMC date, CPI release, and OpEx Friday onto your calendar. Mark every earnings date for every underlying in your approved stock list. These dates are your volatility landmarks. They determine when to open, when to hold, when to close, and when to simply wait. A trader without this calendar is flying blind in fog. Build it in thirty minutes at the start of each month.

The Four Volatility Regimes: Matching Your Strategy to the Environment

Markets do not simply have 'high' or 'low' volatility. They move through four distinct regimes, each requiring a different strategic response. Identifying the current regime before entering any trade is as important as identifying the six market conditions.

Regime	VIX Range	IVR Signal	Best Strategies	Worst Strategies
Low & Stable	VIX 12-16	IVR < 20	Calendars, diagonals, long options for direction. Premiums are cheap — buy time.	Iron condors (premium too low to justify risk). CSPs (income barely covers commissions).
Rising / Expanding	VIX 16-25	IVR 30-60	CSPs on quality names (premium is getting rich). Start building income positions. Vertical spreads for direction.	Long straddles (IV is expanding but may not continue). Naked short strangles (risk is growing).
Elevated / Crisis	VIX 25-40	IVR > 60	Maximum premium selling: iron condors, CSPs, covered calls. Every short option benefits from eventual IV contraction. Hedge with long puts.	Buying any options outright (IV crush will destroy your position even if direction is right). Removing hedges.
Extreme Spike	VIX 40+	IVR > 90	Cash. Reduce all position sizes by 50%. Only sell premium with very wide wings and small size. This is survival mode.	Increasing position sizes. Removing stops. Assuming the spike is 'the bottom.' VIX spikes can sustain for weeks.

The regime determines your sizing, not just your strategy. In Low & Stable, you can run 6-8 simultaneous positions comfortably. In Rising, reduce to 4-5. In Elevated, reduce to 3-4 with wider wings. In Extreme Spike, reduce to 1-2 or move to cash entirely. The regime is not a suggestion — it is a throttle on your risk engine.

VIX Term Structure: Reading the Market's Fear Timeline

The VIX itself is only the 30-day reading. Professional traders also monitor the VIX term structure — the curve of implied volatility across multiple time horizons (VIX, VIX3M, VIX6M). The shape of this curve tells you whether the market expects volatility to increase, decrease, or stay constant.

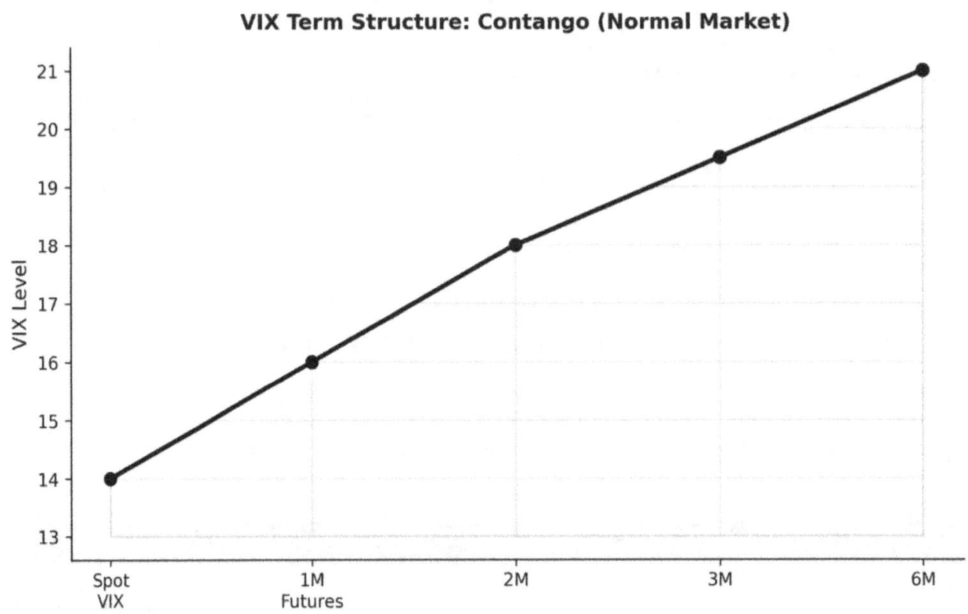

Figure 16.7 — VIX Term Structure: Contango. Normal market — sell options, futures overpriced.

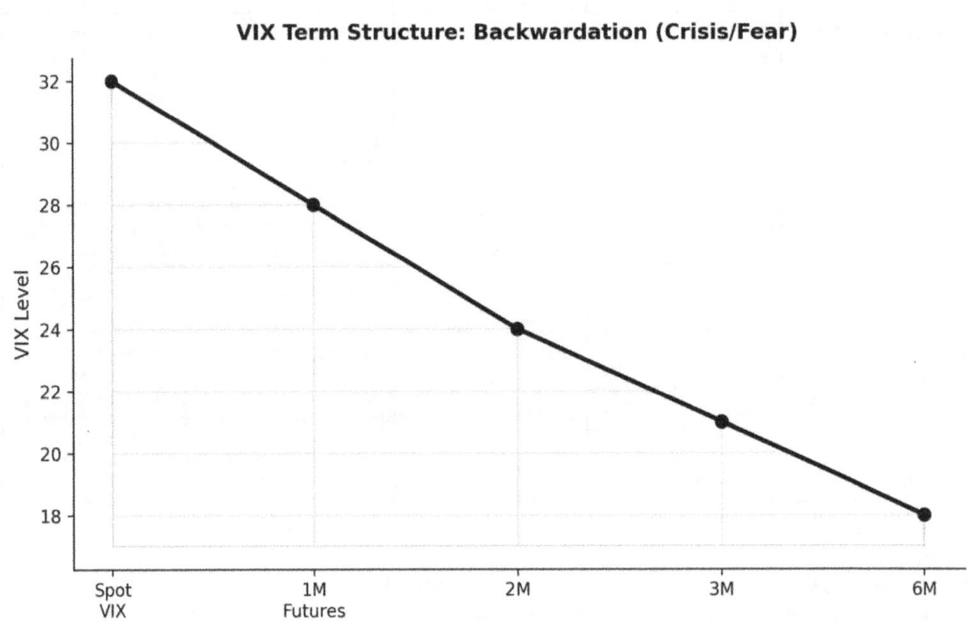

Figure 16.8 — VIX Term Structure: Backwardation. Fear spike — consider buying options.

- Normal Contango (VIX < VIX3M < VIX6M): The market expects near-term volatility to be LOWER than long-term. This is the default state — present about 80% of the time. Income strategies work well. Calendar spreads benefit from the differential;
- Backwardation (VIX > VIX3M): The market expects near-term volatility to be HIGHER than long-term — a fear signal. This occurs during sell-offs, crises, and extreme uncertainty. Reduce position sizes. Add hedges. Do not sell premium without protection; and
- Flat curve (VIX ≈ VIX3M): Transition state. The market is uncertain about the direction of volatility itself. Often occurs before a regime change. Reduce new entries and wait for the curve to resolve.

VIX TERM STRUCTURE RULE

Check the VIX term structure every Monday morning. If it is in contango — proceed with your normal income strategy. If it flips to backwardation — activate your defensive protocol: close any position at 75%+ profit immediately, add a SPY put hedge if you do not have one, and do not open any new short premium positions until contango resumes. Backwardation has preceded every major market decline of the past 20 years.

IV Contraction and Expansion: Strategy Performance Across the Volatility Cycle

The most important practical skill in volatility analysis is knowing precisely how each strategy performs during IV expansion versus IV contraction — and how to exploit the difference. The volatility cycle is predictable: uncertainty builds, IV expands, the event resolves, IV collapses. Your job is to be positioned on the right side of that cycle for every trade you hold.

Strategy	IV Expanding	IV Contracting	Best Entry Timing	Worst Entry Timing
Long Call / Long Put	Profits — Vega helps	Loses — IV crush hurts even if direction right	IVR < 20, before catalyst	Into earnings or VIX spike
Cash-Secured Put (CSP)	Loses — position marked down as IV rises	Profits — IV contraction collapses put value = profit for seller	IVR 40-70, after initial spike	At IV peak (overbought fear)
Bull/Bear Call Spread	Neutral to slight loss (net Vega near zero)	Slight profit from IV contraction on spread premium	Any IVR, confirmed direction	Against the weekly trend
Iron Condor	Loses — expansion breaks short strikes	Profits — contraction collapses both wings toward zero	IVR > 50, range-bound market	During trend or crisis
Calendar Spread	Profits — near-term IV rises faster than far-term	Neutral to slight loss	IVR 40-60, pre-event	Post-event after IV crush
Long Straddle	Profits — both legs increase in value	Loses — IV crush destroys both legs	IVR < 30, pre-earnings if cheap	At peak IV before event
Covered Call	Loses — stock may be called away + marked-to-market loss	Profits — short call decays rapidly as IV collapses	IVR > 40, stock at resistance	During breakout / momentum

The most powerful insight from this table: the strategies that hurt most during IV expansion (CSP, iron condor, covered call) are exactly the strategies that profit most during IV contraction. This means that if you are forced into an IV expansion event on a short premium position, the correct response is almost never to close at a loss — it is to evaluate whether the underlying direction is still intact, hold through the expansion if it is, and let the inevitable contraction restore your position's value. Panic-closing during IV spikes is one of the most expensive recurring mistakes in options trading.

Practical Volatility Dashboard: Your Weekly Pre-Trade Checklist

These five volatility checks should be completed every week before opening any new positions. They take less than 10 minutes and prevent the most common volatility-related mistakes.

#	Check	Bullish / Proceed Signal	Bearish / Pause Signal
1	VIX Level	VIX below 20 (calm market, premium-buying conditions). VIX 20-30 (elevated — income seller's window). Note: above 30 = crisis mode.	VIX above 40 (extreme fear). Reduce all sizes by 50%. No new positions without hedges.
2	VIX Term Structure	VIX < VIX3M (contango — normal, stable conditions). Income strategies working.	VIX > VIX3M (backwardation — near-term fear exceeds long-term). Defensive protocol activated.
3	IVR of Target Underlying	IVR 40-70 for income strategies. IVR < 25 for debit/directional.	IVR > 80 (extreme fear on this stock — check for specific news). IVR < 10 (premiums too cheap for income).
4	HV vs IV Comparison	IV > HV by 20%+ = options expensive = sell premium. IV near HV = fairly priced.	IV < HV = options cheap relative to actual moves = buy premium, not sell.
5	Upcoming Volatility Events	No FOMC, CPI, OpEx, or earnings within your expiration window. Clean runway for income strategies.	FOMC, CPI, or earnings within DTE. Avoid new short premium unless expiration is specifically before the event.

VOLATILITY IS THE AXIS, NOT THE SIGNAL

Volatility does not tell you what direction the market will move — it tells you how much the market expects to move. A high-VIX environment with a bullish chart is Condition 2, not a reason to avoid trading. A low-VIX environment with a bearish chart is Condition 3, not a reason to buy calls. The VIX sets the volatility axis of your six-condition read. Direction sets the other axis. Both are required. Neither one alone is sufficient to determine your strategy.

Layer	Who	Speed	Strategy	Options Impact
Layer 1 — HFT	Market makers; prop firms.	Microseconds.	Market making; arbitrage.	Sets bid/ask spreads; affects fill quality.

Layer 2 — Stat Arb	Quant/hedge funds.	Milliseconds.	Pairs trading; mean reversion.	Creates S/R levels; drives IV mean reversion.
Layer 3 — Portfolio	Institutions; mutual funds.	Seconds to minutes.	Rebalancing; hedging.	Moves underlying; creates options flow.
Layer 4 — Retail AI	Individual traders.	Minutes to hours.	Sentiment; momentum.	Follows others; least market impact.

6-CONDITION FRAMEWORK ▸ ALL SIX CONDITIONS — algo behavior changes execution, not the condition

Algorithms do not change which of the six conditions you are in — they change how quickly conditions shift and how efficiently prices reflect them. Understanding algo behavior protects your execution across all six.

The markets you trade in today are not the markets of twenty years ago — or even ten. More than 80% of all trading volume on U.S. equity and options exchanges on any given day is now generated not by humans making deliberate decisions, but by algorithmic systems executing in microseconds, responding to price patterns, order flow, news sentiment, and each other. Artificial intelligence has accelerated this transformation. Understanding the landscape you are operating in is not optional — it is part of your risk management framework.

This chapter does not teach you to build algorithms. It teaches you to recognize their behavior, anticipate their patterns, and structure your trades so that algo-driven volatility works for you rather than against you.

THE STAT THAT CHANGES EVERYTHING

Algorithmic and AI-driven systems account for more than 80% of all daily trading volume. This means that for every 10 trades placed in the market, 8 are placed by machines — not people. They don't have emotions, they don't have opinions, and they don't care about your thesis. They react to signals, patterns, and each other. The human trader's edge is not speed — it's judgment, patience, and the ability to hold a position through algo-generated noise that has no fundamental meaning.

The Three Layers of Algorithmic Activity

Not all algorithmic trading is the same. There are three distinct layers operating in the market simultaneously, each with different objectives, time horizons, and impacts on options traders.

Figure 17.1 — The Three Layers of Algorithmic Activity

Layer	Who	Speed	Strategy	Options Impact
Layer 1 HFT	Market makers Prop firms	Microseconds	Market making Arbitrage	Sets bid-ask spreads; affects fill quality
Layer 2 Stat Arb	Quant hedge funds	Milliseconds	Pairs trading Mean reversion	Creates S/R levels; drives IV mean reversion
Layer 3 Portfolio	Institutions Mutual funds	Seconds to minutes	Rebalancing Hedging	Moves underlying; creates options flow
Layer 4 Retail AI	Individual traders	Minutes to hours	Sentiment Momentum	Follows others; least market impact

Figure 17.1 — The Three Layers of Algorithmic Activity. HFT, statistical arbitrage, and portfolio rebalancing.

Layer	Who Operates It	Time Horizon	Impact on Options Traders
HFT — High Frequency Trading	Specialized prop firms (Citadel Securities, Virtu, Jane Street)	Microseconds to milliseconds	Sets bid/ask spreads, provides liquidity, creates sudden micro-moves that trigger stop orders and cause brief IV spikes.
Systematic / Quant Funds	Hedge funds running stat-arb, momentum, and mean-reversion strategies	Minutes to weeks	Drives trends and reversals at the day/week level. When quant funds de-risk simultaneously, they create correlated selloffs across unrelated assets.
AI-Driven Portfolio Systems	Large asset managers and banks using ML models for allocation and hedging	Days to months	Creates persistent directional pressure. AI rebalancing around index events (options expiration, quarterly rebalancing) produces predictable flow patterns.

Recognizing Algo Patterns in the Market

Algorithmic systems leave fingerprints. Once you know what to look for, you will start seeing them everywhere — and more importantly, you will stop being surprised by moves that previously seemed random.

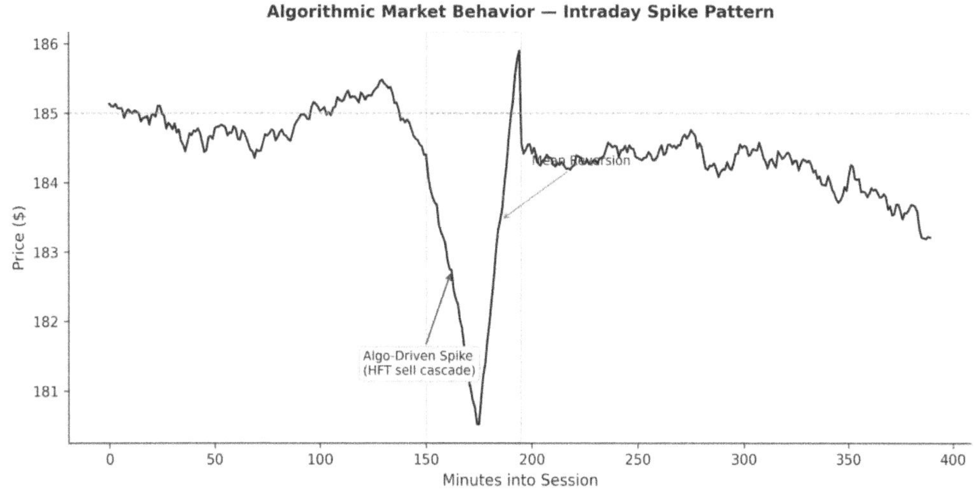

Figure 17.2 — Algo-Driven Intraday Spike. HFT cascade and mean reversion — how to read it.

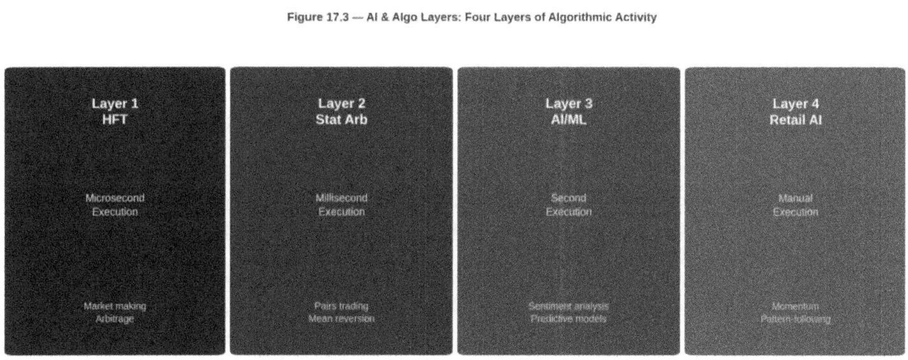

Figure 17.3 — AI & Algo Layers. Four layers of algorithmic activity and their market signatures.

- Stop hunts — A sudden sharp move through a well-known support or resistance level that immediately reverses. Algos are programmed to sweep stop orders clustered at obvious levels. The reversal is not a coincidence — once the stops are triggered and the liquidity absorbed, price snaps back. Lesson: do not place stop orders at obvious round numbers or exact prior highs/lows;
- VWAP magnets — The Volume Weighted Average Price (VWAP) acts as a gravitational center for intraday algo activity. Many systems are programmed to buy when price is below VWAP and sell above it. Price frequently oscillates around VWAP during low-momentum sessions;
- Options expiration pin risk — As major expirations approach (especially monthly and quarterly), market makers and dealers hedge their gamma exposure by buying and selling the underlying. This creates a gravitational pull toward the strike price with maximum open interest — the 'max pain' level. Understanding where max pain is on expiration week gives you an edge in strike selection;
- Momentum ignition — An algo rapidly buys or sells a large quantity to trigger other momentum algorithms, then reverses. Creates sudden spikes on no

news. Characterized by a violent move with no follow-through and immediate mean reversion. Do not chase these moves — wait for resolution; and
- Correlated deleveraging — When risk-off conditions trigger simultaneously across multiple quant funds running similar models, correlations go to 1 and everything falls together. SPY, QQQ, individual stocks, even 'defensive' positions all decline. This is the environment that blindsides traders who believe diversification always protects them.

AI-Driven Volatility Spikes: What's Different Now

Artificial intelligence has changed the speed and character of volatility events. Modern ML-based trading systems can process news sentiment, earnings transcripts, Fed statement language, and even social media in real time — reacting to information before human traders have finished reading the headline. This creates a new category of volatility risk that did not exist in previous market eras.

Use Case	Prompt Template	What AI Returns
Pre-Trade Screening	Analyze [TICKER] for options trade setup. Check trend, IV rank, key S/R levels.	Condition read; IV environment; suggested strategy; key levels to watch.
Risk Calculation	Given this trade: [DETAILS]. Calculate max loss, position size for account, probability of profit estimate.	Complete risk math; position size for account; probability of profit estimate.
Trade Management	My [STRATEGY] on [TICKER] is at [P&L]. Should I close, roll, or hold? T-[DTE] remaining.	Management recommendation based on T-21 rule; position size; and market conditions.
Post-Trade Review	Review this closed trade: [DETAILS]. What did I do right/wrong? Key lessons?	Objective trade analysis; rule adherence check; improvement suggestions.

Figure 17.4 — AI Prompt Framework for Traders.

- Sentiment-driven IV spikes — AI systems reading news sentiment can cause IV to spike on an underlying within seconds of a news release, even before price moves significantly. By the time retail traders notice the IV expansion, the premium has already repriced;
- Earnings surprise amplification — AI models increasingly predict earnings surprises and pre-position in options markets. This drives IV higher into earnings events than historical patterns would justify — and the subsequent IV crush is more severe when the expected surprise doesn't materialize;
- Flash crashes and recovery — AI systems that share similar risk models can all de-risk simultaneously, creating flash crashes that recover within minutes or hours. These events are dangerous for stop-order holders but often irrelevant to 30–45 DTE options positions that don't expire that day; and
- Machine-generated noise vs. real signals — Not every sharp intraday move is meaningful. AI-driven noise is a significant portion of intraday volatility. Options traders with longer time horizons (30–45 DTE) are naturally buffered from this noise — a key structural advantage over day traders.

THE ALGO ADVANTAGE

> You cannot beat HFT algorithms at their own game — microsecond execution is not available to retail traders. But you don't need to. Your advantage is time horizon and defined risk. An algo can't take your money if your maximum loss is defined, your position is sized correctly, and you don't have a stop order sitting at an obvious level waiting to be swept.

Zero Days to Expiration (0DTE) — The New Market Force

Perhaps no development has reshaped the options market more dramatically than the explosion of zero-days-to-expiration (0DTE) options — contracts that expire the same day they are traded. In 2025, 0DTE options accounted for 24% of all U.S. listed options volume, with SPX 0DTE options alone averaging 2.3 million contracts daily — representing 59% of total SPX options volume. On the most active days, retail traders account for half of all options flow.

For the risk-manager trader, 0DTE activity matters in three specific ways:

- Gamma risk is amplified near expiration — market makers delta-hedging millions of near-expiry contracts create sudden, sharp intraday moves in the underlying;
- The T-21 Rule becomes even more important: the final 21 days of any position are now crowded with 0DTE speculation, which can distort your position's mark-to-market; and
- Liquidity windows shift — the best bid-ask spreads on non-zero-DTE options now occur in the morning session before 0DTE volume dominates the tape.

> **THE 0DTE RULE FOR INCOME TRADERS**
>
> Do not compete with 0DTE traders on expiration day. If you hold a short premium position into the final trading day, the gamma environment is not yours to control. The T-21 Rule exists precisely to get you out before this zone. Use 0DTE activity as a sentiment signal — heavy 0DTE put buying signals fear; heavy call buying signals speculative enthusiasm. Neither is a reason to enter a new position. Both are reasons to check your existing positions.

IEX Options: What the SEC Approval Means for Traders

On September 18, 2025, the SEC approved IEX's application to operate a new options exchange — ending a heated regulatory battle that pitted IEX and smaller market makers against Citadel Securities and the existing exchange establishment. IEX Options is expected to launch in 2026 as the 18th U.S. options exchange.

The exchange's defining feature is a 350-microsecond speed bump — a symmetric delay on all incoming orders. This is the same technology IEX uses on its stock exchange, designed to prevent high-frequency traders from front-running quotes before market makers can update them. Citadel argued this would enable 'quote fading' and harm retail investors. The SEC disagreed, siding with the view that the speed bump reduces latency arbitrage and improves displayed liquidity.

> **WHAT IEX OPTIONS MEANS FOR RETAIL TRADERS**
>
> For options income traders using this book's framework, IEX Options represents a long-term positive. Tighter spreads — which result from more competitive markets with better-protected quotes — mean lower entry and exit costs on every spread trade. More exchanges means more competition for your order flow, which your broker should route to the exchange offering the best price. In practice: check that your broker offers smart order routing across all 17+ exchanges, not just the major three. The

difference in fill quality on a 10-contract iron condor can easily exceed the cost of a monthly subscription to any data service.

The Options Expiration Calendar: Algo-Predictable Flow Events

The options expiration calendar creates recurring, predictable flow events driven by dealer hedging activity. These are not random — they happen every month, every quarter, with structural consistency. Understanding the calendar gives you a timing edge.

- Monthly expiration (third Friday of each month) — The largest single expiration event. Max pain gravitational pull is strongest. Avoid opening new positions on expiration Friday — Gamma risk is extreme and algo hedging flows create unpredictable intraday moves;
- Quarterly expiration — OpEx combined with index rebalancing. Largest institutional flows of the quarter. SPY, QQQ, and mega-cap components can show unusual price action in the final week;
- 0DTE (Zero Days to Expiration) — The explosion of same-day options trading, driven largely by retail and algo activity in SPY/QQQ/SPX. 0DTE now accounts for a substantial portion of daily options volume. As a 30–45 DTE income trader, you are structurally on the opposite side of 0DTE noise — this is a feature, not a limitation; and
- FOMC meeting dates — Federal Reserve announcement days create sharp IV spikes before the announcement and immediate IV crush after. Never hold short-premium positions with high Vega exposure through FOMC announcements without a defined hedge.

Adapting Your Strategy for the Algo Environment

The presence of algorithmic trading does not change the fundamentals of options strategy — it changes the execution environment. Here is how to adapt:

Adaptation	Why It Matters in the Algo Era
Use limit orders exclusively	Market orders are prey for HFT. A limit order at the midpoint protects you from being filled at a disadvantaged price during a momentary algo-driven spike.
Avoid stops at obvious levels	Round numbers, prior highs/lows, and exponential moving average crossovers are the most commonly swept stop locations. Place stops at less obvious structural levels or use mental stops managed actively.
Embrace longer DTE for income trades	30–45 DTE positions are structurally buffered from intraday algo noise. A flash crash that reverses in an hour does not trigger a meaningful loss on a spread expiring in 35 days.
Trade during regular market hours	Pre-market and after-hours sessions have minimal liquidity and are dominated by algo order flow. Options spreads widen dramatically outside regular hours — fills are often unfavorable.
Monitor open interest on your strikes	Large open interest at your short strike creates dealer hedging pressure as expiration approaches — this can work for or against you. Know what the max pain level is on your expiration date.
Respect IV expansions around events	AI systems price events before humans process them. When IV spikes suddenly on no obvious news, algos know something. Do

Adaptation	Why It Matters in the Algo Era
	not sell into a vol spike without understanding its source — wait for clarity.

THE RETAIL TRADER'S STRUCTURAL ADVANTAGE

HFT firms spend hundreds of millions of dollars to shave microseconds off execution speed. You cannot compete on that dimension — and you don't need to. Your edge is patience, defined risk, and a time horizon measured in weeks rather than microseconds. The algo's short-term noise is your long-term opportunity. Let them create the volatility. You collect the premium from it.

AI Signal Filtering: Separating Edge from Noise

Artificial intelligence and machine learning are now embedded in every layer of market structure — from the algorithms that set market maker quotes to the natural language processors scanning earnings call transcripts for sentiment signals. As a retail options trader, you are not competing with these systems directly. But you can learn to recognize their fingerprints and filter your entries accordingly.

AI/Algo Behavior	How to Recognize It	Six-Condition Response
Momentum ignition	Stock moves sharply up or down with no news. Volume spikes. Reversal follows within 30–90 minutes as the algo takes profit.	Do not chase the move. Wait for the reversal and re-test of the pre-move level. If the condition was previously confirmed (e.g., condition 2), the algo-driven spike may create a better entry on the re-test.
VWAP pinning	Stock price gravitates back to Volume Weighted Average Price repeatedly throughout the day. Intraday moves fail to hold.	This is algo reversion behavior. It confirms range conditions (5 or 6). Do not trade breakouts that fade repeatedly to VWAP — the range is algo-defended.
Options flow front-running	Unusual options volume in a specific strike appears before a news event. Implied by large OI changes in short-dated OTM options.	Be cautious about selling premium in strikes where unusual flow has appeared. The flow may indicate informed positioning ahead of an event not yet on the public calendar.
Gamma squeeze dynamics	Stock rises sharply as it approaches a large cluster of short-dated call OI. Market makers buying stock to hedge delta as calls go ITM accelerates the move.	Identify high open interest call strikes on platforms like Max Pain calculators. When price approaches those strikes, condition can shift rapidly from 5 to 1. Avoid selling calls at high-OI strikes in momentum environments.
End-of-day momentum reversal	Stocks that have trended strongly all day often reverse in the final 30–60 minutes as algos take profits and rebalance for next-day positioning.	Do not open new directional positions in the last hour of trading. Wait for the next morning's open to confirm whether the intraday move was sustained or reversed. The overnight session often validates or invalidates the intraday trend.

How Algo Behavior Interacts with the Six Conditions

The six-condition framework was built on the premise that price direction and volatility level determine strategy. Algorithms do not change this premise — they change the speed at which conditions transition and the reliability of technical signals within each condition. The practical adjustments are straightforward:

Condition	Algo-Aware Adjustment
1 & 3	Use daily or weekly charts for condition confirmation — not intraday. Algos create false intraday breakouts and reversals that do not reflect actual trend changes. A condition 1 or 3 signal requires confirmation on the daily chart minimum.
2 & 4	Avoid selling premium at strikes that coincide with large gamma clusters (high open interest at nearby strikes). These strikes are algo-defended and can be breached rapidly in momentum moves.
5 & 6	The range boundaries in conditions 5 and 6 are often reinforced by algo VWAP reversion behavior. This can actually improve the reliability of iron condors and calendars — but verify the range is technical, not just algo-driven. True range conditions hold through multiple sessions and multiple news events.

THE ALGO ADVANTAGE FOR THE PATIENT TRADER

Algorithms create short-term noise that punishes impatient traders and rewards patient ones. The algo-driven price whip — the false breakout, the momentum reversal, the VWAP reversion — consistently creates better entry prices for traders who wait for confirmation. Your edge against algo-dominated markets is patience. The machine cannot wait. It executes on its programmed signal. You can observe the false signal, let it resolve, and enter after confirmation at a price the algo's impatient exit created for you.

Putting AI to Work in Your Trading Workflow

Understanding algorithmic activity is the defensive layer of this chapter — knowledge that protects you from being wrong-footed by machine-driven moves. The offensive layer is using AI tools directly in your own trading process. Large language models like ChatGPT, Claude, and Gemini can perform financial calculations, analyze company data, generate strategy scenarios, and review your trade journal — in plain English, in seconds.

AI Can Help With	AI Cannot Replace
Explaining Greeks, skew, and convexity in plain language	Real-time market data — AI has knowledge cutoffs, cannot give live prices or current IV
Calculating breakeven, max risk, max reward, R/R for any described position	Guaranteed accurate calculations — always verify outputs on complex multi-leg structures
Screening a stock against the Ten Indicators — you provide data, AI analyzes it	Personalized financial advice — AI provides frameworks, not licensed investment recommendations

AI Can Help With	AI Cannot Replace
Generating strategy ideas for a given market outlook, DTE, and IV environment	Your judgment — AI is a research assistant, not a trading system. You decide.
Reviewing your trade journal and identifying behavioral patterns	Access your brokerage or execute trades — no connection to trading platforms

The AI Prompt Library for Options Traders

Using AI effectively is a skill, not a shortcut. The difference between a trader who uses AI well and one who does not is not which AI they use — it is the quality of input they provide and how they interpret the output. Each prompt below follows a standard three-part structure: context (what you give the AI), output (what it returns), and interpretation (what you do with the result). Master the interpretation step. AI output is a second opinion, not a directive.

HOW TO READ AI OUTPUT

AI responses for trading analysis should always be verified against your own observation of the live market. If the AI identifies a Condition 2 environment but your two-step read (chart + VIX) shows Condition 5, trust your read. The AI synthesizes what you fed it — your live observation synthesizes what the market is actually doing. Use AI to confirm and challenge your thinking, not to replace it.

These prompts are structured for maximum output quality. Copy them directly, fill in the bracketed variables with your specific trade data, and paste into any major AI assistant.

Prompt 1 — Trade Setup Analysis

"I am considering selling a cash-secured put on [TICKER]. Stock is at $[PRICE]. Target strike: $[STRIKE] put, [DTE] days to expiration. Current premium: $[AMOUNT]. IV Rank: [IVR]. Stock is above its 200-day EMA. No earnings within 35 days. Please: (1) calculate breakeven, maximum risk, and annualized return on reserved capital; (2) evaluate whether this is a favorable setup given the IV environment; (3) suggest the T-21 management plan for this specific trade."

Prompt 2 — Ten Indicators Stock Screen

"Evaluate [COMPANY / TICKER] for a cash-secured put strategy using the Ten Indicators: [paste EPS trend, revenue trend, P/E, PEG, dividend history, debt-to-equity, short interest, market size, barrier to entry, political profile, optionable status, megatrend alignment]. Score each indicator 1 (favorable) or 0 (unfavorable). Total out of 10. Rationale for each score. Recommend: High Conviction / Reduce Size / Avoid."

Prompt 3 — Greeks Calculation for a Multi-Leg Position

"I have this options position: [describe each leg — buy/sell, call/put, strike, expiration, quantity, current premium]. Calculate: (1) total position Delta, (2) total position Theta, (3) total position Vega, (4) maximum profit, maximum loss, and breakevens. Then identify: what market scenario causes maximum loss, and what adjustment reduces my Delta exposure by 50%?"

Prompt 4 — Trade Journal Pattern Analysis

"Here are my last 20 options trades: [paste journal — entry date, ticker, strategy, entry price, exit price, P&L, outcome]. Analyze: (1) win rate by strategy type; (2) average win vs. average loss ratio; (3) behavioral patterns in my losing trades; (4) three specific adjustments that would most improve my edge based on this data."

Prompt 5 — Strategy Selection for Current Market Conditions

"Current conditions: SPY is [above/below] its 200-day EMA. VIX is at [LEVEL]. BPI for [SECTOR] is [LEVEL] and [rising/falling]. Target stock [TICKER] has IVR of [IVR] and is [above/below] its 50-day EMA. No earnings for [DAYS] days. Recommend the three most appropriate options strategies, ranked by expected risk-adjusted return, with entry parameters (strike delta, DTE, target premium) for each."

Prompt 6 — Iron Condor Strike Selection

"I want an iron condor on [TICKER / ETF] at $[PRICE], [DTE] days to expiration. I want: short strikes at approximately 0.16 delta each side; long strikes providing $1.50 of protection per side; net credit of at least $0.80. Give me specific strike prices to check, expected probability of profit, and breakeven prices on each side."

Prompt 7 — Roll Decision Analysis

"Short put position: [TICKER] $[STRIKE] put, originally sold for $[CREDIT], currently worth $[CURRENT PRICE], [DTE] days remaining. Stock at $[STOCK PRICE]. I have captured [X]% of original premium. T-21 review triggered. Analyze: (1) close, roll out, or roll out-and-down? (2) if rolling, optimal next strike and expiration? (3) what new credit should I target to justify the roll?"

Prompt 8 — Earnings Risk Pre-Trade Check

"I am considering a [STRATEGY] on [TICKER] with [DTE] days to expiration. Next earnings date: [DATE]. Last four earnings moves: [+X%, -Y%, +Z%, -W%]. Analyze: (1) does my expiration overlap with earnings? (2) what is the average expected move? (3) is my short strike far enough from the stock price to survive the average historical earnings move? (4) if not, what adjustment — different strike, earlier expiration, or defined-risk spread — protects me?"

AI WORKFLOW RULE

Use AI as your pre-trade checklist, not your decision-maker. Run Prompt 1 (setup analysis) before every new income trade. Run Prompt 4 (journal review) once per month. Run Prompt 5 (strategy selection) when you are uncertain which structure fits current conditions. AI eliminates preventable calculation errors. It does not replace judgment, discipline, or the risk management framework in this book.

Prompt 9 — The Six-Condition Daily Read (Your Most Important AI Prompt)

The most powerful AI prompt in this book is the one you run before the market opens every single day. It takes 60 seconds to complete and gives you a systematic six-condition reading with strategy confirmation. Make this your pre-market ritual.

"Today's market data: SPY is at $[PRICE] and is [above/below] its 50-day EMA and [above/below] its 200-day EMA. Over the past 10 trading sessions, SPY has made [higher highs and higher lows / lower highs and lower lows / oscillated between $X and $Y support/resistance]. VIX is at [LEVEL]. IVR on SPY options is [IVR LEVEL]. Based on the six-condition framework — where direction has three states (bullish, bearish, range-bound) and volatility has two states (high IV above 20 / low IV below 20) — which of the six conditions is currently active? Confirm with one sentence of supporting evidence for each axis. Then state the approved strategy for that condition and what I should NOT be doing today."

Run this prompt every morning. Cross-reference the AI's output with your own two-step condition read (Chapter 15). If they agree — high confidence. If they disagree — investigate the discrepancy before opening any position. The AI does not override your judgment. It provides a second read on the same data.

How AI Is Changing the Options Market — And What That Means for You

Algorithmic trading now accounts for more than 80% of daily U.S. equity volume. For the options trader, this creates both hazards and opportunities. The hazards: sudden, sharp, apparently irrational price moves that are actually systematic responses by algorithms to technical levels, options flow, or news sentiment. The opportunities: these moves are often mean-reverting, predictable in pattern if not in timing, and frequently create temporary mispricing in the options market that disciplined sellers can exploit.

The three algo patterns most relevant to premium sellers are: the volume spike with no follow-through (algorithms buy or sell aggressively on a signal, price spikes, then reverts within minutes — do not chase), the implied volatility manipulation near expiration (market makers and algos push IV higher on large positions near expiry — recognize this as a gamma-related phenomenon, not a directional signal), and the earnings whisper trade (algorithms buy options in the days before earnings as they detect institutional flow, inflating IV above fundamental levels — this is the ramp that premium sellers exploit by entering calendar spreads 10–14 days before the announcement).

The democratization of AI tools has changed options market dynamics in ways that matter directly to retail traders. Here is what is happening and how to use it to your advantage rather than become a casualty of it.

AI/Algo Development	Effect on Markets	Your Response
Large language models now interpret Fed statements in milliseconds. By the time you read the FOMC headline, algorithmic traders have already priced the move.	Markets reprice macro events faster than ever. The first 30 seconds after a data release are chaotic and algo-dominated.	Never trade the initial reaction. Wait 5–15 minutes for price to stabilize and algo order flow to clear before evaluating the new condition. The second-move is more tradeable than the first.
AI-powered earnings analysis tools read earnings transcripts and analyst notes instantly. 'Beat and raise' or 'miss and lower' is priced before retail traders finish reading the headline.	Post-earnings IV crush is sharper and faster than a decade ago. Options premium evaporates in minutes, not hours.	Your protection: never hold short premium through earnings. The IV crush that once played out over a trading day now plays out in 10 minutes — and the risk of being on the wrong side is higher than ever.
Sentiment analysis AIs scan millions of social media posts, news articles, and options flow data in real-time, identifying crowd positioning before the crowd realizes it is positioned.	Option flow anomalies — large unusual buys in puts or calls — are detected and amplified faster. Unusual options activity is less 'unusual' and more quickly incorporated into prices.	Use unusual options activity as a secondary signal only — not a primary trigger. By the time you see the alert, institutions and their AIs are already aware of it. The edge comes from the six-condition system, not from following smart money that has already moved.
Market-making algorithms now adjust bid/ask spreads dynamically in real-time based on order flow. Wide spreads narrow in high-demand strikes. Thin strikes get wider instantly when large orders arrive.	Execution quality is more dynamic. The midpoint price may shift significantly in the few seconds between when you evaluate a spread and when you submit the order.	Always use limit orders. Never chase a spread. If the price moved before your fill, cancel and reassess. The trade that fills above your limit is often the trade the algo wanted you to be in — not the trade you planned.

THE RETAIL TRADER'S PERMANENT EDGE

Algorithms compete on milliseconds. Institutions compete on capital. Neither competes on patience, discipline, and defined risk — the three things a retail trader in the six-condition system deploys as their edge. You don't need to be faster than an algo. You need to be in the right condition, in the right structure, at the right size — and let the math work. That is not an edge algorithms can take from you.

Recognizing Algorithmic Manipulation Patterns

Not all algo activity is legitimate market-making or institutional execution. A subset of algorithmic behavior is designed to create artificial conditions that trigger retail stop-losses, flush out weak hands, or manufacture the appearance of momentum that does not exist. Recognizing these patterns protects your positions — and prevents you from being the liquidity that algos are hunting.

Pattern	What It Looks Like on the Chart	How to Protect Your Positions
Stop Hunt / Liquidity Sweep	Price spikes sharply below a well-known support level or above a well-known resistance level — sweeping the stops clustered there — then immediately reverses. The candle has an extended wick with a small body. Volume spikes on the wick.	Never place stop-losses at the obvious round number or the exact prior low/high. Use offsets — 1–2% beyond the obvious level. Better: use mental stops and manage manually, or use defined-risk options structures that don't need stop orders.
Spoofing / Order Book Manipulation	Large bid or ask orders appear on Level 2, creating the illusion of support or resistance. When price approaches, the large orders disappear before being filled. This tricks retail into trading in the direction of the 'support' that never actually exists.	Ignore Level 2 data as a primary signal. Spoofed orders are canceled in milliseconds. Trade what the chart confirms over multiple candles — not what the order book shows in one moment.
Momentum Ignition	A rapid burst of small orders creates artificial momentum to attract trend-following algos and retail traders. Price accelerates beyond fundamental justification. After retail and momentum algos pile in, the initiating algo exits into the manufactured move.	If you see price move 2–3% in under 5 minutes on no news, treat it as a potential momentum ignition. Wait for the move to complete and consolidate before evaluating the new condition. Do not chase the initial move.
Gamma Squeeze Engineering	On stocks with heavy call open interest, large buyers push the price up through key strikes, forcing market makers to buy shares to hedge their short calls. This creates a self-reinforcing squeeze that can be engineered deliberately.	Monitor open interest levels above current price on high-IV, heavily shorted stocks. If you are short calls on such a stock and price approaches your strike with unusual velocity, close or roll before gamma squeeze dynamics activate.
End-of-Day Mark Painting	In the final minutes of the session, large orders push prices to specific levels — either above a key level for the weekly close, or below a level to trigger stop-losses after the close.	Avoid placing market orders in the final 5 minutes of the session. Use limit orders. Do not make position decisions based solely on closing price action — evaluate the entire day's context.

THE SIX-CONDITION SYSTEM IS MANIPULATION-RESISTANT

The six-condition framework reads the VIX and the daily chart — two inputs that are extremely difficult to manipulate sustainably. A stop hunt lasts minutes. The daily trend lasts days or weeks. The VIX level reflects the aggregate pricing of thousands of options contracts — not a single order. By operating on the daily timeframe with clearly defined condition reads, you sit above the layer of the market where most algorithmic manipulation operates. The system is not perfect — but its timeframe is its protection.

Your Weekly AI-Assisted Trading Workflow

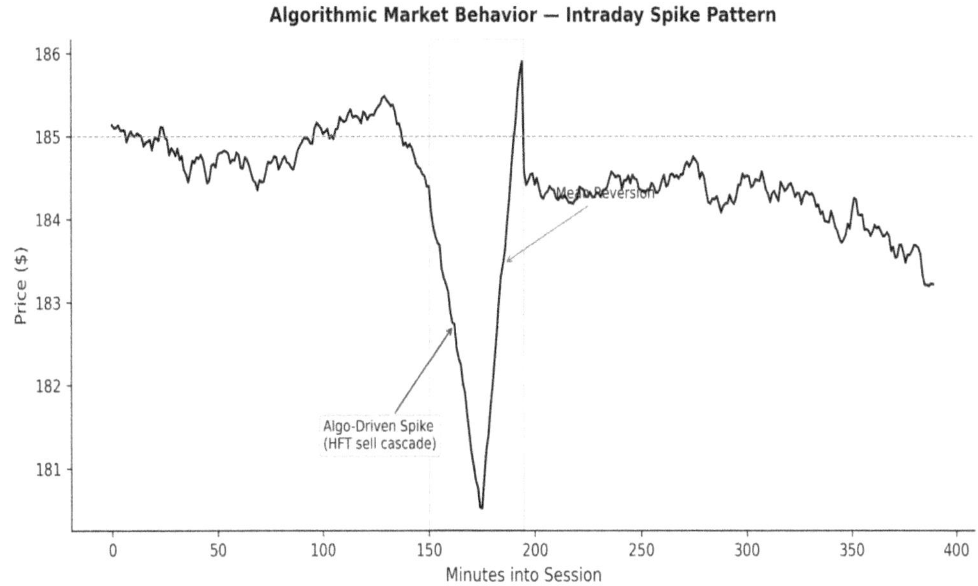

Figure 17.1 — AI-Assisted Weekly Trading Workflow — How to integrate AI tools into your pre-market routine for faster condition reads.

AI-Assisted Weekly Trading Workflow — How to integrate AI tools into your pre-market routine.

The options trader who uses AI will replace the one who does not. Here is a practical weekly workflow that integrates AI tools into your existing process — not as a replacement for judgment, but as a force multiplier for analysis.

Sunday Evening (10 minutes): Feed your open positions into an AI tool and ask it to calculate current Greeks, identify T-21 management dates, flag earnings events within 14 days, and recommend hold/close/roll for each position with reasoning. The AI does in 30 seconds what takes 15 minutes manually. You still make the decision — but with better data.

Monday Morning (5 minutes): Ask the AI to assess the current market condition based on VIX level and SPY's position relative to its 50-day EMA. This gives you a second opinion on your condition assessment — not to override your judgment, but to check it against systematic analysis.

Before Any New Entry (2 minutes): Ask the AI to calculate maximum loss, breakeven, probability of profit, annualized return, and whether the stock has earnings within your DTE window. This pre-trade check catches errors and ensures you have not missed an earnings date — the single most common income-trader mistake.

After Every Losing Trade (3 minutes): Describe the trade to the AI and ask it to analyze which of your rules were followed and which were violated. This turns every loss into a documented lesson without the emotional bias that clouds self-analysis.

Monthly Review (15 minutes): Feed your entire month of trades into the AI and ask for win rate, average winner/loser, profit factor, total P&L, and PPD achieved versus target. The AI creates your monthly scorecard in a fraction of the time — letting you spend energy on analysis rather than arithmetic.

Total weekly AI time: approximately 35 minutes. Manual equivalent: 2-3 hours. The time savings is valuable, but the real edge is consistency — the AI never skips a step, never forgets to check earnings, never lets emotional bias color the analysis. You provide judgment and experience. The AI provides speed and thoroughness. Together, you operate at a level that neither could achieve alone.

THE AI BOUNDARY RULE

Never let AI make a trade decision for you. Always let AI do calculations for you. AI handles math, data lookup, and pattern identification. You handle thesis development, risk assessment, and the final go or no-go. When the AI says a trade has a 72% probability of profit, your job is to decide whether 72% is sufficient given your portfolio exposure, the market condition, and your experience with this stock.

NEW TO FUTURES? START HERE

A futures contract is an agreement to buy or sell an asset at a predetermined price on a specific future date. Unlike stocks — where you own a piece of a company — a futures contract is an obligation to transact. S&P 500 futures (/ES) give you leveraged exposure to the S&P 500 without buying shares. Options on futures are options contracts where the underlying is a futures contract. The mechanics — calls, puts, strikes, expirations, Greeks — are identical to equity options. The differences are contract size, settlement, margin, and tax treatment. If you are comfortable with equity options from Chapters 2–15, you are ready for this chapter. If you are brand new to options, complete those chapters first.

FUTURES OPTIONS ▸ The institutional arena — where index income, commodities, and volatility converge

Options on futures extend the Seller's Philosophy into the deepest, most liquid, and most tax-efficient markets in the world. This chapter builds the professional bridge between equity options income and futures-based premium selling.

Most options traders stop at equity options. They sell cash-secured puts on Apple, run the Wheel on NVDA, and manage iron condors on SPY. That is a complete, legitimate income system — and everything in this book to this point applies to it without modification. But there is a parallel universe of options liquidity, leverage efficiency, and tax advantage that most retail traders never enter: options on futures.

Options on futures are not more complicated than equity options in any meaningful way. The mechanics — premium, strike, expiration, Greeks, the seller's edge — are identical. What changes is the underlying, the leverage structure, the trading hours, the settlement rules, and in many cases, the tax treatment. Each of these differences can work powerfully in your favor once you understand them.

This chapter is not an introduction to futures trading. It is a professional extension of the premium-selling framework you have already built — applied to the instruments where institutional capital operates at scale.

---

1. Why Trade Options on Futures?

The case for selling options on futures rests on five structural advantages that equity options simply cannot match. These are not marginal improvements — they represent a fundamentally different risk/reward architecture.

Advantage	What It Means in Practice
Section 1256 Tax Treatment	60% of all gains taxed as long-term capital gains, 40% as short-term — regardless of how long you held the position. For a trader in the 32% bracket, this alone can reduce effective tax rate on index options income by 8–12 percentage points annually.
24-Hour Market Access	Futures markets trade nearly around the clock — Sunday 6 PM ET through Friday 5 PM ET, with only a one-hour daily break. Equity options close at 4:15 PM. Overnight events — Fed decisions, geopolitical news, foreign market moves — can be managed in real time, not reacted to the following morning.
Cash Settlement (Index Futures)	S&P 500 futures and index options settle in cash. There is no risk of being assigned stock you cannot afford. No shares change hands. You close positions in dollars. For the premium seller, this eliminates the most operationally complex risk in the equity options world.
Unmatched Liquidity	The E-mini S&P 500 (/ES) is one of the most liquid instruments on the planet. Bid-ask spreads on at-the-money options are among the tightest available to retail traders.

Advantage	What It Means in Practice
	Institutional volume ensures fills are clean and slippage is minimal — a critical advantage for spread traders.
Leverage Efficiency via SPAN Margin	Futures options use SPAN (Standard Portfolio Analysis of Risk) margin rather than Reg-T. SPAN calculates margin based on the actual risk of your portfolio rather than per-position rules. A properly structured multi-leg position requires less capital than the equivalent equity options trade — improving capital efficiency without increasing risk.

There are also structural risks that must be stated plainly. Futures carry inherent leverage — a small adverse move in the underlying can produce large losses in the futures position itself. Margin calls on futures can be immediate. Commodity futures carry physical delivery risk if positions are held past First Notice Day. These are manageable risks with proper education and position sizing, but they are not the risks of an equity options account, and they demand respect.

THE PREMIUM DESK RULE ON FUTURES OPTIONS

Apply the same risk-first framework here that governs every other strategy in this book. Futures options do not require you to trade futures. You can sell credit spreads on /ES or SPX options without ever touching an outright futures position. Start with defined-risk structures. Build toward undefined risk only after demonstrating consistent profitability in spreads.

The Data Behind the Seller's Edge: What the CME's Own Research Reveals

The Seller's Philosophy is not built on intuition or trading folklore. It is built on a structural market fact documented by the exchange that created the product: the majority of options — and an overwhelming majority of put options specifically — expire worthless. The buyer who holds options to expiration loses. The writer who holds positions to expiration collects. This is not a claim. It is exchange-published data.

Figure 18.2 — OTM Commodity Options Expiry Reference: Key Dates and Delta Ranges by Commodity

Commodity	Symbol	Expiry Style	Last Trading Day	Delta Target	Notes
Crude Oil (WTI)	CL	American	3rd business day before 25th	0.20–0.30	High IV; avoid earnings periods
Natural Gas	NG	American	3–4 business days before last day	0.15–0.25	Seasonal IV spikes; winter/summer
Corn	ZC	American	Last Friday of month prior	0.20–0.30	Harvest season IV elevated May-Jul
Gold	GC	American	4 business days before last day	0.15–0.25	Flight-to-safety spikes on VIX moves
S&P 500 (/ES)	ES	European	3rd Friday of month	0.20–0.25	Index options; no physical delivery

Figure 18.2 — OTM Commodity Options Expiry Reference. Key dates and delta ranges by commodity.

Figure 18.3 — /ES Futures Contract Specifications: Full vs. Micro Contract Comparison with SPY Options

Spec	E-mini S&P 500 (/ES)	Micro E-mini (/MES)	SPY Options
Multiplier	$50 × index	$5 × index	$100 × SPY price
Notional Value (SPX @ 5,000)	$250,000	$25,000	~$500,000 (100 sh)
Tick Size	0.25 points = $12.50	0.25 points = $1.25	0.01 = 1.00
Margin Required	~$12,000 (SPAN)	~$1,200 (SPAN)	Premium paid or collateral
Settlement	Cash — no delivery risk	Cash — no delivery risk	Cash (SPY) or physical
Tax Treatment	60/40 rule (Section 1256)	60/40 rule (Section 1256)	Short-term or long-term

Figure 18.3 — /ES Futures Contract Specifications. Full vs. Micro contract comparison with SPY options.

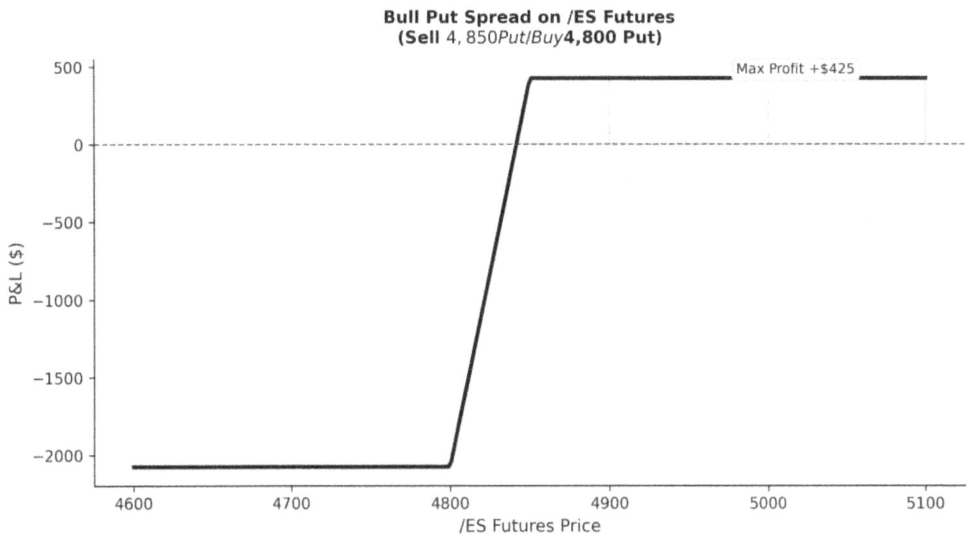

Figure 18.4 — Bull Put Spread on /ES Futures. Credit spread mechanics with $50 multiplier.

In the year 2000, the Chicago Mercantile Exchange published a landmark analysis covering January 1997 through December 1999 — examining more than 83,000 S&P 500 futures options contracts held to expiration. The study appeared in Options on Futures: New Trading Strategies (Wiley & Sons, co-authored by Lawrence McMillan), and it remains the most precisely sourced public breakdown of options expiration rates by product and by side — puts versus calls — that the CME has ever released.

The study's findings are unambiguous: across three consecutive years, more than 94 percent of S&P 500 futures put options held to expiration expired worthless. Overall, approximately 83 percent of all S&P 500 options expired out of the money — and roughly 77 percent of all CME options across the broader futures complex did the same. For the precise year-by-year breakdown, readers are directed to the original source: Options on Futures: New Trading Strategies, CME Group / Wiley & Sons, 2000 (Exhibit 1.1, Chapter 1).

The asymmetry between puts and calls in that study is the key insight: S&P 500 puts expired worthless at 94 percent. S&P 500 calls expired worthless at approximately 55 percent. Both are seller's advantages — but the put side was decisively more favorable, and the reason is structural: equity markets have a long-run upward bias. A put option is a bet that prices fall sharply. Every year the index does not experience a significant drawdown, the put buyer loses. The writer collects. The CME study quantified what practitioners had always understood to be true.

What the 2020–2024 Period Confirms

As of 2026, the CME has not published an updated equivalent study. The explosion in daily-expiry options (0-DTE contracts now represent nearly half of all SPX weekly volume), the commercial sensitivity of granular expiration data, and the sheer volume growth — U.S. options total volume exceeded 15 billion contracts in 2025, up 26% from 2024 — have made a direct replication of the original methodology difficult to produce and commercially sensitive to release. The CME no longer publishes this breakdown publicly.

However, The Premium Desk's internal research team constructed 2020–2024 proxy estimates using three authoritative data streams: OCC broad market open interest settlement patterns, CBOE strategy index performance (the PUT Index, BXM, and WPUT), and Lawrence McMillan's Option Strategist open interest research on CME S&P 500 futures expiration patterns. The results, with appropriate confidence ranges to reflect the proxy methodology, are presented below.

Year	All CME Options OTM at Expiry (Est.)	S&P Options (Proxy %)	S&P PUTS Expiring OTM (Proxy %)	S&P 500 Market Direction
2020	~70–76%	~78–83%	~80–88%	+16.3% (Bull)
2021	~72–78%	~80–85%	~87–92%	+26.9% (Bull)
2022	~65–73%	~70–78%	~60–70%	−19.4% (BEAR)
2023	~72–78%	~80–86%	~87–92%	+24.2% (Bull)
2024	~73–79%	~81–87%	~88–93%	+23.3% (Bull)
Avg 2020–24	**~70–76%**	**~78–84%**	**~80–91% avg**	**Net Bull (4/5 years)**

* CME Study findings cited from Options on Futures: New Trading Strategies (CME Group / Wiley & Sons, 2000, Exhibit 1.1). Year-by-year data not reproduced — see original source.

Source: The Premium Desk Research Memorandum #12, March 2026. Proxy methodology: OCC broad market settlement patterns + CBOE PUT/BXM/WPUT Index performance + Lawrence McMillan / Option Strategist CME open interest research. No official CME annual breakdown has been publicly released for 2020–2024. 2022 figures highlighted reflect bear-market compression of put-worthless rates.

Four years of the five-year period align with the original CME baseline. In 2020, 2021, 2023, and 2024 — all bull markets, each returning between 16% and 27% — proxy estimates place S&P 500 put expiration rates in the high-80% to low-90% range. Sellers who consistently sold put premium across those four years collected the majority of the premium they received. The CBOE PUT Index — which systematically sells one-month at-the-money cash-secured puts — returned +2.1%, +21.8%, +14.3%, and +17.8% in those four years respectively, confirming the realized profitability of the strategy.

2022: The Bear Year — What It Teaches

The exception is 2022. The S&P 500 fell approximately 19.4% as the Federal Reserve executed its fastest interest rate hiking cycle in four decades. In that year, put-worthless rates compressed to an estimated 60–70% — still a majority, but meaningfully below the historical baseline. Put sellers experienced losses. The CBOE PUT Index fell 7.7%.

Here is what the 2022 data actually teaches, and it is not that the Seller's Philosophy failed. It is that the Seller's Philosophy is exposed to sustained directional moves — and that the risk management rules governing every strategy in this book exist precisely for years like 2022. A seller who applied the 2% rule, maintained defined-risk structures, closed positions at predetermined stop-loss levels, and reduced position count as volatility elevated would have taken losses in 2022, but would have survived intact to collect the outsized premiums available in the recovery year of 2023.

There is also a second insight from 2022 that the data makes explicit: when puts stopped expiring worthless at high rates, calls took over. In 2022, call-worthless rates are estimated at approximately 70–80% — sharply above the historical 55.3% call-average from the CME baseline. Market direction determines which side of the options market holds the structural advantage. In bull markets, put sellers win. In bear markets, call sellers win. In both cases, the seller — the disciplined, risk-managed premium collector — wins more often than not.

Metric	CME Study Finding (1997–99)*	Proxy Estimate (2020–24)
All CME Options Expiring Worthless	76.6%	~70–76% (est.)
S&P 500 Options (All Sides)	83.3%	~78–84% (est.)
S&P 500 PUTS Expiring Worthless	94.0%	~80–91% avg (bear year: ~60–70%)
S&P 500 CALLS Expiring Worthless	55.3%	~50–62% avg (bear year: ~70–80%)
Market Trend During Period	Strong Bull (dot-com run-up)	Mixed: 4 bull years + 1 bear year (2022)

The CME's own published data — covering more than 83,000 S&P 500 futures options over three years — confirmed that more than 94 percent of all put options held to expiration expired worthless. This is not a trading legend. It is exchange data. No comparable study has been officially updated for the 2020s; the CME no longer publishes this breakdown publicly, and the explosion of daily-expiry options has made the original methodology harder to replicate cleanly. But the structural dynamic it revealed has not changed. In the four bull market years between 2020 and 2024 — when the S&P returned between 16% and 27% annually — proxy analysis consistently suggests that S&P 500 put options expiring worthless remained in the high-80% to low-90% range. The writer's structural advantage is well intact. And in 2022, the one bear year of the period, calls expired worthless at an elevated rate instead — confirming the other side of the same coin: market direction is not the seller's enemy. Volatility, as always, belongs to the seller's advantage.

★ **THE NUMBER EVERY PREMIUM SELLER SHOULD KNOW BY HEART**

94% — the percentage of S&P 500 futures put options reported as expiring worthless in the CME's published study, as cited in Options on Futures: New Trading Strategies (CME Group / Wiley & Sons, 2000). In four of the five years from 2020–2024, proxy analysis from CBOE strategy indices and OCC settlement data suggests this figure held in the 80–92% range. The seller does not need to be right every trade. The seller needs to be disciplined, properly sized, and consistently positioned on the right side of the structural advantage the exchange's own research confirms.

2. S&P 500 Futures Basics

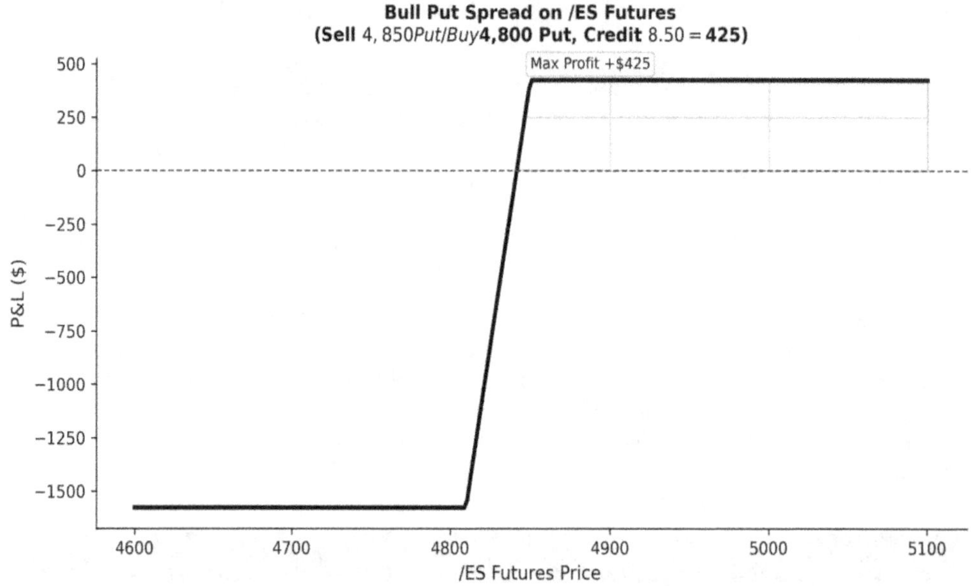

Figure 18.1 — Futures Credit Spread — Applying bull put spreads to ES futures with defined risk and no assignment exposure.

Futures Credit Spread — Applying bull put spreads to ES futures with defined risk.

The S&P 500 futures complex is the professional benchmark for understanding how options on index futures operate. Before trading options on them, you must understand the underlying contracts precisely.

Contract	Ticker	Multiplier	Key Facts
E-mini S&P 500	**/ES**	$50 × index	The institutional standard. At index = 5,000, one contract = $250,000 notional. Minimum tick = 0.25 pts = $12.50. Quarterly expiration (March/June/September/December). Most liquid futures contract in the world.
Micro E-mini S&P 500	**/MES**	$5 × index	1/10th the size of /ES. At index = 5,000, one contract = $25,000 notional. Tick = $1.25. Ideal for smaller accounts and precise position sizing. Same expiration calendar as /ES.
S&P 500 (Standard)	**/SP**	$250 × index	The original full-size contract. Rarely traded by retail; bid-ask spreads are wide. Mentioned for reference only — retail traders use /ES or /MES exclusively.

Contract Mechanics You Must Know

Futures contracts have expiration dates. The front-month contract is the nearest expiration and carries the highest volume and tightest spreads. As expiration approaches, traders 'roll' their position to the next quarter — closing the expiring contract and opening the next one. The price difference between the two contract months is called the 'roll spread' and reflects the cost of carry (interest rates minus dividends).

S&P 500 futures are cash settled — on expiration, the final settlement price is calculated from the opening prices of all 500 component stocks (the 'Special Opening

Quotation' or SOQ on quarterly expiration Fridays). No shares are delivered. Your profit or loss is credited or debited in cash. This is the critical structural feature that makes index futures ideal for premium writers.

Term	Definition — Master These Before Trading
Notional Value	The total market value controlled by one futures contract. /ES at 5,000 = $250,000 notional. One contract controls this amount regardless of the margin required to hold it.
Initial Margin	The deposit required to open a futures position. Set by the exchange (CME Group) and typically 5–10% of notional value. For /ES, approximately $12,000–$15,000 per contract. Subject to change based on volatility.
Maintenance Margin	The minimum account balance required to hold the position. If your account falls below this level, you receive a margin call requiring immediate deposit or position closure.
Mark-to-Market (Daily Settlement)	Futures positions are settled in cash at the end of every trading day. Profits are credited immediately; losses are debited immediately. Unlike stocks, there is no unrealized gain/loss — it is all realized daily.
Contango	When far-month futures prices are higher than near-month prices. Normal for equity index futures (cost of carry > dividends). Has significant implications for VIX futures products.
Backwardation	When near-month futures prices are higher than far-month prices. Signals near-term supply stress in commodities, or fear and demand for immediate protection in VIX futures.
Rollover Date	The date before expiration when most traders move from the front-month to the next contract. For /ES: approximately 8 days before expiration (on the Thursday preceding expiration week).

3. Understanding S&P 500 Options

The S&P 500 options universe gives traders three distinct instruments — SPY, SPX, and /ES options — that track the same underlying index but differ fundamentally in structure, settlement, tax treatment, and strategic application. Choosing the right instrument is not a trivial decision. It determines your capital requirements, tax efficiency, and assignment risk profile.

Feature	SPY Options	SPX Options	/ES Futures Options
Underlying	S&P 500 ETF (shares)	S&P 500 Cash Index	/ES E-mini Futures Contract
Multiplier	$100 per contract	$100 per contract	$50 per contract
Settlement	American-style / Shares	European / Cash (no early exercise)	American / Delivers /ES position
Assignment Risk	Yes — assigned 100 SPY shares	No — cash settled at expiration	Yes — assigned /ES futures contract
Tax Treatment	Standard short/long term	Section 1256 (60/40)	Section 1256 (60/40)
Trading Hours	9:30 AM – 4:15 PM ET	9:30 AM – 4:15 PM ET (standard)	Nearly 24 hours (Sun 6 PM – Fri 5 PM ET)
Expirations	Daily, weekly, monthly	Daily (XSP), weekly (SPXW), monthly	Weekly (/EW), monthly (/ES)
Typical Spread	1–2 cents ATM	$0.10–$0.25 ATM	$0.10–$0.25 ATM

Feature	SPY Options	SPX Options	/ES Futures Options
Best For	Small accounts, defined-risk, familiar structure	Income selling, spreads, tax efficiency	Largest accounts, overnight exposure, SPAN margin efficiency

For most premium writers, SPX options represent the optimal starting point in the index options universe. The combination of cash settlement (eliminating overnight assignment risk), Section 1256 tax treatment, and European-style exercise (no early assignment possible) creates a structurally clean instrument. The Seller's Philosophy applied to SPX credit spreads is one of the most repeatable income frameworks available — and it requires no futures account.

The /ES options route adds the advantages of SPAN margin and near-24-hour access, but introduces futures account requirements and the technical complexity of a futures-settled instrument. It is the natural progression for the experienced SPX trader who wants to deploy more capital with greater efficiency.

CRITICAL: THE MINI-SPX (XSP)

For traders with accounts under $50,000, SPX options can be prohibitively large — a 50-wide spread represents $5,000 of capital at risk. The Mini-SPX (XSP) is 1/10th the size of SPX — ideal for precise position sizing at smaller account levels while retaining cash settlement and Section 1256 tax treatment. Treat XSP as your entry point into index income selling.

4. The Long and Short of an S&P 500 Credit Spread

A credit spread on the S&P 500 is the Seller's Philosophy applied to the deepest liquidity pool in the options market. The structure is identical to equity credit spreads — sell an out-of-the-money option, buy a further out-of-the-money option for protection. The differences are scale, settlement, and tax efficiency.

Element	Bull Put Spread (Bullish / Neutral)	Bear Call Spread (Bearish / Neutral)
Structure	Sell OTM put + Buy lower-strike put	Sell OTM call + Buy higher-strike call
Market View	Bullish to neutral — index stays above short put	Bearish to neutral — index stays below short call
Max Profit	Net credit received × $100 (SPX) or $50 (/ES)	Net credit received × $100 (SPX) or $50 (/ES)
Max Loss	(Width of spread – credit) × multiplier	(Width of spread – credit) × multiplier
Break-Even	Short put strike – net credit received	Short call strike + net credit received
When to Use	Conditions 1 (Bull Low IV) and 2 (Bull High IV). After pullbacks. When VIX spikes above 20.	Conditions 3 (Bear Low IV) and 4 (Bear High IV). When index is extended above resistance with declining breadth.
SPX Example	SPX at 5,000. Sell 4,850 put / Buy 4,800 put for $2.50 credit. Max profit: $250. Max loss: $2,750. Break-even: 4,847.50.	SPX at 5,000. Sell 5,150 call / Buy 5,200 call for $2.00 credit. Max profit: $200. Max loss: $2,800. Break-even: 5,152.
Close Rule	Close at 50% of max profit (T-21 or time target)	Close at 50% of max profit (T-21 or time target)

Position Sizing for S&P 500 Spreads

The index multiplier and spread width determine your dollar risk. SPX spreads of 25, 50, and 100 points are common — each representing $2,500, $5,000, and $10,000 of maximum risk per spread respectively (before credit received). The Premium Desk 2% Rule applies here identically: risk no more than 2% of your account on any single spread trade. An account of $50,000 allows a maximum of $1,000 at risk — a 25-wide SPX spread at full width is therefore your ceiling, and you should be collecting enough credit to close at 50%, reducing realized risk further.

Account Size	2% Risk Limit	Spread Width	Typical Credit	Net Max Risk
$25,000	$500	25-wide SPX	~$1.50–$2.50	$2,500 gross / ~$2,000 after credit
$50,000	$1,000	25-wide SPX	~$1.50–$2.50	$2,500 gross / ~$2,000 after credit
$100,000	$2,000	50-wide SPX	~$2.50–$4.50	$5,000 gross / ~$4,500 after credit
$250,000	$5,000	50-wide SPX × 2	~$2.50–$4.50	$5,000 × 2 gross / ~$4,000 net each

The iron condor — simultaneous bull put spread and bear call spread — is the natural extension on the S&P 500. In low-volatility, range-bound conditions (Condition 5 or 6), the index tends to oscillate within a defined band. An iron condor on SPX collects credit on both sides, with the maximum loss limited to one side of the spread. The six-condition framework tells you exactly when an iron condor is appropriate and when it is not — never enter a condor into a confirmed trending market.

5. Commodity Futures and Options Characteristics

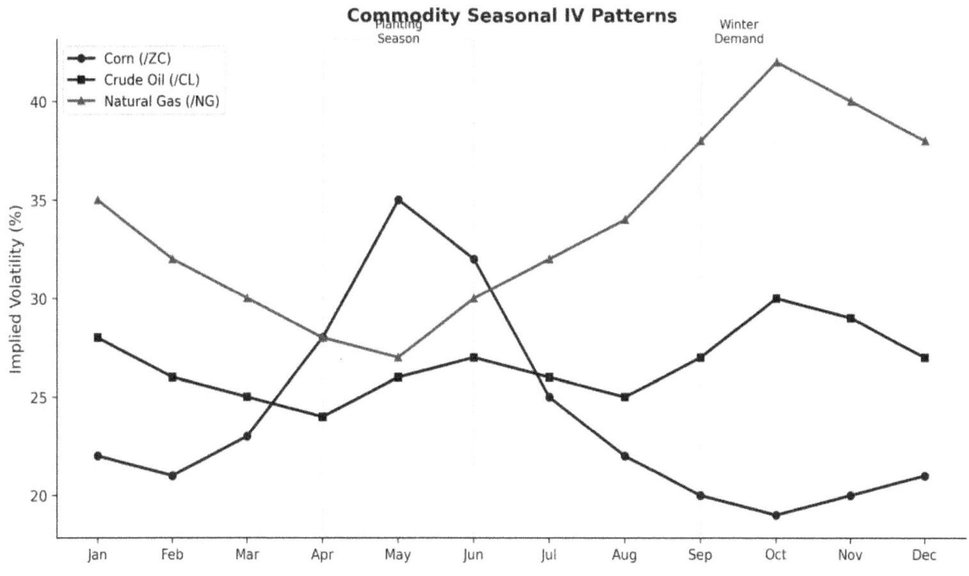

Figure 18.2 — Commodity Seasonality Patterns — Historical IV cycles across major commodity markets by quarter.

Commodity Seasonality Patterns — Historical IV cycles across major commodity markets by quarter.

Commodity futures represent fundamentally different behavior from equity index futures. Where the S&P 500 has a structural long-term upward bias (corporate earnings compound over time), commodities are mean-reverting assets governed by supply and demand cycles, seasonal patterns, weather events, geopolitical disruptions, and currency dynamics. Each of these factors creates volatility spikes — and volatility spikes are premium writers' opportunities.

Before trading options on commodity futures, you must understand the physical delivery mechanism that governs them. Unlike index futures, most commodity futures contracts can result in the delivery of the actual commodity — barrels of crude oil, bushels of corn, troy ounces of gold — if held through expiration. The First Notice Day (FND) is the date before expiration on which the seller of a futures contract can serve notice of intent to deliver. Holding a futures options position past FND can result in assignment into a futures contract that is days away from physical delivery. This is not a theoretical risk — it has happened to uninformed retail traders.

Commodity	Symbol	Exchange	Multiplier	Settlement	Premium Seller's Notes
Crude Oil (WTI)	**/CL**	CME/NYMEX	$1,000/pt ($10/tick)	Physical	Highest volatility of the major commodities. IV spikes during OPEC decisions, geopolitical events, inventory reports. Sell credit spreads after volatility spikes. Never hold through FND — exit positions 2–3 weeks before expiration.
Gold	**/GC**	CME/COMEX	$100/troy oz	Physical	Mean-reverting over medium term. Strong seasonal pattern (Q4 typically strongest). IV spikes during Fed decisions and global risk-off events. Ideal for cash-secured put equivalents (selling puts on /OG micro gold options) during fear-driven selloffs.
Natural Gas	**/NG**	CME/NYMEX	$10,000/MMBtu	Physical	Extremely volatile — seasonal swings can be massive (heating/cooling demand). IV regularly exceeds 50–80%. Spreads are wide. Suitable only for experienced commodity options traders with defined-risk structures only.
Corn	**/ZC**	CME/CBOT	$50/bushel	Physical	Strong seasonality: planting (April–May) and harvest (September–October) create predictable IV expansions. Iron condors during post-planting, pre-harvest windows (June–August) are a classic seasonal strategy.
Soybeans	**/ZS**	CME/CBOT	$50/bushel	Physical	Similar seasonal pattern to corn. Watch USDA crop reports (planted acres, WASDE reports) — these are scheduled events that function like earnings for agricultural commodities.
Silver	**/SI**	CME/COMEX	$5,000/oz	Physical	Higher volatility than gold; industrial demand component adds sensitivity to economic cycles. More difficult to trade for income than gold. Use defined-risk structures only.
Copper	**/HG**	CME/COMEX	$250/lb	Physical	Considered a leading indicator of global economic health ('Dr. Copper'). Moves with PMI data and

Commodity	Symbol	Exchange	Multiplier	Settlement	Premium Seller's Notes
					China demand. Useful for macro-informed options strategies in Materials sector exposure.

The Micro contracts — /MCL (Micro Crude Oil), /MGC (Micro Gold), /MHG (Micro Copper) — provide smaller account traders access to commodity options with more precise sizing. A Micro Gold contract (/MGC) represents 10 troy ounces versus 100 for the standard /GC — a tenfold reduction in capital requirement with identical market exposure per unit.

6. Selling Strategies for Commodities Options

The Seller's Philosophy translates directly into commodity options markets with one critical modification: seasonality replaces the six-condition market framework as the primary context layer. Commodity markets have well-documented, recurring annual patterns driven by planting cycles, harvest cycles, demand seasonality (heating oil in winter, gasoline in summer), and inventory cycles. Understanding where you are in the seasonal pattern tells you when volatility is likely to expand (creating selling opportunities) and when it is likely to contract (determining exit targets).

Strategy	Best Commodity	Optimal Season	Execution Notes
Selling OTM Puts (Fear Spike)	Gold (/GC, /MGC)	Q3–Q4, Fed decisions, geopolitical events	Gold experiences sharp IV spikes during risk-off events. Sell OTM puts 1–2 standard deviations below market during these spikes. Target 30–45 DTE. Close at 50% of max profit. The structural gold bid during uncertainty makes these spikes mean-revert rapidly.
Short Strangle (Seasonal Range)	Corn (/ZC)	June–August (post-planting / pre-harvest)	After spring planting reports are absorbed and before fall harvest uncertainty begins, corn often enters a period of reduced volatility and defined range. Sell OTM strangles on /OZC with 45 DTE. This is a defined-seasonality play — avoid around USDA WASDE report dates.
Iron Condor (Post-Event Calm)	Crude Oil (/CL)	2–3 weeks after OPEC decision	OPEC announcements create sharp IV spikes in crude oil. Post-announcement, when supply uncertainty is resolved, IV often collapses rapidly. Enter iron condors on /LO (crude oil options) 2–3 days after the OPEC event. Target 21–30 DTE. Use wider wings than equity condors — crude oil can gap.
Covered Call Equivalent (Contango Harvest)	Crude Oil (/CL) in contango	When front-month futures trade at discount to second month	When the oil futures curve is in contango (far months > near months), selling calls against a long futures position harvests the contango premium in addition to options premium. This is a carry trade structure — profitable when oil prices remain stable or fall slightly.
Selling Puts After Demand Shock	Natural Gas (/NG)	Post-winter spike (Feb–March), post-summer spike	Natural gas experiences seasonal demand spikes that can be violent. Post-spike, when inventory rebuild begins and demand normalizes, selling OTM puts captures the elevated IV premium with the fundamental tailwind of mean-reversion. Size very small — natural gas volatility is extreme.

THE COMMODITY OPTIONS SURVIVAL RULE

Every commodity options position must have a hard exit date that is no later than 21 days before expiration — and for physically delivered commodities like crude oil and grains, you should target exit no later than 30 days before expiration. Build this date into your trade setup before you enter. A calendar alert the day you place the trade. Missing this date in a commodity options position is not a management failure — it is a structural error.

7. Using the Put-Call Ratio (P:C) Analysis to Find Timeless Entries

The Put-Call Ratio (PCR) is one of the oldest and most consistently reliable sentiment indicators in options analysis. At its core, it measures how many put options are being traded relative to call options. When more puts are being bought than calls, the market is hedging and expressing fear. When more calls are being bought, the market is expressing greed and complacency. Both extremes historically precede reversals — and both create defined entry opportunities for the disciplined premium writer.

The CBOE publishes three versions of the put-call ratio daily: the Total Ratio (all options), the Equity Ratio (stock options only), and the Index Ratio (index options including SPX and OEX). Each has a different baseline reading and a different interpretation. The Index Ratio runs structurally higher than the Equity Ratio because institutional investors use index options for portfolio protection — this is normal put-buying for hedging purposes, not fear-driven speculation.

Ratio	Ticker (CBOE)	Baseline Reading	How to Use It
CBOE Total P/C Ratio	$CPC	~0.85–0.95 (neutral)	Broadest measure. Includes all listed options. Spikes above 1.20 historically signal capitulation and near-term bottoms. Drops below 0.70 signal complacency and elevated reversal risk for bulls. Smooth with a 10-day or 21-day exponential moving average to filter noise.
CBOE Equity P/C Ratio	$CPCE	~0.55–0.65 (neutral)	Best pure sentiment gauge — removes institutional index hedging. Spike above 0.80 = extreme fear among retail/equity traders = contrarian buy signal for CSPs and bull put spreads. Drop below 0.45 = excessive bullish speculation = tighten positions and raise stops.
CBOE Index P/C Ratio	$CPCI	~1.30–1.50 (neutral)	Structurally elevated due to institutional hedging. Extremes are less informative for timing entries. Most useful for understanding the general institutional hedging level — a collapsing index P/C into 1.0 signals institutions removing protection, which often precedes complacency-driven selloffs.

The Premium Seller's PCR Entry Framework

The put-call ratio does not tell you where the market will go. It tells you what traders are betting it will do — and in extreme readings, it tells you that those bets are becoming overcrowded. Overcrowded positions unwind violently. The premium writer's advantage is that these unwinds are precisely the conditions under which selling options becomes most profitable: IV spikes, crowds reverse, and premium deflates rapidly.

Equity P/C Signal	Market Sentiment	Premium Seller's Action
$CPCE > 0.80 (single day)	Acute fear spike	ALERT — elevated conditions for selling puts. Confirm with VIX > 20. Consider entering bull put spreads or cash-secured puts on

Equity P/C Signal	Market Sentiment	Premium Seller's Action
		quality names. Premium is elevated; the crowd is wrong at extremes.
$CPCE 21-day EMA crosses above 0.70	Sustained fear / defensive positioning	HIGH-CONVICTION ENTRY ZONE — the most consistent timing signal for deploying premium-selling capital. Markets historically bottom within 1–3 weeks of this signal.
$CPCE 0.55–0.65	Neutral / balanced	Standard operating conditions. Execute normal premium-selling plan. No sentiment edge in either direction.
$CPCE < 0.50	Elevated greed / complacency	CAUTION — tighten positions. Avoid adding new bullish premium. Consider taking profits on existing positions early. The crowd is buying calls; when they reverse, it will be sharp.
$CPCE < 0.45 (sustained)	Extreme complacency / speculative excess	REDUCE EXPOSURE — take profits, widen stop distances, hedge with modest put exposure on SPX. This reading preceded the corrections of 2000, 2007, and 2021 Q4.

One practical note on data access: the CBOE publishes put-call ratio data for free on cboe.com with a one-day lag. Both thinkorswim (TD Ameritrade/Schwab) and TastyTrade display the equity PCR in real time as a charting indicator ($CPCE). Chart the 21-day exponential moving average and set alerts for readings above 0.75 and below 0.50 — these are the entry and caution triggers that have provided consistent timing signals across three decades of market data.

8. Using the VIX and Options on Futures

The VIX is the most important single number in options trading. You have already encountered it throughout this book as the primary volatility signal for the six-condition framework. This section goes deeper — into what the VIX actually measures, how the VIX futures term structure informs your strategy, what options on VIX futures provide, and how the Volatility Risk Premium (VRP) explains the long-run profitability of the Seller's Philosophy at a structural level.

What the VIX Actually Is

The CBOE Volatility Index (VIX) measures the market's expectation of 30-day volatility for the S&P 500, derived from real-time prices of SPX options across a range of strikes and expirations. It is not derived from historical price movements — it is forward-looking, market-priced, and updated every 15 seconds during market hours. The VIX represents the annualized standard deviation of expected S&P 500 returns over the next 30 days, expressed in percentage terms. A VIX of 20 implies the market expects the S&P 500 to move approximately ±20% over the next year — or roughly ±5.8% over the next 30 days.

VIX Level	Market Regime	Premium Seller's Strategic Position
< 13	Extreme complacency	Premium is thin — the market is pricing almost no risk. Spreads are narrow. Consider reducing position count and waiting for better entry conditions. This is Condition 5 or 6 on the six-condition framework. Do not force trades.
13–17	Low volatility / calm	Standard income-selling conditions. Normal premium levels. Execute the standard plan — CSPs, covered calls, iron condors in range-bound names. Widen your strikes slightly compared to high-IV environments.
17–25	Normal / elevated	Preferred operating range for income sellers. Premium is meaningful without being extreme. The six-condition framework is most reliable in this range. This is your optimal ongoing income zone.

VIX Level	Market Regime	Premium Seller's Strategic Position
25–35	Elevated fear	Begin premium selling aggressively. IV is elevated; the options market is paying a premium for protection that history suggests will not be fully needed. SPX bull put spreads 1–2 standard deviations OTM are the primary vehicle. Scale in — don't deploy all capital at once.
35–50	High fear / near panic	Maximum premium-selling opportunity. Deploy full allocation to bull put spreads and CSPs on quality names. This range has historically produced the highest returns for premium sellers. Keep defined-risk only — volatility can stay elevated for weeks.
> 50	Crisis / capitulation	The highest-premium environment possible — and the highest risk. Options on quality names and indexes are pricing extreme outcomes. Defined-risk only. Size at 50% of normal. History shows these VIX extremes resolve in premium sellers' favor — but they can get worse before they get better. Patience and discipline over aggression.

The VIX Futures Term Structure

The VIX itself measures spot (30-day) implied volatility. VIX futures (/VX) allow traders to express a view on what the VIX will be at a specific future date. The term structure — the curve of VIX futures prices across different expiration months — is one of the most informative signals available to a sophisticated options trader.

Term Structure Shape	What It Means	Strategic Implication
Contango (Normal) Near-month < Far-month	The market expects current calm to continue but prices in uncertainty further out. Front-month VIX futures are cheaper than longer-dated ones. This is the normal state — observed approximately 75–80% of the time.	Premium-selling-friendly. Low near-term realized risk. Products like SVXY (short volatility) benefit. VXX/UVXY holders lose money daily through roll costs. Continue normal income-selling plan.
Backwardation (Fear Regime) Near-month > Far-month	Immediate danger is priced higher than future uncertainty. The market is paying a premium for protection right now. Occurs during crises, major news events, or acute market stress.	High-IV premium-selling opportunity — but approach with caution. Backwardation often persists during genuine deteriorations. Defined-risk spreads only. Begin scaling into bull put spreads. Do not sell naked positions.
Flat Curve Near-month ≈ Far-month	The market has no strong view on whether current volatility will persist or normalize. Often seen during genuine uncertainty — when the outcome of a major event (election, Fed decision, geopolitical development) is genuinely unclear.	Neutral — reduce exposure, tighten spreads, raise strike selection standards. Wait for curve to develop a clear shape before deploying full capital.

The Volatility Risk Premium — The Structural Foundation of the Seller's Edge

Behind every principle in this book — every cash-secured put, every iron condor, every T-21 rule — is a single structural market phenomenon: the Volatility Risk Premium (VRP). Understanding the VRP is understanding why premium selling works across decades, across instruments, and across market regimes. It is not a strategy. It is a structural feature of how options are priced.

The Volatility Risk Premium is the persistent, measurable gap between implied volatility (what the market prices into options) and realized volatility (what the market actually does). Implied volatility — as measured by the VIX for the S&P 500 — has historically exceeded realized volatility by 3 to 5 percentage points on average over rolling 30-day periods. This means options have, on average, been overpriced relative to what actually happened. The premium writer who consistently collects this overpriced premium is harvesting the VRP — capturing the difference between what the market feared would happen and what actually did.

Metric	Historical Average (1990–2024)	What It Means
VIX (30-day Implied Vol)	~20.0%	What options buyers paid for — the market's forward expectation of S&P 500 volatility.
30-day Realized Volatility	~15.5%	What actually happened — the actual magnitude of S&P 500 price movement over the same period.
Volatility Risk Premium (Gap)	~4–5 pts	The structural overpayment by options buyers — harvested by options sellers. This gap has been positive in approximately 75–80% of all rolling 30-day periods since 1990.

The VRP is not a guarantee. It compressed sharply in 2008, 2020, and during extended crisis periods when realized volatility exceeded implied volatility. In these windows, premium writers experience losses. The risk management rules throughout this book — the 2% rule, T-21, defined-risk structures, position sizing, and stop disciplines — exist precisely to ensure you survive these windows and remain in position to harvest the VRP when it normalizes.

Commodity Futures Options: The Seller's Advantage

Commodity futures options offer a structural advantage that equity options traders rarely encounter: deeply embedded volatility premiums driven by supply shocks, seasonal uncertainty, weather events, and geopolitical disruptions. Unlike equity options, where fear is the primary driver of elevated implied volatility, commodity options can carry elevated IV simply because the range of possible price outcomes is genuinely wide. Grains, energy, metals, and agricultural softs all exhibit periods of extreme premium inflation — and when those periods coincide with high IV percentile readings relative to historical volatility, the conditions for option writing are exceptional.

Seller Bias: Calls vs. Puts by Commodity Class

One of the most important risk management principles for commodity options writers is that the directional bias of the position matters more than in equity options — because commodity markets can experience violent upside shocks driven by weather, planting failures, freezes, and supply disruptions. The practical rule: naked put options on grain markets (corn, soybeans, wheat) carry more risk on the upside than the downside, because prices can spike dramatically on supply shocks. For this reason, experienced commodity writers have historically preferred selling calls — or call ratio writes — on grains rather than selling puts outright.

Commodity Class	Primary Risk Direction	Preferred Write Structure	Volatility Profile
Grains (Corn, Soybeans, Wheat)	Upside (supply shock spikes)	OTM call ratio write (1×2 or 1×3)	Seasonal IV peaks at planting/harvest; USDA report spikes

Commodity Class	Primary Risk Direction	Preferred Write Structure	Volatility Profile
Agricultural Softs (Coffee, Cocoa, OJ)	Upside (weather, disease)	Naked OTM put (safer) or call ratio spread	Structurally high IV; excellent ratio write candidates
Energy (Crude Oil, Natural Gas)	Both directions; macro-driven	Ratio write with delta-neutral management	High IV relative to HV during geopolitical events
Metals (Gold, Silver, Copper)	Moderate both directions	Credit spreads or ratio write when IV/HV gap is wide	Lower skew than grains; IV/HV gap is the primary filter

Volatility Skew in Commodity Options: The Ratio Writer's Edge

Many commodity option chains exhibit a pronounced volatility skew: implied volatility increases as you move farther out of the money. This skew is not random — it reflects the asymmetric risk embedded in physical markets. For the ratio writer, this skew creates a systematic edge: by selling a greater number of the more deeply OTM options (which carry higher IV) against a smaller number of closer-to-the-money longs, the trader is selling the most overvalued part of the chain while partially hedging with less overvalued long strikes.

The selection criterion: identify the strikes where implied volatility is highest relative to ATM IV, and where that level significantly exceeds historical volatility. Those are the strikes to sell in the ratio structure. The long leg is selected at a strike where IV is relatively lower — typically the first OTM strike. The ratio of short to long ranges from 1×2 to 1×3 depending on the degree of IV inflation. Maximum position size per commodity market: 20% of account equity.

THE RATIO WRITE SELECTION RULE

Search for commodity markets where: (1) Current IV is in the top quartile of its historical range. (2) Current IV is at least 30% above recent historical volatility. (3) OTM options carry materially higher IV than ATM options (the skew is present). When all three conditions are present, you have the ideal ratio write candidate — a market where you collect the overvalued premium and the skew premium simultaneously.

Put-Call Ratio Analysis: Timing Your Entries

The put-call ratio is one of the most reliable contrarian timing tools for premium sellers — particularly for S&P 500 futures and index options entries. The core principle is contrarian sentiment: when the crowd becomes excessively bearish (too many puts), the market is likely near an intermediate bottom. When the crowd becomes excessively bullish (too many calls), the market is likely near an intermediate top. These extremes are precisely where credit spread and ratio write entries offer the best statistical advantage.

The most effective application uses a 10-day exponential moving average of the equity put-call ratio (10DEMA). A 10DEMA reading above 0.47 signals excessive bearishness and suggests the market is near a bottom. A 10DEMA below 0.39 signals excessive bullishness and suggests the market is near a top. These are not standalone entry signals — they are sentiment context that, combined with the oscillator confirmation, identifies the highest-probability entry windows.

The volume-weighted put-call oscillator provides the confirming signal. Formula: [(Daily put-call ratio − 0.44) × total options volume] / 1,000. A result above +100 indicates extreme bearishness (excessive put-buying volume); below −100 indicates extreme bullishness. When two consecutive oscillator spikes occur in the same direction — especially above ±200 — and the 10DEMA simultaneously confirms the extreme, you have the dual confirmation signal that historically identifies strong credit spread entry points.

Indicator	Threshold	Signal	Action for Premium Seller
10DEMA Put-Call Ratio	> 0.47	Excessive bearishness	Consider OTM bull put spread or cash-secured put
10DEMA Put-Call Ratio	< 0.39	Excessive bullishness	Consider OTM bear call spread or call ratio write
P/C Oscillator	> +100 (two spikes)	Crowd fear at extreme	High-probability entry for deep OTM put credit spread
P/C Oscillator	< −100 (two spikes)	Crowd greed at extreme	High-probability entry for deep OTM call credit spread
Dual Confirmation	10DEMA + Oscillator aligned	Highest probability window	Enter at maximum approved size within the 2% rule

THE PUT-CALL RATIO PRINCIPLE

The put-call ratio does not tell you exactly when to enter — it tells you where sentiment has become stretched enough to justify an options-selling entry. The crowd is consistently wrong at extremes. When put-buying volume overwhelms call-buying volume to an unusual degree, fear has become the dominant emotion — and fear is consistently overpriced in the options market. The dual-confirmation signal (10DEMA + oscillator spike) provides the statistical framework to identify when fear pricing has reached levels that have historically produced mean reversion.

THE UNIFIED THESIS

Everything in this chapter — options on S&P 500 futures, commodity options, the put-call ratio, VIX term structure — points to the same underlying principle: the market consistently prices more risk than it delivers. The premium seller's job is not to predict the market. It is to identify where implied volatility is elevated relative to likely realized volatility, sell that premium with defined risk, and collect the difference with discipline. That is the professional framework. That is the Seller's Philosophy in its fullest expression.

Section 4 — Understanding Nasdaq 100 Options

The Nasdaq 100 (NDX) is the technology and growth benchmark, tracking the 100 largest non-financial companies listed on the Nasdaq exchange. For options traders, the Nasdaq represents higher volatility, more pronounced IV crush cycles, and stronger correlation with earnings from mega-cap technology companies — Apple, Microsoft, Meta, Alphabet, Amazon, and Nvidia collectively account for more than 40% of the index weight.

The Nasdaq trades in two contract forms. NDX is the full-size index option — European-style, cash-settled, with a notional value of approximately $500,000 at current prices. QQQ is the ETF-based alternative tracking the same index at roughly 1/40th the notional value, with American-style exercise and higher liquidity for spread strategies. For retail traders, QQQ is the primary vehicle.

The Nasdaq's volatility premium is structurally higher than the S&P 500. The VXN (Nasdaq Volatility Index) typically runs 2–4 points above the VIX. This means premium sellers collect more per contract on Nasdaq-based positions, but carry greater gamma risk. The same 6-condition framework applies: in Condition 2 (up fast, high IV), covered calls and bull put spreads on QQQ capture elevated premium while maintaining bullish positioning.

Position Sizing for Nasdaq Spreads

Because QQQ trades at roughly $480–$500, a 5-wide put spread (e.g., sell the 490 put, buy the 485 put) requires $500 of buying power reduction and generates approximately $80–$120 in credit depending on IV rank. For NQ (E-mini Nasdaq futures options), a single contract controls $100 × NQ price ≈ $190,000 notional at current levels. MNQ (Micro E-mini Nasdaq) is 1/10th the size at roughly $19,000 notional — the preferred vehicle for accounts under $50,000 trading Nasdaq futures.

Instrument	Ticker	Multiplier	Typical Margin/BPR	Spread Type	Spread Credit	Max Risk	Contracts per $10K Block	Account Min.
QQQ ETF Options	QQQ	$100 per point	$400–$600 (5-wide spread)	Bull Put Spread (5-wide)	$90–$140 credit	$360–$410 max risk	2–4 spreads	$10,000
Instrument	Ticker	Multiplier	Typical Margin/BPR	Spread Type	Spread Credit	Max Risk	Contracts per $10K Block	Account Min.
E-mini Nasdaq (NQ) Futures Options	/NQ	$20 per point	$3,000–$5,000	Bull Put Spread (10-wide)	$400–$600 credit	$1,400–$1,600 max risk	1 spread	$25,000
Instrument	Ticker	Multiplier	Typical Margin/BPR	Spread Type	Spread Credit	Max Risk	Contracts per $10K Block	Account Min.
Micro E-mini Nasdaq (MNQ) Futures Options	/MNQ	$2 per point	$300–$500	Bull Put Spread (10-wide)	$40–$60 credit	$140–$160 max risk	3–5 spreads	$5,000

Section 5 — Understanding Dow Jones Options

The Dow Jones Industrial Average (DJIA) is the oldest U.S. equity index, comprising 30 large-cap blue-chip companies. Unlike the S&P 500 (market-cap weighted) or Nasdaq 100 (technology-heavy), the Dow is price-weighted — a $500 stock has 5× the index influence of a $100 stock regardless of market capitalization. This structural quirk means the Dow is more susceptible to single-stock events in high-priced names such as UnitedHealth Group or Goldman Sachs.

For options traders, the Dow is accessed primarily through DIA (the SPDR Dow Jones ETF, tracking 1/100th of the index) or through /YM futures options (E-mini Dow, $5 per point) and /MYM (Micro E-mini Dow, $0.50 per point). The Dow's implied volatility is generally lower than the Nasdaq and comparable to the S&P 500. It is well-suited for income strategies in Conditions 2, 5, and 6 — where the blue-chip composition provides stability and predictable premium decay.

The Dow's composition makes it a useful sector read: heavy exposure to financials, industrials, healthcare, and consumer staples makes it a leading indicator of the broader economy's health beyond the technology sector. When the Dow diverges from the Nasdaq — rising while tech sells off — it signals rotation into defensive and cyclical names, which changes the premium strategy landscape significantly.

Position Sizing for Dow Jones Spreads

DIA trades at approximately 1/100th of the DJIA level. At a Dow of 42,000, DIA trades near $420. A 5-wide put spread on DIA generates approximately $70–$110 in credit with $390–$430 of buying power reduction. For futures options, /MYM is the accessible vehicle — at $0.50 per point and a Dow near 42,000, a single MYM contract controls approximately $21,000 in notional value.

Instrument	Ticker	Multiplier	Typical Margin/BPR	Spread Type	Spread Credit	Max Risk	Contracts per $10K Block	Account Min.
DIA ETF Options	DIA	$100 per point	$350–$550 (5-wide spread)	Bull Put Spread (5-wide)	$70–$110 credit	$390–$430 max risk	2–4 spreads	$10,000
Instrument	**Ticker**	**Multiplier**	**Typical Margin/BPR**	**Spread Type**	**Spread Credit**	**Max Risk**	**Contracts per $10K Block**	**Account Min.**
E-mini Dow (/YM) Futures Options	/YM	$5 per point	$2,500–$4,000	Bull Put Spread (100-wide)	$350–$500 credit	$1,500–$2,000 max risk	1 spread	$20,000
Instrument	**Ticker**	**Multiplier**	**Typical Margin/BPR**	**Spread Type**	**Spread Credit**	**Max Risk**	**Contracts per $10K Block**	**Account Min.**
Micro E-mini Dow (/MYM) Futures Options	/MYM	$0.50 per point	$250–$400	Bull Put Spread (100-wide)	$35–$50 credit	$150–$200 max risk	3–5 spreads	$5,000

Section 6 — Understanding Russell 2000 Options

The Russell 2000 (RUT / /RTY futures / /M2K micro futures) tracks 2,000 small-cap U.S. companies and is the primary benchmark for small-cap exposure. The Russell behaves differently from large-cap indexes: it is more sensitive to domestic economic conditions, interest rate changes, and credit availability. Small-cap companies have less access to international revenue and greater reliance on bank financing, making the Russell a leading economic indicator during tightening cycles.

For options traders, the Russell offers some of the richest volatility premiums in the index options market. RVX (the Russell Volatility Index) consistently trades above VIX, often by 4–8 points. This premium exists because small-cap stocks are more volatile individually and the index is less diversified by sector. The practical implication: iron condors and credit spreads on RUT or IWM (the iShares Russell 2000 ETF) generate higher premium for the same capital allocation than comparable S&P 500 strategies.

The Russell is particularly effective for income selling during Conditions 5 and 6 (sideways markets). Small-cap stocks tend to consolidate during periods of macro uncertainty when large-cap growth leads the market. The wider bid-ask spreads on RUT options require the use of limit orders priced at or near the mid-point. IWM is preferred over RUT for traders under $100,000 — better liquidity, tighter spreads, and more strike granularity.

Position Sizing for Russell 2000 Spreads

IWM trades at approximately 1/10th of the Russell 2000 level. At an index level of 2,100, IWM trades near $210. A 5-wide put spread on IWM generates approximately $60–$100 in credit with $400–$440 of buying power reduction — a slightly higher premium-to-risk ratio than comparable SPY spreads due to elevated volatility. RUT options (full index, cash-settled) require larger accounts but offer Section 1256 tax treatment (60% long-term / 40% short-term capital gains) like other broad-based index options.

Instrument	Ticker	Multiplier	Typical Margin/BPR	Spread Type	Spread Credit	Max Risk	Contracts per $10K Block	Account Min.
IWM ETF Options	IWM	$100 per point	$400–$450 (5-wide spread)	Bull Put Spread (5-wide)	$60–$100 credit	$400–$440 max risk	2–4 spreads	$10,000

Instrument	Ticker	Multiplier	Typical Margin/BPR	Spread Type	Spread Credit	Max Risk	Contracts per $10K Block	Account Min.
Russell 2000 Index Options (RUT)	RUT	$100 per point (cash-settled)	$4,000–$6,000 (50-wide spread)	Iron Condor (50-wide)	$600–$900 credit	$4,100–$4,400 max risk	1 spread	$50,000

> 6-CONDITION FRAMEWORK ▸ **CONDITIONS 1 & 3 — directional debit strategies for confirmed trends**
> Swing trading with options is a condition 1 (bullish, low IV) or condition 3 (bearish, low IV) discipline. You buy premium when IV is cheap and the trend is confirmed. This chapter gives you the entry protocol for both.

Swing trading occupies the space between day trading and long-term investing — positions held for days to weeks, capturing directional moves within a larger trend. For the options trader, swing trading is not about holding through entire trends. It is about identifying a specific window of price movement, entering with a defined-risk position sized for that window, and exiting when the move delivers — or when it proves wrong.

The options structure gives the swing trader a fundamental advantage over stock swing traders: your maximum loss is defined from the moment you enter. A stock swing trader who gets their direction wrong and holds too long can watch a position erode indefinitely. An options swing trader knows their worst case before they click submit.

The Three Core Swing Trading Environments

Every market — and every individual stock — spends time in one of three conditions. Your strategy must match the condition. Trading a trending strategy in a range-bound market, or a range strategy in a trending market, is the most common way swing traders lose money.

Condition	How to Identify It	Best Options Strategy	Avoid
Trending Up	Higher highs and higher lows. Price above 50-day EMA. MACD positive. BPI rising.	Bull call spreads, long calls (LEAPS), diagonal spreads on sector ETFs	Short calls, bear spreads — fighting the trend is expensive
Trending Down	Lower highs and lower lows. Price below 50-day EMA. MACD negative. BPI falling.	Bear put spreads, long puts, short call spreads on weak sectors	Cash-secured puts on falling knives — wait for stabilization first
Range-Bound	Price oscillating between defined support and resistance. Bollinger Band squeeze. Low BPI movement.	Iron condors, short strangles (defined risk), calendar spreads, credit spreads within the range	Long directional positions — you pay premium for a move that doesn't come
Volatile / Choppy	VIX elevated. Large daily candles in both directions. No clear trend. IV high.	Short premium strategies (spreads, iron condors) to capture IV contraction. Defined risk only.	Naked positions of any kind. Leverage. Chasing intraday moves.

The 5-Step Pullback Entry Protocol

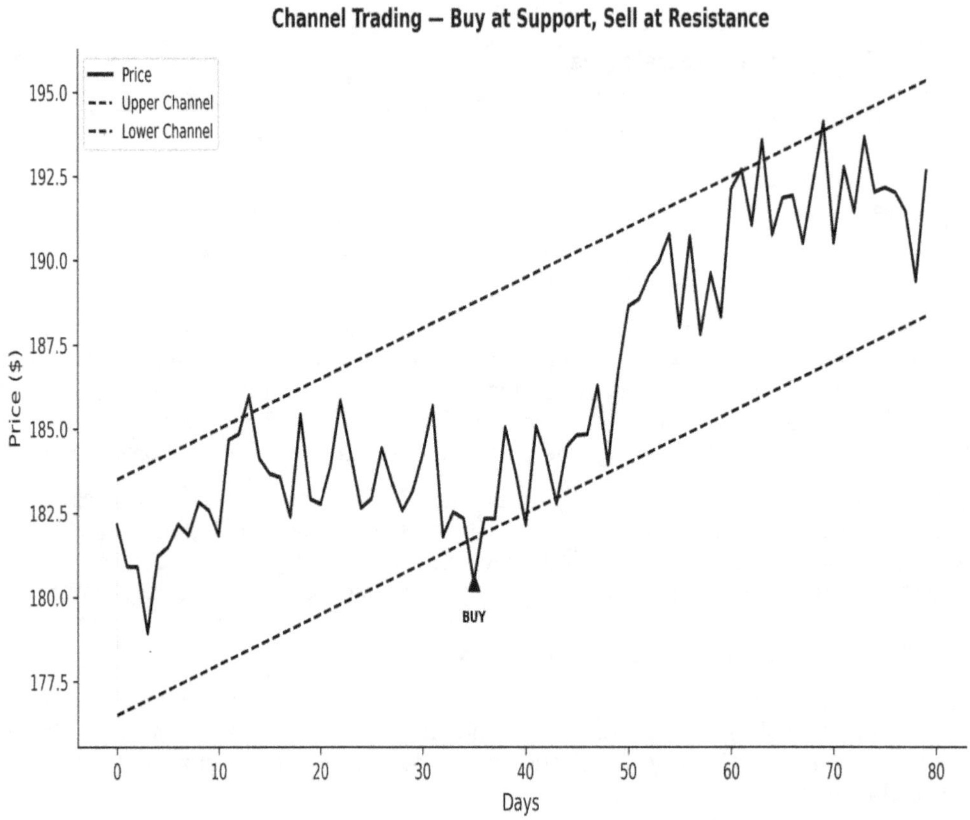

Figure 19.1 — Pullback Protocol — Entry criteria for buying the dip within a confirmed uptrend using EMA confluence.

Pullback trading — entering a trending stock after a brief consolidation — is the most reliable trend-following technique for swing traders. The entry follows a precise 5-step iterative process:

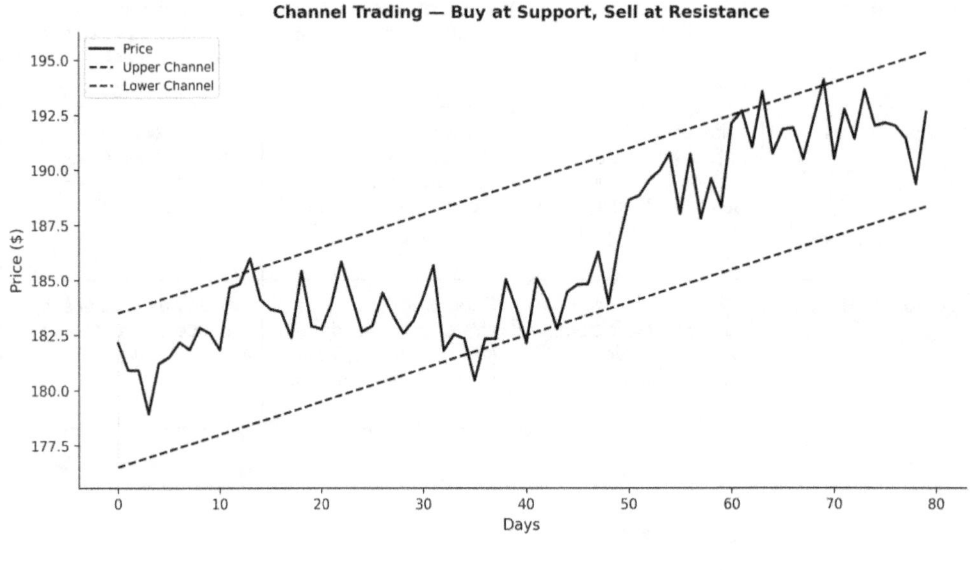

Figure 19.1 — 5-Step Pullback Entry Signal. Entry, stop-loss placement, and trailing stop protocol for pullback trades within a confirmed uptrend. [Chart to be inserted]

- Step 1: Identify a strong uptrend (higher highs, higher lows, price above 50-day EMA). Wait for a pullback from a new high — a brief pause or retracement is your trigger to watch;
- Step 2: Set your buy stop price just above the intraday high of the most recent bar in the pullback. If price exceeds this, the trend is resuming;
- Step 3: If the stock trades above your buy stop → order executes. If not → order cancels end of day. Reset to the new bar's high and reenter. Repeat each day until triggered;
- Step 4: Once filled, immediately place a stop-loss just below the intraday low of the lowest bar in the pullback. Maximum risk defined before the trade begins; and
- Step 5: As the trade progresses, trail your stop-loss daily to just below the intraday low of the most recent bar. This locks in profits as the trend continues.

Real example: Stock makes a new high at $30.44. Pullback occurs. Buy stop triggered at $29.44 when price breaks the pullback high. Stop-loss set at $28.74. If trend continues 10 days, trailing stop locks in gains throughout. If trade reverses immediately, the $28.74 stop limits loss to $0.70/share. This is defined-risk swing trading in practice.

SWING TRADING IS RISKY

Swing trading demands significant time — you must monitor the market actively. Profits are often small relative to capital deployed, and slippage is real. The edge comes from consistency across many trades, not any single large win. Some argue swing trading combines the worst of position trading (overnight risk) and day trading (small profits). Know this going in.

Channel Trading: The Structured Swing

A price channel is defined by two parallel trendlines — one connecting a series of higher highs (the resistance line), one connecting a series of higher lows (the support line). In an upward channel, the support line is the buy zone and the resistance line is the profit target. The options expression of this setup is a long call entered when price touches the support line, targeting a move to resistance. The expected move defines your strike selection: buy the call at or just below the current price (delta 0.45–0.55), with an expiration that gives you 2–3 times the expected time for the move to complete.

Channel breakdown rule: if price closes below the support line by more than 0.5 ATR, exit the position immediately. The channel is broken. Do not average down. Do not wait for a bounce. The thesis is invalidated the moment the channel fails.

CHANNEL TRADING ENTRY PRECISION

The entry for a channel trade is at the support line, not near it. A price that is 2% above the support line is not a channel entry — it is a chase. Wait for the line. If the stock bounces off support before you can enter, the opportunity passed. There will be another channel touch. Patience at the entry point is the most underdeveloped skill in swing trading.

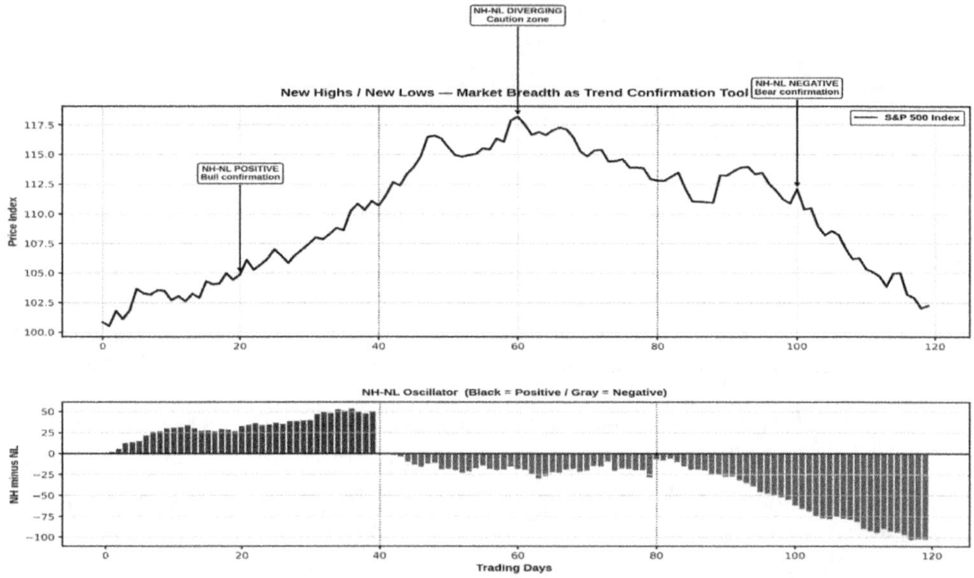

Figure 19.2 — Swing Trading Setups — Entry criteria and chart patterns for multi-day options positions across all six conditions.

Swing Trading Setups — Entry criteria and chart patterns for multi-day options positions.

A price channel forms when a stock makes consistent highs and lows within a defined band. The upper boundary is resistance, the lower is support. Channel trading gives you precise entry, exit, and stop levels — making position management mechanical rather than emotional.

Channel entry and exit protocol:

- Entry (long): As stock approaches the LOWER/SUPPORT channel line, take a long position. Stop-loss just below the support line;
- Exit (long): When stock approaches the UPPER/RESISTANCE channel line, exit. Consider a short position or bear call spread with stop just above resistance;
- Ascending channel — Buy support, target resistance. Bull call spreads with short strike near the upper channel line;
- Horizontal channel — Sell iron condors anchored to the channel walls. Both short strikes inside the range, wings just outside;
- Channel breakout — When price closes outside the channel on volume, the channel is broken. Close channel-range trades immediately and follow the breakout direction;
- Options sizing: Target 30–45 DTE, position strikes just outside the channel boundaries for credit spreads. The channel walls do the risk management for you;

Range-Bound Strategies: Making Money in Sideways Markets

Most traders treat sideways markets as dead money — nothing to do, nowhere to go. The premium writer sees it differently. A range-bound market is an income-generation machine. Every week the stock stays within its range, theta decays in the seller's favor. The range is the profit zone.

- Iron Condor — Sell an OTM call spread and an OTM put spread simultaneously on the same underlying. Collect premium from both sides. Maximum profit if stock stays between the short strikes through expiration. Best deployed when VIX is above 20 and the stock has clear technical boundaries;
- Short Strangle (defined risk) — Sell an OTM call and an OTM put. Buy further OTM options as wings to cap the risk. Wider profit zone than iron condor but more premium collected. Requires larger price movement to breach the tent; and
- Double diagonal — Sell near-term strangle, buy longer-dated strangle at wider strikes. Combines time decay benefit with volatility exposure management. Advanced but highly efficient in persistent range markets.

THE RANGE TRADER'S RULE

Before selling a range-bound structure (iron condor, short strangle), ask: Is there a known catalyst inside this expiration window? Earnings announcements, FDA decisions, FOMC meetings, and index rebalancing events can all destroy a range trade in one session. Check the calendar before you sell the range.

Volatility Setups: Trading the Expansion and Contraction Cycle

The volatility squeeze is one of the highest-probability swing setups available to the options trader. It occurs when Bollinger Bands contract to their narrowest range in 20–30 sessions — a condition indicating that the market has consolidated range to a decision point. Energy is coiling. The breakout, when it comes, is often sharp and sustained. The options play: buy a straddle or strangle when the bands are at their narrowest (ATM straddle when you have no directional bias, or a directional spread if the prior trend gives you a bias), target a 100–150% gain on the long option as the breakout extends, and exit the losing side immediately when direction is confirmed.

Figure 19.2 — Volatility Squeeze → Breakout. Bollinger Band compression precedes the directional breakout. [Chart moved here from pullback section]

The squeeze entry rule: the BB width must be at its lowest reading in at least 20 sessions. Do not enter a straddle on a normal consolidation. The setup requires a genuine volatility compression, not simply a slow day. Use the TTM Squeeze indicator or the BB width metric on your platform to screen for this condition.

Volatility itself is a tradeable phenomenon. IV doesn't stay elevated forever — it mean-reverts. And it doesn't stay suppressed forever — it eventually expands. The trader who understands this cycle can position for the expansion before it arrives and profit from the contraction after it peaks.

- Pre-event long volatility setup — Before a known catalyst (earnings, FDA, macro data), IV rises as the market prices in the uncertainty. Buy a straddle or strangle 7–10 days before the event when IV is still rising. Sell before the event — capture the IV expansion, avoid the IV crush;
- Post-event short volatility setup — After a catalyst event passes, IV collapses regardless of how the stock moved. If the stock moved less than the market expected, both calls and puts lose value simultaneously. Sell premium (credit spreads, iron condors) immediately after major events when IV is still elevated;
- Bollinger Band squeeze breakout — When the bands compress to historically narrow levels, a volatility expansion is imminent. The direction is unknown. Buy

a straddle on the squeeze. Let the breakout determine your directional winner and close the losing side quickly to harvest the gain on the winning leg;
- VIX spike reversal — When VIX spikes above 30 on a market selloff, premium sellers who deploy defined-risk structures during the panic historically profit as VIX reverts toward its mean over the following weeks. Size small, defined risk only, and do not rush the entry — let the spike fully develop before selling into it;

Swing Trade Management: The Three Exit Rules

Opening the trade correctly is half the job. Managing and closing it correctly is the other half. Every swing trade — regardless of strategy — should have three exit conditions defined before entry:

- Profit target exit — For credit spreads and income trades (iron condors, CSPs, covered calls): close at 50% of maximum profit. Do not hold for the last 50% — gamma accelerates and a single adverse move can erase weeks of decay. For long directional positions (long calls, long puts, debit spreads with high-conviction theses): allow the position to run toward maximum profit, using a trailing stop once the position exceeds 50% gain. Collect the efficient portion on income trades and redeploy; let directional winners run;
- Stop loss exit — Define a maximum loss before entry. For debit spreads: lose no more than 100% of debit paid (full loss is already defined). For credit spreads: close if the spread reaches 2× the credit received. For single long options: close if premium drops 50%. No exceptions, no rationalizing; and
- Time exit — If a position has not reached its profit target and has not hit its stop loss but has consumed 50–60% of its time to expiration with no movement, close it. Time is now working against you on long positions and the thesis has not materialized. Free the capital.

The Swing Trader's Entry Signal Checklist

Discretionary swing traders lose money when they trade on feeling. The professional swing trader uses a structured checklist — every entry must clear every item before a position is opened. If any box is unchecked, the trade does not happen. The next setup is always coming.

	Signal	How to Verify	What Failure Means
✓	Trend confirmed on the daily chart	Higher highs and higher lows visible over 20+ days. Price above 50-day EMA for bullish. Below for bearish.	No trend = no swing trade entry. Range-bound strategies only.
✓	Pullback is shallow — less than 38.2% of prior swing	Measure the retracement from swing high to pullback low. Keep it above the 38.2% Fibonacci level.	Deep retracements signal potential trend reversal — wait for a new base to form.
✓	Volume contracted during the pullback	Pullback on declining volume = healthy consolidation. Volume	Selling on high volume means institutions are exiting. Do not buy into institutional selling.

	Signal	How to Verify	What Failure Means
		surge on pullback = distribution.	
✓	MACD is positive (bullish) or negative (bearish) and not diverging	MACD line above signal line for bullish swing. No negative divergence between price and MACD.	MACD divergence often precedes reversal. Divergence = pass the trade.
✓	IV Rank is below 50 for debit strategies	Check IVR on your platform. Below 50 = buy options. Above 50 = sell options or use spreads.	High IVR makes bought options overpriced. You pay too much and theta works against you faster.
✓	No earnings within the trade window	Check earnings calendar on your broker platform or earningswhispers.com. Confirm no report before expiration.	Earnings can gap the stock in any direction. Never hold a directional swing trade through earnings.
✓	Risk/Reward is at least 2:1	Calculate: (Target − Entry) ÷ (Entry − Stop). Must be 2.0 or higher before placing the trade.	Below 2:1 means you need a 67%+ win rate just to break even. That is not a sustainable edge.
✓	Position size is within 2% risk rule	Calculate: (Entry − Stop) × contracts × 100. Must be ≤ 2% of total account.	Oversizing is the number one cause of swing trader account destruction. No exceptions.

Options Structures Mapped to Swing Setups

The swing trading environment determines not just direction — it determines which options structure provides the best risk/reward for that specific setup. Buying the wrong structure for the right directional call still loses money. Here is the complete mapping.

Market Condition	Direction	Best Structure	Why It Fits	Real Example
Strong Uptrend	Bullish	Bull Call Spread	Buy ATM call, sell OTM call. Reduces cost vs. outright long call. Profits from moderate move — does not need a runaway rally.	AAPL at $190. Buy $190 call, sell $200 call, 35 DTE. Cost: $3.00 debit. Max profit: $7.00 (133%). Max loss: $3.00. Target: 50–75% of max profit.
Strong Uptrend — High Conviction	Bullish	Long Call (ATM or slightly ITM)	Full participation in a large upward move. Higher cost but uncapped upside above breakeven. Use when BPI and MACD both strong and IV below 30.	NVDA at $480. Buy $475 call, 45 DTE. Premium $18.00. Breakeven $493. Target: $510+ in 3 weeks for 100%+ gain on option.
Strong Downtrend	Bearish	Bear Put Spread	Buy ATM put, sell OTM put. Reduces cost vs. outright long put. Profits from moderate	SPY at $450. Buy $450 put, sell $440 put, 30 DTE. Cost: $3.50 debit. Max profit:

Market Condition	Direction	Best Structure	Why It Fits	Real Example
			decline. Lower theta cost than single long put.	$6.50 (186%). Requires less than 2.5% move to be profitable.
Weak Stock in Strong Market	Bearish	Long Put or Bear Put Spread	Stock showing relative weakness vs. sector. Sector rotation away from its industry. Short-duration put captures the divergence.	XYZ at $85, sector ETF at all-time high but XYZ below 50-day EMA. Buy $82.50 put, 21 DTE. Pure bearish thesis on relative weakness.
Range-Bound	Neutral	Iron Condor	Sell OTM call spread + OTM put spread simultaneously. Profit if stock stays within the range. Ideal when IV elevated and BPI flat.	AMZN between $175–$195 for 6 weeks. Sell $195/$200 call spread, sell $175/$170 put spread. Collect $1.80 net credit. Max profit if AMZN stays in range.
Pre-Breakout Squeeze	Directional (unknown)	Long Straddle or Strangle	Buy ATM call and ATM put simultaneously before an expected volatility expansion. Profit from the breakout in either direction.	TSLA Bollinger Bands compress to 6-month low. Buy $245 straddle 21 DTE for $8.50. Need $8.50 move in either direction to profit — close the losing side after breakout.
Post-Earnings IV Crush	Neutral	Short Iron Condor	After earnings, IV collapses. Sell premium while IV is still elevated. Stock has already moved — now it tends to consolidate.	GOOG reports earnings, stock gaps up 4%, IV drops 40% from 65 to 38. Sell iron condor at new post-gap price level. Collect elevated residual premium.

A Complete Swing Trade Walkthrough: AAPL Bull Call Spread

The following is a complete trade from identification to exit — every step documented. This is how a professional swing trader thinks through a setup. Read it once. Then use it as a template for documenting your own trades in the journal.

Stage	Detail
Market Context	S&P 500 in confirmed uptrend. BPI at 68 (bullish zone). VIX at 16 (calm). Tech sector (XLK) leading the market. Favorable macro for bullish swing trades on large-cap tech.
Stock Selection	AAPL at $192. 3 consecutive earnings beats. Price above 200-day EMA ($178) and 50-day EMA ($186). Pulled back 4.2% over 5 days from recent high of $200 on light volume (healthy). MACD positive, no divergence. IV Rank: 22 (low — buy options, don't sell them here).

Stage	Detail
Checklist	Trend confirmed ✓ | Pullback shallow ✓ | Volume declining on pullback ✓ | MACD positive, no divergence ✓ | IVR below 50 ✓ | No earnings within 35 days ✓ | R/R target ≥ 2:1 ✓ | Position size within 2% rule ✓
Structure Selected	Bull call spread: Buy $192.50 call / Sell $202.50 call. 35 DTE (monthly expiration). Spread width: $10.00. Cost: $3.40 debit. Max profit: $6.60. Max loss: $3.40. R/R: $6.60 ÷ $3.40 = 1.94:1 — slightly below target. Adjust.
Adjusted Structure	Bull call spread: Buy $190 call / Sell $200 call. 35 DTE. Cost: $4.20 debit. Max profit: $5.80. Max loss: $4.20. R/R: $5.80 ÷ $4.20 = 1.38:1 — too low. Use spread width $10 and go tighter on cost.
Final Structure	Buy $192.50 call / Sell $205 call. 35 DTE. Cost: $3.00 debit. Max profit: $9.50. Max loss: $3.00. R/R: 3.17:1 ✓. Breakeven: $195.50. Requires +1.8% move from current price of $192.
Portfolio Margin	A margin calculation system for options accounts that determines collateral requirements based on the actual risk of the portfolio evaluated across 10 price intervals — not the theoretical maximum loss per position. Available to accounts approved for naked option trading with a minimum of $100,000–$150,000. Produces significantly lower margin requirements for hedged positions (collars, iron condors, covered calls) vs. standard Reg-T margin. Managed by the OCC and CBOE. Relevant when running a full multi-condition book simultaneously. See Appendix E.
Position Sizing	Account: $100,000. 2% risk rule: max loss per trade = $2,000. At $3.00 debit × 100 shares × 1 contract = $300 per contract. 2,000 ÷ 300 = 6 contracts maximum. Choose 5 contracts = $1,500 max loss = 1.5% of account.
Entry	Monday open. Place limit order at $3.00 debit (midpoint of $2.80 bid / $3.20 ask). Filled at $3.05 — slightly above mid on open. Acceptable. 5 contracts × $3.05 × 100 = $1,525 total cost.
Management Plan	Profit target: 50% of max profit = $4.75/spread. Trigger at $7.00 spread value. Stop: spread drops to $1.50 (50% loss of debit). Time stop: close at T-14 regardless of outcome. T-21 reminder set.
Trade Outcome	Day 18: AAPL rallies to $199.40 after positive product news. Spread now worth $6.40. That is 68% of max profit — above 50% target. Close the spread. Sell to close the $192.50/$205 call spread at $6.40. Net: 5 × ($6.40 − $3.05) × 100 = $1,675 profit. Return on capital: $1,675 ÷ $1,525 = 110% in 18 days.
Post-Trade Review	What worked: entry on pullback with checklist, correct structure for IV environment, disciplined profit target exit. What to improve: initial structure calculation required two adjustments before R/R was satisfactory — build a spreadsheet for this. Next: find next setup in tech sector rotation.

DOCUMENT EVERY TRADE THIS WAY

The walkthrough above is not just an example — it is the template. Every swing trade you place should have all eleven stages documented in your journal before and after. Traders who document this thoroughly are building a personal edge database. After 50 trades, patterns emerge: which setups work for you, which checklist items you skip that cost you, and which exits you take too early or too late. The journal is where edge compounds.

Swing Trading Position Sizing: The Kelly-Adjusted 2% Framework

Position sizing is the single variable most under-discussed in retail trading education and most responsible for the difference between traders who survive and traders who blow up. The 2% rule is your floor — never risk more than 2% of your account on any single swing trade. But within that ceiling, you can scale position size up or down based on setup quality.

Setup Quality Score	Risk Allocation	Example ($100K account)	Qualifying Criteria
A+ Setup (8/8 checklist)	2.0% of account	$2,000 max loss	All 8 checklist items pass. R/R ≥ 3:1. Strong sector tailwind. High-liquidity underlying (AAPL, MSFT, SPY). Low IVR (< 25). Clear technical setup with defined catalyst.
A Setup (7/8 checklist)	1.5% of account	$1,500 max loss	Seven checklist items pass. R/R ≥ 2.5:1. Good liquidity. Minor reservation on one item (e.g., IVR slightly elevated at 35 or MACD borderline).
B Setup (6/8 checklist)	1.0% of account	$1,000 max loss	Six items pass. R/R ≥ 2:1. Acceptable liquidity. Two items require judgment calls. Use smallest allowed position in this category.
Below B (5 or fewer)	Do not trade	$0	Five or fewer items pass. The setup does not meet minimum standard. Passing on a trade is a trading decision. The next setup is always coming.

The formula for number of contracts is always: (Account × Risk%) ÷ (Max Loss per Contract). For a $100,000 account on an A+ setup with a $3.00 debit spread: ($100,000 × 2%) ÷ ($3.00 × 100) = $2,000 ÷ $300 = 6.67 → round down to 6 contracts. Always round down. Never round up on position sizing.

SWING TRADER'S CREED

A swing trade is a thesis with a time limit. You are not married to the position. You are renting the directional move for 30–45 days. If the move doesn't come in that window, close the trade, take your defined loss, and find the next setup. The market will always give you another opportunity. Your capital won't regenerate itself if you blow it waiting for a stale trade to work.

Entry and Exit Timing: The SPY Swing Trade Protocol

Swing trading options is not about holding for days hoping the stock moves. It is about identifying confirmed condition 1 or condition 3 setups, entering at the optimal point in the momentum cycle, and exiting with discipline before the move exhausts. The protocol below gives you a repeatable timing sequence for both conditions.

CONDITION 1 SWING ENTRY — QQQ Bull Flag Example

QQQ at $445. Uptrend confirmed (price > 50MA > 200MA). Bull flag forming — 3-day consolidation above $440 support after a sharp 8-day rally.

VIX = 14. IVR = 19. LOW volatility confirmed. Six-condition read: Bullish + Low IV = Condition 1. Buy premium approved.

Entry: Buy QQQ $450 Call, 21 DTE. Premium: $2.85. Delta: 0.44. Target: 50% gain ($4.27). Stop: 40% loss ($1.71).

Time stop: close if 50% of DTE passes with no 25% gain. Do not let theta erode a non-performing position.

Day 8: QQQ breaks $450, rallies to $456. Call worth $6.10. Gain: +$3.25 (+114%). Exit at target — do not wait for the exact $4.27. Lock the gain.

Timing Rule	Condition 1 (Bullish, Low IV)	Condition 3 (Bearish, Low IV)
Optimal entry window	First pullback to rising 20-day EMA after a confirmed breakout above prior resistance	First dead-cat bounce to declining 20-day EMA after confirmed breakdown below prior support
Ideal DTE	21–35 DTE — enough time for the move, not so much that theta is irrelevant to position sizing	21–35 DTE — same logic. Avoid < 14 DTE swing trades: gamma risk and time pressure force poor decisions
Strike selection	5–7% OTM call. Delta 0.35–0.45. High enough delta to participate meaningfully. Low enough to keep cost manageable.	5–7% OTM put. Delta 0.35–0.45. Mirror of condition 1 selection logic.
Profit target	50–75% of premium paid. Exit before the move becomes the news.	50–75% of premium paid. Bear moves are faster and more violent — take profit sooner rather than later.
Stop loss	40–50% of premium paid. Never let a swing position lose more than half its cost.	40–50% of premium paid. Same rule. If the bounce is stronger than expected, the bearish thesis may be broken.
Time stop	Close at 50% of DTE elapsed if no 25% gain has materialized. Theta is accelerating.	Close at 50% of DTE elapsed. Bear moves that don't develop quickly often reverse — exit before time decay compounds.

THE SWING TRADER'S DISCIPLINE

A swing trade has three defined exits set before entry: (1) the profit target, (2) the stop loss, (3) the time stop. All three must be set as GTC orders the moment the position fills. The trader who sets exits at entry and lets the orders work is executing like a professional. The trader who watches the position and decides when to exit based on feel is gambling with a time premium on top.

Complete Swing Trade Walkthrough: NVDA Pullback Entry

Abstract swing rules become real with a step-by-step walkthrough. This example follows a pullback trade on NVDA from identification through exit — applying every rule from this chapter in sequence.

Step 1 — Identify the Trend: NVDA is trading at $870, above both the 50-day EMA ($820) and 200-day EMA ($740). MACD is positive. RSI is 58 — not overbought. The primary trend is confirmed bullish. Condition: Bull Trending (Condition 1).

Step 2 — Wait for the Pullback: Over four days, NVDA pulls back to $835, touching the 50-day EMA. Volume on the pullback is 30% below average — this is a low-volume retracement, not a trend reversal. RSI drops to 42 — approaching oversold but not there yet.

Step 3 — Confirm the Bounce: On day 5, NVDA prints a bullish engulfing candle at $838 on volume 20% above average. The 50-day EMA holds as support. This is the entry signal.

Step 4 — Build the Position: Buy the $850/$880 bull call spread at 35 DTE. Cost: $12.00 per spread ($1,200 for 1 contract). Maximum profit: $18.00 ($1,800) if NVDA above $880 at expiry. Maximum risk: $12.00 ($1,200). R/R ratio: 1.5:1 — above the 1:1 minimum.

Step 5 — Set Management Rules Before Entry:

- Profit target: Close at 50% of max profit ($900 gain) or if NVDA reaches $870 (the pre-pullback level);
- Stop loss: Close if NVDA closes below the 50-day EMA ($820) on a daily basis — this invalidates the pullback thesis; and
- Time stop: If the position has not reached 50% profit by T-21, close regardless of P&L. Do not hold a directional trade through accelerating theta decay.

Step 6 — The Outcome: Over the next 8 trading days, NVDA rallies from $838 to $875. The bull call spread is now worth $18.50 — 54% of max profit. Close the position for a $650 gain.

Day	NVDA Price	Spread Value	P&L	Action
Entry	$838	$12.00	$0	Buy 1x $850/$880 BCS
Day 2	$845	$13.40	+$140	Hold — trend intact
Day 4	$855	$15.20	+$320	Hold — approaching pre-pullback high
Day 6	$862	$16.80	+$480	Hold — momentum increasing
Day 8	$875	$18.50	+$650	CLOSE — 54% of max profit reached

Total time in trade: 8 days. Return on risk: 54% ($650 / $1,200). The trade worked because every step of the protocol was followed: trend confirmed, pullback waited for, bounce confirmed, position sized correctly, management rules written before entry, and profit taken at target without greed.

Three Swing Environments and Their Optimal Strategies

Not every market environment supports swing trading. Forcing swing trades in the wrong environment is one of the most common mistakes intermediate traders make.

Environment	Swing Strategy	What to Avoid
Trending (clear direction, VIX 12-18)	Pullback entries with the trend. Bull call spreads in uptrends, bear put spreads in downtrends. 30-45 DTE. This is the ideal swing environment.	Counter-trend trades. Trying to pick tops in an uptrend or bottoms in a downtrend. The trend is your edge — trade with it.
Choppy (no clear trend, VIX 18-25)	Range-bound strategies: iron condors, calendars. Avoid directional swing trades entirely. Wait for the range to resolve.	Directional swing trades — they will get stopped out repeatedly as the market whipsaws. Chop destroys directional traders.
Volatile crisis (VIX 25+)	Reduce swing size by 50% or sit out entirely. If trading: use wider stops, smaller positions, and expect larger adverse moves before your thesis plays out.	Normal-sized positions. Standard stop widths. In high-volatility environments, your normal 5% stop will trigger routinely on noise alone.

THE SWING ENVIRONMENT CHECK

Before entering any swing trade, check two things: (1) Is the VIX environment suitable? (Below 25 preferred, below 20 ideal.) (2) Is the stock trending or chopping? Use a 20-day exponential moving average — if price is crossing the 20-day EMA repeatedly within a 2-week period, the stock is chopping and you should not swing trade it. Wait for a clean trend to emerge.

Channel Trading with Options: Capturing Range-Bound Income

When a stock is trading in a defined channel (bouncing between support and resistance for weeks or months), swing traders have a unique advantage: the channel itself tells you exactly where to enter, where to exit, and where to place your stops. Options make this setup even more powerful because you can sell premium at both boundaries of the channel simultaneously.

Setup identification: A tradeable channel requires at least three touches of support and three touches of resistance over a minimum of 30 days. The channel width should be at least 8% from bottom to top — narrower channels do not generate enough premium to justify the trade. Draw the lines on your chart and verify that recent touches have been clean (the stock reached the boundary and reversed, rather than drifting through it).

The Options Channel Strategy: Sell a bull put spread when the stock touches channel support. Sell a bear call spread when the stock touches channel resistance. If the stock is in the middle of the channel — do nothing. Wait for a boundary touch. Patience is the entire edge.

Entry at support (bottom of channel): When the stock touches the lower boundary and shows a bullish reversal candle (hammer, bullish engulfing, or morning star), sell a bull put spread with the short strike at or just below channel support. DTE: 30-35 days. Width: $3-$5. The channel support acts as your thesis — if the stock bounces (as it has three times before), the spread profits from theta decay while the stock moves away from your short strike.

Entry at resistance (top of channel): When the stock touches the upper boundary and shows a bearish reversal candle, sell a bear call spread with the short strike at or just above channel resistance. Same DTE and width parameters. The channel resistance acts as a ceiling — premium decay works in your favor while the stock remains below your short strike.

Management: Close either spread at 50% profit or T-21, whichever comes first. If the stock breaks through either boundary on heavy volume (close above resistance or close below support on volume 50%+ above average), close the losing spread immediately — the channel is broken and your thesis is invalid. Channel breaks are not rollable situations. Close, reassess, and wait for a new pattern to form.

The dual-entry approach (selling at both boundaries across multiple cycles) can generate 4-6 income entries per quarter on a single stock — each with defined risk and each with the structural advantage of the channel boundary acting as your thesis. Over a year of disciplined channel trading on 3-4 stocks, this strategy contributes meaningfully to your total PPD income.

6-CONDITION FRAMEWORK ▸ ALL SIX CONDITIONS — adjusted options can corrupt any strategy
A corporate action can turn any clean six-condition trade into an illiquid, non-standard contract overnight. The adjusted options check is part of the universal pre-trade filter — it runs before you execute any condition.

Adjusted options are one of the most dangerous surprises in options trading — and one of the most preventable. An adjusted option is a contract that has been modified from its original standardized terms due to a corporate action: a stock split, reverse split, merger, acquisition, special dividend, or spin-off. When these events occur, the OCC adjusts the terms of existing options contracts. The result is a non-standard contract that can be illiquid, difficult to price, and nearly impossible to manage effectively.

This chapter gives you the rules to identify, avoid, and manage adjusted options risk before it costs you money.

What Causes Options Adjustment?

Corporate Action	What Happens to the Option	Risk to the Trader
Stock Split (e.g., 2-for-1)	Contract adjusted to reflect new shares: 1 contract = 200 shares at half the strike. Still one contract, different deliverable.	Options become non-standard. Market makers widen spreads dramatically. Liquidity collapses on the adjusted contract.
Reverse Split (e.g., 1-for-10)	Contract adjusted to reflect fewer shares at higher strike. Often signals company distress.	Extremely illiquid. Wide spreads. May become untradeable as open interest collapses. The underlying may continue to deteriorate.
Merger / Acquisition	Target company options adjusted to reflect acquisition terms — cash, stock, or combination. Strike and deliverable both change.	Options become cash-settled or reflect the acquirer's stock. Price discovery becomes complex. Exit immediately on announcement.
Special Dividend	Strike prices reduced by the dividend amount on ex-date. Changes the P&L math of all open positions.	Subtle but meaningful impact on profitability calculations. Particularly dangerous for short call holders facing early assignment risk.
Spin-off	Parent and new spun-off company shares both become part of the contract deliverable.	One contract now delivers two different securities. Pricing and hedging become complex. Liquidity deteriorates significantly.

Why Adjustments Happen: The Two-Reason Framework

The OCC does not adjust options arbitrarily. Every corporate action adjustment is driven by exactly two objectives — and understanding them makes the entire system logical rather than mysterious.

Corporate Action	When It Happens	Options Impact	Action Required
Stock Split (2:1, 3:2, etc.)	Record date announced.	Strike halved; shares doubled — non-standard.	Review contract terms; consider closing before.
Special Dividend	Ex-dividend date.	Strike reduced by dividend amount.	Monitor OCC adjustment; check new deliverable.
Merger / Acquisition	Deal close date.	Contract converts to cash or acquirer shares.	Close position before deal close — high risk.
Spinoff	Distribution date.	Deliverable changes to parent + spinoff.	Extremely complex; close before ex-date.
Bankruptcy	Filing date.	Options may become worthless immediately.	Close immediately; do not hold through.

Figure 20.1 — Adjusted Options Risk Calendar. Key corporate action dates and their options adjustment triggers.

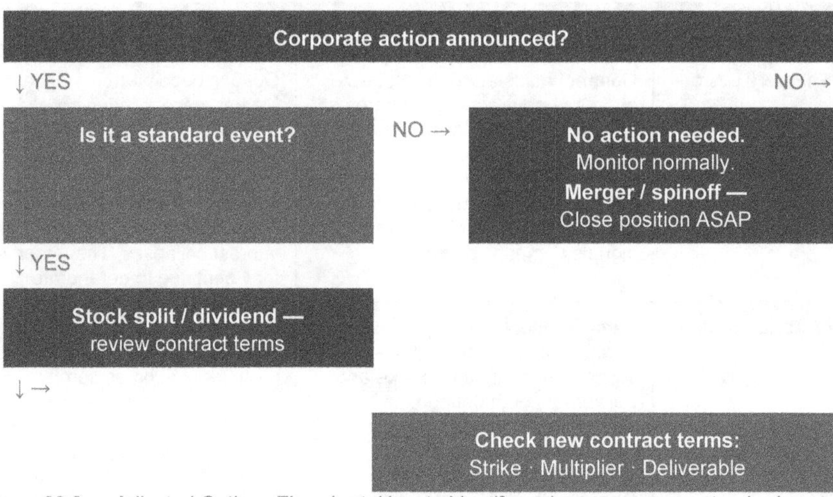

Figure 20.2 — Adjusted Options Flowchart. How to identify and manage a non-standard contract.

Objective	What It Means in Practice
Ensure existing contracts retain their proper economic value	If a stock splits 2-for-1 and the option contract were NOT adjusted, the $100 strike call would immediately become worthless on a stock now priced at $50 — even though nothing fundamentally changed. The adjustment preserves the contract's fair value through the corporate action.
Ensure the contract reflects the correct deliverable package	Options are contracts to buy or sell the underlying. When the underlying changes — through a merger, spinoff, or split — the deliverable changes too. The adjustment makes the contract

Objective	What It Means in Practice
	accurately represent what the holder actually receives or delivers upon exercise or assignment.

Without these adjustments, every major corporate event would create instant windfalls for one side of a trade and catastrophic losses for the other — not from market movement, but from mechanical contract mispricing. The adjustment system is what makes listed options tradeable across corporate events.

The Mechanics of Stock Split Adjustments

Stock split adjustments are the most common type and the easiest to understand — but the math changes significantly depending on whether the split ratio is standard or non-standard. The distinction is critical because non-standard splits create non-standard contracts that are far more difficult to manage.

Split Type	Contracts Held	Shares per Contract	Strike Price	What Changes
2:1 Standard Split	Doubles (1 → 2 contracts)	Stays at 100 (standard)	Halved ($100 → $50)	Contract count doubles, strike halves. The economic value is preserved. This is a clean, standard adjustment — liquidity remains intact.
3:2 Non-Standard Split	Stays the same (1 contract)	Increases to 150 shares	Multiplied by ⅔ ($100 → $66.67)	The multiplier changes from 100 to 150. The contract is NOW NON-STANDARD. This is where the problems begin.
3:1 Standard Split	Triples (1 → 3 contracts)	Stays at 100 (standard)	Divided by 3 ($90 → $30)	Contract count triples, strike thirds. Still a standard contract — still liquid. Manageable.
Reverse 1:10	Stays the same (1 contract)	Decreases to 10 shares	Multiplied by 10 ($5 → $50)	Non-standard contract on a stock already in distress. Liquidity collapses. Exit immediately.

THE NON-STANDARD SPLIT DANGER

A 2:1 split creates standard contracts. Your 1 contract becomes 2 contracts — both with 100 shares at half the strike. Market makers quote them normally. Liquidity is maintained. A 3:2 split is different: your 1 contract now has 150 shares in the deliverable. The multiplier is no longer 100 — it is 150. Market makers are less comfortable quoting non-standard deliverables. Spreads widen. Liquidity deteriorates. Your Greeks calculations — which assume 100 shares — are now wrong. Exit before the split effective date whenever the ratio is non-standard.

How to Value a Split-Adjusted Non-Standard Contract

If you find yourself holding a non-standard contract after an atypical split — for example a 3:2 split creating a 150-share deliverable — the valuation process requires four specific steps. Work through them before attempting to close, roll, or exercise the position.

Step	Action	Example (3:2 Split — XYX 60 Call, 150-share contract)
1	Calculate the exercise value using adjusted strike and multiplier	Strike price × new multiplier: $60 strike × 150 shares = $9,000 exercise value
2	Determine deliverable value using current market price	150 shares × current stock price of $62 = $9,300 deliverable value
3	Subtract exercise value from deliverable value to find intrinsic value	$9,300 − $9,000 = $300 intrinsic value
4	If the current option premium is $3.00, calculate extrinsic value by applying the non-standard multiplier	$3.00 × 150 = $450 total option value. Extrinsic = $450 − $300 intrinsic = $150 time value remaining

The key insight: once the deliverable is non-standard, your platform's automated Greeks and P&L calculations may be unreliable — they often default to the 100-share multiplier. Always calculate manually using the adjusted multiplier when managing a non-standard contract. Call your broker to confirm the exact deliverable specifications before making any decision.

Merger, Spinoff & Dividend Deliverable Changes

Mergers, spinoffs, and large special dividends do not just change the number of shares in the deliverable — they change what is delivered entirely. When a company is acquired, spun off, or pays a large special dividend, the option contract's deliverable package is modified by the OCC to reflect the new economic reality. Understanding the four possible outcomes is essential for managing any position in a company undergoing a corporate event.

Corporate Event	New Deliverable Package	Management Action
Merger (Stock Deal)	100 shares of original company + shares of the acquiring company, per the merger ratio. Example: 100 shares ABC + 0.75 shares XYZ per share acquired.	Exit before the merger closes. Once the deliverable includes the acquirer's shares, pricing the option requires modeling two different stocks simultaneously. Market makers widen spreads

Corporate Event	New Deliverable Package	Management Action
		aggressively. Exit is often the only practical option.
Merger (Cash Deal)	No Original Stock + Cash Amount equal to the acquisition price. Options become effectively cash-settled.	Intrinsic value is fixed at the acquisition price. There is no more movement. The option becomes a binary — exercise if ITM, expire if OTM. Close at fair value and redeploy capital.
Spinoff	100 shares of original company + allocated shares of the new spun-off entity. Both securities in one contract.	The spun-off company's shares may have no options chain and limited liquidity. The combined deliverable is difficult to price. Close before the spinoff effective date.
Special Dividend	100 shares of original company + the cash dividend amount (or the strike is reduced by the dividend amount on ex-date).	For call sellers: monitor early assignment risk. If dividend exceeds remaining time value in an ITM call, expect early exercise from the call buyer. Close or roll before ex-dividend date.

The critical rule for all merger and acquisition situations: the moment an announcement is made, the normal relationship between the underlying's price and your option's Greeks breaks down. The stock gravitates toward the deal price. IV behavior becomes irrational. Do not apply standard management rules to a position in an announced deal. Exit the position, take your P&L, and move on.

How to Detect an Adjusted Option: The CBOE Tool

Adjusted options do not always look different on the surface — the same ticker, the same strike, the same expiration may be showing in your account. But the underlying contract has changed. The fastest way to verify whether any option you hold or are considering has been adjusted is to check the CBOE's daily adjustment postings.

Detection Method	How to Use It
CBOE Adjustment Memos (www.cboe.com)	The CBOE publishes daily memos listing every adjusted option series — including exact changes to symbols, share count per contract, multipliers, and strike prices. If you hold a position in any company undergoing a corporate event, check CBOE.com immediately. Search the underlying ticker in the adjustment database. The memo will tell you exactly what changed and when the adjustment is effective.
Symbol Change in Your Account	A standard XYZ call becomes XYZ1 or XYZW or a variant with a number suffix after adjustment. If you see a suffix appear on a position overnight, a corporate action has occurred. Do not trade the adjusted contract without first reading the CBOE adjustment memo for that symbol.
Unusual Bid/Ask Spreads	An adjusted contract that was previously trading with a $0.05 spread may suddenly show a $0.50–$2.00 spread. Market makers are pricing in the complexity of the non-standard deliverable. Widened spreads on a contract

Detection Method	How to Use It
	you were not expecting to change is a warning sign — investigate before acting.
Open Interest Collapse	When a contract is adjusted, new traders stop opening positions in it — they trade the new standardized series instead. If you notice open interest on your contract dropping significantly while open interest on nearby strikes is rising, an adjustment has likely occurred. The market has moved to the new series; your contract is now the legacy adjusted version.
Your Broker's Corporate Actions Notice	Most brokers send account notifications when positions are affected by corporate actions. These arrive by email or in-app notification. Do not ignore them. Read every corporate action notice the moment it arrives — it describes exactly how your position has been modified.

NEVER OPEN A NEW POSITION IN AN ADJUSTED CONTRACT

Experienced traders — and algorithmic systems — are extremely familiar with how to value adjusted options. If you see an option chain with a contract that looks underpriced relative to what you'd expect, you may have found an adjusted contract, not a mispricing. There is no free money in adjusted options. The apparent discount reflects the complexity of the non-standard deliverable that you may not have fully priced in. Contact your broker. Read the CBOE adjustment memo. Understand it completely before touching it. If in doubt, leave it alone.

The Earnings Rule: The Most Important Avoidance Discipline

Earnings announcements are the single largest source of adjusted IV and unexpected price gaps in the options market. The options trader's primary protection against earnings-related catastrophe is a simple, non-negotiable rule: do not hold short premium positions through earnings unless the position is specifically structured as an earnings play with defined risk.

- Short premium positions (CSPs, covered calls, iron condors) held through earnings face IV crush on one side but catastrophic directional moves on the other. A stock that gaps 20% down through your short put strike can produce losses that exceed weeks of collected premium in a single session;
- The earnings rule: close or roll short premium positions at least 5 trading days before the earnings announcement date. Do not let earnings risk sneak up on you — calendar it when you open the trade;
- Earnings play exception: if you are specifically trading earnings, use defined-risk structures only — long straddles, long strangles, or debit spreads. Collect the IV expansion going in, close before the crush comes out; and
- How to find earnings dates: your brokerage platform shows upcoming earnings dates in the options chain. Always check before opening any position with an expiration that spans the earnings date.

THE EARNINGS CALENDAR IS YOUR RISK CALENDAR

Every options trade you open should be cross-checked against the earnings calendar. If an earnings announcement falls within your expiration window, you have three choices: (1) close before earnings, (2) roll to an expiration after earnings, or (3) structure the trade specifically for the earnings event with defined risk. There is no fourth option.

Support, Resistance & Regression Channels as Risk Filters

Technical structure does not just identify trading opportunities — it identifies risk zones. Using support, resistance, and regression channels as risk filters before entering any options trade prevents a large category of preventable losses.

- Never place your short strike inside a known support or resistance cluster. If the level breaks, your strike is immediately threatened. Place short strikes beyond the nearest significant technical level — that level becomes your first line of defense;
- Linear regression channels define the statistically normal price range for a stock over a given period. Price trading at the outer boundary of a regression channel is statistically extended — mean reversion is more likely than continuation. Avoid selling options in the direction of the extension;
- Dynamic support: the 50-day and 200-day moving averages act as dynamic support in uptrends and dynamic resistance in downtrends. Short put strikes below the 200-day EMA in a downtrend are not protected by a technical floor — the EMA is already broken;
- Avoid trading options on stocks in confirmed downtrends for income strategies. The Wheel requires a stock that recovers. A stock in a structural downtrend may never give you that recovery — your cost basis keeps rising while the stock keeps falling;

Additional Risk Avoidance Rules

- No earnings within the expiration window — covered above. Non-negotiable;
- No stocks with upcoming binary events (FDA decisions, DOJ rulings, merger votes) inside the expiration. These events can gap a stock 30–50% in either direction. Options cannot protect against moves of that magnitude on short premium positions;
- Avoid stocks with very low float or high short interest for income strategies. A short squeeze can take a stock from your short call strike to 3× that level in days. Short interest above 20% is a yellow flag. Above 30% is a stop sign;
- Check for upcoming index additions and deletions — when a stock is added to the S&P 500, forced buying from index funds can create rapid price moves. When deleted, forced selling can be equally dramatic; and
- Avoid options on stocks under $15 per share for income strategies — the absolute dollar premium is too small to be meaningful and the percentage moves are amplified. The bid/ask spread as a percentage of premium is also much wider on low-priced stocks.

Dividend Risk: The Silent Assignment Trap

Dividends create a specific, predictable risk for call sellers: early assignment. When you sell a covered call or call spread on a dividend-paying stock, the call buyer may exercise early to capture the upcoming dividend. This happens when the dividend amount exceeds the remaining extrinsic value of the call option.

If you sold a call that is $2.00 in-the-money with only $0.30 of extrinsic value remaining, and the upcoming dividend is $0.50, the call buyer has a financial incentive to exercise — capturing $0.50 in dividend while surrendering only $0.30 in time value, for a net gain of $0.20 per share. You are assigned overnight and forced to deliver shares.

Dividend Situation	Your Risk as Call Seller	Action Required
ITM call with extrinsic < dividend	High early assignment probability before ex-dividend date	Close the short call before ex-date or accept assignment and deliver shares
ATM call approaching ex-date	Moderate risk — extrinsic erodes quickly as ex-date nears	Monitor extrinsic daily in the week before ex-date. Close if extrinsic < 0.5× dividend
OTM call on dividend stock	Low risk — extrinsic is high relative to dividend	No action needed — maintain normal T-21 management

Merger & Acquisition Risk: Exit on Announcement

When a company announces it is being acquired, options chains freeze, spreads widen dramatically, and the normal relationship between Greeks and price breaks down. The target company's stock gaps to near the acquisition price. The rule is absolute: exit all options positions in the target company the moment a merger or acquisition is announced — before the market fully adjusts.

For the acquirer's stock: covered call holders face specific risk if the acquisition closes and their calls are still open. Calls may be adjusted to reflect the merged entity's share structure, creating non-standard contracts that are difficult to exit. Close all short call positions on the acquiring company as well — do not wait for expiration.

Support/Resistance and Technical Level Rules

Your short strike should never be placed at a recognized technical level. It should be placed beyond the technical level — with support or resistance acting as your buffer, not your line in the sand.

- Short puts: place the strike at least 5% below the nearest support level. If support is at $95 and the stock is at $100, your strike belongs at $88–90, not $95;
- Short calls: place the strike at least 3–5% above the nearest resistance level. If resistance is at $110, sell the $115–117 call, not the $110 call; and
- Regression channels: do not sell puts at the channel's lower boundary. Channels break — and when they do, the move is typically 1.5–2× the channel width. Your strike must survive a channel break, not just normal oscillation.

The Complete Adjusted Options Avoidance Checklist

✓	Check	Action Required
☐	Earnings announcement within 35 days?	Close or roll all short premium positions at least 5 days before the event
☐	Ex-dividend date within 14 days?	Check extrinsic on all short ITM calls. Close if extrinsic < dividend amount
☐	Merger, acquisition, or buyout rumored or announced?	Exit all positions immediately — do not wait for confirmation

✓	Check	Action Required
☐	Stock split or reverse split announced?	Exit before the effective date — adjusted contracts are illiquid
☐	Short strike placed at a recognized support/resistance level?	Move the strike at least 5% beyond the technical level, not at it
☐	FDA, FOMC, or CPI report within 7 days on a macro-sensitive name?	Close or hedge before the catalyst fires
☐	Short interest above 15% on the underlying?	Avoid short calls — high short interest creates violent squeeze risk

THE AVOIDANCE RULE

The cost of exiting a good trade early because a catalyst is approaching is one lost premium cycle. The cost of holding through an unanticipated catalyst is often 5–10 lost premium cycles. The math is overwhelming. When in doubt, close it out.

THE RISK AVOIDANCE CHECKLIST

Before any trade: (1) Is there an earnings announcement within the expiration window? (2) Is there a binary event (FDA, merger vote, DOJ) within the window? (3) Is short interest above 20%? (4) Is my short strike beyond the nearest significant support/resistance level? (5) Is the stock in a confirmed downtrend? Five checks. If any answer raises a red flag — restructure or wait.

Three Adjusted Options Disasters: Real-World Cases

These composites of real trading situations show what happens when traders ignore the warning signs.

Case 1: The Dividend Trap

A trader sells a covered call on a $75 stock at the $80 strike for $2.10 premium. The stock goes ex-dividend with $1.50 three days before expiration. At $80.50, the call buyer exercises early to capture the dividend. The trader loses shares at $80 AND misses the $1.50 dividend — netting less than if they had simply held the stock.

The rule: Never sell covered calls with less than 21 DTE on stocks with an ex-dividend date inside your expiration cycle.

Case 2: The M&A Surprise

A trader sells a CSP on a $45 stock at the $40 strike for $1.80. Two weeks later, the company is acquired for $38 cash. The put is deep ITM. The options contract is adjusted to a non-standard deliverable — $3,800 cash instead of 100 shares. The contract has no liquidity, massive spreads, and cannot be rolled.

The rule: The moment M&A rumors appear — not confirmed, rumors — close all short options on that name within 48 hours.

Case 3: The Stock Split Confusion

A trader holds a bull call spread on a $700 stock. The company announces a 20:1 split. After the split, each contract now delivers 5 shares at adjusted strikes. Open interest evaporates. The bid-ask widens from $0.30 to $2.50. The trader cannot close without surrendering most of their profit to the market maker.

The rule: Close all options positions before the effective date of any stock split. Re-enter after with standard contracts.

ADJUSTED OPTIONS SURVIVAL

Three situations require immediate closure regardless of P&L: (1) earnings inside your expiration cycle when short premium, (2) M&A rumored or announced, (3) stock split/reverse split/special dividend inside your contract period. No premium is worth being trapped in a non-standard contract.

6-CONDITION FRAMEWORK ▸ ALL SIX CONDITIONS — validate each strategy before deploying it live

Backtesting confirms that your six-condition response actually performs in historical data before you risk real capital. Each condition should be backtested independently — what works in condition 2 may not work in condition 4.

A strategy that has not been tested is not a strategy — it is a hypothesis. Backtesting is the process of applying a trading strategy to historical data to evaluate how it would have performed. Paper trading is the process of running a strategy in real market conditions without real capital at risk. Together, they are the laboratory where you validate your edge before putting real money on the line.

Most retail traders skip this step entirely. They hear about a strategy, fund an account, and start trading. The first drawdown surprises them. The second tests their discipline. The third often ends their trading career. Backtesting and paper trading don't guarantee future profits — but they build the conviction and the operational fluency that surviving real markets requires.

Understanding Trading System Types

Before you backtest, you need to know which type of system you are testing. Trading systems fall into two broad categories based on how they interact with the trader — and two further categories based on how they treat market trends. Understanding which type you are building determines how you design your tests:

System Type	Definition	Best For
Discretionary System	Presents trading candidates but leaves the final trade execution decision to the trader. Human judgment determines the ultimate entry.	Experienced traders who can read context and override rules based on qualitative factors
Mechanical System	Computer-based — automatically generates buy and sell signals that are always traded without human override. The rule IS the trade.	Systematic traders who want to remove emotion entirely and test pure statistical edge
Trend-Following System	Identifies trade entry and exit points for new or existing trends. Uses moving averages, MACD, ROC as primary signals.	Bull markets, sector rotation plays, momentum strategies
Countertrend System	Identifies entry and exit by finding tops and bottoms — trades against the prevailing move. Mean reversion logic.	Range-bound markets, IV-elevated environments, oversold bounce setups

NO SYSTEM WORKS IN EVERY SITUATION

Keep that fact firmly in mind when developing your personal trading system. Your goal is to design a system useful to you across a large number of stocks and a large number of situations — not one that works perfectly for one stock in one market condition. Whenever you try to tailor a system too narrowly, you run trouble. Ensure your system works across long periods of time and throughout many different market conditions.

Why Backtesting Options Is Different

Backtesting options strategies is more complex than backtesting stock strategies because options pricing depends on multiple variables that change over time — not just price. A complete options backtest must account for all of the following:

Metric	Minimum Threshold	Target	What It Measures
Win Rate	> 55%	65–75%	Percentage of trades closed profitably.
Expectancy	> $0.50 per 1 risked	> $1.00	Average $ earned per dollar risked.
Profit Factor	> 1.3	> 1.6	Gross profit ÷ gross loss ratio.
Max Drawdown	< 20% of account	< 12%	Largest peak-to-trough equity drop.
Sharpe Ratio	> 0.8	> 1.2	Return per unit of volatility (risk-adjusted).
Walk-Forward Efficiency	> 60%	> 75%	Out-of-sample ÷ in-sample performance ratio.

Figure 21.1 — Backtesting Validation Metrics. Win rate, expectancy, Sharpe, and walk-forward efficiency.

Stage	Name	What You Do	Output
1	Data Collection	Gather historical price, IV, and options chain data for target ticker.	Clean OHLCV + IV history for 2+ years.
2	Rule Definition	Write entry, exit, and size rules exactly as you would trade them live.	Written strategy rules; no discretion allowed.
3	In-Sample Testing	Apply rules to first 70% of data. Optimize parameters if needed.	Baseline win rate, expectancy, Sharpe.
4	Out-of-Sample Validation	Apply rules to held-out 30%. No re-optimization allowed.	True performance estimate — the real test.
5	Walk-Forward Analysis	Roll forward test window quarterly. Re-optimize each period.	Robustness score; confirm edge persists.

Figure 21.2 — Options Backtesting Framework. The five-stage process from data through walk-forward validation.

- Historical implied volatility — not just price, but what IV was at the time of entry. Selling premium when IVR was 15 vs. 65 produces dramatically different results for the same strategy;
- Bid/ask spreads at the time of entry and exit — historical options data should include realistic bid/ask spread assumptions. Assuming mid-price fills on illiquid options produces fictional results;
- Dividend and ex-dividend dates — affect short call positions and assignment risk calculations;
- Corporate actions — splits, mergers, and spin-offs in the historical data can distort backtest results if not properly adjusted; and
- Greeks at entry — delta, theta, and vega at the time of entry affect the expected behavior and risk profile of the position through its life.

The best free resource for options backtesting for retail traders is the TastyTrade platform, which offers historical options data and built-in backtesting tools. OptionAlpha and Tradier also provide backtesting environments. For serious strategy validation, a subscription to ORATS (Options Research and Technology Services) provides institutional-grade historical options data.

What to Test: The Core Validation Metrics

Metric	What It Measures	Target / Benchmark
Win Rate	Percentage of trades that reached the profit target before hitting the stop	Premium sellers: 65–80% target. Debit spread buyers: 40–55% is acceptable with strong R/R.
Average Winner	Average profit on winning trades	Should be at least 50% of the maximum potential profit on each strategy.
Average Loser	Average loss on losing trades	Should not exceed 2× the average winner. If losers dwarf winners, the strategy has no edge.
Expectancy	(Win Rate × Avg Win) − (Loss Rate × Avg Loss)	Must be positive. Even a small positive expectancy compounded over hundreds of trades builds wealth.
Max Drawdown	The largest peak-to-trough decline in account equity during the test period	Should not exceed 20–25% of starting capital. Beyond this, recovery requires disproportionate returns.
Max Adverse Excursion (MAE)	The worst intra-trade loss on any single position before it recovered or was closed	Helps set realistic stop levels. If MAE consistently exceeds your planned stop, your stop is too tight.
Sharpe Ratio	Risk-adjusted return: (strategy return − risk-free rate) ÷ standard deviation of returns	Above 1.0 is acceptable. Above 1.5 is good. Above 2.0 is excellent for an options strategy.

Paper Trading: The Live Laboratory

Paper trading — simulated trading in real market conditions with no real capital at risk — is the bridge between backtesting historical data and trading real money. Before you trade a single dollar of real capital, you must spend time in a simulator. This is not optional. It is the professional prerequisite. The good news: there are excellent free paper trading platforms available to any trader with an internet connection.

The Paper Trading Platforms: Where to Practice

Platform	URL	What It Offers
Investopedia Stock Simulator	www.investopedia.com/simulator	The most widely used free simulator in retail trading education. Provides $100,000 in virtual cash, real-time stock and ETF quotes, and a full trading interface. Ideal for new traders learning order entry, position sizing, and portfolio tracking before touching real capital. No options trading in the free version — use it for stock and ETF mechanics first, then graduate to an options-capable platform.
MarketWatch Virtual Stock Exchange	www.marketwatch.com/game	MarketWatch's free simulator supports stocks, ETFs, and mutual funds with real-time prices. What makes it unique: you can create private games with custom rules — set your own starting capital, leverage limits, and scoring parameters. Excellent for group challenges (trading clubs, cohorts, study groups) where you compete against others under identical rules. The competitive element adds psychological realism that solo simulators lack.
ThinkOrSwim Paper Trading (Schwab)	Download the ThinkorSwim platform	The gold standard for options paper trading. Full options chain access, real-time Greeks, simulated multi-leg order entry, risk graphs, and all the analytics available in the live platform. Data is real-time and the paper trading environment is identical to live trading. This is the platform to graduate to once you are ready to practice options specifically. Free with any Schwab account (no minimum balance required to open).
TastyTrade Paper Trading	TastyTrade.com	TastyTrade's paper trading is built specifically for options income traders. The platform is options-first by design — the interface is built around premium selling, position Greeks, and income tracking. If your primary strategy is the Wheel (CSP → Covered Call), TastyTrade's paper trading environment is the closest simulation to how you will actually operate. Free with account creation.
IBKR Paper Trading (Interactive Brokers)	interactivebrokers.com	Interactive Brokers offers a standalone paper trading account with access to global markets, full options chains, and professional-grade analytics. Most sophisticated of the free options — recommended for traders planning to run

Platform	URL	What It Offers
		a larger, multi-position portfolio. The platform learning curve is steeper, but the simulation fidelity is the highest available to retail traders.

WHICH SIMULATOR TO START WITH

If you are brand new to trading: start at www.investopedia.com/simulator to learn basic order entry and portfolio tracking with no complexity. Once you understand how to buy and sell positions, move to www.marketwatch.com/game to add competitive pressure and practice against other traders. When you are ready to practice options specifically — which is the primary focus of this book — open a ThinkOrSwim or TastyTrade paper trading account and begin running the full strategy: CSP entries, T-21 management, covered call follow-through. Do all three in sequence. Each level prepares you for the next.

Paper trading accomplishes things that backtesting cannot:

- Real-time execution experience — you practice entering multi-leg orders, managing positions, and closing trades in real market conditions with live bid/ask spreads;
- Emotional rehearsal — even without real money at risk, watching a paper position move against you generates useful psychological feedback. Notice where you want to break your rules. Notice when you feel the urge to chase. Paper trading reveals your behavioral tendencies before they cost you real money;
- Platform fluency — you learn where every button is, how to enter spread orders, how to read the Greeks in real time, and how to set conditional orders. Fumbling with platform mechanics during a live trade is expensive; and
- Strategy refinement — real-market conditions often reveal edge cases and scenarios your backtest did not capture. Paper trading gives you a low-stakes environment to encounter and solve these edge cases.

THE PAPER TRADING RULE

Paper trade a new strategy for a minimum of 30 trades — not 30 days, 30 trades — before committing real capital. Thirty trades gives you a sample size large enough to observe the strategy's win rate, average winner/loser, and drawdown characteristics in current market conditions. Fewer than 30 trades is not a representative sample.

→ *See also: The 90-Day New Trader Protocol (Chapter 22, page 389) — a structured live-trading ramp from single positions to full portfolio management.*

Using Trading Systems for Consistent Execution

A trading system is a complete set of rules that defines every aspect of a trade: entry criteria, position sizing, management rules, and exit conditions. It is the written expression of your strategy, specific enough that two different people following it would make the same decisions. Systems prevent emotion from contaminating execution.

- Entry system: Define exactly what conditions must be met before you open a trade. For a CSP income system: IVR > 40, stock above 200-day EMA, no

earnings within 35 days, delta between 0.15–0.25, DTE 30–45. All five conditions must be true. If any are absent, no trade;
- Sizing system: Define position size in terms of max dollar risk, not number of contracts. For a $50,000 account: max 5% risk per trade = $2,500. For a $90 CSP, that means a maximum of 2 contracts ($9,000 cash reserved per contract = $18,000 total reserved on 2 contracts — within the 5% risk framework on the premium itself);
- Management system: Define the exact conditions that trigger management actions. Close at 50% profit. Roll if tested within 21 DTE. Close if loss exceeds 2× credit received. No judgment calls — the system decides;
- Exit system: Define all three exits before entry — profit target, stop loss, and time exit. Write them down for every trade in your trade journal;

Drawdown: Understanding and Surviving It

Drawdown is not failure. It is the inevitable rhythm of any trading system. No strategy — no matter how well-tested — wins every trade. Drawdown periods are when discipline is tested and when undercapitalized or emotionally unprepared traders exit the market.

- Maximum drawdown is the largest peak-to-trough decline in your account during a given period. If your account grows from $50,000 to $60,000 then drops to $48,000, your drawdown is $12,000 — or 20% from the peak;
- Recovery math: a 20% drawdown requires a 25% gain to recover. A 33% drawdown requires a 50% gain. A 50% drawdown requires a 100% gain. This asymmetry is why the 20–25% maximum drawdown rule is not arbitrary — it is mathematically protective;
- Behavioral rule during drawdown: reduce position size, do not increase it. The instinct to 'make it back faster' by trading bigger is the most reliable path to turning a manageable drawdown into a catastrophic one; and
- Statistical drawdown is expected: a strategy with a 70% win rate will, by random chance, produce losing streaks of 4–5 trades in a row regularly. This is normal. The system's edge is in the aggregate — not in any sequence of individual trades.

DRAWDOWN IS DATA

Every drawdown tells you something about your strategy and yourself. Track every trade, every drawdown period, and every recovery in your trade journal. The patterns you find in your own data — the market conditions where your strategy struggles, the emotional triggers that cause you to break rules — are the most valuable intelligence you will ever collect as a trader.

Maximum Adverse Excursion (MAE): Adding Risk Management to Your Backtest

Maximum Adverse Excursion — MAE — is one of the most powerful and most overlooked metrics in options backtesting. MAE measures the largest loss a trade experienced at any point during its life, even if the trade ultimately ended profitably. It is the answer to the question every risk manager must ask: 'How much pain did I have to endure to collect this profit?'

A strategy that wins 70% of the time sounds excellent. But if the average winning trade experienced a 35% unrealized loss at some point before recovering, the trader holding that position through the drawdown needed to exercise extraordinary discipline — and many would not. MAE reveals the psychological cost hidden inside the statistics.

MAE Metric	What It Measures	How to Use It
MAE (per trade)	The maximum unrealized loss at any single point during the trade's life — the deepest the P&L went negative before the trade closed.	Plot MAE for every trade in your backtest. If your winning trades regularly show MAE of 50%+ of max profit, your stop-loss threshold may need to be wider — or the strategy may be creating unnecessary psychological pressure.
Average MAE (winners)	The average maximum adverse excursion across all winning trades.	If winners average 20% MAE, you can calibrate your live stop-loss to trigger at 25–30% — tight enough to protect but wide enough not to stop out trades that would have recovered.
Average MAE (losers)	The average maximum adverse excursion across all losing trades.	Compare to winning trade MAE. If losing trades show dramatically higher MAE before closing, you are likely holding losers too long. The data will show you when the inflection point is.
MAE % of Max Profit	(Maximum adverse excursion) ÷ (maximum possible profit on the trade).	A ratio above 100% means the trade went underwater for more than its maximum potential gain before you could profit. These trades have extremely poor risk/reward experienced profiles.
Reasonable Stop Calculation	Use average MAE of losing trades to set a stop-loss that cuts losers before they reach their worst point.	If losing trades average 45% MAE, set your stop at 40% of max loss — you close before the average losing trade reaches its worst drawdown. This trims average loss without eliminating recoverable trades.

THE MAE STOP-LOSS CALIBRATION RULE

Do not set stop-losses based on round numbers or gut feel. Set them based on MAE data from your backtest. Run 50–100 backtested trades. Plot the MAE of every winning trade and every losing trade. The stop-loss that maximizes your win rate without cutting winners prematurely will be found in that data — not in a textbook. Your MAE average for losing trades is the single most important number for calibrating your stops.

Backtesting Across All Six Conditions: Condition-Specific Validation

The most important backtesting principle in the six-condition system is this: backtest each strategy separately in the condition it was designed for. A strategy that performs brilliantly in condition 2 (bullish, high IV) may perform terribly in condition 1 (bullish, low IV) — because in condition 1, you should be buying premium, not selling it. If you backtest a CSP strategy across all market conditions combined, you will get a blended result that masks both its strengths and its weaknesses.

#	Condition	Strategy to Backtest	Key Metrics to Validate
1	**Bullish, Low IV**	Long calls, bull call spreads	Win rate, average winner size, average MAE on winners, IV level at entry
2	**Bullish, High IV**	CSP, covered call, bull put spread	Premium collected, win rate, average days to 50% profit, MAE on losing trades
3	**Bearish, Low IV**	Long puts, bear put spreads	Win rate in confirmed downtrend, average move captured, time to target
4	**Bearish, High IV**	Bear call spreads only	Credit collected, win rate, average MAE, frequency of max loss
5	**Range-bound, Low IV**	Butterfly, iron condor	Percentage of time stock stayed in range, average premium per day, MAE frequency
6	**Range-bound, High IV**	Calendar spread, diagonal	Calendar P&L at expiration vs. at midpoint, IV differential captured, average daily theta

Condition-specific backtesting is what separates a validated strategy from a hoped-for strategy. If condition 4 (bearish, high IV) always produces your worst results in backtesting, you have two options: refine the strategy further until the numbers improve, or accept that condition 4 is your weakest area and deploy minimum size there. The data tells you where your edge is strongest. Listen to it.

Backtesting Walkthrough: 12-Month CSP Strategy on AAPL

The walkthrough covers January through December of one calendar year, trading cash-secured puts on AAPL with the following fixed rules: sell the 0.20–0.25 delta put, 30–45 DTE at entry, close at 50% of max profit, stop at 2x credit received, one position at a time, no entries within 14 days of earnings. No discretion. Every trade executed mechanically when rules are met.

Results over 24 trades: win rate 79.2%, profit factor 2.31, maximum drawdown 2.8%, annual return 29.7% on deployed capital. The two losing months (May and September) both involved defensive rolls that reduced the loss from full max to approximately 1.5x credit. The three assignments were managed through the Wheel — each generated additional covered call income that reduced the effective cost basis before the stock recovered.

What the backtest validates: the 50% profit close rule for income trades (CSPs, credit spreads, iron condors) was the single highest-impact rule in the system. Trades closed at 50% profit had an average hold time of 18 days, freeing capital for the next position.

Trades held past 50% target (in a test run without the rule) showed a win rate decline from 79% to 61% and doubled the average hold time. The rule is not arbitrary — it is mathematically optimal for this structure.

What the backtest does NOT validate: forward returns. A backtest proves that the rules produced a specific historical outcome on a specific underlying in a specific year. It does not guarantee the same outcome in a different year, different underlying, or different market regime. The backtest is the starting point for conviction, not the ending point. Paper trade the validated system for 90 days on multiple underlyings before going live.

THE THREE BACKTESTING TRAPS

Curve fitting: optimizing parameters to fit historical data produces rules that fail forward. Avoid any rule that was added specifically because it would have prevented a specific past loss. Survivor bias: backtesting only on stocks that exist today ignores companies that failed during the test period. Use index ETFs (SPY, QQQ) as primary backtest vehicles — they cannot go to zero. Overfitting to one market regime: a strategy that worked exclusively in a bull market or exclusively in high-IV environments is not validated — it is regime-specific. Test across at least one bear year and one low-IV year before calling a strategy validated.

Backtest Results Dashboard — Equity curve, win rate, and key validation metrics from strategy testing.

Setup: $50,000 account. Sell 1 CSP monthly at 0.25 delta, 30-35 DTE. Close at 50% profit or manage at T-21. Skip earnings weeks.

Month	AAPL	Strike	Premium	Days	Result	Cumul. P&L
Jan	$182	$170 P	$3.20	14	50% profit	$160
Feb	$186	$174 P	$2.90	18	50% profit	$305
Mar	$178	$166 P	$3.50	12	50% profit	$480
Apr	$185	$173 P	$2.80	—	Skip: earnings	$480
May	$190	$178 P	$3.10	16	50% profit	$635
Jun	$195	$183 P	$2.60	21	T-21 close	$726
Jul	$188	$176 P	$3.40	—	Skip: earnings	$726
Aug	$192	$180 P	$2.90	15	50% profit	$871
Sep	$185	$173 P	$3.60	28	Rolled at T-21	$871
Oct	$178	$166 P	$4.20	—	Skip: earnings	$871
Nov	$180	$168 P	$3.00	22	Assigned	$871+shares
Dec	$175	CC $180	$2.50	—	Wheel: sold CC	$871+shares

Results: 8 entries / 12 months (3 earnings skips, 1 roll). Win rate: 75%. Total premium: $871 on ~$17K capital = 5.1% annual return from premium alone. One assignment transitioned to Wheel. The key insight: skipping earnings reduced income 25% but eliminated the highest-risk entries.

Strategy Comparison: Which Approach Fits Which Market?

After backtesting individual strategies, the next level is comparing strategies against each other in different market environments. This comparison table summarizes backtested performance across the six conditions — showing which strategies thrive and which suffer in each environment.

Strategy	Cond 1: Bull Trend	Cond 2: Bull Vol	Cond 3: Neutral	Cond 4: Bear Vol	Cond 5: Bear Trend	Cond 6: High IV
CSP (0.25 delta)	Strong	Good	Strong	Poor	Very Poor	Excellent
Covered Call	Good	Poor	Strong	Fair	Fair	Good
Iron Condor	Poor	Poor	Excellent	Poor	Poor	Good
Bull Call Spread	Excellent	Good	Poor	Very Poor	Very Poor	Fair
Bear Put Spread	Very Poor	Poor	Poor	Good	Excellent	Fair
Calendar Spread	Fair	Poor	Excellent	Poor	Fair	Very Poor
Long Straddle	Poor	Excellent	Very Poor	Excellent	Poor	Good
Collar	Good	Good	Fair	Good	Good	Good

Two insights from the comparison: (1) No single strategy works in all six conditions. The trader who only knows CSPs will suffer in Conditions 4 and 5. The trader who only knows iron condors will suffer in Conditions 1, 2, 4, and 5. You need at least 3-4 strategies to cover all environments. (2) The Collar is the only strategy rated 'Good' or better in all six conditions — but its return is moderate in each. This is the risk/return tradeoff: versatility costs performance. The specialist outperforms in their condition but fails outside it. The generalist survives everywhere but dominates nowhere.

Your strategy selection should match your assessment of the current market condition. Follow three steps:

- Step 1 — Identify the condition: run your six-condition read (Chapter 1);
- Step 2 — Look up approved strategies: find which strategies are rated 'Good' or better for that condition; and
- Step 3 — Select and size: choose the strategy that matches your account size and risk tolerance.

This three-step process eliminates the guesswork from strategy selection entirely.

The Paper Trading Protocol: Before You Risk Real Capital

Paper trading is not optional for new traders — it is the mandatory prerequisite for going live. But most traders do paper trading wrong: they place trades without consequence, skip the management discipline because 'it's not real money,' and declare themselves ready after two or three winning trades. That is not paper trading — it is rehearsing overconfidence.

Effective paper trading mimics every aspect of live trading except the cash transfer. You execute the same management rules, the same journal discipline, the same monthly review process. You measure the same metrics. The only thing you are testing is the strategy — not your risk tolerance, which can only be calibrated with real money.

Phase	Duration	What You Are Testing — Go Live When
Phase 1 — Mechanics	30 days minimum	You can find, evaluate, enter, manage, and close a CSP without looking up how to do any step. You can read a risk graph, calculate breakeven and max loss, and identify your T-21 date at entry. Go live when all mechanics are automatic.

Phase	Duration	What You Are Testing — Go Live When
Phase 2 — System Discipline	60 days, minimum 20 paper trades	You closed 100% of positions at 50% profit target without holding for more. You triggered T-21 reviews on schedule. You did not open positions that violated your criteria. Go live when your rule compliance rate is 90%+ across 20 trades.
Phase 3 — Drawdown Behavior	Until you experience a losing month in paper trading	You managed a trade that went against you without breaking rules. You executed a defensive roll correctly. You closed a position at stop loss without overriding it. Go live only after you have managed at least one losing trade in paper trading exactly as your plan requires.

Paper trading does not prepare you for the emotional intensity of real money. It does prepare you for the mechanics and the discipline. Those two things — mechanics and discipline — are the controllable variables. The emotional calibration comes from the first six months of live trading at minimum position size.

THE PAPER TRADING RULE

Paper trade for a minimum of 90 days before going live. But do not paper trade indefinitely to avoid the discomfort of real money. The 91st day is for live trading at minimum size. The lessons you cannot learn from paper trading — how you feel watching a position move against you with real capital — cannot be acquired any other way. Paper trading builds the system. Real trading builds the trader.

6-CONDITION FRAMEWORK ▸ ALL SIX — build your complete personal response system for each condition
Mastery is not knowing more strategies. It is having a tested, written, internalized response for each of the six conditions — and executing that response without hesitation when the condition is identified.

Every trader in this book has learned the same tools. The same Greeks, the same strategies, the same risk management framework. But the trader who masters this material is not the one who knows the most — it is the one who knows themselves the most. Mastery is the intersection of knowledge, discipline, and self-awareness applied consistently across market conditions.

This final chapter gives you the framework for building and operating your personal strategy — the specific, written, tested system that reflects your capital, your risk tolerance, your time availability, and your psychological makeup. There is no universal strategy that works for everyone. There is a universal process for finding the strategy that works for you.

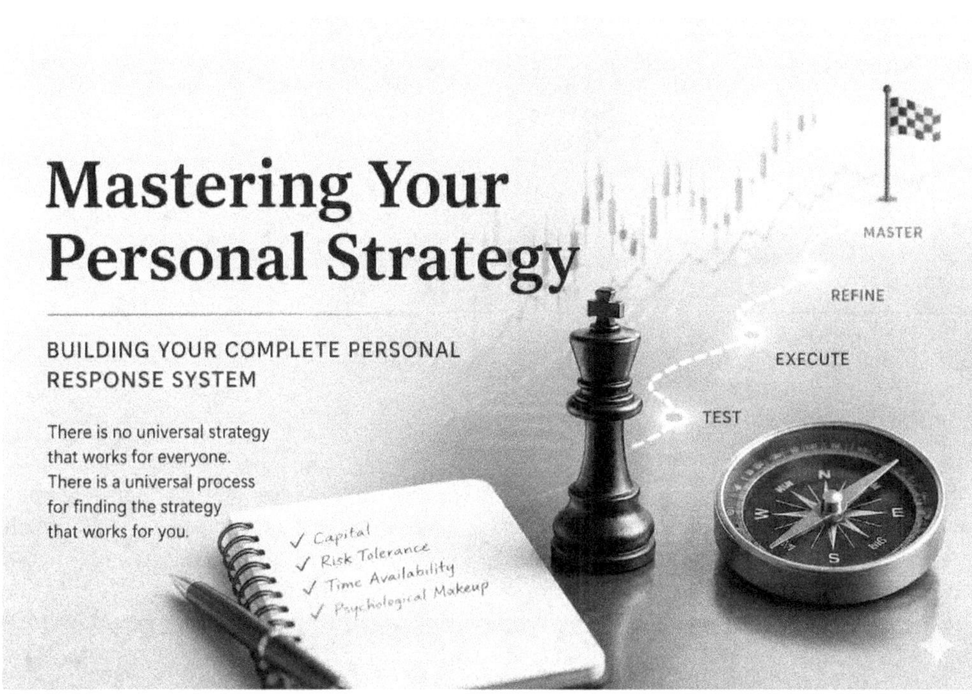

→ See Figure 2.1 — Moneyness Ladder — Call Options (Chapter 2 — Options Contracts Explained)

The Six Market Condition Frameworks

Markets present themselves in six distinct conditions. A master trader has a defined response for each. Before you trade any session, identify which condition the market is in — and make sure your open positions and planned trades are aligned with that condition, not fighting it.

#	Condition	Key Signals	Strategy Alignment
1	**Strong Uptrend**	Price above 50/200-day EMA. MACD positive. BPI rising. VIX low.	Long calls, bull call spreads, diagonal spreads on leading sectors. Covered calls for income on long stock. Avoid bear positions — trend is your tailwind.
2	**Weak / Choppy Uptrend**	Price above 200-day EMA but below 50-day. Whipsaw candles. Mixed MACD.	Reduce position size. Calendar spreads and iron condors in range. Wait for trend clarity before adding directional debit trades. Patience is the strategy.
3	**Sideways / Range-Bound**	Price oscillating within 5–8% range. Bollinger Band squeeze. Low BPI movement.	Iron condors, credit spreads anchored to support/resistance. Cash-secured puts at strong support. Theta is your income. Do not buy premium — it decays without a move.
4	**Weak / Choppy Downtrend**	Price below 50-day EMA but above 200-day. Lower highs. MACD negative but not extreme.	Reduce long exposure. Bear call spreads on weak sectors. Protective puts on existing holdings. No new income strategies on individual stocks — use index ETFs only.
5	**Strong Downtrend**	Price below 200-day EMA. MACD deeply negative. BPI below 30. VIX elevated.	Bear put spreads, long puts on weak sectors. Cash-secured puts only on mega-cap quality names with strong support well below current price. Hedge portfolio with SPY/QQQ puts.
6	**High Volatility / Crisis**	VIX above 30. Large daily candles. Correlations spike to 1. News-driven gaps.	Defined-risk short premium on quality names only. Size at 25–50% of normal. Let the first wave of volatility exhaust itself before deploying. Patience in crisis pays the highest premiums.

The Premium Desk Six-Strategy Framework

The six market conditions described above map directly to six specific strategy families — one approved approach for each combination of directional bias and volatility environment. This is the core of the Premium Desk method: you do not guess which strategy to use. You read the condition. You execute the assigned strategy. You avoid everything else.

Condition	IV Environment	Primary Strategy	IVR Target	DTE Target
C1 — Bullish / Low IV	IVR < 30	Long Call / Bull Call Spread	< 30	30–45 DTE
C2 — Bullish / High IV	IVR > 50	CSP / Bull Put Spread	> 50	30–45 DTE

C3 — Bearish / Low IV	IVR < 30	Long Put / Bear Put Spread	< 30	30–45 DTE
C4 — Bearish / High IV	IVR > 50	Bear Call Spread	> 50	21–35 DTE
C5 — Neutral / High IV	IVR > 50	Iron Condor / Short Strangle	> 50	30–45 DTE
C6 — Neutral / Low IV	IVR < 30	Calendar Spread / Long Straddle	< 30	45–60 DTE

Figure 22.3 — Strategy Matching Matrix. Six conditions mapped to six strategies with IVR and DTE parameters.

The biggest influence on which strategy you choose is your financial goal — some strategies are built for capital gains, some for income, and others for hedging. But regardless of your goal, the condition comes first. The strategy must match the market you are actually in, not the market you wish you were in.

#	Condition	IV Level	Approved Strategies	Why This — Not Something Else
1	**BULLISH**	LOW VOLATILITY	Long Call | Bull Call Spread (debit spread)	Low IV means options are cheap — this is the time to BUY premium, not sell it. A long call gives you leveraged upside at a low cost basis. A bull call spread reduces cost while defining maximum risk — ideal when the move is anticipated but conviction is moderate. Do not sell covered calls in Condition 1 — you cap your upside exactly when the trend is your strongest ally.
2	**BULLISH**	HIGH VOLATILITY	Covered call (on existing long stock) | Bull put spread / Cash-secured put (credit)	High IV means options are expensive — this is the time to SELL premium. A covered call generates income on stock you already hold while IV is elevated. A bull put spread or CSP collects maximum credit in a bullish direction. Do not buy calls here — you overpay for premium that will IV-crush against you.
3	**BEARISH**	LOW VOLATILITY	Basic long put | Bear put spread (debit)	Low IV means puts are affordable — buy them for downside capture. A long put gives leveraged exposure to the decline. A bear put spread reduces cost while still participating in a moderate downward move. Do not sell puts in a bearish environment — you collect a small credit

#	Condition	IV Level	Approved Strategies	Why This — Not Something Else
				and accept large directional risk against you.
4	**BEARISH**	**HIGH VOLATILITY**	**Bear call spread ONLY — sell OTM call / buy further OTM call (credit received)**	**High IV + bearish direction = sell credit spreads on the CALL side. You collect elevated premium for the bearish thesis. The spread caps your risk. Do NOT use long puts here — high IV makes them expensive and IV crush destroys them after the catalyst fires. Do NOT use naked short calls — undefined risk. Credit spreads only.**
5	**RANGE-BOUND**	LOW VOLATILITY	Butterfly spread | Iron condor (defined-risk)	Low IV in a range means options are cheap — but the range itself is the edge. A butterfly concentrates profit at a single target price. An iron condor captures premium on both sides of the range. Do not buy directional premium — there is no trend to profit from, and theta decay will erode it.
6	**RANGE-BOUND**	HIGH VOLATILITY	ATM calendar spread | Diagonal spread	High IV in a range creates an income opportunity through time decay differentials. A calendar spread sells near-term elevated IV and buys longer-dated IV at a relative discount. A diagonal adds a directional tilt while preserving the time decay advantage. Do not sell iron condors with wide wings in high IV — the wings may be too close to the money after a vol spike.

⚠ STRATEGY #4 VERIFIED: BEARISH + HIGH VOLATILITY = CREDIT SPREADS ONLY

When you are bearish AND volatility is high, the only approved structure is the bear call spread — a credit spread on the call side.

• Sell an OTM call at your target strike • Buy a further OTM call as your defined-risk cap • Collect the net credit.

Why not long puts? High IV inflates put premiums — you overpay and IV crush destroys you after the catalyst. Why not naked short calls? Unlimited risk. There is no scenario in which an undefined-risk bearish position is acceptable in this system.

Adjusted Options Filter: Applied to All Six Strategies

Before executing any of the six strategies above, one cross-cutting rule applies without exception: confirm that the underlying is not subject to a pending or announced corporate action that would create an adjusted contract. This check takes thirty seconds and protects you from one of the most preventable losses in options trading.

#	Strategy	Specific Adjusted Options Risk	Pre-Trade Confirmation Required
1	**Bullish Low IV — Long Call / Bull Call Spread**	A pending merger or acquisition can freeze the call's intrinsic value at the deal price, eliminating upside. A stock split adjusts the contract non-standardly if the ratio is not 2:1 or 3:1.	Check CBOE.com for pending adjustments on the ticker. Confirm no merger rumor or announcement. Confirm no split announcement within the option's expiration window.
2	**Bullish High IV — Covered Call / CSP**	A special dividend reduces the strike price on ex-date, changing your P&L math. An ITM covered call faces early assignment risk if the dividend exceeds remaining extrinsic value.	Check ex-dividend date. If dividend is upcoming and call is ITM, calculate: is extrinsic value > dividend? If not, close or roll the call before ex-date. Never hold an ITM covered call through a large special dividend.
3	**Bearish Low IV — Long Put / Bear Put Spread**	A cash merger sets a price floor on the underlying — the stock will not fall below the acquisition price. Your put or put spread loses its value if the stock is acquired at a price above your strike.	Before buying puts on any underlying, confirm there is no pending acquisition at a price above your put strike. A stock being acquired at $95 means a $90 put is permanently worthless — the stock will not go there.
4	**Bearish High IV — Bear Call Spread ONLY**	An unexpected acquisition at a price above your short call strike forces your spread to maximum loss. Post-announcement, the stock does not retrace — it stays at deal price.	This is the highest adjusted-options risk for this strategy. Always screen for M&A rumors before selling a bear call spread. If an acquisition is announced after you open the spread and the stock gaps above your short strike, close immediately — the spread will not recover.
5	**Range-bound Low IV — Butterfly / Iron Condor**	A stock split on either boundary of your condor changes the strike values of all contracts simultaneously. Non-standard splits (3:2) make the Greeks on your wings unreliable.	Confirm no split announcement within the expiration window. On a 2:1 split the condor adjusts cleanly. On a 3:2 split, the contracts are non-standard and the condor's risk profile must be recalculated manually.
6	**Range-bound High IV — Calendar / Diagonal**	A merger or acquisition eliminates the price movement the calendar spread depends on. A stock locked at deal price has no IV, no movement, and no theta differential between legs.	Calendar and diagonal spreads require ongoing price movement to generate profit. A company in an announced deal becomes a static price. Close all calendar and diagonal spreads immediately on any merger announcement.

Spinoff Events: The Fourth Adjusted Options Risk Category

A corporate spinoff occurs when a parent company separates a subsidiary into an independent publicly traded entity, distributing shares of the new company to existing shareholders on a defined record date. From an options perspective, spinoffs are one of the most disruptive corporate events: existing options contracts on the parent stock can become adjusted to deliver a combination of parent shares AND spinoff company shares, fundamentally changing the position's risk profile. Greeks become unreliable, bid-ask spreads widen dramatically, and your broker's automated risk calculations may use incorrect assumptions.

The four categories of adjusted options risk that every pre-trade checklist must address are now: (1) Earnings events — binary outcomes that can gap the stock far beyond any short strike; (2) Merger and acquisition activity — which can cause options to misprice instantly at announcement; (3) Ex-dividend dates — where early assignment risk on ITM short calls destroys the income trade; and (4) Spinoff events — where the deliverable changes and the position becomes unmanageable. All four must be checked before every new entry. Not three. Four.

SPINOFF AVOIDANCE RULE

If a company you are trading announces a spinoff with a record date within your current options cycle — exit all positions immediately. Do not roll. Do not wait for clarity on the adjusted deliverable. Exit and move to a different underlying. Spinoffs routinely catch experienced traders off guard because they occur with shorter advance notice than earnings calendars provide. Check SEC EDGAR filings and company investor relations pages for any pending spinoff disclosure before entering any new position on any single-stock underlying.

THE PRE-TRADE ADJUSTED OPTIONS CHECK — 30 SECONDS

Before opening any position on any of the six strategies: (1) Go to www.cboe.com and check the adjustment memo for the ticker. (2) Check your brokerage for any corporate action notices on the underlying. (3) Confirm the option symbol has no suffix (XYZ1, XYZW = adjusted — do not trade). If any flag appears, find a different underlying. The pre-trade check costs you thirty seconds. An adjusted option discovery after you are already in the position can cost you weeks of premium income.

Building Your Personal Strategy Document

Your personal strategy document is not a trading plan in the generic sense. It is a precision instrument — specific to your account size, your approved options tier, your available trading hours, and your psychological profile. It answers the questions that the market will ask you every single day.

- What is my primary strategy? (e.g., CSP income on large-cap stocks with IVR > 40, 30–45 DTE, 0.20 delta — this is the engine of my account);
- What is my secondary strategy? (e.g., bull call spreads on sector ETF leaders in confirmed rotation — this is how I deploy excess capital in trending conditions);
- What market conditions will I NOT trade in? (e.g., I do not open new positions within 5 days of FOMC meetings or earnings announcements on any position in my account);
- What is my maximum number of open positions at any time? (e.g., maximum 5 simultaneous positions — concentration protects my attention and my capital);
- What is my weekly and monthly income target? (e.g., 2–3% monthly on deployed capital — realistic, sustainable, compounding); and

- What is my maximum monthly drawdown before I stop trading and review? (e.g., if I lose more than 8% in a single month, I stop trading, review every open position, and do not open new trades until I understand what happened).

The Professional Edge: What Separates Lasting Traders

After everything in this book — the Greeks, the strategies, the frameworks, the SCR system, the Wheel — the lasting traders all share the same set of non-negotiable habits. These are not strategies. They are operating principles.

Principle	What It Looks Like in Practice
Protect capital above all else	Never risk money you cannot afford to lose. The first rule every session. The last rule before every trade.
Trade with a written plan	Every trade has a written entry thesis, profit target, stop loss, and position size before the order is submitted. No exceptions.
Manage with discipline	50% profit? Close it. Stop triggered? Close it. No negotiating with the rules you wrote when you were calm.
Journal every trade	Entry, exit, thesis, Greeks at entry, outcome, lesson. The journal is where mediocre traders become excellent ones.
Review weekly	Every Sunday: review open positions, upcoming catalysts, IVR environment, market condition framework. You are running a business — conduct yourself as the CEO of it.
Learn continuously	Markets evolve. Algo behavior changes. Volatility regimes shift. The trader who stops learning stops having edge. Commit to ongoing education as a permanent operating cost.
Separate trading from identity	A losing week does not make you a bad trader. A winning week does not make you a genius. The system's results over hundreds of trades is the only valid performance measure.
Do love the game	The traders who last are the ones who genuinely love the intellectual challenge of the market. Not just the profits — the process. If you love the process, the profits follow.

You now have the complete framework. The markets are open every weekday. The opportunities are available to anyone with the knowledge, discipline, and capital to pursue them. The edge is not in the tools — it is in you. Work the system. Protect the capital. Trust the process.

The Trader Self-Assessment: Know Yourself Before You Trade

Before selecting strategies, honestly assess four dimensions of your trading profile. Each determines which strategies are structurally compatible with your life.

Dimension	Score 1 (Low)	Score 2-3	Score 4-5 (High)	Determines
Capital	Under $10K — spreads only	$10K-$50K — 3-5 positions, some CSPs	$50K+ — full toolkit including Wheel, Long/Short	Which strategies you can physically execute

Dimension	Score 1 (Low)	Score 2-3	Score 4-5 (High)	Determines
Time	Under 30 min/day — set-and-forget	30-60 min/day — manage income positions	2+ hours/day — active scanning, swing trading	How many positions you can manage
Risk Tolerance	5% loss causes stress	Can tolerate 10-15% drawdowns	Comfortable with 20%+ if thesis intact	Position sizing and hedge allocation
Experience	Under 50 live trades	50-200 trades, refining	200+ trades, survived a drawdown	Which strategies are safe for you

The Strategy Matching Matrix

Figure 22.3 — Strategy Matching Matrix: Six Conditions Mapped to Six Strategies

Condition	IV Environment	Primary Strategy	IVR Target	DTE Target
C1 – Bullish Low IV	IVR < 30	Long Call / Bull Call Spread	< 30	30-45 DTE
C2 – Bullish High IV	IVR > 50	CSP / Bull Put Spread	> 50	30-45 DTE
C3 – Bearish Low IV	IVR < 30	Long Put / Bear Put Spread	< 30	30-45 DTE
C4 – Bearish High IV	IVR > 50	Bear Call Spread	> 50	21-35 DTE
C5 – Neutral High IV	IVR > 50	Iron Condor / Short Strangle	> 50	30-45 DTE
C6 – Neutral Low IV	IVR < 30	Calendar Spread / Long Straddle	< 30	45-60 DTE

Figure 22.1 — Strategy Matching Matrix — Which strategy to deploy for each of the six market conditions at each account tier.

Strategy Matching Matrix — Which strategy to deploy for each of the six market conditions.

Your self-assessment scores map to compatible strategies. If ANY dimension is below the minimum, that strategy is not appropriate yet.

Strategy	Capital	Time	Risk	Experience
Vertical Spreads	1 — Any	1 — Minimal	1 — Any	1 — Beginner OK
Iron Condors	2 — $10K+	2 — 30 min	2 — Medium	2 — 50+ trades
Cash-Secured Puts	3 — $15K+	2 — 30 min	2 — Medium	2 — 50+ trades
The Wheel (CSP+CC)	3 — $20K+	2 — 30 min	3 — Med-High	3 — 100+ trades
Swing Trading	2 — $10K+	4 — 1-2 hrs	4 — High	3 — 100+ trades

Strategy	Capital	Time	Risk	Experience
Calendar / Diagonal	3 — $15K+	3 — 60 min	3 — Med-High	4 — 200+ trades
Long/Short Portfolio	5 — $50K+	5 — 2+ hrs	5 — High	5 — 200+ trades

Your weakest dimension is your binding constraint. A trader with $100K capital but only 30 trades of experience should NOT run Long/Short — the capital is there but the experience is not.

YOUR STRATEGY STATEMENT

Write this down: 'I am a [Capital score] / [Time score] / [Risk score] / [Experience score] trader. My compatible strategies are [list from matrix]. I will not trade above my level until I prove consistency for 90 consecutive days.' This prevents ambition from overriding capability.

The Five-Tier Drawdown Protocol: Systematic Response to Losing Periods

Every trader experiences drawdowns. The difference between surviving them and being destroyed by them is not luck — it is having a pre-written, rehearsed protocol that activates automatically when losses reach specific thresholds. This protocol removes decision-making from the most emotionally charged moments of your trading career.

Tier 1 — Normal Operating Drawdown (0-3% of account). This is business as usual. A 1-2% drawdown in any given week is expected and healthy. No action required beyond your standard management rules. Continue executing your plan. Do not reduce size. Do not skip planned entries. A 3% weekly drawdown should be logged in your journal with a brief note on the cause — was it market conditions, strategy selection, or execution error? The answer determines whether any adjustment is needed.

Tier 2 — Elevated Drawdown (3-5% of account in 30 days). Something is not working. The market may have shifted conditions without you recognizing it, or your recent entries may have violated your criteria. Action: review the last 10 trades against your entry checklist. If more than 2 violated criteria, the problem is discipline — activate the behavioral protocol. If all followed criteria, the problem is market fit — check whether the six-condition framework still supports your open strategies. Reduce new position entries by 50% until the drawdown stabilizes.

Tier 3 — Concerning Drawdown (5-8% of account in 30 days). This is no longer routine. Action: close your two weakest positions immediately (lowest conviction, highest risk). Increase your hedge allocation by 50%. Reduce position sizes on all remaining trades by 25%. Schedule a full portfolio review — not a quick check, a sit-down, two-hour analysis of every open position, every closed position from the past 30 days, and your market condition assessment. Something is structurally wrong and you need to find it.

Tier 4 — Serious Drawdown (8-12% of account in 60 days). This is a crisis. Action: close all directional positions. Keep only your highest-conviction income positions (max 2) with reduced size. Move to 50% cash. No new positions for 2 weeks minimum. During those 2 weeks, conduct a complete system audit: is your strategy still valid for current market conditions? Is your position sizing consistent with the 2% rule? Are your entry criteria working or have market dynamics changed? Return to trading only after completing the audit and developing a written recovery plan.

Tier 5 — Critical Drawdown (12%+ of account in any timeframe). Full stop. Close ALL positions. Move to 100% cash. Take one week completely off — no platform access, no market watching, no financial media. After one week, review your entire year of trading data. This level of drawdown indicates either a fundamental system failure, a major discipline breakdown, or an extraordinary market event. Before re-entering live trading, paper trade for 2-4 weeks to recalibrate your execution and rebuild confidence.

The protocol works because each tier is predetermined. When you are in a 10% drawdown, you are not making decisions — you are executing a plan you wrote when you were calm, rational, and not losing money. The plan does not feel right in the moment. It never does. That is exactly why it must be written in advance and followed without negotiation.

THE DRAWDOWN TRUTH

A 10% drawdown requires an 11.1% gain to recover. A 20% drawdown requires 25%. A 30% drawdown requires 42.9%. A 50% drawdown requires 100%. The math is merciless and asymmetric — losses are always easier to create than to recover from. This is why the drawdown protocol activates early (at 3%) rather than late (at 15%). By the time a drawdown feels serious, the recovery math has already turned against you. Protect capital. The profits will follow.

Manage Risk First. The Profits Will Follow.

The 90-Day New Trader Protocol

The first 90 days of live trading are the most important and most dangerous of your career. The account is small, the mistakes are inexpensive, but the habits formed in this period will define your trading psychology for years. Here is the specific protocol that gives new live traders the best foundation.

- Days 1–30: One position at a time, maximum. Open a single CSP on your highest-conviction, most liquid underlying. Manage it by the rules. Close it. Write the journal entry. Open the next one. Do not diversify before you have demonstrated you can manage one position correctly;
- Days 31–60: Maximum two simultaneous positions, in different sectors. Your only goal is executing two clean trades — entry, management, exit — with full rule compliance. Track the time you spend managing each position. If you are spending more than 15 minutes per day on two positions, your management process needs simplification;
- Days 61–90: Maximum three simultaneous positions. Begin running the monthly review framework from Chapter 23. By the end of day 90, you should have a baseline win rate, average P&L per trade, and one clear behavioral pattern you need to improve; and
- Go-live income target in Year 1: not a dollar amount. Your goal in Year 1 is a positive expectancy and a rule compliance rate above 85%. The dollar income is irrelevant — the system validation is everything.

The Drawdown Protocol: Specific Action Steps at Each Threshold

Every trader must have a written drawdown protocol before their account reaches a single penny of loss. Without a protocol, decisions made during drawdowns are made by the emotional brain — the part that specializes in panic, rationalization, and revenge trading. The drawdown protocol is your pre-commitment device: instructions written by your rational self for your future emotional self.

Drawdown Level	Label	Mandatory Actions — Non-Negotiable
−3% in a month	Yellow Alert	Review all open positions. Check for rule violations — did any trade deviate from your written entry criteria? No action required on compliant positions. Log the review in your journal.
−5% in a month	Orange Alert	Reduce maximum position count by one. Do not open any new positions until at least one current position is closed profitably or at the planned stop. Review IVR environment — if broad market IV has spiked, widen all short strikes on open positions.
−8% in a month	Red Alert — Pause	Stop opening new positions entirely. Manage existing positions to close — take 40% profit instead of 50% to accelerate exits. Once all positions are closed, conduct a full forensic review: every losing trade, what rule was broken or what environmental factor was misjudged. Do not re-open until review is complete.
−12% in a month	Full Stop	Close all positions immediately regardless of P&L status. Do not trade for 30 calendar days. Use the 30 days to paper trade the same strategy and verify the system is intact. If paper trading confirms the strategy is sound, resume live trading at 50% of previous position sizes.
−20% peak to trough (any period)	Capital Protection Protocol	This level of drawdown indicates either a fundamental strategy failure or an extreme market event (2020, 2008 type). Contact your broker, review your account tier and margin requirements, and do not re-enter the market until you have a written assessment of what happened and a specific change to prevent recurrence.

From Growth to Income: The Capital Transition Plan

Many traders arrive at income trading from growth trading — they have been running directional debit strategies, building their account with defined-risk bull and bear spreads, and now want to transition to the more consistent income model. This transition has a specific risk: applying growth trader psychology (tolerance for big swings, excitement-seeking, conviction-driven position sizing) to income strategies that require the opposite — patience, consistency, and indifference to individual outcomes.

Milestone	Growth Strategy Focus	Income Strategy Transition Signal
Capital: $5K–$20K	Long calls, long puts, debit spreads. Learn mechanics, build account. Directional bias is your primary skill.	Not yet ready for income strategies at meaningful scale. Continue growth trading. Begin paper trading CSPs.
Capital: $20K–$50K	Directional debit spreads as primary. Begin small CSP income positions (1–2 at a time) to build income trading	Allocate maximum 30% of capital to income strategies. Your primary returns still come from directional

Milestone	Growth Strategy Focus	Income Strategy Transition Signal
	experience alongside growth positions.	trades. Income trading is your training ground.
Capital: $50K–$100K	Balanced portfolio: 50% income strategies, 50% directional. The income base provides consistency while directional trades provide growth.	Begin treating income strategies as the core of your portfolio, not the experiment. Set a monthly income target and track it seriously.
Capital: $100K+	Income strategies as primary engine (70–80% of capital). Directional trades as secondary, sized at maximum 5% of account per position.	Full transition complete. You are an income trader. Growth trades are supplements, not the strategy. Your account's job is to generate monthly income — not to find the next big winner.

Performance Benchmarks: What Good Looks Like

Most traders have no objective benchmark for measuring whether they are performing well. They compare individual trades to perfect outcomes — the premium they left on the table by closing early, the gain they missed by not holding longer. These are the wrong benchmarks. The right benchmarks measure the system's performance over hundreds of trades and multiple market conditions.

Metric	Year 1 (Learning)	Year 2 (Developing)	Year 3+ (Proficient)
Win Rate	55–65% — learning to select quality setups	65–75% — consistent setup quality, better entries	70–80% — systematic approach producing repeatable results
Monthly Return on Capital	0.5–1.5% — early losses and learning costs	1.5–2.5% — system becoming reliable	2–3%+ — full system maturity with capital efficiency
Rule Compliance	70–80% — occasional emotional overrides	85–90% — strong discipline with rare lapses	95%+ — rules are habits, not reminders
Largest Single-Month Loss	Acceptable up to −8%	Acceptable up to −5%	Target max −3%; Red Alert at −5%
Average Win vs. Average Loss	Win = 2× loss — basic positive expectancy	Win = 2.5× loss — improving expectancy	Win = 3×+ loss — mature positive expectancy
Positions Closed at 50% Target	50–60% — learning to close early	70–80% — discipline developing	85%+ — systematic profit-taking is reflexive

The Mental Game: Handling Losing Streaks Without Abandoning the System

Every income trader will experience a losing streak. Three, four, five losing trades in a row — or a full month where every position seems to find the one outcome the strategy was designed to avoid. This is not evidence that the system is broken. It is the statistical reality of any probabilistic edge: even a strategy that wins 75% of the time will produce runs of 4–5 losses in a row with regular frequency.

The mental game during a losing streak has three phases, and each requires a different response:

- Phase 1 — The First Loss: No response needed. Review the trade for rule compliance. If rules were followed, log the outcome and move on. A single loss on a compliant trade is data, not diagnosis;
- Phase 2 — Two or Three Consecutive Losses: Review each trade individually for rule compliance and setup quality. If rules were followed on all of them, the streak is statistical — not structural. Reduce position size by 25% as a precautionary measure. Do not change the strategy; and
- Phase 3 — Four or More Consecutive Losses, or Monthly Drawdown Reaching Orange Alert: Initiate the drawdown protocol. Review whether market conditions have changed (VIX elevated, cycle phase shifting, macro catalyst introducing persistent directional pressure). Determine whether the strategy needs a temporary adaptation or whether you need to reduce exposure until conditions normalize.

The most dangerous response to a losing streak is the one that feels most intuitive: change the strategy. Traders who change their entry criteria, their management rules, or their underlying selection after a losing streak are fitting the system to recent outcomes — not to long-term statistical edge. The system was tested across many market conditions. A four-trade losing streak is not sufficient evidence to override that testing.

> **THE LOSING STREAK RULE**
>
> When you are in a losing streak, do less — not differently. Reduce position size. Increase selectivity. Tighten entry criteria temporarily. But do not change the fundamental structure of the strategy that was built and validated before the streak began. The trader who rebuilds their entire approach after every difficult period never accumulates the consecutive trade runs that produce compounding. Systems need time to express their edge. Give yours the time it earned.

The Six Conditions in Real Markets

How each of the six conditions appeared in actual market history — and what traders who recognized them made

---

The six-condition framework is not theoretical. Every single condition has appeared repeatedly in real market history — some multiple times in a single year. Learning to see them in hindsight trains your eye to recognize them in real time. The following case studies trace each condition through actual market events, showing the VIX level, the chart structure, the approved strategy, and the outcome for traders who executed it correctly.

These examples use SPY and QQQ as the primary underlyings because they offer the deepest liquidity, the most predictable behavior, and the purest expression of each condition. Individual stocks will show the same conditions — but index ETFs are where to learn the pattern recognition before applying it to single names.

CONDITION 1 — BULLISH + LOW IV

Strategy: Long Call / Bull Call Spread | Case Study: S&P 500 Recovery, November 2020 – December 2021

After the COVID crash lows of March 2020, markets entered one of the most sustained condition 1 environments in modern options trading history. SPY climbed from the $220s to $470 over 21 months. The VIX — which had spiked to 82 during the crash — fell steadily through 2021 and traded below 20 for much of the recovery, often dipping to 12–15 during the strongest uptrend phases.

The chart read was unambiguous: SPY made higher highs and higher lows every single month for 14 consecutive months from November 2020 through December 2021. The 50MA pulled well above the 200MA (a Golden Cross) in June 2020 and stayed there through 2021. Any trader running the two-step condition read every morning would have seen the same thing every day: direction UP, VIX LOW = Condition 1.

What the condition read showed	Approved strategy	What it produced
VIX: 16–19. SPY above 50MA and 200MA. Higher highs weekly. IVR: 18–25. Condition 1 confirmed every morning for months.	Long SPY calls (3–5% OTM, 30–45 DTE) or bull call spreads (buy $5–10 OTM, sell $10–15 OTM). Entered on any pullback to the 21-day EMA.	A December 2020 SPY $370/$380 bull call spread (SPY at $366) purchased for $3.20 would have been worth $10.00 by January expiration — a 212% return on a defined-risk trade. Every month offered similar setups as the trend continued uninterrupted.

CONDITION 1 LESSON

Condition 1 does not need to be predicted. It needs to be recognized and executed every day that it persists. Traders who built the discipline to run the condition read every morning through 2021 placed 12–15 monthly bull call spread trades in a straight uptrend — and were not tempted to sell premium into a low-IV bull run. They knew the condition. They ran the approved strategy. The trend did the rest.

CONDITION 2 — BULLISH + HIGH IV

Strategy: Cash-Secured Put / Bull Put Spread | Case Study: Post-Election Uncertainty, November 2016

November 2016 presented a textbook condition 2 environment. Following the U.S. presidential election, SPY had already been in a confirmed uptrend for months — but the election uncertainty caused VIX to spike to 22–25 in the week before election day, elevating IVR to 65–75 across most equity ETFs. The chart still showed SPY above its 200MA. The direction was bullish. The volatility was elevated.

Condition 2 confirmed: bullish trend + high IV. Approved strategy: Cash-secured put or bull put spread. Premium sellers who ran the condition read in the first week of November 2016 found themselves in the optimal income environment — the trend was in their favor (the put was unlikely to be tested) and elevated IV meant the premium they collected was at a meaningful level. The VIX contracted sharply the week after the election results, rewarding sellers with rapid IV crush profits on top of their theta decay.

Condition read	Approved strategy	Outcome
VIX: 22–25. IVR on SPY options: 68. SPY above 200MA. Uptrend intact. No earnings. Condition 2.	SPY $205 CSP (SPY at $213, 5.5% OTM), 30 DTE. Credit collected: $1.85 ($185/contract). Reserved capital: $20,500.	SPY rallied to $220 by expiration. Put expired worthless. Full $185 collected. PPD: $6.17/day. IV crush boosted the premium collapse — the put lost value faster than pure theta alone. 50% profit reached in 11 days.

CONDITION 2 LESSON

Uncertainty events — elections, Fed meetings, earnings seasons — are not dangers to premium sellers. They are gifts. Elevated VIX means elevated premium. The condition read tells you whether the uncertainty is occurring in a bullish or bearish backdrop. When the backdrop is bullish and IV is high, condition 2 gives you the single best risk/reward setup in options trading: selling puts in the direction of the trend at elevated premium levels.

CONDITION 3 — BEARISH + LOW IV

Strategy: Long Put / Bear Put Spread | Case Study: Tech Sector Correction, September 2020

September 2020 saw a sharp correction in the tech-heavy QQQ ETF — from $303 to $258 over 28 days, a 15% decline. Critically, this correction occurred with VIX remaining relatively contained below 30 (it started at 26 and only briefly touched 38 at the low before recovering). IVR was in the 30–40 range throughout — elevated but not extreme. The chart was clearly breaking down: QQQ made lower highs and lower lows every week of the correction. Below the 50MA. The trend was confirmed bearish.

The condition read: Direction DOWN + VIX in the 30–40 range. This was a condition 3/4 transition environment — close enough to condition 3 (bearish, lower IV) to justify debit put strategies, particularly bear put spreads to reduce cost. The approved strategy was the bear put spread: buy a put at or near the money, sell a lower put to offset cost.

Condition read	Trade structure	Outcome
VIX: 28–32. IVR: 35. QQQ below 50MA. Lower lows confirmed. Bearish thesis: tech rotation selling underway. Condition 3.	QQQ bear put spread: Buy $285 put / Sell $270 put. DTE 30. Net debit: $4.20 ($420 per contract). Max profit: $10.80 ($1,080 per contract) if QQQ below $270 at expiry.	QQQ closed at $262 at expiration — below the $270 short put. Max profit achieved: $1,080 on $420 debit. 157% return on defined risk. The bearish thesis confirmed by condition read. Direction paid the full spread width.

CONDITION 4 — BEARISH + HIGH IV

Strategy: Bear Call Spread ONLY | Case Study: Rate Hike Cycle, January–March 2022

The first quarter of 2022 is one of the clearest condition 4 environments in recent market history. The Fed began signaling aggressive rate hikes. SPY fell from $477 to $428, then to $416, making lower highs and lower lows throughout the quarter. The

VIX traded between 25 and 38 for the entire period — consistently elevated, never truly spiking to panic levels but never relaxing to calm. IVR was above 60 throughout January and February 2022.

This was condition 4 — bearish trend, high IV. The critical insight: this was NOT a condition for buying puts. IV at 25–38 meant put premiums were expensive. Buying expensive puts in a declining market feels intuitive — but it is the wrong strategy. The approved move was bear call spreads: sell elevated call premium above the market, buy protection further OTM, collect the credit. The trend keeps the stock below your short strike. The high IV delivers maximum credit on entry.

Condition read	Trade structure	Outcome
VIX: 28–35. IVR: 65. SPY below 50MA, below 200MA. Lower highs every two weeks. Confirmed bearish. Condition 4.	SPY bear call spread: Sell $460 call / Buy $470 call. DTE 35. SPY at $437. Credit: $1.45 ($145). Max risk: $855. Short strike 5.3% OTM.	SPY continued to fall — closed at $428 at expiration. Short call never threatened. Full $145 credit collected. 0% of max risk realized. IV contracted from 32 → 22 after Fed meeting, accelerating premium decay. Closed at 70% profit in 18 days.

CONDITION 4 LESSON — THE MOST IMPORTANT ONE

Condition 4 is the condition that separates disciplined six-condition traders from everyone else. In a falling market with elevated VIX, the most tempting trade is to buy puts. It feels right. The market is going down — buy downside protection. But high IV makes puts expensive, and buying expensive options in a declining market means IV crush destroys your profit even when you are right on direction. The approved trade — the bear call spread — earns the trend AND the IV contraction. Discipline over instinct, every time.

CONDITIONS 5 & 6 — RANGE-BOUND MARKETS

Iron Condor (Condition 5) / Calendar Spread (Condition 6) | Case Study: Mid-2023 S&P 500 Consolidation

After the strong recovery rally of early 2023, SPY entered an extended consolidation phase from late July through October 2023. During this period, SPY oscillated between approximately $420 and $450 — a 30-point ($30) range — for nearly 3 months. The 50MA flattened. The 200MA caught up. No new highs. No new lows. A textbook range-bound market.

The VIX during this period oscillated between 13 and 20 — elevated briefly in August (touching 18) but mostly calm. Condition 5 (range + low IV) was the dominant condition through July and early August. When VIX briefly rose above 18 with IVR pushing toward 50, condition 6 (range + moderate-high IV) emerged for short windows.

Condition	Trade Structure	Key Numbers	Outcome
Condition 5 Low IV / Range	SPY Iron Condor: Short $415 put / Long $410 put + Short $450 call / Long $455 call. DTE 30.	Net credit: $0.95. Range between $415–$450. VIX: 14. IVR: 22.	SPY stayed between $430 and $445 through expiration. All four legs expired worthless. $95 credit collected. Max risk never approached.

Condition 6 High IV / Range (brief window)	SPY Calendar Spread: Sell 30-DTE $438 call. Buy 60-DTE $438 call. Net debit: $2.10.	VIX spiked to 18. IVR hit 52 briefly in August. Near-term IV elevated vs. far-term.	Near-term call decayed 65% in 20 days as VIX contracted from 18 → 14. Closed calendar for $1.65 profit on $2.10 debit. 78% return in 20 days on the IV differential.

CONDITIONS 5 & 6 LESSON

Range-bound markets feel boring. They are not. They are the income seller's vacation — consistent, predictable premium collection with no directional risk. The iron condor earns from the market doing nothing. The calendar spread earns from the IV differential. Both strategies require one thing: a confirmed range. The BPI confirming flat sector breadth, Bollinger Bands squeezing, and the VIX below 20 — all pointing to conditions 5 or 6. Boring is profitable. Embrace it.

The condition is always there. The question is whether you are reading it.

Practice the two-step condition read every morning until it is automatic. The market tells you which of six conditions is active every single day.

PART IV

THE COMPLETE TRADER'S EDGE

FROM TRADER TO PORTFOLIO MANAGER

Parts I, II, and III built a trader. Part IV builds a portfolio manager. The distinction matters: a trader manages positions. A portfolio manager manages a book — the total architecture of all positions working together, each serving a specific role, each sized to the overall risk budget, each timed to the income cycle. Part IV is where the pieces connect into a complete professional system. You are no longer asking 'what is the best trade?' You are asking 'what is the right portfolio structure for the current market environment?' That is the complete trader's edge.

The edge is not complexity. It is identifying the condition and executing the single correct response — every time.

6-CONDITION FRAMEWORK ▸ CONDITIONS 2 & 4 — active management of short premium positions

Rollovers are the management tool for conditions 2 and 4. When a short premium position needs to be extended or adjusted, the rollover protocol — centered on the T-21 rule — keeps the income engine running without breaking the six-condition discipline.

Rolling a position is one of the most powerful — and most misunderstood — tools in the options trader's toolkit. Most traders discover rolling by accident: a position moves against them, expiration is approaching, and they scramble to extend the trade. Done reactively, rolling is a crutch. Done proactively, as a planned strategy, rolling is how professional income traders stay in winning positions longer, adjust their risk profile without closing trades, and extract maximum value from every position they open.

This chapter defines every type of roll, establishes the rules for when to roll vs. when to exit, and introduces the T-21 framework — the systematic approach to rolling that keeps you ahead of Gamma risk and in control of every position.

The T-21 Rule: The Rolling Trigger

T-21 means 21 days to expiration. It is the single most important date in every short premium position you will ever manage. Not the entry date. Not expiration. T-21. This is where the Seller's decision happens — and understanding exactly why this date was chosen, and not any other, is the difference between a trader who follows a rule and a trader who owns it.

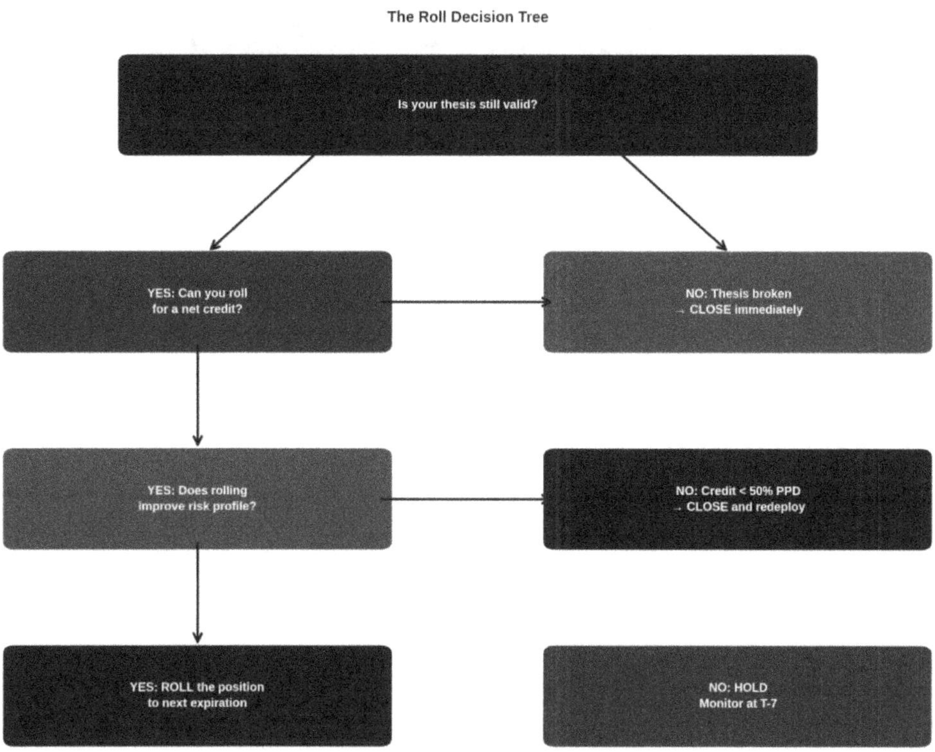

Figure 23.1 — The T-21 Roll Timeline. Entry, management windows, T-21 trigger, and exit zones.

First: Understand What the Theta Curve Actually Does

Theta decay — the daily erosion of time value from an option's price — is not a straight line. It is a curve. And that curve has three distinct phases that every income writer must understand before they can truly appreciate why T-21 is the Goldilocks window.

Phase	DTE Range	What Theta Is Doing	Daily Decay Rate	What This Means for the Seller
Phase 1 — Slow Burn	45 DTE to 30 DTE	Theta decaying slowly. Premium is still mostly intact. The soda bottle is barely touched.	\$0.05–\$0.08/day on a \$3.00 premium	You opened here. The position is working, but the real income has not arrived yet. This is setup, not harvest.
Phase 2 — Acceleration	30 DTE to 21 DTE	Theta accelerating. Each day removes more value than the day before. The bottle is being drunk steadily now.	\$0.10–\$0.18/day — doubling from Phase 1	This is the Seller's harvest zone. The position opened at 45 DTE is now paying its fastest daily return. This is why you opened here.

Phase	DTE Range	What Theta Is Doing	Daily Decay Rate	What This Means for the Seller
Phase 3 — Gamma Danger	21 DTE to 0	Theta still accelerating — but Gamma is now rising just as fast. A small stock move can produce a large position loss, wiping out the remaining premium and more.	Theta: $0.20+/day — but Gamma risk now rivals theta income	The remaining premium is a trap. The daily income looks attractive. The risk is not. Past T-21, you are no longer in the theta business — you are in the Gamma casino.

Read that table again. Phase 2 is green because it is where the Seller lives. Phase 3 is red because it is where the Seller gets hurt. T-21 is the exact boundary between them — the last moment the Seller is working the theta business before the Gamma business takes over uninvited.

The Three Windows: Too Early, Too Late, and Just Right

Young traders often ask: why not roll at T-30? Why not wait until T-10? The answer is in the math of each window. Each choice has a real cost — and only one of them puts the Seller in the optimal position on both sides of the roll simultaneously.

Roll Window	What You Gain	What You Lose	Verdict
Too Early — Roll at T-35 or T-30	You get into the next expiration early. Next month's premium is fresh and full.	You abandon Phase 2 — the fastest-decaying portion of your current position. You leave 30–40% of your maximum profit uncollected. The closing buy is expensive because the current position still has significant time value left.	✕ Inefficient. You are paying full price to exit a position that had more to give. Your net credit on the roll is compressed because the buy is costly.
Too Late — Roll at T-10 or T-7	Maximum premium captured from the current position. The last 10% of decay is yours.	Gamma is now dominant. A 2% move in the underlying can produce a 15–20% swing in your position value overnight. The next expiration's premium has also shrunk — you are rolling into a position with only 3–4 weeks left, not 4–5. And if the stock is near your strike, you may not be able to roll for a credit at all.	✕ Dangerous. The remaining premium does not compensate for the Gamma exposure. This is where income traders get surprised by losses they did not see coming.
Just Right — Roll at T-21	You have captured 50–65% of the original premium — the full Phase	The last 35–50% of the premium. But that last portion takes the longest	☑ Optimal. Your current position has done its job. The next expiration is 30–

Roll Window	What You Gain	What You Lose	Verdict
	1 and Phase 2 harvest. The closing buy is inexpensive because most of the value has already decayed.	to collect at the highest risk. It is not abandoned — it is deliberately left on the table as the price of Gamma protection.	35 DTE — priced at full value, entering its own Phase 2 window. You collect a fresh credit and reset the clock at the exact moment the risk/reward tips.

What a T-21 Roll Actually Looks Like: The Full Number Walk

Abstract concepts become real when you see the dollars. Here is the complete lifecycle of a $3.00 premium CSP opened at 45 DTE — showing exactly what the position is worth at each key date, why T-21 is the right moment to act, and what happens to the Seller who waits.

Day	DTE Left	Premium Left	Profit Captured	Daily Theta	Gamma Level	What the Seller Should Be Thinking
0 — Entry	45 DTE	$3.00 (100%)	$0 (0%)	~$0.04/day	Low	Opened the position. T-21 reminder set in calendar for Day 24. Mission: collect premium, manage at T-21.
Day 10	35 DTE	$2.55	$0.45 (15%)	~$0.05/day	Low	Position working. Theta slow but consistent. No action. The soda bottle is just starting to drain.
Day 17	28 DTE	$2.00	$1.00 (33%)	~$0.08/day	Low-Moderate	Theta accelerating. One-third of the premium captured. Still in Phase 1 tail / Phase 2 entry. No action.
Day 24 — T-21	**21 DTE**	**$1.35**	**$1.65 (55%)**	**~$0.12/day**	**Moderate — rising**	**T-21 reminder fires. 55% profit captured. This is the decision point. Evaluate: close for profit, or roll to next month for fresh credit? The position has done its job.**
Day 31	14 DTE	$0.90	$2.10 (70%)	~$0.15/day	High	If still holding: Gamma now rising sharply. A 1.5% adverse move in the stock produces a $0.25+ position swing — erasing two days of theta in one session.
Day 38	7 DTE	$0.45	$2.55 (85%)	~$0.18/day	Very High	If still holding: Gamma is now dominant. The daily theta income ($0.18) is now smaller than the potential daily Gamma loss on a moderate move. The math has flipped against the Seller.

Day	DTE Left	Premium Left	Profit Captured	Daily Theta	Gamma Level	What the Seller Should Be Thinking
Day 45 — Expiry	0 DTE	$0.00	$3.00 (100%)	$0	Maximum	Full premium collected — IF the stock stayed above the strike for 45 days without a single bad session in the final week. The last $0.45 took 7 days of maximum Gamma risk to collect.

The green row is T-21. The red rows are what happens to sellers who wait. Notice that collecting the final $1.35 — from T-21 to expiration — requires staying in the position through the period of highest Gamma risk, the period when a single bad news day on the underlying can erase that $1.35 and add a loss on top. The T-21 Seller captured $1.65 in 24 days. To collect the next $1.35, the waiting Seller needs 21 more days of a cooperative stock — and accepts Gamma risk that grows larger every single day.

THE T-21 MATH

At T-21 on a standard 45 DTE position, the Seller has captured approximately 50–60% of the maximum premium in the first 55% of the trade's life — during the lowest-risk phase. The remaining 40–50% of premium requires the final 45% of the trade's life — during the highest-risk phase. The Seller who closes at T-21 is not leaving money on the table. They are making an explicit, rational decision: the risk of the final 21 days is not worth the premium remaining. That is not timidity. That is the risk manager's calculation.

Why T-21 Is Also the Best Moment to Roll Into the Next Expiration

T-21 is not only the right time to exit — it is simultaneously the best moment to enter the next position. This is the insight that makes the T-21 roll so powerful: both sides of the transaction are optimized at the same time.

- Your current position's closing buy is cheap — with 55–60% of premium already decayed, the buy-to-close cost is $1.20–$1.40 on a $3.00 original premium. You are not paying full price to exit;
- The next expiration at 30–35 DTE is priced at full value — it is entering Phase 2, the acceleration zone, with maximum time value intact. You are selling into the fattest part of the next cycle;
- Your net roll credit is real — the difference between a cheap close and a full-premium open produces a meaningful net credit, not a marginal one. This is the Seller collecting income on both sides of a single transaction; and
- Your capital stays working — there is no gap between closing one position and opening the next. The roll is simultaneous. The PPD clock never stops.

Compare this to rolling at T-10: the closing buy is now expensive (only 30% of the premium has decayed), and the next expiration has only 25–28 DTE left — already past its entry sweet spot. The net credit on that roll is thin, the new position starts with less time to work, and the capital efficiency is degraded on both sides. T-21 is the only moment where both sides of the roll are simultaneously at their optimal pricing.

THE T-21 ROLL INSIGHT

Rolling at T-21 is not one decision — it is two decisions executing perfectly at the same time. Decision 1: close the current position while the buy-to-close is still cheap, having captured the best portion of the decay curve. Decision 2: open the next position while the next expiration's premium is at its fullest, entering a fresh Phase 2 window. Any other roll timing optimizes one side at the expense of the other. T-21 optimizes both. That is why it is the rule.

The T-21 Decision Framework: Close, Roll, or Exit?

When your T-21 calendar reminder fires, the decision is not automatic — it is systematic. Run through these three questions in order. Every time. No exceptions.

#	Question at T-21	If Yes	If No
1	Is my original thesis still valid? Is the stock fundamentally sound, above key support, and behaving as expected?	Proceed to Question 2. The trade has a valid reason to continue.	Close the position immediately. Do not roll a broken thesis. Take the profit or loss that exists today and redeploy capital into a trade with a valid thesis.
2	Have I captured at least 50% of the original premium?	Either close for profit OR roll to next month for fresh credit — both are correct outcomes. Your choice depends on market conditions and PPD comparison.	Roll to next expiration immediately — same or lower strike — for a net credit. You need more time for this position to reach profitability. The roll buys that time while adding to your total chain credit.
3	Can I roll for a net credit of at least $0.25 after all transaction costs?	Execute the roll. Close the current position and open the next month's position simultaneously as a single order. Set a new T-21 reminder immediately.	Close the position regardless of profit/loss. A roll that generates no credit means the market is not paying you to extend this position. Redeploy the capital where the market will pay you.

- At T-21, evaluate each short position: How much of the premium have you captured? (Target: 50% minimum);
- If less than 50% profit: roll to the next cycle immediately — collect fresh premium and reset the clock;
- If 50–75% profit: close the position and redeploy in a new trade at the current market environment;
- If above 75% profit: close immediately — the last 25% is not worth the Gamma risk in the final 21 days; and
- T-21 is a rule, not a suggestion. The market does not care that you want to hold for the last few dollars.

T-21 MANAGEMENT RULE

Every short premium position should have a T-21 calendar reminder set at entry — the moment the trade is placed, before you even confirm the order. When that reminder fires, you stop what you are doing and evaluate. Not after lunch. Not tomorrow morning. Now. The T-21 window is where the Seller's discipline lives. Miss it consistently and you will find yourself managing positions in the Gamma danger zone, reacting instead of deciding, and wondering why your results don't match your system. Set the reminder. Honor the reminder. That is the entire rule.

The Six Types of Rolls

Roll Type	What Changes	When to Use	Net Effect
Roll Out	Expiration only — same strike, move to next month	At T-21, position is profitable, thesis still valid. Extend the trade without changing the strike.	Collect additional credit. Reset theta decay clock. Same directional risk.
Roll Up	Strike only — higher strike (calls), same expiration	Short call position — stock has risen above or near your short strike. Adjust upward to stay OTM.	May be done for debit or small credit. Reduces assignment risk. Gives stock more room.
Roll Down	Strike only — lower strike (puts), same expiration	Short put position — stock has fallen toward your short strike. Roll lower to widen your cushion.	Usually done for a credit. Increases cash required. Accepts more downside risk for more premium.
Roll Up and Out	Both strike and expiration — higher strike, next month	Covered call: stock running above your short call. Capture some upside AND collect more time premium.	Collects credit. Maintains the position. Lets you participate further in the rally.
Roll Down and Out	Both strike and expiration — lower strike, next month	Short put near breach: stock fell toward strike with time remaining. Buy to close and open next month at lower strike.	Collect additional credit. Lower strike = more margin of safety. Resets T-21 clock.
Roll for Debit	Moves to a significantly better position at a net cost	Rarely used in income trading. Justified when the strike being threatened is critical to avoid assignment.	Pay a net debit to improve the position. Only makes sense if the improvement in risk profile justifies the cost.

Rolling as a Strategy vs. an Afterthought

There is a critical distinction between rolling as a proactive strategy and rolling as a panic response. When rolling is planned — when you define your roll criteria at the time of entry, just like your profit target and stop loss — it becomes a legitimate extension of your trade management system. When rolling is reactive — when you roll to avoid taking a loss — it often compounds the problem.

- Proactive roll (strategy): At entry, you write down: 'If this position reaches T-21 with less than 50% profit, I will roll to next month at the same strike or lower for a credit.' This is a planned outcome;
- Reactive roll (afterthought): The position has moved against you significantly. You are underwater. You roll to next month hoping the stock reverses. This is not a strategy — it is extending a losing thesis without re-evaluating whether it is still valid;

- The roll test: before rolling any losing position, ask — 'If I were starting fresh today with no position, would I open this trade at this strike?' If the answer is no, do not roll. Close and redeploy capital more efficiently;
- Maximum rolls: do not roll the same position more than twice. Three rolls on the same underlying signals that the thesis was wrong. Each additional roll increases total risk and ties up capital that could be deployed more productively;

Deep ITM → ATM Double Quantity: Putting Profits to Work

This is an advanced roll technique for situations where you have accumulated significant profit in a deep in-the-money long position and want to extract capital while increasing your position's return potential. The mechanic: close a deep ITM long call (which is now mostly intrinsic value, little time value), extract the profit from intrinsic value, and redeploy into a larger quantity of ATM calls at the same or later expiration.

- Example: You hold 2 deep ITM calls on XYZ with $15 of intrinsic value each = $3,000 total value. You close them and open 4 ATM calls at $8 premium each = $3,200 cost. You now hold 4× the directional exposure for roughly the same capital;
- Why ATM vs. ITM: ATM calls have maximum gamma — they respond most aggressively to further stock movement. Deep ITM calls move dollar-for-dollar (like stock) but carry large capital commitment per contract with limited leverage;
- Capital extraction: if your original position has grown to 3× its cost, you can sell half the position to extract your original capital and run the remaining position 'for free' — risk is now zero on the house money; and
- Risk: ATM calls have pure extrinsic value — they decay to zero if the stock does not continue moving. This is a high-conviction continuation trade, not a risk-free upgrade.

Rolling by Strategy: CSP vs. Covered Call vs. Iron Condor

Not all rolls are created equal. The mechanics — and the rules governing when to roll — differ significantly by strategy type. Applying the same roll logic to every position is one of the most expensive habits in options income trading.

Rolling a Cash-Secured Put

The CSP is the most forgiving position to roll because it has a defined directional thesis: you are bullish or neutral with willingness to own the stock. When rolling a CSP, you are extending that thesis — so the first question is always whether the thesis is still valid.

Situation	Roll Type	Exact Mechanic & Credit Target
T-21, 30–45% profit, thesis intact	Roll Out (same strike, next month)	Buy to close current put. Sell next month's same strike. Target: new credit ≥ 50% of original premium collected.
T-21, 15–30% profit, stock drifted lower	Roll Down and Out	Buy to close. Sell next month at a strike $2–5 lower. Target: net credit of at least $0.25 after the closing debit. Wider cushion.

Situation	Roll Type	Exact Mechanic & Credit Target
Stock within 3% of short strike, 10+ DTE remaining	Roll Down and Out immediately — do not wait for T-21	Execute before the stock reaches your strike. Every day you wait increases Gamma risk and worsens the roll credit available.
Stock has breached your strike — you are ITM	Roll Down and Out for credit if available; accept assignment if not	If a credit roll exists: take it. If not, compare the cost of a debit roll against the unrealized loss of accepting assignment. Run the numbers — do not guess.
Already rolled once and still threatened	Close and redeploy — do not roll again	Two rolls on the same position is the maximum. The third roll is hope masquerading as strategy. Close. Take the lesson. Redeploy capital.

Rolling a Covered Call

The covered call roll has a unique challenge: your stock may be running away from you. When the stock rises above your short call strike, you face a choice between accepting assignment (selling the stock at your strike) or rolling the call higher to keep participating in the rally. This is the decision where traders most often let emotion override discipline.

- Assignment is not a loss. If your covered call is called away at the strike, you collect the premium AND the stock appreciation up to that strike. That is a successful outcome — not a mistake to fix;
- Roll up and out only when: (a) the roll generates a net credit after the closing debit, AND (b) the stock is above a confirmed technical breakout level on strong volume — not just a one-day spike; and
- The cost math on rolling up: if moving from a $50 to $55 strike costs $0.50 net debit, you are paying $50 per contract for $5.00 of additional upside potential. That bet only pays off if the stock actually reaches $55. If it reverses, you paid the debit and still get called away below it.

COVERED CALL ROLL RULE

Never roll a covered call for a net debit unless the stock has broken out of a multi-month base on high volume and the fundamental thesis has meaningfully strengthened. Rolling for a debit because you 'don't want to miss the rally' is one of the most common ways traders erode the income advantage of covered call writing. When in doubt — let it be called away. The capital is yours to redeploy immediately.

Rolling an Iron Condor

The iron condor roll is the most complex because you have two short strikes to manage simultaneously. When the stock moves strongly in one direction, one side becomes threatened while the other side is deep OTM. The wing adjustment — rolling only the threatened side — is the defining skill of condor management.

Condor Situation	What to Roll	Exact Action
Short call threatened — delta above 0.30	Roll call side up and out. Leave put side alone.	Buy to close the entire call spread (both legs). Sell to open new call spread at higher strikes in next month. Target:

Condor Situation	What to Roll	Exact Action
		new credit on call spread offsets the closing debit.
Short put threatened — delta above 0.30	Roll put side down and out. Leave call side alone.	Buy to close the entire put spread (both legs). Sell to open new put spread at lower strikes in next month. Same credit-targeting logic.
Threatened side approaching 2× original credit collected	Close the entire condor. Do not roll.	When one side reaches max loss, rolling extends bad exposure. Close the full position, accept the loss, and reassess whether the underlying is suitable for a condor at all.
Both sides threatened simultaneously — breakout move	Close the entire condor immediately.	A condor challenged on both sides means volatility exploded well beyond your original range thesis. This is a close-and-reassess, not an adjust.

The Roll Chain: Tracking Net Credits Across Multiple Rolls

Professional income traders do not evaluate each roll in isolation. They track the total net credit collected across all rolls of the same position — the roll chain. The roll chain tells you whether you are actually profitable when you account for every debit paid and credit received across the life of a trade.

Roll #	Action	Strike / Expiry	Credit/(Debit)	Running Net	Status
0 — Open	Sell CSP	$175 put / Jan 17	+$3.20	$3.20	Entry. AAPL at $195. IVR 64.
—	AAPL dips to $182. T-21 reached. 38% profit captured.				Roll triggered.
1	Buy Jan $175, Sell Feb $172	$172 put / Feb 21	+$0.65 net	$3.85	Roll Down + Out. Wider cushion. Fresh 35-day clock.
—	AAPL stabilizes at $186. Feb position reaches 55% profit.				Target hit.
— Close	Buy to close Feb $172 put	At $0.80	(−$0.80)	$3.05 final P&L	+$305 on $17,200 reserved. 1.8% return, ~55 days.

The individual roll looked like a small $0.65 credit — barely worth the commissions. In context of the full chain, it transformed a 38% partial winner into a complete 55%-profit close at a more conservative strike. That is the compounding power of systematic roll management.

Journal rule: log every roll as a continuation of the same trade row, not as a new trade. Your P&L on the chain is what matters — not the P&L of any single leg.

Three Roll Scenarios — Complete Walk-Throughs

Scenario A — The Clean Roll (Proactive, Profitable)

Setup: MSFT at $430. You sell the $400 CSP, 35 DTE, for $4.10. IVR 62. Stock drifts to $415 over 14 days — position at 42% profit. T-21 arrives. Thesis intact: MSFT above all major MAs, no earnings for 40 days.

- Action: Buy to close Jan $400 put at $2.40. Sell Feb $395 put at $3.05. Net credit on the roll: +$0.65;
- New position: $395 put — now 7.5% OTM instead of 6.9%. More cushion. 35-day clock reset;
- Outcome: Feb $395 put reaches 50% profit in 18 days. Close at $1.52. Total chain P&L: $4.10 − $2.40 + $3.05 − $1.52 = $3.23 ($323/contract). Clean, systematic, repeatable;

Scenario B — The Defensive Roll (Stock Moving Against You)

Setup: ETSY at $70. You sell the $60 CSP, 30 DTE, for $2.20. Stock drops to $64 in 12 days — delta has expanded to 0.28. You are now at 12 DTE — T-21 has already passed. This roll is defensive, not proactive.

- Position now worth $1.85 — only 16% of premium captured. The T-21 window was missed when the stock was at $67 and the roll would have been much cleaner;
- Best available roll: close $60 put at $1.85, sell $55 put next month at $2.10. Net credit: $0.25. Marginal — barely covers transaction costs;
- But: holding through the final 12 days with delta expanding toward a threatened strike risks a much larger loss. The marginal roll is still the correct call;
- The lesson in Scenario B is not the roll decision — it is the missed T-21. The same roll at T-21 would have generated a $0.80+ credit. Systematic management creates better options at every decision point;

Scenario C — The No-Roll Close (When Rolling is Wrong)

Setup: RIVN at $16. You sell the $12 CSP, 35 DTE, for $1.80. RIVN drops 22% to $12.50 on a negative earnings miss and production guidance cut. Position now worth $2.40 — a $60 unrealized loss. DTE: 17 days.

- Temptation: roll down and out to the $10 put next month for a small credit and hope for a recovery;
- The roll test applied: If you had no position right now, would you open a new CSP on RIVN — a company that just missed earnings, cut production guidance, and broke a major technical support level? No;
- Correct action: Close at $2.40. Net loss: $0.60 per share ($60/contract). Finite and knowable; and
- Why the roll is wrong: rolling extends exposure to a stock whose fundamental thesis has changed. The original thesis was RIVN stable above $16. It is not. Rolling to $10 bets on a company in distress stabilizing further down — with

more capital reserved, more time at risk, and weaker fundamentals than when you entered.

Two Live Roll Examples: Offensive and Defensive

The following two rolls were executed from a live account within the same month. One is an offensive roll — locking in profit while staying in a winning trend. The other is a defensive roll — converting a losing position into a profitable one. Both use the same roll mechanics. The difference is the reason for rolling and the strike selection.

VERIFIED ROLL 1 — MU $310 CALL: OFFENSIVE ROLL (PROFIT EXTRACTION)

- January 5, 2026 — Entry: Buy 2 MU $310 Calls, Feb 20 expiration, at $30.10 avg. Total cost: $6,020. MU trading near $315 — near-the-money entry, Condition 1, AI/HBM momentum confirmed.
- February 19, 2026 — 45 days later: MU has rallied to ~$420. The $310 Call is worth $104.25. The position has gained +246% on premium.
- Instead of closing — ROLL: Sell $310 Call at $104.25 → +$20,850 credit (2 contracts). Buy $390 Call at $48.70 → −$9,740 cost (2 contracts).
- Net credit extracted: $11,110. Realized profit on $310 leg: +$15,065 (+260.42%).
- Position kept alive: $390 Call Mar 20 now open at a net credit.
- Result: The roll extracted $11,110 in net credit while maintaining full exposure to continued MU upside. The thesis was intact. The position continued.

VERIFIED ROLL 2 — IBRX: DEFENSIVE ROLL (LOSS CONVERSION)

- January 20, 2026 — Entry: Buy 1 IBRX Feb 20, 2026 $4.5 Call at $3.30. Total cost: $330.
- February 6, 2026 — Position under pressure: IBRX has moved against the position. The $4.5 Call is now worth only $1.47 — a −55% loss on premium.
- Defensive Roll: Sell Feb 20 $4.5 Call at $1.47 → +$147 credit. Buy Mar 20 $4.5 Call at $1.78 → −$178 cost. Net roll cost: $31. Position kept alive at dramatically lower premium.
- March 19, 2026 — Recovery: IBRX has recovered. The Mar 20 $4.5 Call is worth $4.10. Sell to close.
- Roll leg P&L: +$232 (+130.3%). Net position after full roll: +$49 — PROFITABLE.
- A −55% losing position, rolled defensively, converted to a net profitable outcome. That is the roll defense in action.

These two rolls illustrate the complete spectrum of roll mechanics. The MU roll was proactive — take extraordinary profits off the table, reduce cost basis to zero, stay in the trend. The IBRX roll was reactive — stop the bleeding at a manageable level, extend the runway, wait for the thesis to play out. In both cases the outcome was superior to simply closing the position when the moment of maximum pressure arrived.

This example reflects a real trade executed and recorded in real time.

The Earnings Trap: The Roll You Must Never Make

One of the costliest roll mistakes in income trading is rolling a short premium position into an expiration window that contains an earnings announcement. Traders do it for two reasons: the elevated pre-earnings IV makes the roll credit look attractive, or they are managing a losing position and the higher premium helps the math look better. Both are traps.

When you roll into an earnings expiration, you are no longer managing a premium-selling strategy. You are running a binary event trade — with premium collected as your entire buffer against a potentially unlimited gap move. A stock can gap 15–25%

through your strike on earnings in a single overnight session, eliminating months of accumulated premium instantly.

- The rule: never roll into an expiration that contains an earnings announcement for the underlying. Verify the earnings date before selecting every roll target expiration;
- The fix: if the nearest available expiration contains earnings, roll to the expiration after it — even if it means collecting less credit. A smaller, safer roll is always better than a larger roll into a binary event; and
- The exception: if you specifically intend to trade the earnings event as a defined-risk structure, set it up as a fresh trade with explicit earnings sizing rules. Do not slide into it accidentally through a defensive roll.

THE EARNINGS ROLL TRAP

The premium that makes the earnings-window roll look attractive is precisely the premium that prices in the large expected move — the move that will happen. Collecting elevated pre-earnings IV on a short premium position is not edge; it is the risk. Check the earnings calendar before every roll. Every single time. This rule has no exceptions.

The Seven Most Common Roll Mistakes

#	Mistake	Why Traders Make It	The Fix
1	Waiting until deep ITM before rolling	Avoidance — hoping the stock reverses	T-21 calendar alert at entry. Act on the alert, not on panic.
2	Rolling for a net debit	The new position looks better on paper	Only roll for a minimum net credit of $0.25. Debit rolls require explicit justification.
3	Rolling the same position three or more times	Sunk cost fallacy — too much invested to close	Maximum two rolls per position. Third roll = close and redeploy.
4	Rolling into an earnings expiration	Pre-earnings IV makes the credit look attractive	Verify earnings calendar before every roll. Never roll into an earnings window.
5	Rolling only one leg of an iron condor — leaving the other at a different DTE	Mismatched position becomes unmanageable	When rolling an IC, close the entire spread and re-open both sides simultaneously in the new expiration.
6	Rolling to an expiration that is too short — 2 to 3 weeks	Immediate re-management pressure	Roll to at least 30–35 DTE on the new position. You need time value to justify the reset.
7	Not tracking net credit across the roll chain	Each roll looks profitable in isolation; the full chain is not	Maintain a roll chain log in your journal: every debit and credit from open to final close.

PPD: The Roll Decision's True Arbiter

Most roll decisions are made on credit alone: 'Can I collect at least $0.25 on this roll?' That is a necessary condition but not a sufficient one. The question that actually determines whether a roll is worth making is whether the PPD (Profit Per Day) on the new rolled position exceeds the PPD you could achieve by closing and redeploying into a fresh trade.

Stage	DTE Window	Action	Rule
1 — Entry Zone	30–45 DTE	Open position; collect premium.	Enter only with condition confirmed.
2 — Watch Zone	22–30 DTE	Monitor P&L; no action needed.	Let theta work; ignore noise.
3 — T-21 Trigger	21 DTE	Evaluate: at 50% profit? Close. If not, roll.	T-21 Rule: at 21 DTE, position at profit close or evaluate roll for credit.
4 — Final Week	0–7 DTE	Close or let expire. Avoid pin risk.	Never hold through expiration unless fully OTM with no risk.

Figure 23.2 — The Roll Decision Tree. Close, roll, or exit — a systematic decision framework.

A roll that looks attractive on a credit basis can be a PPD destroyer — extending capital in a position that is generating a fraction of what a fresh, well-selected trade would produce. Conversely, a roll with a modest credit on a fast-decaying short strike can outperform redeployment on a PPD basis because the time already elapsed has 'seasoned' the position.

The Roll vs. Redeploy PPD Calculation

Before executing any roll, run this comparison:

Option A — Roll the Position	Option B — Close and Redeploy
Net credit received on the roll: $0.65	Premium available on best new trade: $3.20
New position DTE: 35 days	New position DTE: 35 days
PPD on roll: $0.65 ÷ $17,500 ÷ 35 = 0.011%/day	PPD on new trade: $1.60 ÷ $17,500 ÷ 18* = 0.051%/day
Capital stays committed for 35 more days	Capital freed immediately, redeployed at full PPD
Roll PPD is 78% lower than fresh trade PPD	Redeployment PPD is 4.6× better than rolling

* Estimated days to 50% profit on the new trade.

In this example, rolling produces a PPD of 0.011%/day — barely above zero. Closing and redeploying produces 0.051%/day. The roll feels 'free' because you are only collecting $0.65 to extend the position — but you are locking $17,500 of capital into a 35-day commitment that generates a fraction of what a fresh trade would produce. The credit is real; the opportunity cost is larger.

When is rolling the better PPD choice? When the new roll strike is meaningfully higher in premium relative to what the market offers in fresh trades, or when the underlying has moved in your favor and the rolled position now sits further OTM than any fresh trade you could open at a comparable delta. In practice: run the numbers before every roll. The math tells you which choice is actually better for your portfolio.

THE PPD ROLL RULE

Before rolling any position, calculate: PPD of the roll credit vs. PPD of your best available fresh trade. If the roll PPD is less than 50% of your fresh trade PPD, close and redeploy — the roll is destroying capital efficiency. If the roll PPD is within 80% of fresh trade PPD, the roll may be justified by position continuity, tax considerations, or thesis conviction. Make the comparison explicit. Never roll on credit alone.

→ See Figure 6.4 — Moneyness Ladder: Put Contract (Chapter 4 — Options Valuation)

Figure 23.3 — Moneyness Ladder: Put Contract. For puts, the relationship is inverted — strikes above the stock price are ITM, strikes below are OTM.

THE ROLL DECISION TREE

Ask in sequence: (1) Is my thesis still valid? (2) Can I roll for a net credit? (3) Will rolling improve my risk profile? (4) Have I already rolled this position once? If any answer is no — close the position. Rolling is a tool for extending good trades, not for rescuing bad ones.

6-CONDITION FRAMEWORK ▸ CONDITIONS 1, 2, 5, 6 — advanced architecture for premium buyers and sellers

Layering and convexity engineering are available in any condition — but they are most powerful in conditions 1 (amplified upside), 2 (stair-layered income), 5 and 6 (time-decay laddering). They magnify the advantage of your condition read.

The stair-layered approach and convexity planning represent the next level of options strategy sophistication — moving beyond single-entry, single-exit trades into architectured position structures that generate torque on winning moves while preserving capital on adverse ones. These are the techniques used by professional options desks and institutional traders to create asymmetric payoff profiles: limited downside, amplified upside.

You do not need to master these concepts on Day 1. But once you have 50–100 trades of experience with the foundational strategies in this book, layering and convexity become the upgrades that significantly increase your return per unit of risk.

Stair-Layered Convexity — How layered entries create asymmetric reward as the trade moves in your favor.

The Stair-Layered Approach: Building Positions Gradually

The stair-layered approach means entering a position in multiple tranches — at different strikes, different expirations, or both — rather than committing your full position size at a single entry point. Each tranche is a 'step' in the staircase, added as the trade thesis confirms itself through price action.

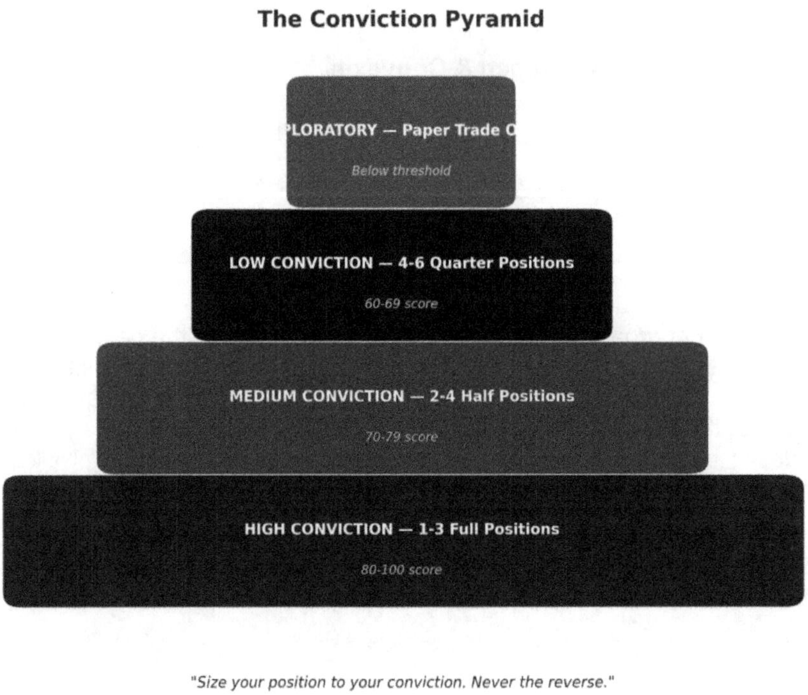

Figure 24.2 — The Conviction Pyramid. Position size scales with score — never the reverse.

- Layer 1 — Initial entry at 25–33% of your planned full position size. You are testing the thesis. If the trade moves against you immediately, your exposure is small;
- Layer 2 — Add 25–33% when the trade confirms: the stock moves in your direction, technical signals strengthen, or the first layer reaches 25% profit. You are now averaging into a winning position, not a losing one; and
- Layer 3 — Final addition at 33–50% when the trade has strong confirmation: multiple signals align, sector rotation is confirmed, or the position is up 40–50%. Your full position is now on, but your average cost is improved because you added into strength.

The critical rule: layers are added only when the trade is winning, never when it is losing. Adding to a losing position — 'averaging down' — is not stair-layering. It is hope disguised as strategy. The staircase goes up with the trade, not down against it.

Strike Laddering: Multiple Strikes, Same Thesis

Strike laddering uses the same directional thesis but spreads exposure across multiple strikes to create a graduated payoff structure. Instead of selling one CSP at the $90 strike, you sell multiple positions at $95, $90, and $85 — each generating income, each with a different breakeven and probability profile.

Layer	Strike	Delta	Premium/Contract	Role in the Structure
Layer 1	$95 Put	0.30 delta	$3.50 ($350)	Highest probability. Closest to money. Collects most premium. First line of income.

Layer	Strike	Delta	Premium/Contract	Role in the Structure
Layer 2	$90 Put	0.20 delta	$2.00 ($200)	Medium probability. 10% buffer from stock. Second income layer at a more conservative strike.
Layer 3	$85 Put	0.12 delta	$1.10 ($110)	Lowest probability. 15% buffer. Speculative income layer — very high chance of expiring worthless.

Total premium collected on 3 layers: $660. If the stock stays above $95, all three expire worthless — full $660 profit. If the stock drops to $92, only Layer 1 is challenged — Layers 2 and 3 still expire worthless. If the stock drops to $87, Layers 1 and 2 are assigned — but Layer 3 buffers the $85 level. The staircase provides three lines of defense rather than one.

Convexity: Engineering Asymmetric Payoffs

Plain-English first: convexity means your position gains value faster than it loses value as the underlying moves. A convex position earns more per point when it wins than it loses per point when it is wrong. This asymmetry — more upside per dollar risked than downside — is the mathematical property that separates professional structures from amateur ones. Everything in this section teaches you to build this property into your positions deliberately.

Convexity in options refers to the non-linear relationship between the option's value and the underlying's movement — specifically, the ability to structure a position where gains are amplified disproportionately relative to losses. A convex position makes more money as the stock moves in your direction than it loses if the stock moves against you by the same amount. This asymmetry is the holy grail of options trading.

Convexity planning means deliberately engineering this asymmetry into your position structure from the start — not hoping for it accidentally.

- Long convexity (debit structures): Long calls, long puts, long straddles, debit spreads. These positions gain value faster as the stock moves in your direction than they lose as it moves against you. The curve of P&L vs. stock price is concave upward — gains accelerate, losses decelerate;
- Short convexity (short premium): Short calls, short puts, iron condors, credit spreads. These positions have limited gains (the premium collected) but losses that can accelerate if the stock moves sharply. The P&L curve is concave downward;
- Convex hedge: Adding a small long convex position to a larger short convex income position. Example: an iron condor with long OTM strangles at wider strikes. The income trade collects premium from the inner structure; the convex hedge provides explosive upside if a large unexpected move occurs;

Calculating Convexity for Torque vs. Protection

'Torque' in trading means the degree of acceleration in your position's value relative to the underlying's movement. Maximum torque = maximum convexity = positions near

ATM with significant gamma. Protection means limited downside regardless of stock movement. Here is how to calibrate:

- For Torque: concentrate position near ATM, high gamma, shorter DTE. Accept higher premium cost in exchange for explosive responsiveness to stock movement. Best when you have high conviction on direction AND magnitude of move;
- For Protection: use wide spreads (OTM long legs far from the money), longer DTE (lower gamma), and multiple layers at different strikes. Accept lower potential return in exchange for resilience to adverse moves; and
- The Convexity Ratio: calculate the maximum gain divided by maximum loss for any structure. A ratio above 2:1 means the position has positive convexity — you gain at least twice as much as you can lose. Below 1:1 means negative convexity — you risk more than you can gain. Most income (credit) trades have negative convexity ratios — this is why win rate and probability of profit are their primary metrics.

Convexity in Practice: A Real Trade Example

Convexity means your position gains value faster than it loses it as the underlying moves in your favor. You manufacture convexity by structuring multiple legs so that winning moves amplify returns while losing moves are capped. Here is how it works with real numbers.

Scenario: you are bullish on NVDA at $800. Instead of buying a single ATM call (high cost, rapid theta decay), you build a layered long call structure across three strikes:

Layer	Action	Strike	Cost	Delta	Role
1	Buy 2×	$800 Call	$28.00 ($5,600)	0.50	ATM anchor — highest probability of participating in any upside move
2	Buy 1×	$850 Call	$14.00 ($1,400)	0.35	OTM acceleration — adds torque if stock reaches $850+
3	Buy 1×	$900 Call	$6.50 ($650)	0.20	Deep OTM — low cost, explosive payoff above $900

Total cost: $7,650 maximum risk. Compare to a simple 4× ATM call purchase at $28 each ($11,200 total cost):

NVDA at Expiry	4× ATM Call P&L	Layered Structure P&L	Advantage	Why Layering Wins
$780 (−2.5%)	−$11,200 (full loss)	−$7,650 (full loss)	Saves $3,550	Lower max loss — OTM layers reduce total cost basis

NVDA at Expiry	4× ATM Call P&L	Layered Structure P&L	Advantage	Why Layering Wins
$830 (+3.75%)	−$3,200 (loss)	−$1,050 (small loss)	Saves $2,150	ATM layers recover faster on smaller moves
$870 (+8.75%)	$5,600 profit	$9,350 profit	+$3,750 more	$850 layer now in-the-money — acceleration kicks in
$920 (+15%)	$16,800 profit	$28,950 profit	+$12,150 more	All three layers fully ITM — maximum convexity torque

The convex structure does three things simultaneously: reduces maximum loss (lower entry cost), accelerates gains on moderate moves (the $850 layer kicks in before the $900 layer becomes relevant), and delivers explosive upside on large moves (all three layers compound above $900). The simple 4× ATM trade is linear, expensive, and all-or-nothing.

CONVEXITY RULE

Never spend more than 60% of your convex structure's budget on ATM or near-ATM options. Allocate the remaining 40% across OTM strikes that add acceleration. A smaller ATM anchor with OTM acceleration is structurally superior to a larger ATM position with no convexity. Size down the anchor — never the architecture.

CONVEXITY IN PRACTICE

Before entering any multi-leg structure, calculate: (1) What is my maximum gain? (2) What is my maximum loss? (3) What does the P&L curve look like at expiration — does it accelerate positively or negatively as the stock moves? A risk graph answers all three questions visually. Run it on every position before you trade.

The MU Conviction Pyramid: A Documented 10-Month Stair

The following is not a hypothetical. It is a documented, brokerage-confirmed trade series executed over ten months on a single underlying — Micron Technology (MU) — as it moved from $102 to $420+. Each entry represents an increase in conviction as the thesis was confirmed by price action. Each roll represents capital efficiency — extracting profit while staying in the trend.

VERIFIED MU STAIR-LAYERED SERIES — JUN 2025 – MAR 2026

STEP 1: Jun 5, 2025 • MU $105 Call • Entry: $2.20 • Cost: $220 Condition 1 entry. MU at $102. Low IV. Clean uptrend. 1 contract.

STEP 2: Nov 17, 2025 • MU $185 Call 2/20 • Entry: $72.70 • Cost: $7,270 Conviction increased. MU still Condition 1. Deep ITM for high delta exposure. Closed Dec 30, 2025 at $110.34 • +$3,764 • +51.78% • 43 days

STEP 3: Jan 5, 2026 • MU $310 Call 2/20 • Entry: $30.10 • Cost: $6,020 MU now $315. Near-the-money for maximum torque. 2 contracts. Rolled Feb 19, 2026 • $310 closed at $104.25 • +$15,065 • +260.42% • 45 days Rolled to $390 Call 3/20 at $48.70 — net credit extracted: $11,110

STEP 4: Jan 23, 2026 • MU $340 Call 3/20 • Entry: $77.00 • Cost: $15,400 MU trending through $340 zone. Deep ITM position, 2 contracts. Closed Feb 25, 2026 at $97.00 • +$4,000 • +25.98% • 33 days

STEP 5: Feb 4, 2026 • MU $420 Call 3/20 • Entry: $42.70 • Cost: $4,270 MU at $420 range. Conviction at maximum. 1 contract. Rolled Mar 18, 2026 to $460 Call Apr 17 • +$584 extracted • +13.7% TOTAL VERIFIED CLOSED PROFIT: +$22,829 TOTAL CAPITAL DEPLOYED: $28,690 BLENDED RETURN: +79.6%

Study the structure of this series. The first entry was $220 — the smallest possible position, testing the thesis with minimal capital at risk. As each step confirmed the trend, position size increased: $7,270, then $6,020, then $15,400. This is the conviction pyramid working exactly as designed. Early entries are small and exploratory. Later entries are larger and more confident because the thesis has already been confirmed by price action.

THE TORQUE PROOF — MU $310 CALL

Stock move: MU went from ~$315 to ~$420 during the $310 Call hold period.

Stock return: +33.3%.

Option move: $310 Call went from $30.10 to $104.25.

Option return: +246.3%.

Torque ratio: 246.3% ÷ 33.3% = 7.4×.

The option delivered 7.4 times the return of the underlying stock on a defined-risk position. This is convexity. This is why professional traders use options instead of stock for directional exposure when conviction is high and IV is reasonable. The stock could have gone to zero — maximum loss was $6,020. The stock gained 33% — the option gained 246%.

The torque ratio of 7.4× was not engineered in advance. It emerged naturally from the position structure: a near-the-money call with 46 days to expiration on a high-beta AI-driven semiconductor stock in a confirmed Condition 1 environment. The system created the conditions for torque. The market delivered it.

As with all examples in this book, this trade is drawn from a real, executed position. Position sizing in this example reflects my account structure and risk tolerance and is not intended as a universal model.

Income Layering: The Seller's Stair-Layered CSP Strategy

Everything discussed so far applies to directional trades. But the stair-layered approach is equally powerful — and arguably more important — for the income writer running the Wheel. Instead of committing your full capital to a single CSP at one strike and one expiration, the income seller builds a layered position across multiple weekly expirations, creating a rolling income engine that generates PPD consistently regardless of which week the stock moves.

The concept is simple: instead of selling one large CSP with 30 DTE, you sell smaller CSPs across three consecutive weekly expirations — each a 'stair' in the income ladder. Each week, one position expires or is closed, and a new position is opened at the next expiration. Capital is always working. Income never stops.

Stair	Expiration	Strike	Premium	Capital Reserved	Status on Entry
Stair 1	This Friday (7 DTE)	$190 Put	$0.85 ($85)	$19,000	Active. Fastest theta burn. Will expire or close by Friday. Capital freed immediately after.
Stair 2	Next Friday (14 DTE)	$188 Put	$1.40 ($140)	$18,800	Active. Mid-term income. More conservative strike — slightly deeper cushion. Closes next week.
Stair 3	Two Fridays out (21 DTE)	$185 Put	$1.65 ($165)	$18,500	Active. Most conservative strike. Longest runway. Provides the base layer of weekly income.

Total weekly premium across three stairs: $390. Each Friday, Stair 1 closes and a new Stair 3 opens at the next available expiration. The system is self-renewing. Annualized: $390/week × 52 weeks = $20,280 on approximately $56,300 of reserved capital = 36% annualized on capital deployed.

THE STAIR-LAYERED INCOME RULE

Never concentrate your full income position in a single expiration. Spread across at least two — preferably three — consecutive weekly expirations. If a single Friday brings a sharp selloff, only one stair is maximally challenged. The other stairs have more time and deeper strikes to absorb the move. Income continuity is the goal. The staircase provides it.

Time Layering: Calendar Laddering for the Income Seller

Time layering means opening positions at the same strike but across multiple expirations — deliberately harvesting theta at different speeds. The near-dated position burns theta fastest. The far-dated position provides stability and a larger credit that decays more slowly. Both serve different roles in the same income architecture.

Layer Type	DTE	Strike	Premium	Daily Theta	Strategic Role
Near-Term Layer	7–14 DTE	$190	$0.85	~$0.12/day	Fast income. Maximum theta burn rate. Opened and closed every 1–2 weeks. The engine of the weekly PPD.
Mid-Term Layer	21–30 DTE	$187	$1.65	~$0.08/day	Steady income with more cushion. Renewed monthly.

Layer Type	DTE	Strike	Premium	Daily Theta	Strategic Role
					Provides the structural backbone of the income position.
Far-Term Layer	45 DTE	$183	$2.80	~$0.06/day	Slow burn. Deepest strike. Opened once per month to start the decay clock on the best portion of the theta curve.

Combined daily theta across all three layers: $0.26/day per contract triplet. On a five-contract ladder across all three layers: $130/day PPD reached on $56K of active capital — 36% annualized. The layered structure achieves target PPD while distributing risk across three expiration windows. No single bad week destroys the engine.

The Convexity Ratio Table: Evaluating Any Structure Before You Trade

Every options structure has a convexity ratio — maximum gain divided by maximum loss. Calculate it before every trade. A positive convexity ratio (> 1.0) means you gain more than you lose on a maximum move. A negative ratio (< 1.0) means you gain less than you risk. Neither is inherently good or bad — but you must know which game you are playing before the trade begins.

Structure	Max Gain	Max Loss	Convexity Ratio	Best Use Case
Long Call (ATM)	Unlimited	Premium paid	∞ theoretically	High conviction bullish, low IVR. Maximum positive convexity.
Bull Call Spread	Spread width – debit	Debit paid	1.5:1 to 3:1	Moderate bullish. Capped positive convexity — lower cost than outright call.
Long Straddle	Unlimited	Both premiums paid	∞ theoretically	Pre-catalyst vol expansion. Positive convexity in both directions.
Cash-Secured Put	Premium collected	Strike – premium	0.03:1 to 0.06:1	Income generation. Negative convexity — managed by quality selection and T-21 discipline.
Covered Call	Premium + upside to strike	Stock decline below breakeven	0.04:1 to 0.08:1	Income on existing position. Negative convexity on the call — capped upside.
Iron Condor	Net credit	Spread width – credit	0.20:1 to 0.50:1	Range-bound market. Defined but real loss risk on breach.
Layered Call Structure (3 strikes)	All layers compound on large move	Total debit paid	2:1 to 5:1+ on large moves	High conviction directional with convexity engineering. Best asymmetric payoff.

Structure	Max Gain	Max Loss	Convexity Ratio	Best Use Case
Stair-Layered CSP (3 expirations)	Sum of all premiums	Largest strike − total credit	0.05:1 to 0.08:1	Income with distributed risk. Negative convexity — but probability of profit is high across all stairs.

THE CONVEXITY DECISION

Before any trade: what is my convexity ratio? Positive convexity (debit structures) — ensure IVR is below 40 and your directional thesis is strong. Negative convexity (credit structures) — ensure IVR is above 30, the underlying is A-class quality, and your position is sized to survive assignment. The convexity ratio tells you which game you are playing. Know the game before the first dollar goes in.

Applying Stair-Layering Across the Six Conditions

Stair-layering is not exclusively a premium-selling tool. Every condition in the six-condition framework has a stair-layering variant — a way to amplify income or directional exposure by running multiple layers simultaneously across expirations or strikes. The architecture changes by condition. The principle is the same: never concentrate all your exposure in a single expiration window when a layered approach offers better risk distribution and higher total theta.

#	Condition	Stair-Layering Application
1	**Bullish / Low IV**	Layer bull call spreads across 3 expiration cycles: Open a 15-DTE spread (fast gain if move is immediate), a 30-DTE spread (core position), and a 45-DTE spread (slow participation if move is gradual). Each layer uses a different strike range to capture different price targets. As the near-term expires, open a new far-term layer — building a self-renewing directional ladder.
2	**Bullish / High IV**	Classic CSP income ladder: 7-DTE, 21-DTE, and 45-DTE puts on the same quality underlying. The 7-DTE generates the highest daily theta but requires active management. The 45-DTE is the slowest but most resilient layer. All three layers working simultaneously compound PPD. This is the Premium Desk income engine structure described in Chapter 9 — applied systematically across all three layers every month.
3	**Bearish / Low IV**	Layer bear put spreads across 2 expiration windows: near-term (21-DTE) for the immediate down move, and far-term (45-DTE) for sustained trend continuation. If the down move is already underway and IV is still low, the near-term spread provides faster profit. If the move has not yet materialized, the far-term spread gives you more time for the thesis to develop without paying excess time decay.
4	**Bearish / High IV**	Layer bear call spreads with staggered short strikes: near-term (21-DTE) at the first resistance level, far-term (45-DTE) at a higher resistance level. The near-term spread earns faster if the stock stays below resistance immediately. The far-term spread is insurance if the stock temporarily bounces — you collect credit there as well while the trend eventually reverses.
5	**Range / Low IV**	Iron condor ladder: run two iron condors simultaneously — one expiring in 30 DTE and one in 45 DTE. The 30-DTE condor has tighter wings (closer to current price) and earns faster. The 45-DTE condor has wider wings and provides a buffer if the stock drifts. This structure keeps continuous premium collection active across two expiration cycles at all times.
6	**Range / High IV**	Calendar ladder: sell near-term options (7-DTE) against longer-dated longs (45-DTE) each week. As each short leg expires, sell the next week's option. This creates a weekly income

#	Condition	Stair-Layering Application
		stream from IV differential — 4 short legs per month harvesting the elevated near-term IV against a single long-dated anchor that you roll forward once per month.

THE MASTER ARCHITECTURE

The complete six-condition income trader runs all six ladders simultaneously — one for each condition that is active. In a typical mid-expansion month (condition 2 dominant, condition 5 secondary), you run the condition 2 CSP ladder on your highest-quality large-caps AND the condition 5 iron condor ladder on SPY for the range-bound periods. Both engines generate theta. Each is managed by its own protocol. The discipline is in never letting one ladder's management bleed into the other's rules.

Convexity Worked Examples: Building Asymmetric Payoff Profiles

Convexity in options means structuring positions so that gains accelerate faster than losses accumulate. A convex position makes more when you are right than it loses when you are wrong — by the same magnitude of move. This asymmetry is the mathematical expression of good risk management, and it can be engineered deliberately using the six-condition framework.

CONVEXITY EXAMPLE — AAPL Condition 1: 1×3 Call Ratio Backspread

AAPL at $195. Condition 1 confirmed (bullish, low IV). Strong conviction on a move to $210+.

Standard call: Buy 1× $195 Call for $5.20. Max loss: $5.20. Gain if AAPL → $210: ~$9.80 (1.9× return).

Convex structure: Sell 1× $195 Call ($5.20) + Buy 3× $205 Call ($1.60 each = $4.80 total). Net debit: $4.80 − $5.20 = −$0.40 (credit received).

If AAPL → $210: Short $195 call worth $15.00 (−$15). Long 3× $205 calls worth $5.00 each (+$15). Net P&L: $15.00 − $15.00 + $0.40 credit = +$0.40. Break even at $210.

If AAPL → $220: Short $195 call worth $25.00 (−$25). Long 3× $205 calls worth $15.00 each (+$45). Net P&L: +$20.40. The 3× long contracts accelerate gains above $210.

If AAPL stays at $195: All options expire worthless. Net P&L: +$0.40 (keep the credit). Max loss occurs between $195 and $210 — limited by the spread structure.

Convexity achieved: lose small in the middle, gain large on a significant move. The structure is designed for high-conviction, large-move condition 1 setups.

Calendar Laddering: Time-Decay Income Across Multiple Expirations

Calendar laddering is the income writer's version of the stair-layered approach: instead of entering the same strategy at different price points, you enter the same strategy at different expiration dates. Each layer matures on a different date, creating a steady income stream rather than a single monthly income event.

Layer	Entry Date	Expiration	Strike	Premium + Target
Layer 1	Week 1	Week 4 (25 DTE)	5% OTM CSP	$1.40 credit. Close at $0.70. Renews immediately — Layer 5 entered.
Layer 2	Week 2	Week 5 (25 DTE)	5% OTM CSP	$1.35 credit. Close at $0.67. Renews — Layer 6 entered.
Layer 3	Week 3	Week 6 (25 DTE)	5% OTM CSP	$1.30 credit. Close at $0.65. Renews — Layer 7 entered.
Layer 4	Week 4	Week 7 (25 DTE)	5% OTM CSP	$1.45 credit. Close at $0.72. Renews — Layer 8 entered.
Result	**Ongoing**	**Weekly income**	**Staggered**	**Average $1.37 credit per layer. Weekly income: ~$137/layer. 4 active layers = ~$548 weekly gross income on deployed capital.**

LAYERING IS DISCIPLINE, NOT COMPLEXITY

The stair-layered approach looks complex in a table. In practice, it is four simple positions entered one week apart. The complexity is in the planning — the execution is mechanical. Set up the calendar ladder at the start of each month, mark the expiration dates, set the GTC close orders at 50% profit for each layer, and let the system run. Weekly income from a monthly plan.

Calendar Spread Layering: Time-Decay Architecture Across Expirations

The calendar spread is the purest expression of time-decay engineering: you sell near-term theta and buy longer-dated theta at a differential. Layering calendar spreads across multiple expirations creates a time-decay income stream that is more stable than any single-expiration position — because at least one layer is always in the optimal theta harvest zone at any given time.

This structure is the six-condition system's most sophisticated tool for Condition 6 (Range-bound, High IV). You are not betting on direction. You are not betting on a large move. You are engineering a multi-layer income machine that runs on the simple, inevitable fact that near-term time passes faster than long-term time.

Layer	Sell (Near)	Buy (Far)	Net Debit	Daily Theta Collected (Est.)
Layer A	14 DTE ATM Call	45 DTE ATM Call	$1.20 debit	~$0.08/day (near-leg decays faster)
Layer B	21 DTE ATM Call	52 DTE ATM Call	$1.35 debit	~$0.06/day
Layer C	28 DTE ATM Call	59 DTE ATM Call	$1.50 debit	~$0.05/day
Combined	Staggered weekly	Staggered weekly	$4.05 total debit	~$0.19/day combined theta

Layer	Sell (Near)	Buy (Far)	Net Debit	Daily Theta Collected (Est.)
At Layer A expiry	Layer A closes at profit	Layer A's long leg now becomes Layer D near-leg	Cycle renews	Income is perpetual while condition 6 persists

The key mechanical insight: when Layer A expires, the 45 DTE long leg you originally bought is now a 31 DTE contract. Instead of buying a new 45 DTE contract, you sell a new 14 DTE contract against the existing 31 DTE — recycling the long leg as the anchor of a new spread. This dramatically reduces the ongoing capital required to run the ladder, because your long legs are perpetually recycled rather than re-purchased.

Exit the entire calendar ladder when the condition changes — specifically when the range breaks and a clear directional trend emerges. A stock that was Condition 6 (range, high IV) and transitions to Condition 2 (bullish, high IV) requires you to close the calendars and deploy a CSP or covered call instead. The calendar structure earns from stability — it bleeds when direction asserts itself.

CALENDAR LAYERING IS CONDITION 6's SIGNATURE TRADE

When IVR > 50 and the stock has been range-bound for 10+ sessions with defined support and resistance — that is the ideal setup for a 3-layer calendar ladder. The elevated IV makes the near-term options expensive to sell. The range keeps both legs near ATM where theta is maximum. The layering smooths the income so you earn every week, not just at one expiration. This is the six-condition system performing at its highest architectural level.

Stair-Layered Income: Building a Three-Tier CSP Position

The stair-layered approach applies to income selling just as powerfully as directional trading. Instead of selling one large CSP, you layer three smaller CSPs at different strikes — creating a more resilient income position with better average pricing if assigned.

Example — AAPL at $190. Instead of selling 1× $180 put for $3.50:

Layer	Strike	Premium	If Assigned	Cost Basis
Top (closest)	$185	$4.20	Assigned first if AAPL dips to $185	$180.80 effective
Middle	$180	$2.80	Assigned second if AAPL drops further	$177.20 effective
Bottom (furthest)	$175	$1.60	Assigned third — only in a significant pullback	$173.40 effective
All three assigned	**—**	**$8.60 total**	**300 shares at layered prices**	**$178.13 average**

Compare to the single CSP approach: selling 1× $180 put gives you 100 shares at $176.50 if assigned. The layered approach gives you up to 300 shares with an average cost of $178.13 — slightly higher, but with three separate premium payments and the flexibility to manage each layer independently.

The real advantage emerges in management. If AAPL dips to $183 and bounces, only the $185 layer is at risk. The $180 and $175 layers expire worthless — pure profit. With a single $180 CSP, the entire position profits or loses together. The layered structure gives you partial wins in scenarios where a single position gives you an all-or-nothing outcome.

Layered Directional Entries: The Conviction Pyramid

The conviction pyramid is the antidote to two of the most expensive trading behaviors: entering a full position immediately (before confirmation) and averaging down into a losing position (chasing a broken thesis). The pyramid solves both by tying position size to evidence, not emotion.

Tier 1 entry (25% of planned position): the initial signal fires. Condition is identified, stock passes Ten Indicators, technical setup is present. You enter with 25% of your planned size. At this stage you are paying for optionality — the right to add more if you are right, with limited damage if you are wrong.

Tier 2 entry (+50% of planned position): the trade is working. Price has moved in the predicted direction by at least 0.5 ATR, and the condition read still confirms the thesis. Now you add 50% of planned size. You are scaling into a winner, not chasing — the market is validating your read.

Tier 3 entry (+25% of planned position): strong momentum, trend is accelerating, no signs of reversal. Add the final 25% to complete the position. At full size you have an average entry that is better than a single full entry would have been, because each add-on was at a more confirmed price.

THE PYRAMID RULE: NEVER ADD TO A LOSER

The conviction pyramid only works in one direction: adding to winning positions. Adding to a losing position is called "averaging down" and it is one of the most destructive habits in trading. If the trade is going against you after Tier 1, the market is telling you your thesis is wrong. Exit the Tier 1 position. Take the small loss. Do not buy more of something the market is rejecting.

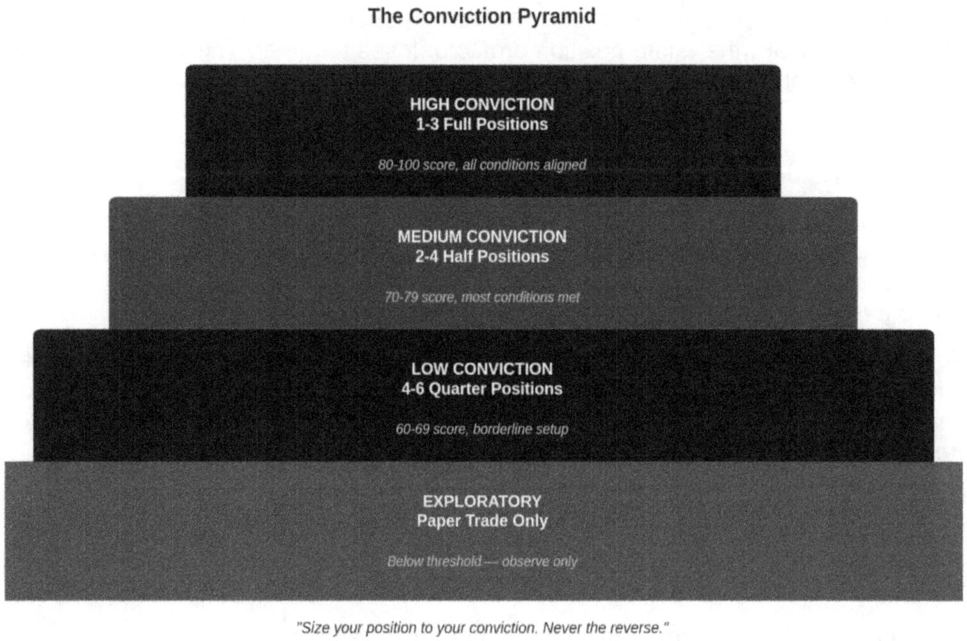

Figure 24.2 — Conviction Pyramid — Position sizing tiers based on setup quality, market alignment, and confirmation sequence.

Conviction Pyramid — Position sizing tiers based on setup quality and market alignment.

For directional swing trades, the stair-layered approach builds position size as the thesis confirms — not all at once based on hope.

- Layer 1 (50% of intended size): Enter when the initial setup triggers (pullback to support, 50-day EMA touch, technical confirmation). This is your 'test' position;
- Layer 2 (30% of intended size): Add when the price confirms the direction — moves 2-3% in your favor with volume confirmation. This proves the setup is working; and
- Layer 3 (20% of intended size): Add when the trade breaks through the next resistance level or hits your acceleration trigger. This is your 'conviction is confirmed' layer.

If the trade fails at Layer 1, you lose only 50% of what you would have lost with a full-size entry. If it succeeds, you end up with full size at a slightly higher average cost — a small price for the insurance of scaling in. Over hundreds of trades, the savings from failed Layer 1 entries far exceed the extra cost on successful entries.

LAYERED ENTRY RULE

Never enter your full intended position size on the first signal. Always reserve at least 30% of your allocation for confirmation adds. The market rewards patience and punishes urgency — especially on directional trades where the first signal is wrong 40% of the time.

Convexity Thinking: Why Small Bets on Large Moves Create Wealth

Convexity is the mathematical property that defines how your position's profit accelerates as the underlying moves further in your favor. A linear position (like owning stock) gains $1 for every $1 the stock rises. A convex position (like a layered call structure) might gain $1 for the first $1 move, $1.50 for the next $1, $2.20 for the next $1, and $3.50 for the next $1. The further the stock moves, the faster you make money. This is the architecture of outsized returns.

The income strategies in this book — CSPs, covered calls, iron condors — are concave. They make money consistently but with bounded upside and exposed downside. Concave strategies are the foundation of your income. Convex strategies are the foundation of your wealth. A complete portfolio includes both: the concave base generates monthly income while the convex layer captures the rare but powerful moves that transform accounts.

The practical application: allocate 80% of your trading capital to income (concave) strategies and 20% to convex opportunities. The income layer pays the bills — covering your monthly expenses, funding your lifestyle, and generating the steady compounding that builds wealth over decades. The convex layer captures the 2-3 events per year where a stock or sector makes a move large enough to deliver 3x, 5x, or 10x returns on the premium invested.

Example of the 80/20 allocation on a $50,000 account: $40,000 allocated to income strategies (CSPs, Wheel, iron condors) generating $800-$1,200/month. $10,000 allocated to convex positions (stair-layered calls on AI stocks, long straddles before major events, LEAPS calls on conviction names). In a typical year, the income layer generates $9,600-$14,400 (19-29% return on allocated capital). The convex layer might lose $3,000-$5,000 in most months (the cost of the asymmetric bets) but capture one or two moves that generate $8,000-$20,000. Net result: the convex wins more than offset the convex losses, and the income layer provides a steady base regardless of whether the convex bets pay off.

The psychological key to convexity: you must be comfortable with many small losses in exchange for occasional large gains. Most traders are psychologically wired for the opposite — many small gains and occasional large losses (which is exactly what unmanaged concave strategies deliver). Training yourself to accept the convex payoff profile — losing small, losing often, and winning big when it counts — is one of the most valuable psychological shifts in this book.

> **6-CONDITION FRAMEWORK ▸ ALL SIX — management rules adapt to the active condition**
> Daily management is not the same in condition 2 (income, wait for theta) as it is in condition 1 (directional, trail the move). This chapter shows you how to manage live positions according to the condition that was active when you opened them.

Opening a trade is the beginning of the job, not the end of it. Once a position is live, it requires active monitoring, periodic evaluation, and disciplined response to changing conditions. Most retail traders open trades and then either check obsessively throughout the day (creating emotional noise) or ignore them entirely until expiration (missing critical management opportunities). Neither extreme is correct.

This chapter gives you a structured trade management framework — the exact metrics to check daily and monthly, and the specific actions each metric can trigger. The goal is to make management systematic and unemotional, driven by data rather than fear or hope.

The Daily Management Routine

Daily management does not mean trading every day. It means reviewing every open position against a defined checklist once per day — ideally in the morning before the market opens, and briefly at the close. The pre-market review sets your decisions before emotion enters. The end-of-day review confirms whether any conditions were triggered.

Metric	What You Track	Frequency
Open Positions	Count, delta, days remaining, current P&L.	Daily.
PPD Tracker	Profit Per Day vs. target for each position.	Daily.
T-21 Alert	Positions within 21 days of expiration.	Daily.
Win/Loss Rate	Rolling 20-trade win rate vs. 60% target.	Weekly.
Monthly P&L	Gross premium, fees, net return on capital.	Monthly.
Max Drawdown	Deepest peak-to-trough decline this month.	Monthly.
Expectancy	Avg win × win rate − avg loss × loss rate.	Monthly.

Figure 25.1 — The Trade Management Dashboard. Daily and monthly metrics for a multi-position portfolio.

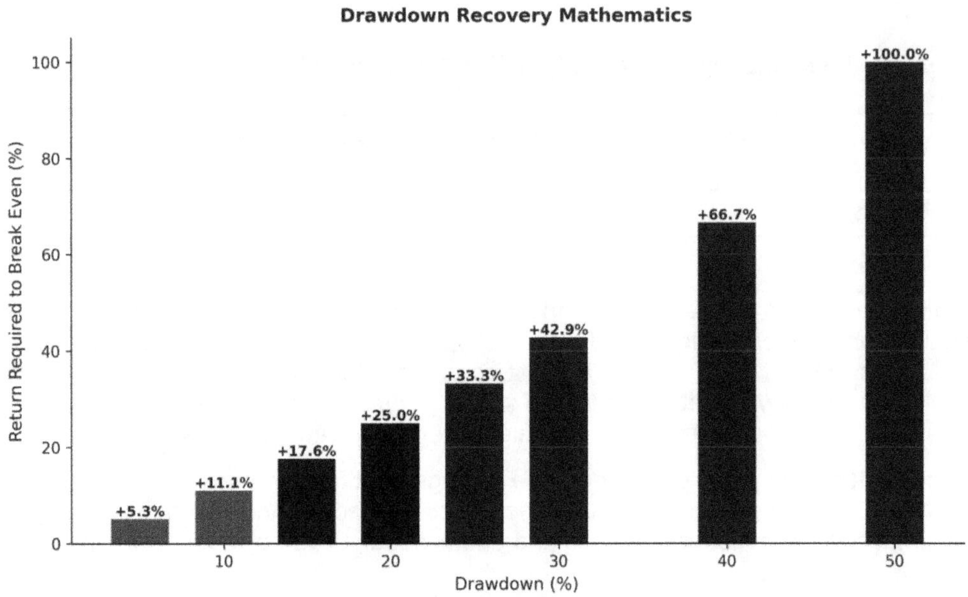

Figure 25.2 — Drawdown Recovery Mathematics. A 50% loss requires a 100% gain to break even.

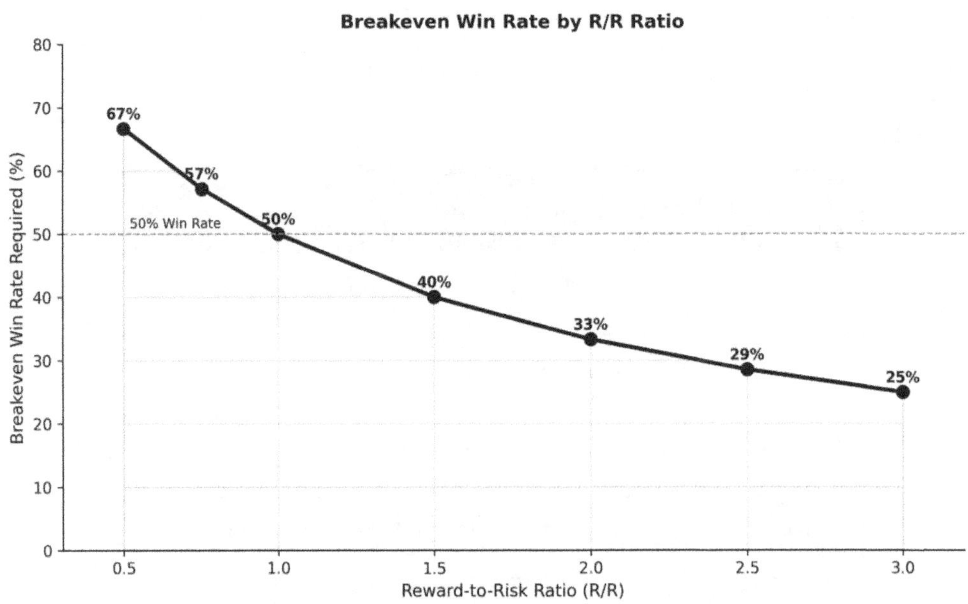

Figure 25.3 — Breakeven Win Rate by R/R. Higher R/R means profitability with fewer wins.

Daily Metric	What to Check	Action Trigger
P&L vs. Target	Current position P&L as % of maximum profit	At 50% profit: prepare to close or set a limit GTC order. At 75%+: close immediately.
Days to Expiration	How many calendar days remain on each position	At T-21: evaluate roll or close. No exceptions — set a calendar alert at entry.

Daily Metric	What to Check	Action Trigger
Delta Drift	Has the short strike's delta moved beyond 0.35?	Delta above 0.35 on a short position means increasing directional risk. Evaluate roll down/up.
Underlying Price vs. Strike	How far is the stock from your short strike?	Stock within 3–5% of short strike: elevate monitoring. Stock at or through strike: immediate management.
VIX Movement	Has VIX moved more than 3 points since entry?	VIX spike: short premium positions face Vega headwinds. Evaluate closing before further IV expansion.
Upcoming Catalyst	Any earnings, FDA, FOMC, or macro event within the next 7 days?	If yes: close or roll short premium positions before the event. Do not hold through binary catalysts.
Stop Loss Breach	Has the position reached your pre-defined maximum loss level?	Close immediately. No deliberation. The stop was set when you were rational — honor it.

THE 5-MINUTE DAILY REVIEW

Total daily management time for a 3–5 position income portfolio: 5 minutes. Open your platform. Check each position's current P&L %, DTE, and distance from short strike. No catalyst in the next 7 days? No stop breach? No T-21 alert? Close the tab. You are done. Discipline means not over-managing — checking obsessively creates noise that leads to breaking your own rules.

The Monthly Review Framework

Once per month — on the Sunday before the monthly options expiration — conduct a complete account and strategy review. This is your business review: you are the CEO of your trading account, and this is your board meeting. The monthly review identifies what is working, what is not, and what adjustments are warranted for the next 30-day cycle.

Monthly Metric	What to Measure	Action / Adjustment
Monthly P&L	Total net profit/loss for the month in dollars and % of account	Compare to monthly target (2–3% on deployed capital). If below target: review strategy selection and IVR timing. If above: review whether outsized wins came from excess risk.
Win Rate	Trades closed as wins ÷ total trades closed this month	Target: 65–80% for income strategies. Below 60%: review strike selection and catalyst exposure. Above 85%: possibly taking too little risk — are premiums worth the capital deployed?

Monthly Metric	What to Measure	Action / Adjustment
Average Winner / Loser	Average profit on wins, average loss on losses	Losers should not exceed 2× average winner. If they do: review stop discipline and position sizing.
Maximum Drawdown	Largest peak-to-trough account decline this month	If drawdown exceeded 8% this month: stop trading for 2 weeks. Review every losing trade. Identify systemic issue before redeploying.
IVR Environment	Average IVR at entry across all trades this month	If average IVR at entry was below 30: you were selling premium in a low-IV environment. Adjust: wait for higher IVR, or shift to debit strategies in low-IV months.
Sector/Underlying Mix	Which underlyings generated most profit? Most loss?	Concentrate future exposure on highest-quality underlyings. Eliminate or reduce exposure to consistently losing underlyings.
Capital Efficiency	Total premium collected ÷ total capital reserved	Target: 2–3% monthly yield on reserved capital. If below: increase IVR filter or select higher-premium underlyings.
Open Position Review	Review all positions still open: DTE, P&L %, distance from strikes, upcoming catalysts	Identify any positions that need early management in the coming week. Set your management alerts for the next cycle.

The monthly review is also when you make macro-level decisions: Does the current business cycle phase still support my strategy mix? Is sector rotation signaling a shift that changes which underlyings I should trade? Is IVR expanding or contracting, and should I shift between income and debit strategies for the next cycle? These are the CEO decisions. Make them monthly, in writing, in your trade journal.

Monthly P&L Journal Template

Every trade closed during the month gets logged with these seven fields. The discipline of logging forces clarity — you cannot write 'I don't know why I lost' in a structured journal. You must identify the specific decision that cost you money, which is the only way to avoid making it again.

Ticker	Strategy	Entry / Exit	P&L $	IVR	DTE	Lesson / Adjustment
AAPL	CSP $180	$3.20 / $1.55	+$165	68	32	Closed at 51% profit at T-24. Textbook exit.
XLF	Iron Condor	$0.90 / $1.80	−$90	41	28	Entered below IVR 50. Rule broken. Do not enter iron condors below IVR 50 regardless of thesis.
MSFT	CSP $400	$4.10 / $1.85	+$225	72	35	Clean. Held to 55% profit, closed 3 days before T-21.

Adding PPD to Your Journal: The Trade Scorecard

The monthly P&L journal template in this chapter tracks absolute profit and loss. To run your income portfolio as a business, add two PPD columns to every trade row. This single addition transforms your journal from a record of outcomes into a performance optimization tool.

Ticker	Strategy	Entry/Exit	P&L $	Days	IVR	PPD $	PPD %/day
AAPL	CSP $175	$3.20/$1.55	+$165	18	68	$9.17/day	0.052%
XLF	Iron Condor	$0.90/$1.80	−$90	28	41	−$3.21/day	−0.023%
MSFT	CSP $390	$4.10/$1.85	+$225	22	72	$10.23/day	0.058%
NVDA	CSP $720	$8.50/$4.20	+$430	16	84	$26.88/day	0.037%

The PPD columns reveal what raw P&L obscures. NVDA shows the highest absolute PPD at $26.88/day — but the lowest PPD on capital at 0.037%/day, because it ties up $72,000 of reserved capital. MSFT produces only $225 in absolute profit but the highest capital-efficiency PPD at 0.058%/day. The XLF condor loss is visible in both columns, but the negative PPD shows exactly how much the position was costing per day while it deteriorated.

Monthly review metric: calculate your portfolio average PPD on capital across all closed trades. This becomes your month-over-month performance benchmark — more meaningful than total P&L because it adjusts for how much capital was deployed and for how long. A month where you ran 3 positions and averaged 0.06%/day PPD is objectively better than a month where you ran 8 positions and averaged 0.03%/day PPD, even if the second month produced more total dollars.

THE MONTHLY REVIEW RULE

Five years of trades without a journal is five years of anecdotes. Five years of trades with a systematic monthly review is five years of compounding improvement. The traders who last longest are not the ones with the best instincts — they are the ones who know exactly why each trade worked or failed, and never make the same mistake three times. The monthly review is how that discipline is built.

THE MONTHLY REVIEW RULE

Your trading journal entry for each month-end review should answer four questions: (1) Did I follow my system? (2) Did the system work? (3) What would I do differently? (4) What is my plan for next month? If you cannot answer all four, your system is not written down clearly enough. Write it down.

Condition-Specific Trade Management Rules

This is the section most books skip: how trade management changes depending on which of the six conditions was active when you opened the position. A position opened in condition 1 (bullish, low IV) is not managed the same way as a position opened in condition 4 (bearish, high IV). The structure is different. The profit driver is different. The danger signals are different. The management protocol must reflect all of this.

#	Condition	Strategy In	Primary P&L Driver	Management Rule
1	**Bullish ↑ / Low IV**	Long call / bull call spread	Delta — you need the stock to move up	Trail the position as it gains. Move stop to breakeven once +30% profit. For debit spreads: close at 50–75% of max profit — the remaining upside carries disproportionate gamma risk. For long calls and puts: allow the position to run toward maximum profit at expiration, protected by a trailing stop. Exit if stock closes below entry support level — thesis broken.
2	**Bullish ↑ / High IV**	CSP / covered call / bull put spread	Theta — time decay earns your premium	Set-and-monitor. Close at 50% of premium collected (not expiration). T-21 check: close or roll. Stop at 2× credit collected. Do not adjust unless strike is tested.
3	**Bearish ↓ / Low IV**	Long put / bear put spread	Delta — you need the stock to move down	Same as condition 1 in reverse. Trail the put as stock falls. Move stop to breakeven at +30%. Exit if stock closes above entry resistance — thesis broken.
4	**Bearish ↓ / High IV**	Bear call spread (credit)	Theta + distance from short strike	Set-and-monitor. Never adjust by selling additional calls. If stock rallies toward short strike, close the spread and accept the loss. Do not turn a defined-risk spread into an undefined-risk position by removing the long call.
5	**Range ↔ / Low IV**	Butterfly / iron condor	Theta + stock staying in range	Daily check: is stock still inside the range? If stock moves to within 2 strikes of either short wing, close that wing and re-evaluate. Do not hold to expiration hoping for recovery. Condors win by defending early, not by praying.
6	**Range ↔ / High IV**	Calendar / diagonal spread	IV differential contraction + theta on short leg	Monitor IV of both legs independently. If near-term IV collapses sharply (IV crush event), close the trade — your edge has been harvested faster than expected. Roll short leg each expiry. Close if stock breaks range by > 3%.

When the Condition Changes Mid-Trade

You opened a bull put spread in condition 2 — bullish, high IV. Two weeks later, the VIX has dropped to 14 and the chart has turned sideways. You are now in condition 5 or 6. Your position was opened in condition 2 and the structure is still condition 2. What do you do?

The answer depends entirely on where your position is in its P&L and time cycle. Here are the four scenarios:

Scenario	Condition Change	Action
Position profitable (>40% of credit collected). Condition changes.	Condition 2 → Condition 5 or 6 (range, lower IV)	Take the profit now. The IV drop means your remaining premium will decay slower than when you entered. The edge is reduced. Bank the gain and redeploy in the new condition.
Position near breakeven. Condition changes to range.	Condition 2 → Condition 5 (range, low IV)	Hold if stock is well above your short put strike and DTE > 21. IV drop hurts future earnings but position remains structurally safe. Set stop and monitor.

Scenario	Condition Change	Action
Position at a loss (<50% of credit remaining, spread widened). Condition turns bearish.	Condition 2 → Condition 3 or 4 (bearish, any IV)	Exit immediately. Your bullish thesis has been invalidated by the condition change. A bull put spread in a bearish condition is a liability, not a recovery opportunity. Accept the loss. Redeploy in condition 3 or 4.
Position profitable. Condition shifts bearish. Stock approaching short strike.	Condition 2 → Condition 4 (bearish, high IV)	Exit the bull put spread and redeploy into a bear call spread. You are now in condition 4. Do not hold a bullish structure in a bearish market hoping for a reversal. The market has told you the condition. Trust it.

THE CONDITION CHANGE RULE

When the six-condition read changes, your open positions must be evaluated immediately against the new condition. A position built for condition 2 in a condition 4 market is misaligned. Misaligned positions bleed slowly and fail suddenly. The market tells you the condition every single day. Your job is to listen — and to manage your book accordingly.

The Weekly Trading Dashboard: Your 7-Day Management Cycle

Professional traders do not manage positions reactively — they manage them on a schedule. The weekly dashboard below is the exact weekly management cycle used by The Premium Desk's income traders. It takes approximately 45 minutes per week and prevents both over-management (the compulsion to adjust constantly) and under-management (the failure to act when action is required).

Day	Task	Six-Condition Tie-In
MON	Weekly condition read: VIX + SPY/QQQ chart. Identify active condition for the week. Review the earnings calendar for all open positions and watchlist stocks.	This is your condition lock for the week. If condition is the same as last week, maintain existing strategy. If condition has changed, review all open positions against the new condition — any that were opened under the old condition may need to be managed or closed.
MON	Review all open positions: DTE check, delta drift check, proximity to short strikes.	Any position with DTE < 21 enters T-21 management protocol: roll or close. Any position where the short strike has been tested (stock within $2) triggers the three-question adjustment protocol.
WED	Open new positions for the week: one or two positions maximum, sized per cap tier rules.	Use the weekly condition read from Monday as the basis. Execute only condition-appropriate strategies. All five pre-trade checklist items confirmed before submission.
FRI	Weekly P&L review: total premium collected, total premium paid, net P&L for the week, win/loss count.	Log in the trade journal (Appendix B). Calculate your PPD for the week. Compare to your annual target. If below target, identify whether the gap is strategy selection, sizing, or market conditions — not all three simultaneously.

Day	Task	Six-Condition Tie-In
FRI	Volatility calendar update: mark next week's FOMC, CPI, earnings, and OpEx events on the trading calendar.	Identify any event that falls within the DTE window of your open or planned positions. No new income positions within 48 hours before a binary event for that underlying.

Monthly P&L Review Protocol: Learning from Every Cycle

At the end of every month, before you open any new positions, run the monthly P&L review. This is not an accounting exercise — it is a performance intelligence session. The data you collect here is what separates the improving trader from the stagnating one.

Metric to Calculate	Where to Find the Data	What to Do With It
Monthly win rate (winners ÷ total trades)	SCR journal — count wins and total trades	Below 60%: review losing trades for pattern. Were they condition violations? Sizing errors? Earnings trades? Each losing trade should have a root cause.
Average premium per winning trade vs. average loss per losing trade	Journal — compare average credit collected vs. average loss taken	The ratio should be at least 1:1 (lose as little as you win) — ideally 1.5:1 or better (win more per winner than you lose per loser). If inverted, your exit discipline needs review.
PPD for the month (total net P&L ÷ 22 trading days)	Brokerage P&L statement	Compare to your PPD target. If you generated $3,200 net and your target is $200/day, you ran at 73% of target. Identify which week underperformed and why.
Six-condition accuracy (how often did you correctly identify the condition?)	Journal — compare your Monday condition read to actual weekly price action	If you were correct 70%+ of the time but still lost money, the issue is execution. If you were correct below 60%, the issue is the condition read itself — review the VIX + chart protocol.
Position sizing compliance (were any positions opened above the cap tier size limit?)	Journal — check each entry against the cap tier table	One position over the size limit that produced a loss can wipe out multiple well-sized winning trades. Size compliance is non-negotiable.

MANAGE BY SCHEDULE, NOT BY EMOTION

The trader who checks positions every 20 minutes is not managing more effectively — they are creating more opportunities to override their plan. The weekly dashboard and monthly review replace continuous monitoring with structured decision points. Outside of those scheduled reviews, your job is to let the positions work. The GTC orders are set. The T-21 calendar is marked. The system runs. You do not need to watch it every hour to confirm it is running.

The Weekly Dashboard: One Page, Every Monday Morning

The weekly dashboard is your single-page operating view of your entire book. It is completed every Monday before the market opens — not during it. It replaces ad-hoc position checking with a structured, scheduled assessment that gives you a clear picture of every position and one action to take (or not take) on each.

Ticker	Strategy	DTE	P&L %	IVR Now	Delta	Action This Week	Notes
SPY	CSP $510	28	38%	64	−0.18	**Hold — on track for T-21 in 7 days**	IVR healthy. No threat to strike.
AAPL	CC $215	14	62%	58	−0.22	**Close — exceeded 50% target**	Book profit. Reset next cycle.
QQQ	Bull Put Spd	21	22%	71	−0.12	**Hold — early, monitor**	IVR elevated. Let theta work.
MSFT	CSP $400	7	49%	55	−0.25	T-21 this week — evaluate roll	Strike $40 OTM. Safe to hold or close.
XLF	Iron Condor	18	−15%	38	+0.05	**Monitor — IVR slipped below 40**	Consider closing if IVR drops further. Condor entered near-limit IVR.

This dashboard takes 15 minutes to complete on Monday morning. It gives you one clear action per position: Hold, Close, Roll, or Monitor. Once complete, you set your GTC orders accordingly and do not revisit positions until the following Monday — or until a pre-set alert triggers (T-21, 50% profit, or 2× premium stop).

The six-condition column is deliberately absent from the weekly dashboard. The condition read is done once — at trade entry. If the condition has dramatically changed, you will know from your Monday macro review of the VIX and chart — and you address affected positions under 'Action This Week.' You do not re-assess the condition on every position every morning. That is a path to overtrading.

THE WEEKLY DASHBOARD IS YOUR DECISION FIREWALL

Every action you take on a position should appear in the Action column before you take it — never the other way around. If you find yourself closing a position that says 'Hold' on your dashboard, you are making an emotional decision. Write down why before you act. If you cannot write a clean risk-management reason, do not act. The dashboard is not a suggestion. It is the system speaking. Listen to it.

The Sunday Evening Pre-Week Review: 15 Minutes That Change Everything

The most impactful habit in this book takes 15 minutes every Sunday evening. It is the difference between a trader who walks into Monday reacting to whatever happens and a trader who walks in with a plan for every position and every scenario. Here is the exact protocol:

Min	Review Item	What to Write Down
1-3	Open positions status	For each position: current P&L, DTE remaining, T-21 date, any earnings or events this week. Flag positions that need action Monday.
4-5	Greeks snapshot	Total portfolio delta, theta, and vega. Is your delta within your target range? Is your theta generating enough daily income? Is your vega exposure acceptable for current VIX?
6-8	Earnings & events	Which stocks on your watchlist report this week? Any FOMC, CPI, or NFP? If an event affects an open position, write the specific action you will take.
9-11	Market condition assessment	Check SPY trend, VIX level, VIX term structure. Which of the six conditions is active? Has it changed from last week? If so, which positions need adjustment?
12-14	Planned entries for the week	Which new positions meet your criteria? Write the exact entry: stock, strategy, strike, DTE, max risk, profit target, stop loss.
15	Rule commitment	Write your one non-negotiable rule for the week. Pick the rule you violated most recently. This is your focus.

The Sunday review turns Monday from the most stressful day of the trading week into the most prepared. Every action you take on Monday was decided on Sunday, when the market was closed and your emotions were calm. This one habit, practiced consistently, is worth more than any strategy in this book.

End-of-Month Performance Scorecard

At the end of each month, complete this scorecard. It takes 10 minutes and gives you a clear, honest picture of your trading business.

Metric	This Month	3-Month Avg
Total P&L	$______	$______
Win Rate (%)	______%	______%
Average Winner ($)	$______	$______
Average Loser ($)	$______	$______
Win/Loss Ratio	______:1	______:1
Total Trades Taken	______	______
Rule Compliance Rate (%)	______%	______%
Largest Single Loss	$______	$______
Days Without Trading (by choice)	______	______
PPD Achieved vs. Target	$___/$___	$___/$___

The two most important numbers on this scorecard are Rule Compliance Rate and Win/Loss Ratio. If compliance is above 90% and your W/L ratio is above 1.5:1, your system is working — regardless of what the raw P&L says in any single month. If compliance is below 80%, fix that before trying to improve anything else. Discipline comes before strategy optimization.

6-CONDITION FRAMEWORK ▸ ALL SIX — portfolio construction across simultaneous conditions
A long/short book may have positions open in multiple conditions simultaneously: longs in condition 1, income in condition 2, hedges in condition 4. Portfolio management means holding all six condition responses in balance at the book level.

The most sophisticated applications of options combine directional thesis, fundamental analysis, and portfolio management into a unified system. This chapter moves beyond individual trade setups into portfolio-level thinking: how to construct a book of long and short ideas, how to align them with sector rotation and business cycle positioning, and how to manage the overall portfolio's risk exposure as conditions evolve.

These frameworks are used by professional long/short equity fund managers. With options, you can implement the same ideas with defined risk — without the unlimited downside exposure that stock-only short sellers face.

The Long/Short Framework

A long/short portfolio holds bullish positions (long calls, bull spreads, CSPs on quality names) on companies and sectors expected to outperform, and bearish positions (long puts, bear spreads, bear call spreads) on companies and sectors expected to underperform. The combination creates a portfolio that can generate returns in both rising and falling markets, with reduced correlation to the broad market index.

Long Positions (Bullish Exposure)	Neutral Core (Market-Agnostic Income)	Short Positions (Bearish Hedge)
Condition 1 or 2 names.	Iron condors on SPY/QQQ.	Condition 3 or 4 names.
Strong Ten Indicator scores.	Calendar spreads.	Bear call spreads.
CSPs, long calls.	Short premium — Condition 5.	Long puts on laggards.
Sector leaders.		Sector underperformers.
Goal: Positive P&L regardless of market direction through disciplined balanced exposure.		

Figure 26.1 — Long/Short Portfolio Structure. Bullish and bearish positions offsetting each other for income.

Rotation fundamentals: the 1–3 month time horizon aligns perfectly with standard options expiration cycles. Positions are entered with 30–60 DTE, managed through the cycle, and closed or rolled based on fundamental catalyst developments. The thesis drives the entry; the options structure defines the risk.

- 90% Fundamental Analysis with catalyst + Technical Analysis and Price Action (TA & PA): Every position should have a clear fundamental thesis AND a technical confirmation. The fundamental thesis tells you WHY the stock should move. The technical setup tells you WHEN and HOW FAR;
- Position sizing: long ideas receive full position sizing when both fundamental and technical signals align. Short ideas receive 50–75% of normal position size — short positions can squeeze violently, requiring more cushion; and
- Portfolio balance: target a rough 60/40 long/short split in bull markets, 40/60 in bear markets, and 50/50 in neutral/transitioning markets.

Why Options L/S Is Superior to Stock L/S

Professional long/short funds that use stocks face a structural disadvantage on the short side: unlimited risk, borrow costs, locate requirements, and forced buy-ins. Options eliminate every one of these constraints while preserving the same directional thesis. Understanding this advantage explains why institutional money is migrating from stock-based L/S to options-based L/S — and why you should never short a stock when you can buy a put spread instead.

Dimension	Stock Short	Options L/S
Maximum Loss on Shorts	Unlimited — stock can rise to any price	Defined — capped at debit paid for puts
Borrow Cost	0.5%–10%+ annually on hard-to-borrow names	None — no stock borrow required
Forced Buyins	Broker can recall shares at any time	No recall risk — you own the option contract
Margin Requirement	50% of position value minimum	Option premium only (debit spreads)
Leverage	1:2 maximum on margin	Implicit leverage via delta exposure
Income from Shorts	None — you pay borrow costs	Bear call spreads generate premium income
Tail Risk on Shorts	Catastrophic if stock gaps up on news	Contained — max loss is debit paid
Short Squeeze Exposure	Full — unlimited P&L destruction	None — defined risk regardless of squeeze

THE SHORT SQUEEZE IMMUNITY RULE

In a stock-only L/S fund, a short squeeze can destroy months of gains in hours. GameStop 2021 is the definitive example: rational short sellers with correct fundamental theses were wiped out by a coordinated gamma squeeze. In an options L/S portfolio, your maximum loss on any bearish position is the debit paid for the put or put spread — the squeeze cannot exceed that number. You are always long the volatility, short the direction. The squeeze actually increases the value of your long puts in the early stages. Use defined risk exclusively on the short side.

The Long/Short Ratio by Six-Condition Framework

The single most important portfolio-level decision in a long/short book is how much gross exposure to allocate to the long side versus the short side at any given moment. This ratio should not be fixed — it should respond dynamically to the current six-condition framework read. A 60/40 long/short ratio in a Condition 4 market (Bearish, High IV) is not a balanced book — it is a mismanaged book.

Condition	Direction	IV	Long %	Short %	Primary Strategy
C1	Bullish	Low	70–80%	20–30%	Maximize long exposure. Small shorts as hedges only. Long calls, bull call spreads dominate.
C2	Bullish	High	60–70%	30–40%	Long bias with income overlay. CSPs and covered calls on longs generate income from elevated IV.
C3	Bearish	Low	30–40%	60–70%	Short bias. Long puts and bear spreads. Minimal new long entries — maintain only highest-conviction positions.
C4	Bearish	High	20–30%	70–80%	Maximum short exposure. Bear call spreads collect premium. Longs hedged aggressively with index puts.
C5	Neutral	Low	45–55%	45–55%	Near market-neutral. Iron condors and calendars replace directional positions. Balance is the strategy.
C6	Neutral	High	45–55%	45–55%	Near market-neutral with income overlay. Straddles and iron condors profit from IV

Condition	Direction	IV	Long %	Short %	Primary Strategy
					contraction. Hold.

THE RATIO RULE

Never operate at 80/20 long/short in any condition except C1 and C4, and even then only when the condition has been confirmed for three or more consecutive trading days. Conditions can shift in one session. The cost of being positioned 80/20 when the condition flips is larger than the benefit of being maximally exposed when it holds. Tilt aggressively — but never absolutely.

Long Ideas: Four High-Conviction Templates

LONG IDEA 1 — Classic Sequentially Positive Earnings Growth (Cyclical)

The cleanest long setup: a cyclical stock (Consumer Discretionary, Industrials, Technology, Financials) with three or more consecutive quarters of sequential EPS growth, revenue growth above sector average, and improving operating margins. The stock is in a confirmed uptrend above both the 50-day and 200-day EMA. MACD is positive. Sector rotation confirms the sector is in the leading phase of the business cycle.

- Options play: bull call spread, 30–45 DTE, long strike at or near ATM, short strike at 1× the expected move above ATM. Target 2:1 reward-to-risk minimum;
- Catalyst requirement: upcoming earnings beat expectation, sector ETF BPI rising, or macro data supporting cyclical outperformance;
- Example template: JPMorgan (JPM) in early expansion phase — rising net interest margin, sequential EPS beats, financials sector rotating in — bull call spread on JPM or XLF with 35 DTE;

LONG IDEA 2 — Sequentially Positive Revenue Growth, High R&D Component (Cyclical)

Applies to growth companies investing heavily in R&D — revenues are rising fast, earnings are intentionally suppressed by reinvestment. The thesis: the R&D spending is building a moat that will generate disproportionate future earnings. Used for technology, biotech (post-Phase 3), and emerging megatrend companies. Requires higher risk tolerance because EPS may be negative — the trade is purely on revenue momentum and forward multiple compression.

- Options play: longer-dated bull call spread (60–90 DTE), LEAPS call as stock substitute to limit capital at risk;
- Risk management: use defined-risk structures only. Do not sell puts on high-R&D names with no earnings — assignment risk on a company with negative earnings is substantially higher;
- Catalyst: revenue beat or upward guidance revision is the trigger. Watch for analyst upgrades that follow strong revenue quarters;

LONG IDEA 3 — EG Positive Above Sector Average (Defensive)

A defensive stock (Healthcare, Consumer Staples, Utilities) that is growing earnings faster than its sector peers — the best-in-class defensive. In a late-cycle or recessionary environment, defensive rotation flows into the entire sector. But within the sector, the fastest-growing names attract disproportionate capital. This idea captures the intersection of sector rotation and within-sector relative strength.

- Options play: cash-secured put for income during the rotation entry, bull call spread for directional participation as the sector gains momentum;
- The Wheel is highly appropriate here: quality defensive names with growing dividends are exactly the underlyings you want to own at a discount if assigned;
- Example: UnitedHealth Group (UNH) in late expansion — healthcare earnings growing above sector average, defensive rotation beginning — sell OTM CSP with strike below key support, collect premium, prepared to own;

LONG IDEA 4 — Believable Turnaround Story with Aggressive MOP & Catalysts (Cyclical)

Management of Problems (MOP) refers to a company that has identified its problems, installed new management or a restructuring plan, and is executing credibly. The stock is typically deeply beaten down — the market has priced in the worst. The trade is on the gap between the market's pessimism and the improving reality. CVNA (Carvana) is the textbook example: written off as near-bankruptcy, then executed an extraordinary operational turnaround. These are high-risk, high-reward — position size accordingly.

- Requirements: clear identification of what went wrong, credible new plan with specific milestones, sequential improvement in financial metrics for 2+ quarters, short interest beginning to decline (shorts covering = additional buying pressure);
- Options play: long calls (LEAPS) to capture the re-rating with limited downside. Do NOT sell puts on turnaround names — if the turnaround fails, the stock can go to zero; and
- Size at 25–50% of normal position size. Two or three sequential quarters of confirming data before adding to position.

Short Ideas: Four Templates for Bearish Conviction

SHORT IDEA 1 — Classic Sequentially Negative Earnings Growth (Cyclical)

The mirror image of Long Idea 1: a cyclical stock with sequential EPS declines, revenue contraction, and deteriorating operating margins. The sector is in the outgoing phase of the business cycle. Institutional money is rotating out. The stock is below its 50-day EMA and testing the 200-day. This is the clearest short setup — the fundamental deterioration is confirmed and the macro backdrop is turning negative.

- Options play: bear put spread, 30–45 DTE, long put near ATM, short put 1× expected move below. Or bear call spread to collect premium with stock below key resistance;
- Avoid: initiating short positions into a stock that has already fallen 30–40%. The easy money is gone and short squeeze risk is elevated. Short the early deterioration, not the rubble;

SHORT IDEA 2 — Flat Then Going Negative EG Below Sector Average (Defensive)

A defensive stock that was growing below sector average (already a yellow flag) and is now showing the first signs of sequential earnings decline. In a late-cycle environment where capital was flowing into defensives, this name is the weakest link — the first to face outflows when the cycle turns. The setup: earnings growth rolling from flat to slightly negative, revenue growth decelerating, and the stock trading near the top of a multi-year range.

- Options play: bear call spread just above the current price range resistance. Collect premium as the stock fails to break higher and begins to fade;
- This is a high-probability setup because the stock is not in crisis — the options market has not priced in deterioration yet. You are early, which means better pricing on the short premium side;

SHORT IDEA 3 — Negative EG Then Less Negative (Defensive)

This seemingly counterintuitive setup targets companies that have reported terrible earnings — and the next quarter's terrible-but-slightly-less-terrible earnings produces a 'beat' of lowered expectations. The stock rallies on the 'improvement' narrative. You use that rally to initiate or add to short positions at better pricing. The fundamental deterioration has not reversed — it is simply decelerating. The trend remains down.

- Options play: sell the rally into resistance using bear call spreads. Do not short the gap-up — wait for the stock to test overhead resistance and fail;
- Risk: if the company surprises with a genuine turnaround (see Long Idea 4), this position moves against you sharply. Use defined risk only. Stop if the stock closes above the 50-day EMA on volume;

SHORT IDEA 4 — Early Ex-Growth Cyclical, Large Cap, Negative Momentum (Tail Risk)

An ex-growth cyclical is a large-cap company that has reached maturity — it grew explosively in its early phase, and now faces market saturation, competitive disruption, or regulatory pressure that structurally limits further growth. The stock may still be richly valued on historical multiples, but forward growth cannot justify that valuation. The re-rating from 'growth stock' to 'value stock' multiple is the trade — it happens slowly, then suddenly.

- Requirements: market cap above $20B (smaller positions harder to short efficiently), P/E above 2× sector peers with decelerating EPS growth, increasing competitive threats or regulatory overhang;
- The Credit Suisse (CS) tail risk example: an institution with persistent structural problems where the market kept 'buying the dip' — until suddenly it couldn't. Tail risk shorts use small sizes of long puts on these names: the premium is cheap when nothing appears wrong, and the payoff is asymmetric if the thesis materializes; and
- Options play: long puts on high-premium, high-visibility names at risk of tail events. LEAPS puts allow holding through noise. Size very small — these are lottery-ticket structures for a low-probability, high-impact event.

Pairs Trading: Long the Strong, Short the Weak

Pairs trading is the purest expression of long/short portfolio management. Rather than betting on the broad market direction, you simultaneously buy the strongest stock in a sector and sell (via options) the weakest — capturing the spread between their relative performances while eliminating broad market risk. If the sector rises, your long outperforms and your short underperforms. If the sector falls, your short drops faster than your long. The market direction is irrelevant — the pair's internal spread is the trade.

For options-based pairs trading, the mechanics are straightforward: buy a bull call spread on the long leg (defined risk, bullish exposure) and buy a bear put spread or bear call spread on the short leg (defined risk, bearish exposure). The total debit or credit of the combined structure defines your maximum risk. The spread between the two stocks' returns defines your profit.

Sector	Long Leg (Strong)	Short Leg (Weak)	Pair Rationale	Options Structure
Financials	JPM (expanding margins, sequential EPS beats)	CS-equivalent (persistent structural problems, declining ROE)	Best-in-class vs. structurally impaired within same sector. Eliminates rate risk — both affected equally.	Buy JPM 45-DTE ATM call / Bull call spread. Buy bear put spread on weak leg.
Technology	NVDA (AI infrastructure dominance, revenue acceleration)	Legacy chip co. (declining PC cycle, no AI exposure)	AI cycle vs. commodity cycle within tech. Spread captures the megatrend vs. the disrupted.	NVDA: bull call spread 60 DTE. Weak leg: bear call spread just above key resistance.
Energy	XOM (integrated, dividend growing, buybacks accelerating)	Marginal producer (high break-even, leveraged balance sheet)	Quality vs. leveraged exposure to same commodity price. Quality wins in any scenario.	XOM: CSP below support for income. Weak leg: long puts, 60 DTE, limited size.
Healthcare	UNH (earnings consistency, moat, growing membership)	Single-product biotech near patent cliff	Durable compounder vs. binary event risk. Patent cliff = predictable earnings collapse.	UNH: bull call spread or CSP. Patent cliff co.: LEAPS puts — time is on your side.
Consumer	COST (membership model, pricing power, global expansion)	Traditional retailer (declining traffic, margin compression)	Structural winner vs. structural loser in same consumer spending pool.	COST: bull call spread 45 DTE. Retailer: bear call spread above falling 50MA resistance.

Three rules for pairs trading that protect the structure's integrity:

- Both legs must be in the same sector or sub-sector. Long NVDA / Short an airline is not a pair — it is two unrelated directional bets. The sector relationship is what eliminates the market risk;
- Size both legs equally in dollar terms. If the long leg is a $500 bull call spread, the short leg should also be a $500 bear spread. Unequal sizing reintroduces directional bias; and
- The pair lives and dies as a unit. Close both legs simultaneously when the fundamental thesis resolves — do not let one leg run while the other expires worthless.

Net Delta Management: Running the Book as One Position

Every individual position in your L/S portfolio has a delta — the approximate dollar change in position value per one-point move in the underlying. The net delta of your entire book is the sum of all individual position deltas, weighted by the number of contracts and the share price of each underlying. A professional portfolio manager monitors net delta as the single most important real-time risk measure of the entire book.

Net delta tells you: if the broad market moves one percent, how much does my entire portfolio move? A net delta of +$500 means your portfolio gains approximately $500 for every one-point rise in SPY. A net delta of -$800 means your portfolio gains $800 for every one-point decline. A net delta near zero means your portfolio is market-neutral — gains and losses depend on relative performance of your longs versus your shorts, not on overall market direction.

Net Delta Range	Market Exposure	Risk Profile	Action
+500 to +2,000	Bullish tilt	Profits if market rises. Losses if market drops. Appropriate for Conditions 1 and 2.	Monitor closely. Reduce delta if conditions shift to 3 or 4.
+200 to +500	Mildly bullish	Small positive correlation to market. Good default for mixed-condition environments.	Acceptable. Review weekly.
-200 to +200	Market neutral	Returns driven by relative performance of longs vs. shorts, not direction.	Ideal for uncertain or transitioning markets. Target this range in Condition 5 or 6.
-200 to -500	Mildly bearish	Small negative market correlation. Appropriate for Condition 3 or 4.	Acceptable. Review weekly.
-500 to -2,000	Bearish tilt	Profits if market falls. Losses if market rises. Appropriate for Conditions 3 and 4.	Monitor closely. Reduce delta if conditions shift bullish.

How to calculate your book's net delta: for each position, multiply the option delta by the number of contracts by 100 (shares per contract) by the underlying price. Sum all long position deltas (positive) and all short position deltas (negative). The result is your net dollar delta — the approximate change in portfolio value per one percent move in the market.

NET DELTA REBALANCING RULE

Rebalance net delta when it drifts beyond ±$1,000 per 1% market move on a $50,000 portfolio (equivalent to ±2% of account). Rebalancing tools: add a long or short position to offset the drift, close the position with the largest contributing delta, or use a small SPY/QQQ hedge position to neutralize the excess. Do not let delta drift compound — a $50K portfolio with +$3,000 delta is effectively running a $300,000 directional equity position. That is not a portfolio. That is a leveraged bet.

Position Lifecycle Management: From Entry to Exit

A long/short position does not manage itself after entry. Each template — long idea or short idea — has a predictable lifecycle: thesis development, entry, monitoring, adjustment, and exit. Understanding where each position is in its lifecycle tells you what action to take today. The most common amateur mistake is treating all positions the same regardless of where they are in their lifecycle — holding a position at T-21 with 80% profit the same way as a position at T-40 with only 20% profit.

Lifecycle Stage	Timeline	Position State	Monitoring Focus	Action
Thesis Formation	Pre-entry	Watchlist — monitoring fundamentals	Sequential earnings trend, sector BPI, business cycle phase, short interest direction	Build position in journal. Define entry trigger, target, and max loss before entry.
Entry	T-45 to T-30	New position — full size or Tier 1	Confirm condition, IV level, technical trigger. Verify earnings calendar — no events within DTE.	Enter at limit. Record six-condition read, delta, max risk. Set alert at 50% profit and 100% loss.
Early Stage	T-30 to T-21	Position developing. 0–30% profit or loss.	Fundamental thesis holding? Sector rotating as expected? No adverse news?	Hold if thesis intact. Close immediately if a rule-breaking event occurs (earnings surprise, restructuring, FDA news).
Active Management	T-21 to T-10	Position in final decay zone. Gamma risk elevated.	Delta drift, gamma exposure, time value remaining. Is the position at 50%+ profit?	At 50% profit: close or roll. At T-21: evaluate roll to next expiration if thesis remains.
Resolution	T-10 to expiration	End of lifecycle — close, roll, or expire.	Cost of closing vs. remaining time value. Risk of holding into settlement.	Do not hold to expiration for the last few dollars. Close at 75–80% of max profit or roll.
Post-Trade Review	T+1 after close	Position closed — journal entry	Did the thesis play out? Were the rules followed? What would you do differently?	Journal the outcome. Update your condition read. The lesson is worth more than the profit.

The thesis-invalidation rule governs every position regardless of lifecycle stage: if the fundamental thesis that justified the entry is materially disproven — an earnings miss that reveals the growth story was overstated, a competitor announcement that destroys the moat thesis, a regulatory ruling that eliminates the addressable market — close the position immediately. Not at the next target. Not at breakeven. Immediately. The options structure limits your dollar loss. Your discipline limits your psychological damage.

Hedging the Book with Index Options

Individual position hedges are inefficient — buying a put on each long position multiplies costs and creates a fragmented hedge structure that is difficult to manage. Professional portfolio managers hedge at the book level using index options: a single SPY or QQQ put spread protects the aggregate long exposure of the entire portfolio against a broad market decline. This is the most capital-efficient hedging tool available to the individual options trader.

The hedge ratio determines how much index protection you buy relative to your aggregate long delta. A portfolio with net long delta equivalent to 200 SPY shares needs a put spread that generates approximately $200 per point of SPY decline to be fully hedged. Most managers run a partial hedge — 50–75% coverage — accepting some market risk in exchange for lower hedge cost.

Hedge Type	When to Use	Structure	Cost Profile
SPY ATM Put Spread	Moderate concern about market pullback (C2 shifting toward C3). Hedge against 3–8% decline.	Buy SPY ATM put, sell put 5–8% lower. 30–45 DTE. Cost: $1.50–$3.00 debit.	High protection per dollar in the strike zone. Zero value below the short put. Ideal for measured corrections.
SPY OTM Put Spread	Tail risk hedge. Low-cost protection against 10–15% crash.	Buy SPY 5% OTM put, sell put 10–15% lower. 60 DTE. Cost: $0.50–$1.50 debit.	Very cheap. Only pays off in a significant crash. Good portfolio insurance in C4.
VIX Call Spread	Hedge against volatility spike rather than price decline. VIX and SPY highly inversely correlated.	Buy VIX call at current level + 5 points, sell call at current + 15 points. 30 DTE.	Cheap in low-VIX environments. Pays off dramatically in C4. Does not expire at VIX spot — uses settlement value.
QQQ Put Spread	Tech-heavy long portfolio hedge. QQQ more volatile than SPY — larger moves, cheaper relative hedge.	Same structure as SPY put spread but on QQQ. Use when long book is overweight technology sector.	Higher beta means more protection per dollar but also more noise. Use when tech exposure exceeds 35% of long book.
Collar on Single Name	Single large position that cannot be reduced (tax, concentration). Protect without selling.	Buy OTM put on the concentrated position, sell OTM call to fund it. Net zero or small credit.	Funded by the call sale. Caps upside but floors downside. Ideal for LEAPS positions with large gains.

THE 2% HEDGE RULE

Allocate 1–2% of total portfolio value per month to book-level hedges. At $50,000, this is $500–$1,000 per month in hedge premium. Think of it as portfolio insurance — not a trade, not a profit center. Run the hedge continuously. In months where nothing happens, the premium expires worthless. In the month where the market drops 10%, the hedge pays 5–10× its cost. The traders who resist paying the 2% because 'the market won't crash this month' are the same traders who have no protection when it does.

Rotation Fundamentals: Managing the 1–3 Month Portfolio

The 1–3 month time horizon is not arbitrary. It aligns with the standard options cycle, the typical lag between economic data releases and market price response, and the duration of most sector rotation moves. At the portfolio level, you are managing a book of ideas that ages and refreshes every 30–60 days.

Rotation Action	When and How
Add to Longs	When sector BPI is rising, fundamental data is improving sequentially, and technical signals confirm momentum. Add in layers — not all at once.
Trim Longs	When the position reaches 50–75% of maximum profit, or when the fundamental thesis shows the first cracks (EPS miss, guidance cut, sector BPI topping). Discipline over conviction.
Add to Shorts	When sector is confirmed in outgoing rotation, fundamental deterioration is evident in two or more consecutive quarters, and the stock fails to hold a key technical level on multiple tests.
Cover Shorts	When short interest drops sharply (squeeze risk elevated), when the company announces a credible restructuring with management commitment, or when the position reaches your profit target. Do not overstay a short.
Rebalance	Monthly — adjust the long/short ratio based on current market condition framework (Ch. 19). Bull market: increase long exposure. Bear market: increase short exposure. Neutral: 50/50.
Exit All	When a macro shock changes the regime entirely (unexpected recession, geopolitical crisis, liquidity crisis). In a regime change, correlation goes to 1 — everything falls. Defined-risk positions limit the damage; unlimited-risk positions do not.

Sample Live L/S Portfolio: A Complete Book Snapshot

Abstract portfolio construction principles are only useful when you can see them applied to real positions. The following is a complete six-position long/short book in a Condition 2 environment (Bullish, High IV) — the most common income-generating condition for the professional options trader. Each position has a defined role, a defined risk, and a defined exit plan. The aggregate book shows how individual positions combine into a managed, intentional system.

Market environment: SPY trending above 50MA and 200MA. VIX at 22 (IVR: 65). Condition 2 confirmed. Long/short ratio target: 65/35. Sector read: Technology and Financials leading. Energy and Consumer Discretionary lagging.

#	Role	Underlying	Position	Delta	Rationale
1	**LONG INCOME**	AAPL	Sell $175 Put / 35 DTE / CSP. Credit: $2.80. Max risk: $17,220.	+42	C2 — Bullish + High IV. Apple 9/10 Ten Indicators. IVR 68. CSP below key support. Collect elevated premium with bullish trend as tailwind. Prepared to

#	Role	Underlying	Position	Delta	Rationale
					own at $172.20 effective cost.
2	**LONG DIRECTIONAL**	NVDA	Buy $820/$860 Bull Call Spread / 40 DTE. Debit: $1.85. Max risk: $185.	+28	C1 momentum within C2 book — NVDA in confirmed AI upcycle, sequential revenue beats. Low debit cost in high-IV environment via spread structure. Target: $860 by expiration.
3	**LONG PAIRS**	JPM	Buy $195/$210 Bull Call Spread / 35 DTE. Debit: $2.10. Max risk: $210.	+22	Long leg of Financials pair. Rising NIM, sequential EPS beats, sector BPI rising. Mid-expansion phase. Pairs against Short Leg #5.
4	**INCOME / NEUTRAL**	SPY	Sell $530/$520 Bull Put Spread / 30 DTE. Credit: $1.40. Net Max Risk: $860.	+18	C2 income position. SPY above all key MAs. Short put spread 3% OTM — well below S1 support. Premium income while broad market holds. T-21 rule governs exit.
5	**SHORT PAIRS**	Regional Bank ETF (KRE)	Buy $45/$40 Bear Put Spread / 35 DTE. Debit: $1.20. Max risk: $120.	-18	Short leg of Financials pair. Regional banks facing NIM compression, CRE loan exposure, deposit flight to money market. Pairs against Long #3. Spread captures JPM outperformance vs. regional banks.
6	**BOOK HEDGE**	SPY	Buy $525/$510 Put Spread / 45 DTE. Debit: $1.60. Max risk: $160.	-32	Book-level hedge. Protects aggregate long delta against 3–5% SPY decline. Cost: $160 per unit. Hedge ratio: covers approximately 60% of aggregate long delta. Monthly renewal as part of 2% hedge budget.

Portfolio Metric	Value	Assessment
Net Delta	+(42+28+22+18)−(18+32) = +60	Mildly bullish. Appropriate for C2 environment. Within ±200 target range.
Long/Short Ratio	4 long / 2 short = 67/33	Within C2 target range of 60–70% long. ✓
Sector Diversification	Tech (NVDA), Financials (JPM/KRE), Consumer (AAPL), Broad (SPY×2)	Four sectors represented. No single sector >40% of book. ✓
Total Capital at Risk	\$185+\$210+\$120+\$860+\$160 = \$1,535 debit + \$17,220 CSP obligation	CSP is secured by cash held. Total options debit: \$1,535 on a \$50K account = 3.1% at risk.
Hedge Coverage	SPY put spread covers 60% of aggregate long delta	Appropriate for C2. Increase to 75–80% if conditions shift toward C3.
Monthly Theta	Est. +\$180/week from CSP and bull put spread income	Positive theta — time working in our favor on income positions while debit positions are directional.

READING THE PORTFOLIO AS A SYSTEM

Look at the six-position snapshot above and notice what is not there: no overlapping sector bets, no uncovered directional exposure, no positions without a defined maximum loss, no hedge-free long book. Every position has a role. The CSP (Position 1) generates income while the directional spread (Position 2) captures momentum. The pair (3 and 5) is self-hedging within Financials. The book hedge (Position 6) protects the aggregate. The income spread (Position 4) pays while the market holds. This is portfolio management — not position management.

THE PORTFOLIO MANAGER'S EDGE

The difference between a trader with a collection of positions and a portfolio manager with a book is intentionality. Every position in a well-managed book has a role: income, growth, hedge, or speculation. The portfolio manager knows the aggregate delta, the aggregate vega, and the aggregate theta of the entire book — not just the individual trades. Build your book with intention. Review it as a whole. Manage it as a system.

> 6-CONDITION FRAMEWORK ▸ **CONDITIONS 2, 5 — Earnings create the highest-volatility events of the year**
> Earnings season is where most retail options traders make their largest gains — and their most devastating losses. The difference is preparation. This chapter gives you the complete system.

Four times per year, the market enters a six-week period where roughly 90% of S&P 500 companies report quarterly results. During these windows — typically the last two weeks of January, April, July, and October — implied volatility surges, options premiums inflate by 40–200%, and stocks move 3–15% overnight on results. For options traders, earnings season is both the greatest opportunity and the greatest danger of the year.

This chapter gives you a complete, rules-based system for trading earnings — not a collection of tips, but a structured framework that tells you exactly what to do before, during, and after every earnings event on every stock you trade.

The Earnings Calendar System: Your Pre-Season Preparation

Before any earnings season begins, you need a calendar — not just of when companies report, but of how those reports affect your existing positions and your planned entries. The calendar system has three layers:

Layer	What to Track	When to Do It
Layer 1 — Defense	Every stock you currently hold or have short options on: when does it report? If earnings fall inside your expiration cycle, you must act BEFORE the report.	The Sunday before earnings season begins. Check every open position. Mark any position with earnings inside its cycle for early closure or roll.
Layer 2 — Offense	Your watchlist of 10–20 quality names: when does each report? What is the market expecting (consensus EPS, revenue)? What is the expected move priced into options?	Two weeks before each company's report date. Research consensus estimates and calculate the expected move from current options pricing.
Layer 3 — Post-Earnings	Companies that just reported: did results beat, meet, or miss? What was the stock's reaction? Is there a post-earnings continuation or mean-reversion setup?	Within 24 hours of each report. Log the result in your journal. Evaluate whether a post-earnings trade meets your criteria.

Layer 1 is non-negotiable. Every Premium Desk trader checks their earnings exposure every Sunday during earnings season. A single unchecked position that catches an earnings report can erase a month of income.

Pre-Earnings Strategies: Profiting from the IV Ramp

In the 7–14 days before a company reports earnings, implied volatility on its options rises steadily. The market is pricing in the uncertainty of the upcoming report. This IV ramp is predictable, repeatable, and tradeable — if you understand the mechanics.

→ See IV Skew & VIX Relationship — How volatility skew shifts with market fear (Chapter 16 — Volatility: The Hidden Driver)

Figure 27.1 — Pre-Earnings IV/Skew/VIX Dynamics. The interaction of IV, skew, and VIX heading into earnings.

The IV ramp creates a natural profit opportunity for traders who own options before the ramp begins and sell them after IV has inflated. The key is entering early enough to capture the ramp but exiting BEFORE the earnings report — because after earnings, IV collapses.

Pre-Earnings Strategy 1 — The Calendar Spread Play

Buy a calendar spread (sell near-term, buy longer-term at the same strike) 14–21 days before earnings. The near-term option's IV inflates more aggressively than the longer-term option as earnings approaches. The spread widens in your favor.

- Entry: 14–21 days before earnings. ATM or slightly OTM calendar spread;
- Exit: The day BEFORE earnings — close the entire position. Do NOT hold through the report;
- Expected return: 15–30% on the debit paid, driven by the differential IV ramp between the two expiration cycles;
- Risk: The stock moves sharply before earnings (catalyst leak, sector event). Maximum loss is the debit paid;

Pre-Earnings Strategy 2 — The Long Straddle (Momentum Play)

Buy an ATM straddle 10–14 days before earnings on a stock with a history of large pre-earnings moves. The thesis: the stock will move enough before earnings to offset the time decay, and the IV ramp will increase the value of both legs.

- Entry: 10–14 days before earnings. ATM straddle;
- Exit: 1–2 days before earnings. You are selling the inflated IV, not holding for the earnings move itself;
- Best candidates: stocks with historical pre-earnings drift (TSLA, NVDA, NFLX, META) — check the stock's 10-day average move into earnings over the last 8 quarters; and
- Danger: stocks that go flat into earnings. The straddle bleeds theta with no IV ramp to offset. Only use on historically volatile names.

The IV Crush: Why Most Earnings Trades Lose Money

The IV crush is the single most common source of options losses for traders who buy options into earnings. The pattern is consistent across hundreds of stocks every quarter: in the 10–14 days before an earnings announcement, implied volatility on the near-term options chain climbs steadily as traders and institutions buy options for directional bets and hedges. By the day before the announcement, IV may have risen 30–60% above its baseline level. Then the announcement happens. The event that was being priced passes. IV collapses the following morning — sometimes within minutes of the market open — returning to or below baseline levels.

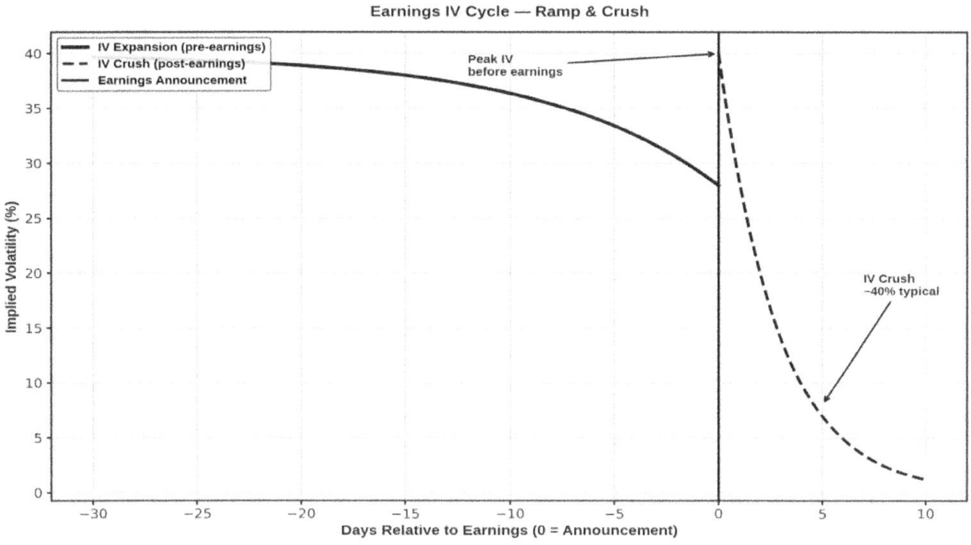

Figure 27.2 — Earnings IV Ramp & Crush. IV expands into earnings, then collapses after announcement.

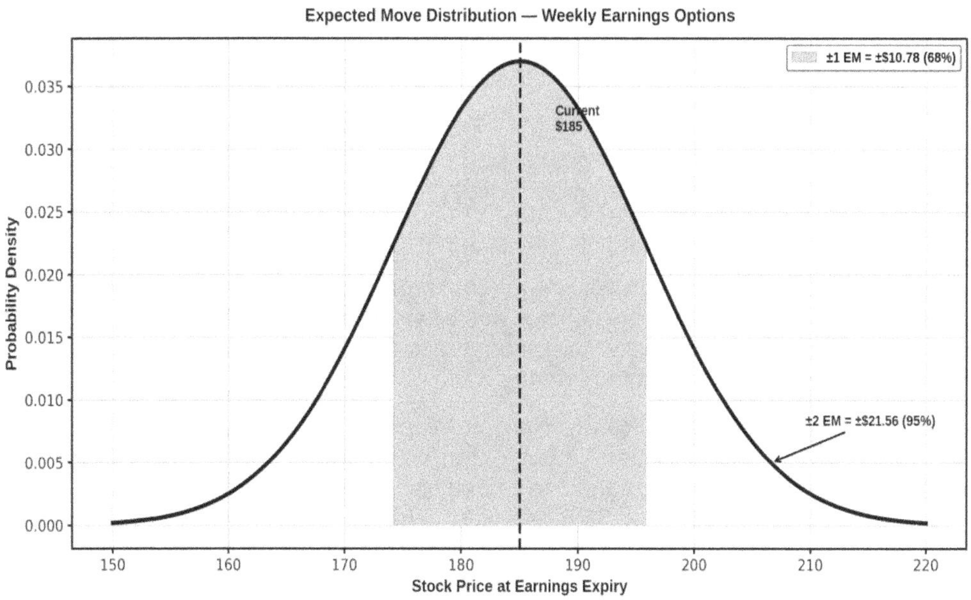

Figure 27.3 — Expected Move Distribution. Probability distribution of outcomes at earnings expiry.

A trader who bought calls 3 days before earnings, was right on direction (the stock beat estimates), but still lost money has experienced the IV crush firsthand. The stock moved up $4. The call they owned lost $1.20. How? The IV contraction from 62% to 28% destroyed more option premium than the intrinsic value gained from the stock move. This is mathematically precise: a 1% move in the stock adds delta-weighted value to the option, but a 34-point IV collapse subtracts vega-weighted value. When vega loss exceeds delta gain, the option loses value despite the correct directional call.

THE IV CRUSH RULE FOR BUYERS

> Never buy options in the final 5 days before an earnings announcement expecting to profit from the move. The IV premium you pay at entry will be partially or fully destroyed by the crush regardless of direction. If you want a directional earnings play, enter 15–20 days before the announcement when IV has not yet fully inflated, and close the position the day before the announcement. Take the IV ramp profit before the crush arrives.

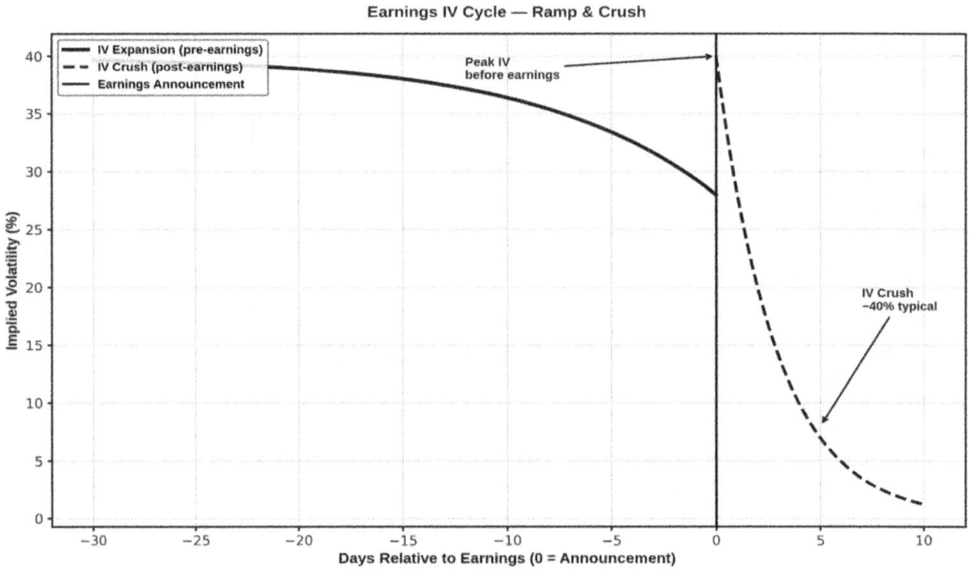

Figure 27.1 — Earnings IV Cycle — IV expansion into earnings and the collapse pattern after announcement. The seller's edge.

Earnings IV Cycle — IV expansion into earnings and the collapse pattern after announcement.

The single most important concept in earnings trading is IV crush — the rapid collapse of implied volatility immediately after a company reports results. Understanding IV crush is the difference between the trader who profits from earnings season and the trader who loses every quarter wondering why.

Here is what happens: in the days before earnings, IV on a stock's options might be 65%. This elevated IV is pricing in the expected earnings move — say, ±7%. The moment the company reports and the market digests the results, the uncertainty is resolved. IV drops from 65% to 35% overnight. This 30-point IV collapse destroys the extrinsic value of every option on that stock — calls AND puts.

The math is devastating for option buyers. Even if you are RIGHT about the direction — even if the stock moves 5% in your favor — the IV crush can still make your option lose money. A 5% move in your favor minus a 30-point IV drop can result in a net loss on a long option position.

Scenario	Stock Move	IV Before	IV After	Option P&L
Buy call, stock rises 3%	+3%	65%	35%	LOSS — IV crush exceeds directional gain
Buy call, stock rises 8%	+8%	65%	35%	SMALL WIN — large move barely offsets crush

Scenario	Stock Move	IV Before	IV After	Option P&L
Buy call, stock rises 15%	+15%	65%	35%	WIN — move large enough to overwhelm crush
Buy put, stock drops 5%	−5%	65%	35%	LOSS — same IV crush destroys put value
Sell iron condor, stock flat	±1%	65%	35%	BIG WIN — you sold expensive IV, it collapsed
Sell CSP, stock drops 4%	−4%	65%	35%	WIN — premium collected exceeds unrealized loss

The table reveals the structural truth of earnings trading: option SELLERS have a massive edge over option BUYERS during earnings. The writer collects inflated premium before the report and profits from the IV crush after. The buyer must overcome both the IV crush AND time decay just to break even. This does not mean never buy options into earnings — it means if you do, the expected move must be large enough to overwhelm the crush, and you should size the position assuming you will lose.

THE IV CRUSH MATH

Before buying any option into earnings, calculate the expected move and compare it to the breakeven. If the stock needs to move 8% for you to break even but the average earnings move over the last 8 quarters is 5%, you are making a negative-expectancy bet. The math does not care about your conviction. Only take long earnings trades when the expected move exceeds the breakeven by at least 1.5×.

Worked Pre-Earnings Trade: NFLX Calendar Spread

NFLX reports earnings in 14 days. The stock is at $680. You want to profit from the IV ramp without holding through the earnings report. Here is the complete execution:

Day 1 (14 days before earnings): NFLX 30-DTE $680 call is trading at $28.00. NFLX 60-DTE $680 call is trading at $42.00. You buy the calendar spread: sell the 30-DTE, buy the 60-DTE. Net debit: $14.00 ($1,400 per contract). Maximum risk: $1,400. Current IV on the 30-DTE option: 38%. Current IV on the 60-DTE option: 32%.

Day 5 (9 days before earnings): IV on the 30-DTE option has risen to 48% (the earnings ramp). IV on the 60-DTE has risen to 36%. NFLX is still at $678. The 30-DTE call is now worth $32.00 (up $4 from IV expansion). The 60-DTE call is now worth $45.50 (up $3.50). Your spread is now worth $13.50 — still slightly underwater because the near-term IV expanded more than the long-term.

Day 10 (4 days before earnings): IV on the 30-DTE option has reached 58%. IV on the 60-DTE is at 38%. NFLX is at $685. The 30-DTE call: $36.00. The 60-DTE call: $48.50. Your spread is now worth $12.50 — you are losing on the spread itself because near-term IV is expanding faster than long-term.

Day 12 (2 days before earnings — YOUR EXIT): This is the key day. The 30-DTE call is now priced at $38.00 (IV at 62%). The 60-DTE call is at $50.00 (IV at 40%). Your spread value: $12.00. But here is what most traders miss — you can capture the IV differential by closing the SHORT leg only. Buy back the short 30-DTE call for $38.00 (loss of $10.00 on that leg). Your long 60-DTE call is worth $50.00 (gain of $8.00). Net P&L: -$2.00 on the spread — a small loss. BUT: you still hold the long 60-DTE call, which will benefit from any post-earnings move while the near-term IV crushes the options you already closed.

Alternative exit (simpler): Close the entire spread 2 days before earnings for $12.00. Net loss: $2.00 ($200). This sounds like a losing trade — but the thesis was wrong. NFLX did not move enough pre-earnings to make the calendar profitable. The lesson: pre-earnings calendars work best on stocks with historical pre-earnings drift. NFLX in this cycle was flat — not ideal for the strategy. Your loss was $200 on a $1,400 risk — 14%. Defined, manageable, and informative.

The key takeaway: pre-earnings calendar spreads are not guaranteed winners. They are defined-risk positions that capture IV differential when the underlying cooperates. When it does not, the loss is bounded. Track your pre-earnings trades by stock over multiple quarters — you will quickly learn which names consistently drift before earnings (ideal candidates) and which go flat (avoid).

Post-Earnings Strategies: Trading the Aftermath

The 3–5 trading days after an earnings report offer some of the cleanest setups of the quarter. IV has collapsed, pricing is rational again, and the market has given a clear verdict on the company's results. There are three post-earnings patterns to watch for:

Pattern 1 — Earnings Gap and Go (Continuation)

The stock gaps up or down on earnings and continues moving in the same direction over the next 3–5 days. This happens when the earnings surprise is significant enough to change the fundamental thesis — analysts revise estimates, funds rebalance, and momentum traders pile in.

- Setup: Stock gaps 5%+ on earnings. The next day, it holds above the gap (for longs) or below the gap (for shorts). Volume confirms the direction;
- Options play: Bull call spread (for gap up) or bear put spread (for gap down), 30 DTE, strikes bracketing the new trading range;
- Edge: IV is now low (post-crush), so spreads are cheap. You are buying options at the lowest IV of the quarter;

Pattern 2 — Earnings Gap and Fade (Mean Reversion)

The stock gaps on earnings but reverses within 2–3 days, filling most or all of the gap. This happens when the initial reaction was overdone — either the market misread the report, or algorithmic trading amplified the move beyond what fundamentals justified.

- Setup: Stock gaps 5%+ but within 2 days has retraced 40%+ of the gap. RSI divergence confirms the fade;
- Options play: Fade the move with a vertical spread in the opposite direction. 30 DTE, defined risk;
- Caution: Do NOT fade a gap on the first day. Wait for the retracement signal. Many gaps that look like fades on day 1 turn into continuations by day 3;

Pattern 3 — The Post-Earnings Volatility Reset (Income Play)

After the earnings event, IV resets to its base level and the stock enters a 10–12 week period of relatively predictable behavior (until the next earnings report). This is the ideal window for income strategies — CSPs, covered calls, iron condors — because you have 10+ weeks of runway before the next binary event.

- Setup: 3–5 days after earnings. Stock has settled into its new range. IVR has dropped below 30;
- Options play: Cash-secured put at 0.20–0.25 delta, 30–35 DTE. Or iron condor if the stock is range-bound; and
- Edge: You are selling premium in a low-IV, low-uncertainty environment. No earnings surprise for 10+ weeks. This is the income trader's sweet spot.

THE POST-EARNINGS WINDOW

The best 10 weeks of the year for income trading are the 10 weeks between earnings reports. During this window, your short premium positions face no binary event risk, IV is stable, and theta decay is predictable. Structure your income calendar around this rhythm: close positions before earnings, wait 3–5 days for the dust to settle, then re-enter for the next 10-week income cycle.

The Earnings Checklist: Before Every Report

Print this checklist and complete it for every earnings event that affects your portfolio. No shortcuts. Every line item exists because a trader skipped it and paid the price.

#	Check	Action If Failed
1	Do I have any open positions on this stock?	If yes: decide NOW whether to close, roll, or hold. Do not wait until report day.
2	Is my expiration cycle AFTER the earnings date?	If yes AND you are short premium: close the position before earnings. The risk is not worth the remaining premium.
3	What is the expected move priced into options?	Calculate: (ATM straddle price ÷ stock price) × 100 = expected move %. Compare to the stock's average earnings move over 8 quarters.
4	Is the expected move larger than the historical average?	If yes: options are expensive. Favor selling strategies (iron condors, CSPs). If no: options are cheap — possible buying opportunity if you have a directional thesis.
5	What is consensus EPS and revenue?	Know the numbers the market expects. A 'beat' that is below whisper numbers can still sell off. Context matters more than the headline.
6	Is this stock in a sector that has already reported?	If sector peers have already reported and the trend is clear (beats across the sector), this stock is more likely to follow the pattern. Sector context reduces surprise risk.
7	What is my maximum acceptable loss on this position?	Write the number down. If the position can lose more than 2% of your account on an adverse earnings move, reduce size or add a protective hedge.
8	Do I have a post-earnings plan?	Write down your response to three scenarios: beat (what you do), miss (what you do), in-line (what you do). Having the plan before the report prevents emotional decisions after.

The Expected Move Calculation: Your Edge in Numbers

The expected move is the market's consensus estimate of how far a stock will move by expiration, implied by the current options pricing. Formula: Expected Move = Stock Price × IV × √(DTE/365). For a $150 stock with 45% IV and 1 day to expiration (earnings night): Expected Move = $150 × 0.45 × √(1/365) = $3.53. This means the market is pricing in approximately a plus or minus $3.53 move by tomorrow's close.

The practical application: if the expected move is $3.53, sell your short options at strikes that are at least 1.5× the expected move away from the current stock price. At $150, your put strike should be below $144.70 ($150 − $5.30) and your call strike above $155.30. This positions you outside the market's own consensus estimate of where the stock will go — a statistical edge in your favor.

The expected move is also directly visible in your options chain. Look at the ATM straddle price (ATM call + ATM put). The sum of those two premiums approximates the expected move. If the ATM straddle costs $7.20, the market expects approximately a $7.20 move by expiration. Your iron condor wings should clear this number with margin to spare.

The expected move is the market's best estimate of how far a stock will move on its earnings report. It is derived directly from options pricing — specifically, the price of the ATM straddle for the nearest expiration after earnings.

The formula: Expected Move = ATM Straddle Price × 0.85. The 0.85 multiplier accounts for the portion of the straddle price that represents non-earnings time value. If AAPL is at $190 and the ATM straddle (nearest weekly expiration after earnings) is priced at $12.00, the expected move is $12.00 × 0.85 = $10.20, or approximately ±5.4%.

How to use it: if you are selling an iron condor into earnings, place your short strikes OUTSIDE the expected move. If the expected move is ±5.4%, your short call should be at least 6% above the current price and your short put at least 6% below. This gives you a margin of safety beyond what the market is pricing.

How NOT to use it: do not treat the expected move as a guaranteed range. Stocks move more than the expected move approximately 30% of the time. The expected move is a probability-weighted estimate, not a ceiling. Size your positions assuming the stock WILL exceed the expected move — because eventually, it will.

Building Your Earnings Season Calendar

The quarterly earnings cycle follows a predictable rhythm. Mapping your trading activity to this rhythm keeps you in the right strategies at the right times.

Week	Phase	Your Action	Strategy Focus
Week -3	Pre-Season	Audit all open positions for earnings exposure. Close or roll anything at risk. Build your watchlist of 10–20 earnings candidates.	Defense: protect existing positions. Offense: research candidates.
Week -2	IV Ramp Begins	Enter pre-earnings calendar spreads or straddles on watchlist names. IV is starting to inflate but hasn't peaked.	Pre-earnings plays only. No income positions on names reporting soon.

Week	Phase	Your Action	Strategy Focus
Week −1	Peak IV	Exit all pre-earnings long positions by Wednesday before Friday earnings (or Thursday before Tuesday earnings). Maximum IV means maximum exit value.	Close pre-earnings trades. Prepare post-earnings plans for each watchlist name.
Weeks 1–2	Earnings Peak	Reports flood in. Execute your post-earnings plans: gap-and-go, gap-and-fade, or wait for the volatility reset.	React to results. No new income positions until IV settles (3–5 days post-report).
Weeks 3–4	Post-Earnings Reset	IV has collapsed. Stocks are in their new ranges. Enter income positions: CSPs, covered calls, iron condors.	This is the income sweet spot. Maximum 10-week runway to next earnings.
Weeks 5–12	Income Season	Manage income positions through their cycles. Close at 50% profit. Roll at T-21. No binary events ahead.	Pure income mode. The most profitable and lowest-stress period of the quarter.

This 12-week cycle repeats four times per year. The disciplined trader maps every quarter to this rhythm and never gets caught holding unprotected short premium through an earnings report. The undisciplined trader treats every week the same — and eventually learns the hard way why earnings weeks are different.

THE EARNINGS SEASON MASTER RULE

Earnings season is not a time to be aggressive. It is a time to be surgical. The trader who makes money during earnings season is not the one who bets big on every report — it is the one who defends existing positions first, captures the IV ramp second, and enters clean income positions after the dust settles. Defense, then precision, then income. In that order, every quarter, for the rest of your trading career.

Sector Earnings Patterns: Who Reports When and Why It Matters

Earnings season does not hit all sectors equally or simultaneously. Understanding the reporting sequence gives you a structural edge — the first companies to report in a sector set the tone for the rest. If the first three banks beat estimates, the fourth bank is more likely to beat too. Sector sentiment cascades.

Reporting Week	Sectors	Bellwethers to Watch	What Their Results Tell You
Week 1	Financials	JPM, GS, BAC, WFC	Credit conditions, loan demand, net interest margin. If banks beat on NII, the economy is still expanding. If loan loss provisions spike, recession is closer.
Week 2	Healthcare, Transport	UNH, JNJ, UPS, FDX	Defensive demand + shipping volumes. UPS/FDX are leading indicators — shipping volume predicts consumer and industrial activity 2-3 months forward.
Week 3	Big Tech	MSFT, GOOGL, META, AMZN	Cloud growth (MSFT Azure, AMZN AWS), ad spending (META, GOOGL), consumer

Reporting Week	Sectors	Bellwethers to Watch	What Their Results Tell You
			behavior (AMZN retail). These four companies reveal the health of the entire digital economy.
Week 4	Consumer, Industrial	AAPL, MCD, CAT, DE	Consumer spending (AAPL, MCD), capital expenditure (CAT, DE). If CAT raises guidance, industrials have 6+ months of tailwind. If AAPL misses on iPhone units, consumer discretionary is weakening.
Week 5-6	Energy, Small/Mid Cap	XOM, CVX, then broad reporting	Commodity demand, small business confidence. The tail of earnings season fills in the remaining picture. By week 6, you should have a complete macro view.

The actionable insight: if Week 1 banks report strong earnings and healthy credit conditions, you can increase confidence in your cyclical long positions for Weeks 2-4. If banks report deteriorating loan quality, reduce cyclical exposure before the rest of the sector reports. The earnings calendar is a real-time economic diagnostic — use it.

The Earnings Trade Journal: Tracking What Works Across Quarters

After every earnings season, the most valuable 30 minutes you can spend is reviewing your earnings-specific trades. This builds a database of what works for YOUR trading style — not what works in theory, but what generates real P&L in your account.

Ticker	Strategy	Entry IV	Exit IV	Stock Move	P&L	Lesson
AAPL	Pre-E calendar	42%	28%	+2.1%	+$185	IV ramp captured. Closed day before report. Perfect execution.
TSLA	Long straddle	68%	35%	+8.5%	-$90	IV crush destroyed both legs despite large move. TSLA straddle was overpriced.
MSFT	Post-E CSP	22%	18%	Gap +4%	+$310	Entered 3 days post-report. Low IV, 10-week runway. Ideal income entry.
NFLX	IC into earnings	55%	30%	+12%	-$450	Stock exceeded expected move. IC short call breached. Should have used wider wings.
JPM	Post-E bull call	24%	20%	Gap +3%	+$220	Sector earnings cascading positive. Entered on WFC beat, rode JPM sympathy.

After 4 quarters of this journal, patterns emerge. You will discover which stocks your earnings strategies work on, which strategies suit your risk tolerance, and — most importantly — which earnings trades you should stop taking because they consistently lose money despite feeling like good ideas at the time.

The December Playbook — End-of-Year Seasonal Setups

December is the one month where the market gives income traders a clear seasonal edge — if they know which edges to take and which to leave alone. The combination of suppressed implied volatility, a historical upward drift bias, tax-loss selling pressure on quality names, and the year's largest OPEX event creates five distinct, repeatable setups. Each one aligns with a Six-Condition entry and follows the same risk management rules as every other trade in this book.

Here is how the Risk Manager approaches December — not as a spectator of 'what pros do,' but as a systematic trader matching the seasonal environment to a defined condition and executing with discipline.

Figure 27.5 – The December Options Playbook: Five Risk-Management Rules

Rule	Action	Why
1 – Calendar Check	Run earnings calendar every Sunday in Nov/Dec	One missed earnings report can erase a month of income
2 – Reduce Size	Cut position size by 25–50% during holiday weeks	Lower liquidity = wider spreads and harder exits
3 – Avoid Holiday Week	No new entries Thanksgiving week, Christmas week	Thin markets magnify moves; premium not worth the risk
4 – OPEX Opportunity	Sell premium BEFORE Dec OPEX spike (W1–W2)	Collect elevated IV before the seasonal crush
5 – Year-End Close	Close all open positions by Dec 28–29	Avoid gap risk from year-end rebalancing flows

Figure 27.4 — The December Options Playbook. Five risk-managed setups aligned to the Six-Condition Framework. December OPEX week is the only period in the calendar where the standing rule is: reduce size, roll open positions, do not open new ones.

The Five December Setups

Setup 1 — Iron Condor (Condition 5 or 6): Between Thanksgiving and the second week of December, implied volatility on the major indexes tends to compress while the market drifts sideways to mildly higher. This is the highest-probability environment of the year for a short-premium iron condor on SPX or QQQ. Enter at 30-45 DTE, sell the 20-delta strikes on both sides, collect the credit, and manage per the T-21 Rule. The trade has a seasonal tailwind: realized volatility in December is structurally lower than implied volatility, meaning the volatility risk premium is wide.

Setup 2 — Bull Put Spread or CSP (Condition 2): The historical December drift — the so-called Santa Rally — is not a myth. S&P 500 December returns have been positive in roughly 75% of years since 1950. That is not a trading signal on its own, but when Condition 2 (bullish, high IV) is also active, a bull put spread or cash-secured put on a quality large-cap name has both the seasonal and the systematic edge behind it. Enter only when the Six-Condition Framework confirms.

Setup 3 — CSP on Tax-Loss Names (Condition 2): Every year in late November and early December, institutional funds and retail investors sell their losing positions for tax purposes. This mechanical, non-fundamental selling temporarily drives down high-quality stocks that have had a bad year — not because the business deteriorated, but because the calendar forced a sale. These names score well on the Ten Indicators but show elevated IV due to recent price weakness. A cash-secured put at or below a major support level collects premium while the assignment price represents a genuine value entry. Run the full Ten Indicator screen first.

Setup 4 — Calendar Spread, Sell December / Buy January (Condition 1 or 2): December options expire faster than any other month relative to January because the short-leg is burning theta at maximum velocity while the long-leg retains significant time value. A Dec/Jan calendar spread near ATM on a stable, high-quality underlying captures this differential decay. The short December leg funds the January long. Use the T-21 Rule: when the short leg hits 21 DTE (early December), evaluate rolling to January.

Setup 5 — December OPEX: Roll, Don't Open. The third Friday of December is not just a regular expiration. It is the quarterly expiration (quad witching) plus year-end index rebalancing, creating the largest single-day gamma flow of the calendar year. Institutional hedges roll, fund managers rebalance, and market makers run massive hedging programs. The intraday moves can be sharp and directional without fundamental cause. The Risk Manager's rule: in the week of December OPEX, reduce position size, do not open new positions, and roll any existing positions approaching their management trigger out to January or March. This is not a week to be a hero.

Question	YES Path	NO Path
Is earnings within 5 trading days?	Proceed to next question.	Normal conditions apply. Use Six-Condition Framework.
Do you hold a position in this name?	Proceed to next question.	No action needed. Monitor normally.
Is the position profitable?	Consider holding with reduced size or protective hedge.	Close before earnings. Do not take directional risk.
Is the position at 50%+ profit and low risk?	Hold through earnings with documented plan.	Close. Protect capital. Re-enter after the report.

Figure 27.5 — December IV Seasonal Pattern. IV typically suppresses from Thanksgiving through mid-December (prime entry window), spikes around OPEX (reduce exposure), then resets into the new year.

THE DECEMBER RISK MANAGER CHECKLIST

Before any December trade: (1) Confirm the Six-Condition Framework — do not trade seasonality alone. (2) Check the distance to December OPEX — if within 5 trading days, wait or roll. (3) Verify IV Rank — are you selling premium when IV is elevated or merely normal? (4) For tax-loss names, run the full Ten Indicator screen — temporary selling creates opportunity only if the business is still intact. (5) Apply the 2% Rule regardless of seasonal conviction. The calendar is one input. Risk management is non-negotiable.

The Earnings Decision Tree: Every Situation, One Framework

The earnings decision tree is the single tool that replaces all ad-hoc thinking during earnings season. Before touching any position — existing or planned — run it through this tree. The tree produces a specific, actionable output for every situation: close, hold, enter pre-earnings, enter post-earnings, or take no action.

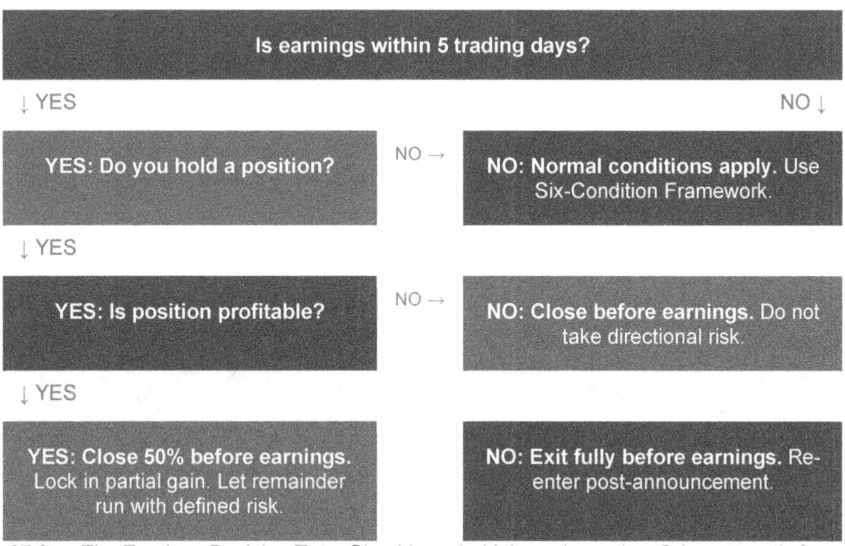

Figure 27.6 — The Earnings Decision Tree. Should you hold through earnings? A systematic framework.

Use this tree every Sunday during earnings season for every open position and every watchlist name with a report in the next 30 days. It takes 3 minutes per stock. Over a full quarter, those 3-minute checks save hours of damage control.

Complete Earnings Trade Walkthrough: AAPL Earnings Cycle

The following is a complete, real-time walkthrough of how a Premium Desk income trader manages an Apple (AAPL) position through an earnings cycle. This is not theory — it is the exact sequence of decisions, calculations, and actions from the Sunday before the report through the post-earnings income entry. Follow this walkthrough as a template for every earnings cycle you navigate.

Scenario: You currently hold a short AAPL $175 Cash-Secured Put, 35 DTE, entered three weeks ago at a $2.80 credit. AAPL is trading at $189. Earnings are in 11 days. The report falls inside your expiration window.

Phase 1 — The Sunday Review: Identifying the Earnings Conflict

You open your earnings calendar every Sunday during earnings season. Today's check reveals: AAPL reports in 11 days. Your $175 Put expires in 35 days. The report falls INSIDE your cycle — this is an earnings conflict.

First calculation: What is the current value of your position? The $175 Put that you sold for $2.80 is now worth $0.90 (AAPL has rallied since entry). Your unrealized profit is $1.90 per share, or $190 per contract — 68% of maximum profit.

- At 68% of maximum profit with 11 days to earnings: the decision is straightforward. You have captured the majority of your edge. The remaining $0.90 of premium is not worth the binary risk of holding through an earnings report;
- The math: closing now locks in $190 profit per contract. Holding to expiry risks the entire premium and the obligation to buy 100 shares if AAPL drops sharply on earnings. The risk-reward of continuing to hold is extremely unfavorable; and
- Action decision: CLOSE the position before earnings. Place a buy-to-close order at $0.90 (the current ask) or slightly above mid-price. Target fill: $0.85-$0.95.

Phase 2 — Pre-Earnings Analysis: Preparing for the Report

Your existing position is closing. Now switch to offense: what does the earnings setup look like for AAPL? Run the pre-earnings analysis checklist.

Pre-Earnings Check	AAPL Finding
Current IVR	IVR at 58% — elevated. Options are pricing in significant uncertainty. This favors selling strategies, not buying.
Expected Move	ATM weekly straddle (expiring 2 days post-earnings) = $9.50. Expected move = $9.50 x 0.85 = $8.08, or ±4.3% on a $189 stock.
Historical Average Move	AAPL's average earnings move over the last 8 quarters: ±3.8%. The expected move ($8.08) slightly exceeds the historical average — options are fairly priced, not cheap.
Consensus EPS	Wall Street consensus: $1.43 EPS. Revenue: $89.5B. Whisper number (from earnings whisperers): slightly above consensus, $1.46 EPS.
Sector Context	Alphabet (GOOGL) reported last week: beat on revenue, strong AI monetization. Meta beat. Positive sector tone heading into AAPL.
Pre-Earnings Strategy Eligibility	IVR 58% + earnings in 11 days = calendar spread or wait. NOT a straddle (options are fairly priced, not cheap for directional bet). Possible: sell iron condor with wings beyond the expected move.

Pre-earnings decision: The sector context is positive and IVR is elevated — conditions favor an iron condor. However, AAPL is a notoriously unpredictable earnings mover and the expected move is already slightly above historical average. Decision: no pre-earnings position this quarter. Wait for the post-earnings reset. Missing a trade is not a loss.

Phase 3 — The Earnings Report: Reacting Without Emotion

AAPL reports after the close. Results: EPS of $1.51 versus $1.43 expected (beats by 5.6%). Revenue: $91.2B versus $89.5B expected (beats by 1.9%). Services revenue sets a new record. Management guidance is in-line with expectations. Stock gaps up 5.8% to $200 in after-hours trading.

Your response to the gap: NOTHING. You have no position. You wrote down a post-earnings plan before the report (Phase 2). Now you wait. Do not chase the after-hours move. Do not buy calls because 'it will keep going.' The plan is: wait 3–5 days for IV to collapse and the stock to find its new range, then evaluate a post-earnings income entry.

- Day 1 post-earnings: AAPL opens at $199, closes at $197. Volume heavy. IVR has dropped from 58% to 24% in one session — the IV crush is complete;
- Day 2-3: AAPL consolidates between $195 and $200. Volume declining. No new catalysts. IV continues to settle lower; and
- Day 4: AAPL trading at $197. IVR at 18%. Weekly chart: uptrend intact, above 26-week EMA. Daily chart: price in value zone between 13-day and 26-day EMA. Six-condition read: Condition 1 (bullish/low IV). 10 weeks until next earnings.

Phase 4 — Post-Earnings Entry: Rebuilding the Income Position

Day 4 post-earnings. AAPL at $197. Condition 1 confirmed (bullish/low IV). Ten Indicators: AAPL scores 9/10 — A-Class. Now build the post-earnings income position.

Strategy selection: Condition 1 with strong quality stock — CSP or bull call spread. Since IVR is low (18%), CSP premium will be modest. Bull call spread offers better leverage in low-IV environment. Strategy: 30 DTE bull call spread targeting the continuation of the post-earnings momentum.

Trade Parameter	Specification
Underlying	AAPL at $197
Strategy	Bull Call Spread (Condition 1 — Bullish / Low IV)
Strikes	Buy $195 Call / Sell $205 Call (width = $10)
Expiration	32 DTE monthly expiration — well clear of next earnings
Debit Paid	$3.80 (entering at near mid-price)
Maximum Profit	$10 - $3.80 = $6.20 per share = $620 per contract
Maximum Risk	$3.80 per share = $380 per contract (the debit)
Profit Target	Close when spread value reaches $7.60 (80% of width = $8 minus debit ~50% gain on debit)
Thesis	AAPL confirmed beat, stock in new range above $195, low IV makes debit spread superior to CSP
T-21 Date	Mark calendar: if spread has not reached target in 21 days, evaluate closing

Outcome (21 days later): AAPL rallied to $204 on continued AI services growth. The $195/$205 spread is worth $7.20 — a $3.40 gain on the $3.80 debit, or 89% return in 21 days. Close the spread for a $340 per contract gain. Total for the full earnings cycle:

$190 profit from closing the CSP before earnings + $340 profit from post-earnings bull call spread = $530 per contract across the full cycle.

THE EARNINGS CYCLE SUMMARY

The complete Premium Desk earnings cycle for any quality stock: (1) Close or protect any short premium inside the expiration cycle — 7-10 days before the report. (2) Evaluate pre-earnings opportunity — only if IV and risk-reward are compelling. (3) Do nothing during the report. (4) Wait 3-5 days for IV to normalize and the stock to find its range. (5) Enter the post-earnings income position for the full 10-week runway. Repeat each quarter. This sequence generates income from two sources — the pre-close profit and the post-earnings income position — while eliminating the binary risk of holding through the report itself.

6-CONDITION FRAMEWORK ▸ ALL SIX — your psychology is tested differently in each condition
Every strategy in this book can be learned in weeks. The psychology required to execute those strategies consistently takes months or years. This chapter accelerates that process.

You now have every strategy, every framework, every management rule you need to trade options profitably for the rest of your career. But here is the uncomfortable truth: the strategies are not the hard part. The hard part is executing them when your emotions are screaming at you to do something else.

Every trader who has blown up an account will tell you the same thing: they knew the rules. They had the plan. They just did not follow it — once — and that once was enough. This chapter is about the space between knowing the rules and following them. It is the most important chapter in the book.

> The market does not reward intelligence. It does not reward bravery. It rewards discipline — the boring, unglamorous, day-after-day execution of a tested plan regardless of how you feel.

The Five Psychological Traps That Destroy Options Traders

Trap	How It Feels	What It Makes You Do	The Antidote
Revenge Trading	Anger after a loss. Urgency to make the money back immediately.	Open a larger position than planned, often in the same stock that just hurt you. Skip your entry criteria. Double down on a broken thesis.	After any loss that exceeds your normal average, close your platform for 24 hours. Do not place another trade until the next trading day. The market will be there tomorrow.
Overconfidence	A winning streak makes you feel invincible. Rules seem unnecessary because you are 'reading the market perfectly.'	Increase position sizes beyond your 2% rule. Skip the checklist because 'I already know this one.' Enter trades without a written plan.	Track your win streak in your journal. When you hit 5 consecutive winners, REDUCE your position size by 25% for the next 5 trades. Overconfidence is most dangerous when it feels most justified.
Loss Aversion	A position is losing money and you cannot bear to close it because closing makes the loss real.	Move your stop loss further out. Remove your stop entirely. Average down on a losing position without thesis confirmation. Hold a losing trade for weeks hoping it will recover.	Write your stop loss price in your journal before entry. When the price hits your stop, close the position within 5 minutes. Do not look at it again for 48 hours. The loss was real the moment the stock crossed your stop — closing the position just acknowledges reality.
The Boredom Trap	Nothing is happening. Your positions are flat. The market is quiet. You feel restless and unproductive.	Open new positions you do not need. Adjust positions that do not require adjustment. Check your account 15 times per day looking for something to do.	Schedule a non-trading activity for quiet market days: review your journal, study a new sector, research your next earnings calendar. The most dangerous thing an income trader can do is trade when bored.

Trap	How It Feels	What It Makes You Do	The Antidote
FOMO (Fear of Missing Out)	A stock you were watching makes a massive move without you. Other traders are posting gains. You feel left behind.	Enter a position after the move has already happened, chasing the momentum at the worst possible entry point. Buy calls at the top of a rally because 'it might keep going.'	Write the ticker and date in your journal under 'Missed Trades.' Review monthly. You will find that most FOMO entries would have been losers. The move already happened — your edge is in the next setup, not in chasing this one.

Every one of these traps has a common feature: it feels rational in the moment. Revenge trading feels like determination. Overconfidence feels like skill. Loss aversion feels like patience. Boredom trading feels like initiative. FOMO feels like opportunity. The ability to recognize these disguises — in real time, under pressure — is what separates the trader who survives from the one who does not.

The Behavioral Journal: Tracking Your Psychology

Your trade journal already tracks entries, exits, and P&L. Now add a behavioral column. After every trade, answer one question: 'Did I follow my rules, and if not, what emotion caused the deviation?' This single addition transforms your journal from a performance record into a psychological diagnostic tool.

Trade	Result	Rule Followed?	If No — What Emotion?	Correction for Next Time
AAPL CSP	+$180	Yes	—	—
TSLA Bull Call	-$420	No	FOMO — entered after 8% rally, chased the move	Wait for pullback to 20-day EMA before entering directional trades
MSFT IC	+$95	Yes	—	—
SPY Put buy	-$310	No	Revenge — opened 2 hours after TSLA loss to 'make it back'	24-hour rule: no trades for 24 hours after a loss exceeding $300
AMZN CSP	+$210	Yes	—	—

In this example, the three winning trades all followed rules. The two losing trades both involved emotional overrides. The pattern is obvious after five trades — it would be invisible without the behavioral column. After 50 trades, you will know exactly which emotions cost you money, how much they cost, and what triggers them. That data is worth more than any strategy.

Building Emotional Resilience: The 90-Day Discipline Protocol

Discipline is not willpower — it is habit. You cannot will yourself to follow rules under pressure if you have not built the neural pathways through repetition. The 90-day discipline protocol trains your trading psychology the same way your paper trading trained your strategy execution:

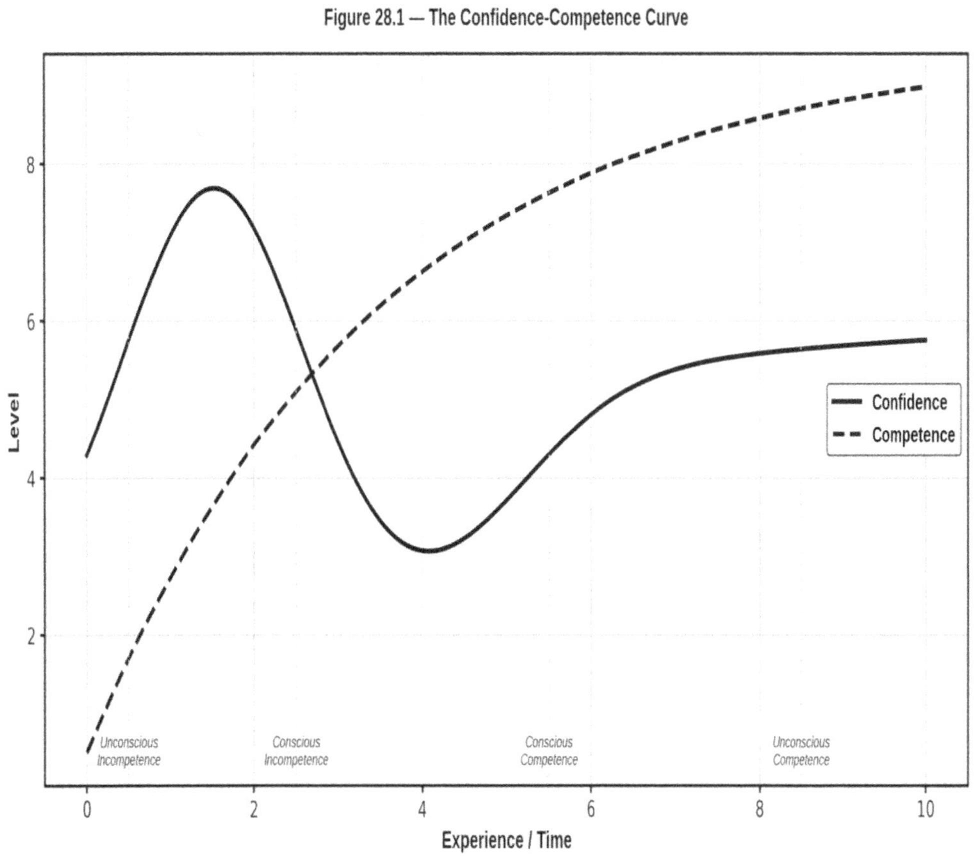

Figure 28.1 — The Confidence-Competence Curve. From unconscious incompetence through conscious mastery.

- Days 1–30: Write your trading plan for the next day every evening. Include specific entries you are watching, position sizes, and stop levels. In the morning, execute ONLY what is on the plan. Nothing else. Log every deviation;
- Days 31–60: Add the 24-hour rule after any loss exceeding 1% of your account. No new positions for 24 hours. Use the time to journal the loss and identify the lesson. If you break the 24-hour rule, restart the 30-day count; and
- Days 61–90: Add the weekly behavioral review. Every Sunday, review your behavioral journal column from the past week. Calculate your 'rule compliance rate' — percentage of trades where you followed all rules. Target: 90% or above. Below 80%? Reduce your position count by half until compliance improves.

Loss Aversion: The Most Expensive Emotion in Trading

Loss aversion is the psychological tendency to feel the pain of a loss approximately twice as intensely as the pleasure of an equivalent gain. In trading, this asymmetry produces a specific and devastating pattern: traders hold losing positions far longer than their rules allow, and close winning positions far too early. The losing position is held because closing it makes the loss feel real. The winning position is closed because taking the profit eliminates the anxiety of watching it disappear. Both behaviors destroy long-term performance even when the trader is right on direction more than 50% of the time.

Psychological Trap	What It Produces	System Override
Fear of Loss	Undersizing; closing too early.	2% Rule enforces correct sizing.
FOMO	Chasing trades; ignoring conditions.	Six-Condition check prevents FOMO entries.
Overconfidence	Oversizing after wins.	Position size tied to account, not feelings.
Revenge Trading	Doubling down on losers.	Stop-loss orders enforce exits mechanically.
Analysis Paralysis	Missing entries; over-researching.	Pre-flight check provides clear go/no-go.
Boredom Trading	Trading when no condition is active.	Rule: No condition, no trade. Period.

Figure 28.2 — The Psychology-Discipline Framework. How emotional triggers map to trading errors and the counter-systems.

The antidote is written rules enforced before emotion enters. Before entering any position, write down three numbers: your profit target (typically 50% of max profit for credit trades), your stop level (typically 2x the credit received), and your maximum hold period. When any number is hit, close the position within five minutes. Do not look at it again. The loss was real the moment the stop was triggered. Closing just acknowledges reality.

THE LOSS AVERSION CIRCUIT BREAKER

Every time you move a stop loss to give a position more room, you are letting loss aversion make your trading decisions. Write your stop before entry. Honor it at the trigger price. If you find yourself negotiating with your stop — 'just a little more room' — close the position immediately. The negotiation is the signal that emotion has taken over.

The Pre-Market Morning Routine: Setting Your Psychological State

Professional traders do not open their platforms cold. Before any screen time, the disciplined trader completes a brief routine that sets the psychological state for the session. The routine takes fifteen minutes and has three components: a review of open positions and their current status relative to rules (not P&L), a condition read using the two-step framework (chart direction + VIX), and a written statement of the day's intention — specifically what you will and will not do today. This is not motivation. It is pre-commitment. Research consistently shows that pre-commitment to specific behaviors reduces emotional override under pressure.

Emotional Circuit Breakers: Hard Rules for When You Are Not Okay

Every trader has days when they are not in the right psychological state to make good decisions. A losing streak, a personal crisis, poor sleep, or simple frustration can all impair judgment in ways that are invisible to the person experiencing them. Circuit breakers are pre-set rules that take the decision out of your hands when your judgment is most likely to be impaired.

Trigger	Circuit Breaker Rule	Duration
Loss > 2x average daily loss	Close platform. No new trades.	24 hours minimum
3 consecutive losing trades	Stop trading for the day.	Rest of session
Hit monthly drawdown limit	Stop trading for the month.	Until next month 1
Personal crisis or stress event	Reduce to half size or stop.	Until resolved
Feeling urgent / must trade	Do not trade today.	Until urge passes

The 90-Day Discipline Protocol

The first 90 days of live trading are the most important of a trader's career. Not because of the money involved — account sizes at this stage are too small for the P&L to matter — but because the habits formed in the first 90 days become the default behaviors under pressure. Every deviation from your written rules in the first 90 days makes the next deviation easier. Every time you honor a rule under pressure, you strengthen the neural pathway of discipline.

The protocol is simple. For the first 30 days: maximum one position open at a time. No exceptions. Close it before opening another. For days 31–60: maximum two positions simultaneously. Full pre-trade checklist required for every entry. For days 61–90: maximum three positions. Begin tracking behavioral patterns in your journal. By day 90, you should have a clear behavioral profile: which emotions cost you money, what triggers them, and what your win rate is by condition. This data is worth more than any strategy.

The Loss-Streak Recovery Protocol

A loss streak is not a sign that your strategy is broken. It is a normal statistical event in any trading system with less than 100% win rate. A system with a 70% win rate will produce runs of 3 consecutive losses approximately 2.7% of the time, and runs of 4 consecutive losses approximately 0.8% of the time. These runs are inevitable. What is not inevitable is how you respond to them.

The loss-streak recovery protocol has four stages. Each stage triggers at a specific threshold and requires a specific response. The stages are not optional — they are the circuit breakers that protect your capital and your psychology before a losing streak becomes a drawdown crisis.

Stage 1 — Two Consecutive Losses

Review each trade against your rules. Were the rules followed? If yes: the losses are statistical noise. Reduce position size by 25% for the next three trades and continue trading. If no: identify the rule broken. Do not trade again until you understand why the rule was broken and have written a specific correction in your trade journal. Name the rule. Name the moment you broke it. Write the fix.

Stage 2 — Three Consecutive Losses (Rules Followed)

Reduce position size by 50% and add a second confirmation requirement to every new entry. From this point forward, only enter a position if both your own six-condition analysis and an AI prompt confirm the same market condition independently. Two inputs, one conclusion. If they diverge, do not trade.

Stage 3 — Four Consecutive Losses

Stop trading for 48 hours. Step away from the screen entirely. Then return and review all four losing trades together — not individually — looking for a common pattern. Is there a shared element? Same sector? Same DTE range? Same market condition? Same time of week? If a pattern exists, you have identified a system edge gap, not a psychological problem. That gap becomes the next rule you add to your checklist.

Stage 4 — Five Consecutive Losses

Return to paper trading for a minimum of 10 days regardless of cause. This is not a punishment. It is a full system reset. Five consecutive losses — whether rule-following or rule-breaking — indicate that something in your read of the market, your execution, or your position management is sufficiently misaligned to require a reset at zero risk. Paper trade the same system, the same checklist, the same sizes. When you produce five consecutive paper trades that follow all rules, you may return to live capital.

LOSSES ARE DATA, NOT FAILURE

Every losing trade that followed your rules is a data point that your system is working correctly. The loss is the cost of doing business — it is the premium you pay for the right to collect income from hundreds of trades over time. The losing trade that broke your rules is the only trade that should concern you, because it represents a failure of process, not a failure of statistics. Track rule adherence, not just win rate.

Condition-Specific Psychological Traps

Each of the six conditions creates a distinct psychological environment that generates its own characteristic mistake. Understanding which trap your current condition is most likely to trigger is part of professional trade preparation.

Condition	Environment	Psychological Trap	Antidote
1 — Bull/Low IV	Rising market, cheap options	Buying too many calls, overleveraging the trend	2% rule per trade, not per direction
2 — Bull/High IV	Income environment, high premium	Selling too aggressively, ignoring assignment risk	Pre-defined assignment plan before entry
3 — Bear/Low IV	Falling market, fear growing	Buying puts at the bottom of the move, chasing	Only enter on failed bounces, not capitulations
4 — Bear/High IV	Fear spike, elevated VIX	Paralysis or panic-selling winners prematurely	Rules-based target: close at 50% of max profit
5 — Range/High IV	Choppy, condor environment	Adjusting condors too early, fighting the range	Only adjust when a short strike is breached
6 — Range/Low IV	Quiet, calendar environment	Over-trading out of boredom, opening bad risk	Calendar minimum: wait for BB squeeze signal

The Trader Self-Assessment: Where Are You Right Now?

Complete this self-assessment honestly once per month, on a neutral day, away from recent trading. Score each statement from 1 (never) to 5 (always). A total score of 40–50 indicates strong execution discipline. A score below 30 indicates the need to reduce position size or return to paper trading until the score improves.

Statement	1–2	3	4–5
I follow my entry checklist on every trade without exception	___	___	___
I close positions at my profit target without second-guessing	___	___	___
I honor my stop-loss levels without moving them	___	___	___
I maintain correct position sizing per the 2% rule	___	___	___
I check the earnings calendar before every new options entry	___	___	___
I complete my morning routine before opening my platform	___	___	___
I can identify the current six-condition read without hesitation	___	___	___
I review my trades in my journal within 24 hours of closing	___	___	___
I trade without significant influence from fear or excitement	___	___	___
When I make a rule violation, I record it and learn from it	___	___	___

The Neuroscience of Bad Trading Decisions

The human brain was not designed for trading. It was designed for survival on the African savanna 200,000 years ago — and the neural wiring that kept our ancestors alive is the exact wiring that destroys trading accounts today. Understanding this is not an excuse. It is a map. You cannot fight a system you do not understand.

Three neurological mechanisms drive the majority of trading errors. The first is the amygdala hijack — when a position moves sharply against you, the amygdala (the brain's threat-detection center) fires before the prefrontal cortex (the rational decision-maker) can process the information. You experience physical fear — elevated cortisol, accelerated heart rate, narrowed attention — and make a decision in that state. That decision is almost always wrong because it is made by a survival system responding to financial data as though it were a predator.

The second mechanism is dopamine anticipation. When you open a winning trade, your brain releases dopamine — the same neurotransmitter activated by gambling, food, and social approval. The dopamine is released not at the win, but at the anticipation of the win. This is why traders hold winning positions too long (chasing the next dopamine hit), add to winners impulsively (the dopamine is flowing), and feel genuine physical discomfort when they close a winner at the systematic target. The system is working correctly. The brain is protesting.

The third mechanism is loss aversion at the neurological level. Brain imaging studies show that financial losses activate the insula — the same region that processes physical pain. A $500 loss is neurologically painful in a way that a $500 gain is not pleasurable. The 2:1 ratio is not a statistic — it is neurology. Your brain will fight you every time you take a loss. The written rule is your prefrontal cortex speaking to your amygdala in advance. Write the rule before the loss — so the prefrontal cortex wins.

THE PREFRONTAL OVERRIDE

The written trading plan — condition read, entry trigger, position size, profit target, stop level — is your prefrontal cortex speaking to your amygdala before the amygdala fires. When a position moves against you and your heart rate spikes, your prefrontal cortex has already lost the argument. The plan wins by arriving first. This is why the pre-trade checklist is not a suggestion. It is your brain's circuit breaker — already in place before the emotional hijack begins.

The Seven Cognitive Biases That Destroy Options Traders

Cognitive biases are systematic errors in thinking — predictable, universal, and invisible to the person experiencing them. Every trader has all seven. The goal is not to eliminate them (impossible) but to build rules that override them before they fire. Each bias below has a specific expression in options trading and a specific structural antidote.

Bias	What It Is	How It Kills Options Traders	The Antidote
Confirmation Bias	Seeking information that confirms your existing thesis and dismissing information that contradicts it.	You find 5 bullish signals and ignore the 2 bearish ones. Your condition read becomes a self-fulfilling prophecy that excludes contrary evidence.	Require one bearish argument in every trade journal entry. If you cannot construct a credible bear case, you do not understand the trade well enough to take it.
Recency Bias	Overweighting recent events and underweighting historical base rates.	After three winning trades, you believe the system has a 90% win rate. After three losing trades, you believe the system is broken. Neither is true — both are recency bias.	Review your trailing 50-trade win rate monthly, not your last 3 trades. Require statistical significance before drawing conclusions about system performance.
Anchoring	Fixing on an initial price point and making all subsequent decisions relative to that anchor.	You bought a call at \$3.20. It is now worth \$1.80. You cannot close it because you are anchored to \$3.20. The question is never where you entered — it is whether you would enter at the current price today.	Replace 'I bought at X' with 'I would buy at the current price: yes or no.' If the answer is no, close the position. The entry price is irrelevant to the exit decision.
Sunk Cost Fallacy	Continuing a losing position because of the resources already committed rather than the future outlook.	'I cannot close this losing CSP — I have already collected the premium and I am not taking a loss.' The premium collected is gone. The question is the current risk, not the past credit.	Write this rule in your trading plan: the cost of a position is the current market value, not the historical entry. Evaluate every position daily as if you were entering it fresh today.
Overconfidence	Overestimating the accuracy of your	After a winning streak, position sizes drift upward. The 2% rule	Lock position sizes to the 2% rule in your plan. After any position

Bias	What It Is	How It Kills Options Traders	The Antidote
	predictions and the strength of your edge.	becomes 3%, then 5%. Conviction overrides math. One large loss destroys three months of disciplined gains.	size increase, require a mandatory 30-day review period before implementing it permanently.
Gambler's Fallacy	Believing that past independent events influence future independent events.	After three losing trades in a row, you increase size on the next trade because 'you are due for a win.' Each trade is statistically independent. The market does not know your streak.	Treat every trade as the first trade in your career. Position size based on current account value and the 2% rule — never on streak history.
FOMO — Fear of Missing Out	Entering trades based on the fear of missing a move rather than a systematic setup.	SPY gaps up 2% at the open. You enter a long call without a condition read because you feel the move is real. You buy at the top of the gap. The gap fills. You lose the premium.	Require a complete pre-trade checklist before any entry. If the checklist is not complete, the trade does not happen. FOMO trades are never on the checklist.

The Four Trader Personality Types — Know Yours

There is no universal psychological weakness in trading — there are four distinct failure modes, each driven by a different personality structure. Most traders have a dominant type with secondary characteristics. Knowing your type does not excuse the behavior — it tells you which rules to write first, which situations to avoid, and where your discipline will be tested hardest.

Type	Dominant Trait	Signature Failure	Tells	Correction Protocol
The Aggressive Trader	High risk tolerance. Thrives on action. Needs to feel in the market.	Oversizing in high-conviction setups. Revenge trading after losses. Adding to losers to 'average down.' Cannot sit in cash.	Multiple positions open simultaneously. Position sizes drifting above 2%. Journal entries that rationalize rule breaks as 'special situations.'	Hard position limit: maximum 3 open positions regardless of conviction. Mandatory 24-hour cooling period after any loss exceeding 1.5% of account. Cash is a position — treat it as one.
The Fearful Trader	High loss aversion. Risk-averse beyond what the system requires. Needs	Taking profits too early (50% of target instead of 75%). Missing entries because	Journal entries with phrases like 'felt uncomfortable,' 'seemed risky,' 'not	Require 3 rules to be violated before closing a position early. If the condition, the

Type	Dominant Trait	Signature Failure	Tells	Correction Protocol
	certainty before acting.	the setup 'does not feel right.' Closing positions on normal volatility before the thesis resolves.	sure about this one.' Consistent underperformance relative to system backtest due to early exits.	fundamental thesis, and the technical structure are all intact — hold. One uncomfortable feeling is not a rule.
The Perfectionist Trader	Cannot tolerate ambiguity. Needs the perfect setup before acting. Overanalyzes.	Paralysis — watching the right setup from the sidelines because one indicator is not aligned. Missing 60% of approved trades because of excessive filtering. Perpetual 'almost' trades.	Journal entries with 'I saw the setup but waited for confirmation that never came.' High paper trading performance but consistent underperformance in live trading.	Define 'good enough' in your trading plan: if 7 of 10 checklist items are satisfied including the condition read and the fundamental filter — the trade is approved. Perfect is not a condition.
The Impulsive Trader	Acts before thinking. Executes before the checklist is complete. Trusts instinct over system.	FOMO entries without condition reads. Increasing size mid-position because 'it is working.' Closing winners at breakeven because 'it might reverse.' Zero patience for the system to play out.	Trades opened within 5 minutes of a market move. Journal entries with no pre-trade checklist completed. Inconsistent results — spectacular wins followed by account-damaging losses.	Mandatory 15-minute waiting period between identifying a setup and executing the trade. During those 15 minutes: complete the full checklist. If the setup is gone after 15 minutes, the setup was FOMO.

IDENTIFY YOUR TYPE — THEN LEGISLATE AGAINST IT

Most traders have one dominant type and one secondary type. The Aggressive-Impulsive is the most common and most dangerous combination — high action orientation with low patience creates a systematic tendency to oversize and overtrade. The Fearful-Perfectionist is the second most common — high loss aversion with excessive filtering creates a systematic tendency to underperform the system's actual edge. Write your type in your trading plan. Then write the three rules that specifically target your type's failure mode. Post them at your trading station.

The Identity Shift: From Speculator to Risk Manager

The single most powerful psychological change a trader can make has nothing to do with strategies, indicators, or Greeks. It is a change in identity. The speculator asks: how much can I make? The risk manager asks: how much can I lose? These two questions produce completely different trading behaviors, completely different position sizes, and completely different long-term outcomes.

The speculator is emotionally attached to the outcome of each trade. A winning trade confirms they are smart. A losing trade confirms they are a failure. This emotional stake means every trade is a referendum on their self-worth — and under that pressure, rational decision-making collapses. The risk manager is emotionally attached to the process. A winning trade is evidence that the process worked. A losing trade that followed all rules is also evidence that the process worked. The outcome and the self-worth are decoupled.

The identity shift is not instant. It happens through repetition — 90 days of journaling process over outcome, 90 days of sizing correctly even when conviction is high, 90 days of closing at the target even when you believe the position could run further. After 90 days of process-first behavior, the identity shifts because the behavior has shifted first. You do not think your way into a new identity. You act your way into it.

The Speculator Thinks...	The Risk Manager Thinks...
"How much can I make on this trade?"	"What is the maximum I can lose, and is that acceptable?"
"This setup feels right — I have a good feeling."	"Does this setup pass the pre-trade checklist? Yes or no."
"I cannot close this loser — it might come back."	"The thesis is broken. I close the position and redeploy the capital."
"I was right on direction but still lost. The system is wrong."	"I followed the rules. The loss is the cost of doing business."
"I need to make back what I lost this week."	"This week's P&L is irrelevant to next week's trade decisions."
"The market is wrong. My analysis is correct."	"The market is always right. My analysis is a probability, not a fact."
"I should have made more — I closed too early."	"I closed at the target. The process was correct. Next trade."

THE IDENTITY DECLARATION

Write this in your trading plan, at the top of every page: 'I am a risk manager. My job is to protect capital and deploy it systematically. The market owes me nothing. My process owes me consistency.' Read it before every trading session. It is not motivation — it is a cognitive primer that activates the risk manager identity before the speculator identity has a chance to take the wheel.

The Winning Streak Trap: Overconfidence Is As Dangerous As Fear

Every trader understands loss streaks are dangerous. Almost no trader understands that winning streaks are equally dangerous — they just destroy accounts more slowly, and more pleasurably. The mechanism: a winning streak triggers dopamine. Dopamine increases risk tolerance, suppresses fear, and creates a sense of invincibility. The trader who has won six trades in a row does not feel like they are taking more risk — they feel like they have found an edge. They are experiencing a pharmacological state that is chemically identical to overconfidence.

The evidence shows up in the trade journal before it shows up in the P&L. Watch for these warning signs in your own journal after any three-consecutive-win streak:

- Position sizes creeping above the 2% rule — 'just this once, because the setup is exceptional';
- Entries without complete pre-trade checklists — 'I know this setup, I do not need to check';

- Extending profit targets beyond the system's defined levels — 'I think it can run further';
- Opening more simultaneous positions than your rules allow — 'I have the capacity for one more'; and
- Skipping the earnings calendar check — 'this name does not have news coming'.

Winning Streak Length	Overconfidence Risk	Mandatory Response
3 consecutive wins	Low — normal statistical variation	Review your last 3 trades for rule compliance. If rules were followed, continue normally.
5 consecutive wins	Moderate — dopamine elevation beginning	Audit your position sizes for the last 5 trades. Confirm each was within the 2% rule. Check your checklist completion rate.
7 consecutive wins	High — overconfidence actively distorting judgment	Mandatory size reduction to 75% of normal for the next 3 trades. Full checklist required without exceptions. Do not open more than 2 simultaneous positions.
10+ consecutive wins	Severe — system review required	Stop and audit the full win streak. Are you in an unusually favorable market condition? Has your edge genuinely improved, or is this an outlier statistical run? Reduce size to 50% until the statistical picture normalizes.

THE SYMMETRY RULE

Apply the same discipline protocol to winning streaks that you apply to losing streaks. After 3 consecutive wins: audit for rule compliance. After 5 consecutive wins: reduce size 25%. After 7 consecutive wins: reduce size 25% further and add confirmation requirements. After 10 consecutive wins: full system review. The market does not care which direction your streak runs. Your discipline must be equally indifferent.

Decision-Making Under Market Stress: Flash Crashes, News Events, and Fast Markets

The most dangerous moments in trading are not quiet drift-down days. They are the sudden, violent moves — the flash crash, the unexpected Fed statement, the pre-market gap, the circuit breaker halt. In these moments, the amygdala fires fully, cortisol floods the bloodstream, and the prefrontal cortex is functionally offline. Every decision made in this state will be emotionally driven, and statistically, emotionally driven decisions in a fast-moving market are wrong.

The professional's response to a fast-moving market is counter-intuitive: do less, not more. The amateur responds to volatility by taking action — covering positions, adding to positions, placing new trades, checking prices every 30 seconds. The professional responds to volatility by returning to the pre-written plan and executing only what the plan already specified.

Stress Event	Amateur Response	Professional Response	The Rule
Flash crash — SPY drops 3%+ in 10 minutes	Panic-close all positions. Sell everything. 'Get out now.'	Check the six-condition read. Has the condition actually changed? Review your stop levels. Execute only pre-planned stops.	No position is closed during a flash move unless it has hit a pre-written stop level. Gut-feeling closes in a flash crash are almost always wrong.
Unexpected Fed statement — hawkish surprise	Immediately buy put protection on all longs. Add shorts impulsively.	Review your existing hedges. Are they in place? Check delta. If book delta is within the defined range, no action is required.	Your book hedge already exists. A news event does not require a new hedge unless the condition has changed and your existing hedge is insufficient.
Pre-market gap against a position	Close the position at market open regardless of price.	Wait for the first 15 minutes of trading. Gaps fill more than 60% of the time within the first hour. Check your stop level against the gap.	Do not trade the first 15 minutes after a major gap. Assess at the 15-minute candle. Execute only pre-planned stops, not emotional reactions.
A position moves 50% against you in one session	Double down — 'it cannot go lower.'	Check the thesis. Is the fundamental case still intact? Is the condition still the same? If yes: hold within stop parameters. If no: close.	The thesis, not the P&L, drives the decision to hold or close. A position down 50% on a still-intact thesis is held. A position down 10% on a broken thesis is closed immediately.
News event within DTE window on an open position	Hold and hope. 'The news is already priced in.'	Close the position before the event if the event represents binary risk. Earnings, FDA decisions, and merger votes are binary events — not options events.	No short premium position is held through a binary event without a pre-defined hedge or a pre-defined exit plan. The plan is written before the event, not during it.

THE STRESS PROTOCOL

When the market moves violently against you, follow this exact sequence before touching anything: (1) Close the trading platform for 60 seconds. Step away from the screen. (2) Return and read your pre-written trading plan for the affected position. (3) Check only two things: has your pre-written stop level been hit, and has the fundamental thesis been broken. (4) If yes to either: execute the exit. If no to both: do nothing. The market's violence is not a mandate for your action. Your plan is.

The Weekend Review Protocol: Psychological Preparation for the Coming Week

Professional traders do not begin their work on Monday morning. They begin on Sunday — reviewing the previous week's psychological performance, assessing their current mental state, and preparing their decision frameworks for the five trading days ahead. The weekend review is not an analytical exercise about the market. It is a psychological calibration exercise about the trader.

The weekly psychological review covers four questions that no market analysis answers: Did I follow my rules last week? Where did I feel the most emotional pressure? What is my current state of mind entering this week? What will I do differently this week based on last week's behavioral journal?

Review Component	What to Do
Rule Compliance Audit	Review every trade from the past week against the pre-trade checklist. Mark each trade: Full Compliance / Partial Compliance / Rule Break. Calculate your rule compliance rate for the week. Target: 90%+. Below 80%: identify which rule was broken most frequently and write a specific correction.
Emotional Pressure Map	Review your behavioral journal column for each trade. Where did you feel the most discomfort? When did you most want to deviate from the plan? These pressure points are your personal psychological risk map — the specific situations where your discipline is most likely to fail next week.
Current State Assessment	Score yourself on five dimensions from 1–5: Sleep quality this week / Financial stress level / Relationship stress level / Confidence in the system / Physical energy level. Total score below 15: reduce position size by 25% for the coming week. Total below 10: paper trade only. You cannot trade well when your life is in chaos.
Six-Condition Pre-Read	Complete your condition read for the coming week before Monday opens. What condition is the market currently in? What is your approved strategy set? What are the key events (Fed, earnings, data) that could change the condition mid-week? Write the plan before Monday so you are executing a pre-written plan, not reacting to live market information.
Next Week's Intention	Write one behavioral intention for the coming week — one specific behavior you will improve based on last week's audit. Not a performance target. Not a P&L goal. A process intention: 'This week I will complete the full checklist before every trade.' 'This week I will close at the 50% profit target without hesitation.' One intention. Specific. Behavioral.

THE SUNDAY RITUAL

Block 45 minutes every Sunday between 4:00 PM and 7:00 PM for the Weekend Review Protocol. Not Monday morning — Sunday. You need to enter the new trading week with a completed plan, a calibrated mental state, and a written behavioral intention. A trader who opens their platform on Monday morning without a completed weekend review is a trader who is reacting to the market instead of executing a plan. The market will present itself on Monday whether you are ready or not. Be ready.

THE PSYCHOLOGY TRUTH

The market does not reward intelligence. It does not reward bravery. It does not reward conviction. It rewards discipline — the boring, unglamorous, day-after-day execution of a tested plan regardless of how you feel. The trader who follows a mediocre plan with perfect discipline will outperform the trader who follows a brilliant plan with inconsistent discipline — every single time. This is not motivational advice. It is statistical fact.

> **6-CONDITION FRAMEWORK ▸ ALL SIX — your strategy options expand as your account grows**
> A step-by-step progression from $5,000 to $50,000 — with exact strategies, position limits, and graduation criteria at each level.

Every strategy in this book becomes available to you at a specific account size. A $5,000 account cannot run the Wheel. A $15,000 account should not attempt a long/short portfolio. Matching your strategy ambition to your capital reality is not conservative — it is survival. This chapter maps the exact progression from your first $5,000 to a $50,000 portfolio, with no ambiguity about what to trade, how much to risk, and when to graduate to the next level.

Level 1 — The $5,000 Account: Learning to Survive

At $5,000, your only job is to not lose money while learning to execute. The strategies available to you are limited by capital constraints, and that is a feature — it forces focus.

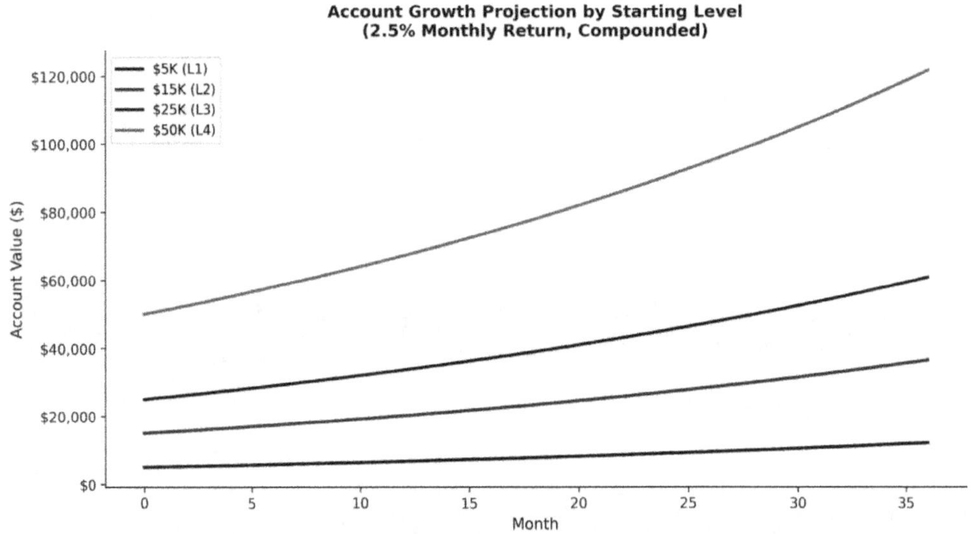

Figure 29.1 — Account Growth Projection. Four starting levels compounded at 2.5% monthly return.

Year	2% / Month	2.5% / Month	3% / Month	Notes
Start	$50,000	$50,000	$50,000	Initial capital.
Year 1	$60,765	$64,068	$68,655	12 months compounded.
Year 2	$73,943	$82,619	$94,025	Accelerating gains.

Year 3	$89,720	$106,082	$128,699	Compounding kicks in.
Year 5	$132,454	$180,544	$241,026	Doubling territory.
Year 10	$350,236	$651,926	$1,159,274	Life-changing growth.

Figure 29.2 — Compounding Table. $50K at 2%, 2.5%, and 3% monthly over 10 years.

Parameter	$5,000 Account Rule
Max risk per trade	$100 (2% of $5,000)
Strategies allowed	Vertical spreads ONLY — bull put spreads, bear call spreads ($1–$2 wide)
Max simultaneous positions	2
Underlying universe	Stocks $20–$50 with liquid options chains. ETFs preferred: SPY, QQQ, IWM, XLF
Position management	Close at 50% profit. Stop at 100% of debit/credit. No exceptions.
Monthly income target	$150–$250 (3–5% of account)
Graduation criteria	20 consecutive trades following all rules. Win rate above 60%. Rule compliance above 90%. Minimum 3 months.

At Level 1, the portfolio looks boring. Good. Boring at $5,000 means you still have $5,000 at the end of the month. Most traders who start with $5,000 and try to make it exciting have $2,500 by month three.

Level 2 — The $10,000–$15,000 Account: Adding Income

Parameter	$10K–$15K Account Rule
Max risk per trade	$200–$300 (2% of account)
New strategies unlocked	Cash-secured puts on stocks $15–$30. Iron condors ($2–$3 wide). All vertical spreads up to $5 wide.
Max simultaneous positions	3–4
Underlying universe	Add individual stocks: BAC, F, T, SOFI, PLTR — stocks under $30 with weekly options
Monthly income target	$300–$500 (2.5–4% of account)
Graduation criteria	40 total trades. Average monthly return positive for 4 consecutive months. No single month below −3%.

Level 2 is where you begin to feel like a real options trader. CSPs on quality names under $30 give you the income experience without requiring massive capital reserves. This is where the PPD mindset starts to compound.

Level 3 — The $20,000–$30,000 Account: The Wheel Begins

Parameter	$20K–$30K Account Rule
Max risk per trade	$400–$600 (2% of account)
New strategies unlocked	The Wheel (CSP → assignment → covered call) on stocks $30–$80. Calendar spreads. Diagonal spreads.
Max simultaneous positions	4–5
Underlying universe	Add mid-price names: AMD, INTC, COIN, SQ, PYPL, XLE, XLF
Monthly income target	$500–$900 (2–3.5% of account)
Graduation criteria	Completed at least 3 full Wheel cycles (CSP → assigned → called away). Monthly income positive for 6 consecutive months.

Level 4 — The $50,000 Account: Full Toolkit Access

Parameter	$50K Account Rule
Max risk per trade	$1,000 (2% of account)
All strategies unlocked	Wheel on stocks up to $150. Stair-layered entries. Swing trading. Earnings plays. Portfolio hedging with SPY/QQQ puts.
Max simultaneous positions	6–8
Underlying universe	Full access: AAPL, MSFT, AMZN, GOOGL, NVDA, JPM, V, EMA — all high-quality large and mega-cap names
Monthly income target	$1,000–$2,000 (2–4% of account)
Next milestone	$100K — which unlocks the long/short portfolio framework from Chapter 24

At $50,000, you have access to essentially every strategy in this book. The constraint is no longer capital — it is discipline, experience, and time. The trader who reaches $50K by following the level progression has the habits, the journal data, and the psychological resilience to handle full-toolkit trading. The trader who deposits $50K on day one and skips levels 1–3 is the one who gives it back to the market.

THE PORTFOLIO GROWTH RULE

Never graduate to the next level by depositing more money. Graduate by growing your account through trading. If you start with $5,000 and your trading grows it to $10,000, you have proven Level 1 competence. If you start with $5,000, lose $2,000, and then deposit $7,000 to reach $10,000 — you have not graduated. You have just added capital to an unproven system. The market does not care about your deposit history. It cares about your trading results.

Beyond $50K: The Roadmap to $100K and Professional-Level Trading

Reaching $50K through your own trading is a milestone that fewer than 10% of options traders ever achieve. It proves your system works, your discipline holds under pressure, and your psychology can sustain extended periods of active trading. But $50K is not the finish line — it is the beginning of professional-level portfolio management.

Account Size	New Unlocks	Monthly Income Target	Key Risk to Manage
$50K-$75K	Wheel on stocks up to $200. Full earnings playbook access. Calendar and diagonal spreads.	$1,000-$2,500 (2-3.5%)	Overconfidence from reaching $50K. This is where many traders increase size too quickly and give back gains.
$75K-$100K	Multiple simultaneous Wheel positions. Sector diversification across 3+ sectors. Portfolio-level hedging with index puts.	$1,500-$3,500 (2-3.5%)	Concentration risk. Monitor sector exposure weekly. No single sector should exceed 35% of portfolio.
$100K-$200K	Long/Short portfolio (Ch. 24). Stair-layered entries on conviction positions. Full 6-8 simultaneous positions.	$2,000-$6,000 (2-3%)	Complexity creep. More positions = more management. If you cannot review all positions in 30 minutes, you have too many.
$200K+	Professional-level portfolio management. Multiple strategy layers running simultaneously. Consider tax-advantaged structures.	$4,000-$8,000 (2-3%)	Complacency. Large accounts feel safe — but a 5% drawdown at $200K is $10,000. The 2% rule matters MORE as accounts grow, not less.

The income percentages stay consistent at every level: 2-3.5% per month. What changes is the dollar amount — and the psychological weight of that dollar amount. Losing $500 at $25K feels manageable. Losing $5,000 at $200K feels devastating, even though both are 2% drawdowns. The 2% rule scales. Your emotions do not scale as gracefully. This is why the psychology chapter comes before the portfolio chapter — you need the emotional infrastructure before you need the capital.

The Compounding Math: What Consistent Income Trading Actually Builds

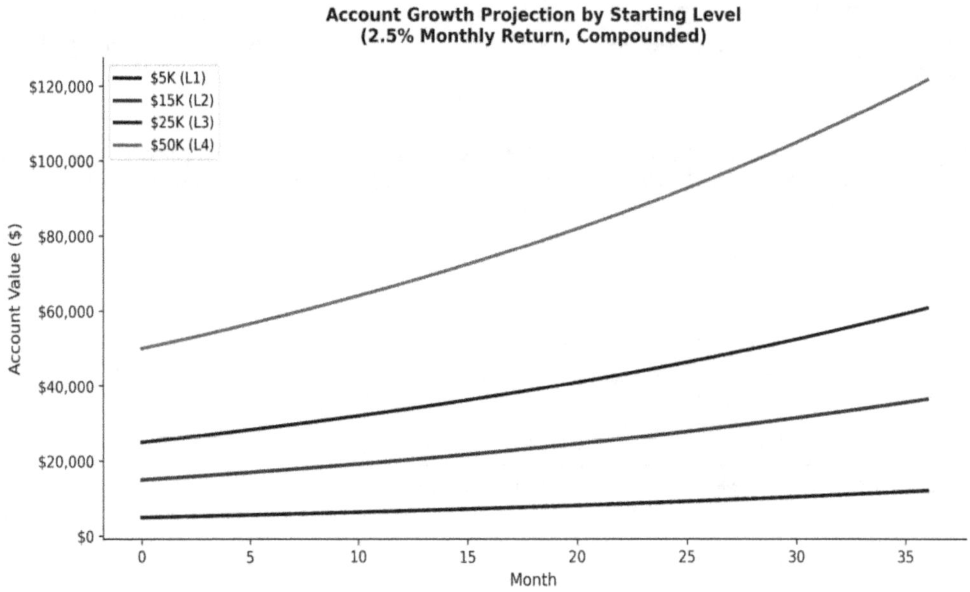

Figure 29.1 — Portfolio Growth Trajectory — Compounding path from $10K to $50K using systematic premium selling over 36 months.

Portfolio Growth Trajectory — Compounding path from $10K to $50K using systematic premium selling.

Traders focus on individual trade P&L. Professionals focus on compounding. Here is what happens when you generate a consistent 2.5% monthly return and reinvest the income into your trading capital — no deposits, no withdrawals, just compounding:

Starting Capital	Year 1	Year 3	Year 5	Year 10
$10,000	$13,449	$24,273	$43,839	$192,186
$25,000	$33,622	$60,684	$109,598	$480,466
$50,000	$67,245	$121,368	$219,196	$960,931
$100,000	$134,489	$242,736	$438,391	$1,921,863

A $50,000 account generating 2.5% monthly becomes $219,196 in five years and $960,931 in ten years — without adding a single dollar of new capital. This is the power of systematic income trading with disciplined reinvestment. It is not exciting on any given Tuesday. It is extraordinary over a decade.

THE COMPOUNDING COMMITMENT

Compounding only works if you do not withdraw. For the first 3-5 years, treat your trading account as a compounding machine — not an ATM. Every dollar you withdraw breaks the exponential curve. Set a rule: no withdrawals until the account reaches 3x your starting capital. Then withdraw only the income above your monthly target, never the base.

The Income Reinvestment Strategy: What to Do with Your Profits

Every month that your options income exceeds your target, you face a decision that has more impact on your long-term wealth than any single trade: what do you do with the excess? Most traders spend it. Professionals follow a reinvestment hierarchy.

Tier 1 — Rebuild the risk budget (first priority). If any of your positions suffered losses this month that reduced your account below the starting balance, the first use of this month's profits is to restore the account to its opening level. Compounding only works on a stable or growing base. Losses must be healed before growth can resume.

Tier 2 — Fund the next position level. If your account has grown enough to unlock a new strategy (e.g., crossing from $20K to $25K unlocks wider spreads and more underlying choices), allocate the excess toward enabling that next level. This is not adding capital — it is earned growth creating new opportunity. The most powerful moment in an options trader's career is the first time their own trading profits unlock a strategy that was previously too expensive.

Tier 3 — Build the hedge fund. Allocate 10-15% of monthly excess income to a permanent hedge position. This is not a trade — it is insurance. Buy rolling SPY or QQQ puts 5-10% OTM with 60-90 DTE, funded entirely by excess income. Over time, this hedge fund becomes self-sustaining: the income from your short premium positions pays for the puts that protect against the next market crash. When the crash comes — and it will come — your hedge fund pays for itself ten times over. The traders who survived 2020, 2022, and every crash before them all had one thing in common: they spent 1-2% of their income on protection every single month.

Tier 4 — Compound the base. Everything remaining after Tiers 1-3 compounds into your trading capital. This is the true growth engine. A $50,000 account that compounds $500/month in excess income (after hedging and reinvestment) grows to $56,000 in one year, $68,000 in two years, and $95,000 in four years — without a single deposit. The math is not dramatic on a monthly basis. Over years, it is transformative.

Tier 5 — Withdraw for life (only after 3x starting capital). Once your account has reached 3x your original starting capital through trading alone (not deposits), you have earned the right to begin withdrawing a portion of monthly income for personal use. The recommended withdrawal rate is 50% of income above your monthly target — keeping 50% compounding and taking 50% as paycheck. This balance allows continued growth while providing tangible reward for the years of discipline that built the account.

A Final Word from the Author

I have watched students come through The Premium Desk who were skeptical, anxious, and uncertain whether any of this would work for them. Teachers. Engineers. Nurses. Retirees. Parents trading from the kitchen table between school pickups. None of them came in with an advantage. None of them had a trading background or a finance degree. What they had was the willingness to learn a system — and the discipline to follow it.

Every one of them who stayed with the process built real income. Not all of them became full-time traders. Most did not want to be. They wanted an income stream that did not require exchanging more hours for more dollars. They built it. The six conditions were the framework. The discipline was theirs. Now it is yours.

You have now read what took me years of real money, real losses, and real lessons to learn. Every table in this book exists because I made the mistake it prevents. Every rule was written after I broke it and paid the price.

The market does not care how smart you are. It does not care how many books you have read, how many courses you have taken, or how confident you feel. It cares about one thing: did you manage the risk? If yes, you survive to trade tomorrow. If no, eventually you will not.

This book gave you a system — the six-condition framework, the Greeks, the strategies, the management rules, the journal discipline. But a system only works if you work it. Every day. Especially the boring days. Especially the days when breaking a rule would feel easier than following it.

Start with paper trading. Graduate to small positions. Prove consistency before you scale. The traders who last decades in this business are not the ones who made the most money in their first year — they are the ones who were still standing in year five, year ten, year twenty. Longevity is the ultimate edge.

The market opens tomorrow. The VIX will give you a reading. The chart will give you a direction. One of the six conditions will be active. You will know exactly what to do.

I wrote this book so you would not have to learn the way I did. Use it. Mark it up. Come back to the chapters that challenge you. And when you have a question the book does not answer — reach out. The Premium Desk community exists for exactly that reason.

Use the tools. Follow the system. Manage the risk.

The rest follows.

— Eddy Alexandre
Master Trader • The Premium Desk
thepremiumdesk.com

A Note to the Reader

You made it to the end of the book.

Take a moment with that. Most people who buy a book about trading never finish it. They read the first few chapters, encounter a concept that requires effort, and return to whatever they were doing before — hoping that a different book, a different course, or a different moment of inspiration will make it click. You did not do that. You stayed with it.

That already separates you from most of the market.

But finishing the book is not the finish line. It is the starting line.

The knowledge in these pages is inert until you apply it. The T-21 rule does nothing sitting on a page. The PPD calculation is theoretical until you open your first cash-secured put and write the number down. The Ten Indicators are just a list until you run a real stock through them, one by one, and make a real decision. The Foreword told you what I hoped to give you. The Afterword is telling you what to do with it.

Here is what I want you to do first: review your trading plan. If you have not written one yet, write it tonight. Not tomorrow. Tonight. Because tomorrow you will find a reason to delay, and that delay is the first trade the market wins before you even open a position. The trading plan is not optional. It is the infrastructure on which everything in this book runs.

Here is what I want you to do second: open a paper trading account. Run the full 90-day protocol described in Chapter 20. Place the trades. Follow the T-21 rules. Journal every position. Do not rush to go live. The market will be there when you are ready. It has been there for centuries. It is not going anywhere. Your capital, however, is precious and finite — protect it through the paper trading phase until the mechanics are automatic.

Here is what I want you to do third: when you do go live, start small. Not as small as you think is appropriate. Smaller than that. The purpose of your first 10 live trades is not to make money. It is to confirm that you can execute the system under the psychological pressure of real capital at risk. Sized small, a mistake is tuition. Sized large, a mistake is a setback that takes months to recover from.

A word about losing trades — because you will have them. Every professional has them. The market does not owe you a winning streak because you read the right book or followed the right rules. There will be positions that go against you. There will be weeks where every trade seems wrong. There will be a month — probably in your first year — where you question whether any of this works.

In that moment, do not change the system. Review it. Audit your trade journal. Check whether you followed the rules — the checklist, the position sizing, the T-21 management, the earnings calendar. If you did, and the system still produced losses, that is statistics, not failure. No edge wins 100% of the time. An edge that wins 60% of the time over 100 trades is a powerful business. Defend the system, adjust the exposure, and continue.

If you did not follow the rules — if you skipped the earnings check, if you oversized a position because you were confident, if you held past T-21 for the extra premium — then you already know what to fix. The answer is always the same: return to the system.

The traders I have watched build real, lasting income from options are not the most brilliant analysts. They are not the fastest or the most aggressive. They are the most consistent. They follow the same checklist on trade 500 that they followed on trade 1. They manage their positions at T-21 when they are tired and when they are excited and when they are sure the stock is about to move. They do not let conviction override the system. They let the system override conviction.

That is the edge. Not the strategy. The consistency of applying it.

One final thought. Financial independence — the ability to generate income from capital you control, on your terms, without depending on an employer or a boss — is one of the most meaningful forms of freedom available in modern life. This book was written to give you the tools to build that freedom. Not to make you a 'trader.' To make you financially free.

Your 90-Day Launch Plan

The transition from reader to active trader is not a leap — it is a sequence. The 90-day plan below is not a suggestion. It is a protocol. Every trader who has gone through The Premium Desk's program and built consistent income followed a structured launch sequence. Skipping ahead accelerates losses, not profits.

Phase	Timeframe	What You Do — And Why
PHASE 1	**Days 1–14: Framework Lock**	Study the six-condition table until it is instinct — not recall. Every morning, open the VIX and the SPY chart. Write down which of the six conditions you believe is active. Write the approved strategy next to it. Do not trade. Do not paper trade yet. Just read the condition and write it down. After 14 days you will have 14 condition reads. Review them. How often were you right? How quickly did you identify the condition? This exercise alone is worth more than most trading courses.
PHASE 2	**Days 15–45: Paper Trading**	Open a paper trading account (ThinkorSwim or TastyTrade, both free). Begin placing the condition-appropriate strategy from your daily read. Execute at least 2 paper trades per week. Run every trade through the pre-trade checklist in Appendix A. Journal every position in the SCR format from Appendix B. Practice the T-21 rollover on every short-premium position. After 30 days you should have 8–12 paper trades. Review them with the same cold objectivity you would apply to a live account. The goal is not to win paper money — it is to identify the weaknesses in your execution before real capital is at risk.
PHASE 3	**Days 46–60: Live Micro Sizing**	Go live — but at 10% of your intended full position size. If you plan to sell one contract CSP normally, sell one contract. Do not scale yet. The purpose is to experience the psychology of real risk: the feeling when the stock moves against you, the discipline required to follow the checklist when your gut says skip it, the emotional pull to close winners too early and hold losers too long. These are the lessons that paper trading cannot teach. At micro size, the tuition cost is minimal.

Phase	Timeframe	What You Do — And Why
PHASE 4	**Days 61–90: System Calibration**	Review your first 30 days of live trades. Calculate your actual win rate, average premium collected, average days held, and MAE on losing trades. Compare to your paper trading results. Where are the gaps? Where did you follow the system and where did you drift? Make three specific adjustments to your execution process — not to the system itself, but to how you execute it. Then scale to 25% of full position size for the next 30 days.
PHASE 5	**Day 91+: Full Deployment**	Full position size. Full strategy toolkit. All six conditions in rotation as the market presents them. By this point the system is not something you are following — it is something you are running. The checklist runs automatically. The condition read happens in two minutes. The T-21 management is a scheduled calendar event, not a decision. This is the state of the experienced options trader — and it is achievable by anyone willing to invest 90 days of structured practice.

What to Expect in Year One

Year one of options trading is not about making life-changing money. It is about building a repeatable process. Here is what a realistic year one looks like for a disciplined trader following the six-condition system:

Period	Realistic Goal	What Success Looks Like
Q1 (Paper)	Zero P&L — process focus	You have 10+ paper trades journaled. You can read a six-condition entry in under 2 minutes. You have executed at least one T-21 rollover correctly.
Q2 (Live micro)	Capital preservation	Your account is within 5% of where you started. You have identified 2–3 execution habits that needed correction. You have not broken the position sizing rule once.
Q3 (25% size)	First consistent income	You are generating 1–2% per month on deployed capital with a win rate above 60%. You have had one losing month — and returned to profit the following month.
Q4 (Full size)	System running	You are generating consistent monthly income. Your PPD target is being met or approached. You have a watchlist, a trade plan, and a weekly review process. You are trading like a risk manager.

The Premium Desk Community

You do not have to do this alone. The Premium Desk exists precisely because trading in isolation — with no accountability, no feedback, and no community of people working through the same challenges — is unnecessarily hard. The community at thepremiumdesk.com is where Eddy Alexandre and the team answer live questions, host weekly market condition reads, review member trades, and provide ongoing education as markets evolve.

The six-condition framework in this book is the core curriculum. The community is where you apply it with support. Markets change. New volatility regimes emerge. AI and algorithmic behavior evolves. The community stays current so you stay current. Join it.

BIBLIOGRAPHY

Selected References & Further Reading

This bibliography comprises verified sources that inform the frameworks, strategies, and principles presented in this book. Entries marked Direct Reference are works whose concepts are substantively discussed in specific chapters. Entries marked Further Reading extend the material for readers seeking deeper expertise in a particular domain. All titles are currently in print or widely available through major booksellers.

I. Foundational Academic Works on Options Pricing

Black, Fischer, and Myron Scholes. "The Pricing of Options and Corporate Liabilities." The Journal of Political Economy, vol. 81, no. 3, pp. 637–654. University of Chicago Press, 1973.

Direct Reference — Chapters 2–5. The foundational paper introducing the Black-Scholes option pricing formula. Essential context for understanding theoretical valuation models and where they break down in practice.

Merton, Robert C. "Theory of Rational Option Pricing." The Bell Journal of Economics and Management Science, vol. 4, no. 1, pp. 141–183. RAND Corporation, 1973.

Direct Reference — Chapters 2–5. Companion paper extending Black-Scholes with rigorous treatment of dividend effects, early exercise, and the continuous-time framework that became the BSM model.

Hull, John C. Options, Futures, and Other Derivatives, 11th edition. Pearson, 2022.

Direct Reference — Chapters 2–8, 19. The definitive derivatives textbook bridging theory and practice. Covers futures mechanics, the BSM model, the Greeks, and exotic options.

Natenberg, Sheldon. Option Volatility and Pricing: Advanced Trading Strategies and Techniques, 2nd edition. McGraw-Hill, 2014.

Direct Reference — Chapters 2–5, 8, 13, 16–17. Widely considered the first book professional traders receive on a trading desk. Covers pricing models, volatility, and dynamic hedging.

II. Practitioner Options Strategy References

McMillan, Lawrence G. Options as a Strategic Investment, 5th edition. Prentice Hall Press, 2012.

Direct Reference — Chapters 2–3, 6–7, 11–13, 15, 22. The comprehensive options strategy reference covering every standard strategy from covered calls to complex spreads.

McMillan, Lawrence G. McMillan on Options, 2nd edition. John Wiley & Sons, 2004.

Further Reading — Chapters 13, 15, 22–23. McMillan's personal trading philosophy with real-world examples, seasonal systems, and volatility-based approaches.

Cohen, Guy. The Bible of Options Strategies: The Definitive Guide for Practical Trading Strategies, 2nd edition. FT Press, 2015.

Direct Reference — Chapters 11–13, 15. Modular, cross-referenced guide covering income, volatility, sideways, and leveraged strategies with step-by-step risk profiles.

Passarelli, Dan. Trading Option Greeks: How Time, Volatility, and Other Pricing Factors Drive Profits, 2nd edition. John Wiley & Sons, 2012.

Direct Reference — Chapters 3, 8, 12. Written by a former CBOE floor trader. Explains how to use Delta, Gamma, Theta, Vega, and Rho for pricing and trade management.

Cottle, Charles M. Options Trading: The Hidden Reality. RiskDoctor, Inc., 2006.

Further Reading — Chapters 9, 13, 22. Advanced guide to position adjustment and hedging featuring 3D graphics and analysis of complex spread configurations.

Rhoads, Russell. Option Spread Trading: A Comprehensive Guide to Strategies and Tactics. John Wiley & Sons, 2011.

Direct Reference — Chapter 13. Practical guide to vertical, horizontal, diagonal, and calendar spreads with guidance on selection, monitoring, and exit.

Augen, Jeff. Trading Options at Expiration: Strategies and Models for Winning the Endgame. FT Press, 2009.
Further Reading — Chapters 12–13, 23. Explores expiration-day pricing dynamics and how to profit from end-of-contract price distortions. Relevant to the T-21 rule discussion.

Ellman, Alan. Complete Encyclopedia for Covered Call Writing, classic edition. The Blue Collar Investor Corp., 2011.
Direct Reference — Chapter 15. The most comprehensive book dedicated to covered call writing, covering stock selection, exit strategies, rolling techniques, and risk management.

III. Volatility, the VIX, and Implied Volatility Dynamics

Sinclair, Euan. Volatility Trading, 2nd edition. John Wiley & Sons, 2013.
Direct Reference — Chapters 16–17, 22, 24. Quantitative guide covering volatility measurement, forecasting, the variance premium, VIX futures, and hedging.

Sinclair, Euan. Option Trading: Pricing and Volatility Strategies and Techniques. John Wiley & Sons, 2010.
Direct Reference — Chapters 2–5, 16–17. Covers option pricing from historical and conceptual perspectives, market structure, and specific hedging techniques.

Rhoads, Russell. Trading VIX Derivatives: Trading and Hedging Strategies Using VIX Futures, Options, and Exchange-Traded Notes. John Wiley & Sons, 2011.
Direct Reference — Chapters 16–17. Comprehensive guide to VIX mechanics, futures, options, and ETNs. The definitive practitioner reference for VIX-based instruments.

Warner, Adam. Options Volatility Trading: Strategies for Profiting from Market Swings. McGraw-Hill, 2009.
Further Reading — Chapters 16–17, 20. Covers VIX behavioral psychology, historical volatility patterns, and strategies for profiting from dramatic market shifts.

Augen, Jeff. The Volatility Edge in Options Trading: New Technical Strategies for Investing in Unstable Markets. FT Press, 2008.
Further Reading — Chapters 16–17, 22. Strategies for identifying and profiting from price distortions arising from volatility changes using statistical analysis.

IV. Technical Analysis and Charting Methods

Murphy, John J. Technical Analysis of the Financial Markets: A Comprehensive Guide to Trading Methods and Applications. New York Institute of Finance, 1999.
Direct Reference — Chapters 8, 20. The definitive technical analysis reference covering chart construction, trend analysis, patterns, moving averages, and candlesticks. Primary CMT certification text.

Pring, Martin J. Technical Analysis Explained: The Successful Investor's Guide to Spotting Investment Trends and Turning Points, 5th edition. McGraw-Hill, 2014.
Direct Reference — Chapter 8. Comprehensive guide covering trend techniques, price patterns, momentum indicators, sentiment, and relative strength.

Elder, Alexander. The New Trading for a Living: Psychology, Discipline, Trading Tools and Systems, Risk Control, Trade Management. John Wiley & Sons, 2014.
Direct Reference — Chapters 8, 20, 28. Updated classic combining market psychology, technical analysis tools, and risk management. Features the Triple Screen and Impulse systems.

Bollinger, John. Bollinger on Bollinger Bands. McGraw-Hill, 2001.
Further Reading — Chapter 8. The definitive guide to Bollinger Bands covering volatility breakout, trend following, and reversal methods.

Nison, Steve. Japanese Candlestick Charting Techniques: A Contemporary Guide to the Ancient Investment Techniques of the Far East, 2nd edition. Prentice Hall Press, 2001.
Further Reading — Chapter 8. The most comprehensive English-language guide to candlestick charting covering all major patterns and their practical application.

Grimes, Adam. The Art and Science of Technical Analysis: Market Structure, Price Action, and Trading Strategies. John Wiley & Sons, 2012.
Further Reading — Chapters 8, 20. Uses statistical analysis to validate which patterns genuinely capture buying and selling imbalances. Rigorous and evidence-based.

V. Business Cycles, Sector Rotation, and Market Structure

Marks, Howard. The Most Important Thing: Uncommon Sense for the Thoughtful Investor. Columbia University Press, 2011.
Further Reading — Chapters 5, 26. Decades of Oaktree Capital wisdom covering second-level thinking, risk assessment, market cycles, and defensive investing.

Marks, Howard. Mastering the Market Cycle: Getting the Odds on Your Side. Houghton Mifflin Harcourt, 2018.
Direct Reference — Chapters 5, 27. Focused specifically on identifying and positioning for market cycles, covering investor psychology, credit cycles, and the pendulum between fear and greed.

Stovall, Sam. Standard & Poor's Guide to Sector Investing. McGraw-Hill, 1996.
Further Reading — Chapter 7. The first comprehensive guide to sector investing explaining how business cycle phases affect sector returns and providing a sector rotation framework.

Pring, Martin J. The Investor's Guide to Active Asset Allocation: Using Technical Analysis and ETFs to Trade the Markets. McGraw-Hill, 2010.
Direct Reference — Chapters 5, 14. Presents the Six Business Cycle Stages framework for rotating among sectors and asset classes using ETFs.

VI. ETFs, Portfolio Management, and Income Strategies

Graham, Benjamin, with commentary by Jason Zweig. The Intelligent Investor: The Definitive Book on Value Investing, revised edition. HarperBusiness, 2003.
Further Reading — Chapters 10, 26, 29. The foundational work on value investing and margin of safety. Philosophical underpinning for stock selection and risk-first portfolio construction.

Swensen, David F. Unconventional Success: A Fundamental Approach to Personal Investment. Free Press, 2005.
Further Reading — Chapters 14, 26, 29. Yale's legendary CIO critiques the mutual fund industry and advocates for diversified portfolios using low-cost ETFs.

VII. Risk Management and Tail-Risk Thinking

Taleb, Nassim Nicholas. Dynamic Hedging: Managing Vanilla and Exotic Options. John Wiley & Sons, 1997.
Direct Reference — Chapters 3, 8, 21, 24. Definitive practical reference for derivatives risk management from a market maker's perspective. Covers the Greeks, volatility surfaces, fat tails, and off-model risks.

Taleb, Nassim Nicholas. The Black Swan: The Impact of the Highly Improbable, 2nd edition. Random House, 2010.
Direct Reference — Chapters 21, 24, 28. Explores the disproportionate role of rare, high-impact events in markets and argues that standard risk models dangerously underestimate tail risk.

Taleb, Nassim Nicholas. Antifragile: Things That Gain from Disorder. Random House, 2012.

Further Reading — Chapters 24, 28–29. Introduces the concept of antifragility and the barbell strategy. Directly relevant to the stair-layered convexity approach and portfolio construction philosophy.

Lo, Andrew W. Adaptive Markets: Financial Evolution at the Speed of Thought. Princeton University Press, 2017.

Further Reading — Chapters 18, 21, 28. Proposes the Adaptive Markets Hypothesis reconciling efficient markets with behavioral economics. Essential context for trading in the age of AI and algorithms.

Brown, Aaron. Red-Blooded Risk: The Secret History of Wall Street. John Wiley & Sons, 2011.

Further Reading — Chapters 21, 25, 28. Covers the Kelly Criterion, Value at Risk, and the philosophy of active risk-taking. Bridges mathematical risk frameworks with practical trading decisions.

VIII. Behavioral Finance and Trading Psychology

Kahneman, Daniel. Thinking, Fast and Slow. Farrar, Straus and Giroux, 2011.

Direct Reference — Chapter 28. Nobel laureate's seminal work on cognitive biases, heuristics, and the two systems driving human decision-making under uncertainty.

Kahneman, Daniel, and Amos Tversky. "Prospect Theory: An Analysis of Decision under Risk." Econometrica, vol. 47, no. 2, pp. 263–291. 1979.

Direct Reference — Chapter 28. The foundational paper demonstrating that people are risk-averse for gains but risk-seeking for losses. Explains why traders hold losers too long and cut winners too short.

Thaler, Richard H. Misbehaving: The Making of Behavioral Economics. W. W. Norton & Company, 2015.

Further Reading — Chapter 28. Nobel laureate's account of how humans deviate from rational-actor assumptions through mental accounting, the endowment effect, and self-control problems.

Douglas, Mark. Trading in the Zone: Master the Market with Confidence, Discipline, and a Winning Attitude. Prentice Hall Press, 2000.

Direct Reference — Chapters 22, 28. Teaches traders to think in probabilities. Addresses the five specific psychological issues that cause trading inconsistency.

Tharp, Van K. Trade Your Way to Financial Freedom, 2nd edition. McGraw-Hill, 2007.

Direct Reference — Chapters 22, 25, 28–29. Covers personalized system development, position sizing via R-multiples, expectancy, and the 17-step trading model.

Steenbarger, Brett N. Trading Psychology 2.0: From Best Practices to Best Processes. John Wiley & Sons, 2015.

Further Reading — Chapters 22, 28. Applies positive psychology to trading, covering creativity, adaptation, and sustained performance. The most modern comprehensive trading psychology text available.

IX. Algorithmic Trading, Backtesting, and Quantitative Methods

Pardo, Robert. The Evaluation and Optimization of Trading Strategies, 2nd edition. John Wiley & Sons, 2008.

Direct Reference — Chapter 21. The definitive guide to designing, testing, and optimizing trading systems. Introduces walk-forward analysis as the key methodology for avoiding overfitting.

Chan, Ernest P. Quantitative Trading: How to Build Your Own Algorithmic Trading Business, 2nd edition. John Wiley & Sons, 2021.

Further Reading — Chapters 18, 21. Step-by-step guide to algorithmic strategy development, backtesting, risk management, and machine learning for parameter optimization.

López de Prado, Marcos. Advances in Financial Machine Learning. John Wiley & Sons, 2018.

Further Reading — Chapter 18. The first comprehensive book on applying modern machine learning to financial modeling. Directly relevant to trading in the age of AI and algorithms.

X. Futures, Commodities, and Supplementary References

Garner, Carley. A Trader's First Book on Commodities: Everything You Need to Know about Futures and Options Trading Before Placing a Trade, 3rd edition. DeCarley Trading, 2017.

Direct Reference — Chapter 19. Practical guide covering commodity market basics, futures contract mechanics, margin requirements, and building a trading plan. The most accessible entry point for options traders moving into futures.

The Core Shelf: Ten Essential Titles

For readers building a focused professional library, these ten titles cover every major domain addressed in this book and provide sufficient depth for professional-level practice:

1. Hull, John C. — Options, Futures, and Other Derivatives (foundational theory)
2. Natenberg, Sheldon — Option Volatility and Pricing (volatility and pricing)
3. McMillan, Lawrence G. — Options as a Strategic Investment (comprehensive strategy)
4. Sinclair, Euan — Volatility Trading (volatility as asset class)
5. Passarelli, Dan — Trading Option Greeks (the Greeks in practice)
6. Taleb, Nassim Nicholas — Dynamic Hedging (professional risk management)
7. Murphy, John J. — Technical Analysis of the Financial Markets (technical analysis)
8. Marks, Howard — Mastering the Market Cycle (market structure)
9. Kahneman, Daniel — Thinking, Fast and Slow (behavioral foundations)
10. Pardo, Robert — The Evaluation and Optimization of Trading Strategies (backtesting methodology)

APPENDIX A

The Premium Desk 90-Day Trader Development Roadmap

A week-by-week learning and execution plan for applying the six-condition framework from Day 1 to live trading

---

The 90-day roadmap below is the exact sequence every Premium Desk student follows from the day they finish reading this book to the day they open their first live position with full confidence. Each week has a specific learning objective, a practice task, and a success metric. Do not skip weeks. Do not accelerate. The sequence is designed to build competence in the right order.

PHASE 1: FRAMEWORK LOCK (Weeks 1–2)

Week	Learning Objective	Daily Practice Task	Success Metric
1	Memorize the six-condition table without reference. Know which strategy belongs to each condition by instinct, not recall.	Morning: read VIX and SPY chart. Write down: (1) VIX level and IVR, (2) direction, (3) active condition number, (4) approved strategy. No trading — observation only.	By Day 7, identify the correct condition in under 90 seconds without opening the six-condition table. If slower, repeat Week 1.
2	Apply the Ten Indicator screening framework to 5 stocks from your preliminary watchlist.	Score each of your 5 stocks using the Ten Indicator worksheet (Appendix A). Classify each as A-class, B-class, C-class, or ineligible. Build your approved underlying list.	End of Week 2: you have a list of at least 3 A-class and 2 B-class underlyings you are comfortable with and have fully researched.

PHASE 2: PAPER TRADING (Weeks 3–6)

Week	Learning Objective	Paper Trading Task	Success Metric
3	Open first paper trade: Condition 2 (CSP) on an A-class underlying in current market condition.	Run full pre-trade checklist (Appendix A). Open 1 paper CSP at 25–30 delta, 30–35 DTE, on your highest-rated A-class stock. Log in SCR journal. Set paper GTC close at 50%.	Trade is entered at mid or better. All five checklist items confirmed. Journal entry complete before order submission.
4	Manage the existing paper position through T-21. Open second paper position.	Monitor week-3 CSP daily. If DTE reaches 21, execute the T-21 decision: roll, hold, or close. Open a second paper position in whatever the current condition dictates.	T-21 decision made and executed according to the three-question protocol. Second position entered. Two active paper positions simultaneously.
5	Add a directional debit paper trade (condition 1 or 3, depending on current market).	If the market is currently in condition 1 or 3, open a paper long call or long put on an A-class underlying. Apply the swing trade timing protocol: entry at pullback, GTC exits at 50% profit and 40% stop.	Three simultaneous paper positions: one income seller, one directional debit, one closing or newly opened. Journal all three current.

Week	Learning Objective	Paper Trading Task	Success Metric
6	Review first month of paper trading. Calculate paper win rate, average premium, PPD.	Month-end review: count paper wins and losses. Calculate average credit collected on income trades. Calculate average gain on directional trades. Compute monthly net P&L.	At least 60% paper win rate. At least 2 clean 50% profit target exits. No position held through an earnings date. All T-21 rules followed.

PHASE 3: LIVE MICRO SIZING (Weeks 7–10)

Week	Objective	Live Task	Success Metric
7	Go live at 10% of intended full position size. 1 contract only, regardless of account size.	Open first live position. Same protocol as paper trading, but real capital. Run full checklist. Log in journal before submission. Set GTC exits immediately after fill confirmation.	First live position opened correctly. All checklist items followed. GTC exits confirmed active.
8–9	Continue at 1-contract sizing. Open 2–3 live positions total over the two weeks.	Open one new live position per week. Continue paper trading in parallel for strategies you are not yet executing live. Note any psychological differences vs. paper.	No position sizing rule violated. No earnings-date trade opened. At least one position closed at 50% profit target using the GTC order.
10	Month-end live review. Compare live results to paper results.	Calculate live win rate, average premium, PPD. Compare to weeks 3–6 paper results. Identify execution gaps.	Live win rate within 10% of paper win rate. No catastrophic loss (> 2× normal position size). Identified 2–3 specific execution improvements.

PHASE 4 & 5: SCALE AND FULL DEPLOYMENT (Weeks 11–13+)

Weeks 11–12	Scale to 25% of full position size (2–3 contracts). Continue weekly dashboard. Apply MAE stop-loss calibration from backtesting data to live positions. Full strategy toolkit available for all six conditions.
Week 13+	**Full position size. All six conditions in rotation. Stair-layered income calendar running. Monthly P&L review every month-end. PPD target tracked weekly. You are now trading like a risk manager.**

The 90-day sequence does not guarantee profitability. It guarantees preparation.

Preparation is the only thing within your control. The market handles the rest.

APPENDIX B

Sample Trade Journals — All Six Conditions

Twelve complete trade records — two per condition — showing the full journal entry from pre-trade to close

A trade journal entry is not a note to yourself — it is a contract between you and your system. It captures your six-condition read, your entry thesis, your risk math, and your exit plan before the trade begins. It captures what actually happened after the trade closes. This appendix shows twelve complete journal entries — two trades (entry & exit) for each of the six conditions — to give you a model for your own record-keeping. Each condition shows one full trade cycle: the entry journal logged before the trade opens, and the exit journal logged when it closes. Twelve entries. Six conditions. One complete record-keeping model.

Copy this format exactly. Adapt the fields to your platform's data. The content changes with every trade. The format never changes.

CONDITION 1 — Trade A: Bull Call Spread (SPY)

Date	March 15, 2025
Underlying	SPY (S&P 500 ETF) at $520.40
Six-Condition Read	VIX: 14.2. IVR: 18. SPY above 50MA ($505) and 200MA ($488). Higher highs for 6 consecutive weeks. → CONDITION 1: Bullish + Low IV ✓
Strategy	Bull Call Spread — debit (approved for Condition 1)
Structure	Buy SPY April 18 $525 Call @ $5.40. Sell SPY April 18 $535 Call @ $2.80. Net debit: $2.60 ($260 per contract).
Max Risk	$260 per contract (debit paid — total exposure)
Max Reward	$740 per contract (spread width $10 − $2.60 debit × 100)
Break-even at Expiry	SPY must be above $527.60 at April 18 expiry
Profit Target	Close at 50% of max reward = +$370 per contract (spread value = $7.40)
Stop Loss	Close if position loses 50% of debit = −$130 (spread value = $1.30)
Time Stop	Close at T-7 regardless of P&L (7 days before expiry)
Pre-trade Checks	Ten Indicators: ETF — bypassed. Earnings: none. FOMC: March 19 (4 days away — decided to enter because spread structure hedges IV spike risk). Adjusted: clean. OI at $525 strike: 12,400 contracts ✓. Size: $260 < 2% of $15,000 account ✓.
Exit	Closed April 3 at spread value $7.40 (50% of max). SPY at $531. 18 days held. P&L: +$480 on $260 debit = 184% return.

Lesson	The FOMC event 4 days after entry caused a brief IV spike that temporarily inflated the long call value. Could have closed earlier but 50% target was the discipline anchor. Let the system run.

CONDITION 2 — Trade A: Cash-Secured Put (MSFT)

Date	January 8, 2025
Underlying	MSFT (Microsoft) at $422.30
Six-Condition Read	VIX: 23.4. IVR on MSFT: 62. MSFT above 200MA. Sector rotation into tech underway. → CONDITION 2: Bullish + High IV ✓
Strategy	Cash-Secured Put — credit (approved for Condition 2)
Structure	Sell MSFT February 21 $390 Put @ $3.85. Reserved capital: $39,000.
Max Risk	Assignment at $390 ($39,000 reserved minus $385 premium = $38,615 net cost basis)
Max Reward	$385 per contract (premium collected)
Break-even at Expiry	MSFT must stay above $386.15 ($390 − $3.85)
Profit Target	Close at 50% of premium = +$192.50 remaining value of $1.93 or less
Stop	Close if put widens to $7.70 (2× original premium)
T-21 Check	February 21 expiry → T-21 review on January 31
Pre-trade Checks	Ten Indicators: MSFT scored 9/10. Earnings: February 29 (after expiry — clean). FOMC: January 29 (within window — sized at 50% of normal because of Fed risk). OI at $390: 3,400 ✓. Position size: 1 contract.
T-21 Result	January 31: MSFT at $436. Put at $0.90 (77% profit). Closed early. Days held: 23. P&L: +$295.
Lesson	MSFT moved significantly higher, accelerating the profit. Closing at 77% instead of waiting for 50% target was a deviation from plan — acceptable when profit > target is available before T-21, but should be documented as a rule-bending deviation.

CONDITION 3 — Trade A: Bear Put Spread (QQQ)

Date	September 5, 2024
Underlying	QQQ at $455.20
Six-Condition Read	VIX: 17.8. IVR: 28. QQQ below 50MA ($462). Lower highs for 3 consecutive weeks. Bearish chart pattern confirmed. → CONDITION 3: Bearish + Low IV ✓
Strategy	Bear Put Spread — debit (approved for Condition 3)
Structure	Buy QQQ October 18 $445 Put @ $6.80. Sell QQQ October 18 $430 Put @ $3.20. Net debit: $3.60 ($360 per contract).
Max Risk	$360 per contract
Max Reward	$1,140 per contract ($15 spread − $3.60 debit × 100)
Break-even at Expiry	QQQ must be below $441.40 at expiry ($445 − $3.60)
Profit Target	Close at 50% max reward = +$570 (position value $9.30)

Stop Loss	Close if spread loses 50% = −$180 (spread value $1.80)
Pre-trade Checks	Ten Indicators: ETF — bypassed. Earnings: none. FOMC: September 18 (within window — structured as spread to limit Vega exposure to Fed). OI at $445: 8,900 ✓.
Exit	Closed September 20 (post-FOMC). QQQ at $432.10. Spread value: $11.80. P&L: +$820 on $360 debit. Held 15 days. FOMC surprised with larger cut — QQQ dropped 4% in 2 days.
Lesson	The spread structure protected against IV crush post-FOMC. A naked long put would have suffered significant time value loss on the announcement day despite the price move. The spread earned the full directional move without the Vega risk.

CONDITION 4 — Trade A: Bear Call Spread (SPY)

Date	February 3, 2022
Underlying	SPY at $437.50
Six-Condition Read	VIX: 31.2. IVR: 72. SPY below 50MA and 200MA. Lower highs confirmed for 5 weeks. → CONDITION 4: Bearish + High IV ✓
Strategy	Bear Call Spread — credit (ONLY approved strategy for Condition 4)
Structure	Sell SPY March 18 $465 Call @ $2.10. Buy SPY March 18 $475 Call @ $1.15. Net credit: $0.95 ($95 per contract).
Max Risk	$905 per contract ($10 spread − $0.95 credit × 100)
Max Reward	$95 per contract
Break-even at Expiry	SPY must stay below $465.95
Profit Target	Close at 50% of credit = buy back spread at $0.48 or less
Stop	Close if spread widens to $1.90 (2× credit)
Pre-trade Checks	Ten Indicators: ETF — bypassed. Earnings: none. FOMC: March 16 (within window — sized at 1 contract only). Short strike $465 is above chart resistance at $458. OI at $465 call: 22,400 ✓.
Exit	Closed February 22. SPY at $428. Spread at $0.45. P&L: +$50 on $905 max risk. 19 days. The spread decayed efficiently as SPY continued lower.
Lesson	The temptation was to buy puts directly (naked long puts) — the instinctive bearish trade in a falling market. IV at 72 would have meant paying an excessive premium for puts that then lost value to IV crush the moment volatility stabilized. The bear call spread collected credit instead. Condition 4 requires discipline over instinct.

CONDITION 5 — Trade A: Iron Condor (SPY)

Date	July 18, 2023
Underlying	SPY at $451.30
Six-Condition Read	VIX: 13.8. IVR: 20. SPY oscillating between $440 and $460 support/resistance. 50MA flat. → CONDITION 5: Range-bound + Low IV ✓
Strategy	Iron Condor (approved for Condition 5)
Structure	Bull put spread: Sell $430 put / Buy $420 put. Bear call spread: Sell $470 call / Buy $480 call. Both August 18 expiry. Net credit: $1.15 total.

Max Risk	$885 per side ($10 spread − $1.15 net credit × 100)
Max Reward	$115 per condor
Profit Zone	SPY between $430 and $470 at August 18 expiry
Profit Target	Close at 50% of credit = buy back full condor at $0.58 or less
Wing Management	Close any single wing if it reaches $2.00 (market approaching that side)
Pre-trade Checks	Bollinger Bands squeezing. BPI flat at 52. No events within window. OI at both short strikes > 5,000. VIX below 15 for 4 consecutive sessions.
Exit	Closed August 4. SPY at $448.20. Full condor at $0.56. P&L: +$59. 17 days. Range held. Neither wing threatened.
Lesson	Condition 5 requires patience — the SPY moved to $453 briefly (close to the call wing) before retreating. No adjustment was needed because $453 was still 17 points from the $470 short call. Rule: do not adjust until the stock is within 2 strikes of the short strike.

CONDITION 6 — Trade A: Calendar Spread (SPY)

Date	August 14, 2023
Underlying	SPY at $447.80
Six-Condition Read	VIX: 17.2. IVR: 58 (brief spike). SPY still in range $440–$455. → CONDITION 6: Range-bound + High IV ✓
Strategy	Calendar Spread (approved for Condition 6 when IV differential favors near-term)
Structure	Sell SPY August 25 (11-DTE) $448 call @ $2.80. Buy SPY September 15 (32-DTE) $448 call @ $4.90. Net debit: $2.10.
Max Risk	$210 per spread (net debit)
Max Reward	Approximately $350–$420 if SPY near $448 at August 25 expiry (IV differential harvest + near-term theta)
IV Differential Check	Near-term (11 DTE) IV: 18.4%. Far-term (32 DTE) IV: 14.2%. Positive differential confirms calendar logic.
Profit Target	Close at 60% of expected max = +$210 when debit recovered plus additional profit
Stop	Close if SPY moves more than 3% from $448 (either direction) before near-term expiry
Exit	Closed August 25 at expiry of short leg. SPY at $449.60 (near strike). Near-term call expired at $0 value. Far-term $448 call worth $4.60. Closed both: P&L: +$180 on $210 debit. 11 days.
Lesson	The VIX spike that created the condition 6 setup resolved quickly — VIX dropped from 17.2 back to 13.8 in 8 days. That contraction in near-term IV accelerated the short leg decay. Calendar spreads earn fastest when the IV spike they were entered on rapidly normalizes.

YOUR JOURNAL IS YOUR EDGE

The traders who consistently outperform over years are rarely the most sophisticated mathematically. They are the most honest — with themselves, about their trades, about their mistakes. This journal format forces that honesty. Every deviation from the plan is recorded. Every lesson is documented. Every trade builds the pattern database that eventually becomes your proprietary edge. Start your journal on your first paper trade. Never stop.

APPENDIX C — The 25 Most Common Options Mistakes

Every mistake below has been made by a real trader — many of them experienced, many of them intelligent, all of them human. This appendix exists so you can learn from their losses instead of creating your own.

#	The Mistake	Why Traders Make It	The Fix
1	Selling puts on stocks they do not want to own	The premium is attractive; they forget assignment is a real outcome.	Only sell CSPs on stocks that pass your Ten Indicators screen.
2	Ignoring earnings dates on short options	They do not check the calendar before entry.	Check earnings date for every stock before every entry. No exceptions.
3	Position size too large (>2% risk)	Overconfidence after a winning streak.	Write position size in journal BEFORE entering the trade.
4	No stop loss or moving stops wider	Loss aversion — they cannot accept the loss.	Write stop level before entry. Execute within 5 minutes of trigger.
5	Trading 0DTE with income strategy rules	They see the high premium and apply income logic to a scalping product.	0DTE requires completely different management. Do not mix frameworks.
6	Holding through earnings when short premium	They think 'it will be fine' or want to capture the IV crush.	Close ALL short premium before earnings. Re-enter after the report.
7	Selling calls too aggressively after assignment	They want to exit the stock immediately regardless of strike quality.	Wait 24 hours. Follow the Assignment Recovery protocol.
8	Trading illiquid options (OI < 500)	They found a stock they like but do not check options liquidity.	Check open interest and bid-ask spread BEFORE evaluating the trade.
9	Overriding the system after 3 winners	Overconfidence: 'I know better than the rules right now.'	Track win streaks. At 5 consecutive wins, reduce size by 25%.
10	Not having a trade journal	They think they will remember the lessons.	You will not. Start the journal today. Every trade, every time.
11	Selling premium when IVR is below 20	They want income regardless of the environment.	Check IVR before every income entry. Below 20 = calendars, not CSPs.
12	Buying options without checking IV first	They see a bullish thesis and buy calls without checking if IV is inflated.	Calculate expected move. If breakeven exceeds expected move, reconsider.
13	Trading too many positions simultaneously	They want to maximize income without considering management capacity.	Max positions = account size / $10,000. $50K account = 5 max positions.
14	Not understanding assignment mechanics	They sell a put and are shocked when shares appear in their account.	Read Ch. 6 on exercise/assignment before selling your first option.
15	Chasing a stock after it has already moved 5%+	FOMO — they see others profiting and rush in.	Log missed trades in your journal. Review monthly. Most would have lost.
16	Rolling a position that should be closed	Hope that the next cycle will work even though the thesis is broken.	Ask the 3 roll questions (Ch. 21). If any answer is No — close, do not roll.
17	Ignoring sector concentration	Three tech positions feel like diversification because they are different stocks.	Check sector exposure weekly. No sector above 30% of portfolio.
18	Trading during the first 15 minutes of market open	They react to the opening move without waiting for the range to establish.	No entries before 9:45 AM EST. The opening range is algorithmic noise.

#	The Mistake	Why Traders Make It	The Fix
19	Not hedging portfolio downside	They collect income month after month and forget that markets crash.	Spend 1-2% of portfolio per quarter on SPY/QQQ put hedges.
20	Confusing correlation with diversification	AAPL and MSFT are different companies but both drop when tech sells off.	Diversify across sectors, not just tickers. Use the sector rotation framework.
21	Trading without a written plan for the day	They open the platform and react to whatever they see.	Write tomorrow's plan tonight. Execute ONLY what is on the plan.
22	Averaging down on a losing position without thesis confirmation	The stock is cheaper so they sell more puts, increasing exposure to a declining name.	Averaging down is only valid if the fundamental thesis is confirmed by new data.
23	Taking profits too early (below 50% target)	They fear giving back gains.	Set alerts at 50% profit. Close at the alert, not before.
24	Not adjusting strategy for the current market condition	They run the same CSP strategy in all six conditions.	Check the six-condition framework weekly. Adjust strategy to match.
25	Treating trading as entertainment instead of a business	The dopamine from winning trades makes trading feel like a game.	Remove alerts that trigger excitement. Reduce screen time. Boring is profitable.

Print this list. Tape it next to your monitor. Every month, circle the mistakes you made. Over time, the circled numbers should change — you should stop making the beginner mistakes and start making the intermediate ones. When you stop making intermediate mistakes, you have arrived. The goal is not to never make mistakes. The goal is to never make the same mistake twice.

APPENDIX D

Frequently Asked Questions

The most common questions from Premium Desk students — answered directly

---

Section 1: The Six-Condition Framework

Q1. Why only six conditions? Are there not more ways the market can behave?

The six conditions are not arbitrary — they are the product of reducing market behavior to its two most actionable variables. Direction and volatility are the only two inputs that determine whether you should be buying or selling premium, and in which direction. Every other market variable — sentiment, fundamentals, macro data, technical patterns — is either captured by these two inputs or is noise that has no deterministic impact on options pricing. The six conditions are six and only six because three directions times two volatility states is the complete decision space. Adding conditions would be adding complexity without adding edge.

Q2. What if the VIX and the chart are sending conflicting signals?

Conflicting signals — for example, a bullish chart with a VIX that just spiked to 28 — are not a condition; they are a transition. The market is moving from one condition to another. The correct response is to wait one to three sessions for the transition to resolve. The VIX spike in a bullish chart almost always resolves in one of two ways: either the VIX retreats and condition 1 is restored, or the chart follows the VIX lower and condition 4 is established. Both resolutions give you a clear condition. Trying to trade the transition itself is a common mistake. The six-condition system rewards patience, not speed.

Q3. How long does each condition typically last?

Conditions vary enormously in duration. Condition 1 (bullish, low IV) can persist for months — the 2020-2021 bull market kept the market in condition 1 for over a year. Condition 4 (bearish, high IV) tends to be shorter because fear is not sustainable — VIX spikes typically resolve within weeks, not months. Conditions 5 and 6 (range-bound) are the most variable: some consolidations last two weeks, others last six months. The system does not predict duration — it identifies the current condition and provides the appropriate strategy for as long as it persists. Run the condition read every morning. When it changes, your strategy changes. Not before.

Q4. My stock is in an uptrend but the overall market (SPY) is in a downtrend. Which condition do I use?

Always start with the broad market condition (SPY/QQQ chart + VIX). The macro condition is the primary condition read. If the market is in condition 4 (bearish, high IV) and your individual stock is holding up, you have a strong relative performer — but you are trading in a bearish macro environment. The appropriate approach is either: (1) use the macro condition 4 strategy on SPY/QQQ, where the condition is clean; or (2) use a reduced-size condition 2 strategy on the strong individual stock, recognizing that macro headwinds increase its risk. Never classify an individual stock's condition as condition 1 when the broad market is in condition 3 or 4 — the correlation risk in a broad market decline is high, and even the strongest stocks often fall in a bear market.

Q5. Does the six-condition framework work on individual stocks or only ETFs?

It works on both — but the sequence is different. For ETFs: read the condition on the ETF itself (SPY chart + SPY IVR). For individual stocks: read the macro condition on SPY first, then confirm the stock's own chart aligns with the macro condition before executing. A stock in a bullish chart within a macro condition 2 environment is the ideal setup — macro and micro aligned. A stock in a bullish chart within a macro condition 4 environment is a relative strength play — possible, but requiring extra caution and reduced size. The six-condition system is most powerful when applied first at the macro level and then confirmed at the individual stock level.

Section 2: Premium Selling and Income Strategies

Q6. Why does The Premium Desk prefer selling premium over buying options?

The statistical edge in options markets favors sellers over buyers in most market environments. Options are priced using implied volatility, which is systematically higher than realized volatility the majority of the time — meaning buyers routinely pay more for options than the actual movement justifies. Sellers collect this excess. Additionally, time decay (theta) works in the seller's favor continuously — every day that passes without the stock threatening the strike is a day the seller earns income. Buyers lose time value every day. The seller has two profit paths: the stock moves in their favor, or it does not move enough against them. The buyer has only one: the stock moves in their favor more than the premium cost. Two profit paths versus one is a structural advantage that compounds over hundreds of trades.

Q7. Is it safe to sell cash-secured puts on any stock?

Absolutely not. The cash-secured put creates an obligation to buy 100 shares at the strike if the put is exercised. This means you are selecting stocks you would be comfortable owning at the strike price. The Ten Indicator screen in Chapter 14 is the quality filter for this exact reason — you should never sell a cash-secured put on a stock scoring below 6 on the Ten Indicators. The risk is not just losing the premium; it is being assigned shares of a declining company at a price above market value, then holding those shares as they continue to fall while you wait for the covered call recovery. The CSP is only safe when the underlying is safe. The strategy quality cannot exceed the underlying quality.

Q8. What is the difference between the Wheel and the six-condition system?

The Wheel is one of the strategies within the six-condition system — specifically a sequenced application of conditions 2 and 1 (or 2 again) on the same underlying. The six-condition system is the complete framework that determines when the Wheel is appropriate, what underlying it should be run on, and when it should be paused. Traders who run the Wheel without the six-condition framework often find themselves wheeling stocks in condition 3 or 4 markets — selling puts on declining stocks while collecting inadequate premium for the risk taken. The six-condition framework prevents this by requiring a condition 2 read before every new put sale in the Wheel cycle.

Q9. How do I handle assignment?

Assignment means the put you sold was exercised and you now own 100 shares at the strike price. This is not a disaster if the stock was properly selected using the Ten Indicators — you were willing to own those shares at that price from the start. The moment you are assigned, do two things: (1) confirm the underlying still passes its Ten Indicator score; if it has deteriorated, close the position and reset. (2) If the stock is still high quality, immediately sell a covered call at or above your cost basis — you have transitioned from condition 2 (CSP) to condition 2 (covered call). The covered call reduces your cost basis every month until the shares are called away at a profit or until you have collected enough premium to justify holding. Assignment is not the end of the Wheel — it is the middle of it.

Q10. Should I trade earnings announcements?

The Premium Desk rule is clear: never hold short premium positions through an earnings announcement. The reason is not the magnitude of the move — it is the IV crush. When a company announces earnings, regardless of whether the result is good or bad, implied volatility collapses immediately afterward. This IV crush destroys the value of options you hold long and rapidly accelerates the profit on options you sold short — but only if you already captured that IV before the announcement, not if you entered after. If your expiration crosses an earnings date, close or roll the position before the announcement. The reward for holding through earnings is a few additional days of theta. The risk is a catastrophic gap that overwhelms the position. The expected value of holding through earnings is negative over a large sample of trades.

Section 3: Risk Management and Position Sizing

Q11. How many positions should I hold simultaneously?

The answer depends on your account size and your management bandwidth. A general rule: hold no more positions than you can review in 30 minutes each morning. For most traders with accounts under $100,000, that means 3 to 7 simultaneous positions. For traders with accounts over $200,000, 7 to 15 positions is feasible with a systematic management protocol. The bigger danger is not holding too few positions — it is holding too many and being unable to manage them when the market moves against you simultaneously. Six positions managed with discipline outperform 20 positions managed loosely. Start with 3. Add a position only when you can demonstrate to yourself that your current 3 are being managed flawlessly.

Q12. What account size do I need to start?

You can paper trade the six-condition system with any account size — including zero. For live trading of CSPs and covered calls on quality underlyings, a minimum of $5,000 is necessary — but the best underlyings (MSFT, AAPL, SPY) require $15,000 to $40,000 of reserved capital per position at typical strikes. With a $10,000 account, focus on the index ETFs (SPY, QQQ, IWM) with narrow spreads to keep required capital manageable. Spreads (bull put spreads, bear call spreads, iron condors) are more capital-efficient and require $500 to $2,000 per position, making them accessible at smaller account sizes. Never risk more than 2% of your account on any single position — this is not a guideline; it is the mathematics of survival.

Q13. What is the 20% drawdown rule and how do I implement it?

The 20% drawdown rule is a circuit breaker: if your account falls 20% from its peak balance at any point during a month, you stop opening new positions for the rest of that month. You do not close existing positions necessarily — you simply do not add new risk. The purpose is to prevent emotional overtrading and loss-chasing behavior, which is most tempting during drawdowns and which consistently makes them worse. When the new month begins, you resume trading — but at 50% of your previous position size until you have recovered to your prior peak. The reduced size forces accountability and prevents the psychological desire to 'make it back quickly.' You make it back slowly, systematically, and without adding additional risk.

Q14. How do I size a spread position versus a CSP position?

For a CSP, calculate reserved capital (the strike price × 100) as the exposure, not just the premium. A $400 strike CSP requires $40,000 of reserved capital. The 2% rule applied to this position means your account must be at least $2,000,000 for a single $400 CSP to qualify as 2% risk — clearly impractical for most. Instead, interpret the 2% rule for CSPs as: the maximum loss from assignment and the stock going to zero is $40,000 minus the credit collected. That is unlikely, but it is the theoretical max. More practically, use the 5% out-of-the-money level as your risk buffer and size accordingly. For spreads, the 2% rule is simpler: max risk (spread width minus credit × 100) must be ≤ 2% of account. A $500 max risk spread on a $25,000 account is exactly 2%. Use this formula for every spread position.

Section 4: The Six-Condition System in Practice

Q15. What if I identify the condition incorrectly?

Misidentifying the condition is the most common mistake in the system — and the most recoverable, because all six-condition strategies use defined-risk structures with known maximum losses. If you enter a bull call spread in condition 1 and discover the market was actually transitioning to condition 4, your maximum loss is the debit you paid — a defined number you knew before entry. The defined risk is what makes wrong-condition trades survivable. What makes them recoverable is the exit discipline: when the condition changes, you close the mismatched position and redeploy in the new condition. You do not hold a condition 1 position in a condition 4 market hoping the chart reverses. The position was built for a condition that no longer exists.

Q16. How long should I paper trade before going live?

The Premium Desk recommendation is 90 days minimum — not 90 calendar days, but 90 days during which you make your daily condition read, execute paper trades using the approved strategy, log every trade in a journal, and review at month-end. The objective is not to prove you can make money on paper — anyone can do that. The objective is to build the habit of the two-step condition read as an automatic morning ritual, to experience the emotional discomfort of watching a position go against you and holding your exit discipline anyway, and to discover your personal behavioral patterns before real money is involved. Traders who skip paper trading and go live immediately are not impatient — they are underprepared. The market is patient. The preparation is the edge.

Q17. How do I know when a condition is 'clear enough' to trade?

A condition is clear when at least four of the six technical indicators (moving averages, MACD, RSI, RS, Bollinger Bands, BPI) are aligned with the same directional read, AND the VIX/IVR reading unambiguously places you in high or low volatility. When fewer than four indicators agree — or when VIX is in the transitional 18-22 range — the condition is not clear. No trade. The market does not pay you for uncertainty. It pays for clarity. The best trades in the six-condition system are the ones where every indicator, every macro backdrop, and the VIX all agree. Those are the high-confidence conditions. They occur more frequently than most traders expect — especially during sustained trend phases in both directions.

Q18. What do I do in conditions where no strategy seems attractive?

You wait. Waiting is a position in the six-condition system. When the condition is transitional, when IV is neither clearly high nor clearly low, when the chart is mixed — the six-condition system has no approved trade. This is not a failure of the system; it is the system protecting you from the category of trade that produces the most losses: the 'boredom trade,' opened not because of a clear condition read but because the account feels idle. Account idleness is not a problem to solve with a trade. It is an opportunity to review your open positions, update your journal, practice your condition-reading skills, or study the next chapter in this book. You trade when the system says trade. You wait when it does not.

Q19. Can I trade the six-condition system part-time?

Yes — and it was designed for exactly that. The income strategies in conditions 2 and 4 (CSPs, bull put spreads, bear call spreads) are the most compatible with part-time trading because they are set-and-monitor positions that only require active attention at entry, at the T-21 checkpoint, and at exit. A part-time trader can run these strategies in 20–30 minutes per day: 5 minutes for the condition read, 10 minutes for position review, and 5–10 minutes for any required entries, exits, or rolls. The directional debit strategies in conditions 1 and 3 require slightly more active monitoring because they depend on price movement. The range strategies in conditions 5 and 6 are the most set-and-forget once entered. For part-time traders, conditions 2 and 6 are the natural home.

Q20. I made money on a trade that was wrong for the condition. Does the six-condition system still apply?

Yes — and this is one of the most important questions a developing trader can ask. A profitable wrong-condition trade is a dangerous event, not a positive one. It reinforces the wrong behavior and creates a false confidence that overrides the system the next time a similar situation arises. The market rewards wrong-condition trades occasionally by chance. It does not reward them consistently over hundreds of trades. Track every trade with a condition tag in your journal. Review monthly: what percentage of your profitable trades were in the correct condition? What percentage of your losing trades were wrong-condition entries? The answer to this question, tracked honestly over three to six months, will be the most powerful education in systematic trading you can receive.

Section 5: The Premium Desk Philosophy

The Premium Desk philosophy is built on one foundational premise: trading options is a business, not a gamble. A business has rules, a repeatable process, defined inputs, and measurable outputs. A gamble relies on luck, emotion, and hope. Every chapter in this book — from the pre-trading flight check through the conviction pyramid to the loss-streak protocol — is designed to help you build a business, not a habit.

The premium seller who survives and compounds is not the smartest trader in the room. They are the most consistent. They check the same two inputs every morning: chart direction and VIX. They apply the same filter to every potential underlying: Ten Indicators. They size every position the same way: 2% rule. They close every winner at the same target: 50% of max profit. They manage every position on the same schedule: T-21. None of these rules are exciting. All of them are profitable, compounded across hundreds of trades over time.

The market will test every rule in this book. It will create conditions where breaking a rule seems justified. The VIX will spike and the premium will look irresistible even though IVR is only 30. A stock will look perfect technically but fail three Ten Indicators. A losing position will look like it needs just one more week. In each of these moments, the rule exists precisely because the moment feels exceptional. Honor it.

Q21. What is 'PPD' and why does The Premium Desk use it instead of monthly P&L?

PPD — Profit Per Trading Day — is the income metric that treats your trading account like a business rather than a speculation. It answers the question: how much income did this account generate per day of market exposure? Monthly P&L is distorted by how many positions were held, how long each was held, and how much capital was deployed. PPD normalizes all of these. A $500 profit over 25 days ($20/day PPD) is a worse business outcome than a $300 profit over 10 days ($30/day PPD) — even though the absolute number is smaller. PPD also creates a daily income target that is traceable to a real-world financial goal: if your target is $100 income per day, that requires $26,000 per year, which requires a specific account size and strategy mix to generate. The PPD framework is how the six-condition system becomes a personal financial freedom plan.

Q22. Why is The Premium Desk philosophy built around premium selling rather than stock speculation?

Because premium selling is income, not gambling. When you sell a cash-secured put on a quality company at a 20-delta OTM strike, you have a statistical probability of approximately 80% of keeping the full premium. You have collected a real dollar in your account that can only leave if the stock falls significantly. The income is real from the moment the order fills — it is not contingent on a future prediction. Stock speculation requires the stock to move in your direction at the right time for the right amount. Premium selling requires the stock to NOT move too much in one direction. Statistically, in most market conditions, not enough movement is more likely than excessive movement. The premium seller is on the statistical winning side of that bet — not in every individual trade, but across hundreds of trades systematically executed in the correct condition.

Q23. What is the single most important lesson from 'Trading Options Like a Risk Manager'?

That the market goes one of six ways — and for each of those six ways, there is one correct strategy. Not two. Not five. One. The discipline of the six-condition system is not learning more strategies. It is learning to execute the single correct strategy for each condition with consistency, patience, and defined risk. Every trader who has studied markets for decades eventually arrives at this simplicity. The six-condition framework puts it on the table on page one — because years of practice, research, and thousands of trades led to exactly this insight. The trader who masters six responses to six conditions will outperform the trader who knows fifty strategies but cannot identify the condition they are in. Simplicity, executed with precision, is the edge.

THE FINAL WORD

> Markets are the most efficient mechanism ever devised for transferring money from the impatient to the patient, from the emotional to the disciplined, from the trader who wings it to the one who follows a system. You now have the system. The rest is execution. Welcome to The Premium Desk.

Have more questions?

The Premium Desk community is at thepremiumdesk.com — where Eddy Alexandre and the team answer questions, host live sessions, and provide ongoing education in the six-condition framework.

APPENDIX E

Portfolio Margin

Portfolio Margin is a margin calculation system for listed stock and index options that determines margin requirements based on the actual risk of your portfolio — not the theoretical maximum loss of each position in isolation. The result is significantly lower margin requirements for hedged and spread positions, and a more capital-efficient way to run a multi-strategy options book.

MINIMUM ACCOUNT REQUIREMENT

Portfolio Margin is available to accounts approved for naked option trading with a minimum account size of $100,000 (if your broker has a real-time margining system) or $150,000 otherwise. Your broker can elect not to grant Portfolio Margin even if you meet the threshold — it is not automatic. Apply directly through your broker's options permissions request.

How Portfolio Margin Is Calculated

Under Portfolio Margin, the risk of an option or stock position is determined by evaluating the position at 10 equally spaced price intervals within a predetermined range. The margin requirement is set at the risk of the most adverse move across all 10 intervals — not at the maximum theoretical loss. The CBOE supplies the essential data for these calculations daily for each underlying entity.

The price ranges used are fixed — not volatility-based. This is a key difference from futures' SPAN Margin, which adjusts for volatility. The fixed ranges are defined as:

- +/−15% for individual stocks, equity options, stock futures, and narrow-based index options;
- +/−10% for broad-based indices that are not high capitalization;
- +6% / −8% for high capitalization broad-based indices (S&P 500, Nasdaq 100, Russell 2000, etc.); and
- Minimum requirement of $37.50 per contract regardless of calculation result.

Because the movements are fixed rather than volatility-adjusted, Portfolio Margin can produce lower requirements than SPAN Margin for index options. For example, selling a naked SPX put is evaluated as if the index dropped 8% — a lower stress scenario than SPAN would apply at high volatility levels. However, this means Portfolio Margin does not automatically tighten when market volatility spikes, which is a risk factor sophisticated traders must manage independently.

Which Strategies Benefit Most

The degree of margin reduction under Portfolio Margin varies substantially by strategy. Truly hedged positions benefit the most because the system recognizes that the long leg limits the maximum loss of the short leg:

Benefit Level	Strategies	Why It Benefits
Most Reduced	Protective put, collar, short calendar, reverse calendar	Risk is fully defined. The long option caps the maximum adverse move — the system

Benefit Level	Strategies	Why It Benefits
	spread, reverse diagonal spread	prices the actual capped risk, not a theoretical naked exposure.
Potentially Large Reduction	Long strangle, long straddle (especially long-term)	The large price movement assumptions used in the calculation make long options appear to have little measurable risk — an assumption that benefits option buyers.
Reasonably Sized Reduction	Covered call, iron condor, index naked option, short strangle, short straddle	Hedged or partially hedged exposure. The covered call is particularly notable: margin drops from 50% of stock price to just 15%, making covered writing on margin viable.
Smallest Reduction	Vertical spreads, long calendars, synthetic long stock	Spreads already have low margin under Reg-T. The improvement is real but modest compared to the above categories.

Covered Call Example: The Margin Difference

The impact of Portfolio Margin on covered writing is dramatic and worth understanding concretely. Suppose a stock is trading at $106 and you write an OTM call at $1.50:

- Old margin (Reg-T): 50% of stock price ($53) minus option price ($1.50) = $51.50 per share, or $5,150 per 100-share contract;
- New margin (Portfolio Margin): 15% of stock price ($15.90) minus option price ($1.50) = $14.40 per share, or $1,440 per 100-share contract.

This 72% reduction in margin requirement fundamentally changes the capital efficiency of the covered call strategy. For a $100,000 account, Reg-T would allow approximately 19 contracts before capital is consumed. Portfolio Margin allows approximately 69 contracts on the same capital — though deploying that level of leverage would be imprudent. The point is that Portfolio Margin allows you to run a properly diversified multi-position book without artificially constraining your capital allocation.

LEVERAGE IS A TOOL, NOT A TARGET

Portfolio Margin gives you more leverage. Leverage is not inherently good or bad — it is within your control. You can always allocate more than the minimum margin requirement to any position, thereby reducing the effective leverage. The Premium Desk framework calls for 2% risk per trade regardless of what margin the system requires. Always size to your risk rules — not to the margin minimum.

Six-Condition Application

Within the Six-Condition system, Portfolio Margin is most relevant at two stages of account development:

- Running Condition 3 (Iron Condor) positions alongside Condition 2 (Cash-Secured Put) positions simultaneously — Portfolio Margin recognizes the net hedged exposure of the combined book and reduces total collateral requirements;

- Scaling Condition 2 positions: Portfolio Margin's 15% stress test (versus Reg-T's 50%) means each CSP requires significantly less capital, freeing buying power to run more positions across more underlyings without increasing total risk.

Portfolio Margin is not necessary for traders running one strategy at a time. It becomes valuable when you have reached the stage of running a full multi-condition book: multiple iron condors, multiple cash-secured puts, covered calls, and calendar spreads simultaneously. At that stage, the capital efficiency improvement is substantial.

RESOURCES

OCC Portfolio Margin Calculator: https://cpm.theocc.com/tims_online.htm

CBOE Portfolio Margin requirements and examples: https://cboe.com/margin.

APPENDIX F

The Ten-Indicator Scoring Worksheet

#	Indicator	What to Look For	Data Source	Score (0–1)	Notes
1	Rising Profits & Earnings Momentum	EPS growth 3+ consecutive quarters; accelerating YoY	Earnings reports, EDGAR, Finviz		
2	Bargain Price Relative to Value	P/E below sector median; PEG ratio < 1.5	Yahoo Finance, Morningstar, Finviz screener		
3	Growing Dividends as Quality Signal	Dividend growth 5+ years; payout ratio < 60%	Dividend.com, Morningstar, company IR page		
4	Megatrend Alignment	Sector exposure to AI, energy transition, aging demographics, infrastructure	Sector ETF analysis, IBD Leaderboard		
5	Sector Tailwinds	Sector in relative strength uptrend vs S&P 500; 3-month RS > 0	Stockcharts.com RRG charts, ETF sector comparison		
6	Rising Institutional Ownership	Institutional ownership increasing QoQ; fund accumulation days	SEC 13-F filings, Finviz, IBD		
7	Strong Balance Sheet	D/E ratio < 1.0; current ratio > 1.5; positive FCF	Balance sheet (10-K/10-Q), Macrotrends.net		
8	High-Quality Management	CEO tenure > 3 years; insider buying > selling; low turnover	SEC Form 4 filings, Glassdoor, company proxy		
9	Competitive Moat	Pricing power, switching costs, network effects, or cost advantage	Morningstar Economic Moat rating, annual report		
10	Liquid Options Chain	Open interest > 500 per strike; bid-ask spread < $0.20 on ATM options	Brokerage platform options chain		
	TOTAL SCORE			/10	

APPENDIX G

The Six Conditions Framework — Combined Reference

Your complete pre-trade decision framework. Identify the condition. Execute the strategy. No exceptions.

#	Condition	Primary Strategy	Entry Signal	Management Rule	Min. Account
C1	**Bullish / Low IV** *(Up Slow)*	**Long Call** Debit Spread	IVR < 30. Trend confirmed up. Buy ATM call or 30-delta debit spread. DTE 30-45.	Close at 50% profit. Stop at 100% loss. Exit at T-21.	**$2,000**
C2	**Bullish / High IV** *(Up Fast)*	**Cash-Secured Put** Covered Call	IVR ≥ 30. Trend up. Sell OTM put at 20-delta. DTE 30-45.	Close at 50% max profit. Roll at T-21 if not closed. Run Wheel on assignment.	**$15,000**
C3	**Bearish / Low IV** *(Down Slow)*	**Long Put** Bear Put Spread	IVR < 30. Trend confirmed down. Buy ATM put or 30-delta bear put spread. DTE 30-45.	Close at 50% profit. Stop at 100% loss. Exit at T-21.	**$2,000**
C4	**Bearish / High IV** *(Down Fast)*	**Bear Call Spread**	IVR ≥ 30. Trend down. Sell OTM call spread above resistance. 20-delta short strike. DTE 30-45.	Close at 50% max profit. Stop at 2× credit received. Roll or close at T-21.	**$5,000**
C5	**Range-Bound / High IV** *(Sideways Fast)*	**Iron Condor** Short Strangle	IVR ≥ 30. No trend. Sell OTM call spread + put spread. 16-delta wings. DTE 30-45.	Close full condor at 50% max profit. Manage tested side if delta exceeds 30. Exit at T-21.	**$10,000**
C6	**Range-Bound / Low IV** *(Sideways Slow)*	**Calendar Spread** Diagonal Spread	IVR < 30. No trend. Sell near-term option, buy further-dated same strike. DTE: sell 21-30, buy 45-60.	Close at 25-30% of max profit. Exit if IV expands sharply. Manage at T-7 on short leg.	**$5,000**

APPENDIX H

The Swing Trader's Entry Signal Checklist

#	Checklist Item	Condition Required	✓ / X
1	Six-Condition Read Completed	Market condition identified (1–6)	
2	Strategy Matches Condition	Entry strategy aligns with current condition	
3	Trend Direction Confirmed	Price above 21 EMA (bullish) or below (bearish)	
4	Dual EMA Value Zone Check (13/26)	Price in the 13/26 EMA value zone or bouncing from it	
5	MACD Confirmation (12/26/9)	MACD histogram turning in direction of trade; signal crossover present	
6	Quick Entry EMA Signal (8/21)	For aggressive entries: 8 EMA crossed above/below 21 EMA	
7	RSI Not Extreme	RSI between 35–65 for trend entries; not overbought/oversold	
8	Support/Resistance Level Identified	Entry near confirmed support (long) or resistance (short)	
9	Volume Confirmation	Entry bar volume above 20-day average; not on thin volume	
10	Fibonacci Level Check	Entry near 38.2%, 50%, or 61.8% retracement of prior swing	
11	Earnings Date Verified	No earnings within the holding period; or risk sized accordingly	
12	IV Rank Checked	IVR appropriate for strategy (>50 for premium selling; any for debit)	
13	Stop-Loss Level Set	Hard stop at prior swing low (long) or swing high (short)	
14	Profit Target Defined	Target at next resistance (long) or support (short); minimum 1:1.5 R/R	
15	Position Size Calculated	2% Rule applied; BPR within account allocation	
16	Channel Trading Setup (if applicable)	Price at lower channel support with reversal signal	
17	Pullback Entry Protocol Verified (5-Step)	All 5 steps confirmed: trend, pull, bounce, candle, trigger	
18	Range-Bound Income Confirmed (if applicable)	Clear range defined; selling near edges of range	
ALL	FINAL GO / NO-GO	All items checked. Trade authorized.	

GLOSSARY OF OPTION TERMINOLOGY

This glossary defines every key term used in this book — covering options contracts, the Greeks, market analysis, fundamental analysis, risk management, and the book's proprietary frameworks. Terms are listed alphabetically. Where a concept appears in a specific chapter, the chapter is noted.

2% Rule The core position-sizing principle of this book. Risk no more than 2% of total trading capital on any single trade. Defines maximum loss per position before entry. The 2% Rule is the first line of defense against catastrophic drawdown.

Adjusted Option An option contract whose terms (strike price, multiplier, or deliverable) have been modified due to a corporate action such as a stock split, merger, acquisition, or special dividend. Adjusted options are non-standard, often illiquid, and must be identified before entry. See Chapter 20.

All-or-None (AON) Order A limit order requiring the full quantity to fill or nothing. Prevents partial fills on multi-leg options orders where a partial fill would create naked risk.

American-Style Option An option contract that can be exercised by the buyer at any time before expiration. Most equity options are American-style. Contrast with European-style options (index options), which can only be exercised at expiration.

Assignment The process by which the seller (writer) of an option is obligated to fulfill the contract after the buyer exercises. A short call writer must deliver 100 shares at the strike price. A short put writer must purchase 100 shares at the strike price. Assignment can occur at any time for American-style options.

Assignment Risk The probability that a short option will be exercised against the writer before expiration. Highest for deep ITM options near ex-dividend dates and in the final days before expiration.

At-the-Money (ATM) An option whose strike price is equal to, or very close to, the current price of the underlying asset. ATM options carry the highest extrinsic (time) value and the greatest sensitivity to changes in implied volatility.

Average True Range (ATR) A technical indicator measuring average daily price range over a set period (typically 14 days). Used to size stop-losses, assess volatility, and determine appropriate option strikes relative to expected daily movement.

Backtesting The process of applying a trading strategy to historical price data to evaluate how it would have performed. Backtesting validates the logic of a strategy before real capital is risked. Paper trading is live-market backtesting with no capital at risk. See Chapter 21.

Backwardation A VIX futures term structure condition where the spot VIX index trades above near-term futures prices, and futures prices slope downward across successive expiration months. Backwardation typically occurs during fear events or market crises when implied volatility is spiking and the market expects volatility to mean-revert lower. For premium sellers, backwardation signals an elevated but potentially short-lived premium environment. See Chapter 16.

Bear Call Spread A credit spread strategy: sell a lower-strike call and buy a higher-strike call on the same underlying and expiration. Profits when the underlying stays below the short strike. Maximum profit is the net credit received. Maximum loss is the spread width minus the credit. A Condition 4 strategy.

Bear Put Spread A debit spread strategy: buy a higher-strike put and sell a lower-strike put on the same underlying and expiration. Profits when the underlying falls below the long strike. Maximum risk is the net debit paid. A Condition 3 strategy.

Beta A measure of a stock's volatility relative to the market (S&P 500). Beta of 1.0 means the stock moves in line with the market. Beta above 1.0 means greater volatility; below 1.0 means less. High-beta stocks generate larger option premiums but carry higher assignment risk.

Bid-Ask Spread The difference between the highest price a buyer will pay (bid) and the lowest price a seller will accept (ask) for an option. Wide bid-ask spreads signal low liquidity and increase transaction costs. Always use limit orders to avoid paying the full spread.

Binary Option A fixed-payout financial instrument that pays a predetermined amount if a specified condition is met, or nothing if it is not. Binary options are not traditional options contracts — they carry no Greeks, no intrinsic/extrinsic value structure, and no secondary market for management. The SEC and CFTC have issued formal warnings about binary options platforms. This book does not teach binary options strategies. See Chapter 2.

Black-Scholes Model (BSM) The mathematical model for pricing European-style options, published by Fischer Black and Myron Scholes in 1973. Calculates theoretical value using five inputs: stock price, strike price, time to expiration, risk-free rate, and volatility. The foundation of all modern options pricing.

Bollinger Bands A volatility indicator consisting of a 20-period exponential moving average with two standard deviation bands above and below. When bands narrow (squeeze), a breakout is likely. When bands widen, volatility is elevated. Used to time entries in trending and mean-reverting markets. See Chapter 8.

Book Value Total assets minus total liabilities, divided by shares outstanding. Represents the net worth of a company on a per-share basis. Stocks trading below book value may be undervalued — or fundamentally impaired. Always analyze alongside earnings and cash flow.

Breakeven Price The underlying price at which an options position neither gains nor loses money at expiration. Long call: Strike + Premium Paid. Long put: Strike minus Premium Paid. Short put (CSP): Strike minus Premium Received. Short call (covered call): Purchase price minus Premium Received.

Bull Call Spread A debit spread strategy: buy a lower-strike call and sell a higher-strike call on the same underlying and expiration. Profits when the underlying rises above the long strike. Maximum risk is the net debit paid. A Condition 1 strategy.

Bull Put Spread A credit spread strategy: sell a higher-strike put and buy a lower-strike put on the same underlying and expiration. Profits when the underlying stays above the short strike. Maximum profit is the net credit received. A Condition 2 strategy.

Business Cycle The recurring pattern of economic expansion and contraction that drives sector rotation and market conditions. The four phases — Early Expansion, Mid Expansion, Late Expansion, and Contraction — each favor different sectors and options strategies. The primary macro framework of Chapter 7.

Buying Power Reduction (BPR) The amount of capital held aside by a broker as collateral for a short options position. For cash-secured puts, BPR equals the full collateral (strike price x 100). For spreads, BPR equals the spread width x 100. BPR determines how many positions a given account can hold simultaneously.

CAGR (Compound Annual Growth Rate) The annualized rate of return that would be required to grow an investment from its beginning value to its ending value over a given time period, assuming profits are reinvested. Formula: CAGR = (Ending Value / Beginning Value)^(1/Years) − 1. Used to compare revenue growth, earnings growth, and portfolio performance across different time horizons. A company with a 5-year revenue CAGR of 15%+ is classified as a high-growth candidate in Chapter 9's Ten Indicators.

Calendar Spread A two-legged strategy: sell a near-term option and buy a longer-dated option at the same strike. Profits from accelerated theta decay in the short leg and slower decay in the long leg. Also called a horizontal spread or time spread. A Condition 6 strategy.

Call Option A contract giving the buyer the right, but not the obligation, to purchase 100 shares of the underlying asset at the strike price on or before the expiration date. The seller of a call is obligated to deliver shares if the buyer exercises.

Cash-Secured Put (CSP) A put-selling strategy where the seller holds sufficient cash to purchase 100 shares at the strike price if assigned. The primary income vehicle of the Seller's Philosophy. Generates premium income while waiting to acquire shares at a target price. See Chapter 15.

CBOE (Chicago Board Options Exchange) The world's largest options exchange, founded in 1973. Home of the VIX, SPX options, and the standardized options contract. The CBOE opened the first standardized listed options market on April 26, 1973.

Collar A protective strategy: own 100 shares, buy a put for downside protection, and sell a call to fund the put cost. Limits both upside and downside. Used on existing stock positions to reduce risk during uncertain market conditions.

Commodity Futures Option An options contract where the underlying asset is a commodity futures contract rather than a stock or ETF. Commodity futures options give the holder the right to enter a futures position at a specified price. They are traded on exchanges such as the CME (grains, metals, energy) and are subject to different margin, tax, and settlement rules than equity options. See Chapter 18.

Contango A VIX futures term structure condition where futures prices are higher than the spot VIX index, and the curve slopes upward across successive expiration months. Contango is the normal state during calm, low-volatility bull markets. In contango, VIX futures prices decline over time even with no change in the index value — this decay is the basis of the premium seller's edge when selling volatility products. See Chapter 16.

Contract Multiplier The number of underlying shares controlled by a single options contract. Standard U.S. equity options have a multiplier of 100. One contract = rights/obligations on 100 shares. Always multiply premiums by 100 to calculate the actual dollar value of a position.

Covered Call A strategy where the owner of 100 shares sells a call option against those shares. Generates premium income but caps upside above the strike price. The second leg of The Wheel strategy. See Chapter 15.

Credit Spread Any options spread where premium received from short options exceeds premium paid for long options, resulting in a net credit. Bull put spreads and bear call spreads are credit spreads. Maximum profit is capped at the credit received.

Daily P&L Attribution The breakdown of daily profit and loss by source: delta P&L from price movement, theta P&L from time decay, and vega P&L from IV change. Essential for understanding whether a trade performs for the right reasons.

Debit Spread Any options spread where premium paid for long options exceeds premium received, resulting in a net debit. Bull call spreads and bear put spreads are debit spreads. Maximum loss is capped at the debit paid.

Debt-to-Equity (D/E) Ratio Total debt divided by shareholders' equity. Measures financial leverage. High D/E increases vulnerability in rising interest rate environments and during earnings contractions. A key metric in the Ten Indicators framework.

Delta (Delta) The rate of change in an option's price for every $1 move in the underlying. Ranges from 0 to 1 for calls, 0 to -1 for puts. Also approximates the probability the option expires in-the-money. A 0.30 delta CSP has approximately a 30% chance of finishing ITM at expiration.

Delta-Neutral A position with net delta near zero, meaning small moves in the underlying have minimal P&L impact. Delta-neutral positions profit from volatility (via gamma) or time decay (via theta). Iron condors can be structured as delta-neutral.

Diagonal Spread A two-legged spread using different strikes AND different expiration dates. Combines elements of a vertical spread and a calendar spread. Allows more flexibility in strike selection and income generation than a standard calendar spread.

Dividend Arbitrage A near-riskless strategy in which a trader buys a deeply ITM put with time value premium less than the upcoming dividend, and simultaneously buys the underlying stock. After the stock goes ex-dividend, the position is closed. The dividend captured exceeds the time value paid for the put, creating a near-riskless profit. Relevant when deep ITM puts are mispriced relative to upcoming dividend events — an edge available primarily to institutional traders with low transaction costs.

Do-Not-Exercise (DNE) Instruction A broker instruction to prevent automatic exercise of an ITM option at expiration. Required when a trader wants to let an ITM option expire without taking assignment. Must be filed before the expiration deadline — typically 5:30 PM ET.

Drawdown The peak-to-trough decline in account value over a given period. Maximum drawdown measures the largest such decline historically. Drawdown recovery requires disproportionately larger gains: a 50% drawdown requires a 100% gain to return to breakeven. See Chapter 8.

DTE (Days to Expiration) The number of calendar days remaining until an option contract expires. The most critical variable in theta decay management. The optimal income-selling window is 30-45 DTE at entry, with positions closed at T-21.

Early Assignment Assignment that occurs before the option's expiration date. Most common for deep ITM short calls just before an ex-dividend date. Can be avoided by monitoring positions and rolling before ex-dividend dates. See Chapter 20.

Earnings Per Share (EPS) Net income divided by shares outstanding. The primary measure of a company's profitability on a per-share basis. Rising EPS over three or more consecutive quarters is the first of the Ten Indicators. EPS growth rate relative to peers determines competitive positioning.

Earnings Season The four annual periods when most public companies report quarterly results, typically January, April, July, and October. Implied volatility reliably rises ahead of announcements and collapses immediately after — creating predictable setups. See Chapter 27.

Edge A statistical advantage that, applied consistently over many trades, produces positive expected value. Without a demonstrable edge, trading is speculation. The Six-Condition Framework, the T-21 Rule, and the 2% Rule are designed to create and preserve edge.

European-Style Option An option that can only be exercised at expiration, not before. SPX (S&P 500 Index) options are European-style. European-style options carry no early assignment risk, making them cleaner for income strategies.

Ex-Dividend The date on which a stock begins trading without the value of its next declared dividend. An investor who buys shares on or after the ex-dividend date does not receive that dividend payment. Options traders must monitor ex-dividend dates because ITM call owners may exercise early to capture the dividend, increasing assignment risk for short call writers. Stocks typically drop by approximately the dividend amount on the ex-dividend date. See Chapter 20.

Exercise The act of the option buyer invoking their right to buy (call) or sell (put) shares at the strike price. Exercise triggers assignment for the option seller. Most options are closed before exercise rather than exercised.

Expected Move The market-implied price range for an underlying over a given period, typically derived from ATM straddle pricing. Expressed as a dollar or percentage range. Used to set spread strikes outside the expected move for a defined probability of success.

Expiration Date The date on which an options contract expires and becomes worthless if not exercised or closed. Standard equity options expire on the third Friday of the expiration month. Weekly options expire every Friday.

Exponential Moving Average (EMA) The average price of an asset over a defined number of periods. The 50-day and 200-day simple moving averages are the primary trend indicators used in this book. Price above both MAs signals an uptrend eligible for bullish strategies.

Extrinsic Value Also called time value. The portion of an option's premium above its intrinsic value. Reflects time remaining, implied volatility, and uncertainty. Extrinsic value decays to zero at expiration — this decay is the foundation of every income strategy in this book.

Fat Tail A statistical distribution with more extreme outcomes than a normal distribution predicts. Options markets exhibit fat tails — large price moves occur more frequently than Black-Scholes assumes. This is why protective options have persistent value.

Fibonacci Levels Horizontal price levels derived from the Fibonacci sequence (23.6%, 38.2%, 50%, 61.8%, 78.6%) applied to a prior price move. Used to identify likely support and resistance zones for pullback entries and stop placement. See Chapter 8.

Free Cash Flow (FCF) Operating cash flow minus capital expenditures. The actual cash generated by a business after maintaining its operations. FCF is the most reliable indicator of real profitability — earnings can be manipulated; cash cannot. A key metric in the Ten Indicators framework.

Front-Month The options expiration nearest in time to the current date. Front-month options have the highest theta decay and the highest gamma. Sellers prefer front-month premium; directional buyers generally prefer back-month.

Fundamental Analysis The method of evaluating a security by analyzing financial statements, economic conditions, industry position, and competitive dynamics to estimate intrinsic value. The 90% component of the 90/10 framework used throughout this book. See Chapter 9.

Gamma (Gamma) The rate of change of delta for every $1 move in the underlying. Gamma is highest for ATM options near expiration. Represents the acceleration of directional risk. High gamma in the final two weeks before expiration is the primary reason for the T-21 exit rule.

Gamma of the Gamma The sixth risk measurement of an option position — the amount by which the gamma will change when the stock moves one point. Positive gamma of the gamma means gamma is growing (option is OTM and approaching the strike — risk is compounding). Negative gamma of the gamma means gamma is shrinking (option has moved ITM — delta is stabilizing toward 1.0 but damage is done). Most critical for premium sellers in Condition 3 (Iron Condor) and Condition 2 (Cash-Secured Put) when the underlying tests a short strike. The T-21 Rule exists in part to exit before gamma of the gamma compounds delta exposure in the final weeks. See Chapter 5.

Good-Till-Canceled (GTC) Order A limit order that remains active until it is either filled or manually canceled by the trader. Used for profit-taking orders placed at the time of entry. Avoids the need to re-enter orders daily.

Greeks The collective term for Delta, Gamma, Theta, Vega, and Rho — the five sensitivity measures that quantify how an option's price responds to changes in the underlying price, time, volatility, and interest rates. The risk dashboard of every position.

Historical Volatility (HV) The actual realized volatility of an underlying asset over a specified past period, calculated as the annualized standard deviation of logarithmic daily price returns. Historical volatility is the risk benchmark against which implied volatility is measured. When implied volatility exceeds historical volatility significantly, the premium seller has a statistical edge. Also called realized volatility or statistical volatility. See Chapter 16.

Implied Move The options market's forecast for how far a stock will move by expiration. Calculated from ATM straddle price: (Call Premium + Put Premium) / Stock Price. Critical for earnings season positioning. See Chapter 27.

Implied Volatility (IV) The market's forward-looking expectation of price movement embedded in an option's premium, expressed as an annualized percentage. IV rises before binary events (earnings, Fed decisions) and collapses after. High IV favors selling premium; low IV favors buying.

In-the-Money (ITM) A call is ITM when the underlying price exceeds the strike price. A put is ITM when the underlying price is below the strike price. ITM options have intrinsic value and a delta magnitude greater than 0.50.

Intrinsic Value (Stock) The estimated true worth of a company based on its fundamentals — earnings, cash flows, assets, and growth prospects — independent of its current market price. The goal of fundamental analysis is to identify stocks trading below their intrinsic value (a margin of safety).

Iron Butterfly A four-legged strategy: sell an ATM call and ATM put (short straddle) and buy OTM call and OTM put (long strangle) for protection. Maximum profit at expiration when the underlying closes exactly at the short strike. Tighter profit zone but higher credit than an iron condor.

Iron Condor A four-legged strategy: sell an OTM put spread and sell an OTM call spread on the same underlying and expiration. Profits when the underlying stays within the range between the two short strikes. A Condition 5 (range/low IV) or Condition 6 (range/high IV) strategy.

IV Crush The rapid collapse of implied volatility immediately following a binary event, most commonly earnings. IV crush reduces option premiums sharply even if the stock moves in the anticipated direction. Selling premium before earnings captures the elevated IV; buying before earnings risks the crush.

IV Rank (IVR) A measurement of where the current implied volatility stands relative to its own 52-week high and low. Formula: (Current IV − 52-week low IV) ÷ (52-week high IV − 52-week low IV) × 100. An IVR of 70 means current IV is at the 70th percentile of its one-year range. IVR above 50 generally signals a favorable premium-selling environment. See Chapter 16.

Kelly Criterion A mathematical formula for optimal position sizing that maximizes long-term growth while avoiding ruin. Kelly Fraction = Edge / Odds. Most professional traders use a fractional Kelly (25-50%) to reduce variance. The 2% Rule is a simplified practical approximation.

LEAPS Long-term Equity Anticipation Securities. Options with expiration dates more than one year away. Used as stock substitutes (buying deep ITM calls instead of shares) or for long-term directional exposure with defined risk.

Limit Order An order to buy or sell an option at a specified price or better. The professional standard for options execution. Never use market orders on options — the bid-ask spread makes market orders unnecessarily expensive.

Liquidity The ease with which an option can be bought or sold without significantly affecting its price. Measured by bid-ask spread width, volume, and open interest. High liquidity is the first filter in options selection — low liquidity means wide spreads and poor fills.

Lognormal Distribution A statistical distribution applied to stock price modeling because it prevents prices from falling below zero while allowing unlimited upside — matching the mathematical reality of equity prices. The Black-Scholes model assumes lognormal price distribution. In practice, actual returns show fatter tails than lognormal predicts — meaning extreme moves (crashes and spikes) occur more frequently. This discrepancy drives volatility skew: OTM puts price in the real-world tail risk that lognormal models underestimate. See Chapter 16.

Long Call Buying a call option, granting the right to purchase 100 shares at the strike price before expiration. Maximum loss is the premium paid. Profit potential is unlimited as the stock rises. The primary Condition 1 strategy.

Long Put Buying a put option, granting the right to sell 100 shares at the strike price before expiration. Maximum loss is the premium paid. Profits as the underlying falls. The primary Condition 3 strategy. Also used as portfolio insurance.

MACD (Moving Average Convergence Divergence) A momentum oscillator calculated from the difference between 12-period and 26-period exponential moving averages, with a 9-period signal line. MACD crossovers signal momentum shifts; histogram divergence signals trend exhaustion. A primary confirmation indicator in Chapter 8.

Margin of Safety The difference between a stock's intrinsic value and its current market price, expressed as a percentage. Value investors require a margin of safety of 20-30% before buying. The larger the margin of safety, the lower the risk of permanent capital loss.

Market Capitalization The total market value of a company's outstanding shares (Share Price x Shares Outstanding). The five tiers — Mega Cap ($200B+), Large Cap ($10-200B), Mid Cap ($2-10B), Small Cap ($300M-2B), and Micro Cap (below $300M) — determine eligible strategies. See Chapter 6.

Market Order An order to buy or sell immediately at the best available current price. Not recommended for options trading. The bid-ask spread means market orders on options routinely cost $0.05-$0.30 per contract more than limit orders.

Mark-to-Market The daily revaluation of open positions at current market prices. P&L shown in brokerage accounts is mark-to-market — it reflects what positions could be closed for today, not the original entry. Unrealized losses do not affect cash until the position is closed.

Max Pain The strike price at which the greatest number of options contracts expire worthless by dollar value. Some traders use max pain as a secondary indicator of where stock prices may gravitate near expiration.

Moat (Competitive Moat) A durable, structural competitive advantage that protects a company's market share and profit margins from erosion by competitors. The term was popularized by Warren Buffett. Types include: network effects (Visa, Meta), switching costs (Microsoft, Salesforce), cost advantages (Walmart, Amazon), intangible assets (patents, brands), and regulatory moats (utilities). Companies with wide moats sustain above-average returns for years — making them the safest underlying candidates for long-term income strategies. Scored in Indicator 5 (Competitive Moat) of the Ten Indicators. See Chapter 9.

Moneyness The classification of an option's relationship between its strike price and the underlying's current price: In-the-Money (ITM), At-the-Money (ATM), or Out-of-the-Money (OTM). Determines premium composition (intrinsic vs. extrinsic) and delta range.

Naked Option An option sold without owning the underlying or holding an offsetting position. Naked calls carry theoretically unlimited risk; naked puts carry risk down to zero. Requires the highest broker approval level. See Chapter 13.

Net Liquidating Value (NLV) The total current value of a trading account if all positions were closed at current market prices. The correct denominator for position sizing (2% Rule) and performance measurement.

Notional Value The total dollar value of the underlying controlled by an options position. For a CSP at a $50 strike: notional value = $50 x 100 = $5,000. Notional value determines real economic exposure and is the basis for calculating position size using the 2% Rule.

OCC (Options Clearing Corporation) The central counterparty clearinghouse for all U.S.-listed options. The OCC guarantees contract performance, eliminating counterparty risk. Every option trade is ultimately a contract with the OCC, not with the individual counterparty.

Open Interest (OI) The total number of outstanding, unsettled options contracts at a given strike and expiration. High open interest signals a liquid market with tight spreads. This book recommends a minimum of 500 open interest at the target strike before entering any position.

Option Chain The full display of all available contracts for a given underlying, organized by expiration and strike price. Shows bid, ask, last price, volume, open interest, and Greeks for each contract. Reading the option chain fluently is a foundational skill.

Option Writer The seller of an options contract. Also called the short option position. The writer collects the premium upfront and assumes the obligation to fulfill the contract if the buyer exercises. The Seller's Philosophy positions the option writer's role as the primary income strategy.

Out-of-the-Money (OTM) A call is OTM when the strike is above the current underlying price. A put is OTM when the strike is below the current underlying price. OTM options consist entirely of extrinsic value. Most income strategies sell OTM options to collect premium with high probability of expiring worthless.

Pairs Trading A market-neutral strategy that simultaneously buys one stock and shorts a historically correlated stock, profiting from convergence of their price relationship rather than market direction. Eliminates broad market beta — profit depends entirely on relative performance of the two stocks. Used as a hedging overlay by portfolio managers and as a standalone income strategy when the spread diverges significantly from its historical mean.

Parity An option trading for exactly its intrinsic value with zero extrinsic (time) value remaining. An ITM option is at parity when its premium equals the difference between the stock price and the strike price exactly. Deep ITM options approach parity as expiration nears and time value evaporates completely. An option trading below parity is called a discount option.

P/E Ratio (Price-to-Earnings) The current stock price divided by earnings per share. The most widely used valuation multiple. A P/E below the sector average may signal undervaluation; significantly above may signal overvaluation. Must be interpreted relative to peers and growth rate.

PEG Ratio Price/Earnings to Growth ratio. P/E divided by the annual EPS growth rate. A PEG below 1.0 suggests potential undervaluation relative to growth. A PEG above 2.0 suggests significant future growth is already priced in. A key metric in the Ten Indicators framework.

PERCS (Preferred Equity Redemption Cumulative Stock) A preferred stock that pays a higher-than-normal dividend but can be called for redemption by the issuing corporation at a fixed call price — economically equivalent to a covered call write. The holder receives enhanced income (the option premium in dividend form) but caps upside at the redemption price. Created by financial institutions as structured income products for yield-seeking investors.

PFOF (Payment for Order Flow) The practice by which broker-dealers receive compensation from market makers for routing customer options and stock orders to them for execution. PFOF is how most commission-free brokers generate revenue. Critics argue it creates a conflict of interest between the broker and the customer. For options traders: understand that your broker may route your order to a market maker who profits from the spread — which is why using limit orders and checking for price improvement matters on every trade.

Pin Risk The risk that at expiration the underlying closes exactly at a short strike, creating uncertainty about assignment. Near-ATM short options held into expiration carry pin risk. The solution: close positions before expiration rather than holding to zero.

Portfolio Delta The sum of all individual position deltas across a trading portfolio, representing the portfolio's net directional exposure. A portfolio delta near zero is market-neutral. Managing portfolio delta is a core risk management practice for multi-position traders.

Portfolio Margin A risk-based margin methodology available to qualified accounts ($100,000+ minimum) that calculates requirements by stress-testing the position across 10 price intervals and requiring only the worst-case loss as collateral. Replaces fixed-percentage Regulation-T with accurate risk-based calculation. Hedged and defined-risk positions see 50–70%+ margin reductions. Requires Level 4 options approval. See Chapter 1.

Position Sizing The process of determining how many contracts to trade based on account size, risk tolerance, and the 2% Rule. Correct position sizing ensures no single trade can cause catastrophic account damage. Oversizing is the primary cause of ruin among retail traders.

PPD (Profit Per Day) The daily theta income generated by a short options position. PPD = Position Theta x 100. Used to benchmark whether a portfolio is generating income at the rate required to meet monthly targets. The operational core of the Seller's Philosophy income tracking system.

Premium The total price of an options contract, paid by the buyer and received by the seller. Premium = Intrinsic Value + Extrinsic Value. For option sellers, the premium received at entry is the maximum possible profit from the position.

Probability of Profit (POP) The statistical likelihood that a trade will be profitable at expiration. Directly derived from the option's delta. A 30-delta short put has approximately 70% POP. Higher-probability trades collect less premium but win more often.

Put Option A contract giving the buyer the right, but not the obligation, to sell 100 shares of the underlying at the strike price on or before expiration. Used for bearish directional trades, portfolio hedging, or income generation when sold (cash-secured put).

Put-Call Ratio (PCR) A sentiment indicator measuring the volume of put options traded relative to call options. Formula: total put volume ÷ total call volume. A rising PCR indicates increasing bearishness (more puts being bought); a falling PCR indicates increasing bullishness. The 10-day exponential moving average (10DEMA) of the PCR above 0.47 signals excessive bearishness (contrarian buy signal for premium sellers); below 0.39 signals excessive bullishness. See Chapter 18.

Ratio Write An options strategy where a trader sells more option contracts than they buy, creating a partially uncovered (naked) position on the excess short contracts. Example: buy one call at a lower strike, sell two calls at a higher strike (1×2 ratio write). Ratio writes are used to exploit volatility skew — the excess short contracts are sold at the most overvalued (highest IV) point on the options chain. Maximum profit occurs when the underlying closes at the short strike at expiration. See Chapter 16.

Realized Volatility The actual volatility a stock experienced over a historical period, calculated from its price returns. When realized volatility is consistently lower than implied volatility, options sellers have a structural edge — the volatility risk premium.

Regulation T (Reg-T) The Federal Reserve rule governing broker extension of credit. Sets standard margin at 50% of stock purchase price for equity positions. For options, Reg-T defines baseline requirements that brokers must meet or exceed. Portfolio Margin is the risk-based alternative for qualified accounts, replacing Reg-T percentages with actual stress-test calculations.

Resistance A price zone where selling pressure has historically exceeded buying interest, causing price advances to stall or reverse. Former resistance, once broken, often becomes support. Resistance levels define the upper boundary for strike placement on short calls and bear call spreads.

Return on Equity (ROE) Net income divided by shareholders' equity. Measures how efficiently management generates profit from equity capital. A consistent ROE above 15% signals a durable competitive advantage and management quality. Screened as part of the Ten Indicators framework.

Revenue Growth The year-over-year or quarter-over-quarter increase in total sales. Sustainable earnings growth requires revenue growth — cost-cutting can improve short-term earnings but cannot drive long-term appreciation. Rising revenue at or above the sector average is the second of the Ten Indicators.

Reversal Arbitrage A riskless arbitrage strategy that involves shorting the stock, selling (writing) a put, and buying a call — all with the same expiration and strike price. The mirror image of a Conversion Arbitrage. Profits when the combined position is mispriced relative to the cost of carry. Primarily executed by market makers and institutional desks with access to short rebates and near-zero transaction costs.

Reverse Strategy The mirror image of a standard options strategy. If a ratio spread involves buying calls at a lower strike and selling more calls at a higher strike, the reverse ratio spread (also called a backspread) sells the lower-strike calls and buys more of the higher-strike calls — creating the opposite risk/reward profile. Reverse strategies typically have unlimited profit potential in one direction and limited risk in the other — the inverse of the original strategy's characteristics.

Rho (Rho) The rate of change in an option's price for every 1% change in interest rates. Most significant for LEAPS and in high interest rate environments. Minimal relevance for standard 30-45 DTE short premium positions.

Roll For Credit Rolling an options position to a new expiration only when doing so results in a net credit — meaning the new position collects more premium than it costs to close the existing one. Rolling for a debit means the trade is working against you.

Rolling Closing an existing options position and opening a new position at a different strike, expiration, or both in a single transaction. Rolling extends duration, adjusts the strike, and collects additional premium. The six roll types and decision framework are covered in Chapter 23.

RSI (Relative Strength Index) A momentum oscillator measuring the speed and magnitude of price changes on a scale of 0-100. RSI above 70 signals overbought conditions; below 30 signals oversold. Used to time entries and identify potential reversals in the context of the prevailing trend. See Chapter 8.

Sector Rotation The movement of investment capital between industry sectors as the business cycle progresses. Technology and Consumer Discretionary lead in early expansion; Healthcare and Utilities outperform in contraction. Aligning strategies with current sector rotation is the macro edge of Chapter 7.

Seller's Philosophy The operational framework of this book. Positions the trader primarily as a seller (writer) of premium, using the statistical advantage of time decay, elevated implied volatility, and high-probability OTM strikes to generate consistent income. Executed through the Wheel, CSPs, covered calls, and credit spreads.

Serial Option A futures option for which no futures contract expires in the same calendar month. The underlying futures contract defaults to the next available expiry. Example: there is no March gold futures contract — March gold options are therefore serial options on April gold futures. Serial options allow traders to fine-tune expiration timing precisely without being constrained to standard futures contract months. See Chapter 18.

Six-Condition Framework The primary market-reading system of this book. Defines six distinct market conditions based on two axes: direction (Bullish, Bearish, Neutral) and implied volatility level (High, Low).

Each condition has a defined strategy set. Identifying the current condition before entry is the first step of every trade.

Slippage The difference between the expected price of a trade and the actual fill price. Most common with market orders and wide bid-ask spreads. Minimized by using limit orders and selecting underlyings with high liquidity and tight spreads.

SPAN Margin (Standard Portfolio Analysis of Risk) A volatility-based margin methodology used for futures and futures options. Calculates margin using volatility scenarios rather than fixed price-movement percentages — making it more favorable than equity Portfolio Margin in low-volatility environments. Contrast with Reg-T and Portfolio Margin, which use fixed stress ranges. See Chapter 18.

Spinoff A corporate action in which a parent company separates a subsidiary into an independent publicly traded entity and distributes shares of the new company to existing shareholders. Spinoffs are one of the four adjusted options risk categories (along with earnings, M&A, and dividends) that require immediate position exit. When a spinoff is announced, existing options on the parent stock can become adjusted to deliver both parent and spinoff shares, making position management unpredictable. See Chapter 20.

SRC System The Sell-Roll-Close system. The three-step management framework for short premium positions: Sell premium at entry (30-45 DTE, OTM strike), Roll at T-21 if profitable or in danger, Close at 50% of max profit or per the T-21 rule. The operational engine of the Seller's Philosophy.

Standard Deviation (σ) In options, the measure of price dispersion used to define expected move ranges. One standard deviation covers approximately 68% of outcomes. Strike selection at the 1-sigma level (approximately 16 delta) gives the seller a ~68% probability of the underlying staying outside that strike.

Straddle A two-legged strategy: buy (or sell) both a call and a put at the same strike price and expiration. A long straddle profits from large moves in either direction. A short straddle profits when the underlying stays near the strike and requires high IV to justify the risk.

Strangle Similar to a straddle but with different strikes: buy (or sell) an OTM call and an OTM put with the same expiration. A long strangle profits from very large moves. A short strangle profits from range-bound price action and is a high-probability income strategy in elevated IV environments.

Strike Price The predetermined price at which the option buyer can buy (call) or sell (put) the underlying asset if they exercise. Also called the exercise price. Strike selection is the single most impactful variable in defining the risk/reward of any options position.

Structured Product A packaged investment that combines a fixed-income instrument (typically a bond) with one or more options into a single tradable security. Structured products trade on exchanges like stocks but have custom risk/reward payoffs — the option component modifies the bond's return profile. Examples include MITTS, TARGETS, BRIDGES, PERCS. Key risk: complex structures can obscure embedded costs and may have limited secondary market liquidity.

Support A price zone where buying interest has historically exceeded selling pressure, causing declines to pause or reverse. Former support, once broken, often becomes resistance. Support levels define the lower boundary for short put strike placement and pullback entry triggers.

Synthetic Put A position that replicates a long put by shorting the underlying stock and buying a call option at the same strike. The combined position has the same profit/loss profile as owning a put — defined risk on the upside, substantial profit as the stock falls. Used when listed puts are unavailable or overpriced relative to the replication cost. Requires a short stock locate and margin.

Synthetic Stock (Synthetic Long/Short) An options position that replicates the risk/reward of owning or shorting the underlying stock without actually holding it. Synthetic long stock: buy a call and sell a put at the same strike and expiration (delta ≈ +1.0). Synthetic short stock: buy a put and sell a call at the same strike (delta ≈ −1.0). Used to gain stock-equivalent exposure with less capital, or when the underlying is unavailable to borrow for short selling.

T-21 Rule The Premium Desk position management rule: close all short premium positions at 21 days to expiration. At T-21, the majority of theta has been captured (50-60% of max profit) while gamma risk is beginning to accelerate. Closing at T-21 locks in gains and eliminates the dangerous final two weeks. See Chapter 23.

T-30 Acceleration Point The point in a contract's life, at 30 DTE, when theta decay begins to accelerate measurably. The Premium Desk harvest window is 45 DTE to 21 DTE — capturing the steepest portion of the decay curve while avoiding the gamma spike below 21 DTE.

Technical Analysis The study of historical price and volume data to identify patterns, trends, and likely future price movements. The 10% component of the 90/10 framework. Used for timing entry and exit, not for determining whether an underlying is worth trading.

Ten Indicators The fundamental quality filter of this book. A ten-point scoring system evaluating: rising profits, rising sales, strong balance sheet, growing dividends or buybacks, competitive moat, insider ownership, megatrend alignment, low debt, strong free cash flow, and bargain price vs. intrinsic value. A score of 8-10 required for full six-condition eligibility. See Chapter 9.

Term Structure The relationship between implied volatility and time to expiration across different expirations. Contango (rising IV for longer expirations) is normal. Backwardation (inverted) occurs in high-fear environments. See Chapter 16.

Term Structure of Volatility The relationship between implied volatility and time to expiration across different maturities on the same underlying. In normal markets (contango), longer-dated options carry higher IV than near-term ones. In stressed markets (backwardation), near-term IV spikes above longer-dated — reflecting immediate fear. Calendar spread entry timing is most favorable when the near-term option is in backwardation relative to the longer leg. See Chapter 16.

The Wheel A systematic, continuous income strategy: sell a cash-secured put on a quality underlying — if assigned, sell covered calls on the acquired shares — if called away, sell cash-secured puts again. The Wheel generates premium income at each stage and is the flagship execution system of the Seller's Philosophy. See Chapter 15.

Theta (Theta) The rate at which an option's extrinsic value decays per calendar day, all else equal. Expressed as a negative dollar amount per day per contract. Theta accelerates as expiration approaches. For option sellers, theta is income — every day that passes, the short option loses value, which is profit for the writer.

Treasury Bill / Option Strategy A capital preservation approach in which approximately 90% of trading capital is held in short-term risk-free instruments (T-bills, money market funds) while only the remaining 10% is deployed in long option positions. Maximum capital loss is limited to the option premium — the T-bill holding preserves the core account. Establishes a hard floor on drawdown. Relevant framework for understanding position sizing discipline in the context of the 2% Rule.

Underlying The asset on which an options contract is based. For equity options, the underlying is the stock or ETF. The underlying's price, volatility, and fundamentals determine which options strategies are appropriate in the current market condition.

Vega (Vega) The rate of change in an option's price for every 1% change in implied volatility. Long options have positive vega (benefit from rising IV). Short options have negative vega (lose value when IV rises). Vega exposure determines how much a position is affected by an IV expansion event.

Vertical Spread Any options strategy combining a long and short option of the same type (both calls or both puts) on the same underlying and expiration, but at different strikes. Defines both maximum profit and maximum loss. The foundational structure for credit spreads (bull put, bear call) and debit spreads (bull call, bear put).

VIX (CBOE Volatility Index) The Chicago Board Options Exchange Volatility Index, measuring the market's 30-day implied volatility expectation derived from a weighted average of S&P 500 option prices across multiple strikes. The VIX is the primary fear gauge in equity markets, with an inverse correlation to the S&P 500 of approximately −0.39. VIX above 25 signals elevated fear and rich premium-selling conditions; below 15 signals complacency and compressed premiums. Also called the fear index. See Chapter 16.

VIX Term Structure The curve showing VIX futures prices at successive expiration months, reflecting the market's expectations for future implied volatility. The two primary shapes are contango (upward-sloping, normal market) and backwardation (downward-sloping, fear event). The term structure is a critical timing tool for premium sellers: steep contango signals caution (low current IV, premiums compressed); backwardation signals elevated fear with potential for mean reversion. See Chapter 16.

Volatility Risk Premium (VRP) The persistent tendency for implied volatility to exceed realized volatility. The VRP is the structural edge that options sellers exploit by collecting premium above what actual movement justifies. See Chapter 16.

Volatility Skew The phenomenon where implied volatility is not uniform across all strike prices for the same underlying and expiration. In equity options, the skew typically slopes downward: OTM puts carry higher IV than ATM options (put skew), driven by institutional demand for downside protection. In commodity options, the skew can be inverted (call skew) when supply shocks drive upside risk. The skew creates a premium-selling edge when the most overvalued strikes are sold in ratio write or credit spread structures. See Chapter 16.

Weekly Options Options contracts that expire every Friday rather than on the monthly cycle. Available on most major ETFs and high-liquidity stocks. Useful for short-duration income strategies and event-driven trades, but carry higher gamma risk than standard monthly options.

Wing The outer protective leg of a spread. In an iron condor, the long call is the upper wing and the long put is the lower wing. Wings cap maximum loss. Wider wings cost less but provide less protection.

Writer The seller of an options contract. The writer collects premium upfront and takes on the obligation to fulfill the contract if assigned. Writing options is the foundation of the Seller's Philosophy.

INDEX

Page numbers refer to chapter references. Final print page numbers are established at layout. Sub-entries are indented. Cross-references appear as "— see [Term]".

www.ingramcontent.com/pod-product-compliance
Lightning Source LLC
La Vergne TN
LVHW060015210926
848481LV00013B/3712